Art and Performance in Oceania

Art and Performance in Oceania

Edited by   Barry Craig   Bernie Kernot   Christopher Anderson

UNIVERSITY OF HAWAI'I PRESS
HONOLULU

A CHP Production

Published in North America by
University of Hawai'i Press
2840 Kolowalu St
Honolulu, Hawai'i 96822

Produced and published by
Crawford House Publishing Pty Ltd
PO Box 1484
Bathurst NSW 2795, Australia

Designed by David H. Barrett
Cover designed by Travis Crawford

Library of Congress Cataloging-in-Publication Data
    Art and performance in Oceania / edited by Barry Craig, Bernie
        Kernot, and Christopher Anderson
                p.   cm.
            Papers presented at the 5th Pacific Arts Symposium held 1993,
        Adelaide, Australia.
            Includes bibliographical references.
            ISBN 0-8248-2283-8 (alk. paper)
            1. Oceania – social life and customs Congresses. 2. Art –
        Oceania Congresses. II. Kernot, B. III. Anderson, Christopher,
        Dr. IV. Pacific Arts Symposium (5th : 1993 : Adelaide, Australia)
        DU28.A78   1999
        700'.995–dc21   99-39638
                                                                  CIP

Printed in China by Everbest Printing Co. Ltd

03 02 01 00 99   5 4 3 2 1

Contents

Preface

Christopher Anderson

This book represents the long-awaited record of the Fifth International Symposium of the Pacific Arts Association. The theme of this event was 'Art, Performance and Society', and it was held from 12 to 18 April 1993, hosted by the South Australian Museum in Adelaide. The symposium was a South Australian contribution to the United Nations Year of the World's Indigenous People. In accordance with UN guidelines, access and active participation by indigenous peoples was a priority. Pacific Islanders, Torres Strait Islanders and Australian Aboriginal artists, scholars and performers joined non-indigenous scholars from around the world attending papers, performances and related activities.

A highlight of the week was the opening event, including welcomes by local Kaurna elder Lewis O'Brien and prominent northern-Australian Aboriginal artist Banduk Marika; performances by a Torres Strait Islander dance group; carvers from New Ireland dancing with masks made especially for the event; and performers from New Britain dancing with a large *hemlaut* headdress, subsequently taken into the South Australian Museum's Pacific Gallery for ceremonial installation.

More than fifty papers were given, along with seven workshops and a highly successful film festival, 'Indigenous Film from the Pacific'. Around 200 delegates attended the conference.

Two significant related events accompanied the symposium. An 'Artists' Week' was organised by Franchesca Cubillo Alberts, Curator of Aboriginal Anthropology at the South Australian Museum, assisted by an Aboriginal working party. The event attracted participation by more than sixty Aboriginal, Torres Strait Islander and Pacific artists.

A unique cross-cultural event, 'The Message Stick', was organised by Pungkai Peter Bertani of the South Australian Museum. This involved Aboriginal dance groups from Arnhem Land, the Kimberleys, and central and southern Australia. Workshops were conducted in which senior Aborigines taught songs, rituals and other cultural practices to more than forty Adelaide Aboriginal youths. In the final performance for the PAA symposium, a message stick (a traditional Aboriginal communication object) was ceremonially transferred, symbolising the cultural connections between Aboriginal groups from north to south.

The Fifth International Symposium of the Pacific Arts Association was generously supported by the Australian Commission for UNESCO, the Commonwealth Foundation, the Kelton Foundation, the South Australian Museum, Tourism SA, the Australian Broadcasting Corporation, Air Niugini, Qantas, Kodak, Southern Pacific Hotel Corporation, The Mansions Hotel, West End All Suites Hotel, and the University of South Australia. Artists from visiting the Pacific region were supported by the

Australian Museum, Friends of the South Australian Museum, the UK Museum Ethnographers Group, and the Sainsbury Research Institute of Asia and the Pacific. 'The Message Stick' event was supported by Foundation SA, the South Australian Department of Aboriginal Affairs, the South Australian Youth Arts Board, and the Australia Council. The 'Aboriginal, Torres Strait and Pacific Islander Artists' Week' was funded by the Aboriginal and Torres Strait Islander Commission, the Australia Council, and the South Australian Department for the Arts and Cultural Heritage, and hosted by Tandanya, the National Aboriginal Cultural Institute. Other Aboriginal and Islander organisations also assisted including the Central, Northern, Kimberley and Pitjantjatjara Land Councils, the Kaurna Heritage Committee, the Kaurna Plains Community School, and the Torres Strait Islander Advisory Board.

I take this opportunity on behalf of the Pacific Arts Association and the symposium participants to warmly thank all those organisations for their support.

The board of the South Australian Museum, the then director of the museum, Lester Russell, and the staff of the Anthropology Department worked tirelessly to make the symposium a great success. In particular, I wish to thank Susan Cochrane, whose vision, drive and commitment kept everyone going from beginning to end. Thanks also go to Barry Craig, Lea Crane, Carmel Dundon, Janine Evans, Susan Jenkins, and Aphrodite Vlavogelakis.

The fifth symposium was a very special one, with the largest indigenous-artist involvement yet. The interweaving of the performance events and the papers was another significant feature. I trust that the papers in this volume reflect the diversity, intensity and excitement of what was for everyone a very enjoyable and fruitful event.

Introduction

Barry Craig

Eric Schwimmer's lucid and perceptive essay (1990), presented at the third Pacific Arts symposium in New York in 1984, falls quite squarely into the theme of the 1993 fifth symposium in Adelaide, 'Art, Performance and Society'. In that paper, titled 'The Anthropology of the Ritual Arts', Schwimmer suggests that there is utility in developing an aesthetic anthropology,[1] and that, in particular (but not only):

> Papua New Guinea would be a highly appropriate venue for such studies because the popular arts there, in the view of their creators as well as the public, are almost totally identified with initiation and with other ceremonies in which the relationship between man and spirit is represented. It is for these occasions that the greatest work in dance, song, theatre, sculpture, painting, architecture, body decoration, instrumental music, ceramics, and so forth is destined … The highest forms of expression occur at the great ceremonies when [the various media] are all massed together. [Schwimmer 1990:6-7]

Picking up on Levi-Strauss's distinction between ritual/myth and art/play, Schwimmer asserts:

> Ritual claims to have as its end result a kind of pre-ordained equilibrium corresponding to certain conditions of life that are fixed and unalterable. This fixity of outcomes is absent from both art and play, where there must exist a plurality of possibilities and an unpredictable course of events. [Schwimmer 1990:7]

And:

> Papua New Guinea art often stands in a mimetic relation to nature, not only when it imitates movements, colors, and habits perceived in nature, but also when it seeks, by its constructed images, to reveal hidden truths about nature … no initiatory performance could be wholly successful unless it was aided by the audience's 'inferential walks' and constructs of 'possible worlds'. [Schwimmer 1990:11]

These ideas parallel Donald Brook's distinction (1977) between art and those activities encompassed by any of the other institutions of human society (science, technology, craft, economics, politics, philosophy, religion, and so on). Brook calls art 'experimental modelling' and likens it to putting one's hand out, not to see if it is raining, but simply 'to see' (Brook 1977:13).

In so far, then, as rituals and performances in tribal societies, such as exist in the Pacific, go beyond the fixed formulae, the dictates of custom, they become *art works*, and, in part at least, what they seek to achieve is a revelation of the spirit world. Schwimmer (1990:7) says:

> this revelation is induced by multiple aesthetic messages emitted by human actors and furthermore … it is the

function of initiatory ceremonies to teach novices how to emit these messages.

Schwimmer reminds us that the 'translatability' of sculpture, painting, masks, dances and body decoration in these societies is 'very low indeed' (Schwimmer 1990:8; cf. Forge 1966:25). This is because the art works are, in Levi-Strauss's terms (1950), the 'floating signifiers' or 'extra ration of sense'.

It is possible to analyse ritual as purposive action that serves to reintegrate dissonant social groups, or that achieves dominance over others through status rivalry, or whatever. However, the music, masks, carvings, paintings, dances, and so on, provide the means for additional information to be conveyed at a deeper level where certainty evaporates and the subject matter becomes, through allusion, elusive.

Only a few of the papers presented at the fifth symposium dealt with this level of analysis, as it is extremely difficult for non-indigenous researchers to elicit the necessary data. It is also difficult for indigenous researchers to stand outside their cultural milieu and conduct analysis; or there may be a disinclination to share such deeper-level meanings, especially if they are part of secret-sacred processes of initiation.

Although researchers yearn to be admitted to the inner circle of understanding at this deep level, most have to be satisfied with the more public understandings available to the non-initiates within these various societies. On the other hand, some researchers choose to seek an understanding of artefacts as material objects resulting from a (changing) set of traditions and skills, or they are interested in the collecting impulse, in the collectors themselves, or in museums and their roles. The papers in this book reflect all of these interests.

The fifth Pacific Arts symposium called for papers in sessions dealing with 'Production and Performance', 'Social and Cultural Context', 'The Record and the Remainder', and 'The Mission of Museums'. In all, some sixty papers were given over a five-day period, and seven workshops were conducted. Three concurrent sessions were scheduled to deal with the number of presentations in the time available. Parallel events included a film festival ('Indigenous Film from the Pacific'), an Artists' Week, with its own program of discussions, workshops and exhibitions, and the Message Stick event (Bertani 1993). There were several exhibitions of Pacific and Australian Aboriginal art organised at various venues to coincide with the symposium (Megaw and Megaw 1993).

Only twenty-four papers have been included in this book, but some presenters have already published material in other places (for example, Bertani 1993; Choulai 1996; Craig 1995; Dutton 1994, 1995a; Gemes 1993; Hereniko 1994; Karen Stevenson 1996), a debate generated by the symposium was published in the Adelaide quarterly arts journal *Broadsheet* (Chance and Zepplin 1993; Craig 1993; Fergie 1994), and several general reports were published in *Pacific Arts*, No. 8, July 1993, and one in *Art and Asia Pacific* (Zepplin 1993).

The first two topics elicited several papers that explored the creative process, including the description and analysis of performance and the taxonomy of objects used (Konishi, Hereniko, Smidt and Eoe, Issac and Craig, Lurang, Gunn, Ewins), the transmission of cultural knowledge (Meredith), and the identity and work of individual artists (Megaw and Megaw, Choulai and Lewis-Harris, Beran). The second two topics provided the opportunity for papers on some significant early museum collectors and collections (Regius, Vargyas), various methods of documenting cultural material (such as photography; Gemes, Quanchi), how cultural material has been and can be exhibited (Kernot, Croft, Fergie, Stanton, Anderson), and the role of museums and cultural centres in Pacific Island countries (Cochrane). Inevitably there were papers that could have been accommodated in more than one session and some that sat uncomfortably in any of them (Stevenson, Pollock, Dark). But all record and advance our understanding of the arts of the Pacific region, and what is of particular note is the increased participation by indigenous researchers in the 1993 symposium.

This book has been divided into four parts, according to the editing task, which conformed to the old quasi-geographical/cultural division of the Pacific into Australia,

Melanesia, Micronesia and Polynesia, and a pan-Pacific section. There will be, of course, critics of such a division, and we agree it is problematic, reflecting more than anything the history of academic research specialisation, but we plead expediency.

Notes

1.   Whether such a subject should be termed 'aesthetic anthropology' is debatable; perhaps the 'anthropology of art' would be more appropriate, since there seems to be a great deal of difficulty with the term 'aesthetics', as indicated in Dutton's review (1995b) of Weiner 1994. Of course, there are disagreements over what is 'art' and how it may be distinguished from 'craft' and other products of human activity, but it is a term that has a wider reference than 'aesthetics'. In effect, 'aesthetics', if it refers to the criteria used for making value judgements about works of art (again, a debatable definition), would become a *part* of the subject matter of the anthropology of art.

PART 1

Art as performance in Micronesia and Polynesia

Bernie Kernot

Art as performance touches on many dimensions of cultural activity. For most of the following papers, art is seen as performing within the political processes of their societies. Two of the papers pick up on aesthetics, though even here aesthetics and politics are intertwined in one of them. The aesthetics of the human body may be taken as an artistic performance in the paper contributed by Nancy Pollock.

In the case of Yapese dance, Konishi is concerned with the relationship between the aesthetics of dance and the Yapese social system. Formal linear dance (*churug*) is owned by local or kinship groups and performed competitively on important peaceful occasions under the aegis of the paramount chiefs.

Aesthetic evaluation of the dance performance is made with reference to the quality of *taqreeb*, meaning 'one', 'one united body' or 'oneness', which Konishi says is the key concept for dance performance as well as for Yapese society. The constraints of Yapese society require strong social bonding, loyalty, and obedience to the authority of chiefs and councils. Unity is thought of as an inner disposition as much as an external manifestation, so that the connotations of *taqreeb* extend to 'virtue'. Participation in a dance performance was, as Konishi observes, an act of allegiance to one's chief. The dance therefore appears to be both a symbolic expression of social and political unity and a means of securing it.

While evaluation of dance performances articulates ideals of unity and beauty, the linear formation of dance troupes refers metaphorically to the network of interactive villages known as *tha'* (literally 'goods tied to a rope'). Villages within the *tha'* network take turns at hosting dance performances, thereby strengthening the *tha'* line, while the dance leader is metaphorically the chief.

Hereniko's paper, reproduced here with permission from the *Contemporary Pacific*, examines the political roles of clowning in traditional and contemporary Polynesian societies. Ritual clowning, once widespread and institutionalised, provided an outlet for satirising and ridiculing chiefs and the power hierarchies they represent, as well as the flouting of established conventions. Ritual clowning, more so than the spontaneous secular clowning, tended to invert the established order, in that clowning roles were usually occupied by those at the lowest social stratum, but both forms were effective as an antidote to the abuse of power. While Hereniko concurs that such 'licensed disrespect' tended to reinforce the status quo and the structures of society, nevertheless clowns 'straddle the interface between order and disorder' and are therefore potentially threatening to the status quo.

This becomes critical in contemporary Polynesia, where changing patterns of political leadership create new tensions between 'chiefs' and people. Ritual clowning has nowadays become secularised and muted, but in the new political climate these old institutions have a vital role as sites for progressive forces in the political struggle, where leaders too easily lose touch with their people. Clowns can become the mouthpiece for the socially oppressed and provide a significant critique of the political process.

Changing politics within the Pacific in recent decades has seen the emergence of an indigenous critique of colonialism, and with it the politics of cultural and political identity. Stevenson contends that indigenous Pacific societies are redefining themselves politically and culturally, and sloughing off the negative values attributed to traditional cultures by colonial agencies.

An important vehicle in developing local and pan-Pacific cultural identities has been the Pacific Arts Festival. Cultural politics of the region has resulted in the canoe, the dance and art production as being at the core of these festivals. The various forms involved have been revitalised, reinterpreted or created anew as symbols of identity for new political communities and a growing consciousness of indigenous Pacific solidarity.

The Tahitian *heiva*, a century-old local festival, has enabled Tahitians to celebrate their traditions as well as generate a unique identity, of which the dance is a key feature. A large contingent of Tahitians participated in the 6th Pacific Arts Festival in Rarotonga in 1992, of which the *vaka* (canoe) was the major theme. Creativity in Tahitian dance and traditional arts, and revitalisation of many of the other arts and traditions of the Pacific, particularly in canoe construction, navigational skills and tattooing, raise questions of authenticity which Stevenson confronts by referring to the dynamism within traditional cultures and the changing cultural context of the contemporary Pacific. She also refers to the cultural politics involved in staging such festivals that bring dominant colonial and commercial interests into relationship with indigenous societies, observing how mixed agendas lie behind the staging of major festivals.

Festival and identity are also the subjects of Kernot's paper, though a festival of a different kind to that discussed by Stevenson. The New Zealand International Exhibition of 1906-07, modelled on the international fairs that followed the Great Exhibition in London in 1851, takes us back to the heyday of colonialism in the Pacific and the emerging national identity of New Zealand within the British Empire. The exhibition incorporated the cultures of British Polynesia, including the New Zealand Maori, Fijian, Cook Island Maori and Niuean, where they were subsumed under the greater glory of the British imperial mantle, represented by New Zealand settler society.

Kernot focuses on the Model Maori *Pa* as a significant feature of the exhibition. The exhibition itself represented a constructed image of the New Zealand nation as British, white and progressive, but with an acknowledgement of the Maori presence. However, as the construction of the *pa* demonstrated, the Maori place in the new nation was to be peripheral and decorative.

Although the Model *Pa* project was under the direction of a group of settler intellectuals, Maori participation in its construction and presentation was significant. Here another politic became apparent as an influential group of mainly young Maori leaders sought to construct an idealised version of the Maori past, and at the same time use the exhibition to promote this new image of Maoridom to other New Zealanders and to the world.

Meredith's paper raises old issues of the place of traditional arts in rapidly westernising cultures. She reviews the place of several traditional arts still current in American Samoa: tattooing, carving, *siapo* and weaving. All of these arts have been affected by modifications, sometimes major, sometimes minor, in media, technique, function and recruitment of experts. Tattooing survives vigorously in Western Samoa but is almost extinct in American Samoa. Furthermore, changes in domestic life now threaten the very transmission of the arts.

There are many echoes and convergences in arguments raised in past symposiums by Hirini Mead and Philip Dark in particular, but there are also significant differences of emphasis. Meredith argues from the subjective experience of an insider for a sense of cultural identity in a world where acculturative processes threaten to swamp traditional identities in tidal waves of westernisation. Her plea arises directly out of the personal experience of loss of contact with one's heritage and cultural roots, an experience she fears will overtake other American Samoans.

Meredith's perspective is that of an acculturated indigenous person. It is not an attack on colonisation as such, and in that she differs from that other indigenous voice, Hirini Moko Mead. She is accepting of the need to become part of the wider world culture, but looks for a distinctive Samoan identity within it. She looks to formal Western educational institutions to bring about a revival in the declining arts, as well as an opportunity for students to recover their artistic heritage. She wants to empower students in the American Samoan educational system to integrate their traditional heritage with the wider world culture that impinges so heavily on American Samoan life. Her paper contributes further to the discourse, already opened in previous symposiums, on the place of traditional arts in changing Pacific cultures.

The critical issue for Pollock is aesthetics rather than politics. Her paper considers the body as an art form in Nauru and Tahiti. Selected individuals were carefully groomed to meet local aesthetic criteria by the fattening and lightening of the skin. The evidence suggests that only high-ranking individuals were selected, but Pollock does not pursue the relationship of social status and aesthetics. She contrasts opposing cultural views, notably the 'fat is bad' view of biological science with the 'fat is beautiful' of local aesthetics. Body enhancement is not merely a biological phenomenon, and she argues it should be included within the discourse on aesthetics. It is a further category within the field of art and aesthetics to be added to those defined by Kaeppler (1989).

The relationship between the evaluations of dance performance and the social system in Yap, Micronesia[1]

Junko Konishi

'To read between the lines' are the words Kiener uses in his essay 'Yap between the lines'. He suggests that although foreign scholars studying Yap culture make, from the Yapese point of view, some laughable mistakes, Yapese do not like to disagree with them. Consequently, to know the Yapese one should leave one's preconceptions behind and keep one's eyes open (Kiener 1978:31). This view is unsatisfactory. If a Yapese is kind enough to tell a lie,[2] we should ask why he does through continual dialogue (Feld 1987). We are required to read the lines as well as to read between the lines, and this should be applied to any study of Yapese dance, though in a slightly different sense. I aim in this paper to read the 'line' of performers in Yapese dance.

'Line' seems to be one of the keys to understanding Yapese aesthetics. We see many aspects of Yapese material culture that are regular and in a line: the length of a grass skirt and the width of a fibre necklace are but two examples. *Malaal* (the traditional dance place) also looks like a line 2 to 3 metres wide. Yapese traditional money (large stone discs) placed in a leaning position on one or both sides of the *malaal*, in one or two rows, accentuates the line (fig. 1.1).

Many of the basic dance formations are in a row (or sometimes two). These lines can be observed by a researcher. But any interpretation of this leading to a definition of an aesthetic for Yapese culture 'should be grasped through the standards recognised by the society' (Kaeppler 1971:176).

Kaeppler also observed rightly 'the importance of the arts as part of culturally constructed social realities' (Kaeppler 1992:313). We may reasonably conclude that the ultimate function of Yapese dance is to present the unification of the community.

Pinsker takes a similar view and describes Micronesian dances as moving in unison, because 'unison dancing requires coordination and rehearsal makes unison performance an index of the viability and political cohesiveness of the presenting community' (Kaeppler 1992:313).

1.1 *Malaal* (traditional dance place) at Balebat village, viewed from the west. At the left side of the *malaal* is the *p'eebaey* (village public house). Beyond the *p'eebaey* is the sea.

1.2 Men's sitting dance *puluwlap* (a legendary spirit) performed on the *malaal* at Falebat village on 2 March 1985. The boy sitting on the far right is about three years old.

However, as Kaeppler pointed out, without an understanding of aesthetic systems, art as socially constructed knowledge or as systems of meaning cannot be understood (Kaeppler 1992:316). The purpose of this paper is to explore the relationships between the line and unity of Yapese dance, and between Yapese aesthetics and society.

Yapese dance in general

Yapese dance (*churuq*) incorporates the text and chanting as well as the body movements of the dance. Most of the dances[3] are performed by a group of men or women who sing at the same time, in leader-chorus form. There are three types of dance: *saak'iy* (standing gesture dances), *puul nga buut'* (sitting gesture dances), and *gamel'* (bamboo-stick dances). Dancers perform sitting or standing symmetrically according to their heights (usually the tallest individual is in the centre; fig. 1.2).

Except for a rhythmic accompaniment on bamboo sticks for *gamel'* and/or body percussion, no musical instrument is used. The performers' singing voices are the main musical element of dance performance. The body movements, as a rule, are made by all performers, although at the beginning of a verse the dance leader starts his or her gesture first to cue the other performers to begin. There is no solo part that attracts the soloist's movements. The melodies of the dance songs consist of repetitions of fixed patterns common to each dance genre.

The text consists of several stanzas. As texts of old dances include archaic Yapese or Ulithian words, or both, even elderly Yapese only understand these partially and have to memorise the text through pronunciation. 'It is clear that most of the songs relate mythological or historical events' (Smith 1980). It is more important to recite the text correctly than to know the content.[4] Accordingly, one could say that Yapese dance is a practice of the 'magical power of words' (Strathern 1995; Tambiah 1968). The vocal performance is of great importance in all ritual contexts and the power of the voice (*lungun*) is connected to the land (Brooks 1988:12-14; Labby 1976:16; Lingenfelter 1975:1; Ushijima 1987:124). It is possible to say, in a sense, that dance is performed to obtain wealth, strength and power from the ancestors, whose voices can be heard through the land (Brooks 1988:64; Montes 1893:21).

However, we should not overlook the fact that Yapese clearly differentiate between the recitation of dance texts and the utterance of conventional phrases in other rituals; the former is called, as mentioned above, *churuq*, while the latter is called *sabaathin* (talk). The difference may be explained by ownership or possession. The voice of a ritual usually belongs to land that belongs to an individual, while dance belongs to a village or kinship group. The notion of possession is strict, and it is interesting to note that a dance can be exchanged between villages for other valuables such as traditional money or goods, or both. Once a dance is 'sold' to another village, the previous owners will never perform it again. Because of this ownership system and the local differences in dialect, performances may be varied. Even a knowledgeable elder cannot always know all the dances in Yap.

The same may be said of *sabaathin* and *taang* (song). *Dulol'oy* (laments for the dead), which are performed by each woman of the kinship group in turn when a person dies and are continued until the deceased is buried, obviously have a melody pattern. However, this is not regarded as *taang* (a song or a chant). Yapese explain that *dulol'oy* is merely *sabaathin* because women talk to the dead about what they are immediately thinking about, whereas *taang* has a fixed text. The important criteria by which Yapese determine *taang* (and also *churuq*) is for 'the text to be fixed', and recognition of the possession of the text. *Sabaathin* can become *taang* when people recognise the owner of a text. To sum up, the recitation of a dance text for the Yapese is to confirm the possession of the villagers, which evokes dance in unison.

In a performance, some performers have individual roles, namely dance leader (*feek churuq*), soloist of the song (*mookol churuq*), and shouting person (*gofal*, also referred to as *ngus*). In some dances, a *ginaeng* (to surprise or startle someone, especially for the *täyoer* performance) or a *gashig* (for sitting dance) recites the text, usually before the solo chant. The performance usually begins with an introductory solo call by *feek churuq*, who is situated at the centre of the performers. This is followed by a strophe of chant by all the dancers. Near the end of the stanza and/or the performance, the *gofal* shouts encouragement and the dance is concluded by a shouted reply from all the dancers.

Traditionally, dance is performed by men or women (but not both together). The dance position, sitting or standing, implies social rank. Sitting is compared with authority, and standing with action (Brooks 1988:92; Müller 1917:257-8; Ushijima 1982:20). Thus, generally speaking, sitting dance is said to represent the higher status of dancers.[5] Such relationships of power can also be seen between performers and the audience (Iwata 1987:102). The audience always sits opposite the line of performers and watches to judge the performance (*teengog*) (fig. 1.3).

However, these descriptions of dance style, contents and semantics fail to account for the inevitable linear position of performers: why and how do Yapese know that their ancestors like to perform dances in a row (or two rows)? In fact, the linear position makes unification more difficult. The distances between *feek churuq*, who is always in the centre, and the individuals at either end (usually the youngest of the performers), means the latter cannot follow the leader's voice and movements.

Lawson has studied the significance of identity in Kiribati dance (1989:79-183). Comparing Yapese with Kiribati dance, one can observe common features, but also see that

the spatial arrangements of the Kiribati dancers – horseshoe, circle and semicircle (Lawson 1989:33-5) – are quite different. As for the semicircular or circular arrangement, she quotes Grimble and mentions that it represents 'canoes' or 'vessels' (Lawson 1989:33-5). Further observations about Kiribati spatial arrangements provide good information for comparison.[6] Here we are getting nearer to the problem of the line as an aspect of Yapese aesthetics.

Yapese evaluations of performances

As in the case of Kiribati, competition functions as the important means of social control in Yap (Lawson 1989:87).

1.3 Spectators gathered to see the events of Youth Week on 27 April 1991. Dance is one of the main attractions, and people gathered from all over the island to see it.

To borrow Lingenfelter's phrase, 'Power struggle is one of the major preoccupations of the Yapese, from the level of estate to that of paramount chiefs' (1975:175). War was one of the important ways for the council of chiefs (*puruy ko bulce'*) and the council of warriors (*puruy ko ulun*) to make decisions. On the other hand, *mitmiit* was one of the important peaceful occasions through which the paramount chiefs and their respective allies could compete openly, working outside the bounds of the cooperative council (Lingenfelter 1975:177). *Mitmiit* was also an important occasion for dance competition, and every dance was evaluated by the audience, especially by the old people. Dance was performed seriously, therefore, being bound in honour.

The Yapese expression for 'good' in its common sense is *maenigiil* or *feal'*. This is used for 'a good dance performance', as in *maenigiil* (or *feal'*) *e churuq*, and for 'a good voice' as *maenigiil* (or *feal'*) *e lungun*. *K'aelay*, which in one word also means 'a good dance performance', is peculiar to dance evaluation. To be evaluated *k'aelay*, all elements of the performance – such as singing voices, movements, ornaments, and the performers' minds – should be *maenigiil*.

The ideal voice for Yapese performance is also derived from a complex concept of their spirit, body sense, and cultural demand for singing (Konishi, in press). It is useful for the definition of the ideal voice to consider the conditions for a good singer. Yapese say that a singer who can pronounce the text clearly (*tamilaeng*, also referred to as *yaram, nga lungun*) with a long breath (*n'uw e nifeeng rok*), and with the correct interval (*ke'kaen e lam*) is good. The first two are, however, contradictory; the longer one's breath is, the richer the ornamentations, but the content of the text becomes unclear. Thus the notion of 'power of voice' or 'power of vocal sound' may be more applicable than that of 'power of words' for Yapese dance performance.

The expression 'correct interval' is different from its Western meaning. In Yap, there were no distinctive words referring to musical intervals before Western solmisation was introduced by Japanese in the middle of the l910s. It is only used to refer to modern types of music. The Yapese concept of musical intervals may be compared to 'wave' (Konishi 1995). Wavy patterns – that is, the upward and downward movements of a melody – which are conspicuous in traditional and modern music, indicate that the correct Yapese concept for interval means the shape of the melody movement rather than the interval.

A singer is required to know the text by heart, and not to become too nervous in a performance. As for range, volume and timbre, there are pairs of opposite words for bad qualities, such as too high and/or too loud, or too low and/or too quiet. One is *kethay/detaw* and the other is *taflang/polpol*. *Kethay* is when a fish is so heavy (big) it bites the bait off a hook; and *detaw* is when a gift is so poor that it does not reach its intended recipient because someone misappropriates it.[7] The latter connotes the *tha'* system. *Tha'* literally means 'goods which are tied to a rope' (fig. 1.4).

It is the network for transmission as 'the main instrument of administration of decision' where the 'enforcing of decisions is done through warfare, determined and organised at the outset by the councils' (Lingenfelter 1975:177). A gift used to be sent through this network but if it was too poor, someone might misappropriate it on the way so that the person could not receive it (*detaw*). *Taflang* and *polpol* are used to refer to ways of sleeping; *taflang* is 'to sleep on one's back', and *polpol* is 'to sleep on one's stomach'. However, a Yapese usually likes to sleep on his or her side, even if a mother lies with a baby. *Taflang*

1.4 The fish, tied to a bamboo stick, were gathered for a dead person.

and *polpol*, therefore, are not seen as being comfortable ranges and volumes of vocal performance.

'A good dancer' is called *tourug*. *Tourug* describes one whose eyes are fixed ahead and all of whose movements of the hands, arms, legs, face and hip are in the same direction without deliberate intention. One who intentionally seeks to be labelled *tourug* is called *kethmour*, which means 'going too far'; he or she is conscious of wanting to be *tourug*. *Tourug* refers to a genius, whereas a hard worker is called *cheag*. The former is considered better than the latter.

Even if there are some good singers and/or dancers in a performance, this is not enough for it to be given a high evaluation, namely *k'aelay*. The most important condition is that performers should be *taqreeb*; this literally means 'one', 'one united body' or 'oneness' (plates 1 and 2).

Thus, all the singing voices should be consistent with the movements of the performers. It is said that a *taqreeb* voice sounds like one person singing. *Taqreeb* is required not only in a unison part, but also in the changing part from *feek churuq* to *mookol churuq,* and *mookol churuq* to other parts. The change should be smooth so that the quality and the quantity of the voices appear the same. The roles of *feek churuq, mookol churuq* and *gofal* are very important because they have to unify more than thirty performers. *Feek churuq* should shout while thinking about the pitch and the loudness of the *mookol churuq*'s voice that follows; and *mookol churuq* should sing just like *feek churuq* but cheerfully, because the others who follow should be able to sing just as he or she does. In addition, singing that includes glissando and crescendo is considered better than that without these effects. Thus, *feek churuq* and *mookol churuq* should be good singers rather than good dancers. Moreover, as the meaning of *feek* ('to take, carry, get, bring, fetch'; Jensen 1977:18) indicates, *feek churuq* is also required to be a person who fetches the audience as well as leads performers. This is considered to be the result of one's good mind.[8]

Yapese believe that when the colour of the performers' skins look *reeqeaq* (bright), the performance will be successful, though even if it is shiny, performers can look *ruumoor* (dim). The reason for this could not be explained.

Reeqeaq could be recognised even by an outsider, as Furness described: 'truly they were a fine looking lot, clean of limb, and smooth and glistening of skin – the declining sun seemed to keep them in a continual barbaric shower of golden spangles' (1910:89). Such a visual effect may have been connected with the performers' yellow make-up of curcuma paste. Local medicine (*fuul 'ay*) and spells (*piig*) were also considered essential for a good performance, before the introduction of Christianity.

Dance performance in the Yapese society

Taqreeb, which literally means 'one', is not only the key concept for dance performance, but also for Yapese society. In Yap,

> individuals are distinguished according to age, sex, and kinship status in the family and are accordingly given access to food resources and space in the household … The relationships of individuals are seen in terms of the mutual exploitation of certain valued resources and the reciprocal obligations of cooperation and sharing. [Lingenfelter 1975:24-5]

The idea of *taqreeb* connotes 'virtue' as well as 'inevitability' for smooth social life. In traditional society, the political power of the paramount chief and two opposite councils of chiefs determined one's feeling of fullness and welfare, and even one's life; and all of the results (for example, the community centre, the road, and the honour brought about by a good dance performance) were eventually shared among all the individuals in the community. To gain rights to, or possession of, all the necessities for living, people had to obey as 'one united body' (*taqreeb*). A treasonable person, on the other hand, could be banished from the village, which meant almost certain death. Thus, participation in dance performance was an act of allegiance to one's chief. In this sense, Yapese dance is, as Brooks put it, 'a product of social practice and labor upon the body' (1988:132).

Before turning to the problem of dance as social labour, we must draw attention to the line as social reality. I have argued from the premise that Yapese dance is basically performed in one or two rows. However, there are descriptions of a 'round dance' on old recordings (Born 1903:9; Müller 1917:346; Senfft 1903:18)[9] (fig. 1.5).

A consideration of these helps to account for the meaning of linear position in the social context. Born's description of *dafell* seems to be that for *dafeal'* (Iwata 1985:9-10). Müller referred to it as *tafel* (1917:446). As Müller describes it, *dafeal'* was performed by a *miispil* (concubine of a men's house) and a group of men surrounding her at a men's house (*faeluw*). This practice disappeared when the Japanese administration (1914 to 1945) imposed a government ban on *miispil*. According to Müller and my informant, *dafeal'* was more a 'council song' than *churuq*, though this was sometimes accompanied by movements of the upper part of the performer's body.[10]

The next description of a round dance (Müller 1917: 346) is as follows: '*dilvaka'k* is a round dance. Boys and girls join hands and sing, dancing around a circle'. I do not believe this was a *churuq* because no-one else has described such a dance. It may have been a dance that was influenced by Europeans by way of the Marianas or elsewhere (Kennedy 1980). However, what can be accepted is that this is a children's play song (*taang ko bitiir*; Iwata 1985:11).

The last description of a 'round dance' was by Senfft (1903): 'There are smaller ones danced in a more intimate circle, for example, by women in memory of dead persons.' This is probably *umman* ('obscene women's dance'). It is referred to as *umon* by Müller (1917:451).

Except for *umman*, the other 'round dances', written about by Westerners in the early 20th century, are not *churuq* in the strict sense; they reflect more private or intensive conditions. *Dafeal'* was performed as an inner performance of young men in a village, for a *miispil* was often a girl stolen from another village. *Taang ko bitiir* can be regarded as out-of-law or more private, because they are out of the caste. *Umman* also may have been private. According to Senfft (1903) and Brooks (1988:138-9), *umman* is connected to a private ceremony (*gatsutsu*; or *kadschudschu* by Senfft) held by a chief. On the contrary, *churuq*, with its linear position, is performed in the more official or more extensive form.

The relationship between the line and unity

In Yap, every person's life is dependent on others, and every person from the youngest to the oldest has his or her role in helping others. A kinship group, or the village, is the unity for all individuals. If one pretends to obey the chief but has some artifice, unity will be broken. Similarly, if a dancer is thinking about something else, like attracting the opposite sex, unity will not be realised. *Feal' e taefnaey* ('good in mind'), which is considered to be the most important concept for Yapese, can be understood in this sense.[11] It is said that a person's behaviour and mind should desirably be *taqreeb* and that a good dance performer should appear to have a good mind. This philosophy is also applied as a standard for a good dance creator and/or teacher. It is said that he or she should be a person whose primary concern is dance, and that if he or she seeks to earn money by creating or teaching a dance, he or she cannot create a good dance or teach well. Thus, *taqreeb* is connected with something like virtue, which is within an individual, but emerges when he or she dances.

Let us now attempt to extend the observation whereby the meaning of *taqreeb* may be seen as 'beautiful'. There are many words that mean 'to gather' or 'gathering'. Jensen lists the following words: 'to gather, meet, collect, haul' – *gachiwor*; 'to pick coconuts, gather coconuts, harvest coconuts' – *fil*; 'to pick, gather, harvest, as coconuts' – *fool*; 'to collect, gather together' – *kunuuy*; 'gathering, group, assembly, collection' – *moekun, muukun*; 'gathering, meeting, collection' – *gachwor*; 'meeting, gathering,

1.5 The square position of *gamel'* (the bamboo-stick dance). *Gamel'* is often performed by groups of four people. However, the basic position is two rows.

assembly, group, collection' – *chowor, möqlung, muqlung*; 'pile, stack, group, collection, gathering, assembly' – *qulung* (Jensen 1977:116-17). Here we should add *cheag*, which is also an essential word for Yapese, to this list. The primary meaning of *cheag* is 'gather for working in one united body'. Other meanings are 'diligent', 'be good at doing something', 'stick with it', 'rich', and 'the same size or length of something'.

As I mentioned at the beginning of this paper, *taqreeb* connotes something beautiful. Things of the same length or size, which are also said to be *taqreeb*, seem to be desirable. Yapese try to gather the same size stones for making the foundation of a house, to cut grass for making a skirt the same length, to braid the mesh of a net for fishing with tight stitches, and so on (fig. 1.6).

In this sense, *cheag* implies almost the same meaning as *taqreeb*. The difference between *taqreeb* and *cheag* can be said to be that the former emphasises the result or purpose of gathering, while the latter emphasises the action of gathering. It must be recalled here that *cheag* is also used for a good dance performer who is not talented but is a hard worker. Thus, 'to gather' seems to be an essential concept for Yapese, and within this *taqreeb* is of prime importance.

Every *taqreeb* village is connected by a line of *tha'*. It can be said that the line of dance performers is a metaphor for the *tha'* network. *Feek churuq*, the dance leader and the person who decides the beginning of the dance, is compared to the paramount chief. It is said that 'nobody acts because his voice is sleeping, until the chief exercises his voice' (Ushijima 1982:51). The linear dance makes the *tha'* line stronger; dance performances should be held at villages in turn. If villagers A perform their dance at village B at the invitation of chief B, some day villagers B should perform at village A. A chief who issues an invitation should prepare food and drink for the performers and guests, and give traditional money or, today, cash as a token of thanks. From the very beginning, dance performance was immaterial 'property' for trade with the outer islands (Smith 1980).

It may be worth noting the concept of *maenigiil* (good) with reference to *kethay* (too high/too loud) and *detaw*

1.6 The stone foundation or platform *(wunbey)* of *p'eebaey* at Balebat village. Stones of the same size are preferred for its construction.

(too low/too quiet). As the meaning of the latter two are clear, *maenigiil* seems to be 'medium', somewhere in between.

Here I would like to outline a *kaakroom* (ancient story) of Walathol. Walathol was a giant (as tall as two coconut trees) who lived on a legendary island. One day, he made friends with a couple of fishermen from the southern part of Yap. Walathol always helped with their work. However, the fishermen were blamed by the villagers because they did not participate in constructing a new house but were absorbed in fishing. They asked Walathol to help and at last it was completed. Walathol was treated to all kinds of delicacies. However, because he needed too much food eventually he was burnt to death by the villagers (Anefal, n.d.).

This tells us about two important Yapese notions: one who does not participate in the work ordered by the chief will be punished; and he who is too big is not good because he needs too much food. Accordingly, the notion of 'medium' as good may be connected with the sharing of the necessities of life; that is, to the optimum way of living on a small island with limited resources.[12] The people had to cultivate gardens so that everyone could eat, and construct roads and meeting houses. Because these tasks were difficult and conducted without the aid of present-day technology, the villagers had to work 'in one united body'. When a Yapese thanks others for doing work, this is expressed in the Yapese term for 'thank you', *ka mu magaer*. Its literal meaning is 'you are tired'. In other words, it could be said that Yapese people are connected by their work. Thus, *taqreeb*, which is the basis for many aspects of life, also supports dance performance 'in line' as an expression of the social system in Yap.

Notes

1. This is an expanded and revised version of a paper read at the Fifth International Symposium of PAA, and Konishi 1993. The field data was collected in 1985, 1990, 1991, 1992 and 1993. I wish to thank the Yapese people, particularly Fanepin (Rull), Falmed (Tamil), Fathebyad (Maap), Gilitomam (Rull), Mangabchan (Fanif), Manngul (Maap), Pong (Tamil), Ruechieng (Tamil), Tethin (Gagir), and others I cannot mention here. I thank Isabel M. Runrgrad, the librarian at Yap State Public Library, for providing me with material, Professor Yamaguti Osamu for reading the entire text in its original form, Dr Margaret McKenzie for valuable advice, and Terence A. Lancashire for checking my English. I gratefully acknowledge helpful discussions and suggestions with and from Dr Barbara B. Smith on several points in the paper.

2. I was disappointed to discover that the following obtained materials were 'counterfeits'; that is, the texts, that had been recorded in the 1930s and edited in *Call of the Morning Bird* (Tatar 1985), were recordings of a Western composer, as were even my previous recordings. I presented a paper about this (Konishi 1995b) and pointed out the necessity of considering the relationship between performers and researchers in a historical context. In addition to this, it is important to bear in mind that what seems to be counterfeit sometimes means 'a different idea' among villages, although Yap is a small land

(approximately 5000 people in 110 square kilometers). To lessen this problem, I put the same questions to several knowledgeable people who were from other villages, whom I list in Note 1. They sometimes gathered in one place to discuss with me, and I then integrated their opinions. I name the informants who give a particular opinion.

3. The modern dances such as *maas* (marching dance, since the late 1930s) and 'discotheque dance' (since the early 1970s) are the exceptions. The accompanying music of *maas* is a series of *teempraa* (Japanese-influenced popular songs) sung by a soloist and/or sometimes the tunes of a harmonica. These are ignored in the following descriptions.

4. *Täyoer* (asking dance), which is created for a particular occasion in the current Yapese, is an exception. The test comes from asking a high-ranking person (for example, the chief of the host village was usual, but now the governor of Yap or even God is included) for goods, money, or providence. The person to whom the dance is addressed should grant the request.

5. This does not always mean that the sitting dance is more worthy than the standing dance (see Smith 1980).

6. Information on Melanesian 'anticlockwise' dance movement has been provided by Crowe (1990).

7. Information provided by Mangabchan.

8. Information provided by Falmed.

9. There are some other descriptions about 'round dance' which obviously mention *gamel*'; for example, Volkens (1901:12), and so on. It is true that some positions of *gamel*' look like a 'round'. However, this is rather square, which is a variation of two rows. All such descriptions are ignored here.

10. Information provided by Pong (1985). Re *dafael*', Marshall (1994:32-3), referring to the description of Born, points out that Born was mistaken in his classification of *dafell* as a *churu*, and that *mespil* would have composed it. I agree with her, but suggest that Müller's following description, which she missed, serves as evidence for our opinions: 'For the *tafel*, the men sit in a circle around a girl and sing in unison' (1917:446).

11. Yamaguti (Yamaguchi) (1986:588) quotes the following saying in Belau from McKnight (1968:11): 'Put out your arm and a man's hand will reach back.' (This is the proper spirit of cooperation and mutual aid.) The Belauan notion of 'back' may be useful for further comparison with the Yapese spirit.

12. Lawson refers to the case of Kiribati (1989:97-8).

Clowning as political commentary: Polynesia – then and now[1]

Vilsoni Hereniko

Every chief needs a clown. Thus, in Tonga and Samoa, two Polynesian societies marked by hierarchy in the social order, chiefs had in their retinue one or two clowns, who were an integral part of their court. Writing of Samoa in 1884, Turner notes that 'court buffoons' amused people at festivals and meetings by their 'dress, gait, or gesture, or by lascivious jokes …'.[2] Gifford's account of jesters who amused Tongan chiefs refers to a man called Kaho from Vava'u who made fun of people and indulged in witty remarks. This same jester, on one hilarious occasion, was carried to a feast tied up like a pig (Gifford 1929:129).

These clowns amused the chiefs (and their subjects) by providing an alternative view of humanity that was normally suppressed in the interest of group harmony and cohesion. Because of their low position in the social ladder, clowns were more in touch with the common folk and their preferred linguistic code and down-to-earth view of society. And they were able to present a populist view (humorous or absurd) that would otherwise be inaccessible to chiefs. In this sense, clowns became mediators between commoners and chiefs. And chiefs were constantly reminded of their subjects and aspects of themselves that they had rejected in favour of power and prestige.

Within the larger social context, ritual and secular clowning, rehearsed or improvised, were avenues through which society inspected itself and commented upon its rules and regulations, and the ways in which the imposition of structure and hierarchy constrained and stifled creativity and individual expression. Through role-reversal and inversion of societal norms, an alternative world view was explored within the frame of play. The message 'this is play' masked the seriousness of important messages that were disguised in laughter but nonetheless experienced and felt. Ambiguity reigned, and individuals who were lampooned through a comic sketch were therefore chastised in a manner that allowed for the saving of face; humour deflected attention to the entertainment aspect of clowning performances.

This paper examines the nature and role of clowning as a critique of indigenous authority and the power structure in Polynesia, which includes the islands within the boundaries of Hawai'i in the north, Easter Island in the east, New Zealand in the south, and Fiji in the west.

I use the term 'clowning' here to refer to public behaviour that causes overt signs of mirth or laughter, and the term 'clown' as a gloss for jester, fool, or comedian. I begin with a description and discussion of clowning performances, in various parts of Polynesia, that criticised authority and foreign influences, followed by a brief analysis of clowning theories and how they relate to Polynesian clowning.

My proposition here is that the indigenous institution of clowning in Polynesia was and is an antidote to the abuse of power. Schweder (1991) expresses this view well when he says that 'every court needs a jester, just as it needs a king, and a loyal opposition'. He adds that the thought of absolute power will eventually go to the head of the king, so to speak; also, there is 'madness in the methods of even the most loyal opposition'. It is therefore most important that the jester not lose his head (Schweder 1991:358). Instead of thinking of the clown as just an oddity, this view challenges us to acknowledge that the clown's role carries an important responsibility, not just to the king's court, but to the chief's retinue, and society.

I do not doubt for a moment that the clown's critical commentary would be valuable for contemporary chiefs. An analysis of the literature on chieftainship, reinforced by personal experiences, reveals much disappointment and dissatisfaction with modern leaders, many of whom are traditional chiefs in their own right. Albert Wendt of Samoa, the Pacific's most perceptive and talented novelist, sums up the general view of chiefs well when he says that corruption is so rife and open in his country today that what he saw in a recent visit made him want to weep (Wendt 1993a). He extends this view to the rest of the Pacific:

> I have watched the euphoria of independence throughout the Pacific degenerate after ten years into political corruption, and how our people become involved in that. Our new leadership, our new elite, of which I am a member, is carrying out a form of colonialism which may even be worse than what we got rid of. [Wendt 1993b]

Epeli Hau'ofa, the Pacific's foremost comic satirist, concurs in his observation:

> It is the privileged who decide on the needs of their communities and the directions of development and whose rising aspirations and affluence entail the worsening conditions of the poor. [Hau'ofa 1987:11]

But chiefs are not wholly to blame for the dilemma they are in. Precariously perched on a crumbling mountain, they are tempted to resort to any means necessary to maintain their balance. Meanwhile, commoners chip away, aided by social, economic, and political forces, within and without. Determined to level out the soil and reconfigure the contours of the mountain, the new educated elite (who are 'chiefs' in the modern sense) are a threat to the power base of traditional chiefs. But these new leaders are not necessarily more humane than their counterparts. This paper therefore includes traditional and modern leaders (many of whom are non-indigenous to the islands) in its broad definition of the word 'chiefs'; this term includes anyone in a political position of influence and therefore susceptible to abuse of power, as well as foreigners, and foreign institutions and practice that are deemed by locals to be in a position of influence.

As evidence in support of my position *vis-à-vis* clowns and chiefs, I cite examples that range back and forth in time and space, dealing with historical descriptions as well as personal observations and academic studies. I also attempt to identify the linkages between these sources as well as the relevant issues.

Secular and ritual clowning

Clowning traditions of Polynesia have survived to the present, albeit in a much diluted and reconstituted form, in Tonga, Samoa, Rotuma, Fiji, Tokelau, and Hawai'i. Contemporary practices of these indigenous forms serve the same or similar purposes and employ the same or similar techniques, particularly in the rural areas. In the urban centers or the cities of the contemporary Pacific, chiefs or their modern counterparts no longer, or rarely, have access to this populist link with the masses. Instead, the role of the clowns or jesters has been taken over by newspapers, television and other media. Sometimes, chiefs resort to suing the press for real or imagined misrepresentation; either that, or they try to legislate censorship and thereby curb opposing or alternative views. A better alternative would have been to encourage an indigenous form of critique that has proven effective in the past. This indigenous form of critique called clowning may be divided into secular and ritual clowning.

Secular clowning occurs spontaneously, a function of our common humanity. Inspired by the prevailing atmosphere of the social occasion, any individual may entertain the assembled company by clowning. Performing ludicrous antics for only a few seconds or minutes, the secular clown – if such a one springs up from among the spectators –

momentarily releases tension: at work parties, weddings, anywhere. The person who is a natural humorist employs wit, irony, parody, punning, gesturing – indeed, any means imaginable – to entertain the assembled company. To limit the occasions when secular clowning can occur or to limit the techniques that may be used is to disregard the spontaneous and fluid nature of secular clowning. Also, in a gathering in which everyone is having a good time, there is no restriction on the number of clowns. In these circumstances, everyone could conceivably become clowns, since the secular clown is self-appointed.

The target of secular clowns may be those in authority, someone in the audience, the values of the dominant class, or anyone and anything. If the clown is an integral part of a formal dance, then he or she usually acts as a kind of master of ceremonies – calling out instructions, weaving in and out among the dancers, livening things up, and acting as a link with the audience. This role existed in the Rotuman traditional dance called *tautoga* and some club or spear dances of Fijians.[3] In the latter case, the clown is called *veli ni meke*, '*veli* of the dance', with *veli* referring to a rustic gnome living in the bush, who supposedly provided the inspiration for the dance. Usually the clown's behaviour contrasts starkly with that of the dignified and orderly arrangement of the dancers. In the Samoan *siva* and Tongan *tau'olunga*, the male dancers who clown around at the periphery pay respect to the dancer(s) at the center. Their disorderly behaviour enhances the gracefulness and the control of the middle dancer(s). (See also Shore 1977:453.) This juxtaposition, with the periphery paying respect to the center through clowning antics, is analogous to ritual clowning.

In ritual clowning, the chief and clown relationship and their dependent yet opposed positions in the social hierarchy, are a recurring theme. Ritual clowning is customary, with the community sharing an implicit set of understandings, one of which is the gender of the clown. For example, in Rotuma, the ritual clown at traditional weddings is always female, chosen by the relatives of the bride, and past child-bearing age. In Samoa and Fiji, the ritual clown is customarily male. Further, in old Samoa, Tokelau, and Tahiti, the ritual clown was a medium of the spirits;

in Fiji and Rotuma, the clown was a representative of the spirits. This link with the supernatural, however, has more or less disappeared, although transvestism was, and is, still typical, and so is the ridiculing of those in authority (particularly chiefs or males) and foreigners or foreign traits. Sometimes the ritual clown deliberately instigates laughter amid serious ritual. This conjunction between the serious and the humorous has various permutations: in Fijian cannibalistic feasting, in Rotuman weddings, and in the comic sketches of Samoa, Tonga, Tokelau, Tahiti, Marquesas, Cook Islands and Hawai'i.

The dramatis persona of a ritual clown is ambiguous: male and female, human and divine, serious and comic. Although the human body is the primary medium of communication in Polynesia, puppets were employed in Hawai'i and New Zealand; also, a type combining strings and rods existed in Mangaia (Luomala 1973:28) and possibly Easter Island.[4] The playful frame in which the clowns or puppets perform, and the costumes of motley and assorted objects they wear or carry, marginalises the clowns from mainstream society, distances their criticism, and makes their biting satire palatable. Criticism is therefore usually accepted in good humour.

Studies of Polynesian clowning concur that this form of licensed disrespect reinforces the status quo and the structure of society. However, because of the inversion of the social order and the ridicule and mockery of chiefs or those in positions of authority, as well as the flaunting of conventions, clowning is potentially a creative and progressive force that threatens to unhinge the foundations upon which society is built. Clowns straddle the interface between order and disorder, a foot in either camp, assembling and disassembling, forever confounding any attempts to decode their true intent and the meanings of their communication. But deconstruction is a must, as long as we are aware that the meanings of clowning are multiple and that there is no single definitive interpretation.

Criticism of chiefs, men and authority

The ritual clowns are often from the lowest stratum in society: in Samoa, the lead comedians in a *fale aitu* ('house of the spirit') sketch are usually young untitled men; in Rotuma, the *han maneak su* ('woman who plays the wedding') is always someone of low rank who is past child-bearing age; in Tahiti, only the lower grades indulged in the so-called 'obscene' practices of the *arioi* (Webster 1968:164-7). In customary frames of 'privileged licence', these common folk lampooned the manners of their chiefs and others who ruled over them. This practice is less prevalent today; when it does occur, the ritual clowns tend to be fearful of the chiefs and reluctant to play their role to the hilt. My study of the Rotuman ritual clown and the records of past practices in different parts of Polynesia (some of which appear below) provide supporting evidence.

Rotuman clowning at weddings (or mat-weaving rituals of old) is improvised and therefore fragmented. I have written extensively about Rotuman clowning elsewhere and will simply reiterate here that the female ritual clown, who dressed like a man in the past but wears a dress in contemporary practice, parodies the behaviour of male chiefs. She prances around wielding a stick and orders people, particularly the chiefs and the men, to do her bidding – she forces them to dance in the sun, kneel on the ground, sit down, stand up, or do whatever she fancies. Having temporarily relinquished his powers to the ritual clown, the district chief, whom the clown would normally obey, becomes a target for the clown's antisocial behaviour. Through ridicule and parody, the district chief and other dignitaries experience being common and being ordered around. Although at the end of the wedding chiefs resume their privileged status while the clown returns to being an ordinary housewife, this role-reversal, theoretically, provides an opportunity in which chiefs can learn humility. Wise chiefs take note of the messages communicated through clowning.

Several accounts of Tahitian clowning also suggest that those in positions of authority were ridiculed in comedic performances. Unlike ritual clowning in Rotuma, Tahitian clowning by the *arioi* society occurred in the frame of a comic sketch driven by a plot. Comprising young men and women, the *arioi*'s members travelled from island to island performing dances and comic sketches. In 1774, Captain Cook saw upwards of sixty canoes of *arioi*

performers as they were leaving Huahine to visit neighbouring islands (cited in Angas 1866:297; see also Andersen 1969:437). Prior to their departure, pig sacrifices and large quantities of fruits were offered to the god 'Oro (Angas 1866:296-7). Oliver, whose descriptions of the *arioi* in the context of Tahitian society is one of the most informative, lists twelve different descriptions for the *arioi*, ranging from 'a society of comedians', to 'human harpies … in whose character and habits all that is most loathsome – earthly, sensual, devilish – was combined' (see Oliver 1974:913-14 for summary).

Amusements of the *arioi* were generally held at night, with fires and candlenut tapers providing illumination. Sometimes performances were held in the open air, or on the canoes as they approached the shore, but more frequently they occurred under the cover of houses erected for public entertainment (Muggridge, cited in Oliver 1974:920; see also Forster 1777:398-9 for another description). High stools and seats for the chief *arioi* of both sexes were positioned on a high platform erected at one end, while the comedians performed at the centre of the building, presided over by the *arioi-hi'o-niao* (master of ceremonies). According to Henry (1928:237-41), 'the actors flattered or ridiculed with impunity people and even priests, from the greatest to the least, and they often did much good in causing faults to be corrected'. Andersen lends support by describing the *arioi* as similar to European medieval minstrels and the actors in the mystery and morality plays (Andersen 1969:437). He adds that in their dramatic performances, the priests and others were 'fearlessly ridiculed' (Andersen 1969:438).

According to Angas (1866:296) and Webster (1968:164-70),[5] a kindred society of the *arioi* existed in the Marquesas, Caroline Islands, New Zealand, Mangareva, Tuamotu, Ladrone Islands (Marianas), Cook Islands (Rarotonga) and Hawai'i.

Like the Tahitians, Samoans performed plotted sketches when they travelled from one village to another during excursions they called *malaga*. Sloan records in 1941 the presence of an acting group in each village in Samoa, and an ability to 'put on any one of a hundred different plays with only a few days' notice' (Sloan 1941:110). Like the *commedia dell'arte* that originated in Italy and was popular from the 16th to the 18th century in Europe (for example, see Caputi 1978), troupes of *fale aitu* actors were a constant source of amusement and a popular way of commenting on society's affairs.[6] As in Rotuma and Tahiti, clowning was often anti-establishment. It occurred within the frame of a *poula* ('teasing night') that was held during a *malaga*, in which there was oratory, dancing, singing, and *fale aitu* sketches.

The gathering of old people at dusk to sing and dance for each other began the *poula*.[7] After dark, when the old people had left, young men and women entered and sat at opposite ends of the *fale aitu*. The singing and dancing, which began slowly, built up in tempo as they also became increasingly ribald and erotic, culminating in the young people embroiled in a wild sexual frenzy. At this point, someone shouted 'I see the ghost; he is coming!' and everyone rushed into the darkness, where they indulged in sexual intercourse. After the sexual act, the young men and women returned to the *fale aitu* for the performance of comic sketches (John Kneubuhl 1993). At the center of these comic sketches that Shore calls a 'Samoan vision, albeit a comic vision, of social disorder' (Shore 1977:333) is the lead comedian, who is male but adopts the ambiguous persona of a ghost and is often referred to as *aitu* (Shore 1977:318). According to Victoria Kneubuhl (1987:167), *aitu* are associated with chaos, wilderness, danger and darkness. Since the lead comedian is a transvestite assuming the persona of a ghost, these dual roles reinforce the marginal position of the comedian on stage, distance him – the roles serve the same function as masks – and free him from taking responsibility for what happens within the comic frame (Shore 1977:333).

Rather than maintain an illusion of being an *aitu* while in role, the lead comedian continually breaks out of role to remind the audience of his real identity (Shore 1977:333). Is he a ghost masked as transvestite, or is he just a man? Is it Petelo the infallible ghost speaking, or is it the fallible man (Shore 1977:365)? This constant shifting in and out of character leads Shore (1977:334) to assert that 'comic virtuosity makes the clown at once admirable, dangerous, and funny'. This ambiguous persona and the sanctioned frame allows the clown to criticise and be able to get away with it.

Commentators on the *fale aitu* attribute the following functions to this social institution. Victoria Kneubuhl (1987:166-76) views *fale aitu* as important for the release of tension through laughter, and the gaining of relief from the constraints of regimented daily routine; Shore (1978:178) highlights the value of the *aitu* in dealing 'with certain kinds of conflict where direct confrontation is culturally impossible or problematical'. Possible conflict in relations of complementarity that overtly deny the possibility of conflict – such as that between chiefs and their subjects or between the sexes – are dealt with covertly in the safe arena of the comic sketch (Shore 1978:197-8). Sinavaiana's work focuses primarily on contemporary practice in Western Samoa, and though she concurs with the prevailing views of Kneubuhl and Shore, she notes that in recent years a lead comedian can be fined for being too skilful at the art of comedy. According to an informant,

> the village pastor was being lampooned so skilfully and accurately, that the pastor himself laughed hard enough to fall from his chair in the audience, and later the comedian was fined. [Sinavaiana 1992b]

The imposition of a fine on a comedian whose role was customarily sanctioned by the spirits is significant. It reflects changes in the way a traditional institution is viewed today.

A brief foray into the early Fijian material reveals practices that are no longer followed but are nevertheless instructive about the role of Fijian clowns, who Clunie and Ligairi prefer to call 'masquers' because of their link with the supernatural (Clunie and Ligairi 1983). In Fiji, the most eagerly anticipated event of the pre-Christian social calendar was the 'invoking of *tabu* harvesting embargoes and … the *i sevu* harvest festival' (Clunie and Ligairi 1983:57). At such festivals, first fruits were offered to the gods and to the chiefs, the gods' representatives on earth.

The yam harvest was regarded as the most important crop, and when yams grew abundantly their harvest signalled a season of plenty. During the months building up to the yam or crop harvest, certain prohibitions were placed on crops, fish and other livestock. Dances were rehearsed and artefacts produced in preparation for exchanges between the hosts and the visitors. There was great anticipation as people looked forward to witnessing the performances of the masquers, who 'on this day could mock earthly authority with a licence normally undreamt of' (Clunie and Ligairi 1983:57).

An 1840s account of a first-fruits *(i sevu)* presentation involving the Roko Tui Dreketi (high chief) of Rewa, records a masque dressed as a sailor who, upon being reminded that he was in the presence of Tui Dreketi,

> immediately asked who Tui Dreketi was, and could not be made to understand, till some of them looked in the direction the king was sitting, when he pointed (which is greatly against the rules), and asked if that was the 'old bloke', walking up to him bolt upright and offering his hand, which the king smilingly shook. The sailor then told him he had better take a whiff or two with him, as it was the best tobacco he had smoked for many a day. The king, willing to make the best of the amusement, took the pipe, the spectators making the air ring again with their shouts of laughter. [Jackson (William Diaper), cited in Clunie & Ligairi 1983:60]

Like ritual clowns in Rotuma, Samoa and Tahiti, the Fijian clown or masque had licence to ridicule his superior. This symbolic inversion of hierarchy allows the clown's superior to display a side of his character that is otherwise hidden from the general public. Here, the chief's elevated position is collapsed as both clown and chief meet as actors in a play who can appreciate and celebrate their shared humanity, of which humour is an integral part.

Apart from clowning during first-fruit festivals, clowning also occurred in cannibalistic feasting. Writing in 1884, Britton describes twenty bodies at a cannibal feast being subjected to all kinds of indignities, then presented at the temple and accepted by the priests as a peace offering to god. The faces of the dead bodies were painted with vermilion and soot to give them a lifelike appearance:

> Next a herald advanced in presence of the multitude, and touching each ghastly corpse in turn in a friendly way, the proudest silence being preserved by the spectators, ha-
> ranguered it in a jocular manner, expressing his extreme regret at seeing such a fine fellow in so sorry a plight, asking if he did not feel ashamed of himself after his recent loud boasting from behind the fortress, and wondering why he should have ventured so far down the hill, unless it was to see his dear friends of Ramaka. Finally the herald expressed them in more excited strains, and wound up by knocking the bodies down like so many ninepins, amid shouts of laughter from the bystanders. [Britton 1884:144]

The bodies were then dragged away to be dissected and consumed. According to Britton, revelry and mirth were very much part of human feasts of this nature, particularly when strong opposing chiefs were captured. Not even death could prevent the Fijian custom of mocking chiefs in the cause of laughter.

Clowning has a levelling effect. Through mocking laughter, imbalances in the power structure can be restored. This example from Adrian Tanner, an anthropologist who did field research in the villages of Savatu in Central Viti Levu in 1986 (in Nagatagata particularly), provides further evidence in support of this observation (Adrian Tanner, pers. comm., Kauai, 1990). According to him, the context was a gift-giving ritual held at the husband's village years after a couple had been married; in this case the couple had had at least three children. As the 'bride' walked across a mat, with her classificatory brothers and uncles following behind her, the women of the 'groom's' *mataqali* ('tribe') mock-attacked the men, who accepted this 'ambush' in good humour.

Tanner observed other women clowning later in the day. He reported two women, dressed in men's overalls, who appeared riding hobbyhorses and displayed mock hostility towards the men who were drinking *yaqona*. Their appearance was sudden, and they paraded in front of the men, goading them to react.

In addition, Tanner described an all-female *yaqona* ceremony that was attended by his wife. The women drank *yaqona* and performed some 'lewd' dancing among themselves. At the very end of the festivities, an elderly woman from the bride's side was seen chasing an old man from the groom's side across the village green, as though to rape him. She then indulged in sexual gesturing, to the amusement of the crowd.

The occasions described above were inverse manifestations of gender and inter-village relations. According to Tanner, these villagers were probably enemies in the past but are now friends; mock aggression or criticism within this context therefore allowed old enemies to express hostility but not threaten the friendship. Women who were usually regarded as inferior to men were able to act out their antagonistic feelings towards men by dressing up and behaving stupidly. After all, men and women have to live together, and women cannot overthrow the men. They can, though, challenge men symbolically. Also, as the bride's side received more than was given away, her classificatory brothers 'paid' for this imbalance by tolerating mock antagonism from the women of the husband's side. Reciprocity is an important feature of Fijian life, although it is possible to be too generous and to appear too pushy. The mock attack restored the balance.

A social-control function is also apparent in the Hawaiian *hula ki'i*, in which ancient Hawaiians used puppets dressed up to represent human beings. The puppets, which were about one-third life size, were held by a performer (or performers) who stood behind a screen.[8] The performer manipulated the movements of the puppet from under its clothing so that its movements were appropriate and in time with the action of the play, while at the same time reciting the words that were apparently being uttered by the puppet. Sometimes human dancers imitated the puppets (Luomala 1984:5). Emerson claims that interest in the actual performances of this type of *hula* was stimulated by byplay and buffoonery:

One of the marionettes,[9] for instance, points to some one in the audience; whereupon one of the hoopaa [members of the hula company who are instrumentalists sitting still] asks, 'What do you want?' The marionette persists in his pointing. At length the interlocutor, as if divining the marionette's wish, says: 'Ah, you want So-and-so.' At this the marionette nods assent, and the hoopaa asks again, 'Do you wish him to come to you?' The marionette expresses its delight and approval by nods and gestures, to

the immense satisfaction of the audience, who join in derisive laughter at the expense of the person held up to ridicule. [Emerson 1965:93]

According to Emerson (1965:94), the songs of the *hula ki'i*

may be characterized as gossipy, sarcastic, ironical, scandal-mongering, dealing in satire, abuse, hitting right and left at social personal vices – a cheese of rank flavour that is not to be partaken of too freely. It might be compared to the vaudeville in opera or to the genre picture in art.

It is not clear if royalty were also ridiculed in such performances; however, it is conceivable that out-of-favour *ali'i* were sometimes targets for ridicule. Luomala (1984:71) lends support:

By means of humor and insouciance the composers of hula ki'i meles [sic] and skits violated everyday restraints on speech and behaviour and delighted in vicarious defiance of them. After all, the puppets were only wooden figures behaving outrageously, and not real people.

According to Luomala (1984:98), the illusion that the puppets were real human beings was maintained sometimes by the puppeteers speaking directly with the spectators. Generally, the puppets provided a distancing effect by becoming personae that were social intermediaries and commentators; their barbs of ridicule and criticism were therefore tolerable. The separation between audience and actors, however, preserved the mysterious aloofness. A member of the audience who was lured onto the stage usually ended up looking ridiculous in a setting in which to behave and look normal is to be out of place.[10] As is typical of the *fale aitu* sketches, a certain amount of improvisation ensured that the acting and dialogue were relevant and dynamic.

Criticism of foreign men and foreign influences

Colonial government brought with it foreign men and institutions that soon became as powerful, if not as oppressive, as the indigenous institution of chieftainship. Subsequently, clowning became a form of anticolonial or counter-hegemonic form of commentary in which that which was foreign became the theme of numerous comic sketches. Using mimicry and parody, Polynesians, like colonised people elsewhere, satirised foreigners or foreign institutions and practices in order to demystify or resist them. Jersey records in 1893 (p. 257) an account in which

> two or three of them [clowns] jumped up and began to act with immense spirit, great contortion of face, and an enjoyment so keen that it could not fail to communicate itself to onlookers. One series of gesticulations was supposed to represent 'German fashion'; the imitation of walk and countenance was hardly complimentary to the supporters of the late Tamasese.

Sloan (1941:78) records a parody of his own behaviour:

> I was ill prepared to see a huge hulk of a man come prancing out into the center of the room, wearing my best white suit, my sun helmet and a pair of tennis shoes – on the wrong feet – all of which he had borrowed from my trunk unknown to me. His face was smeared with white lime, and he was grinning from ear to ear as in mock majesty he strutted out before us, trailing a long heavy rope over his shoulder. Reaching the center of the room, he turned and began to pull and tug on the rope as if it were anchored to a tree. At last he dragged into view a small, protesting boy who had the other end of the rope tied round his neck. Cradled in the boy's arms was a huge basket which the clown took from him and tore open. After peering intently inside for a moment he gave a joyful shout and pulled from it a black box which had been cleverly fixed up to look like my camera.
>
> With great ado he pushed and twisted at imaginary knobs and gadgets on it to satisfy himself that it was ready for the first shot. He then tripped daintily to where I sat and contorted himself into every position imaginable, getting from the crowd a twitter of ill-concealed giggles, before he pressed the trigger of a big bamboo clapper, flattened on one side that was supposed to be the shutter release. It went off with a bang like a firework, and the clown fell down backwards as if he had been bowled over by the kick of a double-barreled shotgun. The crowd roared with laughter, and I joined in too, laughing till my sides ached.

In August 1992, I witnessed a sketch in which masculine Samoan men, dressed in ridiculous modern female attire (complete with lipstick and high heels), vied for first place in a beauty pageant. As they trippingly entered the stage and parodied femininity in front of a mixed audience, the crowd screamed with delight and surprise, if not shock. This comic sketch was an imitation of males imitating females, a phenomenon that the actors associate with modern development, as evidenced by their choice of attire, use of the English language, and the female stars they parodied. When the master of ceremonies asked the lead comedian if he-she had any final comment to make, he replied: 'The University of the South Pacific is full of poofters!'

What is one to make of this comic sketch? On first impression, these brave and masculine men seemed to be satirising modernisation and its concomitant institutions of homosexuality, cross-dressing and pop culture. As each male appeared in drag that displayed individual imagination and attention, he-she portrayed a parodic view of the *fa'afafine* ('the way of women') that was ridiculous, shameful, and therefore negative. Like the Tahitian *mahu*, the equivalent of the Samoan *fa'afafine* (see Levy 1991:16-20; 1993:472-3), these negative images reminded men in the audience of how they were not supposed to behave or dress (see also Mageo 1992:443-59). Also implied was a rejection of homosexuality or transvestism in favour of the indigenous view of the ideal Samoan male.

Unlike Samoa, where the *fale aitu* is a male domain, in Tokelau the women play a role equal to men. The contexts, however, are similar and village-wide events such as weddings, feasts and cricket matches are the preferred occasions. The skits usually involve two characters playing out mock family quarrels. A classic performance is a domestic dispute between husband and wife; Tokelauans find this hilarious because the male and female having the dispute are 'brother' and 'sister' or similarly related.[11]

During the performance of a comedic sketch described by Huntsman and Hooper (1975:415), the women, who are mothers and wives in middle-age or older, wear 'European shirts, ties, coats, trousers and shoes, garments crumpled and filthy, trouser flies gaping open and shoes odd and ill-fitting' as they re-enact scenes from blackbirding days, or parody a medical scene using a 'stethoscope' made from a piece of rope, checking out each other's orifices and exclaiming in amazement, envy or disgust. Women also act as mediators between quarrelling men by clowning to diffuse tension.[12] These accounts suggest that Tokelauan women use clowning as a form of protest in matters involving gender roles and relations. Also, as in other parts of Polynesia, the 'white man' and his 'strange' practices are a recurring theme of local humour.

From Fiji comes an example that is reminiscent of the sketch above, as well as the earlier account of the Samoan clown's parody of Sloan and his camera. In the early 1940s, the Muanivatu people, of an independent kingdom of southern Vanua Levu, presented their first fruits (yams) to their paramount chief, the Tui Wailevu. As the villagers approached the chief's house and stood in file, five pairs of strong men suddenly ran onto the *rara* dragging by their midribs five *waqanidriai* 'canoes' made of *niusawa* fronds. Perched precariously back to back in each vessel, jolting and bouncing as they came, were two *driainisevu* maskers. Halting before the mounds of first-fruit offerings, the burly canoe haulers seized their frantically struggling passengers and carried them one by one, each squirming and peddling his legs furiously in the air, to stand in line before a grotesque trio of *turanai-driai*, officious and vociferous parodies of bossy European overseers, each wearing a khaki shirt over an amply padded paunch, and clopping about on stumpy stilts made from half coconut shells tied to long cords that passed between the big and second toes of their wearers, to be held in their hands (Clunie and Ligairi 1983:64-5).

The unflattering view of Europeans portrayed above is paralleled in a more recent account of Fijian women satirising Indian women by dressing in white bed sheets, plastering their faces with flour, and carrying buckets and pots on their heads. As these 'Indian' women danced a Fijian *meke* dance, they held exaggerated fixed grins on their faces (Arno 1992:44), thereby reinforcing the stereotypical view of Indians as overly serious and surly.

More satires of foreigners appear in these accounts from Hawai'i. Emerson (1965:254) writes that Hawaiians used the *oli*, or lyric utterance 'not only for the songful expression of joy and affection, but as the vehicle of humorous or sarcastic narrative in the entertainment of their comrades'. The *oli* was a favourite form of amusement, even for Hawaiians who ended up as sailors:

> I have heard Mr. Manini, who was the most improvisatore among them, sing for an hour together, when at work in the midst of Americans and Englishmen; and, by the occasional shouts and laughter of the Kanaks, who were at a distance, it was evident that he was singing about the different men that he was at work with. They have great powers of ridicule, and more excellent mimics, many of them discovering and imitating the peculiarities of our own people before we had observed them ourselves. [Dana 1959:117]

Emerson (1965:254) also suggests that the example above is not uncommon:

> If a traveller, not knowing the language of the country, noticed his Hawaiian guide and baggage carriers indulging in mirth while listening to an oli by one of their number, he would probably be right in suspecting himself to be the innocent butt of their merriment.

These various accounts of Polynesians satirising foreigners to their islands, foreign institutions or foreign behaviour, reveal a subversive function of clowning, with the clown figure standing at centre stage, embroiled in an ongoing commentary on important issues of the day.

I now turn to a discussion of theories of clowning that inform and shed light on this important but overlooked indigenous institution.

Analysis

Clowning communicates many messages simultaneously. Contemporary scholarship stresses the polyphonic nature of clowning, in contrast to early studies that reduced clowning to serving limited functions. My own study of the Rotuman *han maneak su*, as well as Sinavaiana's dissertation of the Samoan *fale aitu,* clearly demonstrate that in these two societies the ritual clown mediated between the world of the living and that of the dead (Hereniko 1990, 1992; Sinavaiana 1992a, 1992b, 1992c). Ethnographic accounts of the *arioi* society of Tahiti also reveal the same link with the spirit world of dead ancestors.

Sinavaiana and I both claim that because clowning performances are licensed affairs, they ultimately reinforce the norm (Hereniko 1990; Sinavaiana 1992a). Studies of the Samoan *fale aitu* by Shore (1977, 1978, n.d.) and Victoria Kneubuhl (1987), as well as Huntsman and Hooper's analysis of Tokelauan clowning (1975), support this theory. Earlier commentators such as Eagleton (1981:148), Gluckman (1965:109), Eco (1984), and Nelson (1990: 174) also concur that clowning serves the interests of the dominant culture that it apparently opposes.

But this is not the whole story. Sinavaiana's dissertation on the Samoan *fale aitu* also stresses the mediating role that comic theatre can play as Samoa 'navigates the rickety bridge "betwixt and between" cultural epochs [of] ancient Polynesia and the modern world' (Sinavaiana 1992a:331), as well as the potential for change that is inherent in the subversive nature of clowning.

The potential for influencing social and political change is particularly evident in contemporary practice as Polynesian societies become more fragmented because of competing ideologies and loyalties. The clown, as demonstrated in my study of the Rotuman ritual clown, becomes immersed in the process of transformation and finds her previously 'taken for granted' slot in society questioned, if not undermined. Clowning as an institution has to either make an exit in the imminent future, or to readjust and perhaps become an arena for political expression. The latter course is an exciting possibility that I hope can be fostered.

Clowning shares similarities with carnival, which Bakhtin (1968:109) describes as a 'temporary liberation from the prevailing truth of the established order' and an avenue of 'becoming, change, and renewal'. For Bakhtin, carnival is a festive critique of the dominant class and their values. In a world that is temporarily turned upside down, the material body (what Bakhtin calls 'grotesque realism') accompanied by carnivalesque laughter become the central image for topsy-turvy play that flaunts convention

and the constraints of rules and regulations. In this context that is akin to comic theatre, a multitude of human voices engage in a dialogue that regenerates and revitalises society (Bakhtin 1968:1968).

Clowning and carnival come under the wider rubric of symbolic inversion – what Stallybrass and White call transgression, which Babcock (1978:14) defines as

> any act of expressive behavior which inverts, contradicts, abrogates, or in some fashion presents an alternative to commonly held cultural codes, values and norms be they linguistic, literary or artistic, religious, social and political.

Using this wide-angle lens to view clowning reveals similarities with Pacific literature, particularly the fiction of Epeli Hauʻofa in his novel *Kisses in the Nederends* (1987a), where the primary image is the anus and the narrative about the search for a cure to an ailment in this part of the body that is taboo in normal speech or writing. Hauʻofa's apparent disrespect for the language of propriety and decorum, and his focus on the 'earthy humour' of ordinary Pacific islanders at the bar or marketplace, has led Subramani (1988:50) to say this comic satirist has liberated Pacific literature from a 'narrow-minded seriousness that typifies the early literature'.

But this is assertion more than fact, for it remains to be seen whether other Pacific writers will follow in Hauʻofa's footsteps. The complaints of some of my previous students at the University of the South Pacific about Wendt's use of four-letter words and his graphic descriptions of lovemaking in his early novels (1973, 1977, 1979) suggest transgression in fiction does not necessarily liberate as Subramani and Bakhtin would have us believe. Rather, transgression could conceivably reinforce the moral and spiritual superiority of the reader as Stallybrass and White have suggested in *The Poetics and Politics of Transgression*.

Likewise, Kristeva's proposition that the breaking of formal literary codes of language challenges official law (1980:65) implies that Hauʻofa's focus on obscenity in *Kisses* challenges elitist discourse. I am more inclined, however, to agree with Stallybrass and White, who suggest that political change is possible only when there is control of the major sites of discourse. Challenges within a particular site of discourse – in this case fiction – does not threaten the hierarchy of sites of discourse, and therefore its potential for effecting change may exist only in the political unconscious with no visible shift or realignment in the domain of discourse (Stallybrass and White 1986:201-2).

Many voices have taken up the issue of whether or not symbolic inversions in clowning, carnival, or literature are essentially conservative or progressive. Victor Turner (1982) and now Mitchell (1992a:43; 1992b), among others, see the preoccupation with this either-or question as meaningless outside the realm of specific case studies. Stallybrass and White concur, offering a view that best sums up this controversy. Rejecting the issue of whether or not carnivals are intrinsically radical or conservative, they assert:

> for long periods carnival may be a stable and cyclical ritual with no noticeable politically transformative effects but … given the presence of sharpened political antagonism, it may often act as catalyst and site of actual and symbolic struggle. [Stallybrass and White 1986:14]

The accounts in the early literature of Rotuma, Tahiti and Samoa indicate that ritual clowning in these societies was much more grotesque in Bakhtinian terms. They were also performed to the 'collective ancestral body of all the people' (Bakhtin 1986:19). Carnival, like the *fale aitu* of Samoa or the ritual clowning at weddings in Rotuma, was therefore a locus for recreation and re-creation of seemingly contradictory and opposed elements that encapsulated the complexity of human society. History reveals no revolutions caused by clowning performances in Polynesia. If anything, the evidence indicates that during *arioi* performances, war was forbidden, but resumed as soon as these comedic performances ended. Tokelauan women also clowned to diffuse tension between quarrelling men, and it is probable that humour and laughter in other parts of Polynesia did a lot to maintain harmony between opposing parties. In this sense, clowning was a conservative force.

In the present climate of 'sharpened political antagonism', social institutions such as the *fale aitu* or *arioi* can act as 'a catalyst and site of actual and political struggle'. They can become a mouthpiece for the oppressed in society,

as well as an arena for the exploration of important issues of the day. Through comedy sketches – which, incidentally, are parallel to political cartoonists in Western discourse – chiefs and those in positions of authority can be kept in touch with their subjects and the issues that disturb them. Chiefs can also learn to laugh again and not take themselves too seriously. An example should make my point clearer.

A group of Pacific Islanders attending a university in Marawa were celebrating someone's birthday.[13] Students from five or so different islands from various parts of the Pacific, as well as Caucasian friends, a total of about twenty students, attended. A Fijian woman and her American husband arrived at a late stage during the party with a *tanoa*, bowl of *yaqona,* and the husband proceeded to mix this drink.[14] The atmosphere was very informal, with everyone sitting on chairs, drinking beer, laughing and telling stories.

When the *yaqona* was ready to be drunk, the Fijian woman told the assembled company that the *yaqona* would be drunk informally; that is, without protocol. This seemed appropriate, given the context. But unbeknown to all but one, a chief (who was also a professor) was present. Apparently offended that proper respect to his status was not observed, the chief/professor removed his shirt to reveal his tattoo marks, sat on the floor, refused to drink second because it was demeaning to his position (this he told us in his speech), then stood up and gave everyone an earful of 'authentic' Pacific custom and how he should have been accorded proper respect befitting his title and status.[15]

The exhortation was for Pacific islanders in the room to adhere to tradition which, incidentally, was his version of his country's tradition. Since no-one else in the room was from this individual's country, this 'sermon' was most strange, to say the least. This is a long story; suffice it to say that the evening was ruined. A lesson in humility, through Rotuman clowning, perhaps would be of tremendous benefit to this chief and other status-conscious individuals who impose their assumed authority on other people, irrespective of the context, or the multiracial and therefore multicultural nature of the assembled company. Hau'ofa's observation that 'the privileged often try to force other certain traditions on the poor [those they regard to be of inferior social status] in order … to secure the privileges that they have gained, not so much from their involvement in traditional activities, as from the privileged access to resources in the regional economy' (1987b:12) appears most perceptive.

Conclusion

As performance, clowning in Polynesia communicates through body language, verbal utterances, costume, use of space, colour, and properties. The tropes of irony, parody, caricature and exaggeration are also handy techniques that clowns use to humorous effect.

Clowning performances may be secular or sacred. Secular clowning is usually spontaneous whereas sacred (or ritual) clowning is programmed by society and obligatory. The former is ubiquitous and is a function of the common humanity that we all share; the latter originated in sacred rituals associated with ancestral religions.

Whether secular or ritual, clowning provides avenues for the expression of dissent, as well as alternative ways of being. They are therefore important in the mediation of conflict and the maintenance (or creation) of a humane leadership, particularly in modern Polynesia, where many of its chiefs are losing their sense of humour as they seek (by hook or by crook) to hang onto power and the perks that come with status (for example, see Wendt 1979, 1993a, 1993b; Howard 1986, 1993; Lal 1992).

The techniques and functions of secular and ritual clowning, however, are very similar, particularly in contemporary practice where the sacred element in ritual clowning has been eradicated by Christianity and colonisation, and a marked shift towards secular performance is evident.[16]

Christianity and colonialism destroyed the contexts that allowed ritual clowning to survive or to be effective. For instance, the *poula* nights of ancient Samoa and the *arioi* of Tahiti were regarded by missionaries and their converts as evidence of the devil at work. Their efforts, aided by Western education and Western notions of proper conduct, resulted in the eradication of the *arioi* some time in the first half of the 19th Century (Ellis 1834:169) and

of the *poula* by the 1950s (Mageo 1992:449).[17] Since ancestral religion was at the core of these institutions, the missionaries forbade their practice; subsequently, they coopted these theatrical traditions into acceptable vehicles to serve their own purposes or that of secular society.

With decolonisation and independence in Samoa in 1960, issues of self-determination resurfaced. This growing confidence has resulted in the revival of some of the old institutions, albeit in a more sanitised and acceptable form for Christian converts. For example, the comic sketches of Samoa are now performed in schools and viewed on television. Once a part of boating expeditions between villages, the *fale aitu* is now an institution in its own right (Shore 1977:319).

Many American Samoans experience these sketches vicariously through television; Western Samoans perform *fale aitu* as part of the annual comedy competition during Independence Day festivities. Immigrant Samoans in the United States and New Zealand sometimes use *fale aitu* as a means of earning much-needed cash.

In Tahiti, modern dramatic performances draw from the historical records of *arioi* performances (for costuming and staging), although the religious practices of this once vibrant and dynamic institution have been forgotten or suppressed. Biblical pageants in the Cook Islands, Samoa and Tonga are now big events. As for Rotuma, the ritual clown's link with the supernatural has been lost, and the *han maneak su's* demise is imminent.

In Fiji, first-fruit festivals are now largely a thing of the past, as are the colourful performances of the masquers. The seasonal yam crop has now been replaced by cassava or the ubiquitous white bread. Church disapproval, the tendency to plant cash crops, the subsequent decline in the subsistence surplus, and the growing reluctance of chiefs to properly reciprocate have also contributed to their decline (Clunie and Ligairi 1983:70-1). Even the *veli ni meke* that used to be an integral part of club dances in certain parts of Fiji is rarely seen; in modern eyes, they seem out of place in formal performances directed at royalty or chiefs. Likewise, the likelihood of a revival of the first-fruit festivals and associated performances of the 'spiritual guardians of fertility' (Clunie and Ligairi 1983:71) is slim indeed as Fiji, like her neighbours, aspires to emulate the ways of the modern world.

Yet chiefs remain. Recent events and political developments in Fiji, Tonga and Samoa indicate that many chiefs are now out of touch with the common folk. Ensconced in constitutional politics, living in towns or cities, engaged in the pursuit of power and money, many chiefs (traditional and modern) could benefit by employing a clown or jester as part of their household. And in the evenings, the villagers could arrive with a comic sketch in which they could play out their frustrations and needs, and perhaps, occasionally, parody the oppressive face of authority.

Though ritual clowning has lost its link with ancestral spirits in most of Polynesia, its evolution into a more secular form need not be seen as a loss in potency. Rather, its convergence with secular clowning, albeit in various permutations performed in a myriad of settings, could entail the conscious use of this form as a site for political commentary. The benefits? The restoration of a sense of humour, an awareness of the wishes of the oppressed, and possibly a more humane approach to power and prestige.

Notes

1. This paper first appeared in the Spring 1994 issue of the *Contemporary Pacific* (6(1):1-28), and is reproduced here with permission of the journal's editor. My thanks to David Hanlon, Alan Howard, Epeli Hau'ofa and Edie Bowles for comments on an early draft.

2. See George Turner (1884:126). See also Stair (1897:122), who describes a 'jester' or 'court fool' or 'quick flyer'. On page 123 he mentions 'freelance' clowns who wandered freely and attached themselves to chiefs.

3. Its existence in the *tautoga* was told me by Rotuma's historian Vafo'ou Jiare; see also Hereniko (1977) for a detailed description of this dance. In the case of Fijian dances, see Clunie and Ligairi (1983:55). I also saw this role enacted in a spear dance performed by Queen Victoria School students at the National Gymnasium in 1989.

4. Luomala (1973:28-46) concludes the movable images were strung and worn as necklaces in secular and religious processions and dances, as well as carried in the dancer's hands or arms.

5. According to Webster, the *arioi* version in the Marianas was called *Uritoi*.

6. The *fale aitu* is also comparable to popular theatre, or theatre for community development. It is a form that is popular in many Third World countries, and now has counterparts in Vanuatu and the Solomon Islands. To use this indigenous form to disseminate developmental and educational information is a possibility that is yet to be widely realised in Polynesia.

7. For early reports see Pritchard (1866:78); Williams (1984: 247-8).

8. See Luomala (1984), in which Luomala identifies seven kinds of *hula ki'i*, one of which does not use a screen or wooden puppets.

9. Emerson uses the term marionettes, whereas Luomala uses the term puppets.

10. Usually the defence is to be just as ridiculous as the puppets, and it is possible for the 'victim' to turn the tables.

11. All the information on Tokelauan clowning is from Huntsman and Hooper (1975).

12. Huntsman and Hooper (1975:428). For an earlier example (1840s), see Cannibal Jack Jackson (William Diaper), cited in Clunie and Ligairi (1983:60).

13. Marawa is a fictional island that I use in the play *Last Virgin in Paradise*, which I co-authored with Teresia Teaiwa. I use it here to give this incident some anonymity. The important point is what this incident symbolically represents, and not the identity of the individuals involved. This incident was most disturbing for everyone present; what appears here does not adequately capture the emotional distress it caused students who were present and me. It was this incident that prompted me to write this paper, and to address the question of chiefly status and the need for a more humane leadership.

14. During his speech, the chief claimed that since this man was a *haole* (European), he should not have presumed he could mix the *yaqona*. He added that this *haole* could be killed had he made the same mistake in the chief's country.

15. After this long speech the chief disappeared. We thought he had gone home, and an argument developed among us as we blamed each other for having offended the chief. But he returned about thirty minutes later with a large quantity of liquor. After depositing the evidence of his wealth, he gave us another long speech, all about 'authentic' Pacific custom, which was really his own version of his country's custom.

16.   See Mitchell (1992) for the most comprehensive and up-to-date review of clowning worldwide. This volume also contains essays of clowning in specific Oceanic societies: Wape, Murik, North Mekeo and Lusi Kaliai in Papua New Guinea; Samoa; Rotuma.

17.   Mageo (1992:449) writes that an informant reported spying upon *poula* in his boyhood in the 1950s.

Festivals, identity and performance: Tahiti and the 6th Pacific Arts Festival

Karen Stevensen

The concept of festival is one that has always played an important role in Pacific societies. One need only peruse the ethnographies to find volumes on feasting traditions associated with social, economic, political, agricultural and funeral rituals. If one were to look for an underlying structure that could unify Pacific cultures the festival would suffice. Thus, the South Pacific Commission (SPC) decided to use the concept of festival in their attempts to perpetuate and encourage the traditions and cultures of the Pacific.[1]

It is intriguing that a concept so integrally linked to a very diverse population has not inspired great dialogue. Academicians have, for the most part, remained entrenched in their own disciplines, and have not looked to broader pan-Pacific ideas. Those interested in *kastom* have broken from this mould; such topics as the creation of histories, the invention of traditions, and the formulation of ethnic and political identities have begun a discourse without disciplinary boundaries. However, the role of the festival in the Pacific and how it is associated with these discourses has rarely been addressed.[2]

In contemporary Pacific societies the formation of ethnic identities and political interest groups has created an atmosphere for 'the resistance to colonial domination, racism, and exploitation' (Jolly 1982:338), 'the identification of common cultural themes and the maintenance of tradition' (Tonkinson 1982:309), and 'the emergence of

an objectified concept of indigenous lifeways and more rigid notions of identity' (Linnekin and Poyer 1990:13), all of which lead to the creation and organisation of political structures whose goals are to preserve and develop cultural heritage. As political consciousness develops, culture becomes a subject of public discourse (Linnekin and Poyer 1990:14).

The perceived necessity for this type of cultural affirmation demonstrates a desire 'to retain crucial features of indigenous lifeways and world view' (Linnekin and Poyer 1990:15). Contemporary attempts at cultural affirmation are posited in contrast to colonial and missionary dogma. These beliefs often resulted in negative self-images and cultural images that are now being displaced by the strengthening of positive cultural ideologies. Pacific Islanders now reflect on the strength of their cultural heritage, which, regardless of colonial and missionary zeal, has remained a vital part of contemporary society. Cultural values and traditions have been sustained and supported by means of the festival.

Recently, government agencies have responded to the need for the development and maintenance of indigenous cultural heritage without the grotesque commodification and objectification associated with colonialism. However, the institutionalisation of culture and the presentation of festival requires financial backing. The result is the creation of agencies or offices whose mandates often appear contradictory. Colonial powers, for example, are a major source of cultural aid, and international corporations such as hotels and airlines are usually contributors to the overall budget. Offices of tourism are also involved. This illustrates that conflicting agendas can work together to create an institution (the festival) deemed valuable to all parties. For example, the giving of cultural aid by France prolongs Tahitian dependency, tourism to Tahiti is profitable for multinational corporations, and despite these demonstrations of domination it creates a cultural identity with which the Tahitian people can stand in contradistinction to colonial powers.

The legislation of cultural policy is politically, economically and socially valuable. The concept of cultural policy is intriguing as politicians and governmental officials decide which cultural values, events, and arts are to be spotlighted. The entertainments chosen are those that have remained vital and valuable aspects of contemporary culture. As a result, the *vaka* (canoe), dance and art production are at the core of Pacific festivals.

Authenticity versus tourist art

These core elements are in many cases re-created, reinterpreted, or created anew. For some, this begs the question of authenticity and tourist art. When watching an Aboriginal performance at the 5th Pacific Festival of Arts, I commented to a fellow academic that I thought the paucity of scholars in attendance was unfortunate. His response was that this was not authentic, so why would they want to attend? This is but one of the issues relevant to the festival. Delegations create, choreograph, and share their performances with 'outsiders' – some tourists and academics, but mostly other Pacific peoples. That these performances have been transported to a foreign venue does not deny their authenticity. That governments subsidise these performances does not make them economic pawns in a market economy. Kasfir (1992:53) has suggested that authenticity should be seated in the minds of those who make art, and not those who collect or study it. It is not an award offered up by outsiders, but an essence that expresses and embodies cultural beliefs (Dutton 1994:4).

Another issue concerns tourism and tourist art. There is a growing literature on this topic that was first given credence by Nelson Graburn. We have all experienced tourist shops and the quality of objects, kitsch, that are often found within. This is in great contrast to what can be found in craft and cultural centres, artists workshops and at the festival. Jeffrey Sissons suggests these are not just tourist arts but 'icons of identity' (1995:153), and states:

> carved images of the Cook Islands deity, Tangaroa, with his prominent phallus; Fijian war clubs and kava bowls; Samoan and Tongan tapa cloths – when sold in tourist shops, acquire new or enhanced national value.

This value is imbued with cultural and political identity. The same can be said of performance. Dean MacCannel (1973, 1976) has referred to this as 'staged authenticity'; a glimpse into another past, a tradition like or unlike one's own. Again Sissons (1995:161-2) states:

> When dance represents the community to itself and outsiders, its gestures and choreography participate in creating the nation, imparting their meanings, and taking on new significance in the process. Through dance, the Cook Islands is invoked as gendered and visually appealing, traditional and welcoming. European colonial representations of primitivity, tourist fantasies of a South Seas paradise and expressions of post-colonial indigeneity are brought together in dance as a spectacular display of appearances, an entertaining play of signs available for general consumption.

Using Tahiti and the 6th Pacific Festival of Arts, this paper will demonstrate how the festival venue both highlights and glosses over these salient issues. For example, a cultural spokesperson, within a conference setting, can be addressing the problem of photography *vis-à-vis* cultural property while at the same moment spectators video a performance. Nothing is clear cut except for the cultural and artistic integrity demonstrated by Pacific peoples within the festival venue.

The Pacific Festival of Arts

The notion of festival in the Pacific has gained in importance over the past thirty years as colonial domination (in the political sphere) has lessened. The result is the use of festivals and the arts in the creation of political and cultural identities. The SPC recognised the importance of this phenomenon in their creation of the Pacific Festival of Arts in 1972. At that time, the SPC created a mechanism for the festival to take place every four years sponsored by a different island nation.[3]

The Pacific Festival of Arts has become an important venue for the perpetuation of Pacific arts and cultures. Representatives to the SPC felt that the values embodied in the arts and culture of the Pacific had been neglected during a century of colonisation, and that if left to themselves these island cultures would disappear. As a result it was deemed necessary to highlight those cultural values inherent in, and important to, Pacific communities. The festival, a phenomenon indigenous to all Pacific cultures, seemed a fitting vehicle. The organising principles were noted in the souvenir brochure of the first festival:

> The culture of the South Pacific is a living culture. It shows itself in dance and music, artifacts and handicrafts, in the architecture of their buildings, in their games and in their languages. These are as exciting and as varied as are the islands themselves. In the flurry and the bustle of modern living, where the speed of change has swamped much that was good, the islands remain placid, peaceful oases where lasting values still count. But even in the Pacific change is inevitable, and positive efforts are needed to prevent the age old arts from succumbing to the pervading sense of sameness that exists in much of our society, or being swamped by commercialism, or cheapened to provide facile entertainment for tourists.
>
> We hope that this Festival will not only encourage the preservation of the best in Pacific island culture, but that it will also serve to re-establish much that is in danger of being lost. In particular, we hope that it will re-emphasize the need for the retention of classical art forms, for the best taste, for the highest ideals and dignity. Perhaps it may also enable a recapturing of some of the old chants and dances as they were when they were originally created and in the form they were enjoyed by the peoples of the Pacific long ago.

The result is the institutionalisation of an ideal – the festival – whose goal is to preserve and encourage the arts and cultures of the Pacific.

Each festival has its own theme, and the sixth (the focus of this paper) was the *vaka* (fig. 3.1). These themes often demonstrate the importance of the festival as a cultural and a political event. The *vaka* became a catalyst for the reintroduction of navigational skills throughout the Pacific.[4] In some instances this became a personal quest (Ben Nicholls, pers. comm., October 1992), in others a symbol of national and cultural identity. In this way the festival can promote cultural values and do so in a political arena that reinforces these values, not only in the Pacific, but on a global scale.[5] The sixth festival also highlighted contemporary art production and offered an arts conference where Pacific peoples could discuss those issues of importance to them.[6] Again, the festival offers a consolidated political voice and identity to otherwise unheard voices.

Tahitian participation

The value Tahitians place on the notion of festival derives from their *Heiva*.[7] In Tahiti, festival activity is cultural policy. Ideologies of cultural identity and affirmation are easily transferred from Tahiti's *Heiva* to the Pacific Festival of Arts. Participation as a delegate bestows honour on the individual and pride in one's cultural and artistic heritage.

3.1 Cook Island *vaka*. (Photo: Karen Stevensen.)

3.2 (Right) A member of the Tahitian outrigger canoe team. He is draped with *maire* leaves offered by Cook Islanders upon arrival. Note the tattoos marking his *maʻohi* identity. (Photo: Karen Stevensen.)

3.3 (Far right) Tahitian performers doing the *tamure*. (Photo: Karen Stevensen.)

Due to the importance placed on festivals as a venue for the promotion of cultural and artistic identity, French Polynesia often subsidises quite a large delegation of artists, dancers, and performers.

The structure of the Pacific Festival of Arts mimics that of the *Heiva*. Tahiti's *Heiva* has played a significant role in the genesis of a Tahitian identity and in the perpetuation of Tahitian cultural traditions. The importance the *Heiva* has acquired in Tahitian society reflects the political changes associated with colonisation and the formulation of a Tahitian identity (Stevensen 1990). This identity emphasises the uniqueness of the Tahitian cultural heritage, and it is this heritage that is highlighted during the *Heiva* and the Pacific Festival of Arts.

Tahiti's role in the sixth festival was more than simply as a participating country – Tahiti offered financial, structural and 'relative' support. Due to the financial support given to cultural activities and Tahiti's 'relationship' with France, French Polynesia was able to offer supplemental financial assistance. Tahiti also offered 'lighting equipment for the Cultural Centre auditorium, technicians to work on them and a dozen passenger vehicles' to aid in the transportation of delegates (Takau 1992).

The role of 'relative' was reinforced by the *vaka* theme, which focused on the voyaging 'relationships' of Pacific peoples. Unfortunately the Tahitian government felt that, with the time constraints, it could not underwrite the construction of a canoe (G. Cowan, pers. comm., October 1992). There were those in the festival organisation who felt slighted by this. However, eight young Tahitian men (who were not officially sanctioned) paddled a canoe from Tahiti (fig. 3.2). 'They believed that their ancestors were helping them find their way across the wide ocean' (Kauraka 1993:25). To some this was an exciting declaration of the cultural resurgence sweeping the Pacific, and perhaps more so as it did not carry a political stamp of approval. On the other hand, it also allowed for the romanticisation of the ancestral past, where those witnessing the current event could imagine similar voyages taking place centuries ago.

Tahiti's relationship with the Cook Islands can easily be seen in language, costume, art, music, and dance. This relationship was further reiterated with a firewalk *(umu-ti)* in front of the Tinirao family *marae*. It was noted that 100 years prior a similar performance took place to honour the Tinirao chiefs. The *umu-ti* has been presented by Tahiti in the past three festivals. These theatrical spectacles can be seen as a marked attempt to promote a cultural and political identity – a *maʻohi* identity (Stevensen 1990). These events, however, were on the periphery of Tahitian participation – the focus was dance.

3.4 Male members of the Tahitian delegation sporting tattoos. (Photo: Karen Stevensen.)

Participation in dance is seen as key to Tahiti's cultural identity. The program, choreographed by Coco Hotuhotu, reflected the *vaka* theme, voyaging and the ocean. Polynesian dance and Tahiti have been synonymous for years (fig. 3.3).

The early explorers, especially Cook's men, were quite taken by the 'lascivious motions' (Banks in Beaglehole 1962:326) of Tahiti's dance tradition. Perhaps it is because Tahitian dance has become such an institution that it shoulders more than its fair share of criticism. At Townsville in 1988, comments relating Tahitian dance to 'Las Vegas' or the Folies-Bergère were frequent, as well as a disdain for a Tahitian influence over Melanesian dance, especially the National Theatre of Papua New Guinea. Tahitian dancers are often considered too 'professional', their performances too slick. They are show stoppers, not primitive and/or savage. In attempts to demonstrate virtuosity and precision in dance, hours of practice go unheralded and, to add insult to injury, has been associated with 'Airport Art'. Kaeppler (1977:76) described Tahitian dance as follows:

Today Tahitians dance for entertainment of themselves and others and the deeper meaning of these dances has been lost. What remains is what Euro-American taste has found acceptable and marketable with other airport arts.

This begs the question of created tradition, authenticity, and creativity. The past twenty years has seen a tremendous shift in attitude about these topics, giving the people involved more credit for their cultural performances. But one also finds disdain for the metropolitan islands (Tahiti, Hawai'i, New Zealand), scholars dismissing their traditions as economic responses to tourism. In response to similar criticisms Manouche Lehartel (1989:2) stated:

Scholars tend to exhibit a restrictive, conservative view of the performing arts and sometimes ignore contemporary practices. Individual creativity must be acknowledged, placed within the dynamic traditions of a culture.

She also emphasised that 'Tahitian dance is created and performed first and foremost for the *Tiurai* Festival *(Heiva)*, that is, for a very critical, very knowledgeable audience of fellow Tahitians' (Lehartel 1989:2). This dialogue seems to be part of the creative process, thereby forging an intensity and pride in contemporary dance. In Rarotonga, the predominantly Polynesian audience did not criticise Tahiti's performance; they applauded its beauty, strength and vitality.

Tattoo, criticised for its attempts at authenticity, also deserves attention (fig. 3.4). A large number of Tahitian dancers sport tattoos, and two tattoo artists accompanied the delegation and demonstrated their art form. The desirability of tattoo has grown exponentially in the past decade. Much of this stems, I would suggest, from Tahiti's participation in the 5th Pacific Festival of Arts, in Townsville. There, Ioteve Tehupaia, a young Tahitian with Marquesan ancestry, was spotlighted both for his ability to dance and his full body tattoo. In Townsville a few men from Western and American Samoa bore the marks of their chiefly status, some Hiri Motu women of Papua New Guinea were also tattooed, as were a handful of Tahitian dancers. In Rarotonga, tattoo was seen on hundreds of participants, and in the demonstration areas tattoo artists could barely keep the public at bay.

Tattoo for most of the Pacific clearly is a revived tradition. This accounts for the piecemeal quality of some of the imagery as tattoo artists are learning their craft. Tunui Salmon, Director of Le Centre Métier d'Arts (Tahiti's art school), believes 80 per cent of the young men and women who acquire tattoos do so because it is fashionable. Others, however, associate their distinguished marks with cultural identity (Salmon, pers. comm., July 1990). Within the last decade, tattoo has come to portray not only a political and cultural statement by the wearer, but also the elegance of the art form. Tattoo artists in Tahiti have encouraged people to research the motifs they wish to place upon their body, which has led to both an appreciation of, and knowledge about, their culture and its historic past.[8]

The result is the contemporary creation of images that have significance for the wearer. In Tahiti the importance of the tattoo in relationship to dance is suggested historically by the *arioi*[9] and today by the number of dancers with

3.5 (Below) Member of the Tahitian 'mamas' working on a *tifaifai*. (Photo: Karen Stevensen.)

3.6 (Bottom) Aboriginal design (by Arone Meeks) on Tahitian mother-of-pearl. Etched by David Tapuatea. (Photo: Karen Stevensen.)

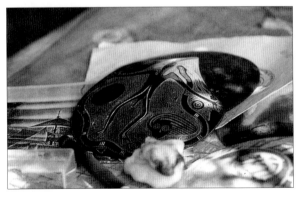

tattoos. This relationship, between tattoo and performance, is often verbalised in the contemporary setting (Tavanna, pers. comm., July 1990). It appears that tattoo is again functioning as a marker of status within the dance community. More important, however, is the use of tattoo to mark one's position within the contemporary cultural movement – *la Culture Ma'ohi* (Stevensen 1992).

The association of art with cultural movements is widespread within the Pacific. The aforementioned *umu-ti* not only reiterated a historical link between the Cook Islands and Tahiti, but its theatricality plays to the re-creation of a traditional past. It is, of course, offered as authentic. Raymond Graff has created the *umu-ti* in its current manifestation. It has become a venue that allows for the gods to be seen in a positive light – as aiding and protecting those who believe. In this way the gods as well as the traditional past are seen in a positive way, thereby reinforcing cultural identity (Stevensen 1992).

This identity was also offered up in the form of contemporary art. As noted above, two tattoo artists practised their work on an interested public. Young artists from Le Centre Métier d'Arts demonstrated some of the new directions traditional carving is taking, working in a variety of media – wood, rock, bone and pearl shell. The 'mamas' rounded out the delegation, exhibiting their skills in plaiting and *tifaifai* (applique) (fig. 3.5).

Within this group, David Tapuatea quietly symbolised the goals of the festival. An artists' village was created for the establishment of relationships among artists from around the Pacific. They could view what each other were doing and in this way reinforce the connectedness within Pacific arts, as well as demonstrate the uniqueness of each artist. In this way Arone Meeks and David Tapuatea were drawn together. Arone, one of the Aboriginal delegates, created a design he wanted David to etch in mother-of-pearl (fig. 3.6). This sharing of ideas, design motifs and artistic endeavour was a central idea behind the creation of the Pacific Festival of Arts.

Tifaifai, introduced by missionary wives in the 19th century, is an important art form in contemporary Tahitian society. It was especially important to have a large delegation of women working in this medium at the Cook

Islands, as *tivaevae* remains at the core of Cook Island culture as well. As an art form it has incorporated new directions and ideas that testify to its vitality and growth. Joyce Hammond (1986:53) stated:

> *Tifaifai* have become symbols of Polynesian tradition because islanders use them to preserve and perpetuate their cultural heritage in three important ways. First, Polynesians use *tifaifai* to replicate some significant functions of indigenous barkcloth. Second, *tifaifai* are used to reinforce traditional cultural principles; and finally, they serve as symbols of cultural identification and pride.

These are not simply women's work or crafts, but an essential link between contemporary and traditional values in central Polynesia. As such they play a large role in the promotion of a cultural identity.

Conclusion

The importance of the festival in contemporary Tahitian society stems from both a celebration of a traditional past and a current politic sweeping the Pacific. Tahiti not only has a history of festival activity dating to pre-contact times, but also has the *Heiva* with its 100-year legacy. Therefore, the continuance of festival activity is itself promoting and perpetuating Tahitian cultural heritage. However, as this heritage becomes objectified and institutionalised it becomes more dependent on political and economic realities rather than cultural ideology. This is clearly seen in the mixed messages and hidden agendas of the agencies involved in the production of these festivals.

These mixed messages present interesting contradictions. People who rue the objectification of culture often associate it with tourism. Since tourist income is being actively pursued, one might find truth in this assumption. However, the Pacific Festival of Art is not a tourist festival, but one put on by and for Pacific peoples. Many of these islands have not yet developed a true tourist industry. Infrequent and expensive flights and a paucity of accommodation allows these festivals to maintain their indigenous integrity.

Also interesting is the political rhetoric underlying these festivals. Often politicians do not admit the manipulation of cultural and political identity as created through festivals. However, the use and creation of composite national symbols (the *vaka*, dance, tattoo) in a multinational festival reinforces the cultural and artistic identities put forth. Using these symbols as a rallying point, diverse groups and agendas can meld in the creation of a cultural and political identity. This is being accomplished through the concept of the fête or festival. This allows the government to promote cultural values – competition, working together, subsistence activities – that will foster the continuity of their culture. The result is a cultural and political identity acknowledged through the venue of festival.

Notes

1. The South Pacific Commission was founded in 1947 when the six colonial governments of the Pacific (US, France, Britain, Australia, the Netherlands, New Zealand) signed an agreement to form the commission. With the process of decolonisation, all independent and self-governing nations were also admitted. There are now twenty-seven members, each of whom has an equal vote. The role of the commission is advisory and consultative.

2. Articles about the Pacific Festival of the Arts have been written by: Carell (1992), Hereniko (1980), Kaeppler (1987), Myers (1989), Simons (1989) and Stevensen (1993). One can also find reference to these festivals in *Glimpses* 20(2):24-31; *Paradise* 26:13-23 and 54:25-8, and *Pacific Islands Monthly* (1972, 1976, 1980, 1985, 1988, 1992). These tend to offer a private view of the festival experience, but no attempt has been made to document methodically the Pacific Festival of the Arts.

3. These have taken place in Fiji (1972), New Zealand (1976), Papua New Guinea (1980), Tahiti (1985), Australia (1988), Cook Islands (1992), Western Samoa (1996).

4. The value of the canoe within Polynesian cultures has been re-established through the efforts of many. The Hawaiian canoe *Hokule'a*, built in the mid-1970s, was the first. Nainoa Thompson was its navigator. He continues to work with the *Hokule'a* and other Pacific navigators.

5. Because the *vaka* were so well-received at the festival, UNESCO followed up by nominating 1995 as the year of the *vaka*. For further information see Lewis-Harris (1994).

6. For further information see Lewis-Harris (1994).

7. It is also from the *Heiva* that Tahiti's delegation is chosen.

8. Derek Lardelli was one of the highlighted New Zealand artists, who during the week of the festival tattooed Bernie Soutar.

A prerequisite of Derek's creative process is a thorough knowledge of the sitter's genealogy. For more on the other tattoo artists at the festival see Kauraka (1993), Lewis-Harris (1994), and Stevensen (1993).

9. The *arioi* were a highly stratified group of professional performers. Each of the eight orders within the *arioi* system was marked by a distinctive tattoo (Oliver 1974; Rose 1970; Stevensen 1988).

Imaging the nation: The New Zealand International Exhibition 1906-07 and the Model Maori *Pa*

4

Bernie Kernot

The public display of human subjects as exotic Others predates international exhibitions possibly by centuries, but according to Raymond Corbey (1995:60) the Paris World Fair of 1878 was the first to exhibit peoples from non-Western cultures in specially constructed pavilions and native villages, which became standard from then onwards. The New Zealand International Exhibition of 1906-07 followed this tradition, where Maori, Cook Islanders, Niue Islanders and Fijians were on display for scientific, ethnological and entertainment purposes.

The importance of international fairs in the construction of national identities has been discussed by Burton Benedict (1983, 1991). He sees them as collective representations of nations, which includes the use of appropriate symbols of unity, invented traditions and reconstituted histories. His more recent discussion (1991) considers the display of dependent peoples by colonial powers that were the major sponsors of world fairs in the later 19th and early 20th centuries, and their different attitudes and policies towards their dependent peoples. By 1906 New Zealand had assumed responsibility for the Cook Islands and Niue Island, as well as its own indigenous Maori population, so any notion of nationhood had to take these peoples into account. The timing of the exhibition was very significant, since it marked the historical juncture of the constitutional transition from colony to self-governing dominion. Nation-building was in the air. As the

Official Record noted, the exhibition 'gave this new land added dignity and mana in the old lands of the North' (Cowan 1910:3) and 'epitomized the story of our nation-making' (Cowan 1910:2).

Symbols of nationhood were still being forged, but the dominant unifying symbol was undoubtedly Britishness. Loyalty to empire had been affirmed in the 1901 Royal Tour by the Duke and Duchess of Cornwall and York (the future George V and Queen Mary). The tour was an extraordinary event, a 'national festival' (Bassett 1987:138) in which many thousands of New Zealanders, European and Maori, were able to participate at local, regional and national levels. Bassett (1987:135) considered the tour 'fascinating evidence of adolescent New Zealand's self-image at that time'. The colony was most loyally British, as the tour demonstrated, but as Bassett (1987:135) observes:

> New Zealand was small, but prosperous. The achievements of the pioneers and the flourishing condition of New Zealand's export industries, the fertility of soil and people, were endlessly celebrated. Maori shared in this progress.

Indeed it is precisely how Maori and Pacific Islands peoples were perceived as sharing in that progress, and their place in the 'imagined [national] community' (Anderson 1983:6) that provides one focus for this paper.

Benedict and Corbey review the presentation of dependent peoples in international exhibitions almost exclusively

37

4.1 Postcard impression of the exhibition site. The 'Wonderland' amusement area and Te Araiteuru *Pa* are both located round the edge of the small lake at centre left. Te Araiteuru is just beyond the pine trees. (D. Thompson Collection, Alexander Turnbull Library, Wellington, NZ. Reference No. F-65386-1/2.)

from the point of view of the sponsoring colonial powers. Corbey's analysis is directed to the display of tribal peoples at these exhibitions as manifestations of a European imperial hegemony over cultural others. The key elements of the colonial master narrative and the panoptic vision of the Western spectator identified by Corbey are clearly evident in the following account, but an examination of Maori participation in this historic national event suggests other narratives and visions were also being formulated.

Recent New Zealand culture historians (Bassett 1987; Blythe 1994; Neich 1977, 1983, 1991; Phillips 1983) have identified the turn of the century as marking the first stirrings of a distinctive national identity. Phillips and Neich in particular have drawn attention to the appropriation of Maori art and culture to serve as symbols of a national identity. Both see only a romanticised image of the Maori as being acceptable to the dominant settler culture, which at the turn of the century delighted in the sobriquet of 'Maoriland' as a romantic alternative to New Zealand. Blythe saw in the Maoriland metaphor an ambiguous term signifying a romanticised world of the European imagination and an acknowledgement of their own cultural displacement in an alien place where the Maori presence was the more authentic. 'Maoriland' involved both romantic appeal and veiled threat.[1] Only Bassett is prepared

to assert colonial society's willingness to include Maoris within the colony's prosperity.

A counter theme to this turn-of-the-century nationalism is provided by historian James Belich, who has argued[2] that the period from 1880 to 1920 marked an essential 'recolonisation', a resurgence of Britishness in which New Zealand saw itself not simply as a Britain of the South (with imperial ambitions in the South Pacific), but as a Better Britain.

The original intention was for a genuinely international fair, but it failed to attract exhibitors from outside the orbit of the British Empire, which gave it a distinctively British focus. This restriction seemed more an advantage than a problem for its sponsors. According to the *Official Record* (Cowan 1910:1), 'it focussed for us the enterprise, the education, and the technical advancement of our own English-speaking peoples'.

The New Zealand International Exhibition of 1906-07 followed closely the model of earlier world fairs, and in particular the 1904 St Louis Fair, where the New Zealand government had been represented by its General Manager for Tourist and Health Resorts, T.E. Donne. As at St Louis, a section of the fairground away from the main display courts but adjacent to the entertainment 'Wonderland' zone had been reserved for the display of native village life (fig. 4.1).

The Model Maori *Pa*

The exhibition was initiated and funded by government, and organised by state-appointed vice-presidents and executive commissioners. Management was by an executive committee assisted by twenty-one subsidiary committees.

One of these subsidiary committees was the Maori Committee, whose function was to support the building and management of a Model Maori *Pa*. The *pa* was the government's own special exhibit, funded by the state and under the ultimate control of the Minister for Native Affairs, the Hon. James Carroll, who was Maori. Carroll appointed the director of the Colonial Museum, Augustus Hamilton, to take charge of the project and to be the government's representative on the Maori Committee. On Hamilton's recommendation, Carroll appointed Gregor McGregor, a pakeha[3] farmer from the Wanganui River, to be the site superintendent, responsible for its daily management. McGregor also became a member of the Maori Committee, which was chaired by the Christchurch magistrate H.W. Bishop. Its ten members included only two Maori, J.H.W. Uru (a Ngai Tahu, South Island, tribal leader) and the young Dr Peter Buck (Te Rangihiroa).

The St Louis Fair had grouped various Native American tribal groups and indigenous Philippine islanders into villages in a particular zone of the fairground. According to Benedict (1983:34), ideas of social Darwinism and historical progress were 'particularly evident' there, and the arrangement of villages was intended to demonstrate an evolutionary sequence. Donne was enthusiastic about by the way the Americans had displayed their colonised peoples, and persuaded the New Zealand government to arrange a similar display.

Despite Carroll having overall responsibility for the Christchurch Model *Pa* project, and the presence of two other Maoris on the committee, its management was largely in the hands of a group of pakeha intellectuals with ethnological interests. Apart from Hamilton, they included T.E. Donne, who was an exhibition vice-president and executive commissioner; Professor McMillan-Brown, an author of books on Maori and Polynesian history; the farmer Gregor McGregor; James McDonald, a photographer and artist; and James Cowan, the official recorder.

This group was primarily responsible for the creation of the *pa* as a particular image consistent with the colonial 'master narrative' (Corbey 1995:71ff.) carried by the whole exhibition. The evolutionary sequence so evident in St Louis was, however, subordinated in Christchurch to the presentation of Maori and Pacific Islands peoples according to colonial images of a mythic 'Maoriland'.

The *pa* was a stockaded area of more than 2 acres at the rear of the showgrounds, adjacent to the entertainment area called 'Wonderland' in the *Official Record*. The basically flat topography, set beside a small artificial lake, prevented the construction of the better-known hill-fort *pa*, but Te Heuheu's Waitahanui *Pa* on Lake Taupo, illustrated by George French Angas in 1843, provided something of a model to follow. The scene within the *pa* was intended to convey the 'semi-barbaric life and colour' (Cowan 1910: 312) that pakeha imagined *pa* life to have been. According to Cowan in the *Official Record* (1910:34), it was a:

> combination of fishing village, waterside stockade, and trenched residential town with its living-houses of various types, its carved and decorated houses for ceremonial purposes, its storehouses and platforms for food, its canoe fleet and all the furniture of the true Maori *kainga*.

Despite this attempt at ethnographic reconstruction, it was in almost every detail a composite construction, with elements drawn from a wide variety of 19th-century sources or created specially for the project. It was less a faithful replication of an historical site than the creation of a particular kind of image:

> The idea reproduced here was from beyond the seas – its origin is lost in the gloom of the untold centuries which have passed since the Maoris' forefathers set sail from Asiatic shores into the unknown Rawhiti – Place of the Rising Sun. [Cowan 1910:321]

It was not only to present Maoris as semibarbaric, but also to locate them in a timeless, romanticised, never-never land of the European imagination. Cowan (1910:5) refers to the:

> singularly picturesque Native Section, where Maori and South Sea Islanders lived side by side in a pallisaded village,

all of the olden times; danced their ancient festive and war dances, and sang their old, old songs – a display that was equally the delight of the ethnologist and folk-lorist and of the ordinary pleasurer.

The *pa* was divided into two segments, referred to as the outer and inner *pas*, by a line of palisades. Access from outer to inner was through a spectacularly carved 22-foot-high entrance, or *waharoa*, carved especially for the exhibition by the Rotorua master carver Neke Kapua and his two sons (fig. 4.2). The model for this *waharoa* was a sketch of an entrance at Maketu done by Horatio Robley about forty years earlier. The public gained entrance to the outer *pa* through another entrance, which was carved by a Wanganui team under Hori Pukehika, according to their own tribal style.

4.2 Entrance to the inner *pa* carved by Neke Kapua and sons. On either side are cemetery posts from Ruato, Rotorua. (Photo: James McDonald; Museum of New Zealand Te Papa Tongarewa. Negative No. C1665.)

The ceremonial buildings mentioned by Cowan included two meeting houses and a richly ornate four-posted storehouse, or *pataka*. The larger meeting house and the *pataka* were set up in the outer *pa*, apparently for the facilitation of staged ceremonials, where, together with an area of open space, they constituted a *marae*. The meeting house (fig. 4.3) was a composite structure derived partly from various pieces held in museums, mainly Hamilton's Colonial Museum in Wellington, but with some panels carved especially for it. Two panels in the porch, which purported to be side-panels or *poupou*, were in fact very large posts taken from a burial ground at Ruato, Rotorua, which had been carved by Neke Kapua some years before. Two other matching posts from the same burial ground were set up at the entrance to the inner *pa*.

The *pataka* was in process of being carved by Neke Kapua and his team for another model village being planned at Whakarewarewa, Rotorua. It was borrowed for the Christchurch project and completed on site under the direction of Hamilton. Several of its parts were copied from the Te Oha and Te Kaha *patakas* in the Auckland Museum, and after the exhibition it was erected in the Whakarewarewa model village for display to tourists (Neich 1977:220-1).

The inner *pa* contained more than twenty dwelling houses, said to be illustrative of all the different dwelling types, grouped round a central *marae*. These dwellings, and a few constructed just outside the *pa* perimeter, accommodated the Maori, Fijian, Cook Islands and Niuean visiting parties that were in residence at different stages of the exhibition. The inner *pa* also included the smaller meeting house, which, although not a composite structure, had nevertheless been personally commissioned by Donne in 1905. According to Neich (1977:215), this house was only 20 feet (6 metres) long by 12 feet (3.7 metres) wide, 'and really only a large model, never intended for actual use'. Donne hired it out to the Maori Committee for £25 for the duration of the exhibition,[4] where it was given the name 'Te Wharepuni-a-Maui' (Neich 1977:215).

A number of canoes had been purchased by McGregor for the model *pa* in the course of a trip he took up the Wanganui River a few months before the opening. These were small named river canoes, but a larger canoe hull

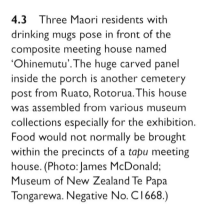

4.3   Three Maori residents with drinking mugs pose in front of the composite meeting house named 'Ohinemutu'. The huge carved panel inside the porch is another cemetery post from Ruato, Rotorua. This house was assembled from various museum collections especially for the exhibition. Food would not normally be brought within the precincts of a *tapu* meeting house. (Photo: James McDonald; Museum of New Zealand Te Papa Tongarewa. Negative No. C1668.)

became the foundation for another composite construction. The one authentic ceremonial canoe was *Taheretikitiki* loaned by King Mahuta. With the canoe came a skeletal crew to supervise manning when it was used to take VIPs on short excursions on the lake or, as on one occasion, for a mock attack on the *pa*.

Other large and small carvings furnished the *pa* in various ways, all arranged with an eye to dramatic representation. Most of the carvings were done especially for the exhibition and under Hamilton's close supervision, either in Wellington or on site in Christchurch. Reviewing these carvings, Neich (1977:217) has commented: 'All these carvings were part of a very self-conscious attempt to reproduce what the European patrons considered was a traditional Maori village.'

Populating the *pa*

Having a model stockaded village was one thing. Giving it life and spectacle was another, and the committee worked hard to ensure there were parties of Maoris present who were able to offer entertainment and craft demonstrations, and participate in formal ceremonies that the public paid to see.

At the opening on 1 November 1906, there were about sixty men, women and children from Wanganui and Rotorua tribes, and a contingent of twenty-five from Rarotonga, Aitutaki and Mangaia. The Maori groups included carvers, craftswomen and entertainers who performed haka and *poi* dances daily. The Cook Islanders included the famous Mangaian carver Daniella Tangitoru,[5] who brought a range of carved objects and craft work for sale, and they performed dances. There were also visits by VIPs, including the governor, the premier, and other notables, which were marked with elaborate ceremonial that the paying public were able to witness.

The Niueans and the first contingent of Fijians also arrived in this early period. The Fijians entertained with dances and weapons demonstrations, and the Niueans demonstrated craft work. There were also public ceremonial exchanges between resident Maoris and the Fijians (fig. 4.4).

Most of the Arawa group returned to Rotorua in late November, while another large Arawa party of seventy-eight entertainers, selected and managed by the pakeha Gilbert Mair, a former soldier, took their place. They returned in mid-December, leaving a small group of Wanganui people for a few days until they were joined by the first of the Turakina School visits. The Turakina girls were very popular with audiences and were kept on till the New Year, a few days longer than originally planned. The second group of Fijians, firewalkers from Beqa, arrived in mid-December for a short season of four performances.

There was a quiet period after New Year, with just the Cook Islanders in residence with Peter Buck before another Wanganui party, recruited by McGregor, arrived in late January. Through February and March, two large parties of Ngati Kahungunu, possibly including a contingent from Ngati Porou, took up residence. About this time also the Turakina *poi* dancers paid their second visit.

A number of notable Maori chiefs and leaders came with their tribal groups or visited the village for long or short periods. Peter Buck from the Maori Committee was there throughout the duration of the exhibition. On occasion he was in charge of the day-to-day management in the sometimes lengthy absences of McGregor. Buck took a very active part in the entertainment and weapons demonstrations, but he was also responsible for the health and hygiene arrangements in the village.

Some of these leaders were employed by Hamilton to perform particular functions. Neke Kapua and his two sons, Eramiha and Tene, were employed as principal carvers from April 1906 until mid-December at the rate of 10 shillings a day, although travel and accommodation expenses were met by the committee.[6] They worked initially at the Colonial Museum in Wellington before going to Christchurch a few weeks before the opening.

Four carvers from Wanganui under Hori Pukehika were also employed, though their rate of pay is not clear. McGregor reported having trouble recruiting Wanganui River women to go to Christchurch, and had to offer them an inducement of 10 shillings a week.

The entertainers, who came in large parties, were paid at the rate of 6 shillings a day. On the other hand, the Turakina Maori Girls' School's *poi* dancers appear to have performed without remuneration, in exchange for keep.

The Ngati Porou chief Tuta Nihoniho was employed, at the express instruction of Carroll at 10 shillings a day, to use his influence to generate support from his tribal area, including the purchase of suitable artefacts. He also took his part in the ceremonial side of things, along with Neke Kapua and other chiefs, in welcoming notable visitors.

Inventing the 'olden times'

In a review of turn-of-the-century New Zealand ethnologists, Neich (1983:255-6) commented how Hamilton and other ethnological experts of the day,

> set up an orthodox doctrine of what 'unchanging traditional Maori culture' should be like … [and] an orthodox account of the traditional Maori discovery and settlement of New Zealand. A basic tennet of both these orthodoxies was that Maori culture had virtually remained unchanged throughout a long history and was only then becoming decadent as a result of European contact. These experts saw their mission to be the preservation of pure Maori culture.

It was Hamilton's intention to recreate in the model *pa* the essence of that orthodoxy, and he went to great lengths to ensure that the residents conveyed his idea of 'the olden times' to the public. They lived in reconstructed traditional *whare* (huts), gave craft demonstrations and cultural and ritual performances, and were expected to be appropriately costumed (fig. 4.5).

Costuming was particularly important. While McGregor was recruiting performers up the Wanganui River he was instructed by Hamilton to tell the people that:

> every man, woman and child who comes down to Christchurch to the *Pa* must have a *piupiu* and a mat of some kind … Everybody must be prepared to wear at certain times only the garments of the Maori.[7]

On another occasion the headmaster of Turakina Girls School, who was also named Hamilton, wrote to McGregor asking for guidance on music for their *poi* performances. He wrote:

> The common custom nowadays is to perform to the music of the mouth organ. Would that be admissible, or should it be the old style of singing by the performers themselves?[8]

The letter was referred to Augustus Hamilton, whose reply is full of unconscious irony:

I think it would be far the best for the girls to sing something in the old style, it does not really matter what. I have heard very good *pois* sung to the Multiplication Tables, and if you can manage something in this way I think it would be best.[9]

Nevertheless, despite his best efforts, reality sometimes intruded in disconcerting ways. Sir John Gorst, who had returned to New Zealand as a special British commissioner to the exhibition after more than forty years absence, commented on the two great receptions given the British

4.4 Fijian party with Chief Ifirimi Qasivakatini, in white uniform and sash, making a ceremonial presentation to Maori residents of Te Araiteuru *Pa*, watched by a large crowd of spectators. The three European males in centre field are, from left, W.A. Scott, Assistant Native Commissioner of Fiji, Captain Gilbert Mair, in charge of the Arawa contingent, and (seated) Gregor McGregor, Te Araiteuru site superintendent. (Photo: James McDonald; Museum of New Zealand Te Papa Tongarewa. Negative No. C1729.)

4.5 A costumed group of mainly Arawa residents. Gilbert Mair is on the extreme left in a suit. The *pataka* behind the group was carved on-site by Neke Kapua and his sons. (Photo: James McDonald; Museum of New Zealand Te Papa Tongarewa. Negative No. C1686.)

commissioners in the *pa*. These were accompanied with ceremonial dances of haka (fig. 4.6) and *poi* followed by speeches of welcome in the 'old style of oratory'. However, he also reported that a few young men 'not of the *haka*', well-educated, well-dressed and speaking in English, wanted him to know there was a new generation who 'were ambitious of seeing their race become in every respect the equals of the Europeans, and taking part in the government and administration of the country' (Gorst 1908:66).

Another exhibition image of the timeless, heroic Maori was presented in a remarkable piece of statuary sculpted by the artist-photographer member of the Maori Committee, James McDonald. This larger than life-size group of Maori figures was located in the Main Corridor, just off the Grand Hall of the exhibition building. The two principal figures were a traditionally costumed young Maori man and woman standing, with the woman carrying a baby on her back. Seated round this family group were four figures representing a youth playing the *putorino* (flute), a carver, a girl making a *poi*-ball, and 'an old warrior, *mere* [weapon] in hand, gazing with introspective eyes far into the past' (Cowan 1910:107). The pedestal base carried a panel on each face, two representing the art of cutting greenstone, and two the art of generating fire by friction. Further decoration involved details appropriated from the Maori artistic tradition.

As a composition, the figures represented no particular personages, nor any event either historical or mythological. They were simply a romanticised image of noble savages whose age was passing. While the old warrior looks backwards into the past, the young family appear to be facing the future, but the air of melancholy that pervades the group suggested there was no future for the Maori except as a decorative embellishment of life in the colony.

Barbarism and redemption

The presentation of Maori and Pacific Islands peoples as exotic Others living out a pakeha fantasy of a timeless, heroic age in a physically bounded village on the fringes of the exhibition represented a utopian Maoriland. James Cowan's *Official Record*, on the other hand, reveals that

other, darker figure in the Maoriland metaphor, the alienated colonist-threatening Maori, referred to by Blythe. Cowan's account is notable for his stress on the savagery of old New Zealand, the progressive civilisation of the colonists, his appeals to the imperial centre of British civilisation, and his invocation of racial superiority.

The Maori as cannibal savage is a recurring theme for Cowan. He extols the exhibition as 'a wonderful record of progress for a land that only three generations ago lay in the hands of the cannibal savage' (1910:2). Again, he comments on 'old New Zealand' as 'peopled by the most desperately savage of brown-skinned races ... who ate human flesh' (Cowan 1910:7).

Contemporary New Zealand was, for him, a land only recently redeemed from savagery by the industry of the white settlers. The purpose of the exhibition, he tells us, was 'primarily illustrating the material progress of New Zealand since it was first redeemed from barbarism by the white man' (Cowan 1910:20).

The exhibition was a manifestation of the success of the civilising mission of British colonisation, as well as a plea for an imperial recognition of the worthiness of colonial society. It was a 'waymark of the short pilgrimage of human endeavour in this part of the Empire' (Cowan 1910:2). Acknowledgement of Maori displacement from prior sovereignty ('domination') over the country and occupation of their lands is justified in terms of the civilising mission of the white race:

> Not only have the brown and white races changed places
> in the domination of Maori Land, but the white has suc-
> ceeded in hewing and building the one-time cannibal islands
> into a peaceful, happy, prosperous State. [Cowan 1910:7]

Cowan saw the exhibition as confirming the superiority of white civilisation in the minds of Maori and Pacific Islanders who came to see it: 'the magnitude of the marvels of the Exhibition impressed them beyond words with the strength and godlike knowledge of the white race' (Cowan 1910:30).

In these passages, Cowan is invoking the doctrine of social Darwinism in asserting the right of white civilisation to dominate other races. The continuing Maori presence appears to be a troubling reality disturbing the peace of mind of settler consciousness. If the Maori would not go away they must be explained away, which for Cowan was in terms of an imputed racial inferiority.

His *Official Record* complements and completes the Maoriland metaphor initiated in the construction of the model *pa*. The *pa* manifested its romantic dimension, but Cowan's text reveals the dark image of the threatening Maori. The Maori as savage must be tamed and contained by progressive British civilisation. The empire is the guarantor of settler peace of mind.

Arai-Te-Uru *Pa* : Maori perceptions

Benedict (1991:8-9) refers to two sorts of tradition-inventing at colonial exhibitions. The first were those promulgated by the colonial powers attempting to represent the position of their dependent peoples within the wider scheme of things. The Model Maori *Pa* was one such example of this kind of tradition-invention. The model *pa,* as a representation of one trope in the Maoriland metaphor, provided the spectacle of romanticised noble savages as fellow citizens existing on the fringes of national life as its decorative element. Cowan's text inverted the

metaphor to suggest ignoble savages whose land was forfeit to a people of superior civilisation.

The second sort of tradition-invention was that of the displayed peoples themselves, 'which promoted their own national and ethnic identities' (Benedict 1991:2). It is to the Maori response that I now turn.

When one asks why Maori would want to participate in an event that presents them so negatively, one is struck by alternative readings of it and different Maori perceptions. Maori responses may be interpreted at economic, political, cultural and ideological levels.

At an economic level the entertainers, carvers, and craftswomen were paid for their services. Many, especially those from Rotorua, were professional performers who were dependent on pakeha patrons and tourists for their livelihood. The *pa* was just another arena to work in.

The politics were more complex. In the first place, only some tribes were actively involved, and these were mainly tribes that were allied with the Crown in the wars of the mid-19th century, namely the eastern North Island tribes of Ngati Kahungunu and Ngati Porou, the Bay of Plenty Arawa Confederation, and tribes of the lower Wanganui River. An exception was Waikato, whose paramount chief, King Mahuta, lent his canoe *Taheretikitiki*, but that seems

4.6 An Arawa team performing a haka in the inner *pa*. Spectators are behind a roped barrier. (Photo: James McDonald; Museum of New Zealand Te Papa Tongarewa. Negative No. C1726.)

4.7 A Maori party in street dress being ceremonially welcomed to Te Araiteuru. This group has probably just arrived off the overnight ferry from the North Island. Their baggage is stacked against the side of the meeting house. There are no paying spectators present, though some people in the amusement area are peering through the fence to catch a glimpse of proceedings. (Photo: James McDonald; Museum of New Zealand Te Papa Tongarewa. Negative No. C1677.)

to have been a personal gesture rather than a tribal commitment. Tribal grievances with the Crown had not been resolved, and quite clearly tribal-Crown politics had a major influence in determining which tribes responded to the government's invitation to take part in the exhibition.

Ngai Tahu, in whose territory the model *pa* was located, played only a minor role in the exhibition. By comparison with some North Island tribes, theirs was a token presence only, which is surprising in view of the strong support they had given the Christchurch Jubilee Festival in 1900,[10] also attended by several North Island tribes. But again there were unresolved grievances against the Crown over land confiscations dating back to 1848, which were particularly sensitive following the passage of the *South Island Landless Natives Act 1906*. Ngai Tahu's partial boycott appears to have been a form of political protest.

On the other hand, the exhibition was the first opportunity for large-scale intertribal contact since the 'Grand Carnival of the Tribes' that greeted the Duke and Duchess of Cornwall and York at Rotorua in 1901. Those tribes that came to the exhibition brought important chiefs who revelled in the chance for tribal interchange and rivalry, and to discuss important political issues of the day.[11]

Memories of the great cultural display at the Maori welcome to the royal couple, and the favourable attention they received from the British press, were still fresh. Maori loyalty to Crown and empire had been shown on that occasion to have been just as intense as that of their pakeha fellows.[12] Just as importantly, the international exhibition offered Maori people another opportunity to present themselves advantageously in an international context. It is clear from the Maori press of the time[13] that they were conscious that they would be displaying their culture and its treasures to the world. The *pa* was an arena in which Maori were able to define a worthy place for themselves within both the New Zealand colonial order and the British imperial family.

What was seen as the Model Maori *Pa* by pakeha became Te Araiteuru *Pa* for Maori, in commemoration of the great canoe of southern tradition. It was named by James Carroll, who was responding diplomatically to tribal sensibilities. The *pa* was erected in the territory of the Ngai Tahu tribe, and naming it after their canoe acknowledged their standing as the senior tribe of the *pa*. More relevant to this discussion, however, is that Te Araiteuru transposed the cultural context from pakeha to Maori and provided a Maori frame of reference.

From the start, the *pa* developed a life of its own, meaningful to its residents and Maori visitors but largely hidden from the public gaze. Shortly after the opening it was consecrated with a *tapu*-lifting ceremony conducted by an Arawa group, who also named the meeting houses located in the outer *pa* 'Ohinemutu' and Donne's house 'Te Wharepuni a Maui'. The matter of ceremonial protocols was a contentious issue among the tribes throughout the life of the *pa*, and in February 1907 another *tapu*-lifting ceremony was performed by members of the Ngati Kahungunu contingent (*Weekly Press* 24 April 1907).

Many ceremonial occasions, including welcomes to visiting pakeha dignitaries, were open to the paying public, and Neich believes these were not taken seriously by Maori participants. On the other hand, some ceremonial occasions were closed to the public out of deference to their importance to the residents (fig. 4.7).

The *tapu*-lifting rites mentioned above were such occasions, as was the welcome given to the Arawa contingent under Gilbert Mair (*Weekly Press* 5 December 1906). Another occasion was the baptism of an infant born in the *pa* to an Arawa couple, appropriately named Araiteuru. Maori and pakeha were present for the christening conducted by the Anglican Bishop of Christchurch, but it was a private ceremony (*Weekly Press* 19 December 1906).

The visiting Fijian dancers and firewalkers excited much pakeha interest, and their public appearances attracted large numbers of spectators. Maori, on the other hand, were much more interested in the presence of the Cook Islanders, whom they considered to be from their ancient homeland of Hawaiki (fig. 4.8). The Cook Islanders brought with them a sacred ceremonial adze called Te Aumapu, which was said to have been used in the building of the *Takitimu* canoe of Maori tradition,[14] which stimulated huge Maori interest. The Cook Islands had only recently (in 1901) come under New Zealand jurisdiction, and this was an early formal contact between Maori and Cook Islands chiefs.

Maori as much as pakeha were given to romanticising their past. The reform movement associated with the Te Aute College Students Association (TACSA), better known as the Young Maori Party, was politically dominant at the time of the exhibition. One of its leaders was the young physician Dr Peter Buck. The reformers sought to bring Maori into the mainstream of social and economic development in the country, and stressed social issues such as health, hygiene, education, the economic development of Maori land, and the moral regeneration of Maori communities. They opposed many of the conservative tendencies in Maori life, but they were also developing their own idealised image of the past, not as an escape from the present, but with the ideological purpose of encouraging their people to think positively of themselves. The idealised past was being put to the service of providing

4.8 Cook Islands dancers entertaining spectators in the inner *pa*. Note the two drummers to the right. (Photo: Samuel Heath Head; Alexander Turnbull Library, Wellington, NZ. Reference No. G-9974-1/1.)

for the future. Maori Land for them was the real world of the contemporary Maori and their struggle to find a place within the colonial order.

Conclusion

The exhibition marked an important closure in the story of the colony. Shortly after the exhibition finished in 1907, New Zealand became a dominion within the British Empire. The period coincided with a developing sense of nationhood and a corresponding search for symbols of identity. The exhibition served this purpose admirably. In the manipulation of symbols, in the construction of a colonial history and in defining traditions, the exhibition was an ideal vehicle for the projection of an image of the nation as it saw itself.

The growing sense of national identity was taking place within a wider British world, wherein the colony and young dominion saw its future and destiny. This identification with the empire and British civilisation led to the colonists' perception of New Zealand as a Britain of the South with imperial ambitions in the South Pacific. As a result of New Zealand lobbying, the Cook Islands and Niue Island had come under its administration in 1901. Thus the exhibition incorporated the cultures of British Polynesia, including Fiji.

New Zealand represented itself in the exhibition as British, white and progressive but nevertheless with an acknowledgement of the Maori presence. The Model Maori *Pa*, the McDonald statuary and Cowan's *Official Record* all point to the Maori presence within the nation as peripheral and decorative. The model *pa*, as a soft 'Maoriland' image, represented pakeha perceptions of the Maori, despite the evidence of other realities observed by Gorst. Cowan's account exposes negative images of racism and social Darwinism.

Maori participation was governed largely by tribal attitudes to the colonial government. All the tribes had demonstrated their loyalty to the British Crown in recent years, but many held grievances against the colonial government going back many years. Those tribes that did attend saw advantages in their involvement. It gave them an opportunity to engage in intertribal activities on a major scale, and to make important linkages with other Pacific peoples. It provided an arena where they were able to affirm their ethnic identity, and to present themselves and their culture to their fellow New Zealanders and to the world. Finally, it allowed the Maori reform movement to reinvent the Maori past in order to promote a reformist political agenda.

At their annual meeting in December 1905, the reformers of the Young Maori Party passed a series of resolutions aimed at reviving traditional arts, architecture and music. They even formed an architecture committee to advance their objectives, and invited Augustus Hamilton to join it (TACSA Report 1905:39). The construction of a model village where traditional arts and crafts and music could be revived fitted neatly into their agenda.

Hamilton's Maoriland may not have been the same as the Maori Land of the Young Maori Party, but in some important respects they overlapped. Likewise, Te Araiteuru was not exactly the same place as the Model Maori *Pa*, but in a number of significant respects they converged.

Acknowledgements

I am indebted to Roger Neich, Dave Simmons, Jan Pouwer and Awhina Tamarapa for comments on an earlier draft. Margaret Orbell kindly supplied Maori texts with English translations from the Maori newspapers *Te Pipiwharauroa* and *Te Puke ki Hikurangi*.

Notes

1. For fuller discussion, see B. Kernot (in press).
2. Macmillan-Brown Lectures, Victoria University, 1994.
3. Common term for European.
4. Letter, Hamilton to Donne, 18 April 1906; Hector Library NZIE 1906-07 File.
5. Janet Davidson, pers. comm., July 1997.
6. Letter, Hamilton to Donne, 5 April 1906; Hector Library, NZIE 1906-07 File.
7. Letter, Hamilton to McGregor, 11 May 1906; Hector Library, NZIE 1906-7 File.

8. Letter, A.G. Hamilton to McGregor, 5 July 1906; Hector Library, NZIE 1906-7 File.

9. Letter, Hamilton to A.G. Hamilton, 10 July 1906; Hector Library NZIE 1906-7 File.

10. *Te Puke ki Hikurangi* 15 April 1901. I am indebted to Margaret Orbell for supplying the translations.

11. The Native Minister James Carroll held a meeting with tribal leaders in the *pa* towards the end of the exhibition, reported in the *Weekly Press*, 10 April 1907.

12. Ngati Kahungunu tribe had been awarded the title 'Duke's Own' at Rotorua. The only tribal group absent from the Rotorua welcome were Waikato, not out of lack of loyalty, but because they were not permitted to hold their own separate welcome to the royal couple on their arrival in Auckland.

13. *Te Pipiwharauroa* No. 95, February 1906. Translation by Margaret Orbell. From Orbell (in press).

14. *Te Pipiwharauroa* Nos 104-6, November 1906 to January 1907. Translations by Margaret Orbell. From Orbell (in press).

5 Art education in Samoa: Acculturated identity

Regina Meredith

The evolution of art is a process of adaptation to suit the time and needs of the society, but those changes in meanings and functions of art must come from within and not be imposed from the outside. Therefore any assimilation of aspects of foreign culture should be highly selective.

To be able to pick and choose, Pacific societies must be confident and have faith in their own cultures and their way of doing things. Only then can the creative process which is firmly based in the past, progress confidently into the future; selecting, discarding, modifying and improving to create a new Pacific, relevant and suitable to present experience. [Vilsoni Tausie 1980:77]

American Samoa is an unincorporated territory of the United States. It comprises seven islands: Tutuila, Aunu'u, the Manu'a group of Tau, Ofu and Olosega, and Rose and Swains atolls. It is located at 13°S 171°E, 4200 kilometres (2600 miles) south-west of Hawai'i and 2900 kilometres (1800 miles) from the northern tip of New Zealand. It is the only US territory south of the equator.

As a territory, American Samoa is the responsibility of the US Department of the Interior. It receives an annual $50 million subsidy from the US government. The American Samoan government is the largest employer and accounts for about 46 per cent of the workforce. Other sources of employment are the tuna canneries and privately owned businesses.

Since 1977, American Samoans have elected their own governor and lieutenant-governor, who hold office for a four-year term. As US nationals, American Samoans have US citizenship rights. They cannot, though, hold office or vote in a US general election. The population of American Samoa has increased rapidly; the 1990 Census taken by the Economic Development Planning Office, recorded 46 773 inhabitants. There are 25 573 American Samoans and 21 200 other nationalities (Western Samoans, Tongans, Fijians, other Pacific Islanders, and other US citizens).

The increase in population, the influence of the American lifestyle, and the presence of other nationalities have swayed American Samoans to the conveniences and modifications of modern living. Acculturation has existed in American Samoa for quite a long time. Intercultural mixing can be observed in something as simple as the use of aluminium foil to replace the use of leaves in cooking a popular Sunday dish called *palusami* (creamed coconut milk and taro leaves steamed in a Samoan *umu* or outdoor oven). The Western-style home replaces many of the thatched *fales* (houses), outboard motors take the place of oars, plastic bags are used instead of woven baskets, and so on.

Nevertheless, the *fa'asamoa* ('Samoan way') remains an integral part of this modern lifestyle. For example, it is still customary in Samoan culture to present guests and dignitaries with a *sua*.[1] This courtesy is extended in appreciation of, and to honour, the recipient.

It is common for a people to be exposed to, and adopt novel ideas and manners from, other cultures, but the supreme test is whether or not they can continue to maintain their identity after sifting through the innovations and selecting what can be integrated into their culture. Samoan culture has proved to be viable, retaining its basic form regardless of outside influences. For example, the *matai* (chief) system. This is composed of related kin and forms an extended-family organisation. Nearly every capable and energetic young man can aspire to hold a family title at some time during his life.

Though Samoan culture has wavered, one aspect maintaining its appearance and status is the native art forms. There are many art forms in Samoan culture: the arts of speaking, singing, cooking, house building and canoe building. Selection of the art forms for this paper, though, is based on the physically pliable visual arts: *tatau* (body tattoo), carving, *siapo* (bark cloth), and mat and basket making. The role of these art forms in the culture and the educational system will be assessed for their significance to the people who consider them a part of the Samoan heritage.

Tatau (body tattoo)

For the Samoan male it was considered honourable to be tattooed. It distinguished him as one entering into the privileges of his mature years. In old Samoa it was usually the youths around the age of sixteen who anticipated the moment when they would fall under the combs of a master *tufuga ta tatau*.[2] Certain designs and patterns were exclusively reserved for the chiefly class, but today they can be worn by anyone who can afford them. There are initially two types of body tattoos:

- the *tatau* or *pe'a* for the males, which covers the area beginning at the lower back down to the knees (fig. 5.1); and
- the *malu* for the women, which covers the region between the thighs and the knees.

Both styles are an elaborate array of patterns and designs reflective of the environment, and have remained consistent.

This art form is performed by a *tufuga ta tatau*. The rank of *tufuga* is usually hereditary, but if an assistant shows

promise, he may be encouraged by his master. Thus an assistant may aspire to the status of an adept *tufuga ta tatau*.

It is believed that the *tatau* originated because of two Samoan females, Taema and Tilafaiga.[3] They were believed to be Siamese twins joined at the back. The twins nonetheless were avid swimmers and there are numerous accounts of their aquatic travels. On one occasion they swam to the Fiji islands, where it was customary in those days for the women to be tattooed. On their return swim, Taema and Tilafaiga carried the tattoo instruments and, while chanting in their native tongue 'the women will be tattooed but not the men', they were distracted by something in the water. This distraction caused them to dive deep and when they surfaced, all the excitement caused them to reverse the chant to 'the men will be tattooed and not the women'.

One can still acquire a traditional body tattoo. It has been mainly the *tufuga* of Western Samoa that have kept

5.1 A few of the traditional Samoan *tatau* symbols.

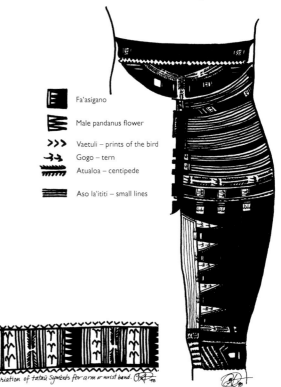

Fa'asigano

Male pandanus flower

Vaetuli – prints of the bird

Gogo – tern

Atualoa – centipede

Aso la'ititi – small lines

variation of tataū symbols for arm & wrist band.

this art alive through the years. Ceremony often accompanies the commencement of a *tatau*. Initially the *tufuga ta tatau* is presented with a *sua*, along with the request or petition for a tattoo. The *tufuga ta tatau* then proceeds to set a commencement date.

To fulfil the request, the *tufuga* will need a selection of items and a team to accompany him. These include assistants to stretch and wipe the skin; six to eight different-sized *'au* (combs) made of turtle shell, wood, bone and sennit; wooden sticks (*'auta*) for tapping the combs; *lama* dye (burnt candlenut mixture) made from the *Aleurites moluccana* tree; clothes to keep the body work area clean; and coconut oil to apply to the tattooed area after a session. A man's tattoo can take up to three months to complete, depending upon the number of sittings with the *tufuga* and the man's tolerance for pain.

There have been a few adjustments in the traditional tattoo, such as new symbols, manufactured ink to replace the *lama* dye, electric tattoo machines, and even fashionable trends such as 'armbands', 'legbands' or 'wristbands'.[4] These changes, however, have not interrupted the Samoan *tatau* heritage. It is still a much sought-after form.

At one time, it was believed by some that the art would eventually disappear because of the incoming new and modern ways:

> It is not likely, however, to stand long before advancing civilisation. European clothing, and a sense of propriety they are daily acquiring, lead them to cover the tattooed part of the body entirely; and when its display is considered a shame more than a boast, it will probably be given up as painful, expensive and useless. [Stanley 1986:40]

Despite this assumption, the *tatau* has survived. The body has become the canvas for the art, and the *tatau* continues to exist as long as the person lives.

The craftsman chooses the instruments and materials to be used in creating the tattoo. His reasons for substituting materials such as Indian ink in lieu of the *lama* dye may include convenience and durability; using the tattoo machine means it takes less time to complete a tattoo. A client's preference for an 'armband' over a full body *tatau* may relate to their level of tolerance for pain and their

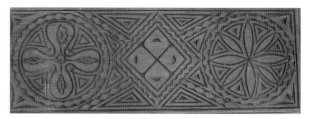

5.2 An example of a wooden *upeti* board; made around the late 19th century by the author's great grandfather.

commitment to suffering. Whatever the individual's choice, traditional *tatau* is still admired and respected greatly.

It is essential that our young people be told of the significance and meaning of *tatau* in our culture, for they may find it desirable to wear the historical tradition of Samoa.

Woodcarving

Woodcarving in Samoa was considered utilitarian rather than decorative. The Samoan carving style parallels those of neighbouring islands, namely Fiji and Tonga. Carved items that are still in use today are the *paopao* (canoe), *tanoa 'ava* (kava bowl), *ali* (headrest), *umete* (food bowl) and the *upeti* board (sunken relief of repeated Samoan symbols used to 'print' designs onto barkcloth; fig. 5.2). Less functional items are the *uatogi* (war club) and the tourist-oriented carvings of *laumei* (turtles), model *fale* (houses) and *paopao* (canoes), kava bowls, figures and the *pate* (wooden gong).

The carvings of these objects is still taught in American Samoa and Western Samoa. In American Samoa there are two male employees of the Jean P. Haydon Museum who work daily at woodcarving. Available for workshops and demonstrations, both men are eager and willing to share their expertise. The overseer of the craft in Tutuila is master-carver Sven Ortquist of Leone.

Woodcarving is not included in the school curriculum, mainly because of lack of materials and instructors. Nevertheless, woodcarving lessons can be provided to the schools on request through the museum. In addition, an annual Summer Cultural Workshop, sponsored by the museum through the American Samoa Council on Art, Culture and Humanities,[5] is offered to students of all ages. The intensive eight-week workshops cover many indigenous art forms, one of which is woodcarving.

Ortquist[6] has kept many students abreast of the traditional carving methods and techniques. He realises the importance of maintaining the supply of carved goods such as the *tanoa 'ava* (kava bowl) because these items assist in the continuation of Samoan culture. At the same time, Ortquist is willing to leave room for innovation in his craft. He hopes to inspire young artists to explore new ideas, as well as to become familiar with traditional ones. Although novel forms may never replace traditional wooden objects in their cultural context, Ortquist is confident that his teachings and his works reflect a Samoa that is dynamic, yet remains connected with its past in terms of techniques, forms and symbolism.

> An important thing to be learned from the cross-cultural study of artists, their personalities, their roles, their degree of freedom, and their conservatism and innovations, is the relationship of the individual to his society and to his culture … Depending to some extent on the degree of freedom allowed by use, by the material, and the technique and demands of cultural norms, the craftsman leaves evidence of his personal style, his personality, on the work. [Hatcher 1985:112]

One of the previously mentioned art forms requiring further comment is the *tanoa 'ava* (kava bowl). The kava bowl is used for special occasions in Samoa, namely the *'ava* ceremony.[7] This ceremony is performed for several reasons, but the *tanoa 'ava* is essential to contain the special drink (*'ava*) which ritually links the participants to one another. Therefore, the kava bowl can be considered to have a dual character: an art form created by the hands of a master carver, and an object necessary for the formal ritual of Samoan protocol. Its exquisite quality and predetermined character assure its continuing existence in Samoan culture.

Siapo

Siapo is the Samoan word for the bark cloth made from the paper mulberry tree (*Broussonetia papyrifera*) in its finished, painted form. In old Samoa, the production of *siapo* was secondary to that of fine mat weaving, but the cloth had many uses, such as for bedding, clothing, partitions for open *fale*, and as mosquito nets. *Siapo* also served as customary gift items for ceremonial occasions such as initiations and dedications. Nowadays, *siapo* is used in several different ways:

- as unmounted *u'a*[8] with an array of asymmetrically painted patterns and designs;
- *u'a* mounted on a flat board, with painted symmetrical patterns and motifs of traditional significance;[9]
- *u'a* rubbed over an *upeti* (wooden relief of carved symbols) and later highlighted with natural dyes;
- in a non-traditional form using silk-screen materials for decoration; and
- as *siapo* symbols on paper, canvas, carving, prints or sculpture.

Much of what has been retained in this art form in terms of its authenticity are credited to a master *siapo* maker, the late Mary J. Pritchard. She preserved her extensive knowledge through her artworks and her collection, as well as in her book *Siapo: Bark Cloth Art of Samoa* (1984). The Pritchard family is devoted to maintaining this art through workshops and demonstrations. Many of Mary's masterpieces are on permanent exhibit in American Samoa, and are illustrated in her book.

There is little information on the origin of *siapo*. Some Samoan songs refer to it, and a few legends speak of women making *siapo*, but its origin remains elusive.

Bark-cloth art requires various steps and procedures to achieve its finished form. These procedures, as well as the design elements and symbols, are fully described by Pritchard. The formalities of traditional *siapo*-making are complex and require many items to sustain the original format. A list of such requirements has seen some changes in the art form. For example, the use of acrylic paint to replace the black *lama* dye, or the use of a polymer liquid to seal the painted *u'a*, and even the concept of mounting *u'a* on boards, have been innovative. As Pritchard (1984:76) notes:

> there have been changes in *siapo* designs, some of which I have made. Changes will be made in the future. If they are rooted in tradition and based on the exploitation of the natural materials, *siapo* will continue as a living art.

The feature of *siapo* that has retained its character, which ties together the old and new ways of making *siapo*, is the symbols. Whether painted on canvas, tattooed, or even printed onto clothing, the *siapo* symbols are recognisable and identified with their original art form. Only the *siapo* symbols have made their way into the curriculum of the arts for both elementary and secondary schools.

Mat-making and basketry

Mat-making is the work of the woman, just as *siapo* used to be. It is still considered a strongly surviving craft in the Samoas, even though the number of people who are learned in the craft is minimal. There are three sources of natural materials for mat-making: the pandanus palms, *laufala* (*Pandanus utilis*) and *lau'ie* (*Pandanus odoratissimus*), and *launiu* (coconut). Mats are classified according to the material used in their making. For example, the *fala moe*, or sleeping mat, is made from the *laufala*. There is a ranking system of mats from low to high according to their usage, which parallels placement in their actual setting. The only mat that will not be used for placement is the fine mat, or *ie toga*, as it is the highest ranking of the mats in Samoa. Types of mats include:

- *polavai* – a coarse mat made of coconut leaves, used for the first layer in a *fale*;
- *fala paogo* – a stiff floor-mat made of *laufala*;
- *fala* – a soft floor-mat made of *laufala*;
- *fala moe* – a sleeping mat made of *laufala*;
- *ie moega* – a chief's sleeping mat made of *lau'ie*;

- *ie toga* – a fine mat used for special occasions, made of *laufala* or *lau'ie*; and
- *fala lau'ie* – a fine mat made of *lau'ie*.

In layering, the *polavai*, *fala paogo*, *fala* and the *fala moe* are placed according to their ranking, with the lowest at the bottom.

Some women in American Samoa continue the mat-making craft with some variation in the finished plaited products. Such alterations include the substitution of the traditional *sega* (*Coriphilus fringilaceus*) bird feathers in the *ie toga* with dyed *moa* (chicken) feathers, the use of decorative yarn, or an elaborate finishing of the mats. Plaiting can be learned through the Jean P. Haydon Museum, the Office of the Territorial Agency on Ageing, and through various teachers who work for the Department of Education. Although the craft is complex and tedious, the products are still used and appreciated. Some women still teach this art form in the home.

Basketry in Samoa, especially the baskets made of coconut fronds, has a short life span. Baskets are easy to make and are biodegradable. Preserving a coconut-frond basket is inconceivable; making a fresh basket is more logical. The types of baskets used today can be identified by the number of braids plaited. Certain baskets are used for certain tasks, such as the *ato filii tasi*, or the single-braided keel-bottom basket, which is mainly used to hold freshly cooked food from the *umu* (earth oven). The basket is made on the day of use for the transport of food. The *ato fili tolu*, or the three-braided keel-bottom basket, is meant for heavy uses like carrying rocks, coconuts or wood. There are other types of Samoan baskets such as the *ato afa* and the *ato lavalava*, but these are not common today.

Plaited items intended to be more permanent are those made from pandanus leaves. Hats, fans, purses, placemats and tableware are among the items made with pandanus basketry techniques. Pandanus plaited items present an array of different styles, and are decorated with shells and patterns using coloured dyes. These items have changed status in Samoa. Before, they were the typical item of everyday use, but now, with widespread use of plastic bags and Western valises and purses, the plaited goods are more community oriented. Basketry in Samoa has been reduced from a wide selection to a limited number of types, mainly due to changing needs in the society. This is the case, as Arbeit (1990:5) has commented, for Polynesia generally:

> Modern day baskets are the products of a circumstance where the makers are no longer the users, and the users are from outside cultures. This results sometimes in lowered quality and often in eclectic design characteristics that are a normal and legitimate part of an on-going evolution of any living craft.

Despite the change in needs, and influence from the outside, the artisans continue to use familiar indigenous techniques and methods.

Art education in Samoa

The state of the traditional arts and crafts of American Samoa is clear. There have been varying degrees of alteration. The authenticity of the art forms in their purest sense has been affected by the wants and needs of the society. The culture has accommodated to the changes. The issue now is to identify an appropriate format by which this cultural knowledge can continue to be transmitted. For example, what are the consequences of taking these arts and crafts out of context and teaching them in an educational setting? Are students receiving a sufficient amount of cultural knowledge to perpetuate self-identity? How much of these art forms is taught at home? Will the use of non-traditional materials and methods change the nature of traditional art forms?

Teaching the native arts in school is one way of preserving them. Historically, cultural knowledge was transmitted or passed on in the home. However, there are many distractions in the home today, such as changes in the way of living and the influence of popular culture. Bringing cultural knowledge into an educational setting, therefore, would achieve a balance between the Western and traditional fields. It would lead to an understanding of society, civilisation, the individual, the nation, and the relationship of that nation to other nations. The outcome can be multicultural consciousness, or an acculturated identity. Cultural knowledge taught as a school subject would ensure its existence.

Art education in American Samoa is intended to suit the needs of the student of the westernised and the indigenous Samoan art forms, even though the art curriculum for public elementary and secondary levels focuses mainly on Western concepts. Samoan visual arts are incorporated through symbols derived from *siapo*. For example, a lesson in block printing requires materials from the United States (linoleum blocks, tools, brayers and ink), but the design carved into the linoleum may derive from *siapo* patterns and designs. The curriculum for the elementary level focuses on combinations so as to prepare the respective levels for the secondary school. At this level, the art class is considered an elective, with a specialised teacher in the classroom, and additional information is offered to strengthen both fields of art, Western and traditional Samoan.

Supplementary programs designed to enrich the set curriculum are offered through the American Samoa Council on Arts, Culture and Humanities. Its goal is to maintain the traditional cultural heritage and the artistic birthright of Samoans while fostering non-Samoan art forms. The council administers four programs, one of which is the Arts in Education Program. This program promotes creativity and enhances the experience of the student through special projects with visiting local and off-island artists. For example, a special project injected into the mainstream of the art curriculum concerns *siapo* symbols and methods, whereas a visiting artist may focus on aspects of creative writing. The program is broad and expansive; it accommodates the needs of all the arts – performing, visual and literary.

To achieve a balance between the two realms of art (Western styles and indigenous art forms), it is suggested that the art curriculum for the schools cover traditional art forms and include the historical and contemporary aspects of those art forms. That way, the students will gain insight into their cultural heritage. Students should have available to them the fundamentals of art education during elementary and secondary schooling. Students who attend the American Samoa Community College should then be able to realise their full potential in the arts and crafts. The college, according to the 1991-93 ASCC

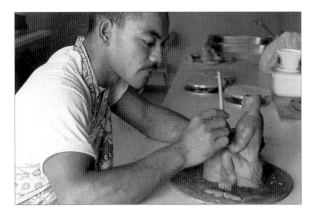

5.3 and 5.4 College students engage in art projects that reflect Samoan culture and integrate Western materials.

Catalogue, 'exists to meet the diverse educational needs of the community and to assist individual students in realising the maximum potential in a setting of cultural change'. Part of the college's goals include assisting 'Samoan youth to integrate their experience in their own culture with their experience in college as a largely Western institution' (ASCC Catalogue 1991:10). Through the Samoan and Pacific Studies Department, students can better understand their place as members of their unique culture and as participants in an ever-changing society.

Recently, a Samoan language course was included in the course selection to enable students to strengthen skills of composition in their native tongue. This will assist them to better understand the relationship between Samoan concepts and English; it also consolidates the richness and competency of the Samoan language. Thus, through the courses offered by Samoan and Pacific Studies and the English Department's inclusion of the Samoan language as part of its curriculum, the transmission of cultural knowledge through the arts has received a positive boost.[10]

Previously, the Fine Arts Department of the college has emphasised Western arts, with few projects offered in indigenous arts. However, the four art forms discussed above have been selected as the subjects of a new course to be labelled 'Indigenous Art Forms'. The intention is to provide a full coverage of both the traditional and contemporary manifestations of these forms. This will provide a rich and beneficial overview of a part of Samoan culture that has experienced changes and promotes balance in the visual-arts program.

This course would be supervised by a teacher knowledgeable in the field, who would then invite indigenous master craftspeople to work with students. All the art forms would be experienced on a first-hand basis, except the *tatau*, which would be accommodated through field observation and research. The course would attempt a revival and acknowledgement of these art forms as utilitarian, aesthetic and vital to the preservation of Samoan culture. The introduction of traditional arts into the Fine Arts Department curriculum should enable the students to identify with their heritage, relate to the outside world and amalgamate the two (figs 5.3 and 5.4).

Awareness of one's acculturated identity is important because a person can expect to be confronted with queries concerning his or her indigenous culture. I experienced this while pursuing an education in the arts. I hope I have conveyed the importance of being fluent in one's culture.

Notes

1. The *sua* consists of: a coconut drink; a length of material; a tray of food; cooked *pua'a* (pig), and; the most treasured gift, the fine mat.

2. *Tufuga*: a craftsman, expert, carpenter, or builder (Allaridge 1989). *Tufuga ta tatau* is a tattooing expert.

3. There are several versions of the story of Taema and Tilafaiga. It is said in one version that Taema introduced the art of tattooing while Tilafaiga went to Savaii.

4. The 'wristband' by itself is a modern form. In old Samoa, however, it was a fashion to tattoo the hand with a wristband design to give the impression of an intricate glove.

5. The American Samoa Council on Art, Culture, and Humanities was established by an executive order from the governor of the territory in 1970. It is funded by the National Endowment for the Arts and an appropriation from the territory. The council is a member of CPAC (Consortium for Pacific Arts and Culture), a regional organisation composed of the arts councils from the Commonwealth of the Northern Marianas and the Territory of Guam. The major role of the council is to exercise leadership in perpetuating Samoan culture, developing programs in the arts and cultivating professional excellence.

6. From an interview with Sven Ortquist on 16 March 1993, acknowledged with thanks.

7. The Samoan word *'ava* can mean the *'ava* drink, or the *'ava* ceremony. The kava plant's scientific name is *Piper methysticum*, and the highly stylised ceremony is an age-old ritual practised throughout the Pacific.

8. *U'a* is the prepared bark of the paper mulberry tree.

9. The permanently mounted *u'a* was initially created by Mary J. Pritchard around the 1970s.

10. I wish to acknowledge the help of Pulefa 'asisina Palauni Tuiasosopo, Director of Samoan and Pacific Studies at the American Samoa Community College, interviewed 10 March 1993. Fa'afetai lava.

6 Fat is beautiful: The body as art form in the Pacific

Nancy J. Pollock

The human body as a living, culturally influenced entity has been underrated as an art form. In painting and sculpture the body has been analysed extensively by artists (see references in Feher 1989), often working from live models. In biology, the human body has been treated as a material form, on which cultural influences have had varying impact, subject to disease and death. In psychology the human body has been treated as a projection of the mind, sometimes appreciated, sometimes negatively valued and leading to medical conditions such as, for example, bulimia and anorexia. But the body itself as an art form, the embodiment of an aesthetic, has not been widely considered.

I am arguing here that the body is culturally manipulated to meet local aesthetic criteria. Enlarging the body and lightening the skin are two significant cultural practices carried out in parts of Polynesia, and in Nauru. Perhaps these practices are even more widespread but awaiting documentation.

In the Pacific, specialised studies of decoration of the human body are increasing; for example, the Stratherns' study of self-decoration in Mount Hagen (1985) and the current work of Mageo, Stevensen and Teilhet-Fisk in Polynesia. But it is noticeable that in her otherwise comprehensive overview of art and aesthetics in Polynesia, Kaeppler (1989) omits discussion of the body as art form.

Social enhancement through bodies is achieved in Polynesian societies by two linked processes. Individuals are fattened and their skin is lightened while they remain in seclusion. The community bears the responsibility for achieving these desired ends, so must direct its efforts and its resources to carrying them out. Intense feeding and sequestering in a special place where the individuals can perform no social tasks are the main means.

The art form produced is thus a result of group efforts towards a communal goal, beauty. All those who participate, the subject of beautification and the beautifiers, share pride in the end product. All members of the social group contribute their share to produce the art form, the beautified body. There is no one particular artist. The person being fattened and beautified is thus the medium. He or she is part of the end product, as moulded by kin and the community. The fattening is not a matter of self-selection, or uncontrolled gluttony by the individual, as is so frequently argued in Western analyses of obesity (Bray 1990). Rather the aesthetic is created by and belongs to the whole social group, which revels in the beautification of one or several of its members.

Fattening rituals for selected individuals, men and women, appear to have been widespread in the Pacific before contact. Many of the early visitors noted the largeness of the Polynesians they met. Among them, Cook noted with amazement the vast amounts of food fed to a Tahitian chief (Beaglehole 1967). They saw these images in terms of their own cultural criteria, namely as large bodies, tall figures by their standards, and implied that the large amounts of food eaten were excessive. The intrusion of alternative value systems, including new ethical principles associated with the body and its uses, was responsible for changing this whole aesthetic. The newcomers sought to eliminate what they considered by their principles to be debauched. Missionaries disapproved of what they called gluttony, as they labelled the prolonged feasting, as well as the 'idleness' associated with these celebrations. Ellis's (1831) strong denouncement of the week-long *opi'o* bakes that drew the Tahitians together for festivities, for eating and dancing, was phrased in terms of the amount of time lost that could have been spent working. He certainly did not appreciate the cultural processes of fattening and lightening of bodies as aesthetic events.

We will examine how this aesthetic has been noted for two societies, Nauru and Tahiti. Records for other societies may be hidden away in the early accounts of visitors who stayed long enough and were able to appreciate values of beauty that were the complete antithesis of values in their society. They could and did admire the end product, the rounded and enlarged cultural form (for example, as depicted in Gauguin's paintings), but decried the process by which that was achieved.

An alternative to viewing the body as fashioned by aesthetic criteria has been much more widespread. According to this second view, a particular body image is the product of biology, derived from genetic and material inputs, with environment playing either a major or a minor role. As I have argued elsewhere (Pollock 1995a), the biological view of a fat body is generally negative for modern populations; it is said to be a risk factor leading to such non-communicable diseases as diabetes, hypertension and coronary heart disease. Obesity itself is sometimes classed as a disease. Fat is bad in this view. This is the flip side to the cultural ethic of the large body as beautiful.

Thus we have two opposed cultural views of the one entity, a large body. The biological view is based on Western cultural perceptions. It has been allowed to predominate, to smother an aesthetic that had significant cultural value,

not only in the Pacific but around the world (see de Garine and Pollock 1995). To consider body size merely a matter of biology is an error, as is to omit the enhancement of the body from consideration along with other aesthetic principles. Modern Western aesthetic criteria need to be questioned. By bringing the two together the 'web of culture' is strengthened.

By considering the body as art form, I am suggesting an additional category within art and aesthetics to those Kaeppler (1989) included in her overview for Polynesia. Adornments such as jewellery, coverings and clothing, and hair treatments (Gordon 1993) are here distinguished from enlargement of the body. Likewise the bodily movements that Kaeppler has studied in much detail are another category. And the body as drafted in wood or stone, on paper, or in some other secondary form is yet another category. Fattening the body and lightening the skin should be included along with tattooing, ear elongation and blackening the teeth as cultural processes that have been valued for the social product. Thereby a new body image is created.

Nauru

Young Nauruan women underwent a period of fattening and seclusion to lighten their skins (Fabricius 1992; Hambruch 1914-15; Rhone 1921). This process was still going on at the time phosphate mining commenced in 1906 with all the modern trappings of colonialism, and continued through into the 1920s. It had obviously been a significant feature of Nauruan culture. With loss of access to traditional sources of food, and the introduction of imported foods available for purchase with money from phosphate, the rituals ceased. New values of the body were being imposed.

Only young women who were of high status were subject to the beautification processes. The daughters of those who were of Nauruan heritage were distinguished in this way from those of in-marrying groups. Gilbertese, Banabans and Marshallese all visited Nauru before mining contracts brought them in as mineworkers but, as they had no rights to membership of a clan on Nauru, they joined the *itsio*, or lowest class of Nauruans, and were given membership of clans set aside for newcomers. Such newly created clans took names such as 'flotsam', 'trash', and so on, that indicated their marginal status in Nauru.

Since Nauru's population was small at the time (less than 1200), the numbers of young women who were honoured by beautification were small. It is likely that the celebration was held infrequently, certainly not every year, since Nauru was prone to long periods of drought and resources were limited. Hambruch photographed those who had been through the celebration in 1910, but he does not specify their exact ages; it is probable that they were in their late teens and early twenties. He records names, such as Babu (meaning 'fat one'), that were given to these women, though whether they were so named before or after the fattening ritual is unclear. The celebration may have taken place around puberty, though nowhere has it been seen as associated with virginity.

The young woman or women were the focus of attention of the whole community. A feast was held to mark the beginning of the celebration. For the next two or three months the women were set aside from the community, kept in a specially built hut. Their relatives brought food to them and took care of their needs. At the end of the period, the women were reintroduced to the community with a major feast and celebration (Kretzschmar 1913). At this time the women wore strings of *ibija* fish around their enlarged bodies, as Dobson Rhone photographed (1921).

That beauty was particularly a mark of the upper classes was noted by observers such as Senfft (1895, cited in Fabricius 1992:268):

Fullness of body is also regarded as beautiful and as in some way denoting high rank. The more corpulent the chiefs' wives are, the prouder they are of them. To prevent their becoming thin, they make sure that they eat as much as they can and take as little exercise as possible. Even at an early age the daughters of the chiefs, who are destined to marry future village headmen, are systematically fattened. For this purpose they are fed almost exclusively on copra and sweet toddy … and permitted to leave their huts only in the morning and towards evening. This way of life means

that by the time they reach their middle years these women can be described only as perambulating lumps of flesh … The greatest chief on Nauru – Jim – has several wives each more corpulent than the other, and as he himself is a man of no mean circumference, to watch him promenading with his wives was an unforgettable sight.

The celebration was held irregularly, in part due to the marginal nature of resources on Nauru. The main food supply was derived from pandanus fruits, which are a seasonal crop, and fish, together with some coconuts. Fish were plentiful in the ocean, but the hazards of launching a boat across the narrow fringing reef were immense. Buada, a small lagoon located in the centre of the upraised part of the island, was thus much prized as the place where milkfish (*Chanos chanos*, known as *ibija*) were raised. Only high-ranking Nauruan families had rights to raise their fish there, and thus they were the only ones who could contribute the *ibija* fish for any feast or celebration.

To wear such strings of fish at the end of her period of confinement thus indicated the status and wealth of a woman's family and tribal group. The fish were hand-raised; the young spat were brought from the Gilberts and carefully nurtured to fingerling size near the household until they were of a size to survive in the Buada lagoon. Young men of the tribe bore the responsibility for raising these fish that held such symbolic importance.

The lightening of the young women's skin resulted from her being separated from normal community activities. Dobson Rhone (1921) suggests that it was a result of their withdrawal from work activities, but with such a minimal resource base this is not a feasible argument. Rather, it appears these young women were kept apart as a mark of their status, a status that became inscribed for all to see when they finally were welcomed back into the community. What their family and tribe saw was a beautiful body that had become fat, with a light skin, resulting from their attentions.

The fattening process could only have been carried out in times when there was enough food available to lavish on the one or two young women chosen. Early accounts of Nauru describe the frequency of drought resulting in the pandanus trees not bearing and a consequent short-age of food for several years. When there was adequate rain and pandanus fruited liberally, the excess over immediate needs was processed into a dried paste that was stored (Kayser 1934).

I have presented elsewhere (Pollock 1995a) a biological argument that is one explanation of the fattening process. I have suggested it was a significant means of ensuring the successful outcome of the first pregnancy of a young Nauruan woman and thus represented a mobilisation of resources to enlarge the social group. Nauruans appear to have been very aware of the risks of the small size of their population and to have taken active steps to seek to increase it. During the early 1900s the population fluctuated between 1000 and 1200 – the Nauruan population reaching the magical figure of 1500 was celebrated in 1932 (see Pollock 1992c). The day of the birth of that 1500th child is still a national holiday for Nauruans. Beautification processes thus resulted in the enlargement of individuals, representing a potential increase in the size of the group, combining material with aesthetic principles.

But enhancing the body had several other significances. The beauty of those Nauruan women was a strong cultural feature that signified their status in the community. It also signified their identity as true Nauruans, with strong ancestral ties to the island. In this matrilineal society they were the representatives of the founders of Nauruan society, carrying forward through their bodies the symbol of ties to the land for the past, present and future.

Tahiti

In Tahiti the concept of *ha'apori* referred to the practice of fattening and lightening the skin of men and women. As Moerenhout recorded (1837 vol. 1:137), selected men and women were fattened to enhance their sexual attractiveness. But others saw these practices in a broader framework, namely that of beautification of selected members of the community.

Young men and young women, usually those of chiefly rank or close to it, were the main participants. Oliver associates these practices with membership in the *arioi* society, a group of Tahitians who moved from place to place entertaining people and living a distinctive lifestyle. Others, such as Moerenhout (1837), suggest the practice was not just confined to *arioi*. Anderson's account of his findings in Tahiti during Cook's voyage tells us that:

> It is a practice, especially among the Erreoes or unmarried men of some consequence to undergo a kind of physical operation to render them fair. This is done by remaining a month or two in the house; during which time they wear a great quantity of clothes, eat nothing but breadfruit to which they ascribe a remarkable property in whitening them. [Anderson 1784, cited in Beaglehole 1967]

These young people were purposely extracted from society:

> They withdrew to a special place in groups where they lay themselves down in the dry grass spread for the purpose … They do not get up except for their bodily necessities; they eat and sleep as much as they can. [Corney 1915:329-30, cited in Oliver 1974:435]

Two special places where *ha'apori* took place are mentioned in the literature: one of the large sheds under which their big canoes were kept was known as 'the gathering spot for the fattening activity' (Corney 1915:329-30, cited in Oliver 1974:435). The other was the atoll of Tetiaroa, which was 'a kind of watering-place for the royal family … and a frequent resort for what might be called the fashionable and gay of Tahiti' (Ellis 1829 vol. 1:173). The latter appears to have been only for the upper classes.

Throughout the time they were away they were specially treated by their community for a period of from 'one moon' to six months (Corney, cited in Oliver 1974: 435). The period of time depended in part on the availability of a food supply, the best time being when there was plenty of breadfruit, the favourite food of Tahitians. *Popoi*, a mixture of fresh and fermented breadfruit, was considered particularly fattening:

> They fed on *popoi*, on fruits, on bananas, on crushed breadfruit mixed in water and taken in an almost liquid state. In the meantime all exercise was forbidden to them. They could not walk, except to go to wash in the river, and before

appearing in public they had to be inspected in a state of complete nudity by the men; but then they became the object of admiration of young people and were sought after afterwards. [Moerenhout 1837 vol. 1:137]

It is not clear to what extent this whole beautification process was one of matchmaking between future partners, or whether it was some form of beauty contest between local groups as an alternative form of battle for prestige.

Those who underwent the *ha'apori* beautification process were collectively known by the term *huapipi*, applied to 'the youth called *pori* [fat] who were fed for some time to make them fair and delicate' (in Oliver 1974:436, 947). Orsmond defines *huapipi* as 'those who sit lazily covered with cloth' (Oliver 1974:1154, n. 47). Thus two distinct groups underwent the process of beautification. Young men and young women, particularly those of high class, were fed and lay around on the grass, their bodies covered in masses of *tapa* cloth.

Chiefs were fed vast amounts of food, at least in the view of their European visitors, whether within these rituals or at 'normal' eating events. Banks's description of what 'their principal people' ate has been much cited, but serves to stress that Tahitians appeared to link the amount eaten with fattening of the body. Banks (1769:141) apologises:

It may be thought that I have given rather too large a quantity of provision to my eater … But this I do affirm, that it is but few of the many I was acquainted with that eat less, while many eat a good deal more.

Lightening the skin is not mentioned in this case as an associated factor that enhanced the chiefs' status.

Oliver's general discussion of this issue separates the fattening process from that of lightening the skin. He suggests the fattening aspect seems to have been more important, as the light pigmentation only had 'aesthetic value' (Oliver 1974:434). This is an important reflection of his views, I suggest, rather than those of the Tahitians at that time. In the light of the argument being offered in this paper, I believe we must depart from our Western attitudes to body size and beauty and take the two factors,

fattening and lightening of the skin, together as significant cultural identifiers.

Conclusion

The body as an aesthetic object in itself has been neglected in the literature. That large body size was accepted as a mark of honour for certain sectors of Polynesian society has become widely acknowledged. But the issue needs further exploration for other parts of the Pacific. The Nauru case shows that it was not just a Polynesian attribute. We need more ethnographic information from the early contact period to establish just how widely the fattening and skin-lightening processes were practised.

The practices associated with body enhancement discussed here have focused mainly on increasing the girth and body fat of the individuals concerned. But it is also apparent that in Western Polynesia, overall size was valued, including height. Predating Darwin's theory of natural selection, it appears 'Uveans and Tongans held the view that 'bigger' was indeed 'better'.

In addition to concerted efforts to increase the girth and plumpness of their high-ranking members, their 'presence' was enhanced by other cultural means. At funerals, Cook and others noted that those of importance bore a significant covering of mats (in various states of array) tied around their bodies with a piece of human-hair rope. They also wore *tapa* headdresses in 'Uvea and Futuna that may have served to increase their height and thus their overall 'presence'.

These mats and tapa adornments would have served to enhance the already enlarged body beneath them. They were only ported on the occasion of major rituals, particularly funerals. But by being so used they became a distinguishing feature of those closely associated with the ritual. They set a kin group apart. They signified status. Their beauty was part of the culturally appropriate behaviour. By displaying the members of a community thus, a strong message was sent to other groups about aesthetic principles and the importance of the body.

The body and its overall size, culturally induced, could thus be further enhanced by using mats and headdresses, by appropriate movements we label 'dance', and by other adornments such as tattooing. Certain sectors of the community could be set apart from the others, such distinguishing features receiving acclaim in the name of beauty. A light skin was a further distinctive feature in such tropical societies. That large size and light skin were transitory did not matter. Beauty changes with time.

The body is an art form in itself. Its value, expressed in Western terms as beauty, can be further enhanced by cultural manipulations, such as corsets or surgical interventions. In the Pacific, the care and effort needed to produce certain symbols of beauty such as large size and light skin was a mark of communal concern. Selected individuals became the centrepiece for such endeavours. The whole community gloried in the display. The beautification process may have been more significant than the final product. The significance did not belong to the individual, but rather to the group that had created that beauty.

Body image is thus an important social representation for some societies. It must be seen as encompassing the cultural attributes discussed here, as well as the biological attributes that have been the focus of discussion elsewhere (for example, Baker and Baker 1986 for Samoa). The body may be manipulated like stone or clay or wood. It may be born in a basic biological form, but from that day of birth it is treated culturally and socialised. Part of the social and cultural manipulation is aimed at enhancing the beauty of the individual; part is aimed at enhancing the social standing of the group of which that person is a member. The biological does not stand alone; it is part of a cultural heritage. The body can be manipulated, adorned, enhanced and enlarged just as any inanimate material can be manipulated in the name of art.

PART 2

Bringing people back into the collections: Indigenous Australians and the presentation of culture

Christopher Anderson

The following six papers deal with the documentation and presentation of culture in a variety of media – object displays, photography, art and performance. Traditionally, museums collected objects and, in both a symbolic and real sense, alienated those objects from the cultures and peoples that produced them. The cultural context was then re-presented by museums in the display of the works. There was thereby a double blow for the originating cultures in some ways: not only was something tangible lost to them, but they also missed out having a say in the post-collecting interpretations. This process marginalised Australian Aboriginal and Pacific peoples as 'Others' who were barely relevant to the museum exercise.

Over the past decade or so, things have changed, and museums have sought wherever possible to involve indigenous people in their activities. The papers in this section of the book present a range of situations and perspectives on this new development.

Vincent and Ruth Megaw – in some ways pioneers in the collecting and interpreting of contemporary Aboriginal art – review the history of the Aboriginal artists-in-residence program at Flinders University in Adelaide. This program was a significant attempt to bring indigenous artists into a collecting and exhibiting institution, and became a catalyst for the careers of a number of Aboriginal artists. The artists – some from remote communities – added to the university's collections, helped set up exhibitions, were

introduced to new media, and interacted with staff and students and among themselves. This active involvement of artists at the collecting and exhibiting end of things (producing works within the art museum itself) was an enriching process for artists and collections (for example, by increasing documentation). The program also initiated relationships between Flinders University and the Megaws on the one hand, and Aboriginal communities and artists on the other. These relationships continue and create a social link and context that is seen as culturally appropriate and desirable by the artists.

Brenda Croft makes a simple but eloquent and powerful plea for museums, galleries, and the art and culture world in general to stop marginalising indigenous peoples through their activities and structures. Croft, an Aboriginal artist herself, was one of the founding members of the Boomalli Aboriginal Artists' Cooperative in Sydney. She describes in her paper the establishment of Boomalli and its role in raising the awareness of non-Aboriginal Australia about urban Aboriginal people and the validity of their art as an expression of Aboriginal Australian culture and history. We can see Boomalli and the activities of Croft and her co-members as successful attempts by Aboriginal artists to play a more active role in the production and presentation of their art.

The recording of culture and cultural events through photography has for at least a century been an important form of documentation for museums. As Juno Gemes reveals, it is also becoming important for indigenous people. Gemes presents here a photographic essay, recording aspects of indigenous peoples' performance roles in the 1993 Pacific Arts Association symposium in Adelaide. In her text, she argues that 'committed photography' provides a more meaningful depiction of Australian Aboriginal life and culture than so-called objective photography. Gemes also discusses the important issue of the use of photographic collections by Aboriginal people for their own purposes, and what implications this (and the related issue of control) has for the future care of collections.

The nature and location of cultural institutions, and the effects of this on attitudes towards indigenous cultures, is the subject of Deane Fergie's paper. Using the History Trust of South Australia and the South Australian Museum as case studies, Fergie critically examines the briefs, policies and, most importantly, the display contents and layouts of the two institutions. She argues that the juxtaposition of indigenous cultures with natural science collections and displays in the museum subtly and unconsciously reinforces racist attitudes in visitors and, more broadly, constitutes a form of state racism. The lack of direct involvement, until recently, of living peoples with cultural representations in the Pacific collections and displays is also, Fergie argues, a form of racist marginalisation and exclusion.

John Stanton, on the other hand, provides us with a counter example of a museum that has worked actively to respond to its indigenous constituents' requests for assistance on cultural projects, including exhibitions and other heritage endeavours. Stanton describes how a small, university-based museum (the Berndt Museum at the University of Western Australia), with very limited resources but very significant collections, can play a vital role for Aboriginal people.

Chris Anderson's paper, 'Old galleries, new people', concludes this section of the book. Anderson discusses how museums have responded to the problem of old-fashioned displays that are expensive to alter, the public desire for 'authentic' experiences, and the demand from indigenous people to play a role in collections and their presentation. Using, as commentary, texts generated by others (in most cases participants or organisers) for other purposes, he critically examines the involvement of indigenous peoples as performers, artists, craftsmen and craftswomen in museum spaces as a means of 'bringing people back into the collections'.

Artists as performers: The Flinders University Aboriginal Artists-in-Residence program re-reviewed

J.V.S. Megaw and M. Ruth Megaw

To the memory of Mitch Dunnet Jr (1964-96) and Lin Onus (1948-96)[1]

On a typical grey Australian July day in 1979, two senior Aboriginal men from the government-established settlement of Papunya, 250 kilometres west of Alice Springs, stepped off the plane at Adelaide Airport. These were David Corby Tjapaltjarri, a well-travelled Ngalia-speaking Warlpiri, and Turkey Tolson Tjupurrula (fig. 7.1), a Pintupi born on Haast Bluff Aboriginal Reserve and sometime-chairman of the Papunya Tula Artists Cooperative, the first and continuing company made up of the now world-famous acrylic painters of Central Australia. At the suggestion of John Kean, then the art adviser at Papunya, both men had come to be guests of the Flinders University of South Australia. They were to work within its Visual Arts Studio in association with its manager, Brian Callen, a graduate of the South Australian School of Art, with experience of teaching art in predominantly Aboriginal schools in Queensland and the Northern Territory.

Just before the Pacific Arts Association's Adelaide symposium, an exhibition entitled 'Desert Fire: Remembrances of an Oodnadatta childhood' opened in the Union Gallery at Flinders. This exhibition was devoted to the work of the two most recent artist-in-residence programs, the main feature being oils by June Kunyi McInerney (fig. 7.2), a qualified general nurse and self-taught painter whose mother was a Yankunjatjarra from the far north of South Australia. In this exhibition were also a number of screen prints by Kerry Giles (fig. 7.3). Kerry, whose art work was

used extensively in the publicity for the Pacific Arts Association (PAA) symposium, was born at Waikerie on the River Murray. Her father was a Ngarrindjeri, a group whose tribal lands are close to the Adelaide region.[2]

There is no longer anything new, of course, in the idea of establishing residencies for indigenous artists in art schools and other tertiary institutions. Here in Australia, the first such program was the appointment in 1978 of the Manggalili bark painters from Yirrkala in north-eastern Arnhem Land, Narritjin and his son Banapana Maymuru, as Visiting Creative Fellows at the Australian National University in Canberra. Here the role of Howard Morphy, who had undertaken postgraduate research at Yirrkala and was then in the Department of Prehistory and Anthropology, was vital. *Narritjin in Canberra*, the film made for Film Australia by Ian Dunlop, one of a series dealing with Narritjin, remains the most useful and detailed record of such an event.

Since the late 1970s, there have been other similarly important developments. At the Canberra School of Art, Theo Tremblay and others have offered tuition and studio space to a varied succession of Aboriginal and Islander print-makers (Lendon 1996). In addition to individual fellowships or residencies, as established most recently at Griffith University in Brisbane, the Associate Diploma of Art for indigenous students. inaugurated in 1984 by Anna Eglitis at the Cairns College of Technical and Further

Education, has produced a remarkable group of artists including Zane Saunders and Pooaraar (Bevan Hayward, who has also worked with Theo Tremblay). Aboriginal print-making is now well and truly established, as witnessed by 'Getting into prints', the symposium on Aboriginal print-making organised in Darwin in April 1993 by the School of Fine Arts at the Northern Territory University and the Association of Northern and Central Australian Aboriginal Artists.

In South Australia alone there have been several residencies aimed at a defined outcome, such as some of the exhibitions at Tandanya, the National Aboriginal Cultural Institute established in 1989, or 'Paintings out of the Desert', literally grounded on acrylics executed in the same period for Christopher Anderson and his colleagues at the South Australian Museum by Warlpiri artists from Yuendumu.

This brief paper is concerned only incidentally with questions of what might, or might not be, practical, let alone politically correct, schemes for training indigenous artists largely in the use of introduced or 'non-traditional' media and techniques. Rather we wish to review what we, the consumers, have learnt of those the creators and to articulate what we see as the purposes, the benefits and the pitfalls of some ten short-term residencies at Flinders University.[3]

A few general principles need to be stated at the outset. All the Flinders residencies have shared a number of elements. The basic aims have remained the same since the 1970s, when Robert Edwards, then director of the Aboriginal Arts Board of the Australia Council, suggested that

7.2 (Below) June Kunyi McInernay at work in the Flinders University Visual Arts Studio, 1992. (Photo: Multimedia Services, Flinders University.)

7.3 (Bottom) Kerry Giles and her son Leslie making marbled paper, Flinders University Visual Arts Studio, 1992. (Photo: Multimedia Services, Flinders University.)

7.1 Turkey Tolson Tjupurrula at work in the Flinders University Visual Arts Studio, 1979. (Photo: J.V.S. Megaw.)

residencies would offer a suitable ancillary development to the introduction of undergraduate courses in ethnographic and prehistoric art. Thus we have attempted to offer training to the artists in answer to a continuing perceived need to establish new sources of income based on their cultural traditions; we have tried ourselves to learn from those whose art it is; and, we have attempted to document each residency, as far as the individual artists were prepared to participate, by sound and visual recording, as well as by descriptions of the work in progress.

All artists have been salaried as graduate research assistants during their stay, since the university has no category for creative scholars or artists as such. New techniques were demonstrated to the artists, though several, notably those from outback communities, generally chose not to take these up. While artists were expected to work to an agreed timetable, visits were arranged to other institutions such as schools of art, the South Australian Museum, Tandanya and – all importantly for those from out of Adelaide – to the downtown shopping centre. As far as possible each residency has ended with a selling exhibition of the works produced, with pricing set by Brian Callen in consultation with the artists. From these exhibitions, the Flinders University Art Museum has since 1979 made purchases for its collection of contemporary Aboriginal art. Finally, the program has relied to a large extent on external grant funding supplied initially by the Aboriginal Arts Board and subsequently by its successor, the Aboriginal Arts Committee.

In a very real sense, all contemporary artists are actors playing out a role that is set for them as an imposed agenda within the consumer ethos of the art market, and at the same time controlled by them to the degree to which they produce images whose content if not form is restricted by their individual and socially-determined rules. In the context of capitalist society, there have been protests from a number of radical white writers who, in their concern to promote a 'hands off' approach to such cross-cultural enterprises, castigate those whom they perceive as making their academic reputations on the back of black culture, and who advocate an immediate and total moratorium on any teaching of indigenous art by non-indigenous teachers. In a first review of our Aboriginal program (Megaw 1980),

we described how the 1979 visit of the Papunya artists sparked a vigorous debate among an active minority whose radical solution to the prevention of what they saw as certain exploitation was to threaten to make a funeral pyre of the seventeen paintings comprising Tjapaltjarri's and Tjupurrula's entire Flinders oeuvre. As we recorded at the time:

> Acceptance that the artists' work was based on tribal traditions and symbolic language, but recognition that it also represented a 'cash crop', introduced points of contact with discussion on the role of 'institutional' and 'institutionalised' art as a whole and the degenerative effect of the introduction of capitalist economics to 'traditional' societies, all of this within the context of a particular philosophy of art representative of some of the teaching of contemporary Western Visual Arts at Flinders. To use [Edmund] Carpenter's expression, the project was seen by a few ethnocentric radicals as manipulative 'misanthropology'. None of this seemed to affect the artists except that too continuous questioning by individual protagonists caused firstly silent incomprehension and secondly obvious physical discomfort. [Megaw 1980:53]

Another area that has given rise to debate has been the preparation of film and video recordings of some of the residencies. Despite attempts to interest successive artists in the use of TV facilities and simple camcorders, there was virtually no interest, although they were happy and indeed eager to see and listen to the results. A recent article by Philip Batty, 'Who told you we wanted to make our own TV?', indicates that the intrusion not only of the technology, but also of the programming of 'Whitefella TV', has not necessarily been regarded by the recipients 'as a direct assault on local languages, customs and beliefs' (Batty 1993:22). We can certainly claim no breakthrough in terms of exchanging white pseudo-objectivity for black control of a process of record, which, frankly, few artists seem to have regarded as more than a useful source of souvenir snapshots of their sojourn at Flinders.

Let us consider, however, some of the perceived benefits, pitfalls and downright failures of the past decade and a half. In the case of the two Papunya artists, their main gain was clearly regarded in terms of a trip 'Down South':

Tjupurrula had never before seen the sea. It was also cash in hand on top of a guaranteed sale of works at rather higher than the prices they could expect to have received through Papunya Tula. We, on the other hand, not only and undeniably accumulated considerable information as well as the works themselves but, much more importantly and lastingly, in subsequent years have gained an entree to Central Australian society which through reciprocal hospitality we have continued to enjoy.

That we have been accorded a 'skin' relationship and attendant 'skin names' through Tjupurrula is no more than happens to any outsider who is accepted into outback Aboriginal society. In turn, through subsequent reciprocal visits, we were able to mount in 1985 'Dot and Circle', a first attempt at a retrospective survey of Aboriginal acrylic paintings consisting of some 100 works, almost all of which had been purchased by Flinders in the years since the first residency (Maughan and Zimmer 1986). Subsequently, of course, there have been other shows, most notably 'East to West: Land in Papunya Tula painting', which surveyed the work of some seven artists.[4] Devised by John Kean, then exhibitions officer at Tandanya, with Kerry Giles as his trainee assistant, and including again the work of Turkey Tolson Tjupurrula, this formed a major contribution to the 1990 Adelaide Festival of Arts.

In parenthesis, we can note that while 'East to West' was opened by Turkey Tolson Tjupurrula, as chairman of Papunya Tula, and Lord Harewood, cousin to the Queen and sometime director of the Adelaide Festival, indigenous artists have been contributing to the festival since the mid 1970s. It was, however, only in 1984 that an Aboriginal art exhibition was included in the official program for the first time, this being another showing of the work of Papunya Tula artists consisting of paintings by three major figures in the movement, including Clifford Possum Tjapaltjarri (Megaw 1984). The contrast between that curious 'whitefella' ritual, the art-gallery opening, which says more about group social dynamics than art appreciation, and the actual context within which the art works are produced, never ceases to surprise.

It is clear that our Papunya Tula artists have never produced works that did not fit into a previously determined pattern of saleable subject matter, with subtle variations to allow for locally perceived preferences. The same factor certainly applied to the short visit to Flinders in 1982 by David Malangi, from Ramingining in Central Arnhem Land (briefly referred to at the PAA New York symposium; Megaw 1990:285). Malangi was also known as 'Dollar Bill' as a result of the – unauthorised – reproduction of one of his bark paintings on the first Australian dollar note issued following decimalisation in 1966. At Flinders, in a series of demonstration classes, Malangi painted and explained the story of Gurrumiringu, the subject reproduced on the dollar bill, and one that has particular significance to the Malangi's Urgiganjdjar clan.

On the other hand, Malangi's two daughters were happy to spend time in the Visual Arts Studio producing works in a very different style: the 'informal' mission or school-based art whose ubiquitous nature in contemporary Aboriginal society has not been fully appreciated. One such example is the series of rough drawings on paper executed by various central-desert artists while visiting Flinders. On occasion, these make obvious reference to the standard bush iconography of the Arrernte watercolourists, beginning at Ntaria or Hermannsburg in the 1930s with Albert Namatjira. Our work on the exhibition and accompanying monograph, *The Heritage of Namatjira* (Hardy, Megaw and Megaw 1992), has made clear the many cultural as well as stylistic links between the varying groups who have lived at Hermannsburg, Haast Bluff and Papunya, all three settlements either established by Lutherans or with a strong Lutheran influence.

Turkey Tolson has recounted how he met Albert at Papunya during the latter's two-month custodial sentence following conviction for supplying liquor to a kinsman. While it is generally accepted that the now ubiquitous 'hegemony of the dot', to use Jenny Green's phrase, in contemporary Aboriginal art often makes important statements about the essential association of indigenous peoples with their ancestral land, it has taken much longer to recognise that the Hermannsburg watercolourists, so long dismissed as the producers of merely skilful European-influenced hackwork, do much the same. This point is nowhere more clearly demonstrated than in a 1989 work

7.4 Adrian Marrie with women from Indulkana in the Flinders University Visual Arts Studio, 1981. (Photo: J.V.S. Megaw.)

by Doug Abbott in the Flinders collection, in which the same kangaroo and emu Dreaming site of Anyarle (Haast Bluff) is depicted in watercolour landscape and dot styles, a subject with its obvious geographical framing device that was developed by the artist during 1988, the bicentenary of white settlement in Australia.

In our opinion, it is unfortunate that, in response to market pressures, so many watercolourists are virtually giving up the medium for acrylic dot paintings, often of dubious quality. This point was demonstrated during a short visit to Flinders in 1989 by one of Namatjira's surviving granddaughters, Elaine Namatjira (Hardy, Megaw and Megaw 1992:18-20, figs 0.5-7).

Because the Flinders Studio is primarily equipped for the production of graphics, it is only natural that we should have attracted those with an expressed interest in such non-indigenous processes as linocut, woodblock or screen-printing, lithography and etching. In 1980, the artist in residence was Bede Tungutalum, accompanied by his schoolteacher wife, Francine. Bede, a Tiwi from Bathurst Island, had gained his training in woodblock and screen-printing in the 1960s from Madeline Clear, training that was to lead to the establishment of Tiwi Designs and the renowned fabric-printing enterprise known as Bima Wear. Previously, Bede had produced a pair of woodblock prints for Festival '78, the arts and cultural program of the XIth

Commonwealth Games held in Edmonton, Alberta. At Flinders he returned to the technique, a natural extension of the traditional Tiwi carving skill. Bede also proved an adept teacher of his peoples' traditions, as well as an excellent storyteller. More recently, Bede has produced large-scale works combining screen printing and acrylic paint, the subject matter as always being drawn from Tiwi traditional lore.

The following year an interesting but not wholly successful experiment was initiated by Adrian Marrie, at the time completing a double honours degree in visual arts at Flinders and ethnomusicology under Catherine Ellis at the University of Adelaide. Observing the 'informal' art produced in their spare time by the male Pitjantjatjara tribal elders and their families from Indulkana, in the north of South Australia, who were visiting Adelaide's Centre for Aboriginal Studies in Music, Marrie encouraged some of the women also to spend time learning linocut and screen-printing in the Flinders Studio (fig. 7.4), the former technique having again obvious affinities with traditional carving. The subsequent establishment of a print workshop at Indulkana, and its only intermittent success in being absorbed into the women's traditional routines, reflects other attempts to introduce a new media for 'cash crop' art at centres such as Ernabella and Fregon.[5] Such enterprises seem almost entirely conditioned by the success

7.5 Banduk Marika at work on a linocut in the Flinders University Visual Arts Studio, 1986. (Photo: Multimedia Services, Flinders University.)

of (non-Aboriginal) craft advisers in persuading the local communities of the value in economic terms of such novel and time-consuming processes.

Other artists who have developed, rather than learnt, their graphic skills while at Flinders include Banduk Marika (fig. 7.5), the well-known member of a well-known and important Yolngu family from Yirrkala, in Arnhem Land. Banduk, who describes her work as 'contemporary traditional', studied print-making with Theo Tremblay in Canberra, and was one of two artists-in-residence at Flinders in 1986, both of whom again provided students willingly with highly articulate descriptions of their life and work. Indeed, it must be observed that, far from proving a nuisance to the artists, students at Flinders have usually been if anything over-reticent in seeking information from those who almost without exception seemed to regard themselves as cultural ambassadors for their people.

The second artist who spent time at Flinders in 1986, South Australia's sesquicentennial year, was Byron Pickett. Born in Quairading, Western Australia, but with connections through marriage to South Australia (a factor seen clearly in the subject matter and accompanying texts that form his graphic art), Byron learned screen-printing during 1984-85 when he was a trainee community artist with the Eyre Peninsula Cultural Trust at Port Lincoln, where he now lives. As Jubilee 150 Artist-in-Residence, he was

7.6 Mitch Dunnett Jnr working on his painting *The Death of the Tasmanian Devil*, Flinders University Visual Arts Studio, 1988. (Photo: J.V.S. Megaw.)

one of the main contributors to 'The Dreamtime Today: A survey of contemporary Aboriginal Arts and Crafts' (Maughan and Megaw 1986), which, with major state funding for the purchase and commissioning of works, enabled Flinders to make a significant contribution in demonstrating the diversity and richness of the indigenous element in Australia's multicultural society.

Two years later, in 1988, Australia celebrated its bicentenary, an event during which some First Australians said they had 'nothing to celebrate'. However, the bicentenary marked a time when indigenous Australian art received exposure and international recognition as never before, a point we have discussed during the previous PAA symposium. For us, 1988 was equally problematic. For the first time, two Nunga, or South Australian urban-based artists were in residence. For Kerry Giles, born on the Murray and associated through marriage with the 'Top End' of Australia, this was her first association with Flinders, an event that can best be described as the right offer at the right time. We met Kerry at a National Aborigines Day barbecue at the Port Adelaide Aboriginal Community College, an institution that has done much to foster the artistic talent of students of varying ages and cultural backgrounds. The previous year an arson attack at her home had destroyed much of the work that Kerry was preparing for her graduation portfolio at the North Adelaide School of Art, forcing her to withdraw from the course. She found the Flinders environment conducive to the production of her first work in acrylics, in which she continued to illustrate varying aspects of the complex issues of what it is to be a single parent of 'Irish-German-Aboriginal descent' as she has described herself. Since 1988, our students and we continued to learn from Kerry, through her art and her willingness to talk, about the issues which most concern her, issues she illustrated through a wide range of media and subject matter (Britton and Wright 1990:82).

The second artist for the bicentennial year was Mitch Dunnett Jr (fig. 7.6). Born in 1964 in Ceduna, a South Australian country town with an often unhappy history of racial conflict, Mitch had natural talent as an artist, which had been recognised at school. A sportsman of considerable talent, like many of his people, Mitch had

had more than one brush with the law. As a result of one of these he found himself in 1987 in Adelaide Gaol in a cell adjacent to that of Kingsley Dixon, whose suicide, an event recorded by Mitch in a painting now in the South Australian Museum (Sutton 1988:32, figs 45-46), was to lead to the establishment of the Royal Commission into Aboriginal Deaths in Custody. When, following his release, we were approached by Mitch's probation officer to see whether we could offer him a residency, it was again a happy circumstance that Kerry Giles was present to act as teacher and support. Both artists had come to Flinders from traineeships at Co-Media, a print and poster workshop in Adelaide, where Mitch illustrated stories he had learnt from his Pitjantjatjara grandmother. These were continued in a striking series of acrylics and somewhat less successful screen-prints where he found the repetitive process and need for careful registration irksome. Recurrent themes in Mitch's work are the need to conserve the environment, the fight indigenous peoples have everywhere to regain their traditional lands, and the conflict within his life between tribal law and 'whitefella law'. The exhibition, curated by Kerry on behalf of Flinders for NAIDOC Week 1988, 'The Cutting Edge: New art of the Third and Fourth Worlds', was the first such exhibition at the university to be curated by an artist-in-residence, and included recent examples of her work and Mitch's (Giles, Megaw and Megaw 1988).

At the beginning of 1989, Mitch was approached to return as artist-in-residence in his own right, without the support of any other members of the Nunga community. This was an arrangement that broke with our rule of inviting, wherever possible, an accompanying artist or other member of the immediate family. It was also an arrangement that in Mitch's case we should have realised from the outset would be fraught with difficulty. After a few weeks, and following discussion with the Aboriginal Arts Unit, the residency was terminated. There had been a patent unwillingness to keep to a more or less regular work schedule, and we had refused Mitch's demand to pay over to him his entire salary in a lump sum; it was, as he put it, up to him as the artist what he did with his life. After this event, Mitch drifted between Ceduna and Adelaide, painting only occasionally between further confrontations with the law – whitefella law.

The replacement of Mitch in 1989-90 by Peter Dabah from north Queensland demonstrates again how it is often only those indigenous artists with some similar previous experience who can readily adapt to the necessarily structured life of a working studio without active and continuous support. We must admit, too, that only in the last two years have the obvious problems facing Aboriginal students attending Flinders for the first time been addressed by the setting up of an Aboriginal and Islander section within the university's Language and Learning Unit.

Peter Dabah originally came to Adelaide after having been an art student at the Cairns TAFE college, following a period at the Port Adelaide Community College studying creative writing. While at Flinders he continued to develop a style that is an amalgam – some might say a legitimate appropriation – of rock art and other traditional Aboriginal design elements, a feature shared by many of the Cairns associate-diploma students (see Hogan 1990). Peter spent much time in the University Library to extend his awareness of his north Queensland tribal culture and language. As he said, 'Painting and language and everything else is one – it can't be divided' (Britton and Wright 1990:83).

Finally, to the work of Kunyi, June Kunyi McInerney. She was brought up in the far north of South Australia and started work at Flinders at the end of 1992, when she overlapped with a second residency by Kerry Giles. This followed Kerry's resignation from the staff of Tandanya, and during this period Kerry held an open workshop in the Flinders Art Museum in the course of the display of another selection of graphic work by a range of indigenous artists from within Australia and beyond. Kunyi's story is the all too familiar one of enforced fostering out of the child of a mixed-blood marriage and a closely regimented early life. Her large paintings illustrate just what it was to be brought up in a segregated mission school. Although she had previously received an Australia Council grant to develop her painting, Kunyi had never before worked in a studio environment. The presence of another Nunga woman – not to mention the vital and non-threatening educative role offered by Brian Callen – did much to break down her reticence and reserve. Kunyi's images of morning 'slopping out' and other vignettes of her childhood in Oodnadatta contrast with her obvious feeling for the richness of the desert flora.

Much remains, however, to be done to educate the consumers rather than the producers of the art of our Aboriginal artist-in-residence program. Too many potential clients for Kunyi's self-taught style, including the new Flinders University School of Law, which has a particular interest in problems of reconciling Aboriginal values, traditional law and Commonwealth legislation, have dismissed her paintings as too European, too 'pretty' and not 'Aboriginal'. Here, indeed, are echoes of the first critical reactions to the Hermannsburg watercolourists of the art establishment of sixty years ago.

What started out at Flinders in 1978 as a professional academic interest in changing cultures and changing art styles soon developed into an enduring respect for the Aboriginal people, the survival of their traditions and their extraordinary artistic talents. Noticing the power of their imagery and recognising the art as a medium for communicating to non-Aboriginal people the many-faceted nature of Aboriginal culture, we have been encouraged to further new ways of developing this medium as a conduit through which something of lasting value can flow. In the future, of course, such whitefella-sponsored projects should become redundant.

For the moment, however, those of us who have been privileged to work with and learn from our indigenous artists, who have been continuously struck by their tolerance, good humour and patience with the often impenetrable stupidity of whitefella ways, consider that something positive has been gained by all involved with the Aboriginal artist-in-residence program. In many ways there has been a feeling of an extended family relationship, extended from them to us, a feeling which can best be summed up by the title of Kerry Giles' first solo exhibition held at Flinders University in September 1992: 'Ooooooh! I feel good . . . !'

Afterword

It is a great sadness to have to record Kerry's passing. 'Kurwingie', as she was known to her people, died suddenly in Adelaide on 21 July 1997. She had many friends at Flinders University, and many of us here are proud to have been regarded by her as friends. We all miss her, and all who came into contact with her learnt something of what it is to be a black face in a predominantly white society. The only consolation we have is her art, which remains as a memorial both to her unrelenting struggle on behalf of her people and to the artistic talent that still had so much to give. For a brief account of Kerry, her life and work, see Megaw and Megaw (1997).

Notes

1.   Untimely death is no stranger to indigenous Australians, but we should like to pay tribute here to two artists who died while this volume was in preparation. Of the two, Mitch had yet to develop fully his obvious talents, while Lin's work, highly regarded in Australia, was only beginning to be recognised adequately by an international audience. We learnt much from both and valued their friendship.

2.   Profiles of many of the artists and organisations cited in this paper are found in Britton and Wright (1990).

3.   For a detailed account of the first two years of residencies and related issues see Megaw (1980).

4.   The most wide-ranging exhibition to concentrate on the new/old art of the desert has probably been that mounted by the National Gallery of Victoria in 1989 (Ryan 1989).

5.   The Indulkana experiment is briefly described in Megaw (1980:59). See also Maughan (1986). A full description and discussion forms the subject of Adrian Marrie's unpublished BA thesis (Marrie 1980, 1982).

8 Speaking as the 'Other'

Brenda L. Croft

I can't quite remember if I chose the title of this paper in a hurry or whether it was chosen for me. As it stands, I have been contemplating this particular choice of words at some length and assessing what speaking as the 'Other' actually means. So as I often do when I'm trying to work out the parameters of something, I referred to the Macquarie Dictionary, which defines 'other' as: additional or further, as in 'he and one other person'; different or distinct from the one or ones mentioned; different in nature.

I can deal with these explanations of Other, as I do consider myself different or distinct (though hopefully not with too much arrogance), and I consider myself different in nature given the context of this symposium and given that we are living in the International Year for Indigenous People. But I think that I am jumping ahead here, and feel that I should provide some background on myself and the area in which I am involved.

I work as coordinator[1] for Boomalli Aboriginal Artists Co-operative which is in Annandale, Sydney. I have been undertaking this role since 1990, and prior to this I was involved in the cooperative on a voluntary basis and as a founding member and artist.

The medium in which I mainly work is photography. Over the past couple of years I have had to juggle being an arts administrator as well as a practising artist. Since 1990, I have also been studying towards a Master of Arts Administration at the College of Fine Arts, University of NSW, on a part-time basis.

Back in 1987, when I first became involved in Boomalli at the invitation of some of the other artists, I was sort of drifting around, doing a bit of this and a bit of that, but with no real focus. That's part of being in your early twenties. I had no inkling that six years down the track I would be as involved in arts administration as I now find myself – and loving it!

When I went back to college in 1990 I had intended to complete my BA. However, I felt I could learn more and contribute more if I had a greater understanding of arts administration and all that entails, and thereby assist in the operation of Boomalli.

Boomalli Aboriginal Artists Co-operative Limited began in 1987 under the impetus of a number of Sydney-based artists. The founding ten members were Bronwyn Bancroft, Euphemia Bostock, Brenda L. Croft, Fiona Foley, Fernanda Martins, Raymond Meeks, Tracey Moffatt, Avril Quaill, Michael Riley and Jeffrey Samuels. These artists' media included print-making, painting, sculpture, photography and film-making. Most of us had met at the various Sydney tertiary art institutions.

The need for an organisation such as Boomalli (a Wiradjuri word meaning 'to strike, to make a mark, to light up, to fight') arose from the artists' frustration at dealing with the inherent racism and ignorance in the mainstream arts industry over the classification of our work. We did not fit the stereotypical image of what then was expected of Aboriginal artists – neither in the work we were creating, nor in our appearance, educational backgrounds and politicism.

The work we were creating was considered by some as 'second-rate "white" art', a passing fad, not 'the real thing' (as in truly 'authentic' Aboriginal art). Boomalli was intended to be a space where we could all work in studio areas, in a mutually supportive environment, and where we could display our work in exhibitions on our terms. The aims and objectives of the cooperative included the promotion of the teaching of arts, and self-management and control by and for Aboriginal people.

Initially, Boomalli was run voluntarily by the members. This presented difficulties, as none of the artists were trained in arts administration. Having to expend a great deal of effort on financial aspects, on keeping records of all our dealings, and on the processes of accessing funding, placed constraints on our artistic development.

In 1989 a non-Aboriginal person was employed part-time to undertake the ongoing administrative duties required by Boomalli. However, the members considered it essential that Boomalli be a totally Aboriginal initiative, and when funding for the position temporarily ceased, administrative duties reverted to a volunteer basis.

In 1990 funds were approved by the Department of Employment, Education and Training under the Training for Aboriginal People scheme, for two positions – coordinator, and assistant/office worker. This enabled Aboriginal people to receive full salary subsidies while being trained in the areas of arts administration. The following year saw the employment of a further two people under the same TAP scheme, as curator and assistant curator. Two of the positions were funded for a period of eighteen months, with the other two positions funded for twelve months.

It cannot be emphasised enough the importance of this funding support in that it enabled consistent administration and the provision of professional services to the artists, and also to our expanding audience. The quality of the organisation and presentation of exhibitions increased substantially due to the curatorial positions.

The curator, Fiona Foley, began a placement as guest curator with the Museum of Contemporary Art, providing her with in-house skills that she then utilised at Boomalli. The coordinator (this writer) was accepted into the Graduate Diploma in Gallery Management at the College of Fine Arts, University of NSW, and was later upgraded to candidacy for a Master of Arts Administration.

This level of training made the wider arts industry realise that Boomalli was serious in its role and long-term goals. By undertaking this training we realised how thin on the ground Aboriginal arts administrators, curators and art workers were, and how the demand for such skilled workers far outweighed the supply. We had to have some say and control over the presentation and marketing of our culture, and to do this we had to become skilled and learn how to break into the arts-administration industry.

People such as Djon Mundine, Art and Craft Adviser at Bulabula Arts at Ramingining, north-east Arnhem Land, provided encouragement as role models and pioneers (for want of a better term) for those who wished to work in this field. Still, being taken seriously by your non-Aboriginal peers often proved elusive, especially if you were working within large arts institutions. There you tended to feel like the token black face, particularly if you were on a traineeship.

I have continually witnessed and participated in seminars and lectures being given by Aboriginal arts workers and artists where non-Aboriginal people in the audience have practically demanded, in a patronising and offensive manner, that the speakers validate their positions and justify their qualifications. It is as if some non-Aboriginal people working in the area of Aboriginal art and culture are afraid that we are going to 'take over' their much-prized field.

Thankfully, this attitude is changing, and major arts institutions around Australia have come to realise that they must take responsibility for ensuring that they employ and consult with Aboriginal arts workers. We are more than capable of making curatorial decisions about our work, and we are more than capable of writing about our histories. We decide the parameters in which we work.

This is where the notion of the Other comes into play. For so long, urban-based Aboriginal people were, and to some extent still are, viewed as different, as apart from not only non-Aboriginal people, but also tradition-oriented Aboriginal people. Along with this view was the inference that we were somehow 'lesser', not as worthy, not capable.

The exhibitions that were created at and through Boomalli over the past six years were created from a need to establish our own agenda and criteria, and to show that all Aboriginal art and culture being practised today is contemporary and multifaceted. We were viewed as 'Others' by the wider – that is, mainstream – society. We never viewed ourselves in this way.

Being categorised as the Other is part of the wider process of marginalisation with which all Aboriginal people can easily identify.

'Wiyana/Persiferia (Periphery)', a Boomalli exhibition recently curated by Hetti Perkins and Liliana E. Correa, involved collaborative work by Sydney-based Latin American artists and Boomalli artists, and was held at the Performance Space, Sydney, in January 1993, as a satellite exhibition of the 9th Biennale of Sydney. The exhibition then toured the regional gallery system of New South Wales. The whole premise of the exhibition deals with being the Other, on the periphery, and is best stated by Boomalli curator, Hetti Perkins in the catalogue:

Marginalisation is a concept, a reality and state of mind. Marginalisation describes the relationship and position of certain groups within a society to a dominant hegemonic power. Indigenous and immigrant peoples can share many similar experiences when they are both in a relationship to another cultural majority. This cultural majority has been termed the 'centre' (here read other). Although all things are defined in relation to the centre, the centre itself avoids definitions – yet has been described by Audre Lorde as 'white, thin, male, young, heterosexual, Christian and financially secure'. The apparent normalcy and ordinariness of the 'mythical norm' is its best defence, rendering it intangible and therefore, immovably and insidiously powerful. It is so accepted it is rarely questioned or even named and, in fact, it may be absurd to do so. The International Year of White People is unlikely to be next on the agenda of the United Nations after the Indigenous, Women, Children, Disabled and Trees.

This centre is relevant to those who are placed, or rather choose to place themselves, within this centre. I, and most of the artists and arts workers who are involved with Boomalli, have sought to redefine this so-called centre. In fact, it may be absurd to consider that there is only one centre, one place of Otherness. I consider there to be many points of reference, many centres, from which our actions create a rippling effect. We create work and exhibitions that invite others to come to us rather than us attempting to go towards others.

'Wiyana/Persiferia' was two years in the planning and emerged from a concern to work with other cultures. It was specifically not Eurocentric. Issues that Aboriginal, indigenous and migrant communities deal with are all too often placed within the realm of Other, of being somebody else's concern, easy to sympathise with and look in upon rather than to deal with or try to comprehend. Hetti Perkins again deals with the notion of defining Otherness in her catalogue essay:

The quite elementary system of 'us and them' encounters immediate difficulties when faced with reality. The artists represented in this exhibition remain outside (Wiyana) of any imposed formulae – as does most of the world it seems. The sphere of the Other is their chosen domain (though not all Aboriginal artists/people subscribe to this statement). Not pursuing a life-style which fits the stereotype of Aboriginal or living outside of the country of their birth or ancestry as a refugee, migrant or exile and refusing to be drawn into the mainstream, they confound the system which seeks to impose a homogeneous identity upon 'other' groups. Under threat, the centre attacks them by questioning their very basic right to their own individual identities.

Furthermore, popular and government practice thwarts their participation in contemporary life on their own terms by placing conditional access on certain rights and privileges. In popular culture any challenge to the current hegemony is hysterically portrayed as apocalyptic; when things fall apart the centre cannot hold, mere anarchy is loosed upon the world.

By choosing to be seen as different, though not necessarily being defined as Other, I am making a statement about who I am as an Aboriginal person and as an Aboriginal woman and as an Aboriginal artist, as are many other Aboriginal people. However, the concept of Otherness, of difference, will broaden as do the parameters defined by those of us operating as cultural activists. We are not outside this place, but rather inherently ingrained in this country and of this country.

I am fair in complexion; I am aware that I am not what people are looking for when they want something authentic, something truly Aboriginal, but I am here. I am aware that as I look through magazines they are not of me, for me. The models are white and pure, or black and foreign or exotic, not from here, not of me. I turn on the television and the advertisements make me feel that I have travelled to some other country, I am not at home. I see reports of our people and we are down again, so far down it is hard to see daylight. When observed, when exposed, we are mere microbes, lucky for some space, alien to white Australians, unknown quantities: sad, sorry, Other, peripheral, not their problem. I travelled overseas and was amazed at how I became the exotic, the foreign, the Other. Displacement can be the other side. By placing myself behind the camera I am taking control of my self-image and images of ourselves. I cannot, do not, take sole responsibility, but challenge and attempt to reverse the expected. My mother marrying my father, white dress, black suit; the negative makes me laugh, the story makes me cry. Reverse roles. Look at me/us and do not see through me/us. Acknowledge me/us. I am right beside you.

Note

1. Ms Bancroft became general manager of Boomalli in 1995. [Editors]

9 Committed photography: Recording history

Juno Gemes

What can a desert be made to do?
  Supply a distance
in which the wrongs
  each heart has nourished
eventually die of exposure
[Robert Harris (1968)]

Communication isn't some quantifiable thing like houses or water bores, where a demonstrated lack is solved by increased numbers. Communication is relational; it brings about relationships between people ... Culture is itself information, and kinship and social structures are communication systems which bring certain people together, but exclude others, protecting communication pathways and the value of information they carry. [Eric Michaels, in Ruby (1991)]

During the past twenty years, Aboriginal and activist white historians have totally recast Australian history. Similarly, photography activists have effected change that has turned a situation of Aboriginal invisibility into one of high visibility in Aboriginal publications, fine-art exhibitions, literary and political publications, and, with difficulty, in the mainstream media. Historical inspection reveals that photographic practice with respect to indigenous peoples has been in a constant state of change.

In 1982 my work of the previous ten years was shown in two simultaneous exhibitions: first, the Apmira Exhibition was mounted to raise awareness and funds for the New South Wales Land Council and the Kimberley Land Council; second, a solo exhibition entitled 'We Wait No More' opened at the Hogarth Gallery, Sydney, and the Bitumen River Gallery in Canberra. The accompanying catalogue essay (Gemes 1982) explained the conceptual basis of the work:

Around 1972 the Aboriginal Embassy was set up in Canberra and Black Theatre was established in Sydney. These were momentous events, the turning point in many people's lives. It was the beginning of a new history and cultural resurgence.

Right up till the 1970s there were very few photographic images produced which represented the realities of Aboriginal life. The living culture of Aboriginal Australia was ignored and kept invisible by the powers within the dominant white culture. The brutal and abhorrent government policies of 'assimilation – genocide' were executed within a mantle of invisibility and silence. The initial impulse and intention of this photographic practice was to make visible the reality of the people from within a true cultural context. The work was produced in conjunction with the communities and individuals represented and is a working articulation with the people in the struggle for justice. As the distinguished poet and activist Oogeroo Noonuccal so generously said, 'I don't blame you for the past but I hold you all accountable for the present and for the future.'

I will give a brief account of how I arrived at this conclusion.

In the late 1960s and early 1970s, I spent six months in Central Australia with Luritja (Loritdja), Pitjantjatjara and Arrente people as a researcher-collaborator on an independent documentary film *Uluru*. After two years of research preparation, I went to the centre six weeks before my partner, experimental film-maker Mick Glasheen. My task was to find the traditional owners and custodians of Uluru, the same elders who in earlier decades had worked with ethnologist Charles Mountford, to ask for their advice and participation in the making of the film. As this was well before the *Pitjantjatjara Land Rights Act 1976*, the locating of traditional owners was no easy matter for me. The people were dispersed over heavily restricted reserves or living in fringe camps under the most difficult circumstances. '*Weya* ['No'], we got nothing, except our culture,' people used to say with a sad laugh.

Racism was deeply entrenched in the Australian psyche. The 'Dying Race' mythology was much in evidence with government authorities and some anthropologists, and was reflected in the media. Police harassment was an everyday fact of life. Yet the people welcomed me with an open generosity.

Eventually I was taken to the fringe camp where the elders stayed. This was the beginning not only of my work in the field, but of my apprenticeship with Aboriginal culture itself. After four weeks the elders began to discuss some aspects of the ceremonial stories depicted in the topography of Uluru. When I noticed that these accounts were substantially different from those relayed by Mountford I asked why this was so. The elder laughed and remarked, 'You can only tell a person what they are ready to understand.'

That we were independent film makers was of the utmost importance. We represented no oppositional authority; we too were outsiders. That I found myself in gaol twice in Alice Springs during this period might indicate that the making of the film became a form of activism for us and the traditional owners, who at that time barely had access to their traditional country. As a result of this collaboration, the film became an insistent statement about the custodial relationship of the people to their country, a proclamation of the strength and resilience of their culture. It was shockingly clear to me that at least 90 per cent of the Australian public neither knew an Aboriginal person nor anything of their history or current circumstances. I therefore felt it was necessary to work in a medium that had a wider reach and more flexible usage than work shown in an art-house cinema, effective though that might be. Photography has a variety of possible usages. It could be used by Aboriginal publications and organisations, in art galleries and in mainstream media. It could be used as an accessible strategy for effecting perceptual change. I saw this as the task at hand.

Catherine de Lorenzo (1981), who has written extensively on the history and changing representations of Aboriginal people in photographic practice, stated:

> I want to show that photographers can go beyond assuming the 'truth' of reportage and can, as Walter Benjamin put it, consciously set out to unmask appearances and even to 'construct' a different way of looking at things'.

Acknowledging that there are many kinds of photographic practices in relationship to indigenous people, how do we distinguish one form from another? I suggest that consideration and analysis of the following questions would be helpful:

- What is the intention of the work? Who commissioned it?
- What is its purpose and its means of construction?
- How has the work been used? For whose benefit?

There is also the difficult question of the cultural background of the photographer.

We all now face a moral crisis, an absence of accurate self-definition. One has to imagine that a white photographer can photograph a white person despite the cultural divergences. One has to imagine that a black photographer can photograph a black person despite the cultural divergences. These are complex and personal questions and there is a multiplicity of possible answers.

*Closing ceremony of Pacific Arts
Association, Adelaide, 1993:
A photo essay by Juno Gemes*

9.1-9.-7 These photographs were
taken by Juno Gemes as a participant
and recorder of the Pacific Arts
Association's closing event. They show
Aboriginal dancers from Elcho Island,
off Arnhem Land in northern Australia,
and Pitjantjatjara people from the
north-west of South Australia. Note
also that audience participation and
learning was encouraged, and that one
photograph at least shows participants
playing an active role in documenting
this event.

Similarly, people now use the word 'culture' or 'cultural production' as if it has a singular meaning – or allude to the possibility that its multiplicity of meanings can be easily located. To quote the distinguished Aboriginal anthropologist Marcia Langton (1981):

> All humans have culture, that culture is a prerequisite of humanness and that identity for any individual is a multivariate composition, non-fixed, situational and constantly maintained and transformed by culture.

In the 1970s a small band of independent photographers emerged who worked with Aboriginal communities, Aboriginal organisations and within specific areas of the Aboriginal movement. These photographers included Wes Stacey, Jon Rhodes, Lee Chidick, Elaine Kitchener and me. I worked as an independent photographer commissioned by Aboriginal organisations and on invitation by Aboriginal communities, mainly on very small budgets.

In 1979, while working with Woomera (Mornington Island Culture Cooperative), I was commissioned to photograph a culture festival. Five people from top-end communities came together to put twenty-four young men through the law. During the first two weeks of my stay, discussions were held with members of the Gunna Amanda Council and clan members regarding what it was we wanted to communicate in this collaboration. The male elders felt it most important to show that 'the culture was still strong', preparation for ceremony, traditional methods of hunting and fishing. The women felt it important to show that their 'ceremonial business' was a very important part of the ceremony. They declared in the strongest terms that their part was seldom given the same importance as the men's role, by anthropologists and government officials alike.

Because I was a young woman, all secret-sacred men's business was out of bounds to me. I photographed no person who suggested they did not want to be photographed. Restrictions involving photographs of people who died later were to be honoured for a period of five years after the death. My suggestion to depict caring, sharing, deep affection between countrymen was greeted with humour and enthusiasm.

It was agreed that the negatives, being my work, would remain in my care, and that the photographs would be used in publications and exhibitions with the intention of changing prevailing attitudes. Many lyric images were produced in this period.

During a return trip (a rare luxury for me) many prints were lodged with the Gunna Amanda Culture Co-operative and are still used in their publications. Many of these images and later works appeared in the exhibition and book *After the Tent Embassy*.

Members of Woomera, coincidentally in Sydney at the time, previewed the exhibition. *After the Tent Embassy* was edited by Marcia Langton who also wrote the hard-hitting text, which acted as a deft tool, prising open each image to an Aboriginal interrogation. It marked the first photographic text of the Aboriginal struggle, and showed the strength of the Aboriginal people and their culture. It was the first publication to locate the urban struggle for social justice within the framework of land rights for all Aborigines.

In 1983 I was commissioned by Aboriginal Hostels Ltd to produce an exhibition celebrating their tenth year of self-management. During the six weeks that followed I stayed in five different hostels around New South Wales, collaborating with the management and students of all ages in the construction and production of images. The resulting exhibition was shown in Canberra during NAIDOC celebrations that year. The *National Times* newspaper gave two pages to the publication of images from this exhibition.

Nevertheless, getting work published in mainstream media was often extremely difficult. This kind of photography, clearly supporting Aboriginal initiatives, goes against the grain of the prevailing fiction called objective reporting. This was particularly the case when I submitted for publication images from land-rights marches showing the protesters as peaceful and the police as aggressive. An example was the work from the National Land Rights Action in Brisbane in 1982. The reporter writing the accompanying piece was sympathetic and even quoted from our media releases. However, when the photographs were taken in to the picture editor, he came rushing out of his office saying, 'This is not objective reporting.' I replied

'No, it's not. There is no bloody fence on the street when women and children and young men are facing 500 Queensland police with batons. You're either on one side or the other and your pictures will reflect that.' During this action I also discovered that a camera focused on the police can cause them instantly to modify their behaviour.

My images have been widely published in Aboriginal publications, *AIM, North Queensland Message Stick, One Nation, Koori Mail, Long Water, Survival, Language and Image 1988, Wiradjari Warrior* by Mary Coe, and mainstream publications including the *Sydney Morning Herald, Social Alternatives*, and *Australian Society*. Some of the images have been used by young Koori artists in the production of posters and fliers for events within their community.

> There are three stages in the perception of truth: At first it is outlawed and declared to be heretical; secondly, it is vigorously debated, and finally, it is declared to be self evident. [A. Schopenhauer, *The World as Will and Idea*, 1819]

Schopenhauer's text gives us a hint as to how we might begin to understand the nature of social change. One danger in rapid perceptual change is that new positions are easily adopted without any recourse or comprehension of the past, or of how the changes have occurred.

In 1984, on request, I helped set up a photographic workshop for young Aboriginal photographers at the Tin Sheds in Sydney. I have regularly badgered organisations such as the National Documentary Festival to invite Koori participation. My studios have always been accessed by young Koori photographers. Tracey Moffatt helped me set up Camera Futura at Kings Cross and used it as a base when filming *Nice Coloured Girls*. My delight in the subtle ingenuity of her work and that of many of her contemporaries continues.

I believe it is essential that the baton of activism be passed on from one generation to the next. It is the young who now set the agenda, building on the greater freedom of expression and expansion of opportunity that characterise this period. However, I cannot support any attempt to recast the history of the 1970s and 1980s on the basis of the present. If we are fighting against the distortion of Aboriginal history by its oppressor, it is very dangerous to fall prey to the same practice ourselves. Curators who take a similar view must eventually find themselves similarly restricted and their collections distorted. The great gap in their collections from the work of the 1970s and 1980s robs all Aboriginal people of their history. It is fine by me for a well-known Aboriginal curator to put together an exhibition titled, 'I shall never become a White Man', in the same year in which he appears in Michael Jackson's video 'It Doesn't Matter if You're Black or White'.

After twenty years of work, my archive contains up to 50 000 negatives. Although the archive is well-maintained, I feel a large responsibility for its care and have begun to cast about for an ultimate resting place that will respect the conditions of its production and its purpose, and maximise accessibility to Aboriginal organisations and communities and genuine researchers.

When I was not yet forty, the Australian Institute of Aboriginal and Torres Strait Islander Studies (AIATSIS) put a form in front of me suggesting I bequeath them my archive. I found the experience quite shocking. Despite them already holding a collection of my work, they have never offered me any kind of assistance or support. Strangely, when I put a submission to them last year for support to catalogue the archive, with the assistance of Sam Wickman (who had assisted Dr Jo Kaminga to recatalogue the Milne collection for the National Museum of Australia), the submission was not successful, despite the strongest possible support from Aboriginal organisations. It seems AIATSIS chooses only to support work it has generated itself.

Looking around at the rate of publication for most bodies of photographic work, one would have to conclude that the most popular photographers with such institutions are usually in the later years of their lives or, more conveniently, dead. I will continue to make accessible the work from my studio until I have found an acceptable and responsive institution for its maintenance.

The complex issue surrounding the eventual location of the archive can only be resolved when its value as a consciously constructed history of the Aboriginal struggle is seen to be beyond partisan politics.

10 Racism and the state: Critical reflections on the organisation of heritage institutions in South Australia

Deane Fergie

This paper[1] is about the transmission of knowledge in my culture. It is about ideas and the imagination. This paper is about the transmission of ideas about indigenous peoples.[2] It is about the contexts in which a goodly number of Australians come to imagine indigenous peoples. This paper is about racism – not acts of racism, but the ideas and imaginings on which such acts are predicated. This paper is about the state of South Australia and the role of the state, despite contrary intentions, in reproducing racism in South Australia.[3]

Racism is built on assumptions of profound and unbreachable difference between imagined communities.[4] These ideas of profound difference are often expressed as natural and 'in the nature of things', and more particularly to be 'in the blood'. This is one of the reasons why supposed differences are understood to be unbreachable – for it is thought not to be possible for human beings to change this sort of natural fact.

Dimensions of Australian racism – distance

As well as this universal characteristic of racism[5] (against any others at any time), Australian racism (perhaps indicative of other Western racisms) has a particular face. In Australia, ideas about indigenous peoples tend to assume profound distance as well as natural difference. This distance is often conceptualised as spatial distance and temporal distance.

In respect of spatial distance, it is useful to examine prevalent ideas about the nature of Australia's indigenous people. There is an abiding assumption that not only is authentic Aboriginality to be found 'in the blood' (and that is assumed to be reflected in the complexion); it is also assumed to be located out there, 'in the outback'. Despite the obvious contrary evidence that 72 per cent of this state's Aboriginal people live close at hand in urban centres, authentic Aboriginality is perceived to be found in outback places and ritual mysteries rather than working in a child-care centre at Port Adelaide. Most Australians believe that 'real' Aboriginality is in distant spaces.

But there is another crucial dimension to the distancing dimension of Australian racism – temporal distance. Here indigenous peoples are positioned as innately and profoundly different from us because they are understood effectively to come 'from another time'. In particular, indigenous peoples are understood in some way to be prehistoric, and most particularly, to come from some 'other kind' of time, often characterised as the Stone Age. Here it is clear that many white Australians have taken on board social evolutionary ideas current in academic circles in the late 19th century but firmly debunked in the first half of this century. Indigenous peoples, in this view, are not really properly 'in' our own historical time; rather they are 'out of time', living fossils of some long-ago human past (cf. Fergie 1991).

It is in this context that we are able to make sense of the profoundly racist appellation about Papua New Guineans that was current among many expatriate Australians during my stays in that country from 1973 onwards. Papua New Guineans were (and often still are) referred to by some Australians as 'rock apes'. This is Australian racism at its most succinct. It represents the profound distancing in which these indigenous people are placed in another time (prehistoric time, at the transition from *Homo erectus*[6] to *Homo sapiens*) and by implication in other spaces (the distant forests where apes might be found). In this expression of racism, Papua New Guineans are set as profoundly and unbreachably different – indeed, from a different time and space.

Heritage institutions in South Australia

What do these disturbing and distressing ideas and appellations have to do with the organisation of cultural-heritage institutions in South Australia?

I argue that the division of labour and focus among the cultural heritage institutions of South Australia reinforces important dimensions of Australian racism. Rather than critiquing these ideas, the organisation of South Australian heritage institutions serves to reinforce and maintain these spurious ideas of spatial and temporal distance between Aboriginal and non-Aboriginal Australians, which are a cornerstone of Australian racism.

South Australia is the home of a number of active and well-respected state-funded and state-administered cultural institutions. They range from our host for the Pacific Arts symposium, the South Australian Museum, to its neighbour, the Art Gallery of South Australia, and include also the institutions under the umbrella of the South Australian History Trust, the Maritime Museum, and the Migration and Settlement Museum. Differently funded and administered, the South Australian government has more recently had a formal and financial relationship with Tandanya, the National Aboriginal Cultural Institute. Each of these institutions has some particular claim to fame.

The South Australian Museum, for instance, boasts the world's 'finest' and largest collection of Aboriginal artefacts, despite being one of the most under-funded state museums in Australia. The Art Gallery of South Australia boasts a collection of 19th-century Australian art 'without rival' (Dicks and Lambert 1992). Tandanya is 'the only' Aboriginal cultural institution of its type and size in Australia.

It is, however, the division of cultural labour between these institutions that is my point of departure. It is clear that there has been a particular division of labour between the art gallery and the museum, which can be characterised as collections of artefacts and crafts on the one hand (understood as more primitive manifestations of culture), and art (high European culture)[7] on the other. However, it is the difference in focus between the human and cultural interests of the South Australian History Trust and the South Australian Museum that is the focus of this paper.

The History Trust deals with the history of South Australia after the arrival of Europeans. The South Australian Museum deals primarily with indigenous peoples[8] and houses the state's 'natural history' collection. My concern is not so much that white faces dominate the exhibits of the South Australian History Trust, while the few faces that are to be found in the South Australian Museum's displays are black. Rather, the model of time with which each institution frames those faces and their cultures is of primary concern to me.

Time frames – temporal distance

The History Trust is quite explicit about its time frame. Not only is it concerned with historic time, but most particularly it focuses on those decades since Europeans first came to these shores. The History Trust then is concerned with 'us' and with 'our' time.

The South Australian Museum, I would suggest, is an entirely different kettle of fish. In particular, I want to suggest that by locating its ethnographic collections and displays about indigenous peoples amid a natural-history collection, the museum facilitates the development and reinforcement of ideas of profound difference and distance.

It is worth tracing the routes by which visitors to the

museum approach displays of humanness here. The main entrance is flanked by the museum's local signature, gargantuan whale bones reminiscent of the dinosaurs (whose modelled remains are on sale in the museum shop). Through the beached bones of long-dead whales the visitor arrives at the world of mammals stuffed and stationary, inviting the kind of inspection impossible at the zoo. Until the past few years, it was then up the stairs that one arrived at the level of human culture – the Pacific Gallery. Stuffed full of undifferentiated, barely interpreted artefacts of savagery (the tools, bows and arrows, spears and clubs, as well as some grotesque trophies: shrunken heads[9] and exotica – *malangan*, Sulka masks and all), the gallery was, until recently, strangely framed.

At the eastern end, just in front of superb masks and sculptures, was a case of tropical butterflies. As one of my students remarked on a research visit in March 1993: 'At least they let you know just where you are – in the tropics down this end, and in the Stone Age down the other.' Indeed, at the far end of the Pacific Gallery, just in front of the large display of *malangan* objects, the museum's mineral collection was located. Such implicit messages about the location of Pacific cultures in space and time have, I would argue, provided powerful food for Australian imaginings. The present and mooted upgrades are none too soon, for otherwise the old gallery would carry this legacy well into the next century.

Yet in all fairness the Pacific Gallery is an anachronism that museum anthropology staff have sought to change for some years. It is only recently that even meagre funds have been made available.

More significant funding has allowed the upgrading of the Aboriginal exhibits. From the acclaimed 'Dreamings' exhibition to an outstanding exhibition of Yuendumu acrylic dot-paintings (exhibitions that have toured internationally) and the in-house Ngurunderi exhibition, the South Australian Museum is developing a formidable reputation for the display of Australian Aboriginal cultures and their artefacts. Indeed the Ngurunderi exhibition is a model of shared vision between museum staff and particular Aboriginal people, and stands in stark contrast to the displays of the Pacific collection.

It is salutary, however, to consider how one gets to these Aboriginal exhibits, for they necessitate passing through a natural-history representation of the world of reptiles, birds and fish. What meanings can be drawn from the placement of coloured faces and the artefacts of indigenous peoples among huge bones, stuffed animals and mineral specimens?

My point here is simple. While clearly the Pacific Gallery is a curatorial embarrassment, the Aboriginal displays are ones of which this state can be modestly proud. These are exhibits where at last indigenous people are represented, and indeed individuals named, and where some attempt has been made to tell their story.

Yet they are presented within a broad and culturally compelling frame: the frame of natural history, which I would argue ultimately thwarts the strengths of the displays in their own right. Aboriginal people, and the indigenous peoples of the Pacific, are framed in this museum by the architecture of social-evolutionary thought.

In that view of the world, indigenous cultures were viewed as living fossils, as representatives of earlier stages of social evolution, where savagery and barbarism, it was baselessly conjectured, characterised the prehistory of civilisation. I suggest such ideas are also imminent in the architecture, layout and contents of the South Australian Museum. It shares this characteristic, I would argue, with all other museums that are forced to present human cultures in the frame of a natural-history museum.

Powerful precincts

These issues would not be so important if the museum was not such a powerful influence on ideas and imaginings. In the first place, the South Australian Museum is located firmly in Adelaide's avenue of state power, North Terrace. In Adelaide, food for the imagination is everywhere.

But my point relates not simply to the powerful frame of North Terrace. It is also important to note that the museum is an extraordinarily popular place to visit in South Australia. It is not simply a popular tourist destination in general; the South Australian Museum is more particularly a popular destination for young South Australians.

Most South Australians can remember the first time they stood in front of the display cases full of savage equipment (spears and clubs), ghastly shrunken heads, and the sort of exotic sculptures I now know as *malangan*. The images of Pacific Islanders that the bus loads of school-children on excursions will carry with them into the 21st century are not the sort of images I would choose to convey to them about Pacific Islanders or Pacific Island cultures.

This is no doubt the reason that the gallery is being updated. But my point is that even when the displays are transformed, and recent works and faces added to materials collected in the 19th and early 20th centuries, the broader time frame of the museum will continue to offer powerful direction to the imaginations of South Australians. We must ensure, for instance, that the 'stuffed' animals do not offer implicit messages about 'stuffed' cultures and feed racist imaginings.

Conclusion

In this paper I make a particular case for the reorganisation of heritage institutions in South Australia. I argue that a distinction should no longer be made between types of cultures in the divisions of labour between heritage institutions.[10] Displays of indigenous cultures should always provoke a questioning of assumptions about us and about them. But most particularly I want to break the physical and conceptual nexus between indigenous (or any) peoples and natural history.

For it is in the framing of indigenous peoples by a natural-history conception of the world that a cornerstone of Australian racism is constantly reinforced. Indigenous peoples are distanced from us, out of space and out of time. The History Trust and the Anthropology Division of the South Australian Museum should be amalgamated, and natural history moved further down North Terrace, where it more logically belongs, between the Botanic Gardens and the Zoo, flanked by science on the university campus and the Royal Adelaide Hospital.

Finally, I argue that the mission of anthropologists in general, and of museum anthropologists in particular, should be not to pursue the curious and emphasise the

exoticness of other cultures. Rather, our mission should be to disrupt ethnocentric and racist ideas and to invite critical reflection upon the taken-for-granted assumptions that underpin our own culture. Anthropologists in South Australia must place increasing pressure on the government to broach the imagined distance between us and them by taking human beings out of natural history. This can be done only through an amalgamation of the human concerns of the museum and those of the History Trust, and a separation of people from the bleached bones of a natural-history conception of the natural world.

Notes

1. I wish to thank the undergraduate students from my Anthropological Approaches to Ritual, Performance and Art course at the University of Adelaide for their critical commentary on this project, and for the astuteness of their observations of the South Australian Museum, the Art Gallery of South Australia, and Tandanya.

2. In this task I benefit from having undertaken intensive and extended fieldwork in island Melanesia (twenty-one months) and my culture in Australia (twelve months), as well as moving between research and teaching functions within universities, and between university and museum anthropology.

3. I would take the opportunity to distance myself from the 'curiosity school' of museum anthropology, which has recently been articulated, and elaborate my position as a defence of the discipline of anthropology. In my view, curiosity is no justification for doing ethnographic field work; nor of appropriating objects from other cultures for display in our own. This is not to say that I believe anthropology is unjustified. Rather, I see the profound contribution of ethnographic field work and anthropological analysis to reside in the opportunity it provides to question our own taken-for-granted understandings of the world. All cultures are ethnocentric. Anthropology allows critical reflections on cultural arrogance. But anthropology that does not use the understanding of other cultures to critically reflect upon our own is indeed open to savage attack. It is as a contribution to such a critical project that this paper is offered.

4. Here I take inspiration from the work of Benedict Anderson and Paul Carter.

5.   And I should hasten to add that I suspect that racism is a universal feature of culture.

6.   As Darwinism would have us understand its origins.

7.   The Art Gallery of South Australia's displays feature representations of Aboriginal people (particularly in its collection of colonial art) and works by Aboriginal people that are 'art' rather than artefact.

8.   The exception is the Egyptian Room, which was obviously important in establishing the cultural credentials of the colony of South Australia in the late 19th century. At that time, any museum worth its salt had its classical exhibits – the Egyptian Room with its mummified feet and Egyptian column, donated to the Museum in 1891, and its date-palms planted 'to make the old Egyptian ghosts who may haunt the column feel more at home' (Dicks and Lambert 1992), at the entrance to the museum clearly served this purpose. Nearly a hundred years later they appear as anachronistic displays of statehood.

9.   Actually, not shrunken heads but overmodelled skulls. [Editors]

10.   For example, a significant Aboriginal presence in the Maritime Museum would be a welcome change.

Ethnographic museums and indigenous peoples: A perspective from Western Australia

John E. Stanton

Museums and their clients (collaborators and visitors) have customarily maintained an ambiguous relationship deriving, in part, from perceived inequalities in the distribution of power and access to resources. Recent critiques of museology and, in particular, the relationship between museums and indigenous peoples (for example, Ames 1992; Clifford 1988; Lavine and Karp 1991), have articulated afresh the element of ambiguity in such relationships. However, consideration of these issues has been taking place for some time. In their different ways, North American anthropologists such as Boas (1907), Burridge (1973) and Stocking (1985) have provided a context for the more recent debate.

The nature of the relationships Australian museums have maintained with indigenous peoples (whether in Papua New Guinea, the Pacific, or within Australia) has been diverse. In many cases, staff remained preoccupied with 19th-century scientism, embedding indigenous peoples (but definitely not themselves) within the 'natural world', falling somewhere between ants, on the one hand, and whales on the other. This imagined scientific approach, allegedly unaffected by cultural bias, aloof from political or moral influences, 'impartial' and 'accurate', served to cloud the underlying preconceptions of their endeavours.

There were some exceptions, however, where elements of a two-way flow existed between the observer and the observed. The South Australian Museum, for example, maintained over many years a program of practical involvement in the museum's exhibition and research activities for members of local Aboriginal groups. These people guided visitors around the galleries, provided demonstrations of boomerang-throwing and spear-throwing, among other things, and were vitally important collaborators in anthropological inquiry. Sadly, such participation was neglected during World War II, and the program of active involvement and participation in the museum's activities by Aborigines was not resurrected for more than thirty years.

Museums and Aborigines in Western Australia

Moving to the Western Australian setting, the state's first museum was established along the lines of a traditional natural-history museum. The Aboriginal collections date from 1892, when some items were presented by the commissioner of police – in today's terms, an inauspicious beginning. Most early collections came from the police or missionaries, or were purchased. However, between 1916 and 1961 most materials were obtained by donation. Since then, collections have been obtained through active fieldwork programs, and through commissions and direct purchases from Aboriginal people.

During this later period, and particularly since the early 1970s, the Department of Aboriginal Sites (operating under statute from within the Western Australian Museum) maintained an extensive site-recording program involving the training through a cadet scheme of young Aboriginal men to become site recorders. Funding problems prevented the scheme from continuing. Nevertheless, at the request of several remote-area Aboriginal communities, prefabricated 'keeping places', or 'sacred storehouses', were erected throughout the state from the early 1970s, paving the way for similar projects in other Australian states.

The museum's reputation suffered, in Aboriginal eyes, an almost irreparable loss of credibility during what became known as the 'Noonkanbah affair' between 1979 and 1982. The trustees of the museum permitted themselves to be overruled by the then minister responsible for Aboriginal matters in Western Australia in the matter of the destruction of a sacred site in the southern Kimberley by mining interests (Hawke and Gallagher 1989). Successive governments have attempted to interfere in the museum trustees' responsibilities for operating the *Aboriginal Heritage Act 1972/81*. In the early 1990s, the Lawrence government sought to seriously diminish Aboriginal rights for protection of Aboriginal sites, removing the Department of Aboriginal Sites from the museum and placing it directly (and vulnerably) under a state-government minister.

Aboriginal involvement in the Berndt Museum

At the University of Western Australia, the Berndt Museum of Anthropology (formerly the Anthropology Research Museum) has vigorously pursued active Aboriginal involvement in its activities. Its smallness and inadequate resourcing belies the scope of education and research initiatives achieved since its formal establishment. Unlike North America and Europe, in Australia university-based anthropology museums are a rarity. The only other similar institution is located at the University of Queensland. Some other universities have museums – for example the Macleay Museum at Sydney – but they are not exclusively anthropological.

The Berndt Museum was founded in 1976 to house the collections stored in the Department of Anthropology at the University of Western Australia. The core collections comprised those obtained by the late Dr Catherine Berndt and the late Emeritus Professor Ronald Berndt. These collections have been augmented with ones made by postgraduate research students, and others affiliated with the department and through an active acquisitions program since the mid-1970s. Today, the museum holds one of the largest and most diverse collections of contemporary arts and crafts in Australia, tripling in its original size to some 8000 pieces today.

The museum operates under its own University Senate-appointed board, which oversees the operation of the museum. The board is assisted by the Aboriginal Advisory Committee. This committee comprises representatives of a number of metropolitan, wheat-belt and south-west based organisations sharing a common interest in issues relating to Aboriginal cultural heritage, as well as several individual community members prominent in this arena. Still in its early phase of operation, requiring more experience and confidence, the advisory committee meets at least three times each year to discuss issues raised by the curator or the board, or to address its own interests. The chairperson attends board meetings, along with (on a rotating basis) another committee member.

The museum is committed to meeting, wherever possible, Aboriginal requests for research and display support, and has directly assisted in a variety of Aboriginal-initiated projects. These include the Moola Bulla local history project at Halls Creek, the Dampierland photographic project at the Broome-based Kimberley Law and Culture Centre (both in the Kimberley), and the establishment of the Marribank Cultural Centre near Katanning, in the south-west. The production of contemporary Kimberley art also has been extensively documented on film and video. In most cases, Aboriginal initiatives focus on requests for copies of historic and ethnographic photographs, of which the museum holds approximately 25 000 (excluding the Berndt Collection, which is yet to be transferred). More rarely, copies of early sound-recordings are requested, and these are made available as required.

Relatively few requests have been made to borrow objects compared with those for photographs, but a number of items of a secret-sacred nature have been repatriated over the years, at the request of individual members of particular communities. The museum has been active also in helping to publicise the provisions of the state act (and more recently the federal act) relating to cultural-heritage material, to dealers, auctioneers and other relevant traders, as well as identifying such items in local and 'colonial' museums and arranging for repatriation where possible.

Having only one-and-a-half permanent staff, and occasional volunteers (along with the support of members of the Aboriginal Advisory Committee and the Friends of the Museum), we have nevertheless been able to maintain an activity profile rivalling that of better-resourced state museums' departments of anthropology. This profile cannot continue indefinitely without additional resources, in funding and staffing. The university has recently rejected our request on economic grounds for a government-funded Aboriginal trainee position (something that would have been a logical step in the development of our museum). It is clear that appropriately trained Aboriginal people will play an increasingly important and direct role in the operations of the museum, and we must identify the means to achieve this goal.

The Marribank Project

The Museum's advice and support for the establishment of the Marribank Cultural Centre has been perhaps its largest and most ambitious project so far.

A government settlement for persons of Aboriginal descent was established near Katanning, in the south-west of this state, in 1915. Named Carrolup, it closed in 1922 but reopened in 1940, and continued to provide a home for Aboriginal people until 1951, when it became the Marribank Family Centre, operated by the Baptist Church. Members of the community approached the Berndt Museum's curator in 1985 for information on the history of the children's art movement, in response to an earlier article we had written (Berndt 1979).

Their enthusiasm led them to seek the museum's assistance in further documenting the original children's art, as well as more recent materials. This involved the curator

participating in a government-sponsored training program for two Nyungar women over a six-month period, teaching basic museological and conservation skills in preparation for their assumption of responsibility for running the centre. Photographic copies were made of the museum's drawings and historic photographs relating to Carrolup. These were lodged with the community. Additional materials were borrowed for copying from local townspeople, former missionaries and teachers and the like, and these copies were catalogued by the trainees. Interviews with elderly former residents were also recorded.

The community obtained funds from the Australian Bicentennial Commission and the Australian Heritage Commission, to restore the former girls' dormitory (a large stone building) and convert half of it into a display gallery, containing wall space for hanging paintings and photographs, as well as cases containing historic artefacts from the area, and contemporary art and craft works made by members of the Marribank community, which was, at that time, producing an original range of pottery, jewellery and batiks. The exhibition was opened at a Back to Carrolup Day in 1988. In 1992, a further gallery of historic photographs was opened, covering the period of the Baptist Ministry at the settlement. A Museum Committee, comprising former Carrolup and Marribank staff and residents, retains responsibility for the cultural centre, opening it to the public during weekends, cleaning the galleries, and continuing the work of salvaging old Nyungar family photograph albums. These are borrowed for copying by the Berndt Museum, and archival prints are then lodged with the centre.

Nyungar Landscapes: a collaborative exhibition

The completion of the most recent phase of the Carrolup Project, which has dominated the Berndt Museum's activities since 1985, came with the launching of a major travelling retrospective exhibition focusing on the art of Carrolup (Stanton 1992). This was mounted in close collaboration with members of the community. The exhibition toured regional venues in Western Australia before travelling to the eastern states.

In the late 1940s, a group of young Nyungar children developed a highly original interpretation of their rural environment with the sympathetic encouragement of their schoolteacher, Noel White. An Englishwoman, Florence Rutter, was highly impressed with these works and took them on an exhibition tour of New Zealand, Britain and Europe. Since then, another generation of artists has emerged, many of these having direct kin-based associations with the original Carrolup artists.

While the art movement was heavily publicised during its emergence in the late 1940s, and the subject of a book by Mary Durack Miller and its promoter Florence Rutter, there has been no critical analysis of the impact this movement had at the time, or of its contemporary significance. The accompanying catalogue essay contextualises this achievement, in sociohistorical terms, and relates the continuing production of this art to the emergence of a powerful Nyungar identity in the south-west.

Museums and Aborigines

The evident success of the museum's long-term collaboration with the Marribank Community is simply one example among a number that point to the increasing level of grassroots interest among members of Western Australian Aboriginal communities in achieving more direct participation in the management and interpretation of their diverse cultural heritage.

The publication in country newspapers of reports concerning the Carrolup Project, as it came to be known, elicited strong responses from members of several Aboriginal communities throughout the state, who sought the museum's involvement in similar projects. All were preoccupied with bringing elements of their community's specific cultural heritage into their local environment, assembling artefacts and historical materials (including photographs, missionary and Department of Native Welfare ephemera, handmade furniture, and so on) to 'tell the story' to their children and grandchildren, and to interested visitors.

The museum's limited resources clearly restrict the number of projects it can take on at any one time. Nevertheless,

advice is given to communities about drawing up submissions for funding support and the like, and lists of relevant items from the museum's collections (such as photographs) are made available. But because the museum lacks funds to make prints, it is often necessary for people to travel to Perth to inspect the photographic records. Although not always an easy task, it is increasingly possible due to improved communications and the need for people to come to Perth to attend the hospital or government meetings, and the like.

This grassroots phenomenon is, of course, not the exclusive preserve of Aboriginal communities; it is clearly evident among the wider Australian society, too. But, given the coercive administration of Aboriginal people in the past (and many would say, today), this is a remarkable demonstration that government (state and federal) policies of assimilation have been largely unsuccessful, even though the fight to withstand them has been a hard one.

The *Report of the State Task Force for Museums Policy* (Stannage 1991) made a number of significant recommendations in this respect. While the full report has remained an internal departmental document, a summarised version (1992) has identified a number of important issues relating to museums and Aboriginal cultural heritage.

Of particular significance were the recommendations of the Aboriginal Interests Working Group, one of three committees of the task force. The working group highlighted the need for the recognition of the primary role of Aboriginal people in the preservation, presentation, continuation and management of their cultural heritage; the promotion of meaningful Aboriginal participation at all levels of this management; and the promotion of respect and understanding for the diverse cultural heritage of Aboriginal Western Australians. It recommended the establishment of an Aboriginal Cultural Heritage Commission, to be responsible for all Aboriginal cultural-heritage materials within the state.

While few, if any, museum professionals could have opposed the establishment of such a commission or general support for the above-mentioned principles, the outright transfer of materials from existing institutions (museum, art gallery and State Archives) proved to be a problem, not the least part of which was the need for appropriate legislation. A more collaborative approach may have been more productive, because the state government did not control the Upper House, and lacked support for the segmentation of the Western Australian Museum from within its own ranks.

Political expediency encouraged the state government to dilute this and other proposals of the task force. Further delays and transformations of proposed legislation were eclipsed by the need for the Labor government to survive the February 1993 election at any cost. So much for political idealism or pragmatism: the Lawrence Government was not returned. The recommendations of the task force expired and are unlikely to be revived in the foreseeable future.

The reality, then, is that it is up to institutions holding significant collections of Aboriginal cultural materials to be responsible for taking the first steps towards a reconciliation, a collaboration between Aboriginal people and their own organisations.

It was 1950 before the first book to seriously promote Australian Aboriginal art was published (Elkin, Berndt and Berndt 1950). It was written by anthropologists. That anthropologists have, until recently, been alone in the promotion of Aboriginal art and have dominated critical writing about it is not surprising, given the orientation of the discipline as a whole. Other disciplines may come to have increasingly important influences on how this art is perceived in the wider community, and we may expect to hear more from the art producers themselves.

In all this, then, I believe anthropologists have something special to offer members of indigenous communities with whom they have worked, over an entire lifetime in some cases. Not only do museum records, photographs, genealogies, tape-recordings and the like provide a rich resource for future generations, but the discipline also provides a means for understanding better some of the processes of change, adaptation and creativity experienced by indigenous societies. Anthropology is interested in the way change is reflected in material performances (Stanton 1989), and how people perpetuate, reinforce and elaborate their cultural identity, quite often in the face of immense government pressure to conform to the dominant culture.

If we have learned anything from the goals expressed in some of the recommendations of the Aboriginal Interests Working Group, it is that museums and their staff must make a much stronger commitment to engaging directly with members of Aboriginal client communities at a collective and an individual level. These issues have been expressed for some time. The 1979 UNESCO-sponsored seminar (Edwards and Stewart 1980) highlighted Aboriginal aspirations in this respect. These reports, and others, present museum curators with a clear challenge for the future. Overseas experiences, particularly in North America and New Zealand will, I have no doubt, provide an inspiration for further achievements.

But more importantly, we have to look to our own resources, our own inspiration, if we are going to develop a much closer collaborative relationship between indigenous peoples and ethnographic museums.

12 Old galleries, new people

Christopher Anderson

Museums are in a curious position. Museum attendance is greater than ever. Interest in the arts and world views of other cultures is at an all-time high. 'Heritage' and 'multiculturalism' are intensely topical notions, and museums embody these for many people. Collections are now being used in ways and by people that previous generations would not have thought possible. Most major museums are today active and positive places, in a scholarly and a public sense.

On the other hand, museums – long considered the poor cousins of 'real' (that is, academic) anthropology and art history – have often been subject to everything from sniping at conferences to sustained critiques from people in those disciplines. The comments range from minor criticism for presentation of inaccurate or outdated information, or old-fashioned displays, through to broad critiques of collections as cultural theft and exhibitions as cultural hegemony.

I have to say that I think much of the criticism is a function of competition for primacy and legitimacy as cultural brokers and interpreters of the exotic. Perhaps there is also worry about a shift of student interest and all that that implies. But it is also a question of envy I believe. Museums are more fun to work in than amid the sometimes petty, bitter, tired and grey struggles in the academic departments of many universities these days.

Museums are now a strange and wonderful mix of scholarly research, writing, politics, entertainment and good fun. This, and the increasing prominence of cultural heritage issues, makes them attractive places for work. We are also getting funds (now and then) that allow us to do interesting things with lots of people, including field work and the opportunity to present our work to a much wider public in a variety of media instead of writing for two or three academic colleagues.

In my view, many of the issues raised in the critiques of museums by academia are now tired remnants of the 1970s, issues that the world has by and large moved beyond. The very people on whose behalf these critics often say they are speaking, and defending from museums, are the ones clamouring most for the use of museums and collections.

The critics are right about several things, however. One of them is the problem, inherited by a new generation of anthropologists working in museums: What do we do with galleries that, while incredibly significant from an historical and anthropological point of view, are demonstrably old-fashioned and one-dimensional, object-oriented and taxonomy-oriented, static, perhaps racist, and sometimes just plain unexciting visually and wrong in terms of information?

The second thing the critics are right about is that material-culture studies as they used to be practised are now largely, for better or worse, dead. People very rarely study objects by themselves. Museum activity in general is not really any longer primarily about collections as objects. Rather, museums are now more about the meanings people attribute to objects and collections, and the interactions between people and objects, past and present. The problem for museums today, though, is how to deal with what has taken the place of traditional material culture studies; that is, people, and in particular the interest of what I call 'origin-culture people', in collections.

In this paper I want to look at these two problems – old galleries and new people – and explore some problems and prospects for both.

Before doing this, I must say that my assumption is that museums will continue to live and, indeed, to thrive. There exists a common view that collections should not be kept, and that somehow indigenous cultural identities would flower everywhere with the simple return of all material and the disestablishment of museums. Apart from this being an insulting notion given the active part indigenous people have had in building museum collections, it is simply not supported by the facts. Museums, what they contain, and how to use them is a major concern of indigenous communities in Australia, as elsewhere.[1]

Another issue raised in academic critiques of museums is that the information gathered and held by sociocultural anthropologists is, in a sense, the structural equivalent of museum activity and collections. There are even greater parallels between museum exhibitions and the presentation of ethnographic 'data' in university courses and academic publications. It is worth noting, though, that claims for repatriation of data gathered by academic anthropologists have met with considerably less success than those made to museums.[2]

Galleries

The South Australian Museum (SAM), like other major state museums in Australia, is a 19th-century, Victorian-era creation. We have Victorian buildings (some of us have Victorian offices!), we have Victorian gallery spaces, and in some cases we have Victorian displays. These are, of course, artefacts themselves, and there is strong pressure to maintain the integrity of such displays and galleries –

for historical reasons as much as nostalgia. SAM's Pacific Cultures Gallery is a prime example.

However, the problem with such displays is that they do not convey accurate pictures of the cultures of the people whose material objects are there: neither past nor present. Rather, they present what people of the Victorian era thought about those cultures. Contra the heritage arguments about the value in maintaining such displays for historical reasons is the valid criticism about the inaccuracies – anthropological, historical and political – often found in the displays; the obsession with certain types of objects (for example, weapons, or *exotica extremis* such as decorated human heads), or the bias towards the male domain; and the taxonomic presumption of the displays, which tacitly supports an evolutionary view of culture.

The total redevelopment of large galleries such as SAM's Pacific Cultures Gallery is a difficult if not impossible task in a period of reduced public funding and tighter private contribution. In addition to the exhibition-mounting costs, the trend towards inclusion of greater context and the need for involvement of contemporary people from the relevant areas (for example, as with SAM's Ngurunderi Gallery) would make the costs for such redevelopment extremely high, especially if the concentration on large areas of the Pacific was to remain.

The South Australian Museum's Pacific Cultures Gallery

I want here to say something briefly about our Pacific Cultures Gallery and talk about what we intend to do with it, given our constraints. The Pacific collection of the South Australian Museum numbers some 15 000 items and is primarily Melanesian. The gallery contains some 3000 objects almost totally devoted to island Melanesia, especially mainland Papua New Guinea. Highlights include: a Trobriand Islands trading canoe; the weapons displays; the New Ireland *malagan* sculptures; masks from the Papuan Gulf, Vanuatu and New Caledonia; carved headrests, skirts and bark-cloth materials from Fiji; and woven materials from Santa Cruz and Vanuatu, among other things. The gallery was 100 years old in 1994, and it has not had a major reworking since 1972, when the light well was filled in to provide more exhibition floor-space. It consists of large old-style glass wall-cases around the perimeter, which contain objects organised on a geographical basis. Table cases in the middle of the gallery are concerned with particular themes, such as tapa-cloth making, betel-nut chewing equipment, fishing gear, and so on. Larger items, such as the Trobriand canoe and a Massim hut, are prominently located. Until a few years ago the museum shop was in the centre of the gallery, and a mineral display dominated one end of the gallery.

The cases contain quite a few mistakes (in information and object attribution), outdated and inaccurate labels, yellowing photographs with little or no identifying information, and almost no broader cultural context information by way of text or visuals. The cultural and political geography was, until recently, outdated. The issue of the display of human remains continues unresolved. The logic of the gallery is not apparent (for example, Micronesia and Polynesia are not included). Even the coverage of Melanesia is not complete (for example, there is little from Irian Jaya, the Papua New Guinea Highlands or Sepik River regions). There is also very little information on the broader picture of the peopling and settlement of the Pacific. Perhaps worst of all, there is nothing on the contemporary life of Melanesian people. The naive gallery viewer has no notion of whether the objects they see are part of a past or present lifestyle. The assumption must be one of timeless primitivism.

Not a pretty picture for any museum. I am being frank here, and am basing these criticisms on my own observations and the complaints of people over the past several years (including our own Barry Craig and visiting museum people such as Soroi Eoe and Chris Issac). What can we do with such a gallery?

Changes to the exhibition have been done in a gradual way over the last few years. With only minor funding, we have been able to move out the shop, rebalance the gallery by shifting the mineral collection to the centre of the space, and correct and upgrade some of the exhibit labels.

Some time soon, I hope, we will provide introductions to the gallery (text, photographs and maps), including material on 'cultural markers' of the Pacific, and on the history and content of the gallery itself. A key part of this will be a focus exhibition on the gallery-as-artefact. Why is this gallery the way it is? What does this display say about the relationships between Australia and Melanesia? Who were the collectors? What were these collectors and the museum trying to say in collecting and exhibiting material in this way?

Two focus exhibitions add new material to complement existing items in the display cases. These are the Sulka and New Ireland *malagan* displays. They result from recent field work by Barry Craig (contracted for the purpose over three months in 1992-93 and appointed Curator of Foreign Ethnology in December 1995), and the purchase of contemporary examples of items of which we have significant older examples. Through projects like this, we aim to re-establish relationships with Pacific communities associated with the cultures of origin for the objects on display in the gallery.

Bringing people into museums

People are right: museums are often disembodied, temples to material objects, independent of people. This was especially true in the past. Museums of late have been subject to a great deal of pressure from origin-culture peoples for greater knowledge of and access to collections relevant to them, their past and their aspirations for the future. I believe that by and large museums are welcoming this interest. Today, museums are attempting to develop relationships between their collections and people in a variety of ways. Some have opted for the ultimate solution of 'giving it all back' and washing their hands of the problems associated with certain types of cultural material. Other museums have been a bit less radical and set up outwardly oriented programs – field research, assisting communities with cultural centres, commissioning new works in the field, promoting the use of collections in the revitalisation of craft traditions, and so on.

Another way of 'peopling' museums is one that, ironically, museums have done for many years: bringing in people of the cultures from which collections were made, as craftspeople or artists; not as viewers but as actors, as performers. Is there any difference between museum 'performances' now and those of the poor indigenes carted off to London, Paris and Washington in the 19th century as 'living exhibits'?

This development is partly a search for ways to involve people without removing objects from museums; partly it is another aspect of the new multimedia emphasis of museums – in addition to interactive CD-ROM computers and multiple video screens, you bring in real people. Partly, though, it is something of real interest to the origin-culture people – sometimes just so they can look at earlier, often technically 'better', examples of material culture from their ancestors. Also, it is often quite natural for them that objects or works of 'art' should have direct correlates in song, dance or ceremony.[3] The key is for museums not only to add living people, but also the other social contexts of meaning related to the objects (song, dance, and so on). How can these be incorporated into displays? What is the 'performance' of an exhibition?

Despite advantages for everyone in having people come into museums to undertake activities culturally relevant to objects on display, and despite the usual enthusiasm of indigenous people for doing this, the whole thing has been subject to intense criticism – often from our old friends, the sociocultural anthropologists.

Let us try to dissect this phenomenon and look at how museums have used performance as a means to solve problems of enlivening their galleries. I want to look at a few examples in my experience, and finish on the Sulka and New Ireland *malagan* performances held as part of the 1993 PAA symposium and our attempts to socially and physically redevelop our Pacific Cultures Gallery.

Performance as exhibition – Brisbane 1975

In 1975, the University of Queensland Anthropology Museum arranged for several Lardil people from Mornington Island in north Queensland to come to Brisbane to work in the public exhibition space and use it as though it was a workshop. This was an attempt by the museum to go beyond the usual material-culture displays, to provide

an opportunity for museum visitors to see objects being made and, further, to create a situation so that the artists would 'choose themselves specific areas of interest and … provide the answers to questions from visitors without an anthropologist acting as a middleman' (Lauer 1975:3). The setting would 'provide a firm and mutually recognisable basis from which as a matter of course further discussions will lead into all other areas of cultural behaviour' (Lauer 1975:3)

The display and workshop generated a great deal of interest from visitors to the museum. It also produced a lot of criticism. The most sustained criticism came from sociocultural anthropologists in the Department of Sociology and Anthropology in the same building as the museum (I was one of these). At least three critiques or review articles were published. Replies were written and there was much department corridor discussion.

One of the critiques, by David Trigger, an anthropologist now at the University of Western Australia, included a detailed and quite devastating ethnography of an encounter between a visitor and a husband-and-wife Laryardil artisan team working in the museum. Trigger (1975) describes the scene:

The … visitor … enters the museum, and finds two elderly Aboriginal people sitting on a raised platform surrounded by cream carpet, wood-panelled walls and glass display cases. As he comes further into the museum, he tries to focus on the two black workers, but they do not offer Western-style social recognition like a nod or a smile. He finds it easier to focus on the interesting objects on the walls and inside the glass cases, but his awareness of the tomahawk being used by the male artisan never ceases. He slowly approaches the woman artisan who appears to be making shell necklaces; he sees the container of Clag glue beside her, leans over towards her and asks: 'Er … is that traditional?'

The woman, most likely unsure of his meaning, remains silent and keeps looking intently downwards at the shell necklace in her hands … the visitor blushes somewhat at not receiving an answer to his seemingly straightforward question. In a rather uncomfortable manner, he once again diverts his focus back to an object on the wall near the stage. After about a minute, he again leans over towards the woman and says slowly: 'I mean … what would have been used instead of GLUE?' He emphasises the word 'glue' to get a clear meaning across. Still looking down, she answers: 'Mm. Glue!' and the male artist also looking down, reiterates: 'Mmm. Glue!'

Both of them perceive the visitor as asking whether the woman is in fact using glue – and of course, they have replied in the affirmative.

The visitor now becomes rather embarrassed. After blushing, and then looking around vaguely at the tools and materials on the stage for a minute or two he starts to move slowly away from the stage back to the wall that is covered with objects. As if to legitimize his visit he spends a few more minutes vaguely looking at more objects … as if attempting to remain … interested until the last moment, he [then] makes a rather hasty retreat out the door.

Performance as exhibition – New York 1988

The second example I want to present is that of Aboriginal artists participating in activities that accompanied the South Australian Museum's 'Dreamings' exhibition in New York in 1988. Several of the artists and curators taking part in the 1993 PAA events were in that group, including Kerry Giles and Djon Mundine. In addition, I was one of the curators of the exhibition and an organiser of the 'people components' of the show.

To supplement the exhibition, we arranged a symposium, which took place over two days. This was open to the public and was held in the Asia Society's main theatre on Park Avenue. Several Aboriginal painters from remote communities took part: Jimmy Wululu and David Malangi from Ramingining, and Dolly Nampijinpa Daniels and June Napanangka Granites from Yuendumu. Formal speeches or 'papers' were given by the artists, mostly in their own languages, with immediate translation by interpreters, on stage with the artists. Papers were also given by Kerry Giles, by non-Aboriginal people (anthropologists such as Fred Myers, Peter Sutton, Francoise Dussart), and by community-arts coordinators such as Djon Mundine

and Felicity Wright. Much of the session was taken up with questions to the artists by the audience.

Artists participated more directly, albeit exclusively through their art, in another supplementary activity, which is the main case I want to describe for you. This was the construction, in the Asia Society theatre, of a large ground design in 'traditional' Central Australian style by Bill Stockman Japaljarri and Michael Nelson Jakamarra.

To tell you about this case, I want to present at length four very different text commentaries. The first is from an Australian artist, Christopher Hodges, then living in New York. Some time after the 'Dreamings' show left New York, Hodges wrote to Peter Sutton, coordinating curator of the Dreamings exhibition, to tell him about something that 'concerned not just me but quite a number of people who attended the "sand painting" by Michael Nelson and Bill Stockman'. Hodges (1988) continued:

> on the Sunday afternoon that I attended the 'sand painting' I was initially confronted with an auditorium of people looking down on the two artists who quietly worked away. I was immediately struck with the feeling of looking at a 19th century 'living exhibit' museum piece akin to the depictions of prehistoric family scenes. This was distressing, but then in front of these were the 'experts' explaining and gesturing to a willing crowd of onlookers, much like a guide at the zoo, or a docent in front of a painting.
>
> I found this disregard for the artists very hard to deal with and left, following my friends who hadn't lasted five minutes and were very shocked. White artists are not asked to do this and wouldn't in those circumstances. I wouldn't.
>
> After some time, looking again at the beautiful exhibition and videotape I went back to see if I felt the same way. This time though I left feeling much worse and very angry as instead of the previous scenario, [two anthropologists] were fielding questions from a capacity audience. Here people were asking questions that Michael Nelson and Billy Stockman could have answered, they could hear the questions, both are most articulate and intelligent, but in front of them ['experts'] were giving answers.
>
> … in the background Michael and Billy painted on, both knowing silently the inaccuracies and folly of what

was going on. Or perhaps they were embarrassed. It certainly was embarrassing to me. I stayed for perhaps twenty minutes.

… I was most upset about the complete dissociation between the artists and the experts and I would have thought with two such articulate artists present a much more desirable scene would have been a completed sand painting as an exhibit and the artists fielding questions about their work, not this image of the artist as tribal beings and silent and the expert waxing lyrical about the noble savage.

I praise you for having artists on the platform with you but I urge you not to let them become another exhibit.

Peter Sutton's response (1988) was as follows:

It seems that presentation always causes more controversy than mere remote representation. In this case, extensive discussions have made it clear however that the performers were: 1) under no pressure to participate, but agreed freely to do so; 2) requested that questions and comments be dealt with by others during the performance, and 3) after the event have gone on record expressing some pleasure at how it all went …

Done in the bush, the making of a sand design is still a performance to be looked at, albeit before a very different audience and with vastly more active participation by all present. Some would argue that the showing of canvas paintings is an even more denuded and objectified representation of Aboriginal performances. They're probably right. This does not, in my view, invalidate the process.

As the organiser of the event, I responded too (Anderson 1988):

We were certainly well aware of the problematic nature of the 'performance' of the sand painting. In fact, I stressed to the audiences over and over the reasons why we were doing it as we did. I have been in many situations where Aboriginal (and other) artists have either attended exhibitions or undertook some aspect of their work there. Not to involve Aboriginal people in this way with exhibitions of their own art seems, at best, to deny both Aboriginal people and exhibition-goers the chance to interact in some form or another. At worst, not to do so is racist and

paternalistic. It is interesting that the artists from the Warlukurlangu Association at Yuendumu always go in large groups to their own exhibitions in the southern Australian cities, and in addition have eagerly performed ceremonies and painted in the galleries of several of their own exhibitions.

… I stress that these events have always been done at the instigation of the artists themselves. The Alice Springs based Jukurrpa group of artists recently had an exhibition in Adelaide. They arranged so that they could do paintings in the grounds of the gallery while their exhibition was on. Despite the '19th century living exhibit' aspect to this (and it may only be in the eye of the beholder anyway), Aboriginal artists are actively creating these situations themselves. We did everything we possibly could in New York to try to break down the atmosphere of an audience watching an exotic incomprehensible performance: having the lights on, having people come down to look more closely at the work, encouraging people to go out and look at the exhibitions and the videos and book and then come back again, having people ask questions, Fred Myers filming the audience and interviewing them, and so on. I might add that all this was radical and new for the Asia Society.

As for your comment about 'experts holding forth … in disregard for the artists'; I have a simple reply: In the many months of planning, discussion and consultation which took place between Papunya Tula, the artists, John Kean and myself, it was very clear that the over-riding motivation for them agreeing to do the work, was to demonstrate to Americans something of their culture and world view. However the actual procedure for how this could be implemented in New York was not worked out in advance. The day before Michael and Bill were to begin the construction, they explicitly asked us, firstly, not to allow people to ask them direct questions while they were working; secondly, to describe what they were doing and to answer questions that came up. How can you possibly think that we would not consider Michael and Bill articulate and intelligent enough to answer their own questions, or that we would not consult them as to how to proceed in such an exercise? The way it went was wholly determined by them. There are many witnesses to this, it is thoroughly documented and I suggest you ask Michael or Bill yourself.

I have to say that we were certainly uncomfortable in our positions as intermediaries. However, I know that Michael and Bill considered it would be quite inappropriate for them to deal with the audience in any way during their painting work. Yet, they did want accurate information to be got across to the people watching. They trusted us and they were very happy with what we did, despite our misgivings. An unprompted comment to me from Japaljarri in the dressing room is indicative: 'Jampijinpa [my subsection name in Central Australia], you're fighting for us out there. That's really good.' They also saw the situation as being part of our culture (we were in America and Fred Myers and I were American) and thus would be better able to deal with it than they (or even John Kean – a non-Aboriginal Australian).

The final commentary on the 'Dreamings' case comes from the two Aboriginal artists involved, Michael Nelson Jakamarra (MNJ) and Bill Stockman Japaljarri. They were interviewed after the trip by John Kean (JK), another of the organisers of the event, and a friend and coworker of the artists (Kean 1989). John is fluent in the language of Papunya.

MNJ: I live at Papunya. I'm an artist. From there we went to America to do our business, the sand painting. We had about three hundred people each day who were very interested in our work. We worked in a big hall to show people from other countries what Aboriginal people are doing in Central Australia. People really enjoyed seeing us do our work. We went to New York to show the world about our culture and our work. Most whites all over the world don't recognise Aboriginal people. But now our work is being spread throughout the world. Now they notice our work and they keep asking about it.

We showed our work in the gallery, a big gallery in New York City. We had already organised materials for our work, to put the Dreamings there by making a sand painting. We did a really good job. Everybody was watching us, people from every place, American people, and people from all over the world.

These people didn't know anything about Aboriginal culture. When we went to America it was the first time all those people saw it … Overseas people had their first chance to see this when we went to America with that exhibition.

Michael and Bill were asked about what story or Dreamings they did in the sand paintings, and MNJ describes these and on what authority he did them. He then adds (Kean 1989):

These are important Dreamings and that's why we showed them to the people in America. They took photographs and they filmed what we were doing. We were pretty happy to be working there. We had a couple of boomerangs and I sang a song with Japaljarri, and he danced. And the dance was really good. We really enjoyed it.

JK: One of the things that people enjoyed seeing the most was seeing Aboriginal people dancing for the first time.

MNJ: Yes, with the red ochre. See we forgot to take Pinkirri, cockatoo feathers and emu feathers. But probably next time, we might be able to take more people to show our culture overseas, it could be to Europe or anywhere, maybe to Africa. We could go to California or Los Angeles, to San Francisco or to Canada or to the Washington area. To show people our culture. It's good to show our culture to different people, overseas.

JK: Why did you choose to dance Jardiwanpa?

MNJ: Because it's an easy one … also we picked out the Snake Dreaming because everybody can look at it. Even in Central Australia when the video comes they can see it. It's clear [that is, has no restrictions].

JK: You were also decorating some boomerangs on stage in New York.

MNJ: Yes, we always do that when we do a sand painting. We decorate boomerangs that represent the same story as in the sand painting. See, people might come [to Australia] from America and ask, 'Where are all the Aboriginal people?' They might tell them. 'They are in Central Australia – go visit Alice Springs, they live in communities in Western Australia, part of South Australia, Top End, and in the centre of Australia. They might ask, 'Have you got any paintings or boomerangs to show us? We can buy them off you.' That will be good to help my people.

MNJ: People can see the paintings that we sell to make our living. We are not selling our culture away, just the paintings, the colourings of our drawings on canvas. They won't take that one [our culture] because we, all the Aboriginal people, have got it in our minds and our heart. They can't take it away. [People just buy the canvas and paint and look at the art] but we are still the owners of the story.

JK: Now I want to ask you about the New York exhibition. In New York, people could look at the exhibition then come down and look at you men doing the sand painting. What does it mean when you were working on a sand painting, then next door to that you have an exhibition?

MNJ: I think that was great, the people would have come and seen the exhibition of canvas paintings and from there they came around to the sand painting. I think it was great as most of the people in America, they have never seen a person doing this job properly. But now they have seen it, what we were doing, me and Japaljarri. They were asking a lot of questions, but that was alright. They asked questions about our work and who we were. Some people thought we were black American, but we are full-blood Aboriginal from Central Australia. We had headbands too. I reckon that looks really good on film and on stage while we were working.

We did it over there. We seemed to get strong in front of everybody. Some Aboriginal people get shy. But not me and Japaljarri.

Performance as exhibition – Adelaide 1993

The policy of the South Australian Museum on exhibition and other projects involving Australian Aboriginal culture is, wherever possible, to make them cooperative efforts. This has worked extremely well with several major projects over the past ten years. The cooperation has extended to joint research, publication and film ventures as well. Partly, this Aboriginal concentration is a function of staff, in that we have a number of staff who are either Aboriginal or have primary interest in Aboriginal culture. It is also a function of geographic proximity.

When it comes to the Pacific, things are a little different. For a start, in 1993 we did not have a curator of Pacific cultures. In addition, the costs of long-term or extensive consultative field work in Melanesia, for example, are well beyond our normal operating budgets. However, it seemed unfair and inconsistent for us to have a policy for one collection that recognised the interests of origin-culture people from one area and not another. In addition, as I have noted above, we sorely wanted to begin the slow but sure redevelopment of our Pacific Cultures Gallery.

We had two display cases that we knew contained spectacular items and collections, but were problematic: these included a case containing a large Sulka headdress and others containing *malagan* sculpture from New Ireland. Barry Craig (then the SA Museum's Aboriginal Family History Research Coordinator) proposed that we mount a trip to PNG to buy or commission new examples of both the Sulka headdress and New Ireland *tantanua* masks. Further, he suggested that we bring to Adelaide two men from each of those areas with the masks, and that they 'dance' them into the gallery. Subsequently, John Telko, Ignasius Sarakie, Edward Sale and Noah Lurang arrived in Adelaide for the opening ceremony on 12 April 1993.

During the event I did not hear any negative comment from audience members (and I received no letters to use as text, as with the New York event). Also, the participants seemed very happy with the way the preparations and the event went. Furthermore, they used the opportunity to examine older works from their areas in the collection (primarily for artistic/craft purposes). I am not naive enough to think that this is all the museum needs to do to re-establish a relationship with PNG communities. However, it is a beginning.

Conclusion

I want to comment briefly on the performance events I have described, and see what was good and what was bad about them.

The University of Queensland Anthropology Museum attempt failed largely because it assumed the universality of 'natural conversation' and avowedly avoided any middle-person involvement. Effectively there was no communication between performer and visitor. As Trigger argued, the normal museum display is probably more effective, in a sense, because the visitor is free to forge his or her relationship with objects in the exhibition. With a people-based exhibit, the visitor is inclined to try to build a social relationship with the performers, and then interpose this between him or herself and the objects around him. The almost universal failure of visitors to do this in the Brisbane exhibit created an uncomfortable frustration.

The case of the symposium in New York for 'Dreamings' was probably the most successful one – at least from the point of view of the audience and the critics. However, it is interesting that this is the one that artists themselves felt most uncomfortable about. The audience and critics felt comfortable because it was a performance they knew all about. They knew the rules for it: a bunch of people sitting in uncomfortable chairs with glasses of water and microphones, in front of people with no glasses of water but with comfortable chairs. Communication was by the normal delivery of speech followed by question and answer. We did provide interpreters for each non-English speaker, and had worked out beforehand, very generally, the topics that the artists wanted to talk about. However the fact remains that this was the most difficult 'performance' for them, and one they did not relish. (Probably the main reason the critics did not cry 'racist living exhibit' was that there were non-Aboriginal people on the stage as well. However, they seemed worried by interpretation on the part of those people and even translation; there seemed to be the notion that information can cross cultural and linguistic boundaries simply by osmosis or through the vibes in the air.)

The 'Dreamings' sand-painting event was a very difficult one, and I would probably do it all differently now. It is interesting that the critics here were much less bothered by the smooth voice, sounds and wonderful landscape pans of the monitors playing the exhibition's video – instead of the awkward, unpredictability of a real, human social scene. Most of the discomfort stemmed from the lack of direct, vocal communication from the artists and the interpositioning of others (the anthropologists).

If we had had the guts, we should have done it as an entirely silent two-day event. However, it was Jakamarra's and Japaljarri's idea that we try to tell the audiences what was going on. The better way may have been to separate out the discussion from the doing, or try to provide audiences with other means (a film seen earlier, or printed materials) to learn about the process and meaning of the event. The artists in the audience saw the event as watching other artists doing their work (something which they seemed to assume is always a private event – a very Eurocentric idea). The artists on the stage knew it was an artificial performance. In watching the film of the final 'ritual' destruction of the sand design, it is readily apparent how Jakamarra and Japaltjarri subtly 'ham it up'. They played the audience for all they were worth in this event.[4]

In the case of the Melanesian event at SAM for the Pacific Arts symposium, we had little or no commentary during the performance. The performers determined the nature of the proceedings; they were very aware of the economic benefits cultural heritage as an activity brings to their local communities these days; they appreciated the prestige that involvement in such projects brings when they return home. Most of all they were proud to demonstrate and promote their culture in an Australian city.

On the other hand, Noah Lurang and Chris Issac presented papers at the symposium (see chapters 14 and 15, this publication) that same day, later in the afternoon, to provide commentary relevant to the performance of the masks from their respective areas. They knew full well that the audience understood little of the performance. They were well aware that the museum, no matter how closely it works with local people, cannot hope to create a full context that will explicate and display totally the cultural meaning and setting for the objects or the performances. However, they know that we must begin somewhere with creating interest and knowledge, not to say deep understanding, in an attempt to cross, however briefly, cultural boundaries. For them, as for us, the real benefit is in the interaction – people and collections – and that the museum recognises the legitimacy and necessity of their involvement in what happens with the depiction of Pacific cultures in Adelaide.

I suspect that such motivations would be insufficient for some critics. However, from the museum perspective it is the only way we can go.

Notes

1.   The primary difference in viewpoints seems to be about the definition of object-meaning: who establishes meaning, where and for what purpose. The 'museum-object-as-dead-wood' theory we have recently heard about seems to be more a problem with some people having too rigid a notion of culture boundedness The theory posits that objects necessarily lose their meaning and all real utility once they leave the culture of their origin. Further, it suggests that their use outside this context is not only meaningless, but a dangerous form of exoticism for the entertainment of a dominant culture. As a Warlpiri man from Central Australia said to me once with respect to the art of his culture, the power of the Dreaming does not cease when things pass through the museum door. The recognition is strong that objects can have new meanings; and that there is a strongly political element to the keenness with which people participate in having elements of their culture put in a museum.

2.   I am not really presenting here an opposition between museum and social-cultural anthropology as this is a false dichotomy. I am part of both, and the overlap between what we all do is considerable, at least in terms of methods and concepts.

3.   I remember being at the Degas exhibition at the Metropolitan Museum of Art in New York in 1988 where Dolly Nampijinpa Daniels, a senior Warlpiri woman from Central Australia, asked what Dreaming or ancestral being and myth complex a particular Degas ballerina was dancing and why she wasn't painted up with the right designs.

4.   See *Market of Dreams*, a film by Kate Kennedy White, shown on Australia's ABC TV in 1990.

PART 3

From performance to museum in Melanesia

Barry Craig

The ten papers in this section of the book cover a wide range of topics embracing field-work studies of the social and cultural context of artworks, taxonomies and technical aspects of ritual objects, the individual artist past and present, and museum collections and documentation. All but one of the papers focus on the cultures of Papua New Guinea; the exception deals with a Fijian topic.

Dirk Smidt and Soroi Eoe describe in considerable detail an end-of-mourning festival in the lower Ramu area of Madang Province, Papua New Guinea. The highlight of the festival is the performance of maskers. Men wear carved wooden masks – embedded in elaborate superstructures of feathers, shells and leaves up to 6 metres tall – representing spirits of the ancestors, of the bush and of the waters. The cultural context of the festival is examined by Smidt and Eoe, who find there are social, political, economic and mythical components that serve to link groups across language boundaries through an ongoing cycle of reciprocal obligations and gift-giving. In the process, individual 'Big Men' confirm and enhance their status as leaders.

Chris Issac and Barry Craig describe the masked ceremonies of the Sulka of East New Britain Province, Papua New Guinea. Of the several types of masks made by the Sulka for weddings, for the initiation of boys and girls, and for funerals, the umbrella-like *hemlaut* masks are the most spectacular. These may be linked through three-dimensional constructed forms to episodes in myths, and

are accompanied by songs of great beauty sung by the women. Not immediately apparent to the outside observer is the importance of the exchange of masks and food to cement relationships between social groups. The dancing of a *hemlaut* mask from Issac's village at the symposium and its installation in the South Australian Museum was an extension of this principle to the relationship between a metropolitan museum, which held a rare *hemlaut* mask collected during World War I, and the indigenous community from which it came.

The significance of the well-known *tantanua* mask within the rich variety of *malagan* masking traditions is explored by Noah Lurang, drawing on his experience as a Tabar Islander of New Ireland Province, Papua New Guinea. *Malagan* is the term[1] applied to the sacred objects made and displayed during funerary feasts; it also applies to the activities themselves. Lurang cites the taxonomy of masks, the stages of their performance, and the songs and ritual calls associated with them. His account demonstrates the rich complexity of the *malagan* tradition, and he points out that there is much still to be recorded.

Lurang brought with him to the symposium several of the masks he describes in his paper. These he displayed, with assistance from Edward Sale (a Tabar Islands carver), during his presentation at the symposium. One mask was presented as a gift and the others were subsequently purchased by the South Australian Museum. Several are now on display in its Pacific Gallery, in association with the display of *malagan* carvings and masks collected in 1918 by Edgar Waite for the museum (Craig 1995).

Michael Gunn's paper dwells heavily on the taxonomy of the *malagan* tradition. He has not done this out of a fascination for taxonomy, but at the request of the people with whom he worked. They dismissed the search for the significance of symbolic or iconographic interpretation of *malagan* as an unhelpful European obsession. They were much more interested in having recorded who owns rights to which of the multitudinous *malagan* images. Lurang's and Gunn's papers complement each other in the same way that Issac's insider knowledge complements Craig's outsider observations in the Sulka paper.

Rod Ewin's discussion of the Fijian *lali* (wooden slit-gong) is primarily a technical analysis of its properties as a sound-producing instrument and how these characteristics are achieved. His report demonstrates the high level of sophistication inherent in the design of these instruments. Slit-gongs (also referred to as slit-drums and *garamuts* in Papua New Guinea) appear to be of Austronesian origin (Niles 1983; Swadling et al. 1988); visitors to Bali will see them hanging in village banyan trees. A comparative study of the slit-gong is long overdue, and description of the technical characteristics would be an important component of such a study.

The next two papers focus on the individual artist. Harry Beran uses the classic methodology of art history to identify works of a master carver named Mutuaga, who lived on Suau Island, Milne Bay Province, Papua New Guinea, during the 19th century. By careful observation of style, Beran has attributed seventy-nine pieces to Mutuaga and five to others significantly influenced by him. Beran's more voluminous treatment of this subject, published in 1996, identifies works by other carvers as well.

Beran demonstrates that the anonymity of individual artists in tribal society is an artefact of our ignorance. While there have been several studies of living artists that have demonstrated this point (for example, Gerbrands 1967), Beran's paper is perhaps the first to do this by reference to the works of a Pacific artist long dead.

Wendy Choulai is an expatriate Papuan artist very much alive and practising her fibre arts in Australia. She bases her work on traditionally female techniques and forms, including those found among her mother's people, the Solien Besena of Central Province. Because she is sensitive to the restrictions of traditional copyright, she has generalised the motifs of Africa, Asia, the Americas and the Pacific to develop her own design repertoire. Her textiles and skirts are cited by her coauthor, Jackie Lewis-Harris, as a form of 'soft wealth' that provides status in an art milieu dominated by men and their products.

The topics of the next three papers relate more to the world of the historian and museum curator. Max Quanchi examines the way photographs from the late 20th and early 20th centuries were used to construct a popularist and stereotyped image of Papua and its inhabitants as primitive savages. Quanchi traces the image of the Koiari tree-house to demonstrate this. He is careful, however, to point out that this constructed narrative was not necessarily the intent of the photographer, nor necessarily inherent in the nature of the image, but rather was developed by the writers and journalists who used the images to illustrate their texts. Contemporary misuse of ethnographic photographs has been sharply criticised by Dutton (1995).

Helena Regius brings us right into the museum with an account of the Melanesian collections in the National Museum of Ethnography in Stockholm, Sweden. She recounts vividly the metaphoric war that was waged among collectors from different countries. Because of Sweden's friendly relationship with Germany towards the end of the 19th century, most of Stockholm's Melanesian material came from the German colonies.

Stockholm's collections include material from Erik Nyman, Fredrich Wandres, Birger Mörner, Rudolph Wahlen, Maximiliam Thiel, Robert Pullaine, Carl Pettersson and Carl Wilhelm Öberg. It is interesting that the South Australian Museum turned down Pullaine's[2] offer of his collection of 4000 Melanesian and Australian Aboriginal pieces for £600 in 1911 on the grounds that 'we already possess many of the articles represented', and in due course they were purchased for Stockholm by Wahlen.

But the South Australian Museum does have a small collection from Pettersson, obtained from him by Edgar Waite when he was travelling through the Tabar Islands in 1918.

Regius analyses the way Melanesian material was exhibited in Stockholm from 1878 until the 1920s. Pettersson's collection of *malagans* were displayed in 1917 in a culturally contextualised fashion, and studios at the museum attracted students of painting, sculpture and textiles. By 1927, ethnographic material was being displayed as 'art for art's sake'.

As for Sweden, Hungary found it convenient to operate in German territories. Gabor Vargyas focuses on the collections from Astrolabe Bay made by the Hungarians, Bíró and Fenichel, now housed in the Ethnographic Museum of Budapest. Elsewhere, Vargyas (1992) has informed us that Fenichel died in New Guinea before he could write up his material, and that Bíró published only the first part of his collections. The major work in

analysing the early material from German New Guinea was done by Bodrogi between 1953 and 1990, though he never set foot in the Pacific. Vargyas combs these sources, and others such as Mikloucho-Maclay and Kunze, for information on the function of the large *telem* sculptures and the wooden masks of the region, but little has been recorded.

Nevertheless, Regius and Vargyas note that museum curators can add considerably to the documentation of their collections by returning to the people from among whom collections have been made, and not only asking about the objects, but also about what is remembered of the collectors.

Notes

1. *Malagan* may also be found in the literature with other spellings: *malangan* and *malanggan*.
2. Spelt Pulleine in South Australian Museum correspondence.

A festival to honour the dead and revitalise society: Masks and prestige in a Gamei community (Lower Ramu, Papua New Guinea)

13

Dirk Smidt and Soroi Marepo Eoe

This paper reports on the course of events and the socio-cultural context of an end-of-mourning festival as witnessed in the village of Damur, Lower Ramu area, Madang Province, in 1979.[1] The performance of maskers proved to be a dominant aspect of the festival (plate 3). Therefore, before focusing on the specific event at Damur we will give some consideration to the significance of masks in general in the region concerned. We will also present a short historical overview of research relevant to the topic, discuss general elements of culture that have a bearing on the festival, and consider some theoretical aspects of the concept 'festival'.

Background of field work

In March 1979, Soroi Marepo Eoe and Dirk Smidt were conducting field work among the Kominimung people of the Goam River, Middle Ramu area (fig. 13.1). It was rumoured that an end-of-mourning feast was to be held in the Lower Ramu area, during which many maskers would perform, and so Eoe went downriver to investigate. In April, Eoe witnessed the majestic opening ritual when in a single day all the participating maskers presented themselves. Eoe then returned to join Smidt among the Kominimung. In April, May and June, the maskers performed regularly in small units, and other activities took place. During the final month, Eoe and

Smidt went to Damur to witness the proceedings, including the closing ritual.

The 130 people of Damur village, and another thousand in seven other villages, speak the Gamei language, which has been classified under the Ottilien Family of the Ruboni Stock, Ramu Super-Stock (Z'Graggen 1975:32-3). The village is situated in a low-lying area, part of the Ramu delta, characterised by intersected waterways, lagoons and lakes. Subsistence crops include sago, yam, taro, bananas and *galip* nuts (*Canarium*). Copra is the cash crop.

General context of masking

Historical perspective

The Lower Sepik-Ramu and adjoining coastal region is known as one of the major art-producing areas of New Guinea.[2] Masks, figures and other types of woodcarving are rendered, by and large, in a distinct style, but not excluding substyles (cf. Kaufmann 1993:587-8). Many museums and private collections hold wooden masks from the area. In books and catalogues we find numerous illustrations of them (for example, Haberland and Schuster 1964:28-9; Kelm 1968; Wardwell 1971:17-23, figs 1, 3, 5-8, 10, 12,13-16).

Until recently it was not widely known that such masks, when used in the context of a festival, were part of an

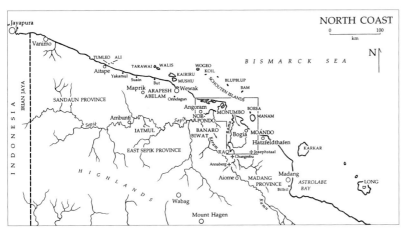

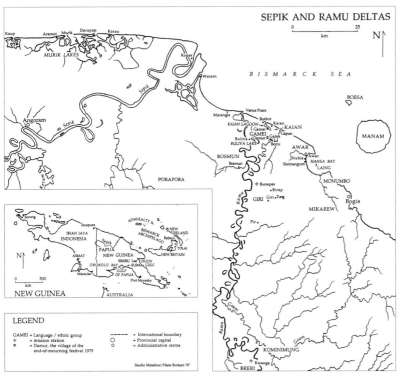

13.1 Map of the north coast and Sepik-Ramu delta showing the Gamei area in its geographical context. (Map: Hans Borkent.)

elaborate costume worn by an initiated male. To some extent this is because usually only the wooden masks as such are displayed in museums and illustrated in publications. Another factor is that in many areas, large-scale festivals in the context of which maskers perform seem to be something of the past; for example, the *Hevehe* festival

of the Elema people, Orokolo Bay, Gulf of Papua (Williams 1940).

Only a few illustrations of complete mask costumes from the Lower Sepik-Ramu area can be traced in the literature. Rare early photographs of huge masks were taken by Albert B. Lewis around 1910 at Awar, Hansa Bay (fig. 13.2), during the Joseph N. Field South Pacific Expedition to Melanesia 1909-13 (Lewis 1922: figs opp. pp. 1, 6, 8; Laufer 1922; Parker 1978).[3] An early photograph of an Awar masker can also be found in Neuhauss (1911:392, fig. 311). Maskers were photographed by Ian Hogbin on Wogeo Island in 1934 (Hogbin 1970: fig. on p. 64; 1978: pl. 'A *tangbwal* spirit monster' between pp. 84 and 85). Some drawings of maskers were made at Murik Lakes by Philipp Osega and Balthasar Sakara, local informants who were commissioned by Father Joseph Schmidt, SVD, to make drawings between 1926 and 1933 (Schmidt 1933a: 322, Tafel I, figs 17, 20, 21; 1933b: figs 24, 29, Tafel II, figs 28, 31). There are scant references by Camilla Wedgwood for Manam Island in 1933-34 (Wedgwood 1934), and by Beatrice Blackwood for Bosmun village, Lower Ramu, in 1937 (Blackwood 1951). Blackwood gives a general descriptive account of a mask costume as she 'was shown some of them being prepared for a ceremony, which unfortunately I could not wait to see' (Blackwood 1951:275).

During the Crane Pacific Expedition 1928-29 (Shurcliff 1930), photographs of mask costumes or feather headdresses kept in enclosures were taken by Sidney Nichols Shurcliff

and Murray N. Fairbank in the village of Darapap, Murik Lakes, on 11 May 1929. These photographs, largely unpublished, are kept at the photographic archives of the Metropolitan Museum of Art, New York. As Shurcliff reports in his diary (11 May 1929, cited in Webb 1996:522):

… we persuaded the men to show us the costumes they are making for a sing-sing or dance. These costumes consisted of the most elaborate headdresses I have ever seen. They averaged about 12 feet in height and at the base of each one was a cleverly carved grotesque wooden mask. Above the mask these headdresses swelled out again [to] a curious shape as shown and this swelling was made entirely out of real feathers of various colors, each feather being tied separately to a bamboo shoot and each shoot being stuck into the bamboo frame of the masks. Beautiful patterns as well as a soft texture were produced with these feathers above the [rolling or swelling]; the design was simple being merely alternate bands of red, white and black cloth with a ball and tassel at the top. It takes two or three years to be ready for a dance and during all of them no women may be allowed to see them. Then in the

13.2 'Religious procession with feather masks leaving the sacred enclosure at Awar, New Guinea', circa 1910. (Lewis 1922: fig. opp. p. 1). (Photo: A.B. Lewis, Field Museum, #44529, Chicago.)

great night they are brought forth in all their glory and destroyed the next day. Very remarkable.

During the same day, the missionary Father Joseph Schmidt, SVD, also saw the feather headdresses, as he reported in his journal: 'We entered the Tambu house and saw about 8 immense feather masks being made' (Webb 1996: 552). Even earlier photographs, including one of 'a line of dancers with the same type of towering feathered headdresses', were taken in a different Murik village (possibly Karau) by Father Kirschbaum (Webb 1996:556). These are kept at the Rautenstrauch-Joest Museum in Cologne.

After a lapse of more than fifty years, photographs of complete maskers in motion taken during performances in the last decade have started to appear again in publications, this time in full colour (Berman 1988:13, 15; Swadling et al. 1988: cover, plates 250, 252-4). More importantly, Marsha Berman and Paula van den Berg cooperated in recording a performance of maskers, as well as preparatory phases, at Birap (located approximately 15 kilometres south of Damur, it belongs to the Giri language) in 1990 (van den Berg 1992).[4] The Birap event was also presented in recent documentary video films (Berman 1995a, 1995b),[5] and in a television documentary (Berman 1995c). Video documents were made of masker performances at Bosmun and Boroi (Berman 1990, 1991).[6] These visual recordings came about in the context of cultural revivals. The decisive factor proved to be the desire, on the part of the men responsible for the events, to provide visual documentation for later generations of their communities, as well as for the outside world (van den Berg 1990:1).[7] Recently the performance of such maskers in the context of a general pan-Papua New Guinean festival, held far away from the local area concerned, has been reported. It was announced that a 'Birap mask of Madang' was to perform during a festival of masks, staged by the National Cultural Commission at the Sir John Guise Stadium at Port Moresby on 17 May 1997 (*Independent* 1997).

Function and symbolic connotations

Wooden masks were not meant to be shown to the uninitiated (women, children, uninitiated male youths).

Masks represent mythical beings or ancestral spirits, and have individual names of their own. This does not imply a static presence. Masks are imbued with the power of the spirit, ranging from 'dormant' to vibrantly alive.

The spirits of the masks are invoked during important occasions such as the building of a ceremonial house, the construction of a ceremonial canoe, the initiation of young men, or in the context of an end-of-mourning festival to honour the dead, as described in this paper. Some masks played a crucial role in warfare. Masks were thought to give strength and protection in battle: enemy spears threatening to reach the guardian of the mask would be magically averted. A mask could also help its people escape from the enemy by making them invisible. Before a headhunting raid, a mask might be consulted and presented with food offerings. Also, it was offered, in a shell, the blood drawn from the penis of an important man of the village. The men were then advised by the mask (that is, the spirit of the mask entered into a man who went into a trance) when and in what direction to go, which village to raid and how many people to kill. After the raid the warriors would bring back the severed head of an enemy to be presented to the mask, which would drink the blood of the victim (Wino Keko to Smidt, pers. comm., Darapap village, Murik Lakes, 1971). During such a ritual, as well as for other consultations and presentations of food offerings, the mask apparently was not attached to a costume worn by a dancer, but was placed on a scaffolding of wood and bamboo inside the ceremonial house (Smidt 1975:53, fig. 53A).

Schmidt describes the inauguration of a ceremonial house, which was not complete without a human head or heads being offered to the masks. The blood was drunk by the masks and smeared on the posts of the house. At a later stage the skulls were displayed in front of the masks. Following this a procession took place: masks and skulls were brought to the lagoon to allow the spirits of the victims to return to their place of origin. The masks and skulls were then brought back to the ceremonial house to be presented with food (Schmidt 1923-24:705).

The spirits of some masks were supposed to have a positive effect on hunting, and of others on fishing. These masks, decorated with shell and other ornaments, were presented with food and invoked before the people embarked on such activities (Böhm 1983:226).

The copyright on the making of a particular mask belonged to a particular clan and village. Other villages could be allowed to acquire a mask, or rather the use of it in a ceremonial context. Information gathered in the Murik Lakes area in 1971 indicates that the Ramu delta is supposed to be the original provenance of several masks kept at Murik. Apparently, masks from Bot Bot, Kaian, Marangis and Bosmun had been acquired by the Murik people in exchange for boars' tusks, dogs' teeth, shell rings and baskets (Marabo, pers. comm., Darapap village, Murik Lakes, 1971). However, masks could also be acquired by force when taken in battle (Wino Kiko and Marabo, pers. comm., Darapap village, Murik Lakes, 1971).

Sometimes a mask will become so dangerous that the illness and death of men, women and children are attributed to it. Apparently, carving a slit-gong for the spirit of the mask and inaugurating it with the appropriate ritual, and building a spirit house or ceremonial men's house to appease the spirit, were considered means to keep the danger in check (Josephides 1990:65). In some cases, however, the owner of a mask would be only too happy to get rid of it before it could do further harm. It was reported that a mask from Bosmun village was thrown away in the water because it was believed to have killed people. The Ramu River carried the mask downstream to its mouth, where it was found by people from Marangis village. However, at Marangis too it killed many people before it was eventually obtained by the ancestors of the Murik people (Daya, pers. comm., Karau village, Murik Lakes, 1971).

When the wooden masks are not being performed in the context of a festival, they are displayed in a standing position inside the ancestral spirit house or ceremonial men's house, sometimes in a partitioned-off section at one end of the house (Ruff 1987:18, Ruff and Ruff 1990:596, fig. 17), placed along part of the side wall (Ruff 1987:12) or longitudinally across the open floor space of the house (Ruff 1987:12-14), or stored in the rafters (Ruff 1987:33). Masks are also known to have been (temporarily?) tied above eye-level to the ornamental posts of the house, along with their feather headdresses, skirts of sago fibre, and shell

ornaments (Höltker 1966: Tafel IV, Abb. 7).[8] As observed by the authors at Damur in 1979, masks that still have a traditional function and are imbued with power may be stored in a small attic underneath the roofing over a ceremonial 'platform'.[9]

Characteristic elements of culture

The North Coast cultural domain

Culturally speaking, the Gamei area is part of a larger domain that stretches from west to east along the north coast, from about Suain (via Murik Lakes, the Sepik-Ramu mouth, and Hansa Bay) as far as Bogia, and including the Schouten Islands and Manam (Kaufmann 1985:39, Map 3, 'Regional styles: coast and lower reaches'; see also Tiesler 1969, 1970).

The cultures in this domain share certain elements in common, notwithstanding local variations (see, for example, Lutkehaus (1990b) for variations in forms of hierarchy). In a thorough and revealing paper on the relationship between language and culture, Welsch, Terrell and Nadolski (1992:592) imply that 'the North Coast comprises a widely shared community of culture marked by a more or less unified culture complex (see Schwartz 1963)'.

Because they have a bearing on the festival at Damur, some characteristic cultural elements of the north-coast region are listed:

- patrilineal descent groups, patrilocal marriage and sister exchange;
- hereditary village leaders of aristocratic rank (called *kukurai* in Melanesian Pidgin);
- hereditary permanent exchange partners;
- the 'platform' institution;
- sacred ritual objects (masks, figures, slit-gongs and flutes) that play an important role in political, social and economic life;
- large-scale end-of-mourning festivals during which maskers perform;
- the loincloth ritual as indicative of male initiation; and
- the grass-skirt ritual to mark the end of first menstruation.

Before dealing with the festival at Damur, it is necessary to provide basic information on some of these cultural elements.

The hereditary clan and village leaders

A crucial role is played by the clan and village leader of aristocratic rank (*kukurai*). His office is hereditary. It is handed down from father to (eldest) son, or from grandfather to grandson. As stated for a comparable type of leadership on Manam Island, the authority of the *kukurai* is based on a combination of sacred and profane factors (Lutkehaus 1990a:299).

The *kukurai* has privileges and obligations. Some of his privileges are:

- he owns a larger piece of land and has larger gardens than other people;
- he has a larger and more beautiful house;
- he is the only one who is allowed to use boars' tusks as ornaments;
- his status is expressed in monumental carvings (carved posts of the spirit house, slit-gongs, a sailing canoe), and he is the guardian of other sacred objects as well (masks and flutes); and
- at initiation and death the sacred musical instruments (slit-gongs and flutes) are played on his behalf.

His obligations are:

- to represent the interests of clan and village *vis-à-vis* the external world;
- to maintain law and order, and resolve quarrels;
- to organise feasts and rituals;
- to be generous; and
- in the past, to decide on matters of warfare and peace.

Although his office is hereditary, a *kukurai* displays certain characteristics of the Melanesian Big Man: 'a specific type of political leadership, characterised by authority derived from personal efforts and abilities through the allocation and reallocation of private resources' (van Bakel, Hagesteijn and van de Velde 1986:1). In a way, a Big Man, or an ascending Big Man, is involved in 'prestige competition' based on 'nurturance – influence over others achieved through generous hospitality and gift giving' (Barlow 1992:64). He is a person 'who by means of his personal skills and abilities achieves a position of renown and power' (van Bakel, Hagesteijn and van de Velde 1986:3). He is dependent, however, 'on the consent of his followers … and upon his possibilities to extract and to distribute resources' (van Bakel, Hagesteijn and van de Velde 1986:3). His prestige then depends to a great extent on his ability to maintain and develop a network of relationships for enlisting the support of other people. He must be self-confident and energetic, and must have persuasive power to 'get things done' and command respect. Moreover, he is deemed to have a special relationship with the spirits, and he might even be associated with sorcery (Lutkehaus 1990a:300).

As mentioned above, the boar's tusk as an ornament serves as a sort of marker or badge to indicate the elevated position of the *kukurai* (Lipset 1990: fig. 1). It is not only a 'symbol of authority', but also a 'sign of history', because it reflects ascribed status that is transmitted from generation to generation and 'must be perpetuated over time' (Lutkehaus 1990b:190). The symbolic value of the boar's tusk is related to the great significance attached to pigs and their relationship to hereditary leadership (Lutkehaus 1990b:190-1).

At his installation as head of his family group, the *kukurai* wears a number of such boars' tusks; see, for example, Michael Somare, the first prime minister of Papua New Guinea, wearing such ornaments on his forehead and around his neck, and attached to an armband and to a ceremonial staff positioned near him, during his installation as head of his clan (Somare 1975a: figs opp. p. 121; 1975b:8-9). Somare was decorated also as head of his wife's family 'because there was no senior man in her line' (Somare 1974:32). This required boars' tusks to be worn on the forehead (but in a different way) and a string bag decorated with boars' tusks to be suspended from the neck to cover the breast (Somare 1974: ill. p. 33).

A mask associated with a *kukurai* also wears such ornaments when performing in the context of a festival as described in this paper. Just as boar-tusk ornaments are attached to the forehead of the man to be installed as a chief, they are attached to the forehead of the wooden mask (plate 4). Other parts of the mask costume may also be decorated with boar's tusk ornaments. One mask costume associated with a *kukurai*, as seen at Damur in 1979, had (at regular intervals) several such ornaments attached along the entire length of the decorated tube rising high above the mask. The young man who goes into the mask costume to parade it through the village may also have a boar's tusk tied to his leg band. Thus, the masked spirit figure has the insignia of the *kukurai* attached to it from top to bottom.

Hereditary exchange partners

It is well known that the larger domain of which the Gamei are a part is characterised by long-term trade or gift-exchange relationships maintained by means of sea voyages (Tiesler 1969, 1970). The network of traditional trade partners has become even more extensive during the colonial era and since independence. Barlow, Bolton and Lipset (1986:17-24) suggest the rationale behind, and the mechanisms of, the trading and exchange network in this part of New Guinea.[10] Trade and exchange should be seen in relationship to the Big Man phenomenon and the motivating force of ritual:

> The importation of traditional valuables … was and still is done for the purpose of developing male political standing and reputation [and] … owning slit-drums, handdrums, masks, shell valuables, ornaments, named Murik baskets, pigs and dance festivals, are all symbols for the accomplishment of having purchased rights to them with great prestations. These inevitably required the coordination of many relationships and were usually associated with the end of mourning'. [Barlow, Bolton and Lipset 1986:20]

An example of a trade and exchange relationship concerns the link between the island of Wogeo and the mainland.[11] Nets and nuts from Wogeo are exchanged for clay pots and baskets of the mainland. Even a ceremony involving an 'ancestral figure called *leo*' (probably a masker) was reported to have been 'imported' from Wogeo to Aitape (Huber 1990:150). Another example is the relationship between Yakamul and Murik: sago, yams and betel nuts from Yakamul are exchanged for fish and baskets from Murik. Slit-gongs from Murik are exchanged for a variety of goods from Yakamul, including spears, pigs, string bags and pots (Huber 1990:36). This is an aspect of Yakamul trade to the east; there is also the relationship between Yakamul and the west – for example, shell rings from Ali and Tumleo Island are exchanged for sago, bananas, taro, betel nuts and 'pepper' (Huber 1990:37). Certain villages are specialised in the production of particular goods, which find their way through the trade network into neighbouring areas and far beyond. In the context of the Damur festival, goods and foodstuffs obtained from other places and areas were distributed and played a role in a long-term scheme of reciprocal obligations. Clay pots from Bosmun and galip nuts from Manam are but two examples of items used in a ceremonial context at Damur.

The 'platform' institution

The term 'platform' (*bet* –Melanesian Pidgin for 'bed') refers to a physical structure that marks the place of residence of a particular village group or subclan, and to the people who form such a group.

Each village may have several platforms. The physical platform itself may or may not have a roof over it, but serves as the meeting place for the men and is considered sacred because it is also the dwelling place of the ancestors and spirits (Meiser 1955:266; Tranel 1952). Each platform:

- has a name of its own;
- as a community is exogamous with membership reckoned patrilineally;
- is associated with a particular animal or plant, which is its protective totem or guardian spirit;
- possesses its own symbols, on which it holds copyright; and
- has its own masks, songs, dances and oral history (Höltker 1964:62).

There appears to be a dualistic tendency in this structure; a division of tasks among platforms along the lines of peace and war can be noted alongside a distinction in rank. In some areas these platforms are called 'war plat-form', ('spear platform', 'murderers' platform') and 'peace platform' ('reception/hospitality platform', 'doers-of-good platform') respectively (Höltker 1964:63-65; Tranel 1952:460-461). The Kaian distinguish between three main types of platforms, which are called 'the doers-of-good', 'the murderers' and 'the thieves' respectively (Meiser 1955:267).[12]

Some platforms have an assisting role; they are 'help-ing platforms'. The physical platform of 'the doers-of-good' functions as a sanctuary. This platform must make friends with other tribal groups and invite visitors to the village, for no harm can come to a person who is under its pro-tection: 'anyone who takes refuge there must not be touched or harmed in any way' (Meiser 1955:269-70). Because the chief of the tribe is always selected from this type of platform, it is higher in rank than the other two types.

The function of the platform of the murderers was to kill; its chief is second in rank (Meiser 1955:271). The physical structure functioned as a trap to unsuspecting strangers. Under false pretences, they were enticed in a friendly manner to come near this platform only to be suddenly killed (Meiser 1955:271).

At Damur there are five major platforms: four are as-sociated with a particular animal (crocodile, eagle, cas-sowary, pig), and the fifth is associated with two animals (crocodile and cassowary), though this probably concerns two visions of the same being.

The loincloth ritual

The loincloth, or *pasim mal* (Melanesian Pidgin, literally meaning 'to put on the loin cloth'), ritual for boys marks the adoption of the wearing of a loincloth for the first time in their lives, at the age of ten to twelve years, in the con-text of an initiation ritual (Höltker 1964:46-50 on this ritual among the Nubia-Awar; Böhm 1983:82-5 on the ritual in the context of a second-stage initiation on Manam Island; Höltker 1962: Tafel VI, fig. 2 for the manner of wearing the loincloth).

In former days this ritual was performed after about six months of seclusion. The ritual has a sacred and symbolic connotation: it is thought that the loincloth is given by a spirit, and wearing it is symbolic for guarding secret knowledge. If somebody has betrayed the secrets, it is said: 'he has taken off (laid down) his loin-cloth' (Meyer 1943: 167). However, a man could take off his loincloth and walk around naked as a sign of mourning the death of a child or a younger brother. Similar action could be taken by a senior man to end arguments or terminate warfare, in particular when close relatives had been killed or many people wounded. This show of defencelessness would result in immediate cessation of hostilities (Meyer 1943:168).

During the second stage of initiation (at the age of about seventeen years), the youth was provided with a tight rattan waist-belt and a hair-basket or wicker cone (Höltker 1964:55-8).[13] The forehead was shaved and the remain-ing hair pushed through the basket to form a mop stick-ing out at the tapering end of the cone. There are many variations in hair-basket decoration, using dogs' teeth, shells, beads and trimmed feathers, reflecting the family group of the wearer.

Some old wooden figures in collections still have a loin-cloth, and sometimes, even more rarely, a hair-basket attached to them (de Grunne 1979:76, fig. 6.1; Haberland and Schuster 1964:30, fig. at left; Smidt 1990:235, cat. no. 89, 239, cat. no. 90; Wardwell 1971:34, fig. 49), but most old figures have lost these elements.[14] These figures have a pointed projection on top of the head for wrap-ping around a wig of human hair covered with a hair-basket (Smidt 1975:54-5, figs 54, 55). In only a few examples, one or the other element is still present, such as a mop of human hair (Beier and Aris 1975:31, figs 10a, 10b; Höltker 1968: Tafel XXIX, figs. at left and right; Smidt 1990:239, cat. no. 90; Wardwell 1971:39, fig. 61).[15]

Some masked performers representing spirits also wear a hair-basket, as observed by Hogbin (1978, illustration of 'A *tangbwal* spirit monster' between pp. 84 and 85) at Wogeo in 1934 and by Eoe and Smidt at Damur in 1979. A bark cloth may be worn below the mask for the attach-ment of valuable ornaments made of *melo* shell.[16] Perhaps this piece of bark cloth signifies the loincloth worn tra-ditionally by initiated males.[17]

The festival at Damur

Functions of the festival

The festival at Damur may be considered primarily a large-scale ceremony in honour of important people who have died, to bid them a last farewell and to end a period of mourning. In this respect, it is significant that in the course of the festival the personal belongings of the dead are burnt and the sacred flutes are played on the graves. For the living who are left behind, a major goal of the festival is to temporarily create 'heaven on earth' and revitalise society in the process. In that regard the performance of many maskers in the course of the festival is a splendid testimony to the ability of the community to draw on all possible resources to create a tangible unity between the world of the living and the ancestral spirits.

The most spectacular impact of the ancestral spirits is made at the opening and closing rituals, the only occasions when all the maskers enlisted for the festival parade through the village in massive groups. At the opening ritual (called *brukim banis* in Melanesian Pidgin) all the participating maskers burst through the fence that has been erected to hide the mask costumes from public view.

In the period between the opening and closing ritual, the maskers perform regularly in smaller units. There are, though, several other activities such as *rites de passage* (van Gennep 1909), installing and lifting food taboos, and transactions strengthening social, economic and political ties between individual people, family groups and villages.

An important motive in organising the prestigious event was to show off to people of a neighbouring village, with whom an antagonistic relationship in connection with a longstanding land dispute existed, and challenge them. From what we were told in Damur, the festival was triggered by grave insults cast upon the Damur people by people from Bot Bot village. These insults suggested that the Damur people were 'rubbish people', that they did not even have a decent spirit house, and that they were weak. This challenge was met by the decision on the part of a major village leader of Damur, Tom Kambek Kumi, to organise a *Tiam*, as the Damur people call the festival concerned. In this endeavour he appeared to have been

13.3   Tom Kambek Kumi, the initiator of the end-of-mourning festival at Damur, and his wife. Damur, 24 April 1979. (Photo: Dirk Smidt.)

greatly supported by his wife (fig. 13.3).[18] The challenge offered him the opportunity to strengthen his position, confirm his status as a Big Man, and give him added prestige. It may well be that in the process he also secured his future position in the ancestral world (cf. Birket-Smith 1965:23). After all, the festival showed him to be influential with the ancestral spirits who accepted the invitation to come to Damur to perform.[19] Apart from honouring the dead and creating 'heaven on earth', perhaps the most essential aspect of the festival was for the Damur people to take up the challenge and win a major victory in the context of the ongoing 'prestige fight' with a neighbouring village.

Phases of the festival

The festival took place during three months in 1979, but preparations began in 1977 and included many phases.[20]

1977

- The Bot Bot people insulted and challenged the Damur people.
- A major village leader of Damur emerged as initiator and chief organiser of the festival.
- A large-scale pig and cassowary hunt was organised.
- The game was distributed to enlist support.

- A meeting was held to obtain cooperation and the *Tiam* festival was announced.
- An ancestral spirit house (*haus tambaran* in Melanesian Pidgin) was built and opened at the end of 1977.

1978

- Mask costumes were made, representing bush spirits.
- Two female masks from Kaian, for which the rights of use were obtained, were brought to the ancestral spirit house.
- In March, a large fence was erected around the major ancestral spirit house, the most important platform (*nambawan bet* in Melanesian Pidgin). This was done to shield from the public eye the festival preparations and particular sacred activities; for example, the construction and storage of the mask costumes of village spirits, the donning of the mask costumes by the dancers, and the playing of the sacred flutes.
- The mask costumes of village spirits were made.

1979

- Food was acquired, particularly sago (which can be stored for long periods).
- Two male masks arrived from Kaian and were installed surreptitiously within the enclosure so as not to draw the attention of women and children.[21]
- In early April the opening ritual took place; the maskers burst through the fence around the enclosure and paraded through the village.
- Pigs were distributed to co-sponsors from neighbouring villages. Then followed a period of regular performances of maskers – single, in pairs, or in small groups. During this time (April to June 1979) various rituals took place involving the maskers (or rather the spirits represented by the maskers):
  - placing and lifting of short-term taboos on the use of betel and coconuts;
  - lifting a long-term taboo on the use of sago from a particular place;
  - putting grass skirts around the hips of a few girls after first menstruation;
  - burning personal belongings of the dead and playing the sacred flutes on their graves;
  - killing of pigs to fulfil obligations or enlist cooperation then and in the future; and
  - hanging a boar-tusk ornament around the neck of a son of the leader of the festival as token of proof (to be shown as an historical 'document' to later generations) that a pig was paid for the commissioning of the two masks from Kaian village (plate 5).
- During this period also, various transactions took place:
  - paying for the use of maskers from another village;
  - enlisting the future help of other people;
  - claiming the use of a particular mask and/or dance for a future occasion;
  - meeting outstanding obligations.[22]
- Towards the end of June the closing ritual took place. For the last time the maskers paraded through the village plaza, forming three long rows. First the spirit maskers of the bush and water took their leave, followed by the maskers representing the spirits of the village. During this last parade, the maskers were presented with baskets containing food (including Western food such as biscuits) to take home with them. They were also presented with gifts of tobacco, newspaper (for cigarette paper) and betel nut. They did not walk normally as they had previously during the festival; they swayed back and forth as if their strength was diminishing and they might collapse at any moment. It was a deeply moving occasion. There was an atmosphere of sadness in the air. Wives of major sponsors of the festival rushed towards particular maskers, holding a coconut and bush knife in their hands. As a token of grief they sliced open the coconut and poured the milk on the ground in front of the masker. Several participants were barely

able to control their emotions and tears welled into their eyes. This was the final farewell of the deceased who were departing for the spirit world. Essential to the proceedings on the closing day of the festival was the proclamation of the final results by the chief organiser (see below).

- By the end of June the mask costumes had been dismantled. The wooden masks had been detached and 'killed' or 'made cold' by throwing lime on their foreheads (during the festival the masks had been regarded as 'hot'; that is, fully imbued with the spirits). This allowed the spirits to go back to their habitations in the bush, the water or wherever. Shell and other ornaments, as well as the feather decorations, were retrieved by their owners for future occasions, and most of the frameworks of the mask costumes were burnt. Some were kept, however, to be used for a festival at another village later in the year.
- In July the fence around the enclosure was pulled down.[23]

Mask costumes: storage and materials

A mask costume is considered merely a shell for the temporary containment of an ancestral spirit. At the conclusion of the festival the spirit is released and its shell – the mask costume, with the exception of the wooden mask, valuable ornaments and feather decorations – is burnt.

For the festival at Damur, thirty-nine mask costumes were prepared. To store and hide these from the eyes of women and children, a huge fence was built enclosing a rectangular space at one of the two longitudinal ends of the village, near the boundary between village and bush. Within the fence, a rectangular ancestral spirit house was built with an annexe behind it (fig. 13.4). In these buildings the mask costumes were hung from the rafters in three parallel rows. In the ancestral spirit house, sixteen mask costumes were stored; in the annexe, fifteen. Under a small lean-to, built against the fence, eight mask costumes were stored. Those included the four leased from Kaian village. For a performance, the mask costumes are donned by initiated young

men who must have undergone a purification ritual, which formerly involved having blood drawn from the penis.[24] They must also abstain from sexual intercourse.

Most maskers have a characteristic arrangement of several plates of *melo* shell hanging on their breast. These shells are attached to either a string bag or a piece of cloth made of beaten bark, the same material used for loincloths. The bark cloth, suggestive of the loincloth worn by initiated

13.4 Schematic plan (not to scale) of the sacred enclosure showing the ancestral spirit house, annexe and lean-to used for the storage of mask costumes. Platforms to sit on or for depositing of paraphernalia, and slit-gongs, are also included. The maskers leave the enclosure through the main entrance and return through it (see arrow). Outside the fence, a pair of maskers associated with music and dance perform (accompanied by the sound of the slit-gong) in front of the most important platform of the village. (Drawn by Anna-Karina Hermkens, based on a sketch by Dirk Smidt.)

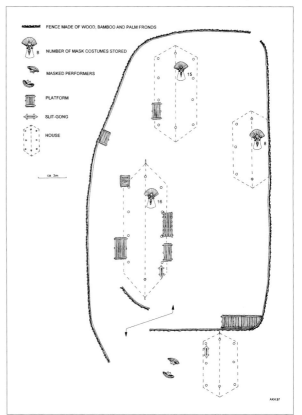

males, may indicate the masker to be male. The manner in which the shell ornaments are arranged differs from mask to mask: either in a rather loose arrangement, or in a more strict pattern; in a vertical row, for example, running gradually from large pieces at the top end to small pieces at the bottom end, or vice versa. There might also be a pattern of several rows side by side. The variations in this patterning of the shell ornaments is indicative of the various family groups, with which the masks are associated.

Imported materials are readily included in the decoration of the masks. The feathers of the headdresses are brightly coloured by application of pink, blue, purple and green chemical paints; the decoration around the mask may include glossy Christmas-tree tinsels, snippets of paper, woollen threads, and even an occasional Chinese lantern of coloured paper. The wooden masks are usually painted (or repainted in the case of an old mask) stark red using oil paint. A masker may have an attribute imported from another part of Papua New Guinea, such as a small string bag on his back made of wool, and apparently obtained from the Chimbu, in the central Highlands.

Classification of spirit masks and music

Schmidt (1933b:663-7) distinguishes eight different types of masks being used among the Nor-Papua (Murik-Kaup-Karau). Vormann (1911:420-6) distinguishes six types of masks among the Monumbo. These appear to be linked to different types of dances or performances. He divides them into two groups: a group of three that is considered of a higher order than the other group of three, which represents certain animals (Vormann 1911:420-1). At Damur, the entire group of masked figures can be considered a family: a primeval mother and father and their children. There are male and female masks, adults and children. Accordingly, mask costumes vary in size: there are very large ones (5 to 6 metres tall), large ones (3.5 metres), of a man's height (1.8 metres), and small ones (1.5 metres). A few masks might be considered hermaphrodites. Some are representations of animals such as cas-

sowary or fish, some of trees or plants such as banana.

The Damur people distinguish masks from: the bush; the water – the Ramu River or the sea; and the village.

Bush spirit masks: Masks representing spirits associated with the bush usually play an important role in the context of hunting. These spirits may show the prey to the hunters of their own group while making it invisible to outsiders, and they make sure that the prey does not run away and will be surely hit. This is particularly applicable

13.5 The largest and most imposing of all the maskers, representing Taikurum, the founder of Damur village. Tied vertically along its 'vertebral column' are three wooden panels. When the masker is in motion, these constitute a mobile version of the main carved post (no longer in existence) of the major platform in the village. The faces and figures carved in the panels constitute the ancestral line of the platform. Damur, 22 April 1979. (Photo: Dirk Smidt.)

13.6 Detail of one of the wooden panels shown in fig. 13.4. Damur, 11 June 1979. (Photo: Dirk Smidt.)

to the pig hunt. From the outside appearance of the masker, especially the materials used to cover the framework of the mask costume, its association with the bush can be recognised. These materials are taken from bush vegetation or from animals living in the bush; for example, sago-leaf fibres and cassowary feathers, respectively. From a listing of the parts of a Birap masker represented in a schematic drawing by van den Berg (1992:34), it can be inferred that a very high, tubelike construction on top of some of these maskers is indicative of a tree. One masker at Damur represented an ancestral spirit associated with the banana: at the top end it had an elliptical red piece representing the flowering part of the banana tree.

Water spirit masks: The mask costumes of the spirits associated with water have, like the ones associated with the bush, characteristic elements to identify them as such. They may be covered with a green material that refers to the growth of a vegetable substance (algae?) found on driftwood. Some mask costumes may have the figure of a fish attached at the top end. A rare type of wooden mask, as seen at Damur, shows a combination of human and animal features, in this case a face with a large beaklike nose is superimposed on a crocodile head. This mask represents a spirit crocodile and its transformation.[25] Hogbin (1970:64) reports how maskers representing spirits of the water/sea arrive and depart by 'canoe' – a platform at the edge of the village.

Village spirit masks: The largest and most important of all the maskers associated with Damur village represents Taikurum, the founding spirit of the village. It shows a most extraordinary feature. At the back, running along the full length of the 'vertebral column' in a single row, are tied three wooden panels, in which masks and a few figures are carved (figs 13.5 and 13.6). This constitutes some sort of family tree, and forms a movable version of the main post of the most important ancestral spirit house, which is named after the same major spirit as the mask.

Examples of such wooden panels have reached museum collections, but their function as part of maskers in motion was not known before to the authors (fig. 13.7).[26] When not used in the context of a festival, such panels may be displayed inside the spirit house. Photographs taken by Father Georg Höltker, SVD, in 1937 of the interior of an ancestral spirit house at Bosmun (Bosngun) seem to suggest this. On these photographs, panels that appear to be comparable to the ones seen at Damur can be vaguely discerned as part of an ornamental wall (Höltker 1966: figs 7, 10).

At the conclusion of the festival, Taikurum plays a most important role when he shows the tallies indicating the major achievements of the festival. This act and the verbal explanation given by the initiator of the festival constitute a publicly announced challenge to the Bot Bot people (see 'Spirit masks as agents in the fight for prestige', below).

13.7 Panel. Provenance not documented. Possibly Bosmun; there are similarities in style between some of the figures carved in this panel and several carved in posts of a ceremonial house at Wemtak hamlet, Bosmun, as recorded by Fukumotu (1976: plates 20-21) and Smidt (1973: unpublished photographs). Probably collected during the 1960s. Wood, red, blue, yellow, black, white, sago-leaf fibre. H. 186 cm. Collection Rijksmuseum voor Volkenkunde, Leiden. RMV 5173-5. (Photo: Ben Grishaaver.)

the hand-drums, beating the slit-gongs, and blowing the sacred flutes.[27] Some of these instruments are played to accompany the dancing of the maskers, and their sound may be thought of as an audible extension of the maskers. The drummers are publicly visible, sitting somewhere near the dancing ground or accompanying the maskers, dancing around them. The slit-gong players are also visible under the roofs of the platforms. The sacred flutes, however – sometimes accompanied by the sound of a small slit-gong – form a different musical category. The flute players are not supposed to be seen by the uninitiated; therefore the flutes are usually played at night within the enclosure housing the mask costumes.

However, on one rare occasion we observed the sacred flutes being played outside the enclosure during the day. Before the flute players moved out of the secluded area, the uninitiated (women and children), who had been signalled to get out of the way, left the village. Upon leaving the fence through the main entrance, the flute players paused in front of the platform of the initiator of the festival, where the most important pig, a huge animal reared in the village, was suspended upside down from a wooden framework in order to be killed. On several other occasions during the festival a masker would kill a similarly displayed pig by thrusting a spear through its heart (in most cases with the assistance of the owner of the mask). On this occasion the spirit represented by flute music symbolically killed the pig; this was physically indicated by the flute player lifting his leg (while playing) and placing his foot against the belly of the animal.

After this rite, the flute players proceeded towards the graves of the important deceased who were being commemorated by the festival. On the graves, located somewhere near the edge of the village, they played the sacred flutes, after which they returned to the enclosure.

The importance and symbolic value of the most sacred music (the music that is produced in a secluded manner) is markedly demonstrated at the conclusion of the festival. When it comes to listing the achievements of the festival, proclaiming them as a challenge to the adversary group, this music is counted as a separate tally element (see 'Spirit masks as agents in the fight for prestige', below).

Audible spirits: The ancestral spirits are not only visible through the medium of maskers, but are also audible through the medium of music: by people singing, playing

This is not the case with the music played publicly to accompany the peacefully dancing maskers.

Major functions of maskers

Maskers perform a variety of roles in the course of the festival. Many rites are of no consequence if not sanctioned by the presence of the ancestral spirits in their temporary abode of maskers. For example:

- food taboos are placed and removed under supervision of a major masker;
- the decorating of the son of the festival leader with a boar-tusk ornament is done in the presence of one of the maskers whose witnessing this act serves as a supernatural seal on the act;
- the burning of the personal belongings of the dead takes place under the supervision of one or more maskers associated with the deceased;
- the grass-skirt ritual is symbolically performed by a masker; and
- the ritual killing of pigs is done by maskers.

The Damur people make a distinction between the maskers of peaceful spirits of music and dance, and aggressive spirits of warfare.

A further etic distinction may be made between female maskers that implement and lift food taboos, female maskers that go around asking for food, and male and female maskers whose main role is to entertain in a comical manner.

This latter classification is not an altogether strict one. It is meant to alert the reader to a number of functions the masks perform; it is not meant to suggest that each function is linked to a different type of mask. These categories may overlap. For example, some masks that go around asking for food may also have a comical role to fulfil; sometimes the two roles may even be performed simultaneously. Furthermore, although by and large there is a strict distinction between aggressive and peaceful masks, in one instance there is overlap. The same mask being aggressive on one occasion may dance peacefully on another. In this case the dual behaviour appears to be linked to the hermaphroditic nature of the spirit concerned. It is male and female, but performs either as a male or as a female, never simultaneously. When it performs as a male aggressive spirit, it carries and throws spears (or at least bamboo shafts); when it performs as a female spirit, it dances around holding a stick in each hand, stooping slightly to push the ends of the sticks against the ground while making stirring movements (fig. 13.8). By this gesture it refers to a phase in a myth when the particular spirit made a hole in the ground, or a well. Photographs of a comparable performance were taken by A.B. Lewis around 1910 at Awar (fig. 13.9). Lewis collected the masks and the sticks; they are displayed at the Field Museum, Chicago (fig. 13.10).

13.8 Pair of maskers, representing the ancestral spirits Boti and Bauwu, performing a dance near the major platform of Damur village. The sticks they hold in their hands refer to a particular phase in a myth when these spirits dug a well or hole in the ground. In the background is the fence around the enclosure with its main entrance. Damur, 20 April 1979. (Photo: Dirk Smidt.)

13.9 Masker manipulating two sticks while dancing, Awar, circa 1910. (Photo: A.B. Lewis, Field Museum, #33519, Chicago.)

The Primeval Mother and Father. The Primeval Mother and Father, called Kobin and Kupapa respectively, are associated with the bush, as can be recognised from the materials that cover their bodies: cassowary feathers and sago-leaf fibres, as well as fibre anklets, and the cuscus skin headband worn by Kupapa (fig. 13.11). Their appearance is unique in comparison to the other masks. Apart from the typical bush materials just mentioned, Kobin stands out because she is made to look fat and stocky. Her mask costume consequently should be donned by a rather stout man. As the lower legs of the person are visible, the legs are of particular importance. In Kobin's case the legs should have fat calves to be in line with the overall figure.

Kupapa, the Primeval Father, on the other hand, is much taller and of more slender build; consequently his mask costume should be donned by a man with slim legs. A

vertical structure superimposed above the wooden mask, which elongates towards the top end, emphasises the impression of slenderness. Most male masks have a similar basic structure. Yet Kupapa shows a marked difference in lacking a most eye-catching element: the large, more-or-less triangular colourful feather headdress (compare fig. 13.11 and plate 3). This makes it possible for him to move with agility among houses and people, while the range of action of the maskers with huge feather head-dresses is naturally restricted to more open areas, particularly the village plaza.

The gender distinction between Kobin and Kupapa shows clearly in the roles they perform. Kobin has a more feminine nurturing role; Kupapa is a more imposing, somewhat dangerous and disciplinary force. His attribute is a

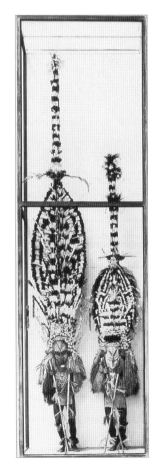

13.10 Display of two maskers holding sticks at The Field Museum, Chicago. Collected by A.B. Lewis at Awar, circa 1910. (Photo: Field Museum, #58765, Chicago.)

13.11 Masker representing Kupapa, the Primeval Father, in front of the sacred enclosure. The materials of the costume – cassowary feathers, sago-leaf fibres and cuscus fur – help to identify the Primeval Father as a being associated with the bush. Damur, 20 April 1979. (Photo: Dirk Smidt.)

Although Kupapa looks the more intimidating and commanding figure, Kobin appears to play a more prominent role. She is an almost ever-present figure, and certainly performs much more frequently than her husband, Kupapa. At the opening ritual she is the first to appear, as she is considered to open the 'door' to the bush. She subsequently goes back inside the enclosure to get her 'children', and accompanies them when leaving the enclosure to perform in the village. She plays a central

13.12 A masker representing Kupapa, the Primeval Father, 'kills' (wounds) a pig, assisted by Barbar, the owner of the pig who presents it as one of his contributions to the festival. He had bought it on Manam Island, apparently in exchange for a lump of sago of approximately the same size as the pig. On this occasion, eight maskers, one after the other, made a similar gesture, the larger maskers (such as the ones parading in the background) pointing the spear without thrusting it. After the symbolic killing by the maskers, this pig was taken down, carried to its owner's house, put on the ground and actually killed by the owner by moving a spear with an iron point around in the inflicted wound. Damur, 12 June 1979. (Photo: Dirk Smidt.)

long stick with attached hook. With this instrument he hooks men while rounding them up during the opening ritual, when men and women try to flee him. He chases women, children and uninitiated youths away if necessary.

Like some other male maskers, Kupapa is also directly involved in the ritual killing of pigs, as these are meant to be killed by the ancestral spirits (fig. 13.12). Although his role is not primarily of a comical nature, he may occasionally do comical things. Thus Kupapa once poked his hooked stick underneath and inside the skirt of a masker representing an unmarried female spirit.

13.13 Burning of the personal belongings of the deceased mother of Andrew Bangi Nake, one of the main organizers of the end-of-mourning festival. In the background, Andrew Bangi Nake and the masker representing Kobin, the Primeval Mother, are watching the fire consume the artefacts. Just before this picture was taken, Kobin had 'lit' the fire by using a torch of dry coconut fronds. (The torch held in Kobin's hand was lit by Andrew Bangi Nake who subsequently took it out of her hand to start the fire.) The personal belongings included: part of a canoe, several wooden food plates, a metal cooking pot plus lid, an eating plate, a basket, a grass skirt, and a canvas bag. The ritual took place during the second-last day of the festival. Damur, 22 June 1979. (Photo: Dirk Smidt.)

13.14 (Top) The masker representing Kobin, the Primeval Mother, crosses a waterway near Damur by canoe (note the stylised crocodile-head prow). Kobin is on her way to Bogia market, a coastal administrative centre. Her wish to go to market was innovative and considered hazardous by some. 15 June 1979. (Photo: Dirk Smidt.)

13.15 (Above) The *tanim saksak* (Melanesian Pidgin, meaning 'to cook sago pudding') ritual. A taboo on a plot of sago is revoked by Kobin, the Primeval Mother. The ritual is attended by a masker representing Gurmbi, a male water spirit (its mask is double-faced, a long-beaked face is superimposed on a crocodile's face) flanked by Tom Kambek Kumi, the initiator of the festival, holding an enamel foodplate containing pork and sago. Kobin holds a piece of sago in her hand, which she moves around above the head of Mr Kumi's wife. This gesture signifies the stirring of the sago pudding. Kobin will subsequently give this piece of sago to the woman, who will put it in her mouth and eat it (after having rejected it the first time). After her, the same procedure will be repeated with her husband. Damur, 12 June 1979. (Photo: Dirk Smidt.)

role in various rituals taking place in the course of the festival; for example, implementing and lifting food taboos, officiating at *rites de passage*, and burning the personal belongings of the deceased (fig. 13.13). She is also considered to have magical healing powers. On one occasion the owner of the mask had been bitten on his leg by a centipede, which caused pain and a swelling. Kobin removed both by chewing a leaf and by spitting the juice onto the particular spot. Moreover, like some other maskers she regularly goes around to demand food, and she may have other functions.[28]

Once Kobin made a remarkable decision that proved she was inclined to keep up with the times. When the Damur people were planning to go to market at the coastal town and administrative centre, Bogia, she indicated that she wished to join them.[29] So she was taken by canoe to cross a waterway before embarking on a trip by truck (fig. 13.14). Like the people she had something to sell: sago in a bamboo container, which had her name written on it to distinguish it from others.

Food taboos and food collecting: It would seem that, in general, food taboos are implemented and lifted by Kobin, the Primeval Mother. We witnessed Kobin supervising the wife of one of the chief organisers of the festival when she attached dried palm-leaf to a betel palm to indicate a temporary ban on the harvesting of betel nut. Kobin's presence ensured the taboo was perceived as a sacred taboo. We also saw Kobin playing an essential role in the lifting of a taboo on sago from a particular spot. In the past, a child of Tom Kambek Kumi, the initiator of the festival, had died after eating sago obtained from this spot. The child's death was attributed to an evil spirit spoiling the sago. Upon the child's death a taboo was put on all sago from the spot in question. During the festival, Kobin performed the act of lifting the taboo. She took a piece of sago from a plate, moved it around above the head of the wife of the initiator of the festival to indicate the process of stirring sago, and put it in her mouth to be eaten. The same procedure was followed with regard to the initiator of the festival (fig. 13.15).

A major function of several masks is to collect food from among the villagers. As indicated above, only particular categories of mask have this function. By and large, this task is not undertaken by the larger type of mask. For example, it is out of the question that the dangerous and aggressive masks, let alone the mask representing the founder of the village, would undertake it. Also, the masks whose main function is to entertain by dancing (to the accompaniment of music) do not go around collecting food.

Demanding and collecting food is done by some of the smaller, female masks, whose behaviour appears to be less restricted to a particular pattern than the types of masks just mentioned. In fact, the role of food collecting is undertaken by some of the comical masks (see below) and, to some extent, by the Primeval Mother Kobin. The task implies the collecting of empty wooden bowls from people involved in the activities taking place inside the enclosure, and returning these filled with food. It is not just a matter of collecting food there and then. Such masks may also anticipate food-procuring activities by instructing people to start pounding the pith of the sago palm to extract the starch. The food collected consists mainly of sago, coconut and galip nuts, and sometimes sago pudding topped with fish or a crab and some greens (fig. 13.16). Also, stimulants like betel nut and tobacco are collected by maskers in the course of the festival.

The most important food, however, is pork, as it has special status and symbolic significance. During several gatherings, pork is presented in palm-leaf baskets or in wooden bowls with sago pudding. This is indicative of important transactions taking place in the course of the festival. It also signifies the considerable sacrifice made by the owners of the pigs that are killed: it is too traumatic for them to attend the slaughter of their pigs, reared so carefully over many years. A connotation between pigs and souls of the dead probably also plays a role here.[30] The killing of pigs is a prerequisite for a successful festival, as it is the major way of sponsoring essential aspects of the festival such as the performance of maskers.

Peaceful and aggressive performances: The peaceful masks of music and dance perform regularly in the village, usually in front of a platform to which one or more major sponsors of the festival belong, in particular the platform

13.16 Masker representing Ambumba – an old, unmarried, female ancestral spirit – who occasionally performs a comical role. Here she has just collected sago pudding, topped with crabs and some greens, in a ceremonial wooden bowl. In her right hand she holds an attribute of hers, a wooden bush-knife. Damur, 19 April 1979. (Photo: Dirk Smidt.)

The aggressive and dangerous masks have spears and spear-throwers as characteristic attributes. They are much feared. In the course of the festival they perform at regular intervals. When they are ready, they burst out through the front entrance in the fence and rush up and down the village plaza in an agitated and rather mechanical manner (rather as if a key in their back has been turned to set them in motion), throwing spears at people they perceive within reach. Of all the masks, they seem to be the most strictly programmed, without room for improvisation. No doubt they would wound and even kill people who got in their way. The authors were clearly warned about them and told not to take any chances. As a rule, people make sure to get out of their way.[32] Nevertheless, a comparatively recent report on a dangerous mask from Boroi (one of the contributing villages to the festival and belonging to the same language as Damur) claimed that the spirit of that mask had killed several people and threatened others (Josephides 1990:65).

Comical performances: In the context of the end-of-mourning festival at Damur, ample opportunity is given for 'performance humour' or 'ritual clowning' (cf. Mitchell

13.17 Two maskers representing Yangdé and Tangru, a pair of ancestral sisters, dance together near the platform with which they are associated. Note the slit-gongs underneath the roofing of the platform. These maskers are in the category of 'peaceful maskers of music and dance'. Their main purpose is to dance in a relaxed atmosphere to the accompaniment of music. By doing so they make people happy. Damur, 20 April 1979. (Photo: Dirk Smidt.)

of the initiator of the festival. They often dance in pairs representing brothers and sisters or husbands and wives (fig. 13.17). They make gentle movements towards and away from each other with their grass skirts swaying to the accompaniment of men singing and beating hand-drums and slit-gong (fig. 13.18). They are watched by an appreciative audience, and when they parade up and down the village plaza they are preceded, followed or surrounded by dancing women, and by men singing and beating hand-drums (fig. 13.19).[31]

13.18 Playing the slit-gong to represent the voice of the ancestral spirit of the performing masker. The slit-gong is placed under the roofing of a platform. Damur, 17 June 1979. (Photo: Dirk Smidt.)

1992:viii, 29-31) by some of the maskers. Mortuary clowning, as a form of comic relief taking place soon after somebody dies, has been reported from various areas of New Guinea, including Murik Lakes, west of the Lower Ramu area (Barlow 1992). As observed by Mitchell (1992:30):

> ritual clowning … usually juxtaposes hilarity and gravity. While relatives grieve over a death, their affinal kin begin a ritual performance of disgusting hilarity that will dissolve grief into laughter and return the aggrieved to everyday life.

Paraphrasing the term 'mortuary clowning', one might refer to the comical performances taking place in the course of the Damur festival as 'end-of-mourning clowning'. Male and female comical maskers perform. The comical masker does various things to entertain the public but 'its efficacy is more than entertainment … Her work is to generate laughter for a reason, a reason far beyond the superficial one of comic relief' (Mitchell 1992:30).

At Damur, the comical maskers imitate their big brothers, even the dangerous aggressive ones, by threatening to throw spears, for example, or by imitating the beating of the slit-gong (Smidt 1996:66, fig. 3). They show the typical behaviour of what in the Western world is known as an *enfant terrible*, or 'little terror'. In contrast to the dangerous, aggressive maskers and the peaceful maskers of music and dance, their performance appears to be less programmed. They seem to have much more freedom to improvise. They may even create impromptu interactions with outsiders like the authors. Smidt was honoured by the attentions of one of these comical maskers, which happened to represent an unmarried female spirit called Ambumba. To the delight of the onlookers, she suggested attraction to this male visitor by swaying her grass skirt and other suggestive gestures. One of her attributes was

13.19 Procession of several maskers along the village plaza, preceded by women (two of them just taking some lime to chew together with betel nut). The two large maskers are accompanied by Kobin, the Primeval Mother, and Mopo, a small comical masker (both facing one of the large maskers). Damur, 16 June 1979. (Photo: Dirk Smidt.)

a wooden knife or club, which aroused phallic connotations by the way she handled this instrument. On one occasion she poked it in Smidt's trousers, which, freshly washed, were hanging on a clothes line to dry in the sun. She also chaffed Smidt in his capacity as a photographer (fig. 13.20).

The authors witnessed the following actions by this particular mask :

- she threw a stick (in imitation of a dangerous spear-throwing masker) in a clumsy manner;

13.20 Masker representing Ambumba comically imitates one of the authors in his capacity as a photographer. In her left hand she holds a wooden knife, an attribute she comically manipulates during her performances. Damur, 19 April 1979. (Photo: Dirk Smidt.)

- she attempted to throw the stick forwards, and it fell behind her back instead;
- she kicked at a small boy but the boy kicked at her also;
- a young man grasped her by her genitals;
- she danced with another masker, Manme, in a comical manner;
- together with another small comical masker called Mopo, she beat a slit-gong in a comical manner;
- she involved herself in a mock fist-fight with Munme, another comical masker;
- she accepted cigarettes from the authors;
- she comically performed the ritual of a soldier presenting arms and saluting;
- she ordered food to be brought: by raising five fingers she indicated five bowls of food, stipulating pounded sago pith;
- she collected food (sago and coconuts) and took it inside the enclosure;
- she refused to accept a bowl with sago until grated coconut had been added;
- she brought back the empty bowl after use;
- she took the 'pepper' (for chewing with betel nut) out of somebody's string bag;
- she hit boys and girls with her stick;
- she hit men against their legs or thighs in passing;
- she hit the roof of a house;
- she pulled stepladders away from houses; and
- she chased a woman after that woman had sliced open a coconut in front of Ambumba as a token of grief at her impending departure.

The grass-skirt ritual.   This kind of ritual also took place in the course of the Damur festival. The grass skirt, or *pasim purpur* (Melanesian Pidgin, 'to put on the grass skirt'), ritual may be seen as the female counterpart of the loincloth ritual (fig. 13.21). The ritual is performed soon after a girl's first menstruation. As in many other cultures in New Guinea, dress may serve to mark a particular phase in life. In this case it marks the change from girl to marriageable woman. Ornaments with which she is decorated,

13.21 *Passim purpur* (Melanesian Pidgin meaning 'putting on of the grass skirt') ritual. The daughter of Alois Bande has received a colourful grass skirt to mark her first menstruation, and to indicate a commitment by the giver to help her in the future. The grass skirt was made and presented to her by people from Bak (Boroi No. 2) in return for the use of a mask her father had allowed them in the past. Prior to the ritual, he had presented a pig to two female relatives (sisters of his mother or his mother's family, and both of them sisters of each other), requesting them to perform the ritual on his daughter. It is believed it is a female ancestral spirit who puts the grass skirt on the girl, the women acting only on her behalf. The girl wears the design of this ancestral spirit on her grass skirt, and receives also the spirit's paint marks on her face. This would also signify that her father now has the right to use these designs and apply them himself. The chain of shell and boar-tusk ornaments serves as a ceremonial seal to the agreement between the parties. Because these ornaments were temporarily worn by the ancestral spirit who symbolically performed the grass-skirt ritual, they have a supernatural aura ensuring the commitments made will be put into practice. Damur, 10 June 1979. (Photo: Dirk Smidt.)

such as feathers, shell rings and dogs' teeth, may indicate the status of her father as a chief (Hogbin 1970:125-36, illustration p. 132).

As was explained to the authors at Damur, perhaps the prime significance of this ritual is that it implies the so-cial security of the girl in the future. The putting on of the grass skirt signifies that the person who does it (often an aunt) will look after the girl in times of need. The girl will be able to call on that particular relative, and be al-lowed to make use of sago plots and fishing grounds owned by this person (or her relatives) who sponsored her 'putting on of the grass skirt' ritual.

The performance of this ritual in the context of the fes-tival at Damur implies the great significance attached to it, as it is done in the presence of certain maskers representing ancestral spirits. It is believed that the grass skirt is received from a female spirit (in this case Kobin, the Primeval Mother), the woman who puts it around the girl's hips acting on behalf of the spirit. Thus it is not just a matter of a promise by human beings, relatives of the girl, to support her in the future; it is a sacred commitment, sealed and confirmed by the act of a supernatural being.

At Damur, the *pasim purpur* ritual was performed on two girls who had reached puberty. In one case it was performed on a daughter of one of the major Damur organisers of the festival by people from Boroi. The act was apparently done in return for a 'gift' by the father of the girl; in the past he had allowed the Boroi people the performance of a mask owned by him. The reverse situation also occurred during the festival at Damur: a man from Buliva assisted his sister's

13.22 A chain of shell and turtle-shell ornaments and a dog-teeth and fibre ornament is temporarily attached to a masker representing an ancestral spirit associated with water and fish. This gesture signifies a solemn pledge of the owner of the mask that in the future the 'putting on of the grass skirt' ritual will be performed by him and a female relative (probably his wife) on an as yet small daughter of the initiator of the festival, acting on behalf of the particular spirit represented by the masker. Immediately following this short ritual, the ornaments are handed over to the father of the girl, who keeps them as a tangible proof of the pledge (see fig. 13.23). Damur, 10 June 1979. (Photo: Dirk Smidt.)

13.23 Tom Kambek Kumi, the initiator of the festival, proudly shows a chain of shell and turtle-shell ornaments, and an ornament of fibre and dogs' teeth worn by his small daughter. He had just received the ornaments from the owner of a mask who acted on behalf of the ancestral spirit represented by the mask. These ornaments serve as official documents confirming a solemn pledge that in future the 'putting on of the grass skirt' ritual will be performed by the donor of the ornaments and a female relative, probably his wife (see also fig. 13.21). By this ritual the social security of the daughter of the recipient is ensured. Damur, 10 June 1979. (Photo: Dirk Smidt.)

Damur husband by providing feather decorations and shell ornaments for a mask costume, and helped put the costume together. This help would be returned in the future by the grass-skirt ritual being performed on the Buliva man's daughter by his sister (see also fig. 13.21).

Apart from the two girls receiving their grass skirts, a solemn pledge was made to perform such a ritual in the future on an as yet small daughter of the initiator of the festival. This pledge was sealed by the highest authority: a masker associated with the promising and giving party acting as a witness. The pledge was symbolically expressed and confirmed by temporarily attaching ornaments of shell, turtle shell and boar's tusk to that particular masker (fig. 13.22). These ornaments were subsequently handed over to the father of the girl, to be proudly kept by him as 'official documents' providing evidence of the safeguarding of his daughter's future (fig. 13.23).

The role of the gift-exchange network

Trading and gift-exchange relationships exist between the people of Damur and places such as Awar, Bosmun, Kaian and Murik Lakes, where people speak related Papuan languages. There are also relationships with Manam Island, which is inhabited by Austronesian-language speakers (Wurm 1981). For the purposes of the festival reported here, people of the villages of Boroi, Buliva and Galek (all speakers of the Gamei language) cooperated closely in the event.

One example of cooperation between Damur and Buliva at the festival, but seen in the wider context of a long-term relationship, is presented here. People from Buliva rendered assistance at the festival by leasing parts of the outfit of a mask costume. Damur people promised to reciprocate in the future by letting the Buliva representatives have the benefit of a particular dance – characterised by a boat made of light materials, which would be carried around – of which the ownership rested at Damur. The promise of this dance was signified by a small model boat that was attached to the back of the particular masker (fig. 13.24).[33]

From the village of Bosmun, clay pots were obtained. Some pots were kept by the Damur people for their own use, but others were exchanged with people from Manam Island for galip nuts, tobacco and bananas.

From the village of Kaian, two pairs of masks were 'leased' (or rather the spirits from Kaian represented by these masks were enlisted to come to Damur). These were of the peaceful type used for creating an atmosphere of happiness while dancing to the accompaniment of music.[34] The organisers of the festival were given the right to have the spirit masks from Kaian perform at their festival, and to use the dances and music associated with them, which they were allowed to learn. Thus the masks were not sold; the original

masks remained with the Kaian people, and for the purposes of the festival new copies were made.

For the right to use the copies of the Kaian masks and to learn the accompanying music, a fee was paid in several instalments:

- The first instalment was paid at Kaian village in 1978. This consisted of one pig and two bags of rice to establish the agreement between the two parties.
- The second instalment was paid after the arrival of the copies of the masks at Damur village in May 1979. This consisted of one pig, plus sago, taro and bananas.

13.24 Small boat model – with hull wrapped in silver paper, and a feather construction indicating mast and sail – attached to the back of a masker representing the male water spirit Gurmbi (after whom the boat model is named). This signifies a promise of the owner of the mask to 'lend' a dance featuring a boat (probably reflecting cargo-cult notions) to people from Buliva at a future occasion. This is regarded as a counter-prestation in exchange for the contribution by the Buliva people of the outfit of the masker on the occasion of the Damur festival. Gurmbi wears a double mask: a face with elongated beak and round eyes superimposed on a face with slit-eyes representing a crocodile (see also fig. 13.15). Damur, 11 June 1979. (Photo: Dirk Smidt.)

- The third instalment was paid at Damur towards the conclusion of the festival in June 1979 (fig. 13.25). This consisted of:
  - fifteen clay pots obtained from Bosmun;
  - five clay pots obtained from Bilbil (near Madang);
  - twelve bunches of bananas obtained from Manam Island;
  - one bundle of taro (eight tubers a bundle);
  - ten packets of sago;
  - four sugarcane stalks;
  - one fish basket;
  - clothes; and
  - rice put in small baskets, which in their turn are put in a large basket, to be carried away by the maskers.
- The final instalment, consisting of one pig, was paid at Kaian upon the return of the masks.[35]

The 'lease' of a mask from a neighbouring village may be part of a long-term relationship that involves a number of transactions over the years. For example, on the occasion of the payment at Damur of the third instalment for the maskers from Kaian referred to above, the Kaian party also presented their Damur counterparts with some gifts: clothes, three baskets made at Murik, and one basket of fish. The 'payment' for the lease of the mask and its performance may be balanced by rendering a particular service to the mask-lending party in the future; for example, sponsoring the 'putting on of the grass skirt' ritual. Thus, the wife of the man who 'borrows' the mask may dress the daughter of the mask-lender in a grass skirt

13.25 Third instalment being paid for the performance of two maskers from Kaian, called Béramb and Katiknate. These maskers, belonging to the peaceful category of music and dance, represent female cassowary spirits (note the carved cassowary head attached above the feather headdress). Damur, 20 June 1979. (Photo: Dirk Smidt.)

13.26 Schematic example of an exchange relationship between Damur and Buliva. The main exchange is between the outfit for a masker performing in the context of the festival at Damur (provided by a woman's brother to her husband) and a future 'putting on of the grass skirt' ritual at Buliva as counter-prestation (provided by a woman to her brother's daughter). These major exchanges are preceded and followed by other exchanges, primarily of pigs being killed and distributed.

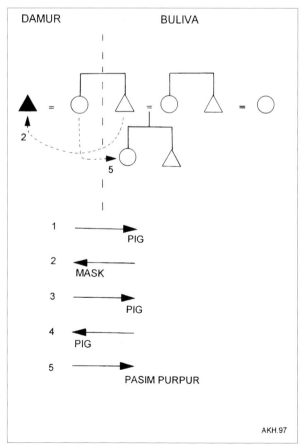

(marking the end of her first menstruation) in the future. The leasing of masks in exchange for the grass-skirt ritual is a major transaction supported and supplemented by other transactions, in particular the exchange of pigs, taking place in the course of time (fig. 13.26).

Leasing a mask costume for a festival, or assisting in assembling an outfit of a mask costume by providing valuable shell ornaments or feathers for its headdress, will have long-term benefits. As one man said: 'Later on, my children are entitled to claim a section of a garden or to obtain the right to fish in waters belonging to the family of my wife, who I have assisted in this festival.' He also explained it in Western economic terms: 'To make shell ornaments and feather decoration available for a masker is like depositing money in a bank account from which I will draw interest later on. It is a kind of insurance in case I go broke.' He compared it with 'being accepted as a member of a club by paying a fee' (Francis Domdom, pers. comm., Sabatmuning village, 1979).

Spirit masks as agents in the fight for prestige

For the proclamation of the final results at the conclusion of the festival, tallies were made of pieces of sago-leaf stem indicating the number of maskers performing (in other words, the number of spirits who visibly honoured Damur with their visit), the music played (in other words, the spirits who manifested themselves audibly), and the number of pigs slaughtered – killed by some of the spirit masks – of which the meat was cut up and festively distributed in portions.

Just before the festival was closed, during the last round of the main village mask Taikurum (the only one with the wooden panels attached to its back representing the main post of the ancestral spirit house Taikurum), the tally presentation took place. When the masker walked away from the enclosure and proceeded along the village plaza, Tom Kambek Kumi, the initiator of the festival, placed the two tallies over its hand. On his way back towards the enclosure the masker halted in front of Kumi's platform. Kumi blew a whistle to call for attention and gave a speech in which he reminded his audience of the insults and the

challenges by the Bot Bot people: how they came to Damur to *tok bilas* (Melanesian Pidgin, 'to ridicule', 'to make a mockery of'), and how they 'rubbished' the ancestral spirit house. He related how the Damur people took up the challenge by organising the festival and in their turn challenged the Bot Bot people to show themselves equal to the Damur achievement. During his speech he took the tallies from the hand of Taikurum, showed them to the audience (fig. 13.27) and hung them again over the hand of Taikurum. He finally took the tallies again from Taikurum's hand and suspended them from the roof of his ceremonial platform, the most important platform (*numba-wan bet*) in the village, to display them as a token of pride. These tallies were to be presented to the people of Bot Bot village as a challenge to them: 'See what we have been capable of! You try to organise something like that and we will see if you will manage to have as many maskers (spirits) attending your feast, and so on.'

Bot Bot and Damur people had not been to each other's village since the insulting visit of the Bot Bot people. No Bot Bot people had attended any part of the Damur festival. Because of the strained relationship between the two

13.27 Presentation of two tallies on the final day of the festival by Tom Kambek Kumi, the initiator of the festival, in the presence of the masker representing Taikurum, the founder of Damur village. The tallies form a listing of the main (sacred) investments and results of the festival: a list of pigs slaughtered and a list of maskers and music (ancestral spirits) who took part (see also fig. 13.24). Damur, 23 June 1979. (Photo: Dirk Smidt.)

13.28 Two tallies (made of pieces of sago-leaf stem) listing the main results are displayed at the main platform at the conclusion of the festival. These tallies constitute a formal challenge to the neighbouring village of Botbot. Each horizontal piece of the tally at left signifies a pig slaughtered; each horizontal piece of the tally at right signifies a spirit or mask. The tally at right is divided into four segments representing (top to bottom): four spirits represented by music; four masks from Galek village; twenty-two masks sponsored by Damur village, including the masks leased from Kaian; and thirteen masks from Buliva and Sabatmuning (located on the Ramu River). Damur, 23 June 1979. (Photo: Dirk Smidt.)

Tom Kambek Kumi's proclamation included references to:

- the number of pigs slaughtered (fig. 13.28, left);
- the number of spirits represented by maskers;
- the number of spirits manifested through sacred music: flutes, slit-gongs, hand-drums and singing; and
- financial expenditure.

One of the tallies presented at the conclusion of the festival consisted of forty-three pieces of sago-leaf stem tied to a rope in vertical order (fig. 13.28, right). Thirty-nine of these pieces were references to the number of masks that performed during the festival. The remaining four referred to spirits whose 'voices' were represented by the sound of musical instruments. The forty-three pieces were divided into four clusters:

- four pieces referring to four spirits represented by sacred music, the first pair of spirits rendered by two flutes, one slit-gong and one hand-drum, the second pair of spirits rendered by two flutes, one slit-gong, one hand-drum and singing;
- four pieces referring to four masks contributed by people from Galek village;
- twenty-two pieces referring to masks contributed by people of Damur, including the masks leased from Kaian but sponsored by people of Damur; and
- thirteen pieces referring to masks contributed by people from the villages of Buliva and Sabatmuning, located on the Ramu River.

Theoretical aspects of the festival

In an introductory chapter to *Time out of Time*, a book of essays on the Festival, Falassi (1987:1) notes that 'festival is an event, a social phenomenon, encountered in virtually all human cultures'. The same author provides us with a definition and a set of characteristics. The definition is of a generalised nature,[36] but the characteristics mentioned are more specific and as a frame of reference bear some relevance to the Damur festival. Thus Falassi discusses several aspects and gives insight into the 'mor-

villages, the tallies would not be presented to the Bot Bot people by Tom Kambek Kumi, nor by any other Damur man. Instead, they would be brought to Bot Bot by a magistrate acting as an intermediary.

phology of festivals'. From the outset, he stipulates that 'a morphology of festivals must indicate their minimal units and their possible sequences' (Falassi 1987:3). These units can be considered 'ritual acts' or 'rites' (Falassi 1987:3). These 'rites' are listed below and in each case their Damur equivalent is indicated.

Opening rite or rite of 'valorisation':[37] The beginning and end of the festival is clearly demarcated in time by a particular ritual characterised by valorisation or modification of the 'usual and daily function and meaning of time and space'. Thus, 'daily time is modified by a gradual or sudden interruption that introduces "time out of time", a special temporal dimension devoted to special activities' (Falassi 1987:4). The Damur equivalent of this is the *brukim banis* ritual, when all the maskers enlisted burst through the fence around the enclosure, one after the other. 'The opening rite is followed by a number of events that belong to a limited group of general ritual types' (Falassi 1987:4).

'*Rites of purification and cleansing:* The Damur equivalent concerns, for example, the purification of the dancers prior to donning the mask costumes.

Rites of passage: These 'mark the transition from one life stage to the next' (Falassi 1987:4). The Damur equivalent concerns the 'putting-on of the grass skirt' ritual to mark a girl's first menstruation, and the loincloth ritual to mark a boy's initiation.

Rites of reversal: For example, 'sex roles are inverted in masquerade with males dressing as females' (Falassi 1987:4). The Damur equivalent concerns male dancers who don mask costumes representing female ancestral spirits.

Rites of conspicuous display: For example:

> in sacred processions and secular parades, the icons and symbolic elements are … moved through space specifically adorned with ephemeral festive decorations … In such perambulatory events, along with the community icons, the ruling groups typically display themselves as

their guardians and keepers, and as depositories of religious or secular power, authority, and military might. [Falassi 1987:4]

The Damur equivalent concerns the spectacular display of maskers with huge feather headdresses and other elements of decoration parading through the village, and the bearing of this on matters of prestige and Big-Manship.

Rites of conspicuous consumption: These 'involve food and drink' which may, apart from the nutritional aspect, be used as 'a means to communicate with gods and ancestors' (Falassi 1987:4). The Damur equivalent concerns the ceremonial distribution and eating of pork, sago and betel nut. Pork, in particular, is of high symbolic significance.

Ritual dramas: These 'are usually staged at festival sites', often in reference to myths. 'Their subject matter is often a creation myth, a foundation or migratory legend, or a military success particularly relevant in the mythical or historical memory of the community staging the festival' (Falassi 1987:5). The Damur equivalent concerns the performance of maskers representing ancestral or mythical spirits; in some instances these enact certain episodes that are recorded in myth.

Rites of exchange: This may involve 'money and goods … exchanged at an economic level … [but] at more abstract and symbolic levels, information, ritual gifts, or visits may be exchanged'. Also 'thanksgiving for a grace received may take place in various forms of redistribution, sponsored by the community or a privileged individual, who thus repays the community or the gods for what he has received in excess' (Falassi 1987:5). The Damur equivalent concerns the distribution of traditional and Western goods (in particular, clay pots and clothes respectively) and food as payment for services rendered, in particular for the loan and performance of masks, or parts of the outfit, from other villages.

Rites of competition: These rites 'in their symbolic aspect … may be seen as a metaphor for the emergence and establishment of power' (Falassi 1987:6). Falassi refers to competitive matches between contestants, yielding winners and losers, and resulting in prize-giving and awards. There is no direct Damur equivalent, but the whole Damur festival is pervaded by a competitive element, as the festival appears to be a most conspicuous weapon in the perennial fight for prestige between Damur and a neighbouring village. As a consequence, the Damur festival is also a manifestation of leadership and Big-Manship.

Closing rite or 'rite of devalorisation':   'At the end of the festival, a rite of devalorization, symmetrical to the opening rite, marks the end of the festive activities and the return to the normal spatial and temporal dimensions of daily life' (Falassi 1987:6). The Damur equivalent concerns the farewell parades of the maskers, divided in groups on two consecutive days, and the subsequent release of the spirits by the 'killing of the masks' ritual.[38]

Thus, almost all the rites presented in Falassi's overview are relevant to the Damur festival, particularly the opening and closing rites. Only the rites of competition have no direct equivalent in the Damur festival, but, indirectly and metaphorically, competition is of paramount importance.

Although Falassi's general scheme appears to be applicable to the Damur festival, this does not imply that his frame of reference should be considered a precise blueprint. After all, the Damur festival is in many ways unique, not only in its visual aesthetics, choreography and music, but also in content.

Conclusion

This paper is a preliminary report on an 'end-of-mourning festival' observed in the village of Damur, Lower Ramu area, in 1979. Rarely have such festivals been reported in detail from this area. It was discovered that, after a lapse of many years, a large-scale festival could still be held under the impulses of traditional cultural, socioeconomic and political processes operating within the community, and between Damur and other communities. These processes were probably indirectly supported by the renewed interest in traditional culture (as a dynamic phenomenon of continuity and change) in the wake of independence in 1975.

The festival strengthened the existing socioeconomic network through which neighbouring groups are linked together in a long-term scheme of reciprocal obligations, including gift exchange. The whole community was temporarily uplifted and revitalised by drawing on economic, social and artistic resources, and channelling these through several rituals taking place in the course of the festival. The ability to launch such a festival, during which no less than thirty-nine maskers performed, was a matter of great pride to the people concerned. An essential characteristic of the whole event was the effort expended to maintain and improve community identity and prestige in response to a challenge from another group, and to impress its representatives with a strong challenge in return.

The initiative to organise the festival was taken by a hereditary clan and village leader. Under his vigorous impulse, people cooperated in making the festival a success. In the process he confirmed and strengthened his status as a Big Man. The initiator of the festival not only showed himself capable as a manager of people and goods on an organisational and profane plane, but by commanding the ancestral spirits to come and perform at Damur he proved he had access to the supernatural world as well. Thus the relationship between political leadership and the world of the ancestral spirits was clearly demonstrated, and, in general, the relationships between human beings, their ancestors and the world of the spirits was strengthened through the festival.

It should be noted that the festival was a matter not only of social processes, but also of human emotions (cf. Mitchell 1992:10-12): sadness about the definitive departure of the dead, happiness because of the visit of the ancestral spirits, pride in achieving a beautiful display of maskers, dance and music in communication with the ancestral spirits, comic relief, anger, and conflict *vis-à-vis* the enemy group. Perhaps the most pervasive feeling was that of *Krismas* (Melanesian Pidgin for any celebration that includes dancing and feasting) as the Damur people put it, or, in other words, 'heaven on earth'.

Acknowledgements

The field work on which this paper is based was sponsored by the Trustees of the National Museum and Art Gallery, Port Moresby. Dirk Smidt is grateful to Soroi M. Eoe for his companionship during field work, and for insights into Damur culture gained from him.

We owe a great debt to the people of Damur, foremost Tom Kambek Kumi, the initiator and chief organiser of the festival, for allowing us to witness the festival, for giving us access to the enclosure and its activities, and for granting permission to photograph and tape-record aspects of it. We wish to acknowledge the friendly and informative cooperation received from other important men, not only from Damur, but also from neighbouring villages participating in the event, such as Andrew Bangi Nake, Tom Bagep and Francis Domdom. We also wish to convey our thanks to the women and to members of the younger generation. The whole community played a positive role in making our stay at Damur a rewarding and pleasant one.

Dr Phillip H. Lewis, Curator of Primitive Art and Melanesian Ethnology at the Field Museum in Chicago, kindly provided information on the mask costumes from Awar displayed at the Field Museum, and facilitated access to the A.B. Lewis photographic archives.

The spelling and interpretation of words and phrases in Melanesian Pidgin is based on Mihalic (1971).

Notes

1. This field work was undertaken on behalf of the National Museum and Art Gallery of Papua New Guinea. Communication between the Gamei people and the authors took place in the lingua franca, Melanesian Pidgin.

2. See Kaufmann (1985:39), Map 3, 'Regional styles: coast and lower reaches', shaded area 2.

3. Field Museum of Natural History, Chicago, has displayed for quite some time, and continues to display, four mask costumes (mounted on naturalistic puppets for realistic impact) collected by Lewis at Awar (see Kaufmann 1993:587, fig. 889). According to emic standards, this approaches an acceptable way of showing masks: as part of a complete outfit worn by a dancer. Such a display is to be preferred above one of wooden masks without costumes. Simet (1976:1-2) with regard to the Tolai

Tubuan society, does not think it right to take one element (the mask) and display it separately from the other elements with which it forms an organic whole: 'Any one of the elements existing by itself has no meaning whatsoever. These elements are: the mask, the society, the rules, the songs and the setting.'

4. In a preliminary statement the reader is alerted that the book contains 'culturally sensitive material'; that is, pictures taken of the construction of mask costumes within an enclosure to prevent the uninitiated from witnessing the proceedings. Thus the responsibility to prevent this information falling into the wrong hands is shifted from the author to the reader. In our opinion, researchers who have recorded sensitive material remain solely responsible and should abstain from publishing it, to avoid the risk of provoking feelings of anger and embarrassment in the culture concerned. As to the filmed version of the proceedings at Birap, the producer adopted a much more cautious and acceptable approach (see note 5). With regard to our field work at Damur, the men in charge of the festival allowed us to take pictures within the sacred enclosure, but made it clear to us that we would not be allowed to publish them. Consequently such pictures are not included in this paper. For the same reason, no pictures are included of men playing the sacred flutes.

5. Of the video film *Singsing Tumbuan (Mask Dance)* three versions were made: a 170-minute version including sensitive material such as the construction of masks within a secluded area and the playing of sacred flutes, acts that are restricted to initiated males – this version is only to be shown in a safeguarded context by authorised institutions such as museums; a 140-minute version that excludes sensitive material to make it suitable for showing to general audiences in Papua New Guinea; and a fifty-minute television version, including sensitive material made unrecognisable by image distortion – the distortion serves as an educational device to make audiences aware of the sensitive and sacred nature of some of the proceedings (Marsha Berman, pers. comm. 1996). There is also a brochure (Berman 1995d) and a booklet giving background information in Dutch (Stichting Ophraeis 1996). An account of this project by Malia Zoghlin, titled *Papua New Guinea: Mask Dance*, may be found on the internet site <http://neog.com/asianow/png/png.html>.

6. The video documents *Singsing Tumbuan Bosmun* (Berman 1990) and *Singsing Tumbuan at Boroi* (Berman 1991) have no subtitles nor spoken English commentary, in contrast to the docu-

mentary video films (Berman 1995a, 1995b) and the television documentary (Berman 1995c).

7.   The Birap performance was recorded on film at the specifc request of the people in charge of the event.

8.   In 1973, one of the authors (Smidt) observed several newly made masks suspended from the rafters inside a ceremonial house at Bosmun village. Once visitors had entered the house, these masks were immediately visible to them, not being hidden in a partitioned-off section. It is surmised that at least some of these masks might have been available for sale, and were therefore made more accessible than the old sacred heirlooms.

9.   In the case referred to, the platform was of modest dimensions and not decorated with woodcarving. Grand-scale and richly ornamented ceremonial houses are known to have existed in the past (cf. Höltker 1966; Fukumotu 1976:figs.20-9; Swadling et al. 1988:figs.172-9; Ruff and Ruff 1990:582-6, figs.13-17).

10.   See also Barlow (1985) on the role of women in Murik trade, Lipset (1985) on aspects of Murik trade, and Lutkehaus (1985) on aspects of Manam trade. For a discussion of trade networks along the north coast, including hypotheses dealing with areal integration, and the outcome of a survey of the Aitape coast, see Terrell and Welsch (1990). For a broad perspective on gift-exchange in Melanesia, including references to Murik, see Gell (1992).

11.   Many more examples can be found in, among others, Tiesler (1969, 1970) and Barlow, Bolton and Lipset (1986).

12.   'Murderers' may not be the appropriate term; perhaps 'killers' is a more neutral alternative. The activities of the 'thieves' not only involved theft of things and food, but also open extortion.

13.   For examples of such a hair basket in use, see Hogbin (1970: ill. on p. 122; 1978: illustration of 'Kawang' between pp. 84 and 85). See also Schmidt (1926:49-54) on various phases of initiation.

14.   In those cases, the lighter colour of that part of the sculpture that used to be covered by the loincloth indicates this item of dress once covered the genitals of the figure.

15.   In more recently made figures, these elements, which used to be rendered in natura, are carved in the wood (personal observation, D. Smidt).

16.   See a mask and additional bark cloth in a photograph taken by Smidt in 1971 and published in Beier and Aris (1975:28, fig. 3).

17.   Some maskers wear a string bag, decorated with shell ornaments, below the wooden mask.

18.   The role played by women in the context of the festival is much greater than the present paper could do justice to. The authors regret that the female perspective is not yet adequately covered. This is due to a male-oriented focus in their research, and the impossibility for male researchers to have as easy access to the female world as they have to the male world.

19.   It is surmised that, in the future, changes in the beliefs and the behaviour surrounding the ancestral spirits will have their bearing on the power and authority of the kukurai, which will also undergo change (cf. Lutkehaus 1990a:307).

20.   The reader should bear in mind that only about one-third of the festival was witnessed by the authors. It is surmised that particular rites must have taken place in their absence, perhaps initiation of boys. There are indications that at least a preliminary ritual heralding a future 'loin-cloth ritual' took place during the festival.

21.   These masks were different from the Kaian masks mentioned above.

22.   Traditional goods, such as pots and food, are still used as 'payment', but Western items – clothes in particular – have also become significant items in these transactions.

23.   A detailed comparison of the festival at Damur and the ceremony at Birap would be of interest but is beyond the scope of this paper. For example, the stylistic differences between the maskers are notable. It might suffice to make some general remarks about the scope of both events. It would seem the Damur presentation constituted a more full-grown festival than the one at Birap, because it lasted much longer (three months), had a larger number of maskers performing (thirty-nine), and included a number of specific rites that took place during the festival but were not recorded at Birap. A major difference concerns the way in which both events came about. In the preliminary discussions of the Damur festival, no outsiders played a role, while at Birap the organizers requested a visual recording to be made. Apparently the short duration of the performance of the maskers (two to three days) and the duration of the total event including preparations (about five weeks) were partly determined by pragmatic considerations arising from consultation between the organizers and the external recorders (van den Berg 1990:1). Three major phases could be discerned: first, the erection of an enclosure around the men's house of the organizing clan, the bringing of the sacred flutes inside the enclosure, the making

of the Mother Mask, and the construction of a house inside the enclosure to store the large masks; second, the construction of the large masks by men, the making of grass skirts and the preparation of food by women, and the initiation of boys, who are bound to remain inside the enclosure for a period of two weeks; and third, the performance of the four large maskers for two to three days (van den Berg 1990:1-3).

24. Considered the male equivalent of menstruation, it is meant to symbolically purify the male from the 'female' blood, which is considered injurious and contaminating.

25. In certain myths it is recounted how such a spirit being changes its outward appearance from human to animal form and vice versa.

26. The Rijksmuseum voor Volkenkunde at Leiden has one panel of this kind in its collections (RMV 5173-5). Field Museum of Natural History, Chicago and the Museum für Völkerkunde, Berlin probably also have such panels.

27. See Gourlay (1975) for general information on distribution, function and symbolic significance of sacred sound-producing instruments in New Guinea.

28. Van den Berg (1992:32) reports that one of the functions of the 'Mother Mask', as it is called at Birap (*Mama Tumbuan* in Melanesian Pidgin), is to enable the younger dancers to practise the dance steps within the enclosure around the ancestral spirit house before performing in public.

29. Behind the scenes there were some arguments about this plan, because the idea was not unanimously applauded. Apparently, some feared there might be repercussions if Kobin moved in the outside world among potential enemies.

30. Cf. Hauser-Schäublin 1984 on similar notions among the Abelam.

31. Compare the scene of an Orokolo *Hevehe* masker surrounded by dancing women called 'A Flock of Mountain Birds' (Williams 1940:plate 51).

32. Because of the dangerous nature of these masks, it was not possible for the authors to take pictures of them while they were in action.

33. There probably is a cargo-cult connotation here; the boat model may refer to a boat loaded with cargo expected to arrive as a gift from the ancestors. In 1973, Smidt saw in a Bosmun ceremonial house a partly-dismantled mask costume that had a large model of a boat, made of plant materials, incorporated in the costume. The boat, named Josep, was positioned above the wooden mask and dominated the whole structure.

34. For an impression of a dancing performance of these masks, see a photograph by Eoe in Swadling et al. (1988:69, plate 254).

35. This payment may be compared with payments for comparable cultural items as reported from neighbouring areas such as Murik Lakes and Beach Arapesh (Barlow, Bolton and Lipset 1986:32). It was also reported that the people of Orindagun/Pariame gave to the people of Murik in exchange for the Simoki dance (including two spirit figures) the following: fourteen pigs, six cartons of beer, one carton of tinned fish, dogs' teeth, nassa shells, four boars' tusks, and K226.40. This dance was staged at Kwekin village during an end-of-mourning ceremony (Barlow, Bolton and Lipset 1986:38). Beer did not feature in the exchanges witnessed at Damur because of the Seventh-Day Adventist ban on liquor. The SDAs are the major religious denomination in the area.

36. The definition referred to reads: 'a periodically recurrent, social occasion in which, through a multiplicity of forms and a series of coordinated events, participate directly or indirectly and to various degrees, all members of a whole community, united by ethnic, linguistic, religious, historical bonds, and sharing a worldview' (Falassi 1987:2).

37. Or 'sacralization' for religious events (Falassi 1987:4).

38. Cf. Williams 1940:372-5 for the 'Slaying of the *Hevehe*'.

14 Sulka masked ceremonies and exchange

Chris Issac and Barry Craig

The Sulka live on the southern shore of Wide Bay in East New Britain Province, Papua New Guinea (fig. 14.1). Their villages are located among the coconut and cacao plantations along the narrow coastal strip at the base of the mountains on which they locate their gardens. Streams tumble out of the mountainous hinterland, which is exploited for its animal and wild plant resources, across the pebble beaches into the deep water of the bay. In the distance to the north-east, the southern end of New Ireland may be seen. Immediately north across the bay is the mountainous territory of the Baining; immediately north of them is the provincial centre of Rabaul,[1] located among the Tolai.

The Sulka speak a non-Austronesian language related to the languages of the Baining and of the peoples of central and southern Bougainville. Their Mengen neighbours along the coast to the south-east share their culture but speak an Austronesian language. Corbin (1990) has provided an overview of the artistic forms of the Sulka on the basis of objects collected and photographs taken between 1900 and 1930, and a review (1996) of continuity and change in these forms. This paper will add to the record of the continuation of the tradition of masked ceremonies into the present.

Masked ceremonies

There are four ceremonies for which the Sulka make *hemlaut* and *susu* masks (figs 14.2 and 14.3):

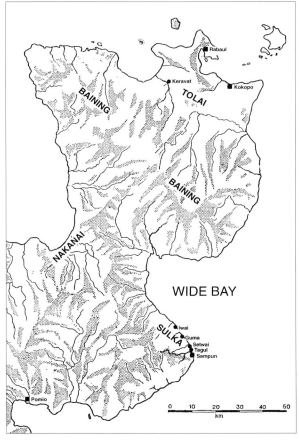

14.1 Map of Sulka area, Wide Bay, East New Britain Province.

14.2 *Hemlaut* mask being painted at Guma village, January 1993. (Photo: B. Craig, courtesy SA Museum.)

- bride-price exchanges;
- initiation of boys by means of circumcision and of girls by the piercing of ears and nasal septum;
- initiation of young men by blackening the teeth before marriage; and
- mourning.

The *keipa* mask (fig. 14.4) is a simple woven vine or cane 'cap' with painted face and a palm-leaf shroud, worn for the purpose of collecting food for the *hemlaut* and *susu* mask-makers, and to exact a physical 'toll' on the beneficiaries of the food exchanges.

The construction and dancing of the masks is an essential complement to the public exchange of food marking these ceremonial occasions. The following description of a wedding ceremony illustrates these exchanges.

A wedding ceremony

Prior to the ceremony, the person who is initiating it must first plan with the person who he will invite to receive his goods; for example, the father of the bridegroom plans with the father of the bride how many gardens will be harvested and how many masks are going to be made, how many pigs and how much bride-price will be needed. As soon as the planning is done, the real work begins.

The bridegroom's father and relatives make two gardens, while the bride's people make one garden. The same applies

14.3 (Top) *Susu* masks dancing at Tagul village, January 1993. (Photo: B. Craig, courtesy SA Museum.)

14.4 (Above) *Keipa* masks whipping recipients of the benefits of the food exchanges, Guma village, January 1993. (Photo: B. Craig, courtesy SA Museum.)

to the *hemlaut* masks – the bridegroom's people should make two masks, while the bride's people make one – and to other bride-wealth exchange items, such as pigs, laplaps (trade cloth) and shell wealth. When the exchange takes place, there must be two lots of food, goods and masks from the bridegroom's people, and one lot from the bride's people. Thus the bridegroom's people invest twice the amount invested by the bride's people.

The bride-price payment feast takes four days. The first day is called *elelotong*, and is a declaration of intention to make the bride-price payment and hold the feast in a particular village.

During the declaration of the feast, the bridegroom will bring his food and pigs to the bride in exchange for hers. The bride's father will pass the exchanged food to the bride's mother, and she will pass it on to her brother (that is, the bride's uncle). The food from the bride will be passed on to the father of the groom, then to his brother (that is, the bridegroom's uncle). Thus the bride-price payments 'follow the name' of bridegroom and bride.[2]

The second day of the feast takes place several days after *elelotong*, to give the bride's and bridegroom's relatives time to harvest their gardens for the feast. When the bride harvests her food she invites the bridegroom's people to come and collect the crops from her garden and carry them to the village where the feast is to be held. Similarly, pigs will be taken from the bride's village to the bridegroom's village. The bridegroom does the same by inviting the bride's relatives to collect his food crops.

The food crops that are harvested from the gardens must not be cleaned up or the tubers cut. The food is taken home and stored on shelves at the back of the village houses.

As soon as the harvest is completed, the next part of the feast takes place, which is called *msirol* ('the cutting of the taro tubers'). The food is taken from the shelves, scraped and cleaned, and placed in heaps in the centre of the village. There will be two heaps from the bridegroom and one from the bride, plus another heap of food that will be cooked the next day for the people who attend the feast. Pigs also will be placed near the heaps of food. There will be dancing by the women only at this stage of the ceremony.

The following day is the third day of the ceremony and is called *elelonpik*. This involves mainly cooking, sharing and eating the food. The bridegroom's relatives bring in the cooked food, including pigs and other meat, for the bride's relatives; the bride's relatives do the same for the bridegroom's relatives.

While this is going on in the village, some men take garden foods and pork to the *haus tumbuan* (Neo-Melanesian: 'mask house'). Here there is another exchange of garden food and meat between the bridegroom's relatives and the bride's relatives. This is when all the men find out who will be dancing the masks the following day. The

persons who share out the food and pork among the men are the ones who will dance the masks. Because there are two different *haus tumbuan* (mask houses), one for the bride's relatives and one for the bridegroom's relatives, the bride's relatives will invite the bridegroom's relatives to their mask house, where they will be given their food and pork, and the young men from the bridegroom's side will share the food. These young men will dance with the mask the next day.

The same process will take place for the bride's relatives, who will be invited to the bridegroom's mask house.

14.5 The *hemlaut* mask 'Bethlehem' being danced at the Guma Catholic mission to commemorate the induction of a Sulka man to the Catholic priesthood, 1982. (Photo: B. Craig, courtesy PNG National Museum & Art Gallery.)

Only initiated men from the sides of groom and bride are allowed into the mask house. All the food brought into the mask house must be eaten there and none taken into the village, otherwise young boys, uninitiated men and women might eat the food and become sick.

In the village, the women will again sing and dance, following which there will be a lot of sharing of cooked food between these two groups of people, the bride's and the bridegroom's. This part of the feast is the preparation for the next day's big event.

The final day of the feast is the main part of the month of feasting and dancing, and is called *palngaem* ('waiting

14.6 The *hemlaut* mask 'Noot' being danced at Tagul, January 1993. (Photo: B. Craig, courtesy SA Museum.)

for this day'). During this day a lot happens; women in the village will be busy cooking while some men will be making palm-leaf shrouds for the masks. Other men will be slaughtering pigs. The food and most of the pigs are cooked, but some pigs are kept alive by both parties for people to take home to their villages as exchange gifts.

After everything is ready, the cooked food and meat is taken out of the earth 'ovens'. Surplus food is distributed among the people who have come to watch the singing and dancing. The women prepare themselves for the dancing. The women have two groups, one for the bride and one for the groom. The bridegroom's women dance first, followed by his mask, which is danced by the man appointed by the bride's relatives; then the bride's women dance, followed by the bride's mask danced by the man appointed by the bridegroom's relatives. Finally, the bridegroom's women dance again, followed by another mask owned by the bridegroom and danced by a man appointed by the bride's relatives. This extra mask is the most important, because the other two balance each other out; this third mask is really a gift to the bride.

When the dances are over, all the cooked food from both sides is taken out and placed in between the heaps of raw food. This is when the exchange between bride and groom takes place. The bride gives her presents to the bridegroom and the bridegroom gives his presents to the bride.

Conclusion

This process of exchanging masks and presents is the same for initiation of boys and girls (including male circumcision, piercing of the ears and nasal septum, and teethblackening) and for mourning. In 1982, when a Sulka man was inducted into the Franciscan priesthood, a masked ceremony took place on the grounds that he was being initiated (into the priesthood), was being 'married' (to the church), and was counted as dead (dead to normal community life). Thus it was entirely appropriate to use the traditional masks for this Christian ceremony (Hill 1982). On that occasion, the *hemlaut* mask named 'Bethlehem' incorporated the figures of Mary, Joseph and two angels kneeling around the baby Jesus in His manger (fig. 14.5).

In January 1993, at the initiation ceremony for older girls witnessed by the authors at Tagul village (Craig 1993, 1995), the main *hemlaut* mask incorporated figures from the traditional story of the brothers Noot (fig. 14.6).

After the ceremonies are completed, the masks are destroyed. Each mask takes several months to make, but is danced for only fifteen minutes or so. To the uninitiated, the mask is the manifestation of a spirit, and such a significant phenomenon is meant to be fleeting. Thus these masks cannot be preserved and displayed in Sulka country. Though permission was given in 1982 to collect and take away the 'Bethlehem' mask to the PNG National Museum, it cannot be displayed there, because it is presumed that uninitiated Sulka could be living in, or might visit, Port Moresby. However, this restriction was not applied to the *hemlaut* purchased by the South Australian Museum in 1993, and that mask (Craig 1993; 1995: fig. 14) is now on display opposite the rare double-headed *hemlaut* obtained by the museum in 1917 from Major H. Balfour Ogilvy (Craig 1995: fig. 15).

Notes

1. Rabaul was devastated by volcanic eruptions in September 1994, and although the hotels and some other functions have been revived there, the administrative centre has been moved to Kokopo. Rabaul's Lakunai airstrip has been abandoned, and the airstrip at Tokua, 20 kilometres distant, is now being used.
2. When a person is born, his or her clan provides a name and so the clan receives the payment of bride-price.

The significance of the *tantanua* dance within the *Verem malagan*

Noah J. Lurang

15

A number of anthropologists have written about *malagan*[1] (see 'Bibliography', Lincoln 1987). They have tried to give their interpretation of the concept as they see it from an outsider's point of view, but because of limited explanations provided by local people, the concept of *malagan* has never been fully understood and explained.

Although quite intricate, *malagan* can be understood if one closely follows the variety of its uses, when it is used, and for what purposes *malagan* masks and sculptures are made. The term *malagan* refers to the mortuary rituals, the masks and sculptures used in those rituals, and the feast during which the *malagan* objects are displayed

I hope this paper on the *Verem* subtradition of *malagan* will help the reader to a better understanding of the *verem malagan* culture as practised on Tabar Islands and mainland New Ireland (fig. 15.1).

The meaning of *malagan*

Malagan can be seen as having deep connections to every Tabar individual's life and status. It adds to an individual's cultural wealth.

- The word *malagan* is given to the sacred objects that are made and displayed during special feasts of remembrance for dead relatives. Most *malagans* are displayed inside special enclosures that women rarely enter.

- It can be used as a singular or plural term referring to a single mask or carving, or to many.

- It is the name given to the sacred practice of making totemic figures and symbols in memory of the deaths of relatives.

- It could also be explained as the medium through which people express their love for their dead relatives.

- You will sometimes hear people refer to a feast as *malagan*. This would mean the sacred objects are displayed, and there is an exchange and sharing of cultural wealth and experiences.

- It is well-known that *malagan* originated in Tabar Islands. The Madar people call these totemic figures and other woven patterns *malaga*. It is believed that the pidgin English word *malagan* originated from the Madar word *malaga*, which means 'elaborately colourful and very powerful'.

Verem malagan – main points

First, *Verem malagan* involves the creation and use of wooden sculptures; wooden masks; and masks constructed from tree fibres and bush vines.

Second, not all the people who own *Verem malagan* use the same *Verem* masks and sculptures; practise the same rituals; or know the same *Verem* songs and addressing calls.

145

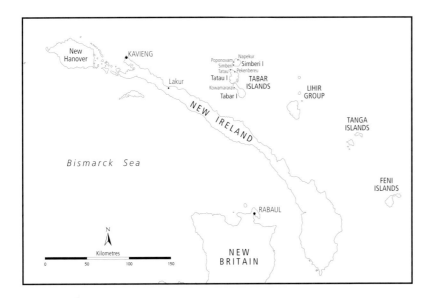

15.1 Map of New Ireland and Tabar Islands.

Third, the terms used in this paper (except *malagan* and *tantanua*) are in the Madar language of the people of the Tabar Islands.

Verem malagan is well-known in Tabar. The term *Verem* covers all types of *vanis* masks, including various *ngeis* and the *tantanua* masks. The masks have specific roles involving dancing, removal of taboos, determining dates for *Verem* feasts, carrying the dead body of *Nguts* (male chief) or *Ngutsu-vevin* (female chief), and various other functions.

Verem also possesses horizontal wooden sculptures called *kobo-kobor,* which feature a row of heads, and vertical sculptures called *ekuar*, which feature full figures.

Not everyone who possesses *Verem malagan* knows and practises the same ritual, or has the same addressing calls (*tatangis*) and *Verem* songs (*paka verem*). Some people possess only one or a couple of masks, with a limited number of songs.

Starting a *Verem malagan* feast

There are several small feasts (fig. 15.2) that take place prior to the final big *malagan* feast. The people start a *Verem* feast just as they do the other *malagans*. *Varam* is the first stage of a *malagan* feast; it is the opening feast that removes all the taboos and allows all the preparatory work to begin.

Varam is followed by the second stage, which is *Chirep*, the collection of materials for making the *malagan* masks and sculptures.

The third stage is *Ba*. During *Ba*, the people indicate the number of pigs that will be slaughtered. They use coconuts (*voturu niu*) to do this. Each clan member puts a coconut in the centre of the village to indicate that he has a pig for the feast, and challenges others to compete with him.

15.2 One of the smaller feasts, preceding the final feast (*Ngabor*). Tatau village, Tabar Islands. Left to right: Nguts Joel Pitsia, Noah Lurang (New Ireland Cultural Officer), and carver Edward Salle. (Photo: Noah Lurang.)

15.3   Nguts Sola Leo, one of the mask makers, getting the team of *ngeis* masks ready. He thinks he has them all under control. Tatau village, Tabar Islands. (Photo: Noah Lurang.)

The fourth stage is *Kendeve mi rongar*, the making of the *vanis* masks. Those who make the *vanis* masks of the subcategory *ngeis* (fig. 15.3) usually first make *Susur-vono*, *Mat-N'na-N'nach* and *Chire-Chirep* to carry out the instructions of the carvers. When the carvers need supplies, they send any of these *vanis* to find and bring the items needed. They collect food, traditional shell money, clothing, cash (kina and toea), cigarettes, tobacco leaves, and so on. When the *vanis* return, the carvers inside the *malagan* enclosure divide the proceeds among themselves. The specific roles of these *vanis* masks are as follows:

- *Susur-vono*: this mask (fig. 15.4) threatens to burn down a house if his appeal for things to take to the carvers in the enclosure is ignored.
- *Mat-N'na-N'nach*: this *vanis* (fig. 15.5) has a similar role to *Susur-vono*, except he just sits and stares into the house he is in front of. If the inhabitants are not quick to attend to his silent plea, he will pretend to cut down the nearest post of the house or attack the front roof of the house.
- *Chire-Chirep*: the role of this mask (fig. 15.6) is to go any garden and harvest food crops for the *malagan* carvers. He is not required to ask permission.

The fifth stage is called *Choka-vono*: During this stage the people proceed with the construction of the *malagan* house in three steps, as follows:

15.4   The *vanis* or *ngeis* called *Susur-vono*; it threatens to burn down houses if the occupants do not provide food. Tatau village, Tabar Islands. (Photo: Noah Lurang.)

- *Tem eii*: the collection of the materials to construct the *malagan* house.
- *Bonto vono*: erecting the framework (*Tsiri-vono*) of the *malagan* house.
- *Choka-vono*: thatching the roof of the *malagan* house.

After this activity the people display traditional shell-money for the payment of the pigs indicated by the number of *voturu-niu* (coconuts) during *Ba*. The people who own *Verem malagan* will then be asked to send their teams of *ngeis* to attempt to spear a coconut hung from a bamboo pole in the middle of the village hosting the *malagan* feast.

This competition determines when the final stage of the feast will be, and which team of *ngeis* will dance the *tantanua* masks at that feast (see below).

While the *ngeis* masks do their part in the village (preceded by a dawn ritual – fig. 15.7), the *Ngeis Niv-Niv* lurk around in the nearby bushes waiting for people who try to run away from the *ngeis* in the village. During this stage of the *malagan* preparations, the women are too frightened to go to the bush to fetch water. This period is called *chur-nda kovo-kovo* ('when empty water bottles gather dust').

During the night, the *ngeis* called *Tono Kuk-kuch* ('the devil who pokes') plays his part. In the old days when there were no lamps, and fire was the only source of light, the *Tono Kuk-kuch* would take advantage of the darkness to enter the houses. He slips into a house and hides under a bed waiting for people to come in. When everyone drops off to sleep he comes out and starts poking them

15.5 (Right) The *vanis* or *ngeis* called *Mat N'na-N'nats* with its basket, in which it puts food collected from the houses. Note the machete in its right hand, with which it attacks the houses of those slow to provide food. Tatau village, Tabar Islands. (Photo: Noah Lurang.)

15.6 (Below) Nguts Joel Pitsia leading the *ngeis* into the village after their performances to receive appreciation fees. The mask *Chire-Chirep* is in the lead, followed by *Bai-i*. Tatau village, Tabar Islands. (Photo: Noah Lurang.)

15.7 (Bottom) A team of *ngeis* lining up on the reef at dawn in readiness for their performance, led by Nguts Joel Pitsia. Tatau village, Tabar Islands. (Photo: Noah Lurang.)

in the ribs. After they all run out of the house, the *Tono Kuk-kuch* leaves and goes to another house or returns to the enclosure.

Other *ngeis* masks are:

- *Baia Kurur*: a mask with big ears, red;
- *Bayang*: a mask with big ears, yellow (Lincoln 1987: fig. 40);
- *Bai-i*: a mask (fig. 15.8) with big round ears, black, which clears taboos on objects or areas owned by the deceased, and is restricted for use in public places;
- *Ngeis Mangeot*: a mask with big round ears, black;
- *Seser*: a mask which uses seashell rattles (*lengleng*).

How *Verem* came into existence

The Tabar people have a legend in song form about how *Verem* came into existence. A group of *Verem vanis*, who were actual people, set out in a canoe to go shark-calling (*tut*):

Sor Cheom (They carry the canoe);
Churan mi Cheom (They push the canoe into the water);
Kesi mi Cheom (They get into the canoe);
Boit i poir-poir (They are in the shallows where seaweed is still visible);
Tou nge won te (They are passing through the part of the reef where they trap fish using stone weirs);
I pot-pot-te (They are before the edge of the reef where the waves break);
Simi Kopokop te (They are at the edge of the reef where the waves break);
Si mi titer-ter-te (Where the slope of the reef begins to drop);
Subu Tupi Mou te (Passing over the sea valleys);
Simi Kichir-Kichir Kotom te (At the beginning of the deep blue ocean);
Simi Raman megeot te (Over the deep ocean where you can no longer see the bottom);
I Rou Leong te (Far out in the open sea);
I pek-te (So far away that they can no longer see the land);
Simi Mou Kap te (They can no longer work out where they are);

15.8 The *vanis* or *ngeis* called *Bai-i*. Tatau village, Tabar Islands. (Photo: Noah Lurang.)

Mi-mur leong a tenga chur worotangi (The storm strikes them);
A teng pot-pot ke mi ngeleu (The wind breaks the canoe into pieces).

At this point the song tells what happened during their struggle until their remains were washed ashore:

One of the *chizko* broke (the piece of wood which holds the outrigger to the canoe);

The other *chizko* broke (the piece of wood which holds the outrigger to the canoe);

One *avarit* (outrigger) broke (joins the canoe hull to the outrigger);

The other *avarit* (outrigger) broke;

The prow carving (*mu-u*) broke;

The stern carving (*mu-u*) broke;

The canoe finally broke into pieces;

The *Verem* (*vanis*) swam and drifted;

Some of them were drowned;

Others were eaten by sharks leaving heads only, which were washed ashore;

All that was left of some of the people were either the heads or limbs;

In some places, whole *vanis* bodies were washed ashore.

On Tatau and Simberi islands of the Tabar group, only the heads were washed ashore, so they now create only the heads of the *vanis*. At Tabar and Mapua Islands of the Tabar group, whole bodies were washed ashore. This is why the complete *vanis* called *Rupu-Mongos* are made there.

On the Tabar Islands the style of *Verem* (*vanis*) is slightly different from that of the mainland of New Ireland in the Nalik, Kara, Noatsi, Madak, Tigak and Lovongai areas.

The major groups of *vanis*

Because of the complexity of the *Verem* (*vanis*) *malagan*, I can give only a few examples. There are many others that need thorough research and recording.

A *vanis* is classified by its origin and what it represents. For example, if a certain part of the *vanis* uses the image of a fish, then the origin of that *vanis* is the sea. Examples of *vanis* originating from the sea are:

- *Mi-chur Tara*: *tara* is red scaly fish with very sharp dorsal fins; it lives under big stones in deep water;
- *Mi-chur Velvelto*: *velvelto* is a stylish flat fish, silver and light yellow, with vertical black stripes;
- *Mi-chur Kurur*: *kurur* is a type of *tara* fish, red with big eyes, which also lives under big stones in deep water;
- *Mi-chur Lep*: *lep* is a type of seabird; and

- *Mi-chur Kenikis*: belongs to the wooden *vanis* and has a representation of a paddle on top of the head.

Other *vanis* come from inland:

- *Mi-chur Silon*: has a carving of a man on top of the mask;
- *Mi-chur Mat-Lala*: represents the morning star; and
- *Mi-chur Keu*: has a representation of a coconut-eating land crab on top.

Mi-chur literally means 'bed' but the word implies 'nest' or 'source' and indicates a grouping of *malagan*.

Summary of the subgroups of *Verem vanis* masks

Vanis is a subgroup of the *Verem malagan* that covers all the masks but mainly refers to the larger wooden masks (fig. 15.9).

Ngeis is a subgroup of *vanis*, and includes *Baii, Bayang, Baia Kurur, Chire-Chirep, Mat-N'na-N'nach, Ngeis Mangeot, Ngeis Niv-Niv, Ngeis Seser, Pii, Susur-vono* and *Tono Kuk-kuch*.

Tantanua (*Sapa*) is another subgroup of *vanis*, and follows on from *ngeis* activity (the spearing of the coconut).

The significance of the *tantanua*[2]

Tantanua (*Sapa* in Madar language) is known as *Man tou bes mi verem*, the dance or dancing mask for the *Verem*

15.9 Nguts Joel Pitsia leads four *vanis* masks at the final feast (*Ngabor*). *Verem* was used as Tatau village is one of the *Aro-verem* or *Mar-ra verem*. (Photo: Noah Lurang.)

malagan. It is perhaps the most interesting of the *vanis* masks in the staging of a *Verem* feast because it is a dance deeply connected with the *Verem* and originated from the team of *ngeis*. *Tantanua* masks are created from wood and tree fibres.

During the *voturu niu* activity, when the people publicly indicate the number of pigs that will be slaughtered, the owner or sponsors of the feast identify which of the *Aro Verem* or *Mar-ra-Verem* (the physical sites of *Verem malagan*) will form a group of *vanis* or *ngeis-sapa* (*tantanua*-to-be) to compete in spearing the coconut hanging from a bamboo pole in the middle of the village.

The villages known as the *Aro Verem* or *Mar-ra Verem* are asked to come group by group to try to spear the hanging coconut. The hitting of the coconut has great significance because it will determine when the feast will be held (the month, and the week of the month). If the coconut is not hit, it will delay the commencement of the feast. The group of *ngeis-sapa* that successfully spears the coconut has the honour of performing the *tantanua* dance for the *Verem malagan* feast.

Ritual addressing calls (*tantangis*)

The ritual addressing calls for the *Verem malagan* differ from place to place, but those who create the same *vanis* would normally use the same ritual calls. The calls go something like this:

> *O Mi-Ngeoch mangeot* (repeat three times)
> *E Vanariu* (repeat three times)
> *E Tarmalo* (repeat three times)
>
> *O E Vanariu* (repeat three times)
> *E Tumelakai* (repeat three times)
> *Mi Variu* (repeat three times)
> *E Pombuamai* (repeat three times)
>
> *O E Vanariu* (repeat three times)
> *E Tumalakai* (repeat three times)
> *Mi Ngeoch mangeot* (repeat three times)

The above are only three of the many varieties of addressing calls for the *Verem malagan*.

Some of the *Verem* sites: *aro verem/ma-ra verem*

See tables 1 to 3, overleaf.

Terms and definitions

Aro verem: The enclosure or sites where the *Verem malagan* was originally introduced and is currently being practised. Also termed *Mar-ra verem*.

Ba: This is the third stage of the series of smaller feasts towards the final big feast, which is called *Ngabor* in the Madar language.

Bai-i: A member of the *vanis* family of masks. It plays a similar role to the *vanis*, clearing up taboos on objects or areas owned by the deceased; it is restricted for use in public places.

Chire-Chirep: This mask's role is to collect food from gardens for the *malagan* carvers. It is not required to ask permission of the gardens' owners before it does this.

Chizko: The poles that join the outrigger to the canoe.

Ekuar: A vertical pole carved with *malagan* figures.

Kobo-Kobor: A horizontal wooden slab or pole carved with *malagan* figures.

Madar: There are three meanings in the language of Tabar:
1. Literally, it means a male person from Tabar Islands.
2. It is also a general term for people from Tabar, and is used when addressing someone who comes from those islands.
3. It refers to the language spoken by the people of Tabar.

Malaga: In the Madar language of Tabar, this term refers to:
- Something admirable, attractive, colourful, and powerful in its appearance, be it wooden carving or hand-woven tree fibres and bush vines.
- An object used during memorial feasts for dead relatives.
- Something that, in its deeper cultural sense, has a very close connection with the life and status of all Tabar persons.

TABLE 1: Some *Verem* sites of Simberi Island

Site name	*Vuna verem* (owner)	*Matabu* (clan of owner)
1. Saba (Simberi)	Tobem and Kuvil (brothers)	Saramangis
2. Lava (Simberi)	Tamun and Lubor (brothers)	Pakila
3. Levenru (Simberi)	Wonono and Sepeli (brothers)	Tupinavono
4. Satav (Lavokulep)	Seten	Keis
5. Pekin-mi-rem (Rubis, Poponovam)	Peket	Saramangis
6. Samat (Napekur)	Kororou Kongkong	Bausevokou
7. Bodar (Kai-Koen)	Sevei and Borom (brothers)	Marantom
8. Bekou	Karke and Pusong (brother and sister)	Rumarik

TABLE 2: Some *Verem* sites of Tatau Island

Site name	*Vuna verem* (owner)	*Matabu* (clan of owner)
1. Tumlum (Marai)	Bonga	Sik-Kor
2. Tauvoi (Tatau)	Aisoli Salin and Pitsia Joel	Saramangis/Kuk
3. Lava	Lovan	Obon
4. Sos	Timi	Tavia
5. Pekenbereu	Levi	Lavakulep
6. Butamut (Mapua)	Karol Mole	Larongo
7. Chibar (Kapatiran, Mapua)	Makou	Sicheom
8. Puek Monmon (Mapua)	Kalu	Rumarik

TABLE 3: Some *Verem* sites of Tabar Island

Site name	*Vuna verem* (owner)	*Matabu* (clan of owner)
1. Pichu (Teripats)	Nalo	Tirapats
2. Tesin (Rakupo)	Makeu (Makou)	Rakupo
3. Sinamin (Mapua)	Francis Kaletau (Carol)	Kokaip
4. Matlik	Sangal	Sicheom
5. Banesa	Galen (Lungisa)	Unduram
6. Koir-Koir Por (old site for the *Verem* that settled at Matlik)	Not known	Sicheom

Plates 1 and 2 *Täyoer* performed on the *malaal* of the Yap Women's Association on 16 August 1992. All the dancers are 'skilled' because their movements are *taqreeb* (unified). (See Chapter 1.)

Plate 3 Masker performing in the context of the end-of-mourning festival at Damur village, Gamei, Lower Ramu area, Papua New Guinea. In the background, part of the fence around the sacred enclosure with its main entrance. 20 April 1979. (Photo: Dirk Smidt.) (See Chapter 13.)

Plate 4 Detail of the central element of a masker: the wooden mask and its decoration of traditional ornaments (boars' tusks, dogs' teeth, shell plates, trimmed feathers) and imported elements (buttons, porcelain rings and paper snippets). Major ornaments are the boars' tusks indicating the chiefly rank of the owner of the mask. Damur, 10 June 1979. (Photo: Dirk Smidt.) (See Chapter 13.)

Plate 5 Kabé, the owner of a mask from Kaian village, hangs a boar-tusk ornament around the neck of Andrew, son of Tom Kambek Kumi. As initiator of the end-of-mourning festival, the latter commissioned the mask to come to Damur to perform. The ornament serves as a token of proof – to be shown as a historical document to later generations – that a pig was killed to pay for the performances of the mask at Damur village. Note the boar's tusk ornaments worn as chiefly symbols on the forehead of the mask, and the row of imitation shell plates, made of plastic, attached to a string bag. Damur, 20 June 1979. (Photo: Dirk Smidt.) (See Chapter 13.)

Plate 6 (Above) Oro Chief with tapa loincloth and *bilum*. (See Chapter 19.)

Plate 7 (Above right) Artist Wendi Choulai in Port Moresby, 1987. (See Chapter 19.)

Plate 8 (Right) Skirt design by Wendi Choulai. (See Chapter 19.)

Malagan: A pidgin English name for *malaga* that refers to:
- The sacred practice deeply connected to the life of an individual Tabar person.
- The sacred objects used in memorial feasts for dead relatives.
- The feasts during which the sacred objects are displayed.

Mat N'na-N'nach: The mask whose role is to collect food for *malagan* carvers. It sits at the doorway of a house from which it wishes to collect things, and stares at its occupants until they hand something over.

Ngabor: The final feast day when a mass slaughtering of pigs takes place, and pig meat and garden food are shared. People return to their homes soon after.

Ngeis: Members of the *vanis* family of masks; they play a minor role as 'security' for the dancing *vanis* mask, acting as scouts or warriors for the dancing *vanis*. The various types of *ngeis* also have other functions relating to the processes of the *malagan* ceremonials.

Ngeis Niv-Niv: Its role is to hang around in the bushes at the outskirts of the village where a *Verem* feast is being staged. If people go into the bush to collect food or fetch water, the *Ngeis Niv-Niv* chases them back into the village. This is the period termed *Chur-nda kovo-kovo*, 'when empty water bottles gather dust'.

Nguts: A male 'chief'.

Ngutsu-vevin: A female 'chief'.

Paka Verem: Special *malaga* songs that are sung during the *Verem malaga* feast. Each type of *malagan* has its own songs that are sung to it.

pidgin: One of the two lingua francas of Papua New Guinea. The other is Motu, which is spoken mainly in Papua.

Pii: A deaf *ngeis* or *vanis*, which is regarded as rebellious and dangerous. It throws stones and lemons at people.

Sapa: In the Madar language, refers to *tantanua*.

Susur-vono: This *ngeis* mask's role is to collect food (cooked or uncooked) for the *malagan* carvers. It threatens to burn down people's houses if they ignore its appeal for food.

Tantanua: The pidgin term for *sapa* in Madar language (see Clay, in Lincoln 1987:63-73). It refers to a particular type of wooden mask and its accompanying dance in the category of *Verem malagan*. It is a dance closely connected to the making of the *Verem malagan* feast.

Tatangis: The name for the ritual calls that address the spirits of the masks of particular *Verem malagan*.

Tono Kuk-kuch: Literally, 'the devil who pokes'. This *ngeis* goes into houses when people are not around, usually in the early hours of the night. It hides under a bed and waits until everyone comes into the house to sleep. Just as people are about to go into deep sleep, the devil goes about poking them in the ribs, or even tries to suffocate them.

Tut: Shark catching using the traditional technique, which involves the use of a rattle to call the shark, and a noose with a wooden, propeller-like float to snare it.

Vanis: Specifically refers to the major group of large carved wooden *malagan* masks that people wear. It is sometimes used as a general name for the family of masks in the *Verem malagan* that includes the *ngeis*. The main role of the *vanis* is to dance. After it has danced, it is then retired to its house for public viewing.

Varam: The first stage of a *malagan* feast. It is an opening feast that removes all the taboos and allows all the preparatory work to begin.

Verem: The 'Big Name' under which most *malagan* masks come. These masks are worn, and each type has a specific purpose within the context of *malagan* feasts.

Vuna: The major owner of *Verem malagan*.

Vuna verem: A *Nguts* who has been initiated into the *Verem malagan* soon after birth.

Notes

1. *Malagan* is a pidgin English term equivalent to *malaga* in the Madar language of the islands of Tabar. It is also spelt *malangan* and *malanggan*.

2. For examples of *tantanua* masks, see Helfrich (1973:20-6, and Abb. 1-45).

16 Taxonomic structure and typology in the *malagan* ritual art tradition of Tabar, New Ireland

Michael Gunn

With their relatively standardised iconographic elements, their broad range of variation of overall design, and the large numbers of examples now in museum collections all over the world, *malagan*[1] art works from northern New Ireland would appear to be a prime candidate for a semiotic study.[2] Material equivalents to phonemes and morphemes can be identified in the elements of an iconographic vocabulary present in the painted and the sculpted designs, and in the relationships between the various elements that can be seen to form coherent patterns.

But when the *malagan* owners of the Tabar Islands were asked about the 'meaning' of the various elements of the iconic vocabulary,[3] or of various combinations of these elements, these owners insisted that the 'meaning' of *malagan* was not to be found in an explication of the iconography of the various elements. Instead, they said, the style elements found within the *malagan* art tradition today are reproductions of designs that were first created many generations ago. The original context has long been forgotten, and although the images are still used, their original symbolic content is lost. These *malagan* owners told me that any patterns I identified, either within the artistic tradition of *malagan* or in the use of the various designs, were most likely the products of a Western analytical process, and were not considered to have any basis in reality on Tabar. Instead, they emphasised to me that the 'meaning'

of any particular *malagan* is 'that this person, as leader of this lineage, owns this particular *malagan*'.

To concentrate my mind further along the lines they defined, a number of Tabar leaders asked me to develop an understanding of *malagan* that would be applicable to them as owners and users of the tradition. So, rather than developing a structural or other paradigm to account for perceived relations between categories and arriving at an entirely artificial resolution that would be of interest only to Western anthropologists, I began to document the extent and distribution of the ownership of *malagan* on Tabar, and to record the context of *malagan* ritual and associated production of sculpture.[4]

Ownership of *malagan*

Ownership of *malagan* on Tabar is not merely the result of possession of a sculptural object, for it involves becoming a source of the ritual world of Tabar. Ownership of *malagan* rights is at the nucleus of *malagan*. Without ownership of *malagan*, or access to ownership, there is no tangible means of honouring dead affines except by erecting a gravestone symbol in lieu of the display of a *malagan* sculpture. And on Tabar a person who does not honour dead affines is a 'rubbish man'.

This social context of *malagan* ritual outlines that the sculptural elements of *malagan* do not operate as words do, carrying implicit meanings, but instead bring with them a history of ownership and patterns of descent. They carry with them very powerful connotations of obligation, indebtedness, sacrifice, love and affiliation. They carry with them the commitments of the bonds of marriage.

Totemism and malagan

A *malagan* image, the primary focus of *malagan* activity, is often mistakenly understood by outsiders to be either an image of the dead person or an image of the spirit of the dead.[5] On Tabar a *malagan* image is understood to originate from the totemic life force that is responsible also for the creation of clanspeople, totemic sharks, and other totemic animals. As such, a *malagan* image is specifically linked to a clan, for a *malagan* sculpture is the material manifestation of an idea of the clan's totemic life force.[6]

To explain to me the concept of a *tadar* life force, people often used the image that a *tadar* is like the rootstock or bole of a tree – that vital part of a tree from which everything grows, the trunk and branches upwards, the roots downwards. As the productive bole, the *tadar* is the mother of all entities that spring from it. These entities can include totemic sharks, other subsidiary totems, the clan, the people living in it, the *malagans* belonging to it. The *tadar* enables these entities to exist in the same way that the life force of a tree enables the branches and leaves to live. Each person on Tabar is understood to be part of one of the *tadar* totemic life forces, for a *tadar* life force manifests itself as a human embryo that becomes a person. When a person dies, the life force is retained by the *tadar* in the same way life is retained by a tree when a dead leaf drops off.

A person's movement from village to village or region to region is understood to be a movement of the totem. When a person settles in a new village and confirms this settlement by negotiating for land-use rights, then the totem is understood to have taken up a new location. As a consequence, the reef in some villages may be owned by the totemic shark of one clan, but the land behind that reef may belong to the totem of another people. The people's relationship to the land is complex and multilayered, and it is not the purpose of this paper to explore this aspect of Tabar life. Very briefly: land on Tabar is owned by individuals as representatives of lineages; these lineages are aspects of the *tadar* totems; lineage land boundaries are delineated by secondary totems; land transactions take place at *malagan* ceremonies.

A wooden *Marumarua malagan* figure is a strictly controlled material representation of an image or idea of the totemic life force that is understood to give life to people and other beings. At *malagan* ceremonies, it represents the bonds of marriage and kinship that link the various totems.

Malagan sculptures are understood by the people of Tabar to be merely wooden pictures, and are not considered 'active' in any way. All of the sculptors and most of the *malagan* owners of Tabar were emphatic that *malagan* sculptures are merely pieces of carved wood, and that the power associated or attributed to them comes from people. In this view, a *malagan* sculpture is not a 'spirit image' in the sense of being a wooden image which somehow contains a 'spirit'. Nor is a *malagan* an 'ancestor figure' in the sense of representing and maintaining a link with some primal ancestor, human or otherwise. A *malagan* sculpture should be understood to be a picture of an idea of the totemic life force of a particular clan, rather than a sculpture of a dead person.

Malagan *ownership and the fragmentation of a ritual tradition*

The nucleus of all *malagan* activity is contained in the rights to produce specific *malagan* sculpture. These rights are named, are subject to ownership, and include a number of other cultural references. The manifestation of these rights in wooden or woven sculpture is undertaken by a *tunumar*, who is usually, but not always, a professional artist.

It is important to note that the rights to all *malagan* designs are enforced by traditional law. If any man counterfeits a *malagan* owned by another man, then he commits a major offence and is liable to attack through the local courts, as well as by public accusation and sorcery. Every *malagan* is owned by someone, and each owner receives the rights to each specific *malagan*, in public, during a *malagan* ceremony. Much care is taken not to infringe the designs owned by another man or lineage, and *malagan* owners try to ensure that the sculptors make an exact manifestation of the *malagan* image – as far as they can remember.

A person may receive the sculptural rights to a particular *malagan* when he is as young as seven or eight years old and may first use these rights some decades later, after he has amassed wealth and influence enough to honour his affines through a *malagan* ceremony. To manifest his sculptural rights, the owner must try to remember what the *malagan* looked like, and in this process of recollection he usually has the sculptor with him to advise and to reconstruct the image. During this process of reconstructing an owner's sculptural rights, the artistic representation of *malagan* undergoes stylistic change, for even though the finished product is meant to be identical to the previous manifestation of decades ago, the sculptor and the owner will be influenced by the hundreds of *malagan* sculptures that they would have seen displayed at *malagan* ceremonies in the interim.

Malagan ownership falls into more patterns than mere presence or absence of the rights to produce sculpture, for the process of transferring *malagan* from one generation to the next over a considerable period of time has produced a distinct fragmentation pattern in the overall tradition of *malagan*. This fragmentation pattern has remained highly organised on Tabar, and can be identified within the 'Big-Name' subtraditions of *malagan*. Although these Big-Names are also found on the mainland of northern New Ireland, it is not yet clear whether the same degree of coherency has been achieved there. Tabar is generally understood by most New Irelanders to have been the source of most *malagan* traditions.

On Tabar a *malagan* sculpture is always considered primarily within the context of its Big-Name, from which it is inseparable. Every *malagan* is part of a Big-Name, just as every person is part of a totemic life force. No sculpture within the *malagan* ritual world of Tabar is known as just a '*malagan*'.

The sculptural element that can be considered the primary or basic unit of *malagan* ownership is called *malaga*.

On Tabar a *malaga* is generally an image that had its artistic origins in the shape of a human or animal life form, although many other types have also been recorded. A *malagan* art work will consist of at least one *malaga*, but may have ten or more *malaga* within it, depending upon the complexity of the image.

At least 450 identified *malagan* names are found today within twenty-one Big-Name subtraditions on Tabar,[7] and judging from the sketchy record left by early researchers[8] it is probable that many more *malagan* rights existed in the 19th century than are found today. The total number of *malagan* sculptural rights in any one subtradition is not known, for although the rights to some of the Big-Names are held by only one or two people, other Big-Names may be owned by tens or even hundreds of people, if mainland New Ireland owners are included. From my record on Tabar, the number of *malagan* sculptural rights and owners in the Big-Name subtraditions varied from one *malagan* in *Karavas* (with 1 owner), through to thirty-four *malagan* names in *Madas* (forty-six owners), forty-six in *Malagacak* (fifty-two owners), and seventy-six in *Verem* (forty-seven owners).[9] The relationship between the number of *malagan* owners and the number of *malagan* names is a product of two opposing factors: a person may own the rights to ten or twelve *malagans* within a single Big-Name subtradition; and many people may share in the ownership of specific sculptural rights. These two factors operate together to produce a balance between owners sharing rights with other owners, and owners accumulating rights.

The number of named *malagan* sculptural rights a person will own may depend upon whether the owner is a *vuna* source of *malagan* (repository of the clan's stock of *malagan* rights), or a minor owner. An owner who is a *vuna* source of *malagan* may own the rights to ten or more *malagan* names from several subgroupings, comprising generic and specific sculptural names. A minor *malagan* owner would be more likely to own the rights to only one or two generic sculptures within one subgrouping of a Big-Name.

Transmission of *malagan* rights within the clan is the accepted mode for transferring a clan's core *malagans*, those that are central to the identity of the lineage. These central clan *malagans* are transferred in clan-owned or individual-owned 'strings' (*tabataba*) or transfer groupings of *malagan*, and the bond these *malagans* have with the clan is termed *mem*. *Tabataba* 'strings' form the basic structural groupings for the transference of *malagan* ownership from one generation to the next. All *malagans* that are owned by the clan are identified and transferred within the structure of these groupings.

When the rights to *malagan* are transferred from one generation to the next, the *tabataba* transfer groupings become important, for it is at this level that the rights to produce individual items of *malagan* sculpture are located, and it is this transference of *malagan* rights that results in the production of *malagan* sculpture.

A number of Tabar people said that many *malagan* rights had their origin when a new lineage was formed at a different location. To mark this genesis and to provide the new lineage with a ritual identity, a new *malagan* would have been created from within a Big-Name owned by the founding clan, and this new *malagan* formed the nucleus of a new *tabataba* transfer grouping of *malagan* owned by the new lineage.

If a woman gives birth outside her clan land, then she and her child take a new lineage name and identity. Part of the identity of a lineage is associated with the *malagan* owned by that lineage, and the character of that *malagan* may take on an aspect of the lineage's new identity. To clarify by way of example, Masol of Sodir village (west Simberi Island) belongs to the lineage Tavia. This lineage began when a woman in Carameges clan gave birth to her child outside clan land at a place where two streams merged. 'Tavia' means 'turbulent water'. The source *malagan* of Tavia lineage is a *Kobokobor* (foundation *malagan*) of the saltwater branch of the *Madas malagan* group. Masol said this *Kobokobor* was specific to Tavia lineage and associated with the origin of the lineage beside the turbulent water.

As transfer groupings are linked to the development of lineages, and the consequent movement and development of the associated totems, so Big-Name subtraditions are comprised of transfer groupings of *malagan*. It is apparent that the development of *malagan* is intrinsically linked to the organic development of lineages and to the associated development of totems. Equally, the system of classification used on Tabar to organise the various *malagan* rights is based primarily on this organic system of *malagan*'s development. At the basis of this organisation are the rights to own, produce, use, and transfer *malagan* ritual and individual *malagan* items of sculpture. In this view, Big-Name subtraditions originated as transfer groupings that have gradually diverged from each other to the extent that today they are recognised as independent but related subtraditions. In this model, the entire structure of *malagan* can be seen to have been shaped by this process of transferring *malagan* from one generation to the next, by the need to keep *malagan* coherent yet to enable it to fulfil its functions and meet its own internal demands.

When considered as a whole, *malagan* is a highly organised tradition. All *malagan* sculpture is located within the context of one or another of the Big-Name subtraditions, and through the medium of the Big-Name subtraditions *malagan* can unite ritual participants from different clans and different regions on Tabar and northern New Ireland.

More importantly, *malagan* ownership involves the rights to display and consolidate delicate affinal links, for the ritual rights allow and enable a person to pay attention to that most fragile of links between kin groups – marriage. *Malagan* is primarily concerned with the maintenance and development of links between affinal clans by honouring the dead in the lineage of the marriage partner. Each *malagan* sculpture that is displayed represents an affinal link, a bond between a man and his wife's and children's people. These are important political links, for they are the connections of alliance and security, and it is for this reason that *malagan* is the key to political stability on Tabar.

Description and partial analysis of the *Madas* Big-Name subtradition of Tabar

Malagan Big-Name subtraditions are distinguished from each other by their names, their characters, the history of use and ownership of the various subbranches of each grouping, and by all the unique aspects of each *malagan* that are associated with the production, display and transference of sculpture. Within each Big-Name subtradition there are a number of distinct subclasses of named *malagan* sculpture. Some names refer to major subgroupings, other names refer to generic types, which may be either sculptural or functional types of *malagan*. Around 60 per cent of *malagan* sculptural names are specific and refer to one particular sculptural realisation in wood.[10] In addition to the wooden sculptural artefacts that end up in museums around the world, the Big-Name subtraditions of *malagan* also include ritual sites, ownership chants, songs, ritual behaviour, and display houses.

The following description of the *Madas* Big-Name *malagan* subtradition is intended more to illustrate the complexity of *malagan* on Tabar than to attempt to define *malagan* through example. It should be noted that this is not a full description of all *Madas* components on Tabar, but merely a list of those *malagans* I recorded from informants. *Madas* is just one of at least twenty-one subtraditions of *malagan* on Tabar.[11]

Malagan *ritual sites*

All *malagan* activity is directed toward an enclosed ritual site (*aro*), and usually takes place within the stone-walled or bamboo-walled confines of these enclosures (fig. 16.1). These ritual sites also serve as graveyards and as focal points for men's activity. A *malagan* owner is buried in the ritual site of his main *malagan* (the one he received first as a child), and this graveyard is generally used by all his matri-clan.

Each ritual site is specific to one Big-Name subtradition, and these ritual sites are maintained as separate enclosures, even if all the clan owners of one particular *malagan* grouping have died out. Unlike totemic sites, *malagan* ritual sites do not appear to accompany the migrations of human owners to new locations. But because it appears that most, if not all, *malagan* Big-Name subtraditions have several ritual sites on Tabar, it is apparent that there must be some as yet undocumented mechanism for developing a *malagan* ritual site at a new location. In the course of my field work I recorded a total of fifty-two *malagan* ritual sites on Tabar, and there are undoubtedly many more

around old village sites. Seven of these sites belonged to *Madas malagan*.

Character of the Madas *Big-Name subtradition*

Judging from its distribution, *Madas* as a name appears to have been used in some very old traditions that predate the *malagan* traditions, for it is found not only throughout New Ireland, but also from non-Austronesian groups in East New Britain. George Corbin recorded from the Central Baining (a Papuan language group) of the Gazelle Peninsula of East New Britain the names *mendas*, or *mandas*, referring to specific masks used in daytime dancing and 'dedicated to female fertility, mourning of the dead, and the celebration of major community events' (Corbin 1979:177). From the *malagan* traditions, Walden in 1907-09 (Walden and Nevermann 1940:24) recorded *mandas* and *mandas si tanua* at Teripats village, north-west Big Tabar Island. Wilkinson in 1970 and 1971 (1978:229) recorded the *malagan* name *Mandeis* at Tatau village. From the mainland of New Ireland, Augustin Krämer (1925:73) recorded *mandas* from Hamba (Notsi region), and Edgar Walden (Walden and Nevermann 1940:24) recorded the same name from Nangama village (Kuot-Panaras region).

16.1 *Malagan* ritual site belonging to *Valik* Big-Name subtradition. *Malagan* owner Songis Lamot (centre) is consulting with a colleague on a mock-up display of a *malagan* snake *simara* belonging to the *Lunet* Big-Name subtradition. Lakavil hamlet, Tatau village, north Tatau Island. (Photo: NGE 1982-11-23.)

In 1983, during a *malagan* ceremony at Panamafei village, in the west-coast Kara-speaking area of northern New Ireland, I recorded *Mendis* as the 'small name' for a *malagan* also termed *Lasisi* (the name of the figure), *Lekeu* (the 'baptised name'), and *Mandasim* (its Big-Name subtradition).

Madas has a strong theme of sexual intercourse, centring around the incest taboo. Current *Madas malagan* activity includes a number of subtle references to incest, or to sex in general. For example, when the Big-Name *malagan Madas* is transferred from one generation to the next, the ritual leader must dance with pigs' bones (*ciribor*) tied to his genitalia, and according to one informant these bones should be tied to the genitalia by the wife's sister. A number of the songs of *Madas* refer to incest, and previous initiation practices are reputed to have involved incestuous activity between a brother and sister, which was terminated by their death through spearing.

Many aspects of *Madas*, such as the 'wild dog' *mi kupuinmucgur*, which is used with fire, spears and bullroarers to 'kill' a dead man's spirit during the night prior to a burial, are today considered by Tabar Christians to be 'no good'. Of all *malagan* funerary practices that I witnessed, *Madas* activities produced the most emotion among people, many of whom would break into weeping during the singing of *Madas* songs.

In a myth that I recorded in Maragon village (west Simberi Island), a *Madas malagan* ceremony was used as a form of reciprocity carried out by the nomadic sea-clan Keis when staying on the beaches and using the land of the landowning bush-clan called Carameges. Periodically, Keis, to compensate for land use, would organise a *malagan* ceremony for the dead in Carameges. After a series of marriages, Carameges were the affines of Keis, so the *malagan* ceremonies were organised for the landowning affinal dead. That *Madas* also deals with incest may not be entirely coincidental. A ritual that punishes incest also promotes cooperation between affinal clans.

Ownership chants

Taŋtaŋias (*taŋtaŋis, taŋtaŋiasa, tarataraŋias, tataŋias, tataŋis*) ownership chants are called out in public by *malagan*

16.2 Young *malagan* owner standing in front of the framework for a 7-metre-tall *malagan* display house from the *Madassitanua* subgrouping of *Madas*. Entire tree trunks are used in many types of display house, the roots alternating with black and yellow spirally striped poles. Pekinberiu village, north-east Tatau Island. (Photo: NGE 1984-11-4.)

owners or their representatives whenever true *malagan* activity takes place. *Taŋtaŋias* ownership chants are one of the determining marks of *malagan* activity: if ritual activity does not include a calling of the ownership chant then it is not *malagan*. A person will only call out an ownership chant for a Big-Name *malagan* to which he belongs; even in private conversation a person will not recite the chant for a *malagan* to which he does not own the rights.

16.3 Ownership chant called out in public before entering the *malagan* ritual site. Tatau village, north Tatau Island. (Photo: NGE 1984-16-9.)

Ownership chants are called out during any activity that involves the use of *malagan* rights (*ciribor*), such as the right to build a certain style of *malagan* house (fig. 16.2), the right to roof the *malagan* house, the right to construct and exhibit specific *malagan* sculpture, the rights to organise particular aspects of funerary behaviour. For example, when ceremonially bringing *malagan* material through the village and into a *malagan* ritual site, the ownership chant for that *malagan* will be called out in the village square by the owners when the procession has stopped at the ritual site entrance (fig. 16.3). These chants are also called out when *malagan* sculpture is placed in a *malagan* display house.

A *taŋtaŋias* ownership chant consists of three to five phrases, each phrase repeated three or more times, called out in front of all the viewers of *malagan* activity, and accompanied by the owner throwing a piece of betel nut onto the ground as each chant is called. Sometimes a chant phrase is the name of a previous *malagan* originator, sometimes it is a reference to an aspect of the character of the *malagan*. Often the meaning of a chant phrase has been lost in time or distance from the original language. Sometimes the chant as a whole may differ under some circumstances; for example, it may be shorter when it is called out at a *malagan* ceremony that is taboo to women.

Each Big-Name subtradition draws upon a repertoire of chant phrases, and each of the transference groupings

(*tabataba*) of *malagan* uses two to five of these phrases. Each chant is specific to a transfer grouping, which is in turn part of a Big-Name subtradition. Ownership chants used for the various Big-Name subtraditions are quite different from each other.[12]

As an example, the following ownership chant phrases were recorded during ceremonial activity involving the *Madas* Big-Name subtradition from seven different *malagan* owners on nine occasions:

- *vuaset*: a name also recorded as a *malagan* figure in the *Madassiteno* and *Madassiut* subgroupings; this phrase was found in six of nine chants recorded.
- *udu*: means 'sago' a reference to the *Da malagan* (see below), which was previously worked on top of the sago tree; this phrase was found in seven of nine chants recorded.
- *keskesbor*: means 'one pig for each section of the sequence of transferral of ownership of *malagan*'; this phrase was found in seven of nine chants recorded.
- *pitmadas*: 'penis', associated with references to incest; this phrase was found in eight of nine chants recorded.
- *a pit mere*: other references to this name were not found – it is possibly a dialect variant for 'red penis'; this phrase was found in one of nine chants recorded.
- *ma pit manget*: 'black penis'; this phrase was found in one of nine chants recorded.
- *madas pakapaka un*: a reference to the sago thatching leaves of the *Madas malagan* display house; also recorded as a reference to the *tabataba* ancestral lineage of the *Madassiut malagan* subgrouping in *Madas*.
- *manibo madas ibo*: means 'women cannot feast, men only'; this phrase was found in one of nine chants recorded.
- *manibo madassiubi*: when called out as part of *taŋtaŋias* of Madas Madassiro *malagan* the name means all *Madas malagans* – with chicken feathers all around the outline; also recorded as a

malagan type of *Malagacak*, where it is referred to as a *Marumarua* figure sculpture, but also as a stick for beating the *garamut*; this phrase was found in two of nine chants recorded.

Ownership Patterns

In total I recorded the names of 215 *malagan* owners (tweny-five of them were women) within 137 lineages among the 2500 people living on Tabar in 1982-84. The *Madas* subtradition appears to be predominantly the property of *Keis* lineages living on Simberi Island. Of the forty-six *Madas* owners I recorded in twenty-one different villages (eighteen owners on Simberi Island, fifteen on Tatau, seven on Mapua, six on Big Tabar Island), fifteen belonged to *Keis* lineages, and the other thirty-one owners were distributed throughout twenty-two other clans or lineages. None of the six sculptors known to have made *Madas malagan* art works belonged to *Keis* clan, although three of these artists owned rights to *Madas*.

Malagan *names*

A total of fifty-six separate descriptions were recorded for twenty-nine *malagan* names in *Madas*. They comprised:
- major subgrouping names: *Madas, Madassiteno, Madassiro, Madassiut*;
- generic sculptural names: *Eikuar, Kobokobor, Kovkov, Marumarua, Kupkup ci malaga*;
- specific sculptural names: *Belel, Cikopic, Curuda, Curudamas, Curudasar, Curudavovo, Curuvuaset, Da, Damas, Dasar, Davovo, Eiboŋamas, Kovacikopic, Madasi, Potoviso, Vuaset*;
- masks: *Tanua, Tonomatmerik, Vudida*;
- display platform: *kokoi*.

Major subgroupings within Madas

The classification of the named *malagans* within *Madas* is dominated by four subdivisions:
- *Madas* proper;
- *Madassiteno* (*Madas* of the life force);

- *Madassiro* (*Madas* of the sea);
- *Madassiut* (*Madas* of the bush).

The nature of these subdivisions is not yet clear to me, for there are a number of specific *aro* ritual geographic sites for each of these four subdivisions, and each of these four groupings has its own form of ritual behaviour. Yet all four share the same or similar ownership chants, and occur as a group in a number of different transference groupings. According to one informant the subgrouping *Madassiut* broke from *Madassiro*, with the implication that *Madassiro* preceded *Madassiut*. This informant, who received *Madassiteno* from his mother's brother and *Madas* from his mother's father, treated these two subgroupings as quite different and said that *Madassiteno* belonged only to *Keis* (his mother's brother's clan) whereas *Madas* belonged to all men.

Madas *proper*: Although *Madas* (*Madas, Mandas, Medis, Mendes,* or *Mendis*) is the parent grouping, *Madas* was also considered to be one of the subgroupings of the Big-Name subtradition by some informants. It was not until the end of my second period of field work on Tabar that I became aware that this taxonomic subtlety was not a misunderstanding on my part, but was in accordance with the general taxonomic system of classification used on Tabar. So a number of *malagan* items that I recorded as belonging to *Madas* may belong to the subgrouping *Madas*, or may belong to the subtradition *Madas*.

Madassiteno: The *Madassiteno* (*Mandasetno, Mandassitano, Mandassiteno, Mandassitanua, Mansetno, Mansitano,* or *Mansiteno*) subgrouping of *Madas* is associated with a dead man's spirit (*tanua*) and 'bush' in origin or orientation. *Madassiteno* differs from the other subgroupings of *Madas* in a number of significant ways. *Madassiteno* is considered to be stronger and to have more power than *Madassiro*. *Madassiteno* has some unique performances; for example, men use wooden hornbill shapes in their mouths to 'eat' *tinibor* ritualised pig's belly. Within *Madassiteno* is performed the dance *tirimadas*, where men and women fasten *ciribor* (pig's bones) to their genitals and dance naked. *Madassiteno* apparently has a type of evil power termed *pitpit*; a person with the source of this power is called *vanavanar*. *Madassiteno* has at least one ritual site on Tabar – at Sunagaramut, which is located at Revar village site above Tupinmida village (west Tatau Island).

Six examples of a *Madassiteno* figure in *Madas* were recorded from a total of six owners (some owners owned more than one example):

1. a seated *Madassiteno* figure with arms raised; has a bark-cloth head (two owners recorded);
2. a seated *Madassiteno* figure with arms raised; has a wooden head and a sago-trunk body (one owner recorded);
3. a standing *Madassiteno* figure wearing a woman's cap (*karuka*) (one owner recorded);
4. a *kupkup ci malaga* standing *Madassiteno* figure wearing a woman's cap (*karuka*) (two owners recorded);
5. a *Madassiteno* figure described as standing up on the ground on its own and positioned in a house made for it (one owner recorded);
6. a *Vuaset* figure of *Madassiteno* on a frame (one owner recorded).

Madassiro: The *Madassiro* (*Mandasiro, Mandassiro, Mandesiro,* or *Mansiro*) subgrouping of *Madas* is associated with salt water (the sea) in origin or orientation. It is considered to have less power than *Madassiteno*, and is less dramatic in its displays. *Madassiro* has a ritual site at Sotobuer, a beach near Poponovam village (north-west Simberi Island) and another at Aro Madassiro in Tokara village (Mapua Island). Several examples of *Madassiro* were recorded for ten owners. Some of these were:

1. one type of what is apparently a number of types of *kupkup ci malaga* in *Madassiro* is portrayed made from a conical bamboo frame with a coconut-like *Da* ritual sculpture[14] placed on top representing the flower of the wild hardwood palm[15] (one owner recorded);
2. a *Madas* figure standing on top of a canoe (one owner recorded);
3. a *Madassiro* figure called *Belel* (see below) (one owner recorded).

Madassiut: The *Madassiut* (*Mandassiot, Mandassiut, Mandassiwota,* or *Mansiot*) subgrouping of *Madas* is associated with a 'bush' origin or orientation (inland-dwelling people, as opposed to 'saltwater' people). *Madassiut* has ritual sites at Sunagaramut at the old village site of Revar, which is located above Tupinmida village (west Tatau Island) and at Pekinlabam, a village site on a mountain close to Tupinmida. Six owners in total were recorded for *Madassiut*.

Generic malagan types within Madas

Malagan owners often use generic names when describing or referring to specific types of *malagan* sculpture. I recorded seven generic sculptural types of *malagan* on Tabar: *Marumarua, Kobokobor, Eikuar, Kovkov, rarau, vanis,* and *kupkup ci malaga*. These functional or generic types are not all of the same class, but have been grouped together here because they cross-cut the Big-Name *malagan* categories.

Marumarua: On Tabar, *Marumarua* (*maromarua, marumaru, moramoru, mormmoru, moromorou, moromoru, moromorua, morumoru, morumorua,* or *mromro*) is the name for the basic human-like figure element in *malagan* sculpture, and is the most common form of *malagan* sculpture found today. It is also the name for a concept that includes what people in Western, English-speaking cultures would call 'spirit' or 'soul', as well as referring to 'image' or 'picture'. But this is not to say that a *malagan Marumarua* figure is a 'spirit figure' in the loose or glib sense of the term, for the connection occurs at a deeper level.[16]

The German MSC missionary Father John Lamers, working on Mapua Island, described the term *Marumarua* to mean 'shadow from a light, silhouette, a drawing' (Lamers 1928-38). William Groves at Tatau village referred to *mi moromorou* as 'the shadow, disappears when life leaves the body' (1935:358). Several of my Tabar informants indicated that *Marumarua* is a synonym for *pacapaca* – a picture or image of a person.

Most typically the sculptural *Marumarua* is a three-dimensional wooden human-like figure made from *saba* (*Alstonia scholaris*) wood, and varies from between 50 and 150 cm tall (fig. 16.4). Generally referred to by its Big-Name, this

16.4 *Marumarua* type figure from the *Malagacak* Big-Name subtradition. Gitarut village, Mapua Island. (Photo: NGE 1983-2-36.)

figure was recorded within the following Big-Name subtraditions: *Dengenasi, Karavas, Kulepmu, Lunet, Madas, Malagacak, Maris, Sisubua, Takapa, Tangala, Valik,* and *Verem*.

Although most figure sculptures in *Madas* were known only by the generic term *Marumarua*, there were several types of *Marumarua* known by their specific names, *Cikopic, Vuaset* and *Madassiteno* (see below).

Kobokobor: As the 'root of the tree of *malagan*', the *Kobokobor* is understood to be the strongest *malagan*. When a *Kobokobor* is transferred to the next generation, people realise they are witnessing a major event for the clan concerned, for its transferral indicates that the weight of

responsibility for a clan's ritual property then lies on the initiate's shoulders.

Kobokobor is also understood to be a platform, the central form around which *malagan* is publicly displayed and understood. Consequently the *Kobokobor* is often portrayed by *malagan* owners as the central and foundation *malagan* for a large display. Generally described as a long horizontal sculptural form, the *Kobokobor* often acts as the horizontal base for vertical *Eikuar* or *Marumarua* sculptural forms. But as around 10 per cent of *Kobokobor* were described to me as vertical in alignment, it must be assumed that *Kobokobor* is not exclusively a sculptural term, but can also be a reference to the significance of a particular *malagan* item. I recorded the term *Kobokobor* within the following Big-Name subtraditions: *Dengenasi, Kulepmu, Madas, Malagacak, Totobo, Valik,* and *Verem*.

Horizontal *Kobokobor* (foundation) *malagan* forms generally contain a number of seated or standing *Marumarua* figure images, each interspaced by a *koltibor* block (see fig. 16.9). *Koltibor* is a *malagan* design feature representing the middle of a pig, and is said to have full power in *malagan*. Generally the *koltibor* has a *kabotoliŋic* design painted on the surface and is used to separate major sculptural design elements. *Kabotoliŋic* is often said to be a painted image of a type of barnacle, but may also be a combined image of clitoris (*boto*) and a type of small betel nut (*liŋic*). The ends of a *Kobokobor* are usually finished with carved wooden pigs' heads, whole fish or fish heads, or with horizontal in-turned spikes termed *or* (which may also refer to the conical fish-trap *ora*, made from pieces of thorned vine). Occasionally one end of the *Kobokobor* would portray a fish, the other a pig's head. Fish-image finials are understood to reflect a 'saltwater' ancestry, whereby the original *malagan* was conceived, or at least owned, by people living on the coast. Their inland counterparts, often their exchange partners, were considered bush people, and their *malagans* displayed pig-head finials. One sculptor told me that if a *Kobokobor* had a fish head at one end and a pig head at the other then it would belong to the *Madassiut* subgrouping. However, the data I collected indicates that a non-symmetrical type could belong to any of the subgroupings of *Madas*.

Veivem struts project horizontally through the image in *Kobokobor malagan* types. Most often the *Marumarua* figures grasp the *veivem* with their hands, and *veivem* finials are sometimes cleverly turned to become *or*. Classic *malagan* sculpture collected in the 19th century is often easily identified by the portrayal of the hands that grasp *veivem*: the hands appear to be transposed, so that the palms face outwards with the thumbs to the top gripping the *veivem*.

Eikuar: The spectacular vertical 'totem pole' type *malagan* termed *Eikuar* is powerful in visual appearance, but is less significant than the *Kobokobor* for *malagan* owners. There may be as many as five or six *Marumarua* images in a column on top of each other in the *Eikuar*, each image separated from the next by *koltibor* (fig. 16.5). At the top of the *Eikuar* stands an image of a bird or human head, and the base is usually a pig's head, although a significant number of *Eikuar* were recorded placed directly on top of a horizontal *Kobokobor*. The sides of the *Eikuar* usually comprise *veivem* vertical struts, which are often incorporated as an element of the overall visual design. The top image in the *Eikuar* is the key to sculptural variation, and in the past clever play was made with this image, producing some of the most remarkable sculpture to come out of the *malagan* traditions.

Eikuar on Tabar were recorded within the following Big-Name subtraditions: *Dengenasi, Kulepmu, Madas, Malagacak, Sisubua, Takapa, Totobo, Turu, Valik, Verem*, and *Vuvil*. From the data collected it appears that *Eikuar* can have subtypes with specific names. A number of *Eikuar* in *Madas* had individual names (see below); unnamed examples are described below under the entry for *Eikuar*.

Kovkov: Solid *Kovkov* (*kaokao, koko, koukou, kovakova, kowakowa*, or *kowkow*) wooden head-only *malagans* on Tabar are quite distinct from *vanis* masks, which are worn on the head. *Kovkov* seem to be disembodied versions of *Marumarua* images, and can be displayed either attached to bodies made of bush materials, or tied individually to a wooden beam. *Kovkov malagan* heads were recorded from the Big-Name subtraditions *Dengenasi, Kulepmu, Madas* (see below), and *Malagacak*.

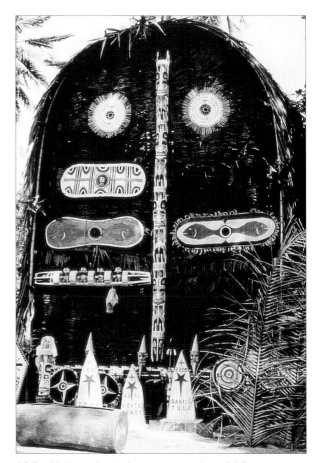

16.5 *Malagan* display featuring a number of different types of *malagan* sculpture. Vertically in the center is an *Eikuar* belonging to the Big-Name subtradition called *Malagacak*. Two large wooden horizontal *Kobokobor* are also featured: at the bottom of the display is a *Kobokobor* of the *Madas* subtradition; above it and to the left is another *Kobokobor* belonging to the *Verem* subtradition. Other Big-Name subtraditions represented in this display are: *Vavara* (top left and right); *Kulepmu* (second row, left); *Lunet* (second row, right). The display house belongs to the *Madassitanua* subgrouping of *Madas*. Pekinberiu village, north-east Tatau Island. (Photo: NGE 1984-33-33.)

Rarau: *Rarau* (*raorao, rarou, raru, rerau, rorou, roru, rurou*, or *ruru*) is a generic *malagan* name meaning 'leaf'. In this context a Big-Name *malagan* subtradition is understood to be analogous to a tree and the *rarau* is a leaf that falls from it. This type of *malagan* is one of a number of 'cloning' types of *malagan*. Other terms referring to cloning *malagans* are: *cur-malaga*, where *cur-* refers to a bed from which many *malagans* get up; *malaga-kapot*, where *-kapot* means 'broken, to have been shared out'; and *mata-rarau*, where *mata-* refers to a well from which an inexhaustible number of *malagan* 'leaves' can be extracted. A cloning *malagan* is one that is sold out of the clan to someone who has need of a *malagan* to show at another man's ceremony, or who needs to embellish his stock for a particularly important showing. The cloned *malagan* is sold without the authority to hand it on to the next generation, but the purchaser is able to reproduce and use the *malagan* throughout his life. On Tabar, *rarau* were recorded within the Big-Name subtraditions *Kulepmu*, *Lunet*, *Malagacak*, *Valik*, and *Vuvil*.

Vanis *masks*:   *Vanis (wanis)* is the generic term on Tabar for a *malagan* mask that is generally worn on the head, but can also be placed on a body made of assembled bush materials (in contrast to carved wood). By examining the usage of *malagan* masks on Tabar, we find that they fall into a number of discrete groupings: burial masks; major taboo-manipulating masks; cleaners and destroyers; and fundraising masks.[17] Most masks on Tabar were recorded in the *Verem* subtradition, and a few were recorded in some of the other Big-Name subtraditions such as *Kulepmu* and *Madas*. Briefly:

- Burial masks were recorded as Tanua barkcloth masks worn by pallbearers in *Madas malagan* or as the *Kakam* white-feather masks worn by pallbearers in *Kulepmu malagan*.
- Major taboo-manipulating masks are usually the large and heavy 'walking' masks, generally made of wood with large ear planks and elaborate superstructure. From my field records they are used by the *ŋuc* ('mouth man, speaker') to manipulate or remove taboos from a village and ritual site during a final commemorative *malagan* ceremony. Although the vast majority of these masks were recorded from the *Verem malagan* subtradition, several 'walking' masks were also recorded in *Kulepmu*, *Malagacak* and *Marada*.

- Cleaning and destroying masks are minor taboo-manipulating masks worn by men acting under the control of the *ŋuc* ('mouth man', speaker), used to remove symbolic barriers either in the village or around the *malagan* ritual site and to destroy the property of the dead. The distinctive *Ges* (*gas*, *geis*, *gis*, *ngeis*, *nges*, or *ngis*) is a subgrouping of this type of mask. *Ges* is a term widespread in New Ireland, and on Tabar refers to a spirit that lives in the jungle, or to a 'wild man' – a legendary psychopathic type of personality. In *malagan* imagery, the *Ges* masked figures are understood as guards or spies moving in front of the major walking masks, wielding spears and rocks to clear the area of people and to remove the influence of the dead. *Ges* may also be represented as a seated mask or as a wooden figure. All versions are said to have originated in *Verem malagan*, and all exhibit the characteristic slanting eyes of the wild *Ges*. *Ges malagan* figures were recorded in *Kulepmu*, *Malagacak*, *Songsong*, *Totobo*, and *Verem* Big-Name subtraditions.
- Fundraising masks are minor masks used by young men under the control of a *malagan* organiser to solicit funds and other necessary items such as food, tobacco, and betel nuts for forthcoming *malagan* activity. A number of these masks were recorded in *Verem malagan*.

Kupkup ci malaga: These are a generic grouping of 'quick-to-work' taboo-clearing *malagans* that were recorded in the Big-Name subtraditions *Kulepmu*, *Lunet*, *Madas*, *Malagacak*, *Marada*, *Sisubua*, *Soŋsoŋ*, *Takapa*, *Totobo*, *Valik*, and *Vuvil*. *Kupkup ci malaga* are most often used at *malagan* ceremonies for taboo removal; for the arrival of a newborn baby; at ceremonies to welcome someone home after a long period of absence; and at small *malagan* ceremonies of a commemorative nature to honour a dead affine.

Kupkup ci malaga refers to a 'fountain of water, fresh and light', the analogy being a fresh sprouting coconut bursting with life and growth in the early dawn of its life.

In many ways these *malagans* are the most powerful of *malagans*, for they begin and end a person's ritual life. This type of *malagan* is the first one given to the next generation of *malagan* owners; the first *malagan* given is often referred to as the 'head of the Big-Name *malagan*'.

Much of the *kupkup ci malaga*'s true nature is camouflaged, for to be a true *kupkup ci malaga*, the image must be made of bush materials, not of wood like a 'normal' *malagan*. Some *kupkup ci malaga* are painted to look like a wooden *malagan* (fig. 16.6), but others, particularly those which carry more power, are natural objects with great symbolic meaning unrecognised by the uninitiated.

The *kupkup ci malaga*'s 'quick-to-work' nature derives from its use when a *malagan* sculpture is needed in a hurry, such as when a taboo has been broken and needs clearing away. As such a *kupkup ci malaga* is generally made from materials found at hand, such as vines, flowers, shells, inverted tree ferns, even a coconut sack or piece of cloth pulled taut across a bamboo or rattan frame and painted. A *malagan* ceremony that uses a *kupkup ci malaga* can be organised within a day or two, and participants are usually from the kin-groups immediately involved. A *kupkup ci malaga malagan* sculpture is usually transferred to the next generation when it is used in a *malagan* ceremony. Many varieties of *kupkup ci malaga* were recorded in *Madas* (see *Madassiteno*, *Madassiro*, *Curuda*, *Curudamas*, *Da*, *Damas*, *Dasar*, and *Tanua*).

Specific named and generic malagans recorded within the Madas Big-Name subtradition

Between 1982 and 1984, I recorded the following *malagans* on Tabar within the subgroupings *Madassiteno*, *Madassiro*, *Madassiut*, or as part of the parent group *Madas*:

Belel: Saltwater *malagan* within the subgrouping *Madassiro*; it originated at *Sotobuer malagan* ritual site on the beach near Poponovam (north-west Simberi Island). This *malagan* was described as follows: made of *saba* wood; under the *malagan* several baby seagulls (*kalai*) are placed to sit on a ritualised inverted tree *auvutun* (called *vut* within the *Madas* ritual system), which is found or positioned

on the beach; this figure is portrayed as sheltering or hiding under the leaves of a *gesev* (wild banana) tree (one owner was recorded).

Cikopic (Chikopits):   *Marumarua*-type figure; the head-only version is called *Kovacikopic* (three owners were recorded).

Curuda (Churu-da, Chur-da, Churun-da, Me-chur-da, Me-churu-da, mi Chur-nda):   Images of *Curuda* in the *Madassiro* subgrouping were described thus:

16.6   *Kupkup ci malaga* (figure with raised arms) from the *Malagacak* Big-Name subtradition; this example was called more specifically *malagaruru si mi Malagacak*. Tatau village, north Tatau Island. (Photo: NGE 1982-11-32.)

1. Cloneable[18] *Da* images were found in *Kobokobor* and on *Eikuar* (one owner recorded);

2. *Curuda* could also be a combination of *Kobokobor* and *Eikuar* with the figures holding *Davovo* 'fresh morning water' containers; on top of the *Eikuar* is a *Marumarua* figure, at the bottom a wooden pig's head, with heads of fish at the ends of the *Kobokobor* (one owner recorded);

3. *Curuda* were said to be *kupkup ci malaga* (see above) (one owner recorded);

4. A *Curuda* type of *Kobokobor* was described as about 3 metres long, with a central *Da* connected on each side by a single *veivem* to another *Da*, then *koltibor*, and finishing with a pig's head at each end (two owners recorded);

5. The name *Curuda* was also recorded as a *Kobokobor* in the Big-Name subtradition *Marada*.

Curudamas *(Churu-damas, Me-chur-damas, Chur-damas)*: Recorded from the *Madassiro* subgrouping as cloneable *Damas* nautilus *kupkup ci malaga* images found in *Kobokobor*. Used only to initiate young children, the *Curudamas* were not used at death ceremonies (four owners were recorded).

Curudasar *(Churu-dasar, Chur-dasar)*: Represents a sea urchin; used only to initiate young children and not at death feasts; probably a type of *kupkup ci malaga* (one owner was recorded).

Curudavovo *(Churu-dawowo)*: A *Kobokobor* of *Madassiut*, featuring *Davovo* images and used to initiate young children; can also be used at normal commemorative *malagan* ceremonies (one owner was recorded).

Curuvuaset *(Churu-vwaset)*: Grouping of small *Vuaset* figures placed in front of the *malagan* display house (one owner was recorded).

Da: Public name for a *malagan*ised image of a coconut water-bottle (figs 16.7, 16.8). In *Madas malagan*, the *Da* occurs in three forms: *Davovo* (water within), *Damas* (water

without), and *Dasar* (edible water?). As a *kupkup ci malaga* the *Da* is most often given to a person at birth, and as a *kupkup ci malaga* the *Da* should stay within the clan. When making this sculpture the carver should not break open a real coconut. When used on its own as a *kupkup ci malaga*, the *Da* is represented by a coconut, or by a piece of sago painted black with a red circumference band embellished with white chicken feathers fastened around the circumference and around the neck. If the *Da* is made as a wooden *malagan*, then it is not a *kupkup ci malaga*, but a true *malagan*, and often a *malagan* head or complete figure forms the stopper to the bottle. *Da* was also recorded in the *Marada*, *Soŋsoŋ* and *Tahala* Big-Name subtraditions (thirteen owners of *Da* were recorded in *Madas*).

Damas: *Malagan* name and image for the *ahgo* chambered nautilus.[19] A powerful *malagan* symbol in *Madas*, the name refers to 'water outside' or 'water is dry'. A *Damas* can be an individual *malagan* used as a *kupkup ci malaga* for clearing taboos; it can also be used as a subunit within a *Kobokobor*. As a powerful *kupkup ci malaga*, the *Damas* should stay within the clan and not be sold or given outside. It should be noted that the *ahgo* is the source of the power, not the *Damas*. *Damas* is regarded as having a stronger power than the related *Davovo*. To inherit the

16.7 *Malagan*ised coconut water-bottle *Da*, from the Big-Name subtradition *Madas*. This example was made by Rorun from *saba* wood and freshly painted with charcoal, lime, and *toromon* seeds (for the red paint). Poponovam village, northwest Simberi Island. (Photo: NGE 1984-8-28.)

16.8 Another version of the *Da* (*malagan*ised coconut water-bottle) in *Madas*. This example was made by Pius Kumau Leugaga from a hardwood (*Calophyllum inophyllum* or *Cordia subcordata*), and features a *malagan* head 'sprouting' from the stopper. Maragon village, west Simberi Island. (Photo: NGE 1982-12-17.)

Damas the rights are given to break it against the *garamut* (slit-drum); the owner of *Damas* cannot drink water from a *Davovo* coconut water-bottle. *Damas* can be displayed supported on a conical bamboo platform called *Da* (six owners were recorded).

Dasar: *Malagan* name and image for the sea urchin *sar*. *Dasar* is a *kupkup ci malaga* used for clearing taboos, and was recorded as part of *Madassiro* and *Madassiteno* sub-

groupings. *Dasar* has a stronger power than *Davovo*. The *malagan*ised version of *Dasar* is made from the soft wood *sebalot* and sago needles, and is placed on the coffin and buried with the dead person. The *sar* sea urchin can be eaten at any time except at a *malagan* feast (one owner was recorded).

Davovo *(*Dawowe, Dawowo*)*: The *malagan*ised coconut water bottle *Da* is referred to as *Davovo* 'fresh morning water' – a symbol of growth and potential, and a centre of much ambiguous imagery. One owner said that the *Davovo* occurred only in the subgrouping *Madassiteno* and not in *Madassiro*; another owner said it was to be found in three subgroupings of *Madas*: *Madassiteno*, *Madassiro*, and *Madassiut*. *Davovo* can be displayed on a *masuvoi* inverted tree platform, or on a *padar* three-branched support. When carried, the *Davovo* is supported on leaves, for the hand should not touch it. This *malagan* is often given to the initiate as the first *malagan* of a series. *Davovo* can also be used as a sculptural subunit within a *Kobokobor* or *Eikuar* (seven owners were recorded).

Eiboŋamas *(*Eboŋamas*)*: In *Madas* the *Boŋamas* was recorded as an *Eikuar* version, the *Eiboŋamas*. One example was described as a column of three *Marumarua* figures, each separated by a *koltibor*, with a pig's head at both top and bottom. The *Boŋamas* was also recorded as a *Marumarua* in *Malagacak* and *Valik*. In all images recorded the figures were described as having had the bellies eaten out (two owners were recorded).

Eikuar *(*Aik-war, Aik-wara, Eik-war, Ek-uar, Ekwa, Ekwar, Ik-wara*)*: Generic *malagan* type found in most Big-Name subtraditions. *Eikuar* can be individually named, or may be known only as '*Eikuar* of *Madas* (or *Madassiro*)'. Within the subtradition *Madas* the following unnamed examples were described:

1. one example of an *Eikuar* in the subgrouping *Madassiro* was recorded as having a column of *Marumarua* figures holding *Da* water bottles, each figure separated from the next by *koltibor*; at the top of the sculpture was a pig's head looking

up, and at the bottom another pig's head looking down (one owner was recorded);

2. another type of *Eikuar* was recorded as having a column of *Marumarua* figures separated by *koltibor*; on the top was a *ci* bird[20] and at the bottom was a pig's head (one owner was recorded);

3. a combination *Eikuar* and *Kobokobor* was described (see '*Curuda*' (2.) above).

Kobokobor *(Kabakabor, Kabkabor, Kabokabor, Kaboka-boro, Kambakambor, Kambakamboro, Kambkambor, Kambokambor, Kambukambor, Kambukamboro, Kam-kambor, Kobobor, Kobokoboro, Koborkobor)*: Generic *malagan* type found in most Big-Name subtraditions. Seventeen *Kobokobor* within the *Madas* subtradition were described to me in some detail, fourteen of which were bilaterally symmetrical and three non-symmetrical.

1. one non-symmetrical *Kobokobor* belonged to the *Madassiteno* subgrouping, and had a pig's head at one end and the head of a fish at the other; in the middle of the sculpture two *Da* were separated from each other and from the ends by *koltibor*; on top of both *Da* were either a wooden head or a *Vuaset* type of *Marumarua* (see below) (one owner recorded);

2. another non-symmetrical *Kobokobor* also belonged to the *Madassiteno* subgrouping, and was described as having a pig's head at one end and the head of a fish (*rahor* = tuna?) at the other; in the center was a *Da*, separated from the end elements by a *koltibor* on each side (one owner recorded);

3. a *Kobokobor* in *Madassiro* was recorded in two versions, one symmetrical (see (10.) below) the other non-symmetrical; the non-symmetrical *Kobokobor* was described as having a pig's head at one end, the head of a fish at the other, then *koltibor*, then a *tatin* fish; the center was a *koltibor* with an *Eikuar* standing on top of it, the base of the *Eikuar* was a pig's head, the top finished with a *koltibor* crowned with *ora*; this example

was half saltwater and half bush in ancestry (two owners recorded).

4. a bilaterally symmetrical *Kobokobor* about 1 metre long consisted of six *veivem* projecting horizontally each side from the perimeter of a central *koltibor* (one informant);

5. a bilaterally symmetrical *Kobokobor* with a central sun, then to each side a *koltibor*, then a *Da*, a seated figure of man, another *Da*, a *koltibor*, finished with a pig's head at each end (one owner recorded);

6. a bilaterally symmetrical *Kobokobor* with a central *koltibor*, then a *Da* water bottle with a *Vuaset* type of *Marumarua* as the stopper, another *koltibor*, and finally with *ci* birds at each end (one owner recorded);

7. a bilaterally symmetrical *Kobokobor* in *Madassiteno* with a central *Da*, on top of which stood a *Vuaset* type of *Marumarua* figure, then on either side of the *Da* was a *koltibor*; the *Kobokobor* was finished at each end with fish positioned tail outwards, their mouths touching the more central *koltibor*; three *veivem* are used for each end, the bottom *veivem* omitted; apparently a *Kobokobor* of *Marada* looks very similar to this one, except pigs' heads are added as finials, separated from the fish by *koltibor* (one owner recorded);

8. a bilaterally symmetrical *Kobokobor* in *Madassiro* with central *koltibor*, a *Marumarua* figure with outstretched forefingers standing on top of the *koltibor*; on either side of the *koltibor* a fish positioned with tail outwards and the mouth touching the central *koltibor*, four *veivem* curving in at the ends enclosing the fish; the *Marumarua* represents a man standing on top of a rock wishing to spear the two fish (one owner recorded);

9. a bilaterally symmetrical *Kobokobor* (fig. 16.9) with three *Da* water-bottles, each separated by a *koltibor*; the stopper of each *Da* is a head wearing a woman's pointed cap[21] and showing a long protruding tongue; each end is finished with a *koltibor* then a pig's head (three owners recorded);

16.9 *Kobokobor*-type *malagan* within the *Madas* Big-Name subtradition. This *malagan* features three *kovkov* heads with protruding tongues, each head represented wearing a woman's *karuka* pandanus-leaf hat. Each head emerges from a *Da* water-bottle and is separated from the next image by a *koltibor* block. Both ends of the *malagan* are finished by pig heads. Poponovam village, north-west Simberi Island. (Photo: NGE 1984-7-4.)

10. two versions of a *Kobokobor* of Madassiro were recorded; one was a bilaterally symmetrical *Kobokobor* with a pig's head at each end, then *koltibor*, then a seagull, then *koltibor*, then a central pig's head, which was the base of an *Eikuar* that was topped by a *kova marumarua* (head of a man); the other version was asymmetric (see (3.) above) (two owners recorded);

11. a bilaterally symmetrical *Kobokobor* in *Madassiteno* with a pig's head at each end, then *koltibor*, then seated man holding a *Davovo*, one hand holding the bottle, the other holding the stopper; the central image was a *koltibor*, which supported an *Eikuar*, which had a pig's head at the bottom and was topped with the *kova marumarua* head of a man (two owners recorded);

12. a bilaterally symmetrical *Kobokobor* in *Madassiut* with a pig's head at each end, then *koltibor*, then seated man holding a horizontal *veivem* and angrily looking to one side; the central image was a *koltibor*, which supported an *Eikuar*, which had a pig's head at the bottom and was topped with an image of a standing man holding *veivem* (two owners recorded).

Then there were two *Kobokobor* in *Madassiro*, each of which had three versions. The first *Kobokobor* featured *Damas*, the second featured *Da*, otherwise they were identical. The three versions of each are:

13. *Curdamas*, or *Curda*, a complete *Damas* or a *Da* on its own (one owner recorded);

14. a bilaterally symmetrical *Kobokobor* with a pig's head at each end, then *koltibor*, then a man seated holding *Damas* (the eye of the *Damas* faces out) or *Da*, then a central *koltibor*; in this case the *Da* or *Damas* is a subunit within the *Kobokobor* (one owner recorded);

15. a bilaterally symmetrical *Kobokobor* with pig's head at each end, then a *koltibor*, then either *Damas* (the eye of the *Damas* faces out) or *Da*, then a central *koltibor* (one owner recorded);

Then there were two other types:

16. a *Kobokobor* in Madassiro was described as two fish heads connected together (one owner recorded);

17. a combination *Eikuar* and *Kobokobor* was described (see *Curuda* (2.) above).

A number of other examples were not described (eight owners were recorded).

Kokoi: The *kokoi* display platform, possibly part of *Madassiteno*, consists of a raised dome supported on a central bamboo post; the dome is covered with the flowers of the black palm;[22] on top of the flowers are a number of fish made of cane; underneath the dome are cane *lako* fish looking out into the *roŋar*; on top of the dome, fastened to a bamboo post, is a *Vuaset* type of *Marumarua* figure (one owner recorded).

Kovacikopic *(Kowa-chikopits)*:   The proper name of a wooden head *Kovkov* type of *Cikopic malagan* sculpture (three owners recorded).

Kovkov *(ko-ko, kao-kao)*:   A generic *malagan* type found within a number of Big-Name subtraditions; in *Madas*, the *Kovkov* head-only-type *malagan* can have names such as *Kovacikopic*.

Madasi *(Mandasi)*:   A seated figure with wooden body and legs and hands raised; has face of man with tall ears and no hair (one owner recorded).

Potoviso *(Put-vis)*:   An *Eikuar* with pig's head at the bottom, and a column of *Marumarua* figures playing bamboo pipes and separated by *koltibor*; the top image is a *Marumarua*; the name *Potoviso* means 'bundle of bamboo, bamboo pipes' with implications that it is flexible, swinging around in the wind (three owners recorded).

Tanua *(Tan-oa, Teno, Tinou)*:   A *kupkup ci malaga* death mask in *Madassiteno* subgrouping, worn by mourners to bury the dead; examples were described made of bark cloth with a face painted black on the front and with holes for the eyes; this type of mask is usually burnt after the burial; *tanua* death masks were recorded only from the *Madas* Big-Name subtradition, and they carry the name of one of the main human spirit types; the *tanua* spirit is understood to leave the body at death, and appears to be portrayed by the white feather *kakam* masks (in *Kulepmu* Big-Name subtradition) worn by chief mourners and pallbearers during the *vavil* funeral procession (four *Madas* owners recorded).

Tonomatmerik: Mask part of *Madas* used to fasten the door of the ceremonial area (one owner recorded).

Vuaset *(Vaset, Vuasit, Vwaset, Waset)*:   Wooden *Marumarua* type of figure *malagan* recorded in *Madassiteno* and *Madassiut*; the name was also recorded as part of *tangtangias* of *Madas* (four owners recorded).

Vudida *(Undida)*:   Recorded in *Madassiro*, the *malagan* consists of the action of two men wearing bark-cloth masks rubbing rotten bananas on top of the head of a newborn child (two owners recorded).

Conclusion

Although the sculptural products of *malagan* have been well-known in the Western world for more than 100 years, and *malagan* ritual context has been documented from several regions, the relationships between the various art works have not been closely examined before. In this paper the *malagan* ritual traditions of the Tabar Islands are considered through terms the Tabar Islanders considered important – the context of ownership. Ownership was the thread that linked each *malagan* art work to its predecessors as well as to other contemporary *malagan* rights owned by the clan. Groups or 'strings' of *malagan* rights are passed from one generation of owners to the next, one item at a time, linking a clan's ritual property during a lifetime of ritual transferral.

Each *malagan* art work is understood to belong to a Big-Name subtradition of *malagan*, which comprises one or more 'strings' of *malagan* rights. No *malagan* sculpture can legally exist outside this framework of ownership. A *malagan* can only be made from *malagan* rights that are either inherited from within the matri-clan, or that have been purchased from outside the clan, usually from the father.

Each Big-Name subtradition on Tabar has its own ritual sites, songs, character, and many other attributes that are used to distinguish one subtradition from another. In this paper several aspects of the subtradition *Madas* were described to illustrate some of the complexity of *malagan* ownership and its manifestation in sculptural rights. Because Tabar was the source of most (but not all) of the *malagan* rights that have produced sculpture throughout northern New Ireland, an understanding of the structure of *malagan* traditions on Tabar may assist in disentangling the history of evolution of *malagan* on the mainland of New Ireland.

Notes

1.   This is the Tok Pisin (PNG Pidgin) spelling of the concept that is usually pronounced in northern New Ireland as *malahgan*, and that has been spelt variously in the literature as *malanggan*, *malangan*, and *mulligan*.

2.   Following the lead taken by Eco (1976).

3.   I carried out field work on the Tabar Islands from May to June 1982, and from December 1983 to March 1984, funded

by the Northern Territory Museums and Art Galleries, in Darwin, Australia, and affiliated with the National Museum of Papua New Guinea and the Institute of Papua New Guinea Studies.

4.   In addition to my own field notes, I also drew upon the work of Albert (1986), Brouwer (1980), Bühler (1933), Clay (1987), Derlon (1991), Fergie (1985, 1989), Gifford (1974), Groves (1932-34, 1934-35), Heintze (1969, 1987), Helfrich (1973, 1985), Jessep (1980), Krämer (1925, 1927), Krämer-Bannow (1916), Küchler (1985, 1987, 1988, 1992), Lamers (1928-38), Lewis (1969), Lincoln (1987), Neuhaus (1962), Parkinson (1907), Peekel (1910, 1926, 1927, 1928, 1929, 1931, 1932), Powdermaker (1931a, 1931b, 1932, 1933), Walden (Walden and Nevermann 1940), and Wilkinson (1978), among others.

5.   An easy mistake given *malagan* sculpture's intimate association with the dead, but harder to understand when it becomes apparent that although around 60 per cent of all *malagan* sculptures feature a human-like figure, the other 40 per cent feature a wide variety of objects ranging from images of coconut water-bottles through to filleted fish.

6.   The totemic life force is called *masalai* in Tok Pisin, and *tandar, tandaro, tandoro,* or *tendar* in the dialect variants found on Tabar. On the mainland of New Ireland it is also referred to as *tandar* around the Namatanai region of central New Ireland, and *randa* in the Madak region further north. See Peekel (1927) and Neuhaus (1962) for further examples.

7.   I recorded information on Tabar about *malagans* within the following Big-Name subtraditions: *Curvunavuŋa, Deŋenasi, Karavas, Kulepmu, Loŋobu, Lunet, Madas, Malagacak, Marada, Maris, Sisubua, Soŋsoŋ, Takapa, Tahala, Tomut, Totobo, Turu, Valik, Vavara, Verem,* and *Vuvil.*

8.   Walden's notes, published as Walden and Nevermann (1940), are the primary early source for *malagan* names on Tabar.

9.   It should be noted that there is a north-south dialect chain of Madara, the Austronesian language spoken on Tabar. For this paper I have used the dialectical variant that most clearly illustrates

the etymology of a word or its usage. Because my field data was recorded from all four dialect areas of the Tabar group of islands (Simberi, Tatau, Mapua, and Big Tabar), it proved impractical to use any one particular dialect, for many words were recorded from one or another village and not elsewhere.

10.   Proper and generic *malagan* names will be distinguished respectively through the use of upper-case and lower-case first letters.

11.   See also Gunn (1983, 1984, 1986, 1987, 1988, 1990, 1992) for further discussion of *malagan* Big-Name subtraditions.

12.   Following the linguist Malcolm Ross, in vernacular terms I have used *c* to represent *ch* and *ts* sounds, which are allophones of the same phoneme.

13.   I recorded at least one set of *taŋtaŋias* ownership chants for each of the following Big-Name *malagan* subtraditions: *Deŋenasi, Kulepmu, Loŋobu, Lunet, Madas, Malagacak, Sisubua, Soŋsoŋ, Tomut, Totobo, Turu, Valik, Vavara, Verem,* and *Vuvil.*

14.   See below for a description of the *Da.*

15.   *Kentiopsis archontophoenix.*

16.   See above section on totemism and *malagan.*

17.   See also Lurang, this volume.

18.   See '*Rarau*', above, for definition of cloneable *malagans.*

19.   *Nautilus tompilius.*

20.   The New Ireland Drongo (*Dicrurus megarhynchus*). It is probably also known as *ciroru,* a bird that is featured on other *malagan* sculpture, such as some types of *Kobokobor* in *Valik,* where a pair of these birds are portrayed eating from the central *tumsiv* (a representation of a shell growing on stone, which is part of the central *mataliŋ* design on *Valik malagan*).

21.   Although gender is distinguished on some *malagan* figures so that males have a *kovage* feather headdress and females wear a pointed woman's hat (*karuka*), the gender of the *malagan* may bear no relationship to the gender of the dead person who is the focus of the ritual.

22.   *Kentiopsis archontophoenix.*

The acoustic properties of the Fijian 'slit-gongs'

Rod Ewins

17

Normally referred to as the drum or slit-gong of Fiji, the *lali* has a form rather like a large wooden trough carved out of a single hollowed-out log.

> The Fijian … has found out that a hollow tree on concussion produces more sound than a solid one … [and that] a hollow tree slightly open will emit more sound than a closed one … [and] a tree stripped of its bark is an improvement on one which has its bark intact. He has likewise marked the fact that some woods are superior to others in resonance. All these … discoveries in acoustics the Fijian has embodied in his lali – an instrument half-drum and half-bell. [Deane 1911]

In most villages, either one or a pair of *lali* are found, varying in length from 0.6 to 1.8 metres (2 to 6 feet) according to the seniority of the chief living in the village, and hence the relative importance of the village. They are normally situated on one side of the village green, frequently near the church, provincial administration office, or other 'official' building, often under a shady tree, or very occasionally in purpose-built shelters that have roofs but no walls. Today their use is limited to calling the faithful to worship, sending the children off to school, and occasionally announcing special village meetings. In early days, however, the *lali* and its beat were invested with great importance, and the *lali* was never beaten without some definite motive or meaning. Beats were regionally distinct

and of great variety, but their significance was easily recognised by those who heard them. The most common reference in the early literature is to the heavy, ominous beat – the *derua* – which signalled the bringing into the village of corpses intended for eating. An early missionary writer, Thomas Williams (1982), described this as 'a peculiar beating of the drum, which alarmed me even before I was informed of its import'.

Large *lali* are not used to accompany dances or *meke* – for this purpose small *lali* called *lalinimeke* are made, similar in concept but usually rather long and slim, with a proportionately smaller cavity, and sometimes with no recess in their ends. Better-made versions, however, are very fair replicas of large *lali* and are made of the same timbers. Typically they are between 30 and 60 centimetres (1 and 2 feet) long. The sound they emit when struck with their little beaters is sharp and piercing but not resonant. In use they are either placed on the floor in front of, across the outstretched shins of, or in the lap of, the player. *Lalinimeke* are used together with long sticks that are beaten with shorter ones, 'stamping tubes' of bamboo, and handclapping, to create the strong rhythm that accompanies a vocal soloist and many-voiced vocal refrain.

This paper is limited to a description of the acoustic considerations employed by the makers of *lali* – in other words, why they have the form they have, what effect the different parts have, and how the makers 'tune' them during

17.1 (Above left) Easi Qalo, master *lali*-maker of Namuka, starts the initial flattening of the top of the *vesi* log.

17.2 (Above) Commencing the hollowing of the *lali*.

17.3 (Far left) The tool kit: two felling-axes; a hollowing-adze made from a large gouge bound to a tree elbow; a chopping/planing adze made from an ancient broad-axe blade; a commercial hole-tanged adze.

17.4 (Left) Two nearly finished large *lali* are tested for sound. More wood will be removed until the correct pitch and tone are achieved. These are *not* a matched pair of drums, which would be of disparate size. The smaller drums to 'mate' with these will be made later, about two-thirds the size of these.

manufacture. A great deal more about the process of manufacture, the traditional exchange networks in which these objects function, and their traditional uses and the various beats related to those, is provided in my 1986 article in the Fiji Museum journal *Domodomo*.

Prerogatives relating to the manufacture of important traditional goods are gender-specific and place-specific in Fiji. Making *lali* is the special male craft of the island of Namuka, in the Lau Group of eastern Fiji. During August 1985, I watched the *matai* (expert maker) Easi Qalo (pronounced Ay-ah-si Ng-ga-law) making a *lali,* from the felling of the tree to the testing of the almost-finished drum prior to final planing and sanding (figs 17.1 to 17.4). He was then aged forty-one, one of two noted *lali*-makers

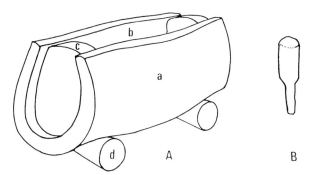

17.5 A. *Lali:* (a) belly; (b) cavity; (c) baffle; (d) roller support. B. Beater. A typical *lali* was measured as follows: L: 100 cm (max.); H: 41 cm; W: 41 cm (centre), 26 cm (ends); wall thickness: 6 cm (centre), 3 cm (ends); baffle thickness: 6 cm (top), 17 cm (bottom); extension of walls beyond baffles: 5 cm; cavity opening: 21.5 cm (max. width), 75 cm (max. length). Dimensions of beaters: L. 40 cm; head diam.: 7 cm; handle diam. 3 cm.

on the island, and his knowledge of the craft and some of his tools are a legacy from his father.

Lali are made only from extremely dense, acoustically resonant timbers, and today the main timber used is that of the *vesi* tree (*Intsia bijuga*, called 'greenheart' in India), which thrives in the forests of limestone islands such as Namuka. *Vesi* wood is so dense that even when dry it floats submerged to water-level. Today, chainsaws are used in the initial tree-felling and chopping-to-length. The latter is dictated by the girth of the tree, as there is an acoustically desirable proportion for the drum, and correct judgement of this is crucial to its ultimate pitch and resonance. All of the other forming is done using hand tools, axes, adzes (store-bought and homemade) and a smoothing plane. The form of the *lali* is as shown in the figure 17.5; it is open along the top, and in cross-section is bellied out between the top and the base. The side walls are slightly thicker at their centre than at the ends, and thinner at the lip than further down. A short recess is let into either end, which exactly continues the interior line of the drum wall, but is separated from the amplifying chamber by a stout straight-sided baffle, called the 'neck' or 'voice' of the drum. The chainsaw, with its round-ended bar, is an ideal tool for creating the end recess while

simultaneously creating the outside face of the baffle. The projection probably affects to some degree the vibration of the walls, and thus also the soundwaves that result, but the effect is probably not great. The top edges of the baffles are in some *lali* a couple of centimetres below the level of the top of the drum wall, and sometimes arc down even further below this level. On all of the Namuka ones I saw, however, the top edges of the baffles were slightly convex, starting at the walls only about a centimetre below the top edges and rising to be virtually level with them in the centre. Their height and shape would probably have some small effect on sound overtones.

There are two beaters, or drumsticks, to each drum, each with a large cylindrical head tapering sharply to the straight cylindrical handle. They must be made of wood that is much softer than the *lali* so as not to damage the lip, on the edge of which they are struck – one *lali* will outlast many beaters. They are made proportional to the size of the drum, and today are both the same size for any given drum, though interestingly this may not always have been the case. A mid-19th-century illustration (fig. 17.6), meticulously accurate in all other details, shows a drummer using a typical beater in his right hand, and a lighter one – in effect a straight stick – in his left.

17.6 'Feejeean Drummer', after illustration in Wilkes (1845:316).

There is a possible logic to this arrangement. Many *lali* beats require that one beater is struck much more lightly, producing a quieter and less penetrating note. The effect of a lighter stick is to produce a note similarly pitched to the heavy beater, struck with the same force, but not as loud or penetrating, and because it emphasises different overtones it has the effect of seeming to be higher-pitched also. This arrangement, therefore, would inherently provide some variation in the volume, and thus the carrying power, of the total beat, and an apparent difference in pitch at the same time. If, however, the small beater were used to strike the drum near to the baffle, then the difference in pitch would be actual, not apparent, with the overall effect of higher notes 'ornamenting' the fundamental deep note that was providing the basic rhythm.

In the following comments, I will try to show that the *lali* is not functioning as either a drum or a gong, which are the common terms applied to it. Typically in drums, a partly or wholly enclosed airspace is covered with a thin tympanum of metal, hide, or fabric. When this is struck, it is the vibration of the enclosed air that generates the sound. Gongs typically are flat plates, and while it is the material of the gong that generates the sound, as it is with the *lali*, the acoustics of flat plates are different from those in play here.

The *lali* is functioning as a wooden bell, with an open-mouthed cavity that serves to maximise the audible effect of the vibrations of its complex form. The acoustics of bells are extraordinarily complex, and even the manufacture of European and Asian cast-metal bells still relies on the maker's experience and judgement rather than scientifically definable data. Since it is the vibration of the whole object that produces the sound, virtually every variable of dimension will have some effect. Any one of these things may be modified without much noticeable effect, but the sum of them all is that which imparts to each instrument its own properties. It is in knowing how to repeatedly achieve a functional and pleasing result that the skill of the maker lies.

The *lali* is first tested for sound before final finishing. To do this it must be properly 'set up' by placing it on two short logs of coconut palm, placed at right angles to the drum and about one-quarter of the way in from either end (fig. 17.4). The use of a coil support was also noted by early observers, but I have never seen it. The vine or rope, being less dense than the palm-wood supports, and the coils creating an enclosed cavity under the drum, would probably have influenced the quality of sound, as does simply lying the *lali* on the ground without support. Ideally, for minimal interference with vibration, the supports ought to be positioned exactly under, or near to, the baffles, which are already creating a node.

Testing consists merely of beating some simple rhythms on the *lali*; if the sound is clear and penetrating it will be judged good. If the sound is muffled, since it is impossible to put material back, adjustment can be made only by judiciously carving some more out of the amplifying chamber and off the baffle, thus thinning the walls and altering the quality of the vibration when the wall is struck (changing the tone and slightly raising the pitch), and also changing slightly the distance between the walls (the nodes), thus the wavelength, and accordingly the pitch.

When it is considered acceptable, the outside is finished off with a normal smoothing plane. Formerly, I was told, it was scraped smooth with a seashell, possibly a *Conus*. Old *lali* were often as smooth inside as out, but these days there is no attempt to finish off the inside surface of the amplifying chamber beyond the rather rough 'dimpled' finish left by the hollowing adze. This must interfere to a small degree with internal reflection, and thus its amplifying effect, but is perhaps not very significant given the reduced role of the *lali* today, with less need for great carrying power.

Qalo asserted that it is incorrect to make single *lali*; they should always be in pairs – one large and deep-pitched, its mate smaller and higher-pitched. In many parts of Fiji, single *lali* are the norm in villages, probably because of their substantial cost. Many traditional beats were 'scored' for two *lali* alternating, rather than the musically more advanced concept of having them playing simultaneously in counterpoint, though some overlapping can occur. Part of the conventional wisdom handed down in such traditional crafts is the judgement of sizes and proportions; the large *lali* is always made first, and the smaller one made later 'to go with it', I was told. Thus the sound of a pair of matched drums is, in my experience, invariably very attractive to the ear. In the case of the two village *lali* in Namuka, the small one was tuned to the same note exactly one octave above that of the larger one.

To establish the relationship between the physical components of the *lali* and the sounds it generates, I questioned the maker closely, and subsequently made some very simple acoustic tests on one medium-sized *lali* and one medium-sized *lalinimeke*, both of which are the property of the Tasmanian Museum and Art Gallery. The drums were beaten and recorded in the open air, as would be the case in normal usage, rather than in an acoustically 'dead' laboratory. The sound analysis was undertaken for me by my colleague David Davies of the Physics Department, University of Tasmania, who is also a musician. The following conclusions, however, are ultimately mine, and I do not implicate Mr Davies in any errors there may be. Bearing in mind that most of us are not musicians, it may be helpful to remember that sound is the effect of vibration, transmitted through the air as waves that are perceived by the delicate mechanisms of the ear. These waves may be schematically charted as a graph, in which the wave oscillates above and below a constant line while it travels through time, and its parts can be measured.

Pitch, tone, and carrying power

The *frequency* is the number of times the wave oscillates in a second. In the case of solid objects being agitated (as is the case with piano strings or the walls of a bell, as here), it is affected by their length, thickness, density and tension – the thicker, longer (that is, distance between the fixed ends or *nodes*) and more dense the material, the slower it will vibrate when struck, the lower the frequency, longer the wavelength and, in sound terms, the deeper the note (or lower the *pitch*). If we strike a random piece of wood or metal, many sounds of different (and/or changing) frequencies are generated simultaneously, conflicting with one another and making what we call 'noise'. The sound generated by striking a *lali* is extremely complex, but the fundamental frequency is dominant, the vibrations rein-

force one another, and thus we perceive the sound as musical.

Low-frequency waves have long wavelengths that possess more energy and decay more slowly, thus carrying further. Also, they are, unlike high-frequency waves, capable of travelling around obstacles – important in heavily forested environments. The fundamental frequency of vibration of the particular *lali* that was tested was in the mid-range, which would not have exceptional carrying power. This is consistent with its average size and function, almost certainly only as a village 'meeting' drum. Certainly it would be more than adequate for its purpose, and would be heard clearly throughout a village and the neighbouring garden and work areas, all of which would typically fall within a radius of 1.6 kilometres (1 mile). The giant *lali* of important villages in old Fiji, some of them three times this size or more, in view of the greater length between the nodes of their baffles, thicker walls, and greater volume of material altogether, delivered a far deeper note, resulting in great carrying power (reported to be more than 16 kilometres (10 miles) in a straight line).

Beaters are held further up the handle (toward the head) than might be expected. This delivers a less 'woody', more mellow, sound. For the same reason, the drum is not hit right on top of the lip but either on the inside angle of the lip nearest to, or on the top of the outside wall furthest from, the drummer. The swing used for the stroke is usually fairly long and deliberate, which makes it easier to maintain a rhythm, and to ensure that each stroke has approximately the same value as the one before, since it is momentum rather than muscular effort that controls the force with which the beater hits the drum. The beater is allowed to rebound cleanly so as not to muffle the sound. Sometimes it is allowed to 'bounce' to create a short sound, but this is only in particular 'tunes'. Striking the drum in the dead centre of its length produces the longest available wavelength and thus the deepest sound. The closer to the node that vibration is initiated, the greater the excitation of shorter wavelengths and the higher the pitch. Thus, in the test, striking near the baffle shortened the wavelength of the vibration so that the drum resonated at B_5, whereas striking at the centre caused it to resonate four notes lower, at E_4. With larger drums the difference could be greater. However, beating directly at the baffle produces little vibration other than that of wood on wood, and thus virtually no musical quality.

Any note produced by a musical instrument is accompanied simultaneously by a number of higher notes, or *harmonics* (overtones). While the fundamental note is the one picked out by the ear as the actual pitch, these harmonics either reinforce or compete with it, altering the *tone*. In manufacturing, the *wall-thickness* will affect the fundamental and the harmonics; that is to say, the actual pitch and the tone, giving the particular *timbre* of the *lali*. In essence, the thicker the wood the deeper the note, but (particularly on small or average-sized drums) thinner walls may deliver a somewhat 'brighter' and less muffled note. Thus there is a 'correct' relationship between the length of the drum (and thus the distance between the baffles) and the thickness of the walls.

The *amplitude* is the distance above and below the constant line that the wave achieves; that is, the distance of deformation of the string, bell wall, and so on. The example of a plucked string can demonstrate this graphically. If it is pulled out a long way and let go, its vibrations will be long and the sound loud. If it is pulled gently only, the vibrations will be short and the sound soft. Thus amplitude is perceived as *loudness*, but because the number of vibrations per second remains the same it does not affect pitch, or the actual note. In the case of the *lali*, this means the harder the wall is hit, the louder will be the note, but it is also a function of the size of the beater and exactly where the wall is struck so as to maximise the deformation and thus the amplitude. It is for this reason that beating is on the side or edge of the mouth of the drum rather than directly on the lip, which would cause little lateral deformation and result in a lot of wood-on-wood noise. The *cavity* has a relatively large mouth, so it does not really function as a resonating – but rather as an amplifying – chamber. It facilitates a connection of the

excited air all around the vibrating walls of the drum, inside and out, and focuses and projects it, thus maximising the sound. If the mouth were more closed, although the internal resonance would favour the lower harmonics and alter the tone of the drum, its carrying power would probably be diminished rather than enhanced.

The *baffles* serve not so much to close the cavity as to provide a physical connection (even to the level of continuous xylem structure) between all parts of the opened 'cylinder', permitting very rapid transmission of the waves through all parts of the drum when it is struck. (As just indicated, the note delivered by the drum is a function of wall vibration rather than of air resonating within a chamber.) Also, since they create nodes, the distance between the baffles determines the wavelength and thus the pitch of the drum – the greater the distance between the baffles, the deeper the note or fundamental frequency of the drum. Thus during manufacture some 'tuning', say from a sharp to a natural note, may be achievable by paring off the inside of the baffle. The operative effect is on the substance of the drum rather than on the size of the internal cavity.

Note on *lalinimeke*

Testing showed that the main characteristics of the small *lalinimeke* are surprisingly consistent with those of the large *lali*. Initial amplitude (which is perceived as loudness) is similar to that of the large drum, but decay is more rapid – to about half in 15 milliseconds as against 25 seconds in the large *lali*. Thus the sound from the *lalinimeke* is loud, but much shorter. Fundamental frequency is high – approximately 1250 Hz (the note E^b_6) – almost exactly two octaves higher than that of the larger drum (which was approximately 333 Hz – the note E_4, or E above Middle C). This relatively high pitch has little carrying power, but is perfectly adequate for its function as the rhythmic accompaniment of dances.

The woodcarvings of Mutuaga, a 19th-century artist of the Massim district of Papua New Guinea[1]

Harry Beran

Mutuaga and his world

Among the most frequently published art works from the Massim district of Papua New Guinea are lime spatulas and human figures carved in a highly distinctive naturalistic style. The handles of the spatulas are carved as human figures or pigs. This paper identifies the artist who created them and attributes some eighty carvings to him.

The style of the anthropomorphic carvings is more naturalistic than that of other traditional Massim artworks. The figures are sculpted three-dimensionally and with a considerable degree of realism. They are the only ones among Massim anthropomorphic carvings that indicate the ankle bones, the bony prominence of the ulna near the wrist joint (the ulna prominence), the vertical groove between nose and upper lip (the philtrum), the groove that runs down the middle of the back (the spinal sulcus), and the musculature of the limbs. Some Massim carvings, not in the same style as the present group, have one or two of these features, but none has all or even most of them. The pigs on the pig spatulas, though less realistically carved than the human figures, are so similar to the latter in their highly sculpted three-dimensional style and their surface decoration that one suspects both groups of carvings to be by one carver or school of carvers. Douglas Newton (1975:6), among others, has suggested that some of these carvings are by one hand.

I have located ninety-seven artworks with a component in the distinctive naturalistic style just described. They fall into the following groups:

- 28 spatulas with squatting human figure handles;
- 1 spatula with a handle carved as a human figure on top of another;
- 1 spatula with a handle carved as a human figure and a pig;
- 20 spatulas with pig handles;
- 1 spatula with a handle incorporating birds and a pig;
- 27 human figures on pedestals;
- 2 human figure fragments;
- 9 staffs with human figure tops;
- 4 staffs with pig tops;
- 1 betel-nut bowl and mortar with a human figure and a pig on the rim;
- 1 headrest with human figure supports;
- 1 pig on a base; and
- 1 club with a human figure finial.

The location of these carvings is recorded in the Inventory at the end of this paper, and representative examples are illustrated in figures 18.2 to 18.10, 18.14 to 18.20, 18.26 to 18.32, and 18.34 to 18.44. The Inventory probably includes the great majority of extant carvings in the naturalistic style, as it is based on a worldwide survey of major collections of Massim art.[2]

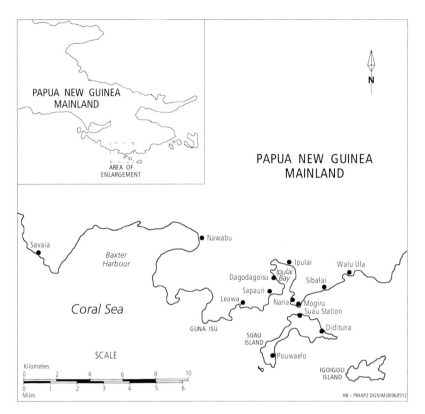

18.1 The central Suau area, Milne Bay Province, Papua New Guinea

The carver of some of these naturalistic artworks is identified as Mutuaga in two catalogues of the P.G. Black Collection of Melanesian artefacts, formed between 1886 and 1916, and held by the Buffalo Museum of Science. One catalogue of the collection, prepared in Sydney in May 1901, lists seven carvings in the naturalistic style and six lime spatulas in various non-naturalistic styles as being from Suau (South Cape)[3] and 'Carved by Mutuaga'. Another catalogue of the by then enlarged collection, dated 1 January 1914, attributes these and another three carvings in the naturalistic style to Mutuaga.[4] Presumably the latter carvings entered the collection between 1901 and 1913. One of the naturalistic carvings can no longer be located. The other nine comprise three anthropomorphic spatulas, two pig spatulas, two independent human figures, one human figure fragment, and one staff (figs 18.2 to 18.10).

The six spatulas in non-naturalistic styles attributed to Mutuaga in the catalogues comprise two anthropomorphic spatulas, two clapper spatulas, one canoe-end spatula, and one spatula of unidentified design. Three of them are shown in figures 18.11 to 18.13.

Information about Mutuaga comes from two informants who knew him. Cecil Abel (1903-94) knew Mutuaga as a visitor to the Kwato Island Mission Station, just off Samarai Island. He was the eldest son of the English missionary Charles Abel, who took over the London Missionary Society Head Station in eastern Papua in August 1891. This station was established by James and Jane Chalmers in 1878 in Suau Island. After his wife's death in 1879, Chalmers left the Suau Island Mission Station in the hands of Polynesian missionary teachers, who were in charge of it until the arrival of another English missionary, Fred Walker, in 1890. In the same year, Walker transferred the head station to Kwato Island, 45 kilometres further east. Cecil Abel was born at Kwato, grew up there, was bilingual in Suau and English, and was married to a Suau woman. At fourteen he went to school in Australia, but regularly returned to Kwato Island for the Christmas holidays. Weibo Mamohoi (1888-1997) of Mogiriu village, near Suau Island, was well-known among the Suau people as an oral historian, and knew Mutuaga well as a member of a neighbouring village. I interviewed Cecil Abel on numerous occasions in Port Moresby and Sydney between 1987 and 1994, and Weibo briefly in 1989 and at great length during a nine-day stay in his village in 1993. From their recollections Mutuaga emerges as the most highly regarded wood carver of his generation in the central Suau area (fig. 18.1).[5] He was born around 1860 and died soon after 1920. His first marriage was without issue. His second marriage produced a son, Saliwowo, born around 1915, too late to acquire carving skills from his father.[6] Mutuaga has no living descendants, as he had no siblings, and his son died around 1980 without offspring.

According to Cecil Abel, his father befriended Mutuaga soon after his arrival in the Suau area, because he admired the artist's carvings. Charles Abel became Mutuaga's patron and accepted all carvings that Mutuaga brought to him at the Kwato Mission. Cecil Abel believed that Mutuaga was already carving anthropomorphic spatulas when Charles Abel arrived in the Suau region and that their production was an established practice there. However, according to Cecil Abel, Mutuaga started producing independent human figures on pedestals as the result of a suggestion from Charles Abel that he do so for trade with Westerners. When Cecil Abel was a youngster the Mission House was full of carvings by the artist.

Weibo reported that Mutuaga was of the *maliboi* (flying fox) clan and lived in Dagodagoisu village, on the mainland opposite Suau Island.[7] He recalled that, in addition to lime spatulas and independent figures, Mutuaga also carved presentation axe handles, house boards, and crescent-topped handles for the presentation of shell money. When Weibo knew the artist, he used metal tools.

Mutuaga walked with a pronounced limp and the help of a long plain staff. He was a kind and cheerful man, and one of the men of highest standing in his village. In recognition of his skill and penchant for carving, his nickname was Oitau, which is the Suau word for the human figures on pedestals he made.

Mutuaga lived in the centre of the area occupied by the people speaking the Suau language (fig. 18.1), who around 1920 numbered about 6000. Their area extends from Mullins Harbour in the west to Logea (Rogeia) Island in the east, and includes Suau Island, Igoigoli Island, and the Brumer Islands. According to an article in the *Papuan Villager* ('Suau Wood Carving' 1929), probably by F.E. Williams, the Suau people were among the finest wood carvers of the Massim district in the first decades of the 20th century.

Four carvings in Mutuaga's naturalistic style are still held by members of the Abel family, and a few more are known to have once belonged to them. The independent figure in figure 18.14 was taken by Charles Abel to England in 1900, and is now held by his grandson Chris Abel. Cecil Abel found the pig spatula in figure 18.19 among his possessions in 1993 (he could not recall how he had obtained it), and it is now also in Chris Abel's collection. Figure 18.16 reproduces a photograph taken in 1930, almost certainly at the Kwato Mission House, of two independent human figures. The figure on the left remained there until 1965, and has since been held by Sheila Abel, a daughter-in-law of Charles Abel. The whereabouts of the figure on the right is unknown. The bowl cum betelnut mortar in figure 18.18 belongs to Badi (Marjorie) Smeeton, the younger daughter of Charles Abel, born in 1909. She cannot recall how she acquired it, but as she lived in Kwato Island until 1949, she may have obtained it while living there. The bowl is referred to below as the Smeeton Bowl.

Robert Abel, an Auckland resident and brother of Charles Abel, donated the human figure spatula in figure 18.15 and the pig spatula in figure 18.20 to the Auckland Museum in 1937. Presumably he had obtained them from his brother.

When Cecil Abel saw Mutuaga for the last time in 1920, shortly before Abel went to England for a few years, Mutuaga gave him a headrest with human figure supports in the naturalistic style and a spatula with a canoe-end handle and told him that they were his own work. Cecil Abel took them to England with a drummer figure spatula by Mutuaga, and a spatula with a clapper handle, perhaps also by Mutuaga. Their whereabouts is unknown, but a drawing of the headrest has been published (Abel 1934:69) and is reproduced in figure 18.17. Cecil Abel believed that the highly stylised canoe-end spatula Mutuaga gave him was of the same style and design as that in figure 18.21.

On two occasions in 1990 and 1991, Cecil Abel viewed pictures of two thirds of the artworks in the naturalistic style in the Inventory and told me which of them he attributed to Mutuaga. He was not asked to do this for illustrations of artworks in the naturalistic style that became available after 1991, because he had by then learnt of my attributions and I wanted to obtain from him only attributions uninfluenced by mine. Of the seventeen art works in the naturalistic style associated with Black and the Abel family, Cecil Abel attributed to Mutuaga those in figures 18.2, 18.4, 18.6, 18.9, 18.10, 18.15, 18.16 (figure on left), and 18.17. When he told me of his discovery of the spatula in figure 18.19 among his possessions in 1993, he said it was also by Mutuaga. He was uncertain whether the pig spatula in figure 18.20 was by Mutuaga, because of the unusual curved shape of its head and extensive scrollwork below the head. He thought the carvings in figures 18.3 and 18.8 were not by Mutuaga, the former because of its low quality, the latter for reasons not recorded. He was not asked to consider the attribution of the carvings in figures 18.5, 18.7, 18.14, 18.16 (figure on right) and 18.18 because no pictures of them were available at the time. In the section 'Attribution', below, only the more important of Abel's attributions are mentioned.

The individuation of Massim carving styles

I claim that the anthropomorphic handles of the spatulas attributed to Mutuaga by Black and Cecil Abel are carved in a very distinctive naturalistic version of the Massim style. This claim is most easily substantiated by comparing this style to other styles in which Massim spatula figures are carved.

The human figure is represented on about a thousand extant Massim lime spatulas. I now recognise among the better-carved spatulas collected in the 19th and early 20th centuries more than a dozen distinct substyles of the Massim

style. The following are five of these substyles, including the naturalistic substyle already described.

For ease of future reference each substyle is said to be that of a master carver or school of master carvers. This is not meant to imply that the carvers had the formal status of master carver in their society or had been trained in an apprenticeship system, although in some cases this may have been the case. It is meant to imply that the carvers produced work of outstanding quality, and that the similarity among the works by members of a school is due to each member's familiarity with the work of at least one other member of it.

If very few stylistically uniform examples of a substyle exist, it is quite likely that a single carver has been identified. If there are many examples of a substyle, with some stylistic variation among them, a number of carvers may have used the style, or one carver may have had a long carving career and modified his style over time. Only a brief description of each substyle is possible in this paper and so the example of each substyle illustrated must, to some extent, speak for itself.

Master(s) of the Concave Back: As the example in figure 18.22 shows, this is the most stylised of the five substyles identified in this paper. The conception of the figure is two-dimensional. Therefore, the figure's body measures only 10 millimetres or less from shoulder to shoulder, but 20 to 35 millimetres from the back of the shoulders to the front of the hands. Its body consists almost entirely of the limbs, with only a hint of the torso. The elbows rest on the knees and the figure's back is very concave. The face is T-shaped (see 'Glossary'), the eyes are circular, and the nose has flared nostrils and a pierced septum. Each bracket consists of one scroll, which probably represents two stylised birds' heads facing each other.[8] There are dozens of examples, including those published in Chauvet (1930: ill. 245) and Wingert (1953: ill. 54), and they are probably from Kitava Island in the Trobriand Archipelago.

Master(s) of the Interlocking Scrolls (fig. 18.23):   The figure is stylised, but a little less so than that of Substyle I. The conception of the figure is more two-dimensional than three-dimensional, but the torso is clearly shown and separates the elbows from the knees. The face is T-shaped, the eyes are circular, and the tip of the tongue is visible between the lips. Usually each side of the torso and each limb shows two interlocking half-scrolls. The brackets include two birds' heads, whose beaks point towards the blade and to its tip. There are at least six clear examples, including those published in Brizzi (1976: 239) and Newton (1975: ill. 18), and a few degraded ones; all of them are probably from the Trobriand Islands or possibly Woodlark Island.

Master(s) of the Realistic Proportions (fig. 18.24): The conception of the figure is three-dimensional and semirealistic. The head, body, and limbs are roughly in realistic proportion to each other, the hands and feet have digits, but the limbs are spindly and rectangular in cross-section. The torso is clearly shown, the limbs are partly free from it, and the elbows rest on the knees. The face is T-shaped, the eyes are circular or oval, and the mouth is placed very close to the chin. There are no brackets. Only four clear examples have been located, including one published repeatedly (Christie's London 1982: Lot 136; Christie's South Kensington 1988: Lot 65; Rubin 1984: vol. II, p. 440). They were probably carved in the 19th century by one carver whose location is unknown.

Master(s) of the Prominent Eyes (fig. 18.25): The conception of the figure is three-dimensional, and the figure is even more naturalistic than that of Substyle III. The higher realism is due to the well-rounded head, shoulders and buttocks, cylindrical conception of torso and limbs, and a face that is approximately V-shaped. However, the legs are disproportionately smaller than in nature and, because of this, the knees do not reach the elbows on squatting figures. The limbs are free from the torso in some examples, and two figures have a loin cover. Very unusually for Massim art, the eyes (with one exception) consist of raised ovals with smaller ovals engraved on them. Usually in Massim art the eye is circular and engraved directly onto the face. Some examples have no brackets, two have brackets featuring two birds' heads with beaks pointing towards the blade and to

the handle, and another two have brackets featuring two birds' heads pointing away from the blade and away from the handle. Eleven examples have been located, including those published in the Baltimore Museum of Art (1956: item 113), Beran (1988: ills 11-13), and Bourgoin (1994: 35, no. 4). They date from the 19th century. Only three have a known or probable place of collection. One was collected in the Trobriands, another in Milne Bay, a third probably in the Suau or Milne Bay region. This and their stylistic similarity to the anthropomorphic spatulas of the next substyle suggest southern Massim production.[9]

Master(s) of the Naturalistic Style (figs 18.2-18.4, 18.15, 18.26-18.29 show spatulas with squatting figures): This is, of course, the style of the anthropomorphic spatulas attributed to Mutuaga by Black and Cecil Abel. The conception of the figure is fully three-dimensional and more naturalistic than in all other traditional Massim substyles. The head is fully rounded and the neck, torso, and the limbs are cylindrical, with the limbs usually partly free from the torso. Some figures hold a drum. Irrespective of this, almost all figures have the elbows resting on the knees. The face is usually V-shaped. The figure usually shows a great deal of naturalistic detail that has already been described. The buttocks of squatting figures show part of the loin-cover men wear; the one standing figure on a spatula (fig. 18.30) shows the complete loin-cover. The brackets often include birds' heads; if they include only two, their beaks point away from the blade and to its tip. On some pieces the beaks of the most prominent birds' heads are elaborated into further birds' heads.

The comparison of these five substyles of spatula figures shows that such substyles can readily be identified within the Massim style, and that the substyles of traditional Massim spatulas range, by gradation, from the highly stylised to the naturalistic.[10]

Attribution

Apart from identifying Mutuaga as one of the Masters of the Naturalistic Style, the main task of this paper is to

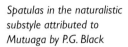

Spatulas in the naturalistic substyle attributed to Mutuaga by P.G. Black

18.2 (Far left) Spatula collected by P.G. Black, 1886-1901 (SV3) (Inv. 17). By Mutuaga. (Photo: Buffalo Museum of Science.)

18.3 (Centre left) Spatula collected by P.G. Black, 1901-13 (SV5) (Inv. 13). Probably by Mutuaga. (Photo: Buffalo Museum of Science.)

18.4 (Left) Spatula collected by P.G. Black, 1886-1901 (SV3) (Inv. 9). By Mutuaga. (Photo: Buffalo Museum of Science.)

Artworks in the naturalistic substyle attributed to Mutuaga by P.G. Black

18.5 (Far left) Figure collected by P.G. Black, 1901-13 (SV3) (Inv. 55). Not attributed. (Photo: Buffalo Museum of Science.)

18.6 (Centre left) Figure collected by P.G. Black, 1886-1901 (SV3) (Inv. 56). By Mutuaga. (Photo: Buffalo Museum of Science.)

18.7 (Left) Staff collected by P.G. Black, 1886-1901 (SV3) (Inv. 82). By Mutuaga. (Photo: Buffalo Museum of Science.)

consider how many of the carvings in the naturalistic substyle can be attributed to him on the basis of style and historical information.

The attribution to Mutuaga of carvings in non-naturalistic styles is beyond the scope of the paper, but is attempted, to some extent, in my book-length study of Mutuaga (1996). In that book I accept Cecil Abel's report that Mutuaga made spatulas with stylised canoe-end handles, such as that shown in figure 18.21, and tentatively attribute this spatula to him. However, again following Cecil Abel, I reject the attribution to Mutuaga of the six spatulas of various stylised designs that is made in the 1901 and 1914 catalogues of the P.G. Black Collection (three of them are shown in figures 18.11 to 18.13). I have made no systematic attempt to locate some of the other types of carving that Mutuaga made according to Weibo Mamohoi, such as presentation axe handles and handles for the presentation of shell money.

Talented tribal artists in many societies in Africa, North America, Polynesia and Melanesia develop personal versions of the art styles of their cultures, and this provides some scope for attributing artworks to artists on the basis of style (Fagg 1963, 1965; Fischer 1963; Gerbrands 1967; Holm 1981, 1983; Neich 1991; Thompson 1973). However, in some cultures there is hardly any difference between the styles of different artists (Fagg 1963:120). And, even in cultures where great artists tend to develop personal styles, attribution of works to particular artists is made difficult by three things: two artists can, at least at times, work in indistinguishable styles (Fischer 1963:166; Holm 1983:30, 46-7, 72, 103-5); an artist's style can change over time (Holm 1983:113; Thompson 1973); and one artist can work in two or more different styles simultaneously (Neich 1991).[11]

'The individuation of Massim carving styles', above, shows that the human figure on Massim spatulas is carved in a range of different styles, and this opens up the possibility that gifted Massim artists develop personal styles. Is it possible to attribute carvings in the naturalistic substyle to Mutuaga on stylistic grounds? The primary yardstick for doing so must be the carvings in this style attributed to him by Black (figs 18.2 to 18.10) and those associated with the Abel family and attributed to him by Cecil Abel (figs 18.15, 18.16 (figure on left), 18.17 and 18.19).[12]

Attribution of carvings to Mutuaga on a stylistic basis is made difficult by two things. First, there is considerable variation of stylistic detail and quality among the naturalistic carvings, especially the anthropomorphic ones. Second, Weibo reports that carvers other than Mutuaga also made naturalistic anthropomorphic carvings. Such spatulas were also made by Banieva (circa 1863 to the early 1930s) of Sapauri village, and Ninia (circa 1880 to circa 1935) of Leawa village; human figures on pedestals were also made by these two and Faivivi (from around 1880 to around 1950) of Savaia village; and walking sticks were also carved by Ninia, and by Taulelegi (from around 1885 to around 1970) of Sibalai village. (All the villages mentioned are shown in figure 18.1.) No one other than Mutuaga was mentioned as having made pig spatulas.[13] Cecil Abel had not heard of these contemporaries of Mutuaga until I mentioned them to him, and was not aware of anyone other than Mutuaga bringing carvings in the naturalistic substyle to the Kwato Mission House.

Banieva was of the same generation as Mutuaga. Ninia and Faivivi represent the next generation of carvers in the central Suau area, but, due to the impact of colonial government and the missions, they also represent the last generation that carved traditional objects or objects for trade on a regular basis. Unfortunately, I obtained no information about the generation of carvers before Mutuaga and Banieva.

Bowl cum mortar

It is best to begin the task of attribution with this carving, because it points to two significant stylistic distinctions that are of help in attributing some of the other carvings. In 1993 Weibo recalled a bowl on four legs with two human figures on the rim, carved by Banieva and used for holding betel nuts while people were sitting together chewing them. Since then Badi Smeeton has shown me the bowl in figure 18.18 (the Smeeton Bowl), which is like the one described by Weibo except that it has a mortar for crushing betel nuts in the centre, and a human figure and a pig on the rim. As already noted, she cannot recall how she acquired it. Although I have a comprehensive knowledge of collections of Massim betel-chewing utensils, I have not seen another bowl cum mortar even remotely like the present one. It is, therefore, possible that this is the bowl Weibo recalls and, if it is not, it probably is another carved by Banieva.

The Smeeton Bowl is unlikely to be by Mutuaga because the scrolling on the top and side of its rim is different in two ways from similar scrolling on the naturalistic carvings that can be attributed to him with the greatest confidence; that is, those attributed to him by Black and those associated with the Abel family and attributed to him by Cecil Abel. The two differences are shown in figure 18.45, in which the white sections represent intaglio filled in with lime. The straight parts of the reverse-side scrolls in panels A and B rise from left to right, while the straight parts of the scrolls in panels C and D fall from left to right. The white filler lines more or less at right angles to the straight parts of the scrolls are straight all the way in panels A and C, while they flare in panels B and D as they approach the straight parts of the scrolls. The two differences create four options for an artist in decorating his creations.

The carvings that can be attributed to Mutuaga with most confidence show that he has a very strong but not complete preference for rising reverse-side scrolls, and a complete preference for straight filler lines. Because the top and side of the rim of the Smeeton Bowl are decorated with falling reverse-side scrolls and flared filler lines, it is unlikely to be by Mutuaga.

Spatulas with squatting human figure handles and independent figures

The attribution of the spatulas with squatting human figures and independent human figures has to be preceded by a classification of the variations in stylistic detail and quality among them. The following features vary together, at least to some extent, and, therefore, permit the identification of seven style variations among anthropomorphic carvings in the naturalistic substyle.[14] The features are: the

degree of naturalism; the shape of the neck, face and eyes (see figure 18.46 for drawings of the various eye-shapes); and the type and extent of scrolling on the figure. Although they are not matters of style, the presence or absence of a drum, the carving's quality, and its collection period are also mentioned, as they seem to be related to the variations in style.

The style variations among spatulas with squatting human figure handles and independent figures are as follows:

- *Style Variation 1*: The spatula figure that is the sole member of this style variation (fig. 18.26) resembles the members of Style Variation 2 in having a straight neck, a flat face, and circular eyes. But unlike almost all other human figures in the naturalistic substyle, the face is T-shaped, there is no philtrum, the ulna prominence is absent on the left hand and only hinted at on the other, the ankle bone is absent on the right foot and only hinted at on the other, and the loop of the loin cover at the buttocks is absent, as are the brackets at the top of the spatula's blade. Uniquely among the thirty spatula figures, it has nipples (but two independent figures of Style Variation 3, including that in figure 18.6, also have them), and its back is decorated with rectangular engravings along its spinal sulcus. Uniquely among the drummer figures, its right hand is placed on its cheek instead of on the drumhead, and the drum is connected to the figure's torso with a bracket, presumably to stop it from breaking off. It was discovered at a bric-a-brac market in Australia, without provenance, in the 1980s. I dub it the Drummer at Rest because the right hand is not on the drumhead ready to beat it.
- *Style Variation 2*: The nine spatula figures of this group, including seven drummers, have a flat or flattish face, mostly with circular eyes, but in three cases with eyes carved in relief and incised in the shape of an almond. The figure's neck is a straight column. Apart from the features mentioned, all the usual naturalistic detail is

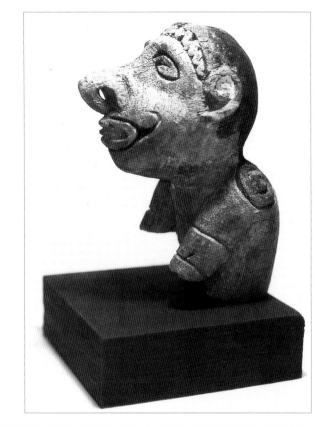

Artworks in the naturalistic substyle attributed to Mutuaga by P.G. Black

18.8   (Right) Fragmentary figure collected by P.G. Black, 1886-1901 (SV3) (Inv. 79). By Mutuaga. (Photo: Buffalo Museum of Science.)

18.9   (Below) Spatula collected by P.G. Black, 1886-1901 (Inv. 31). By Mutuaga. (Photo: Buffalo Museum of Science.)

18.10   (Bottom) Spatula collected by P.G. Black, 1886-1901 (Inv. 32). By Mutuaga. (Photo: Buffalo Museum of Science.)

Spatulas in non-naturalistic styles attributed to Mutuaga by P.G. Black, perhaps erroneously

18.11   (Far left) Spatula collected by P.G. Black, 1886-1901. Buffalo Museum of Science C8340. By unknown carver. (Photo: Buffalo Museum of Science.)

18.12   (Left) Spatula collected by P.G. Black, 1886-1901. Buffalo Museum of Science C8345. By unknown carver. (Photo: Buffalo Museum of Science.)

18.13   (Below) Spatula collected by P.G. Black, 1886-1901. Denver Art Museum 1940.330, ex Buffalo Museum of Science C8342. By unknown carver. (Photo: Denver Art Museum.)

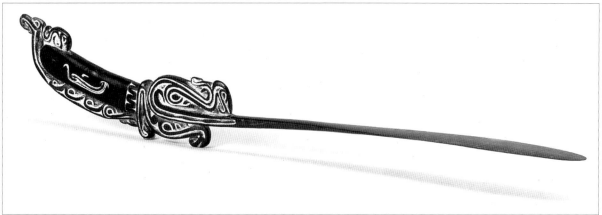

present: V-shaped face, philtrum, ulna prominence, ankle bones, and limbs that are muscular and thick enough to be roughly in correct proportion to the torso. The members of this group are of high quality and include the finest of all the spatulas (fig. 18.28). The group also includes the two anthropomorphic spatulas with the earliest known collection dates: 1884 for one (fig. 18.27), which is transitional in style between Style Variations 1 and 2, and 1886-87 for the other (Inventory 3).

Three independent figures belong to Style Variation 2 (one is shown in figure 18.38). They have a flat face, majestic nose, and comparatively little scrolling on the back. One has eyes formed by two engraved concentric circles, while the other two have raised almond-shaped eyes. All three have the well-muscled limbs absent from Style Variation 1, but present in the other style variations. The two figures whose whereabouts is known are comparable in quality to the finest spatula figures of Style Variation 2.

• *Style Variation 3*: The ten spatula figures of this group, including three drummers, have more or less rounded faces, and necks that widen naturalistically as they meet head and torso. All have a band of zigzags running across their cheeks, and most have much scrolling on their backs. Most have eyes carved as an open scroll with overlapping ends. Their quality is high. The two spatulas collected by Black between 1886 and 1901 (figs 18.2, 18.4) are typical examples of the group. They are also the only ones with a known collection period. Another two pieces included in the group (Inventory 11 and 16) are intermediate in style between Style Variations 2 and 3.

Nine independent figures belong to this style variation; three are shown in figures 18.5, 18.6 and 18.14. They have a rounded face and much scrolling on the back. Eight have engraved scrolled eyes, and another has eyes that consist of two engraved concentric ovals. Six have bands on their cheeks. Eight are elegant sculptures, but the ninth, shown in figure 18.5, is a poor stiff carving. Two of the figures, including that in figure 18.6, have prominent nipples.

• *Style Variation 4*: Of the two spatula figures in this group, one is a drummer (fig. 18.29). They differ from the previous group in having almond-shaped eyes, and perhaps in being not quite as well sculpted. One of the spatulas was accessioned by a museum in 1903, and the other turned up at auction in Sydney in 1976 without provenance.

Four independent figures belong to this style variation; two are shown in figure 18.16. They have rounded faces, almond-shaped eyes, bands on the cheeks, and much scrolling on the back. There is some reduction in quality compared to the previous group.

• *Style Variation 5*: The six spatulas in this group, including one drummer, differ from those of Style Variations 3 and 4 in a number of respects: the figures' engraved almond-shaped eyes have upper eyelids (created by a groove above the eye); there is a considerable reduction in elegance and naturalistic detail in some figures; and the following four spatulas have unusual features. One spatula has unique brackets (Inventory 26), one has a figure positioned in profile relative to the blade (Inventory 25), one has a figure with unusual scrolling on the back and lacks brackets (Inventory 27),[15] and one has a figure that is unique among spatula figures in having a broad chest and belly that are covered in scrolls and zigzags (Inventory 28). One member of the group was collected by Black between 1901 and 1913 (fig. 18.3); another was accessioned by a museum in 1911 (Inventory 26). The spatula with a standing figure on top of a half-figure (fig. 18.30) is also of Style Variation 5, and was collected between 1904 and 1906.

Six independent figures belong to this style

variation; one is shown in figure 18.39. They have almond-shaped eyes with upper eyelids, bands on the cheeks, and much scrolling on the back. Their quality is comparable to that of the independent figures of Style Variation 4.

Style Variation 6: This variation comprises three independent figures and no spatulas. One is a figure standing on a pedestal (fig. 18.40); another is a figure leaning against a chair, all on a pedestal (Inventory 75); the third sculpture consists of two addorsed figures squatting on their feet and surmounted by a relatively large animal, with all three creatures resting on a pedestal (Inventory 74).

Although the third sculpture is totally different in composition from the first two, all three share four features that distinguish them from those already dealt with. First, the figures have ears of equal height and width, whereas the ears of the figures in the previous style variations are always of greater height than width. Second, the figures lack the spinal sulcus that all the independent figures of the previous style variations have. Third, the sculptures are decorated with bands of zigzags whose lines are angled more widely than those on the carvings of the previous variations. Fourth, the bases of the sculptures are decorated with falling reverse-side scrolls with flared filler lines, as shown in figure 18.45D. In this respect the sculptures are reminiscent of the Smeeton Bowl (fig. 18.18). Two of the sculptures consist of single human figures; the reverse-side scrolls that decorate these figures are also entirely of the falling type with flared filler lines.

These two figures are much larger than the two squatting figures that are part of the third sculpture of Style Variation 6, and therefore display their style more clearly than the last. They have lumpy bodies, arms squashed into their bodies, hands with very long spidery fingers fully turned back against the arms, and feet with very large heels. This combination of features

distinguishes them clearly from the members of all other style variations.

- *Style Variation 7*: Although the remaining two sculptures, both independent figures, differ in some details from each other, they share three features that distinguish them from those of the other style variations, and this suggests uniting them in a style variation of their own. One of the figures is shown in figure 18.41. First, their bases are decorated with wavy lines rather than zigzags. Second, the bodies of the figures carry no scrolling and are decorated only with zigzags. Third, and most important, are the ineptly carved hands of the figures. The right hand of the figure in figure 18.41 looks as though it has lost its fingers. It is entirely different from the fine naturalistic hands of the figures of Style Variations 2 to 5, and from the long-fingered hands of the two large figures of Style Variation 6. The figure not illustrated is a squatting figure holding a drum.

Attribution: The carvings of Style Variations 3 and 4 can be attributed to Mutuaga straightforwardly. It is, therefore, best to start with these groups and then to proceed to those whose attribution is less easy.

All except one of the carvings of Style Variations 3 and 4 can be attributed to Mutuaga with full confidence. Nine are shown in figures 18.2, 18.4 to 18.6, 18.14 to 18.16, and 18.29. They exemplify the style that Cecil Abel recognised as Mutuaga's without hesitation. He saw photographs of most of them, and of these he attributed all to Mutuaga except one (Inventory 58). He was uncertain whether to attribute this figure to Mutuaga because of its unusually large size. However, it can safely be attributed to Mutuaga because of its very great similarity to two equally large figures of Style Variation 2 (fig. 18.38 and Inventory 54), which will be shown to be by Mutuaga in the discussion of this style variation.

All the anthropomorphic spatulas and independent figures associated with the Abel family belong to Style Variations 3 and 4; and so do those attributed to Mutuaga

Artworks in the naturalistic substyle associated with the Abel family

18.14 (Far left) Figure collected by Charles Abel, base unfinished (SV3) (Inv. 57). By Mutuaga. (Photo: Christie's South Kensington.)

18.15 (Left) Spatula donated by R.S. Abel to Auckland Museum (SV3) (Inv. 18). By Mutuaga. (Photo: Auckland Museum.)

Figures in the naturalistic substyle associated with the Abel family
18.16 Two figures photographed at the Kwato Mission House in 1930, nose of figure on left chipped (SV4) (Inv. 64, 65). By Mutuaga. (Photo: B. Platt. Reproduced by permission of Paulian New Guinea Arts, Sydney.)

Artworks in the naturalistic substyle associated with the Abel family

18.17 (Top) Headrest given by Mutuaga to Cecil Abel in 1920 (Inv. 94). By Mutuaga. (After a drawing by Frank R. Southard in Abel (1934).)

18.18 (Bottom) Bowl cum betel-nut mortar in Badi Smeeton Collection (Inv. 95). Probably by Banieva. (Photo: Simone Rose and Shalia.)

Spatulas: two in the naturalistic substyle (top and centre), one in a non-naturalistic style (bottom)

18.19 (Top) Spatula once owned by Cecil Abel, pig's snout deficient (Inv. 33). By Mutuaga. (Photo: Cecil Abel.)

18.20 (Centre) Spatula donated by R.S. Abel to Auckland Museum (Inv. 34). By Mutuaga. (Photo: Auckland Museum.)

18.21 (Bottom) Spatula of canoe-end design like that given by Mutuaga to Cecil Abel in 1920. Royal Scottish Museum, Edinburgh 1954.190. Perhaps by Mutuaga. (Photo: Royal Scottish Museum.)

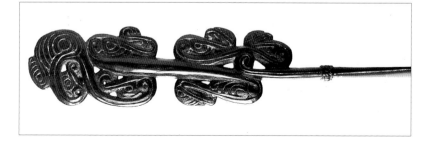

by Black, except for one drummer spatula that belongs to Style Variation 5.

One of the independent figures attributed to Mutuaga by Black (fig. 18.5) presents a puzzle. Cecil Abel did not see a picture of it when he made his attributions. It has the scrolled eyes typical of Style Variation 3, but none of the quality that all the other independent figures and spatula figures of this group have. Because I did not see the figure during my visit to the Buffalo Museum of Science, I am reluctant to decide whether to attribute it to Mutuaga or to one of his followers, despite Black's attribution of it to the former.

The spatulas and independent figures of Style Variation 2 can be attributed to Mutuaga on the basis of circumstantial evidence. Three are shown in figures 18.27, 18.28 and 18.38. The superb independent figure in figure 18.38, with a flat face and almond-shaped raised eyes, clearly belongs to Style Variation 2. It must have been made by Mutuaga, because he is the carver Charles Abel inspired to create such figures. Abel did not arrive in the Suau region until August 1891, and the figure was donated to the Australian Museum in March 1893. Therefore, it must have been made between these dates, too early to be the work of a follower of Mutuaga. The figure is clearly by the same inspired hand as the other two independent figures and the spatula figures of Style Variation 2.

The sole member of Style Variation 1, the Drummer at Rest (fig. 18.26), can also be attributed to Mutuaga, but with less confidence. It is the least naturalistic of the spatulas (and indeed of all the anthropomorphic carvings) in the naturalistic substyle. Interestingly, the Drummer at Rest is closest, stylistically, to the spatula with the earliest known collection date, 1884, shown in figure 18.27. Therefore, the latter spatula provides the stylistic transition between the Drummer at Rest and the spatulas of Style Variation 2.

Also, the Drummer at Rest is the only drummer on which the drum is not supported in an aesthetically satisfactory way. For a dramatic composition the drum has to be free from the drummer's torso, but it must also be anchored well so as not to break off. On the Drummer at Rest the drum's support is provided by the drummer's feet, his left hand, and a clamp from the drum to his belly. His right hand is placed on his cheek. On all other drummers, the right hand is shifted to the drumhead, thus removing the need for the aesthetically unsatisfactory clamp. This provides support for the hypothesis that the Drummer at Rest is a very early work by Mutuaga, carved before he had fully solved the problem of anchoring the drums to his drummers.

The spatulas of Style Variation 2 are such accomplished carvings that they cannot be the first anthropomorphic spatulas Mutuaga carved. Hence, if the Drummer at Rest is not by Mutuaga, there would have to be other anthropomorphic spatulas, perhaps now lost, from Mutuaga's developmental period.

The six independent figures of Style Variation 5 can be attributed to Mutuaga with confidence. One is shown in figure 18.39. Cecil Abel saw illustrations of three others (Inventory 68 to 70) and attributed them to him.

However, the attribution of the spatulas of this style variation is difficult because of conflicting evidence. Three of the spatulas (Inventory 24 to 26) can readily be attributed to Mutuaga and were attributed to him by Cecil Abel. But the other three spatulas (fig. 18.3 and Inventory 27 and 28) are of such low quality that it is hard to believe that they are by the same hand as the masterpieces of Style Variations 2 and 3. The three spatulas clearly are by one hand, but whose? Cecil Abel believed that they are not sufficiently well carved to be Mutuaga's work, but the carver may not have shown his poorest efforts to members of the Abel family. Black attributes one of the three poorest spatulas (fig. 18.3) to Mutuaga, but we do not know the basis of Black's attribution, and it is therefore not beyond challenge. I cannot suggest that they are immature efforts of Mutuaga because I claim below that, if they are by him, they are late pieces.

Production of the three mediocre pieces by a follower of Mutuaga could explain their low quality, but not so easily a particular type of continuity they have with the carvings of Style Variations 1 to 4 already attributed to Mutuaga. The three mediocre spatulas display five features that occur on the spatulas of Style Variations 1 to 4, but each feature occurs only on a small proportion of

Spatulas in various substyles

18.22 (Far left) Spatula by the Master(s) of the Concave Back. Author's collection HB160. (Photo: Simone Rose and Sharia.)

18.23 (Left) Spatula by the Master(s) of the Interlocking Scrolls. Author's collection HB101, ex Hooper Collection. (Photo: Simone Rose and Sharia.)

18.24 (Far left) Spatula by the Master(s) of the Realistic Proportions. Author's collection HB193. (Photo: Simone Rose and Sharia.)

18.25 (Left) Spatula by the Master(s) of the Prominent Eyes. Anthropology Museum, University of Aberdeen VII-87-15. (Photo: Anthropology Museum, University of Aberdeen.)

the latter carvings, and the five features do not occur together in any systematic way. They are: a prominent aquiline nose; powerful cupped hands placed on the cheeks; simple face-like brackets at the top of the blade without the addition of birds' heads; a two-tiered instead of a one-tiered platform to support the squatting figure; and a starlike motif consisting of two concentric circles, with short lines radiating from the outer circle.

The prominent aquiline nose also occurs on two of the mediocre spatula figures (fig. 18.3 and Inventory 27); the powerful cupped hands occur on two of them (Inventory 27 and 28); the simple bracket and two-tiered platform occur on one of them (Inventory 28); and the starlike motif occurs on one of them (Inventory 27). The most plausible explanation of the features of the three mediocre spatulas is that they are by Mutuaga's hand. A follower of Mutuaga is much more likely to have copied features that were used frequently by Mutuaga rather than five different features, each used only rarely by him.

Production of the three spatulas by an old Mutuaga with failing powers would explain why they have his stylistic features but are of low quality. But one of the spatulas was collected by Black before 1914, and Cecil Abel reported that the carvings Mutuaga brought to the Kwato Mission in 1920 were still of good quality. Perhaps the three spatulas are Mutuaga's 'malaria pieces'. Though still of generally good health in his fifties, he may have been unwell for stretches of time, but may still have carved spatulas for the sake of the trade goods he could obtain for them.

The three independent figures that comprise Style Variation 6 are stylistically so different from the members of the previous five style variations that they cannot plausibly be attributed to Mutuaga, and have enough in common to be attributed to a single follower. One figure is shown in figure 18.40. Because all the reverse-side scrolls on the three sculptures are falling ones, the follower is dubbed the Master of the Falling Scroll. Cecil Abel thought the three sculptures were not by Mutuaga.

Some of the features that distinguish Style Variation 6 from Style Variations 1 to 5 can also be found on a few members of Style Variations 4 and 5. For example, a few figures have hands twisted back against the arm (for example, Inventory 65 and 69), and the former of these, shown on the right in figure 18.16, has elongated fingers on one hand. But any single figure by Mutuaga has only one or two of the features distinctive of the figures of Style Variation 6 and, therefore, looks quite different from them. This can be seen clearly at the Australian Museum, which has independent figures of Style Variation 2 (Inventory 53), Style Variation 4 (Inventory 66), Style Variation 5 (Inventory 68), and Style Variation 6 (Inventory 74 and 75).

Informants in the central Suau area mentioned three carvers, apart from Mutuaga, as having made independent figures in the naturalistic substyle. Of these, Banieva is most likely to be responsible for the three carvings of Style Variation 6, if he is indeed the carver of the Smeeton Bowl. This is so because the bowl and the independent figures carry the same falling reverse-side scrolls and the same flared filler lines. The human figure on the rim of the Smeeton Bowl does not display very strong stylistic characteristics, but could be by the same hand as the small figures that are part of one of the carvings of Style Variation 6 (Inventory 74).

The two figures of Style Variation 7 are stylistically so different from the previous style variations that they cannot be attributed to Mutuaga or the Master of the Falling Scroll. One is shown in figure 18.41. They may be by one carver, who is dubbed the Master of the Zigzag, because the figures are decorated with zigzags and zigzag-like wavy lines, and are devoid of scrolling. However, because of their low quality, 'master' is here only a courtesy title. There is no evidence as to whether this carver is Ninia or Faivivi, the carvers mentioned by Suau informants as having made independent figures in the naturalistic substyle, but to whom none has been attributed so far. Cecil Abel did not see pictures of the two sculptures.

Now that the carvings of Style Variations 6 and 7 have been attributed to carvers other than Mutuaga, it is worth returning to the three spatulas of Style Variation 5 that cannot be attributed to Mutuaga with full confidence because of their low quality. Whether their tentative attribution to Mutuaga is correct or not, there are certainly no stylistic reasons to attribute them to the carvers responsible

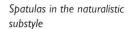

Spatulas in the naturalistic substyle

18.26 (Far left) Spatula, the Drummer at Rest (SV1) (Inv. 1). Probably by Mutuaga. (Photo: Simone Rose and Sharia.)

18.27 (Centre left) Spatula collected by Sir James Erskine in 1884 (SV2) (Inv. 2). By Mutuaga. (Photo: Royal Museum of Scotland, Neg. H7875.)

18.28 (Left) Spatula (SV2) (Inv. 5). By Mutuaga. (Photo: Museum of Mankind, London.)

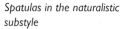

Spatulas in the naturalistic substyle

18.29 (Far left) Spatula (SV4) (Inv. 12). By Mutuaga. (Photo: Ursula Didoni, Linden-Museum, Stuttgart, Neg. p1663/9.)

18.30 (Second from far left) Spatula collected by Sir Hubert Murray, 1904-06 (SV5) (Inv. 29). Probably by Mutuaga. (Drawing: Keith Fyfe, after photos by author.)

18.31 (Third from far left) Spatula with Janus figure (Inv. 30). Probably by Mutuaga. (Photo: John Bayalis and Homer V. Holdren, Field Museum, Chicago.)

18.32 (Left) Spatula with rectangle, birds and pig as handle (Inv. 51). Probably by Mutuaga. (After ill. 244 in Chauvet (1930).)

for the carvings of Style Variations 6 and 7. Thus, if Banieva and Ninia did indeed carve anthropomorphic spatulas in the naturalistic substyle, as Weibo recalls, I have not located them.

Spatulas with pig handles

Massim spatulas with handles carved as complete animals are rare but not unknown. A spatula with a tree-kangaroo handle and another with a praying-mantis handle have been published repeatedly (Beran 1988: ills 35-6; Bounoure 1992:174-5; Gathercole, Kaeppler and Newton 1979: ills 26.2-26.3; Newton 1975: ills 13-14). There are also a few fine bird-handled spatulas (Beran 1988: ill. 34).

Of the twenty-one pig spatulas I have located, only one (fig. 18.33) is not by the Masters of the Naturalistic Style. It was acquired by the Museum of Mankind, London (+3406), in 1886 and collected by the Reverend Samuel McFarlane, perhaps in the Suau-Milne Bay region, because this is the part of the Massim district where he was active. Though its pig is also carved in a relatively realistic style, it clearly differs from the other twenty spatula pigs by having a flared snout and a straight tail, by resting on a curved bar, and by the absence of scrolling.

Among the other twenty pig spatulas, three stand out: one because the pig's body is completely stylised (fig. 18.34); one because it is carved in a yellow wood, and the pig has extended legs and rests on a base (fig. 18.35); and the third because the pig rests at right angles across the top of the blade and seems to have a penis and testicles (fig. 18.36).[16] The wood of the last-mentioned spatula is not known. All, except for the last two, are in ebony or a fine-grained brown wood.

Although the other seventeen pig spatulas vary in minor stylistic details and in size, the differences do not seem to cluster in a way that makes classification into style variations useful. The four pig spatulas associated with Black and the Abel family, which provide the primary yardstick for attributing the other thirteen to Mutuaga, vary just as much in stylistic details and size as these others. Hence, there is no reason not to attribute all seventeen spatulas to Mutuaga.

The spatula whose handle consists of a pig with a stylised body is, in other respects, stylistically identical to the seventeen just discussed, and there is, therefore, no good reason not to attribute it to Mutuaga. The pig's unusual shape may be due to the shape of the piece of ebony (a rare wood) available for it, or to a flaw in the wood that challenged the carver's ingenuity.

The spatula with a pig on a stand is probably also by Mutuaga. It resembles the 45-centimetre-long pig on a stand in figure 18.37, which, for stylistic reasons, can be attributed to Mutuaga. The spatula was collected in the 1880s, too early to be by a follower of Mutuaga. It is much more likely to be a work of his own from the time when he was still developing the design of his pig spatulas. The stand under the pig, perhaps there to prevent its extended legs from breaking off, makes the spatula inelegant. On all other pig spatulas attributed to Mutuaga, the pig's legs are drawn up to its body, which makes the stand unnecessary and constitutes an aesthetically pleasing design for a spatula handle shaped as a pig.

The spatula with a pig across the top of the blade is stylistically related to the nineteen pig spatulas already attributed to Mutuaga.[17] The pig's body is decorated with a horizontal reverse-side scroll framed by two vertical bands of zigzags, just like the bodies of the other spatula pigs. On the other hand, there are so many stylistic differences from them that it cannot be attributed to Mutuaga: the general conception of the spatula is different, the pig is more elongated, its ears are larger, its sex is indicated, and its eyes are carved as single circles instead of two concentric circles. F.E. Williams appears to have drawn (and possibly collected) the spatula in 1925 during his extended stay in the Suau area.[18] Because the reverse-side scroll engraved on the pig's body is a falling one and, as far as one can tell from the drawing, has flared filler lines, the spatula may be by Banieva.

Three spatulas of various design

The spatula with a human figure standing on a Janus figure in figure 18.30 belongs to Style Variation 5. Stylistically, it is as likely to be by Mutuaga as the others of this style

Pig-handled spatulas: two in the naturalistic substyle (centre and bottom), one in another naturalistic style (top)

18.33 (Top) Spatula collected by Samuel McFarlane in the 1870s-1880s. Museum of Mankind, London +3406. By unknown carver. (Photo: Museum of Mankind, London.)

18.34 (Centre) Spatula with pig with highly stylised body, scrolling above pig's snout missing (Inv. 44). By Mutuaga. (Photo: Ric Bolzen, Australian Museum, Neg. 6435m3-8.)

18.35 (Bottom) Spatula with pig on a stand (Inv. 35). Probably by Mutuaga. (Photo: Museum of Mankind, London.)

Artworks in the naturalistic substyle

18.36 (Top) Spatula with pig across the top of the handle (Inv. 50). Possibly by Banieva. (After a drawing in the *Papuan Villager*, 15 April 1931.)

18.37 (Bottom) Pig on a stand (Inv. 96). By Mutuaga. (Photo: Jim Willis Gallery, San Francisco.)

variation already attributed to him. The spatula in figure 18.31 has a handle carved as a Janus figure with a totally stylised torso, naturalistic arms and hands, and a small seminaturalistic head. The figure is surmounted by a small pig. The figure's head is like Mutuaga's heads, but does not clearly fit into any of the style variations that have been identified. The figure's arms, the scrolls on its torso, and the spatula's brackets are identical to those carved by Mutuaga. Therefore, the spatula is probably by him. The spatula in figure 18.32 has a handle composed of a rectangle, birds and a small pig. Because the pig is identical to that on the previous spatula, this spatula is probably also by Mutuaga.

Staffs

Most Massim staffs, usually about 1 metre long, are made for sale to Westerners, but some are used by the Massim people in association with magic. One of the nine staffs with anthropomorphic tops in the naturalistic substyle is shown in figure 18.7, one of the four with pig tops in figure 18.43. Eleven of the staffs can be attributed to Mutuaga on the basis of style and carving quality. Their shafts are decorated with non-interlocking rising reverse-side scrolls with straight filler lines. Such scrolls are typical of the carvings already attributed to Mutuaga, except that Mutuaga uses interlocking and non-interlocking scrolls on these carvings.

The remaining two staffs (fig. 18.42 and Inventory 84) are almost identical in design. The human heads that form their tops have scrolled eyes, and so belong to Style Variation 3. But the carving quality, especially that of the staff shown in figure 18.42, is far below that of all other carvings in this style variation that have been attributed to Mutuaga. This suggests they may be by a follower of Mutuaga.

Moreover, the two staffs differ from the eleven staffs attributed to Mutuaga in a number of ways. First, their shape is different from the staffs attributed to Mutuaga in having spool-shaped sections just below the human heads that form their tops. Second, their shafts are decorated with interlocking falling reverse-side scrolls with straight filler lines. Hence, the scrolls on their shafts conform to panel C of figure 18.45, while most of Mutuaga's conform to panel A, and all of those on the carvings attributed to Banieva conform to panel D. Third, the staff in figure 18.42 carries two types of short reverse-side scrolls that are stylistically quite different from the long reverse-side scrolls just discussed and shown in figure 18.45. These shorter types of scroll are not found on any of the other carvings in the naturalistic substyle. The three types of reverse-side scroll on the staff in figure 18.42 are shown in figure 18.47, drawn to the same scale. Finally, the two staffs are shorter than all the others, except for one whose bottom section may be missing (Inventory 86), and indeed are too short to be used as walking sticks.

It is just possible that these two staffs are by Mutuaga and that they differ so much from the other staffs because they were intended for use by the Suau with magic rather than as walking sticks. But their features are more plausibly explained by their being the work of someone who copied Mutuaga's style, was unable to match his carving quality, and introduced new features to distinguish his work from that of Mutuaga. There is no evidence to determine whether they are by Ninia or Tauledega, two carvers mentioned by Suau informants as carvers of staffs.

Human figure fragments and miscellaneous carvings

The two human figure fragments can be attributed to Mutuaga on stylistic grounds. One (Inventory 80) is clearly the upper part of a figure on a pedestal of Style Variation 5. The second fragment (fig. 18.8), of Style Variation 3 and attributed to Mutuaga by Black, is of great interest because it differs from all other anthropomorphic carvings in the naturalistic substyle in being of a lightweight wood and being painted red, black and white. It may be a figure from a canoe prow. No such canoe prows are known from the Suau area, but the Peabody Museum, Salem, has a canoe prow (E25, 111), apparently from Milne Bay, with a small sitting human figure carved fully in the round.

The headrest in figure 18.17 was given to Cecil Abel by Mutuaga in 1920, and the carver told Abel that it was his work. The quality of the carving and the precise style of the figure supports cannot be judged from the drawing

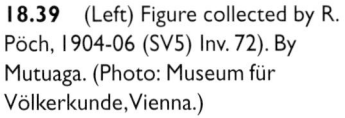

Artworks in the naturalistic substyle

18.38 (Far left) Figure donated by the Reverend W.G. Lawes to the Australian Museum (E3829) in 1893 (SV2) (Inv. 53). By Mutuaga. (Photo: Carl Bento, Australian Museum, Neg. 8266m10-26.)

18.39 (Left) Figure collected by R. Pöch, 1904-06 (SV5) Inv. 72. By Mutuaga. (Photo: Museum für Völkerkunde, Vienna.)

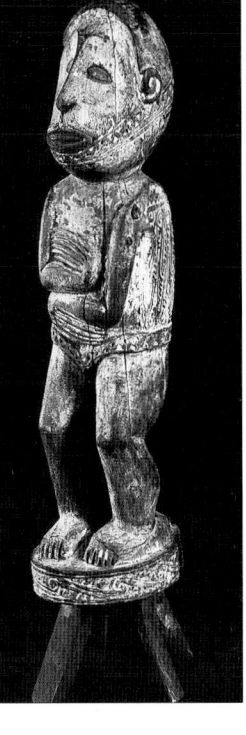

Artworks in the naturalistic substyle

18.40 (Right) Figure (SV 6) (Inv. 76). By the Master of the Falling Scroll (perhaps Banieva). (Photo: Royal Museum of Central Africa, Neg. 126,837.)

18.41 (Far right) Figure (SV 7) (Inv. 78). By the Master of the Zigzag. (Photo: John Bayalis and Homer V. Holdren, Field Museum, Chicago.)

available. I have also physically inspected sixty-nine of the carvings, including that of which no illustration is available, but over a period going back to 1979. A few pieces I have not seen since that year. The opportunity to see all the pieces together might reveal features not noted here that would further support the attributions made, but it might also reveal other features that would lead to revised attributions.

An attempt at a chronology of the changes in Mutuaga's style of anthropomorphic carvings may make it possible to give a coherent explanation of these changes and, thereby, to strengthen the attributions made. The years of collection or accession to a collection of the carvings, recorded in the 'Inventory', provide some support for the hypothesis that the chronological order of the changes in Mutuaga's style is the same as the numerical order, in this essay, of the five style variations in his work. They are certainly consistent with it.

If this hypothesis is correct, the chronology of changes in his style is as follows: he carved figures with semirealistic bodies and stylised heads around 1880 (Style Variation 1); subsequent figures have more realistic bodies, but in the 1880s they still have stylised heads with flat faces and circular eyes (Style Variation 2); from the 1890s he made figures with rounded faces, and in this decade they have scrolled eyes (Style Variation 3); from around 1900 the eyes became almond-shaped (Style Variation 4), and then almond-shaped with an upper eyelid (Style Variation 5). It is, of course, quite possible that the production of the figures of different style variations overlapped to some extent.

If this chronology is correct, then a coherent account can be given of the changes in Mutuaga's style. His earliest known work is seminaturalistic. Then, during forty years of carving human figures, he developed increasing degrees of naturalism. First the body became more naturalistic, then so did the shape of the neck and the head, and gradually over the decades the eyes also became less and less stylised.

The sole example of Style Variation 1 (and the spatula whose handle consists of a pig on a stand) represents Mutuaga's developmental period. Style Variations 2 and 3 show him as mature artist at the height of his powers.

of it, but the figures certainly are in the naturalistic substyle. It is the only Massim headrest I know of with human figure supports.

The animal on a stand in figure 18.37 can be attributed to Mutuaga because in quality and style it is comparable to the pigs that form spatula handles. As the pig's back is too curved to make a comfortable headrest, it is probably a work carved for sale to Westerners.

The club in figure 18.44 shows a Janus head in the naturalistic substyle. At least one of the faces has eyes carved as two concentric circles, which suggests creation by Mutuaga, at an early stage in his career, rather than by one of his followers. This attribution is further supported by the scrolling on the club's shaft, which is identical to that on the eleven staffs already attributed to Mutuaga. The club is probably an all-wood imitation of the extremely rare Massim clubs with pole-shaped shafts and stone heads (see Force and Force 1971:309).

The attributions made above can be summarised as follows. The Smeeton Bowl is probably by Banieva. All the spatulas with squatting human figures in the naturalistic substyle are by Mutuaga, but his authorship of four is only probable. Twenty-one of the independent figures and the two anthropomorphic fragments are by Mutuaga. One independent figure has been left without attribution. Another three independent figures are by a follower of Mutuaga, perhaps Banieva. A further two independent figures are by another follower of unknown identity. Eighteen of the pig spatulas in the naturalistic substyle are by Mutuaga, and another is probably by him. One more is not by him, and is possibly by Banieva. The three spatulas of various designs are probably by Mutuaga. Eleven of the thirteen staffs are by Mutuaga, and the remaining two probably by a follower whose identity is unknown. The headrest is by Mutuaga, and the pig on a stand and the club with an anthropomorphic finial are probably also by him.

The attributions of the ninety-seven artworks with components in the naturalistic substyle are based on historical and stylistic evidence. The latter has been derived from the inspection of photographs or drawings of all except one carving (Inventory 22), of which no illustration is

The lesser examples of Style Variation 4 and all those of Style Variation 5 show him in artistic decline.

Assessment and conclusions

In the Massim district, lime spatulas are, of course, used as spoons for lime, one of the ingredients of the betel-chew. They are also used in association with sorcery and protective magic (Beran 1988). There is limited but clear evidence that some independent human figures are used in association with protective magic, and some anthropomorphic staffs in association with sorcery and healing magic.[19] But all three types of carving have also been made in considerable numbers for trade with Westerners since the late 19th century.

Some of the anthropomorphic and pig spatulas by Mutuaga were made for use by his fellow villagers. This is shown by their village patina and their blades being stained from use as lime spatulas (for example, Inventory 25 and 37). But quite a few of his spatulas seem to have been new at the time of collection, and were probably made as presents for Charles Abel or for trade with Westerners. It has already been noted that all of Mutuaga's independent figures were made for Westerners. Some of his staffs seem also to have been made for Westerners, because they have the flared bottom end and some Western walking-sticks have.

What can be learnt from this survey of the ninety-seven carvings with naturalistic components created by Mutuaga and his followers? (It has already been noted that these artists also carved objects without any naturalistic components, such as canoe-end spatulas and presentation axe handles, but the discussion of these carvings is beyond the scope of this paper.) Even the carvings with naturalistic components show that Mutuaga worked both in a naturalistic and a non-naturalistic style. For example, the handle of the spatula in figure 18.15 is carved as a human figure in the naturalistic substyle, but the bird on the figure's head is carved in a non-naturalistic style. Again, the head of the lower figure on the spatula in figure 18.30 is carved naturalistically, but its arms are completely stylised. The survey reveals the gradual changes in one carver's style over forty years of creative activity. It also shows that

the carver's career can be divided into periods of artistic development, maturity and decline.

The survey provides evidence of the stylistic relationship between a number of carvers. It appears that Mutuaga, a highly talented and original carver, created the naturalistic substyle of much of his work, perhaps drawing on a greater tendency towards naturalism in Suau carvings than in carvings of other parts of the Massim district. Once created, the style was adopted by a number of other local carvers for some of their creations, but with less success. They are referred to as followers rather than apprentices of Mutuaga as there is no evidence that he taught them, even informally. Mutuaga's virtues as an artist include flexibility, originality, and aesthetic sensibility. He was a young man when Christian missions were first established in south-east New Guinea, when the first government station was established in Samarai, not far from his home, and when contact with Westerners became more frequent and more extensive. As a result he became one of the first Papua New Guinea artists to make carvings for trade with Europeans. One of the most astonishing aspects of his work is the flexibility that enabled him to translate the small spatula figures into comparatively massive independent figures, such as that in figure 18.38, without loss of aesthetic quality. He is an exceptionally original sculptor in style and subject matter. The naturalistic substyle he developed for human figures and pigs is probably the most recognisable personal style in Massim art. He was probably not the first to make spatulas with drummer handles and pig handles, but he perfected both designs.[20] He appears to be the only Massim carver ever to have made a headrest with human figure supports, staffs with pig handles, and a pole-shaped club with a wooden striking head.

His aesthetic sensibility is most fully displayed in the large independent figure in figure 18.38 and the drummer figure on the spatula in figure 18.28. The former and its three large companions (Inventory 52, 54 and 58), are among the best independent figures in Massim art; that in figure 18.38 is an especially impressive and powerful sculpture. It has been exhibited at the Australian Museum a number of times, and was published twice before my book on Mutuaga (1996).

Artworks in the naturalistic substyle

18.42 Staff (SV 3) (Inv. 83). By a follower of Mutuaga. (Photo: Queensland Museum, Brisbane.)

18.43 Staff (Inv. 91). By Mutuaga. (Photo: Anthony J.P. Meyer.)

18.44 Club (Inv. 97). Probably by Mutuaga. (Photo: John Bayalis and Homer V. Holdren, Field Museum, Chicago.)

Rising reverse-side scroll   Falling reverse-side scroll

A

C

Straight filler lines

B

D

Flared filler lines

18.45 Four combinations of reverse-side scrolls and filler lines.

Style Variation 1

Style Variation 2

Style Variation 3

Style Variation 4

Style Variation 5

Engraved concentric circles

Engraved concentric circles

Almond-shaped, carved in relief and engraved

Engraved scroll

Engraved almond shape

Engraved almond shape and sculpted

18.46 Variations in the representation of the human eye.

18.47 Scrolls on the staff in fig. 18.42.

Massim lime spatulas (Beran 1988) are probably the finest lime spatulas of all betel-chewing societies. The drummer spatula in figure 18.28 is probably the best of all Massim lime spatulas. The drummer's parts are beautifully balanced. The head is simplified in shape to a semisphere, and given great power by means of a prominent brow and nose and a large mouth. The slightly curved back and feet, and the hand on the drumhead suggest the drummer is about to perform. Its quality has been acknowledged by repeated exhibition at the Museum of Mankind, London, and by frequent publication. The repeated exhibition and publication of Mutuaga's finest works show that they are regarded as masterpieces of tribal art.

These judgements are made from a Western aesthetic viewpoint. Although Mutuaga was regarded as the best carver of his generation by his Suau contemporaries, I do not know to what extant Massim art connoisseurs would agree with my judgements.

Some of Mutuaga's art works are also of historical significance: the list of those who once owned carvings by him includes some of the most important people in the first period of substantial contact between New Guinea and the West. Among these are: the Reverend William Lawes who, with his wife, in 1874 became the first permanent European resident of what was to become British New Guinea; Commodore James Erskine, who in 1884 proclaimed the British Protectorate over Papua; Sir William Macgregor and Sir Hubert Murray, the country's greatest lieutenant governors; and the Reverend George Brown, who in 1891 established the Methodist mission in what is now Milne Bay Province.

Mutuaga produced a greater corpus of naturalistic artworks than any other 19th-century Massim carver, and developed a personal carving style that makes his work recognisable by style alone. But other Massim carvers of his time also approached naturalism in the representation of humans and animals, and it seems highly likely that other talented Massim carvers also developed personal carving styles. Mutuaga's artistic achievement is, therefore, one within the artistic traditions of his culture.

Very few Massim artworks are known to have been collected before the 1880s, and information about the creators of Massim artworks was hardly ever obtained until very recently. Therefore, even after future research on individual Papua New Guinea artists, Mutuaga is likely to remain the greatest traditional Suau artist and one of the finest Papua New Guinea artists whose work we know in some quantity.

Glossary

Head viewed from above

Flat head   Rounded head and rounded face   Rounded head and flat face

Head viewed from front

T-shaped face

V-shaped face

Inventory of carvings with components in the naturalistic substyle attributed to Mutuaga and his followers

This inventory includes only pieces that I have seen or of which I have seen an illustration. All items in the 'Inventory', except number 22, are illustrated in my book on Mutuaga (Beran 1996). Some further pieces of which I have heard, but of which I have not seen even an illustration, are also recorded in this book. The year of collection of carvings or accession to a collection is given only if it is within Mutuaga's lifetime; that is, if it helps in determining when he is likely to have made them. My attribution of each piece is recorded at the end of each entry.

I would appreciate hearing of any carvings likely to be by Mutuaga or his followers not recorded here, or of the location of those recorded here as having unknown whereabouts.

Spatulas with drummer figure handles

STYLE VARIATION 1

1. The Drummer at Rest. Private collection, Australia. Fig. 18.26. Probably by Mutuaga.

STYLE VARIATION 2

2. Royal Museum of Scotland, Edinburgh, 1954.187, collected by Sir James Erskine in 1884. F.ig 27. By Mutuaga.
3. Museum of Mankind, London, +5919, collected by H.O. Forbes 1886-7. By Mutuaga.
4. Museum of Mankind, London, 1935.4-11.15. By Mutuaga.
5. Museum of Mankind, London, 1944.Oc.2.1901. Fig. 18.28. By Mutuaga.
6. Martin and Faith-dorian Wright Collection, New York. By Mutuaga.

7. Carlo Monzino Collection, Milan. By Mutuaga.
8. University of Aberdeen, Anthropology Museum, VII-87-14 (177), collected by Sir William Macgregor 1888-98. By Mutuaga.

STYLE VARIATION 3

9. Buffalo Museum of Science, C8337, collected by P.G. Black, 1886-1901. Fig. 18.4. By Mutuaga.
10. Aaron Furman Collection. By Mutuaga.
11. Private Collection, United Kingdom. By Mutuaga.

STYLE VARIATION 4

12. Linden-Museum, Stuttgart, 29,887, accessioned in 1903. Fig. 18.29. By Mutuaga.

STYLE VARIATION 5

13. Buffalo Museum of Science, C11,026. Collected by P.G. Black, 1901-13. Fig. 18.3. Probably by Mutuaga.

Spatulas with squatting human figure handles

STYLE VARIATION 2

14. Museum of Mankind, London, 1944.Oc.2.1900. By Mutuaga.
15. University of Aberdeen, Anthropology Museum, VII-87-14 (180), collected by Sir William Macgregor, 1888-98. By Mutuaga.

STYLE VARIATION 3

16. John and Marcia Friede Collection, New York. By Mutuaga.
17. Buffalo Museum of Science, C8335, collected by P.G. Black, 1886-1901. Fig. 18.2. By Mutuaga.
18. Auckland Museum, 23,504.8, presented by Robert S. Abel in 1937. Fig. 18.15. By Mutuaga.
19. Museum of New Zealand, Wellington, FE6960. By Mutuaga.
20. Auckland Museum, 16,875.1. By Mutuaga.
21. Auckland Museum, 19,457. By Mutuaga.
22. Whereabouts unknown, viewed in Robert Bleakley Collection in 1987, ex Robert Shaw, Sydney, who obtained it from a South American Museum. By Mutuaga.

STYLE VARIATION 4

23. Author's collection, HB166. By Mutuaga.

STYLE VARIATION 5

24. Museum of Mankind, London, 1944.Oc.2.1899. By Mutuaga.
25. Author's collection, HB323. By Mutuaga.
26. Pitt Rivers Museum, Oxford, 1911.56.3. By Mutuaga.
27. Author's collection, HB580. Probably by Mutuaga.
28. Aaron Furman Collection. Probably by Mutuaga.

Spatulas with various human figure handles

29. Handle carved as a standing human figure on top of a Janus half-figure. Tasmanian Museum and Art Gallery, Hobart, M 224-2676, collected by Sir Hubert Murray 1904-06. Fig. 18.30. Probably by Mutuaga.
30. Handle carved as a human Janus figure with highly stylised torso, topped with a small pig. Field Museum of Natural History, Chicago, 275,978. Fig. 18.31. Probably by Mutuaga.

Spatulas with pig handles

31. Buffalo Museum of Science, C8338, collected by P.G. Black, 1886-1901. Fig. 18.9. By Mutuaga.
32. Buffalo Museum of Science, C8339, collected by P.G. Black, 1886-1901. Fig. 18.10. By Mutuaga.
33. Chris Abel Collection, Alotau, ex Cecil Abel Collection. Fig. 18.19. By Mutuaga.
34. Auckland Museum, 23,504.9, presented by Robert S. Abel in 1937. Fig. 18.20. By Mutuaga.
35. Museum of Mankind, London, +3847, collected by H.O. Forbes, 1886-87. Fig. 18.35. Probably by Mutuaga.
36. Museum of Mankind, London, Q72.Oc.16, collected by Norman Hardy before 1902. By Mutuaga.
37. Author's collection, HB616, collected by W.D. Cross before 1920. By Mutuaga.
38. Pitt Rivers Museum, Oxford, c.15.A. By Mutuaga.
39. Auckland Museum, 8824. By Mutuaga.
40. Kirby Kallas-Lewis Collection, Seattle. By Mutuaga.

41. Cambridge University Museum of Archaeology and Anthropology, 54.89.3. By Mutuaga.
42. National Gallery of Victoria, Melbourne, 013/1979. By Mutuaga.
43. Pitt Rivers Museum, Oxford, 1904.11.128. By Mutuaga.
44. Australian Museum, Sydney, E27,510. Fig. 18.34. By Mutuaga.
45. B.P. Bishop Museum, Honolulu, 08437.001. By Mutuaga.
46. Akio Ohashi Collection, Tokyo. By Mutuaga.
47. National Museum of Ethnology, Osaka, H0137599, collected by George Brown, 1890-1905. By Mutuaga.
48. Field Museum of Natural History, Chicago, 275,980. By Mutuaga.
49. Field Museum of Natural History, Chicago, 275,981. By Mutuaga.
50. Whereabouts unknown. Fig. 18.36. Possibly by Banieva.

Spatula with a handle decorated with birds and a small pig

51. Whereabouts unknown. Fig. 18.32. Probably by Mutuaga.

Independent human figures on bases

STYLE VARIATION 2

52. Squatting figure. Private Collection, France. By Mutuaga.
53. Squatting figure. Australian Museum, Sydney, E3829, collected by W.G. Lawes before March 1893. Fig. 18.38. By Mutuaga.
54. Squatting figure. National Museum of Ethnology, Osaka, H0137338, collected by W.G. Lawes before March 1893. Shown in two photographs contained in album of photographs by Lawes (1874-90) and in Brown (1908: opp. p. 208). By Mutuaga.

STYLE VARIATION 3

55. Standing figure. Buffalo Museum of Science, C11,024, collected by P.G. Black, 1901-13. Fig. 18.5. No attribution.
56. Standing figure. Buffalo Museum of Science, C8334, collected by P.G. Black, 1886-1901. Fig. 18.6. By Mutuaga.
57. Squatting figure. Chris Abel Collection, Alotau, collected

by Charles Abel, probably before 1901. Fig. 18.14. By Mutuaga.

58. Squatting figure. University of Aberdeen, Anthropology Museum, VII-96-3 (1950), collected by Sir William Macgregor, 1888-98. By Mutuaga.

59. Squatting figure. Robert Bleakley Collection, Sydney. By Mutuaga.

60. Squatting figure. Eunice de W. Coe Collection, Ossining, New York. By Mutuaga.

61. Standing figure. University of Aberdeen, Anthropology Museum, VII-96-5 (1951), collected by Sir William Macgregor, 1888-98. By Mutuaga.

62. Two addorsed standing figures. Pigorini Museum, Rome, 103,059. By Mutuaga.

63. Standing figure. Field Museum of Natural History, Chicago, 275,881. By Mutuaga.

STYLE VARIATION 4

64. Figure sitting on a chair. Sheila Abel Collection. Cecil Abel observed Mutuaga bringing this figure to the Kwato Mission Station shortly before 1920. Fig. 18.16 (left). By Mutuaga.

65. Standing figure. Whereabouts unknown. Recorded in photograph taken by B. Platt, around 1930, at the Kwato Mission house in Kwato Island. Copy in author's photo collection. Fig. 18.16 (right). By Mutuaga.

66. Standing figure. Australian Museum, Sydney, E72,828. By Mutuaga.

67. Standing figure. Museum voor Volkenkunde, Rotterdam, 32,951. By Mutuaga.

STYLE VARIATION 5

68. Standing figure. Australian Museum, Sydney, E27,502. By Mutuaga.

69. Standing figure. Robert Ypes Collection, Amsterdam. By Mutuaga.

70. Standing figure. Sheila Rosenberg Collection, Cornwall. By Mutuaga.

71. Standing figure. David Matthews Collection, London. By Mutuaga.

72. Figure sitting on a chair, holding a bamboo pipe. Museum für Völkerkunde, Vienna, 79,471, collected by R. Pöch, 1904-06. Fig. 18.39. By Mutuaga.

73. Figure sitting on a chair, holding a bamboo pipe. Museum of New Zealand, Wellington, FE6231, believed to have been given late 19th century to the grandfather of the person who donated the object to the museum. By Mutuaga.

STYLE VARIATION 6

74. Two squatting addorsed figures topped with an animal. Australian Museum, Sydney, E27,503. By the Master of the Falling Scroll (perhaps Banieva).

75. Figure leaning against a chair. Australian Museum, Sydney, E51,069. By the Master of the Falling Scroll (perhaps Banieva).

76. Standing figure. Royal Museum of Central Africa, Tervuren, 81.34.10. Fig. 18.40. By the Master of the Falling Scroll (perhaps Banieva).

STYLE VARIATION 7

77. Squatting drummer figure. Royal Museum of Scotland, Edinburgh, 1951.392. By the Master of the Zigzag.

78. Figure sitting on a chair. Field Museum of Natural History, Chicago, 275,884. Fig. 18.41. By the Master of the Zigzag.

Human figure fragments

STYLE VARIATION 3

79. Buffalo Museum of Science, C11,025, collected by P.G. Black, 1901-13. Fig. 18.8. By Mutuaga.

STYLE VARIATION 5

80. Queensland Museum, Brisbane, E13,193. By Mutuaga.

Staffs

ANTHROPOMORPHIC STAFFS, STYLE VARIATION 3

81. Horniman Museum, London, 10.64, accessioned 1910. By Mutuaga.

82. Buffalo Museum of Science, C8333, collected by P.G. Black, 1886-1901. Fig. 18.7. By Mutuaga.

83. Queensland Museum, Brisbane, E4024, part of a collection formed in Brisbane 1890-1918. Fig. 18.42. By a follower of Mutuaga.

84. Queensland Museum, Brisbane, E4023, part of a collection formed in Brisbane, 1890-1918. By a follower of Mutuaga.

ANTHROPOMORPHIC STAFFS, STYLE VARIATION 4

85. South Australian Museum, Adelaide, A46,604. By Mutuaga.
86. Institut und Sammlung für Völkerkunde, Göttingen, Oz3076. By Mutuaga.
87. Aaron Furman Collection. By Mutuaga.
88. B.P. Bishop Museum, Honolulu, 11.385, accessioned in 1914. By Mutuaga.
89. Field Museum of Natural History, Chicago, 275,926. By Mutuaga.

STAFFS TOPPED WITH PIGS

90. Leo and Lillian Fortess Collection, Hawaii. By Mutuaga.
91. Author's Collection HB641. Fig. 18.43. By Mutuaga.
92. Colonial Inn Museum, Mudgee, NSW. Probably collected by T.B. Heath, bank agent in Samarai from 1919. By Mutuaga.
93. Field Museum of Natural History, Chicago, 132,535, collected by Robert H. Baker, accessioned 1912. By Mutuaga.

Miscellaneous artefacts

94. Headrest. Whereabouts unknown. By Mutuaga, according to Cecil Abel, who saw Mutuaga bring it to the Kwato Mission Station in 1920. Fig. 18.17. By Mutuaga.
95. Bowl cum mortar. Badi Smeeton Collection, Buderim. Fig. 18.18. Probably by Banieva.
96. Pig on base. Jim Willis Gallery, San Francisco. Fig. 18.37. By Mutuaga.
97. Club. Field Museum of Natural History, Chicago. Fig. 18.44. Probably by Mutuaga.

Notes

1. This is a revised version of a paper given at the 5th International Symposium of the Pacific Arts Association in Adelaide in 1993. I have also written a book-length study of Mutuaga, which was published in 1996. I am indebted to the late Sir Cecil Abel and to the late Weibo Mamohoi for sharing their knowledge of Mutuaga with me. I am grateful to many friends and colleagues who have been kind enough to comment on various versions of my attempts to attribute art works to Mutuaga, including Sir Cecil Abel, Shirley Campbell, Barry Craig, Philip J.C. Dark, Clare Harding, Dudley Jackson, Anthony J.P. Meyer, Roger Neich, Douglas Newton, Michael O'Hanlon, Kevin P. Smith, Jim Specht, Dorota Starzecka, and Robyn Watt. I am indebted to Philippe Bourgoin, Bill Evans, John Friede, Michael Graham-Stewart, Anthony J.P. Meyer, Douglas Newton and Gabor Vargyas for telling me of carvings in Mutuaga's style previously unknown to me, and to Anthony J.P. Meyer for finding the photograph reproduced as fig. 18.16.

2. Since the completion of my book on Mutuaga, I have become aware of another eight carvings that can be attributed to him: one anthropomorphic spatula, one pig spatula, and six anthropomorphic sculptures on pedestals.

3. In the 19th century, Europeans named part of Suau Island 'South Cape' before they realised that there was a narrow passage between the island and the mainland. Objects recorded as having been collected at South Cape may not have been collected in Suau Island, but in the area of which Suau Island is the centre.

4. Although some of the carvings attributed to Mutuaga in the catalogues have been published repeatedly, their attribution to him was not published until 1988 (Beran 1988). This is so mainly because the attribution to Mutuaga of the finest of the carvings did not appear in the records available to those who published them. The Buffalo Museum of Science did not have access to its copy of the 1914 catalogue for many decades, and did not obtain a copy of the 1901 catalogue until the early 1990s.

5. 'Central Suau area' is a term I introduce for the sake of convenience. It covers all the villages in the centre of the Suau region that I visited in 1993 to obtain information about Mutuaga and other woodcarvers of his time.

6. Saliwowo did carve as an adult. He is especially remembered for having carved canoe-end spatulas and a replica of a shotgun.

7. According to the 1914 catalogue of the P.G. Black Collection and Black's field diaries, held by the Buffalo Museum of Science, Mutuaga lived in the village of Naguna. In 1993 I could find no-one who knew of such a village. Since then Ilaiah Bigilale, a Suau Islander, has suggested to me that Naguna may have been

the name of a section of Dagodagoisu village, which was much larger in Mutuaga's time than it is now. I have not had the opportunity to check whether this is so.

8. 'Brackets' refers to the carved projections at the top of the spatula's blade.

9. All eleven spatulas are illustrated in Beran (1997).

10. The claim that these five groups of masters made lime spatulas for the Massim has to be qualified. Of the dozens of spatulas similar to that in fig. 18.22, made by the Master(s) of the Concave Back, some were certainly made for use by the Massim people, but others are likely to have been made for trade with Westerners, because they have no village patina and show no evidence of having been used as lime spatulas.

11. A few walking sticks by the Maori carver Heberley show some human figures in a non-naturalistic style and others in a naturalistic style (Neich 1991: Catalogue Items 3, 61).

12. It is unclear on what evidence Black attributed artworks to Mutuaga. Black's field diaries show that he visited New Guinea in 1893, 1899, 1902 and 1910. The last three journeys included visits to Samarai Island, located right next to Charles Abel's Kwato Mission Station, and the 1902 journey included visits to Kwato Island and to the passage between Suau Island and the mainland, where Mutuaga lived. Black probably visited Mutuaga's homeground in the hope of meeting him, but the visit lasted only a few hours and it is not recorded whether Black met Mutuaga or bought any artefacts while in his home area. Cecil Abel and Weibo Mamohoi reported that Mutuaga visited Samarai and Kwato Island, but, presumably, not very often, because each visit required a 90-kilometre round trip by canoe. Hence it is possible that Black obtained some of the artefacts he attributes to Mutuaga from the artist himself, but it is more likely that he obtained most if not all from the Burns Philp agent in Samarai and Charles Abel.

13. These carvers are well remembered by a number of people in the central Suau area, but only Weibo and two other informants had heard of Mutuaga when I interviewed Suau villagers in 1993.

14. I must explain the terms that are used in this paper to refer to carving style. I take it for granted that most of the woodcarvings of the Massim culture district share a style that is distinct from those of neighbouring culture districts. *Substyle* refers to the identifiably distinct style of a particular carver or school

of carvers within the Massim style. *Style variation* refers to identifiably distinct styles within a substyle. If a substyle is used by only one carver, all style variations within it are his; if a school of carvers share a substyle, some style variations within it may be by one member of the school, and other style variations by other members. I have already described the substyles of five Massim schools of carvers. I am about to distinguish seven style variations within the substyle of the Masters of the Naturalistic Style, and to claim that five of these were used by Mutuaga, one by Banieva, and one by an unidentified carver.

15. The figure is said to be positioned in profile relative to the spatula's blade if it faces in the same direction as one of the blade's edges.

16. The spatula is known to me only from a drawing that seems to show the animal's sex. Two more of the pig-handled spatulas by the Masters of the Naturalistic Style, while stylistically entirely typical, have unusual features. The pig on one spatula (Inventory 49) has two heads, and the pig on another (Inventory 40) seems to have human hands as front and rear paws.

17. The animal on the nineteen spatulas already attributed to Mutuaga is interpreted as a pig because: Black refers to the animal spatulas in his collection as pig spatulas, and this description may have come directly or indirectly from Mutuaga; Weibo interprets the animal as a pig; the carved animal's shape makes this interpretation plausible; and the pig is an important animal in Suau society (Beran 1996:113-14). However, it has to be noted that the animal on the spatula under discussion (fig. 18.36) looks more like a bandicoot than a pig.

18. The drawing first appeared in the *Papuan Villager* of 15 April 1931, a newspaper edited by F.E. Williams.

19. Three different collectors have been told that the figures they obtained in the Massim district had served in protective magic. The figures are: a figure in the Museum of Mankind, London (1950.Oc2.33), collected by Ellis Silas in the Trobriands in the 1920s; a figure in the Queensland Museum (Gerrits Collection No. 2605), collected by Fred Gerrits in Iwa Island around 1970; and a figure in my collection, collected by Peter Hallinan in Normanby Island. Two staffs topped with human figures are known to have been used in sorcery. Both were collected in the southern part of the Massim district, one (author's collection) by Arthur Swinfield in the 1930s, the other (John and Marcia Friede collection) by Peter Hallinan in the 1980s.

Another staff (author's collection) topped with a human figure was used in healing magic. It was collected by Anthony J.P. Meyer and me on Sudest Island in 1990.

20.   So far I have located only one drummer spatula not in the naturalistic substyle (Baltimore Museum of Art 1956: Item 113). It is one of the eleven spatulas by the Master(s) of the Prominent Eyes, but only a borderline example of the style. The only pig-handled spatula not in the naturalistic substyle that I have located so far is illustrated in fig. 18.33. It is possible that both spatulas predate Mutuaga's work.

Women and the fibre arts of Papua New Guinea[1]

Wendi Choulai and Jacquelyn Lewis-Harris

In Papua New Guinea, labour and traditional knowledge is divided along gender lines. In terms of material culture, with little exception, females produce 'soft' materials while men utilise 'hard' media for their constructions (Teilhet 1983:49); for example, string bags and basketry as opposed to sculpture and canoes in the Middle Sepik area, and Collingwood Bay women's tapa cloth and ceramics in contrast to the men's shell money and canoe carving. Annette Weiner (1989) has defined women's textiles as 'soft wealth'. This paper examines 'soft wealth' produced by women in Papua New Guinea, and the sociocultural roles, past and present, in which women's textiles have been utilised, including the role of the individual artist who produces them.

The textiles of Papua New Guinea are as wonderful and varied as the several hundred languages of the country. They have played an essential role in the establishment of personal and group identification as well as status (Barker and Tietjen 1990; Beattie 1973; Lewis-Harris 1994; Mackenzie 1991; Pepena 1994; Weiner 1988). The tapa cloth of Collingwood Bay in Oro Province is readily distinguishable from that of the Mekeo people in Central Province. The elaborately decorated and woven Wosera wedding *bilum* (string bag), when presented to the bride, raised her status among her peers and marked her as a worthy member of the community. In contemporary urban areas, the design on a *bilum*, the materials of which it is made,

and its general shape assist Papua New Guineans in identifying the village or region of the person wearing or possessing it. Politicians, the clergy, and musicians have found it expedient to announce their Papua New Guinean identity by wearing contemporary materials that are printed with designs derived from traditional sources or designs from their home area. As a sign of national pride and status, visiting dignitaries like the Pope are presented with clothing constructed of traditional tapa cloth, or *bilums* designed especially for the occasion (Berman 1990; Lewis-Harris 1994; Mackenzie 1991).

Traditional Papua New Guinean textiles produced by women fall into three major categories: tapa cloth, *bilums*, and skirts. Apart from their importance as utilitarian items, these items often hold ceremonial or ritual importance due to their particular use, the nature of their construction, or the designs placed upon or worked into them.

Bilums are a good example of this (fig. 19.1). They are used for carrying large amounts of food, children, small ritual carvings, human remains, sacred plant-based mixtures, and personal effects and weapons. *Bilums* are looped into specific designs that represent particular animals, stories, or objects. The design 'flying fox in flight' – looped in red, green and natural-coloured threads – is readily identified with the Wosera area, while 'seven brothers' is associated with the middle Sepik River area. The 'centipede' design of the Mendi wedding *bilum* is associated

19.1 Agatha Waramen instructing other women making *bilums*.

Papua New Guinea, in the Madang area, the middle Sepik River area, the Western Highlands, and among the Oksapmin of central New Guinea (Bateson 1958; Lewis-Harris 1994; Mackenzie 1991; Strathern 1972; Winter n.d.).

Tapa cloth is used for clothing, shrouds, sheets, masks and diapers in almost every area in which the raw materials are available. The bark of the paper mulberry (*Broussonetia papyrifera*), fig and hibiscus has been processed by women throughout the main island (Beattie 1973; Christensen 1981; Leonard and Terrell 1980; Lewis-Harris 1994).

Some of the most outstanding tapa is still produced in the Collingwood Bay area of Oro Province (fig. 18.2 and plate 6). The women in this area maintain paper mulberry

19.2 Naomi of Uiaku village, Oro Province, making tapa cloth.

with that particular area of Southern Highlands Province. Other designs, such as '*kundu*' (hand-drum), 'mountains', 'Independence', and 'PNG', relate to specific social groups throughout the country (Agatha Waramen, pers. comm. 1991).

Oral tradition generally attributes the creation of the *bilum* to a female spirit. As women's backs were the major means of transporting produce and other heavy loads in many parts of Papua New Guinea, it would seem fitting that the labour-saving *bilum* would be given to them by a spirit of the same gender. In the middle Sepik River area the women note that the *bilum* stitch was brought to mankind by Kezelaji, the female spirit of creation. She came in the form of a great bird, from the New Guinea coast (*Post Courier* 1979). Mackenzie (1991) noted that among the Telefol in central New Guinea, the first *bilum* was introduced by Afek, the Primal Mother.

Bilums are also a commodity to be bartered and exchanged for other goods. The people of Uiaku village in Oro Province are known for their beautiful tapa and a type of small bush dog that is excellent for hunting. As there is no *bilum*-making tradition in their culture, they trade dogs for *bilums* from their neighbours in the nearby mountains. The rate in 1985 was five medium-sized *bilums* for one puppy (Gideon Ifoki, pers. comm. 1985). Ethnologists have noted this type of exchange of goods and the use of *bilums* in bride price along the north-west coast of gardens specifically for the raw tapa material. The manufacturing process is very personal; the women sleep on the piece of bark each night to imbue the material with 'a little part of ourselves'. Each clan has its own designs, which are passed on from mother to daughter. These designs are often reflected in the full-face tattoos that were given to young women around puberty (Barker and Tietjen 1990). In this case, tapa designs not only identify the clan, but also the female members of that clan. Tapa has provided the women of this area with a significant income by transcending the traditional barter market and thriving in the contemporary cash market.

Skirts are another type of textile that are utilitarian and symbolic. The length, construction, colour and texture combinations, and style in which the skirt is worn, send messages to the viewers. Depending upon the area, they were constructed from sago leaves, possum fur, a variety of tree-bark fibres, raffia palm, pandanus or banana leaves (Christensen 1981; Lewis-Harris 1994; Weiner 1988; Winter n.d.).

Weiner (1988) has documented the use of Trobriand Islands skirts as part of women's special currency. She found that the skirts and banana-fibre money (*yawovau*) had a special role in the *lisaladabu*, the women's mortuary distribution. The textiles provided the economic base for a system of ranking among the clans by providing wealth, status and power; thus the *lisaladabu* enabled women to participate fully in the politics of the mortuary rituals.

The use of skirts as barter items is common in Sepik, Gulf and Central provinces. For several generations, the Solien Besena of Central Province have obtained their dance skirts by trading shell lime, a major component in betelnut use. The coastal villages located between the Brown River and Mekeo areas provide the majority of their skirts. As a consequence of this successful trading system, the Solien Besena women have no history of skirt production.

New materials such as nylon, unravelled plastic from rice and copra sacking, plastic strapping tape, and other imported fibres are being used in the construction of contemporary skirts. Many of these skirts are being sold and exchanged in the urban markets around the country. In association with tourism, skirts are becoming part of the lucrative artefact and crafts market overseas. As the role of 'soft wealth' has begun to change and merge into the international urban market, so has the lifestyle of the textile artist producing the wealth.

The contemporary female textile artist in Papua New Guinea often must bridge the gap between two cultures – the 'traditional' one in which she was raised and the 'Western' one in which she was educated. Wendi Choulai's experiences clearly illustrate this situation. Born of mixed ethnic parentage – her mother of the Solien Besena people and her father a Dyaul (Djaul) Island (PNG) Chinese – Choulai (plate 7) was raised in village and urban centres. She notes (Choulai 1993):

> The contemporary Papua New Guinean female textile artist, while working with imported materials in a multi-ethnic urban environment, must still adhere to the parameters established in traditional trade and usage of textiles and designs.

Choulai, along with other women artists, is acutely aware of the line she must walk when incorporating traditionally derived designs in her work. Faced with the task of submitting a wearable art project as a college class assignment, she created a modern 'grass' skirt of various imported textiles (plate 8). The inspiration for this project came from several different types of skirts found in the Solien Besena area. The 'grass' dance skirts were an essential part of the *gumaroho* dance, a mourning ritual. Choulai had participated in the *gumaroho* since childhood, and it became a major inspiration for many of her designs. According to the artist, this was her first significant contemporary design, made without compromising the integrity of the traditional skirt styles.

The dilemma faced by Choulai when asked to incorporate traditional design into her class assignment is an example of the difficulties faced by many students and artists who have passed through the government education system. Early national education policy encouraged the development of a pan-New Guinean culture that would integrate new media with traditional design sources (Simons 1993:178). This had its greatest effect upon the curriculum of the National Arts School. Stevenson recorded that 'the

Creative Arts Center (now the National Arts School) had a philosophy aimed at assisting individual artists to develop and integrate traditional practices and aesthetics with contemporary materials' (Stevenson 1990:29). This well-meaning policy did not take into account the cultural forces of traditional copyright and taboo associated with copyright violation. This altruistic idealism created problems for those students who were not at liberty to draw from their traditional repertoire. As one of the first female graduates from the National Arts School, Choulai (1993) remembers the difficulties that arose when instructors encouraged the students to derive their personal style and designs from traditional sources:

> The National Arts School of Papua New Guinea employs foreign contract lecturers for three years to instruct the students in graphics, fine arts and textile design. They have no knowledge or training in traditional culture. In an effort to diversify, the results largely ignore traditional 'customs'; for example, the reproducing of women's tapa designs by non-initiates. By not acknowledging these principles, creative images produced in educational institutions will be imaged elsewhere thereby creating conflict with the sensitivities inherent in the Melanesian culture. The complex expression of clanship is an integral part of P.N.G. identity and to ignore it is not only to ignore the cultural origins of creative expression and the inherent ownership of the various art forms but also to contribute to the decline of the culture.

Under the pressure of completing class assignments, many students resorted to copying common designs from other Papua New Guinean groups not related to their own clan systems. Simons characterised their endeavours: 'One element of innovation is in translating the traditional form into an article which will not affront the traditional owners and will appeal to the commercial market'(Simons 1990: 43). Members of the National Theatre Company, the musical group Sanguma, and artists holding architectural commissions explored alternative approaches to integrating traditional art styles into their work by incorporating stylistic devices and subject matter that were commonly found throughout Papua New Guinea. Ruki Fame's wall murals

and gates at the Institute of Technology in Lae and the National Parliament in Waigani are excellent examples of this approach.

Choulai has often remarked that the nature of 'traditional copyright' and the exclusion of females from traditional forms of art have hindered her role as artist and her attempts to transfer traditional designs to fabric:

> Despite the abundance of traditional motifs in P.N.G., I would no sooner fish or even travel through another tribe's traditional land than I would use their designs. It is not only my fear of compensation payment but also an identification with my own Papuan clan and respect for P.N.G. custom that prevents me from doing so … Within P.N.G. there is great importance and pride placed on the cultural group because it gives you an immense sense of belonging … It has its own unique art, rituals, customs, traditional land, burial grounds, hunting areas, rivers and seaways. [Choulai 1993]

She believes that the pervasive fear and taboo against breaking with tradition stifles contemporary self-expression:

> Even working as a commercial textile artist in Australia, I find myself adhering to the unwritten laws of indigenous people. I feel that I do not have the artistic authority or legitimacy to reproduce designs that are exclusive and sacred to Australian Aboriginals. [Choulai 1993]

The strong relationship between magical power, ownership, ancestral connections and clan motifs offers a plausible explanation as to why these taboos play a role in the creation of contemporary art. It is common knowledge that many forms of Papua New Guinean art are covered by traditional copyright and strict ownership guidelines (Bateson 1958; Beattie 1973; Forge 1966; Gerbrands 1990; Gunn 1993 and chapter 16 this volume; Lewis-Harris 1993, 1994; Ter Keurs 1990). In the recent past there have been many disputes over the perceived misuse of clan designs and motifs. Thomas (1995:186) commented upon the contemporary attitude towards copyright in his book on Oceanic art:

> One of the most successful examples of design inspired by traditional styles was David Lasisi's concrete facade panels

for the Papua New Guinea Banking Corporation, drawing on Papuan Gulf masks and shields. It is notable that the artist himself came not from this area but from New Ireland, and that today, sensitivities concerning indigenous copyright in artistic motifs and traditions might preclude an artist making so much use of the style of an area other than his own; the fact that there would at least be controversy itself marks a shift from the optimism that followed independence to a period of deep divisions.

As late as 1986, there were serious disagreements between Kanganaman village and a neighbouring Sepik village in which Kanganaman elders claimed that the particular design of a finial on their men's cult house had been used on another village's cult house without their permission. Choulai's research on National Arts School students' use of traditional designs revealed the serious consequences of recent copyright infringement:

When I was seven … my aunty's husband was speared to death … because he painted the yam mask using another clan's symbol. Had he [sought] permission or paid a huge compensation prior to using the symbol, this killing would not have eventuated. [Name withheld on request, 1994]

Most of the students she interviewed felt they should not use the traditional designs and motifs from their immediate areas, but rely upon more universal designs for their work.

Choulai has found that the laws of design usage were not totally inflexible. She presently has the right to use designs that belong exclusively to her mother's clan. She believes that in the future she may be able to incorporate other traditional motifs into commercial design and textile art through a negotiation process. This process would include arrangements with the clan through the traditional copyright laws, ensuring that the clan would retain ownership of the designs, that the product would bring great esteem to the clan, and that clan members would receive a portion of the profits from the sale of the textiles.

The taboos associated with traditional copyright are doubly threatening to the contemporary female artist. Not only must they respect the general laws of design usage, but they must also cope with the ritually based gender division found throughout the country. Choulai (1993) states:

Coming from P.N.G., a country that has retained so much of its rich and diverse traditional culture, I as a female have not been initiated into the male occupations of carving, weaving, beading, or woodwork. As a female I am not meant to watch these artistic processes for fear that my observation of them will disrupt their creation and produce bad luck.

In most areas of Papua New Guinea, women are still prohibited by custom from viewing particular works of art and utilising certain clan motifs (Chowning 1987; Gerbrands 1990; Narokobi 1980; Thomas 1995). There are numerous myths and stories to substantiate the taboos associated with women's participation in ritual. One of the most common themes is that women original possessed sacred objects that were subsequently taken over by men (Bateson 1958; Brumbaugh 1990; Narokobi 1980; Teilhet 1983; Thomas 1995). In her seminal article 'The Role of Women Artists in Polynesia and Melanesia', Teilhet (1983:49) discussed the basis for female exclusion:

as the sex roles became more defined, the art-making habits developed into political moves and the material that the men initially worked in was given an imaginary power that it did not previously have to enhance and validate the power and status of men over women in the realm of the supernatural … By ritualising the artist's tools, women were barred from using them because, as sources of pollution, women could nullify the efficacy of the tools.

Despite this exclusion, women held important counterbalancing ritual influence within Papua New Guinean societies. Although gender roles were distinctly separate, men and women ultimately shared in a balance of economic and ritual power that was negated by the advent of colonialism. Women lost the majority of their traditional status through the Western patriarchal colonial system. This imbalance is reflected in the menial role in which contemporary female artists are often regarded:

The absence of art works by women is not deliberate, but rather the result of no women having yet chosen the role of individualist visual artist … [they] have preferred to become textile designers, graphic artists, or members of theatre groups. The independence and self-assertiveness required to become successful as an artist in the urban environment is not a role Papua New Guinean women have been culturally conditioned for to date. [Simons 1990:14]

This statement ignores that female artists have been discouraged by their families and their male classmates from continuing their art careers, and excluded from important group exhibits. Artists such as Wendi Choulai have been struggling to overcome this type of discrimination and pressure by promoting their own exhibits within the country, and by exhibiting their work overseas.

Choulai's restrictions and taboos have forced her to look towards non-traditional sources for her designs and to re-evaluate her use of various media:

> Due to my alienation from the male-dominated cultures in P.N.G., all of my fashion drawings are of women, modern universal indigenous women who embody a universal language of geometric symbols. In exploring new mediums to represent the rawness of P.N.G., I started to use monoprints, resist and crayon on fabric. The range of new mediums, tools, and materials that is available today has given the contemporary artist such as myself new avenues to extend the 'feel' and placement of traditional designs. [Choulai 1993]

Choulai also finds inspiration from what she calls 'universal motifs' derived from Africa, Asia, South America, and other parts of the Pacific. They include mountain and water symbols, and woven designs found on basketry, matting and other textiles. She notes:

> I am outside of these cultures and feel free to use these universal symbols in a decorative way. When representing P.N.G., I use the markings of the land, a strong and binding element for Papua New Guineans. My designs represent images of the Hiritano Highway that connects Port Moresby to my family's traditional land. Images include the patterns of the mud along the highway in the wet season. Other designs represent fish, so important to our survival, pigs, snakes, feathers and the geometric designs

of our gardens. The dance ceremonies also are an inspiration as they embody so much rhythm, color, jewelry, and dress. [Choulai 1993]

Choulai is currently utilising the traditional female role as a dance-skirt designer to introduce a new form of 'soft wealth' into her home area. Because her people have no history of making and designing their own dance skirts, she has decided to use her design skills to create a Besena dance skirt. If Choulai is successful in integrating this skirt into the *gumaroho* ceremonies, she will become the first Solien Besena woman to have created a dance skirt that is uniquely their own.

As illustrated in this paper, the role of 'soft wealth' continues to be an important factor in contemporary Papua New Guinean societies. With the disillusionment felt by many Papua New Guineans for development and its diminishing monetary returns, 'soft wealth' and the women who produce it are once again being granted significant status within their cultures. The contemporary female textile artist has the potential to become the urban producer of this wealth through the production of textiles that feature hybrid PNG designs (fig. 19.3). Bought by Papua New Guineans, Air Niugini and other local airlines, tourists, private enterprise and government agencies, these designs represent the continuation of a long tradition of Papua New Guinean textiles as 'soft wealth'.

19.3 Cloth design by Wendi Choulai.

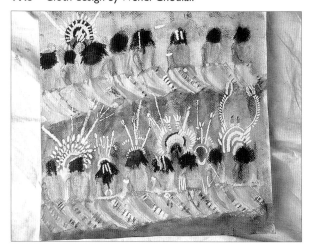

Notes

1.   This paper is a compilation of Jacquelyn Lewis-Harris' research and Wendi Choulai's personal statements and description of her work. The papers were presented individually at the symposium, but have been combined for clarity and continuity. Lewis-Harris provided the general text and Choulai (1993) is quoted extensively. Photographs are by the authors.

Tree-houses, representation and photography on the Papuan coast, 1880 to 1930

Max Quanchi

At the close of the 19th century and early in the 20th century, the Australian, British and American newspaper, magazine and book buying and reading public began to be presented with photographic images of colonial others from the coasts of Papua. These images were the product of the confluence of three arrivals on the Papuan coast: a relatively new apparatus (the camera), a new 'science for understanding the native' (anthropology), and new strangers variously categorised as missionaries, government officials, miners, traders, professors, collectors and travellers.[1]

The published visual images of Papua before the 1880s were either line drawings, pastels, oil paintings or, increasingly, etchings based on photographs. In the mid-1890s, these artistic illustrations and engravings based on photographs were gradually phased out in newspapers, magazines and books, though some remained in use over the next twenty years. Publications on the ethnographic fieldwork of individuals or major expeditions, official reports, and books of reminiscences of residents, travellers and missionaries were soon relying solely on photographs for illustrative material, supplemented by a simple phrase or longer 'ethnographic' caption. For example, the 1901 *British New Guinea Annual Report* included eight photographs in the text and a further thirty-one photographs in a special appendix. The opening photograph was a *lakatoi*. A caption informed readers of construction details, and of the purposes of annual *hiri* voyages, and noted that the photograph had been used in the design of the first issue of British New Guinea stamps (BNG/AR 1901:2). By the early 1900s, books that twenty years before had contained perhaps five or six engravings were now heavily illustrated, sometimes with as many as a hundred full or half-page plates. About thirty to fifty captioned photographs soon became the accepted format.

In the period from 1880 to 1930, the few Europeans outside Samarai, Daru and Port Moresby were at administration posts and missionary stations, and were only slowly being joined by new arrivals headed for scattered plantation projects and gold prospects. The camera, already in wide use in other British possessions (Australia, New Zealand, the Pacific Islands, India and Africa), was part of their baggage. In 1889, the first year that imports of photographic equipment were recorded, one package of photographic supplies worth £3 entered Port Moresby. The next year the value of imported plates, chemicals and papers had increased sixfold. By 1899, photographic equipment worth £104 entered Port Moresby, Samarai and Daru. This was commercially available photographic material sold to private individuals, and was a small fraction of the equipment and materials carried into Papua by travellers as personal or expedition luggage. Although there was no official salaried photographer on the administration payroll in Papua, the value of the colonial government's photographic apparatus was reckoned in the 1886 *British New Guinea Annual Report* at £50 (BNG/AR 1887:35).

When the *Papuan Times and Tropical Advertiser* began publication in 1911, of the half dozen individuals and companies who advertised their services and products, the Eastman Kodak company featured cameras and equipment each week, and continued to do so right through to the 1930s, though the serious photographer and alert reader of the paper's public notice columns could pick up a cheap second-hand 5 x 4 plate or film camera for 50 shillings, a folding Brownie 'fitted with RR lens' as new for 52 shillings and for £5 10 s a 'Victor Magazine Camera, plate holders, stand, red lamp, etc' valued at £15. Amateur photographers could purchase a new Eastman No. 3 Folding Pocket Camera for £4 10 s, or the compact Kodak Folding Austral for £1 10 s. The plate camera remained in use by professional and amateur photographers, while the use of roll film and the hand-held camera, although available since the mid-1890s, was not widespread in Papua until the 1920s. Taken in tropical conditions, which hindered preparation, shooting, developing and the storing of plates or prints, the great majority of photographs of Papua were therefore not snapped, but were carefully and laboriously arranged and posed compositions. Although rarely mentioned in despatches, letters, private diaries or published texts, the intention to photograph Papuans was part of the frontier experience that Europeans expected in the colonies.

The popularity of photography in Papua may be measured by the huge number of photographs extant in archives and other collections, by the level of sales of photographic equipment in Samarai, Moresby and Daru, and by the fact that authors and publishers were able to keep finding for each edition thirty and more illustrations that had not previously been published. Photographs of Papua also appeared in official reports, as postcards, as lantern slides, and as personal memories pasted in private albums or thrown loosely in a convenient cigar box or trade-store carton. The widespread practice of photography at the 'far ends of the earth' is indicated by the Royal Colonial Institute proceedings, where audiences were informed and entertained, for example, by talks on Sierra Leone, the Transvaal, St Helena and Nyasaland, illustrated by a number of 'limelight views', usually about forty. In 1898-99, the Royal Colonial Institute hosted lantern-slide talks about the Malay Peninsula, Trinidad, 'The native races of South Africa', and Queensland; in 1899-1900, on views of Swaziland, Trinidad, the Bahamas, Tasmania and Ceylon; and in 1900-01, on views of Basutoland, Trinidad (again), and Fiji.

In 1895, on the basis of a short trip along the Papuan coast and up the William River with her brother, Dr Balldyce Baildon, and the missionary James Chalmers, Miss Baildon gave a talk at Oxford on 'A visit to New Guinea'. She told the Geography section of the British Association how 'a number of interesting views were taken which served to illustrate the native life and the character of the scenery' (Baildon 1895:96). Her remarks, and those of other visitors to Papua in the 1890s, suggest that the camera was already being carried along for the useful purpose of observing people on the frontiers of the colonial world. Thirty years later, in 1927, the *Papuan Courier* reported that a Seventh-Day Adventist pastor, A.G. Stewart, gave an address in Port Moresby on 'Cannibals and Christians', illustrating his talk on twenty years of mission work in the South Seas with more than 100 'beautifully colourful' lantern slides. A hundred photographs transferred to glass slides and individually coloured were a major investment and a commitment to providing visual detail. This was not exceptional. From the 1890s, black-and-white photographs, later transferred from wet and dry plates and roll-film negatives to glass lantern slides and then hand colored, were eagerly sought in pursuit of Miss Baildon's goal of capturing 'native life and the character of the scenery'. The photographic image quickly changed from a novelty to a necessity. As a supplement to oral delivery on the lecture circuit at universities, learned societies and special-interest associations, time spent on 'limelight' or lantern views partially replaced time allotted to the spoken words of the traveller recently returned from faraway places. In the late 19th and early 20th centuries, the screening of 100 or 200 photographic views of Papua and Papuans, as enlargements of prints or as lantern slides, was not an unusual event in London, the Australian colonies or Port Moresby.[2]

20.1   Tree-house, Koiari village. Photographed by J.W. Lindt in 1885 and published as Plate XIV in his book, *Picturesque New Guinea* (1887).

Two years earlier, during an illustrated lecture at the Royal Colonial Institute, T.H. Hatton-Richards told an audience of London gentlemen and ladies that in the recently mapped and explored British New Guinea, 'each village usually has two or three tree houses with platforms' (Hatton-Richards 1892-93:296). Over the next forty years, a photograph, etching or drawing of a tree-house appeared regularly in illustrated books on British New Guinea (after a transfer of power in 1906, the Australian Territory of Papua). Most of these tree-house images were repro-

ductions of, or replicated, a photograph (fig. 20.1) taken at Sadara Makara, a Koiari village,[3] by J.W. Lindt, a Melbourne photographer travelling with the Sir Peter Scratchley expedition of 1885. Lindt may been replicating a series of unpublished Veibure tree-house photographs taken earlier by the missionary W.G. Lawes, but it was the commercial release of Lindt's photographs and albums that initiated a narrative of what was to become an iconographic misrepresentation.

This long iconographic sequence continued into the 1970s, when the Papua New Guinea government's National Parks Service built a reconstruction or replica of a Koiari tree-house at Varirata National Park on the Sogeri plateau, east of Port Moresby. It became a popular tourist site, much photographed and climbed (fig. 20.2). This suggests that Lawes', then Lindt's, 1885 tree-house photographs were part of a diachronic discourse, including Colonial Institute lectures, book illustrations, lantern slides and modern architectural reconstructions in which the tree-house has become a signifier or photographic representation for Papua in the same way that Baldwin Spencer and Frank Gillen's 1900 photograph of a gaunt, desert Arunta became synonymous for all Aborigines (Mulvaney 1989:116-19), or W.H. Jackson's and E.S. Curtis's mounted Plains Indian warrior or plumed chief wistfully staring to the past, or an uncertain future, became an icon of the alleged disappearing Native American way of life (English 1983; Fleming and Luskey 1988; Goetzemann and Goetzemann 1986). The photographs of Papua are also part of the larger late-19th century and early-20th century colonial discourse, differentiated by the lateness of the colonial incursion into Papua. The purpose of this essay is to outline the development of photographic representation of Papua by reference to a particular image – Koiari tree-house photographs – and to identify the processes through which a small set of photographs became signifiers for Papua.

The second *British New Guinea Annual Report*, printed an account of an expedition to Mount Owen Stanley by H.O. Forbes, in which he noted using a camera on several occasions, and that he 'obtained some good photographs which were of great ethnological interest' (BNG/AR

20.2   Replica of Koiari tree-house, Varirata National Park, Sogeri Plateau. (Photo: by B. Craig, 1979.)

20.3   Tree-houses at Farunumu village. Note photographer with camera on tripod, just left of centre. (Photo: A.J. Dunning. RAI Ig.110.)

1887:31). Forbes's use of the superlative indicates that the particular contribution of the camera was recognised in administration and scientific circles, and prompted the fascination, over the next fifty years, of using photographs to capture for distant readers the human 'types', exotic behaviour and material culture of Papua. Miss Baildon's 'interesting views' and H.O. Forbes's 'great ethnological

interest' would be repeated over and over. In illustrated books on Papua, the phrases 'a native type' and 'a typical village' became commonly used captions for carefully posed and scientifically arranged side, rear and front profiles, and for opportunity-shots of Papuans who stood still long enough for the cumbersome tripod and wet-plate camera to be set up (fig. 20.3).

In the 1890s and early 20th century, there was a ready market for the photographs being carefully posed and later snapped along the Papuan coast, and along the few routes that the administration, prospectors and missions had opened towards inland districts. These photographs have geographic boundaries determined by proximity to coastal anchorages, permanent European presence or regular visitation. The coastal villages of Hula, Aroma, Kerepuna, Tupeselei, Hanuabada and Elevala, and the Koiari villages inland from Moresby, dominate the early photographs. Samarai, Anglican areas out from Wanigela, and villages in the Methodist Mission's island region begin to feature later. As patrols on foot, or using canoes and small launches, edged towards the mountainous interior, the Mafulu and other inland communities, and eventually the Gulf and Fly River peoples to the west, joined the Papuan gallery of types, of sago and pot-makers, belles and dandies, tree-houses, *lakatoi* and marine villages.

The portable Kodak and Eastman roll-film camera later made the snapshot photograph accessible to all who visited or lived in Papua, but photographs 'of great ethnological interest' had been and continued to be taken in Papua by most European residents or visitors. The casual visitor, the resident magistrate on patrol, and amateur ethnographer-photographers shared this interest with the participants of early anthropological expeditions, such as Haddon and Seligman and their colleagues on the Torres Strait and Papua expedition of 1898-99, though without the scholarly purpose of taking a photograph that might shake an opponent's theory apart or substantiate a premise first aired in a Cambridge lecture or Royal Colonial Institute address. The photographic archive these early photographers amassed includes body scarification, mourning attire, penis gourds and nose ornaments, mission converts and the yet-to-be-converted, profiles or types of the newly discovered link in the Great Chain of Being (or branch of the tree of civilisation), and 'frozen moments' in the allegedly disappearing world of the primitive native.

Each photograph can also be seen as a fragment or text within a colonial discourse. However, the placement of an individual photograph is difficult, for photographs lie outside the metaphor, metonymy, irony or figuration that is normally considered when analysing tropes or verbal composition of discourse. The critical analysis of literary texts cannot easily be transferred to a photograph or album of images. A critical reading of individual photographs, separate from their pictorial composition of subject and action, comes from applying the post-structuralist principle that texts (or photographs) usually leave out what they mean to say. Photographs also constitute evidence or proof. The colonial encounter between the people of Papua and the new arrivals – often crossing over the nominal boundaries of photographer, anthropologist, administrator, planter, missionary, traveller – was shaped by the urge to provide visual evidence, as Lindt claimed, direct from 'savage real life' (Lindt 1887:44), or to validate the work of the expedition, mission or administration. Further scholarly and colonial imperatives arose from demands for scientific evidence of the 'others' who were then joining the British community of colonial subjects. Judging these images for their place in the construction of an ideology or a colonising culture adds to our understanding of colonial cross-cultural contacts, and relegates as a minor concern arguments about the frequency of a particular phenomenon, the location of a particular setting or the artificiality of a composed background. Whether these photographs captured reality, as the photographers claimed, is of less interest than how the image was further shaped by the demand of the reading public for texts and images that were popular and exotic, yet factual.

Koiari tree-houses kept appearing in contemporary official reports, works of fiction, ethnographies and histories of this period, but the tree-house photograph did not assume a special status in isolation. It occurred in the context of the general mass of Papuan images and representations, and, second, in the context of the specific images from missionary, scientific, travel or colonial administration discourses. However, there is a difficulty here because the photograph does not always match the supposed viewpoint or ideology of the author of the written text, or the generally attributed characteristics of a particular literary genre. A survey of the illustrations used to supplement texts on Papua suggests that when the photographer was leaning towards the tripod and carefully framing the image, the meaning intended by the composition, setting and central focus of each photograph was different from the messages that, later in Sydney or London, the authors, editors and publishers wanted to convey to readers. What readers memorised and related from their vicarious though intimate visual contact with Papua and Papuans is difficult to establish. Equally uncertain is what readers who did not see the photographs until decades later, in a different intellectual and colonial milieu, thought about the people, events, artefacts or behaviour captured on film.

In the several thousand photographs published in illustrated texts in between 1880 and 1930, a stereotyped image of a Papuan person and a stereotyped inventory of Papuan material culture soon developed, creating a sense of visual sameness across the illustrated texts. This sameness or stereotyping is easily identified as a pattern by 1990s researchers, though perhaps not by the puzzled, smiling London or Brisbane reader in the 1920s, who saw a series of photographs in an illustrated magazine, or who glanced through twenty or so plates while browsing along a library shelf. For the book buyer and borrower or casual reader, the Papuan belle, sago-maker, pot-maker, *lakatoi* and tree-house were a gathered truth.[4] For them the photograph proved the existence of a people, caught by the camera lens somewhere out there in one of those unknown, blank spots only superficially detailed by Europe's map-makers. Although sometimes warned through literary devices in the narrative, readers did not question whether everyone in Papua lived in a tree-house, sailed about in multiple-hulled *lakatoi*, made sago, or perpetually and coquettishly gazed naked and half-naked towards mostly male, fully clad photographers.

Mr T.H. Hatton-Richards, the speaker referred to earlier, informed his Royal Colonial Institute audience that he had lived in Papua. However, he claimed an exaggerated frequency and domain for tree-house construction. In the Port Moresby hinterland he had seen several Koiari tree-houses, and in London he had probably read the annual reports in which European patrols reported seeing tree-houses in their early forays across the Goldie and Laloki rivers and into the Astrolabe Range. In 1880, H.M. Chester had traversed the country inland from Port Moresby and

reported that at the village of Maiari there were 'twenty-two houses, some in trees', at Keremu 'seventy-eight houses some of which are in trees', and that at Munikaila village there were 'several scattered groups of houses built on the tops of ridges within call of each other. Several of the houses are built in the tops of high trees' (Chester 1880:7-8). Ten years later, F.R. Barton and A.C. English reported that among the Doriwaidi tribe at Puneabura village 'there are at present four houses in the enclosure and three tree-houses' and at Mikanigoro village they counted eight defensive enclosures, one hundred houses and eleven tree-houses spaced along a precipitous ridge (BNG/AR 1901:42).

However, William Macgregor in his 1890 'Despatch reporting visit of inspection to the Koiari District' did not think the presence of tree-houses significant enough to be mentioned (Macgregor 1891:26-7), and in Burns Philp's 1886 tourism booklet *British New Guinea with Illustrations of Scenery*, housing at Kerepuna and Hula, and an unidentified 'native house', are included, but not a tree-house. In 1878, the missionary W.G. Lawes had noted the exceptional architectural skills of Papuans without mentioning tree-houses (Lovett 1902a:123-5), and photographer and filmmaker Frank Hurley noted that 'throughout all Papua there are seldom two villages in which the customs and the architectural features are precisely the same' (Hurley 1924:403). In 1928 the administration published a *Papuan School Reader* written by the missionary W.J. Saville, but in a six page section on houses there is no mention of tree-houses. A year later, in the *Papuan Villager*, a local newspaper printed for 'natives', a lead article on Papuan houses, supported by five photographs, did not include tree-houses. In the British New Guinea and later Australian Territory of Papua annual reports, the use of tree-houses was not mentioned in a section devoted to 'Native Houses', though it was acknowledged that 'generally speaking, the native architecture throughout the territory is of a high standard for such a primitive people' (ATP/AR 1909:58). In the 1912 *Annual Report* this was qualified by a subtle word change to a 'fairly high standard for primitive people' (ATP/AR 1912:22). Therein lies a clue to the popularity and regular appearance of Koiari tree-houses in the photographic representation of Papua.

At the turn of the century, Papuans were considered a primitive people, low on the scale of civilisation formulated by scholars keen to place all human occupation in a grand 'map of mankind'. Papuans were a lowly branch of the 'tree of civilisation'. Tree-houses, cannibalism, nakedness, and one other indicator of so-called primitiveness, men with tails, can be found scattered across the pages in textual and illustrative descriptions of Papua in this era. Indeed, in the 1920s, the *Papuan Courier* was still running 'monkey' stories, including one lifted from the Sydney magazine, the *Bulletin*. The inclusion of a photograph or drawing of a tree-house therefore catered for the anticipated expectation of readers that Papuans as primitives, cannibals, head-hunters and savages would occupy the lowest forms of domicile, the tree-house or cave. The release of Lindt's Koiari tree-house photographs, repeated in many forms over the next fifty years, was the opening sign in a narrative of primitiveness, including various forms of representation, which continued to the present through the building of an 'authentic' Koiari tree-house at Varirata National Park. It was also a hegemonic discourse by intruders in which the newly discovered primitives were appropriated by three newly ascribed roles: as British subjects, ethnographic others, and children now under the sacred trust of their colonial and mission masters.

To place photography of Papuans in a regional Melanesian context, New Caledonia, which had been annexed and settled by the French in the 1850s, by 1872 already had been extensively portrayed by photographers. '*Scéne domestique á L'île de Pins*', a '*Maison de Colon*', sugar mills and panoramic views of Noumea were available for sale or publication; and, in the 1890s, studio portraits of *canaques* were being taken (O'Reilly and Poirier 1959). A photograph of the missionary Dourre landing at Balade beach in New Caledonia, attributed to 1843, just a few years after the daguerreotype had been invented in France, indicates how quickly photography had circled the world. Daguerreotypes were made by d'Urville and Seibold during voyages in the Pacific in the 1840s, and the French photographer Gustave Viaud photographed Tahiti in 1859, while another Frenchman, Desire Charnay, photographed Mexico and Central America in the late 1850s, and Madagascar,

Chile, Java, and Yemen in the 1860s and 1870s (Jammes and Sobieszek 1970:6). In the USA in the early 1870s, a travelling 'South Seas' show advertised that a catalogue of prints of chiefs and villages was available for purchase (Thomas 1991:166). By the 1880s, the camera was also in wide use in Australia and New Zealand, and in the Dutch and German portions of the island of New Guinea.

Photography in Papua came well after the camera had intruded on Melanesians and other Pacific Island peoples. It also arrived in Papua in a later and changed atmosphere of philosophical and intellectual debate. By the 1900s, photography was being affected by artistic influences as well as Edwardian interests in pictorialism. Lindt's tree-house photograph fits the pictorialist's demand for attention to aesthetic matters of shape, tone, harmony and proportion. It is placed in the centre of the frame, with surroundings that do not detract from the central feature of the photograph, conforming with the pictorialist principle that composition was more important than attention to minute detail, which had been the earlier Victorian photographers taxonomic and artistic interest (Millar 1984; Newton 1979:4-6).

There is surprisingly little repetition of individual photographs in the hundreds of published works. But it is significant that four or five images were repeated so often that from a perspective in the 1990s it is possible to discern a pattern and see the beginnings of a set of views of Papua. The tree-house was one of these often-repeated images.

Tree-houses were built in Papua by Koiari people and some other Papuan peoples, but their use was not widespread.[5] By measuring the photographic image against the actual presence of tree-houses in Papua, a gap is revealed between the constructed image (a photograph) and the reality (the Koiari tree-house). This gap allows the presumption of other meanings and messages. Colonial observers asserted that tree-houses were part of a broader Koiari defensive strategy including palisades, enclosures, positioning atop precipitous ridges and crags, and the choice of trees without branches in their lower levels. This was a judgement based on the general fear Europeans had of violence or attack by so-called savages, cannibals and head-hunters. Europeans also carried with them a predilection in which primitives were seen as potentially aggressive due to their uncivilised status. After many years in Papua, Hubert Murray concluded, on what appears to be pretty flimsy evidence, that the Koiari were among the fiercest opponents of European contact, having attacked the young journalist Morrison (of China fame) in 1884, H.O. Forbes in 1887, and a private gold-prospecting expedition in 1896. Murray's opinion was that although they lived near Port Moresby, 'they have been but little affected by civilization' (Murray 1925:80-1). The judgements of those who made personal inspections of tree-houses seemed to support Murray's view of the violent nature of Koiari life. Lyne, in 1885, informed readers that tree-houses had been placed in 'their peculiar position in order that the tribe might be better able to withstand attacks from their enemies'(Lyne 1885:44-6). Hatton-Richards advised his Colonial Institute audience that trees houses were 'for fighting purposes. In them are kept reserve stores of weapons and food and in times of warfare they are a decided advantage to those who hold them' (Hatton-Richards 1892-93:296). Resident Magistrate J.A. Blayney reported being attacked by natives heaving stones from a tree-house when trying to make arrests at Makanigoro village (BNG/AR 1901:14), and G. Currie Martin noted in 1908 that many tree-houses had 'fighting platforms below the house and large stocks of ammunition in the form of heavy stones and spears to discharge from these platforms in case of assault' (Martin 1908:25-6).

However, in 1880, H.M. Chester and 'Tamate' (the missionary James Chalmers) reported that they climbed a 30-metre ladder to inspect a strongly built tree-house at Munikaila, with two storeys, 'both of which had earth in one corner to make a fire on, in one end of the top storey the owner had put by a large quantity of yams and three earthenware pots, in the lower one we saw some spears and a couple of net bags' (Chester 1880:7). In 1892, J.P. Thompson 'FRGS, Honorary Secretary of the Royal Geographical Society of Australia (Brisbane)', observed that the Veiburi people, after incessant raids by their neighbours, the Garia and Manukoro, had built a defensive village with two houses on the ground and eleven tree-houses, 'stocked with food and weapons of defence and constantly occupied

by their owners' (Thompson 1892:51). A former serving officer in Papua, W.N. Beaver, included in his book on Papua, a tree-house photograph with a caption that included the advice that 'these houses are used for observation' (Beaver 1920:48). The evidence gathered by observation, mostly from ground level, suggests that the military use of one or two tree-houses within a larger village perimeter was defensive rather than offensive, and that tree-houses, where they were built, were occasional refuges in time of attack, or sentry boxes, and only in rare instances where a small group lived under daily threat were they permanently occupied.

The many tree-house photographs and captions used in published texts do not carry any suggestion of a military or aggressive role, though in a fanciful rendition in *Tamate: The Life and Adventure of a Christian Hero – A Book for Boys*, several Papuans are seen clubbing and spearing each other in a fight sprawling across the ladders and platforms of several adjoining tree-houses (Lovett 1902b:151). This fanciful scenario is an aberration included on the misguided presumption that boys' books needed action scenes and additional gratuitous violence in the illustrations supporting the text. In the 1880 to 1930 period, the captions, a third level of transmitted meaning or subtext, did not support these assertions of violence, aggression and warfare among Papuans. The tree-house photograph captions tended towards self-evident phraseology and brevity and a preference to let the picture stand alone. Captions typically read 'A New Guinea Tree house', 'Tree house in Papua' or 'A typical house in a mountain village'.

Tree-house photographs suggested Papuans built houses that were simple and different, and did not provide evidence of, or suggest, any form of indigenous social or political organisation, or any achievement in arts, crafts or technology, that would attribute to Papuans a degree of sophistication or civilisation. Tree-house photographs clearly placed Papuans in the category of primitives.

J.W. Lindt's trip to Papua in 1885, the publication in 1887 of his book *Picturesque New Guinea*, and the sale over the counter of his postcards, framed prints and folios of photographs of Papua, were the genesis of this tree-house chronology. On his return to Melbourne, Lindt published three photographs of Koiari tree-houses. The most copied was a ground-level composition highlighting three Papuans on a platform above a solitary tree-house, captioned simply 'Tree House' (fig. 20.1). The second was a longer-angled view of a ridge, showing the full area of settlement and several tree-houses. The third was a close-up of a group of 'chiefs' and villagers squatting in an open area before their houses. These photographs were subsequently used by other publishers, with and without acknowledgement. They were also used as a composition model by other photographers, and for direct copying by artists for engravings, etchings and drawings used in book illustration.

James Chalmers and W.W. Gill, in their 1885 missionary tract, *Work and Adventure in New Guinea*, included 'two maps and many illustrations from original sketches and photographs', and their special Presentation Edition contained a further thirty illustrations. This was the first published appearance of a Papuan tree-house. The drawings and etchings, based on photographs, were simplistic and imaginative, with stylised tropical trees and tree-houses drawn according to Western architectural forms, but with a thatched roof and rough-hewn timber walls. In the Presentation Edition, the caption on the Koiari tree-house, from Lindt's photograph, was changed to 'Life in the tree tops; Tree houses showing platform and ladders', but the German edition, *Neuguinea Reisen and Missionstatigfeit*, reverted to the simpler 'Baumhaufer'. This artistic depiction of a Papuan tree-house then disappeared from use.

Later books by Chalmers (without Gill), *Pioneering in New Guinea* (1887), *Pioneer life and work* (1895), and a new edition of Chalmers and Gill's book in 1903, continued to borrow from Lindt's tree-house photograph. These illustrations were engraved by E. Whymper, taken directly from Lindt's photograph, but leaving out the three Papuans on the upper platform. The captions in Chalmers' books contained various combinations of the terms 'tree house', 'Koiari' and *dobu*. In Chalmers' 1887 and 1895 books, a second Whymper engraving, loosely based on all three Lindt photographs of the Koiari, is practically the same but for the addition of a woman climbing the ladder, and another walking past carrying clay pots. Captioned 'a dobo for women at Koiari', this was presumably included in the interests

of gender balance, or merely to provide another illustration, as there is no evidence that Koiari tree-houses were built specifically for women's use. This misrepresentation, repeated by others (Bevan 1890:209), and lasting until the 1970s (Doussett and Taillemite 1974:84), along with the use of the Papuan terms *dobo* and *dobu* interchangeably for the English word 'house', point to a further gap between intention and message in photographic images.

As well as claiming to capture reality and providing visual evidence of his actual presence in Papua, the illustrations offered by Chalmers also carried an ideological intent, and signified a civilising or tutelage relationship between Europeans and the newly discovered 'other', in this case between the missionary and the Papuan heathen, and by inference, converts waiting to be won. A duality of intention and message is also obvious in the 1888 publication of J.S. Macfarlane's missionary tract, *Among the Cannibals of New Guinea: Being the Story of the New Guinea Mission of the LMS*, in which a Hume Nisbet drawing portrays 'a heathen fight' occurring below a tree-house (fig. 20.4). Used as a header for a chapter on mission achievements called 'Results', this fighting scene is captioned 'Then'. It is juxtaposed against a scene captioned 'Now' on the right of the page, in which a European-style, local-material church is being approached submissively by a group of fully clothed native converts (Macfarlane 1888:149). The tree-house is included as a signifier of primitiveness. It connects the reader to, and places the action in, primitive Papua, though geographic location could be mistaken, given the simplicity of Nisbet's interpretation of Lindt's photographs. The European-style clothing, neatness and church construction in the 'Now' scene indicate another Papua, one that was being elevated from a primitive state, and which with mission help was approaching civilisation.

In 1892, two liberally illustrated books, J.P. Thompson's *British New Guinea* and B.F.S. Baden-Powell's *In Savage Isles and Settled Lands*, were published. They included engravings of a tree-house based on a photograph by a Mr H. Barnes and a second unknown source, probably Lindt, judging by the similarity of composition and setting (Baden-Powell 1892:201; Thompson 1892:52). The

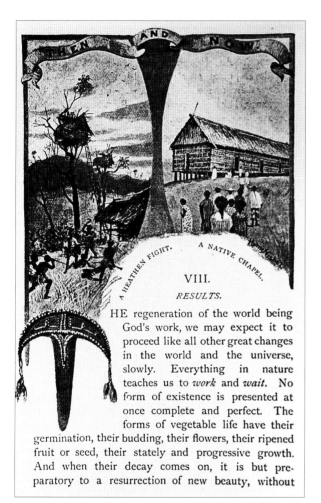

20.4 Drawing for chapter header for J.S. Macfarlane's 1888 missionary tract *Among the Cannibals of New Guinea*, incorporating sketch of tree-house copied from Lindt's photograph (fig. 20.1).

Barnes photograph-engraving is the first by an artist to suggest the actual dishevelled appearance of a Koiari tree-house, built roughly of local materials according to the natural angles and spacing of tree branches rather than any set architectural wall, roof or floor plan.

In 1893, H.M. Romilly, without acknowledging the photographer, repeated Lindt's Koiari village photograph, retitled a 'village in New Guinea' (Romilly 1893:287), and in a series of books published between 1900 and the start of World War I, Lindt's photograph is repeated several

times, usually unacknowledged. In this period there are also seven artistic renditions based on Lindt's photograph, and six tree-house photographs by unknown photographers.

Three of these tree-house photographs appeared in official publications, raising the tree-house to a new level of 'gathered truth'. Although they contained tree-house photographs, the *British New Guinea Annual Report 1900-1901*, and the 1909 and 1912 editions of the *Handbook of the Territory of Papua*, edited by M. Staniforth-Smith, do not refer to the usage or number of tree-houses. The photographs and the captions informed readers that tree-houses could be found at Babakagoro (fig. 20.5), Sogeri, Eriki, and Hombrom Bluff. An alternative reading of their inclusion in the officially sanctioned images of Papua is that in this context tree-houses were an exotic rather than a 'from life' representation of Papuan material culture and domestic life. Knowing that annual reports and handbooks were part of a global and ubiquitous genre of propaganda, self-justification and statistical reporting, by including tree-houses perhaps Papua's administrators were attempting to distinguish Papua from other colonial possessions, to emphasise the transition from primitive to colonised status, or to attract some of the growing number of traveller-cum-tourists.

The engravings, drawings and artists' sketches of tree-houses that appeared during the rush of mission hagiography devoted to the recently martyred James Chalmers were continuations of Lindt's photographic composition (Lennox 1903:86; Lovett 1902a:151; Robson n.d.:78; Seton n.d.:89). These simplistic depictions of tree-houses reinforced the status of Papuans as primitives. In 1911, Frank Fox in *Peeps at Many Lands: Oceania* was the first to portray an artistic likeness of the trees and the house construction (Fox 1911:22), but his setting suggests a flat forest floor rather than the precipitous crags and sparsely vegetated narrow back ridges the Koiari favoured as sites for their tree-houses.

Beginning in the late 1880s, the trading and shipping firm, Burns Philp, ran an advertising campaign and published many illustrated pamphlets, magazines and brochures to promote international tourism using their vessels.

In *Picturesque Travel* in 1920, they included a photograph of a Koiari 'Papuan Tree Residence' and noted that 'the visitor can by a short journey from the township see the Rona Falls, and the tree houses of the Ikeri village'. Later, in *Picturesque Isles of the South Seas*, travellers were informed that 'in contrast to the coastal natives, with their houses built over the water, the inland people sometimes choose the branches of trees wherein to build their homes', though in this edition a tree-house photograph was not included. Tree-house images were being excluded by the 1920s because they were considered not photogenic enough for tourists, or were inaccessible, being too far from the wharves for tourists to go trekking. Perhaps by the 1920s, forty years of government presence had calmed the allegedly warlike and independent Koiari, and tree-houses were no longer being built. Although tree-houses do not appear elsewhere in the liberally illustrated Burns Philp publications, the tree-house's place as a stereotype had been further cemented by inclusion in the modern, tourist snapshot gallery of the 'other' world.

That the tree-house had become a signifier for Papua can be judged by the longevity of Lindt's tree-house photograph. A replica edition of his book, *Picturesque New Guinea*, was published in 1984, and in the same year in the

20.5 Tree-house at Babakagoro village, published in *British New Guinea: Annual Report* for 1901, Appendix, Plate 10. RAI lg.111.

French-language and English-language editions of George Delbos's *Cent ans chez les Papous*, Lindt's tree-house photograph was used as a frontispiece. In the same year, Moore, Griffin and Griffin's *Colonial Intrusion*, a commemorative educational text of photographs, also contained two of Lindt's Koiari photographs. Tree-houses kept appearing – in John Ryan's *The Hotland: Focus on New Guinea* in 1969, in Timothy Severin's *Vanishing Primitive Man* in 1973, Hank Nelson's *Black, White and Gold* in 1977, Doussett and Taillenmite's *Great Book of the Pacific* in 1979, and Snow and Waine's *The People from the Horizon* in 1979. Young children continued to be misled. For example, in 1989, the caption to an artist's depiction of a tree-house in Time-Life's serial encyclopaedia, *The World We Live In*, informed young readers that Papua New Guineans build houses in the air to avoid the muggy ground-level air, to catch the cool breeze and the sunshine, and to live above the insects (Time-Life 1989:12-13). The Museum of Victoria, the Queensland Museum, and the Museum of Mankind, London, still have elaborately mounted oversize enlargements of Lindt's photographs, and although now stored they were on display for much of the 20th century. The corridor of the History Department at the University of Papua New Guinea is decorated with Lindt's Koiari photography, and in 1992 a Port Moresby publication, Coutts's *Looking Back* (1992:19) continued this chronology by including the same Lindt photograph. The building of a replica Koiari tree-house at Varirata National Park in the 1970s was therefore the continuation of a representation of Papua transmitted through several media and several generations.[6]

A similar narrative might be constructed for the other images that formed the iconographic core of books, magazines, lantern-slide shows and postcards of Papua. The Koiari tree-house sits alongside other icons – Papuan types, sago-making, *lakatoi*, pot-making, marine villages, and Papuan belles and dandies – published between 1880 and 1930. These images are an ethnographic and historical window for present-day researchers seeking to contribute to the history of relationships between newly discovered others and Europeans, and the history of European colonial policy and practice. By transmission to reading, exhibition and public-address audiences, these images linked the distant, disengaged reader with the entanglements and encounters of photographers, Europeans and Papuans on the coasts of Papua.

The intention of the image-maker at the moment of taking the photograph, and the often contradictory intention inherent in the image at the time of publication, suggest that tourist publications, colonial reports, memoirs by casual visitors, hagiography, amateur ethnographies and travellers' tales about Papua were powerful forces in constructing public attitudes towards others during an era in which it seemed that one or two new books about Papua were being released each month and yet another explorer, missionary or amateur ethnographer was in town to give a public address. In Miss Baildon's talk, Pastor Stewart's lantern slides, Lindt's folios and postcards, Chalmer's travelogues, Staniforth-Smith's handbooks, and a growing library of ethnographies, 'the native life and scenery' of Papua, and tree-houses, had been appropriated and frozen in a small set of photographic images.

Notes

1. This is a revised version of a paper first presented at the Ninth Pacific History Association Conference, Christchurch, New Zealand, in December 1992, and further revised for the fifth Pacific Arts symposium, Adelaide, April 1993.
2. In December 1927, the Kodak Gallery in Sydney held an exhibition of 200 photographs by Frank Hurley, who had just returned from an Anglican Board of Missions photography trip to Papua. Hurley had taken 1200 negatives during his three-month trip. The board paid Hurley £250 for a separate copyrighted set of 100 coloured lantern slides and 1500 feet of cinema film (later released by the board as *Heart of New Guinea*). Hurley did not include a tree-house, but the other staple shots – a *lakotai*, sago-making, marine villages, men's cult-houses, and Papuan belles and dandies – were featured (Legge and Hurley 1966:113-15; Millar 1984:77-8).
3. Where Lindt took his photographs of Koiari tree-houses is uncertain. His description of the day's events identifies a small, newly built village of twenty houses situated on low scrubby ridges east of Port Moresby. Lindt's topographic references suggest it was not as far east as the Sogeri-Varirata plateau (Lindt

1887:39-40). His description coincides with an 1883 map (printed in the *British New Guinea Annual Report for 1891-92*) by W.E. Armit indicating the Coiari [sic] district, which also notes the villages of Serika, Yenari and Effaro, but not that of Sedara Makara named by Lindt. A village called Sadara Makara was noted on a map by H.O. Forbes after his Mt Owen Stanley expedition in 1887 (BNG/AR 1887:31), but then it disappears from view, probably abandoned as the people distanced themselves from increasing European activity to maintain their Koiari independence.

4. Photographs continue to hold a powerful presence in books but are rarely part of the critical writing process. For example, the text of the first history of the Tokelau Islands (*Matagi Tokelau*) was hotly contested by Tokelauans and the interpretation debated at length to establish equity, parity and 'truth'. But the sixty photographs in the book were apparently accepted as uncontestable evidence of the past, thereby ignoring the knowledge that many early photographs were carefully contrived and therefore misleading in their manipulated messages (Huntsman 1992).

5. Another style of tree-house began to feature briefly in the 1920s, photographed in the upper Fly River, Western Province, Papua, and the Digul River area of south-east Netherlands New Guinea (now Irian Jaya). These large dwellings were supported by a single trunk but with dozens of thin poles supporting the floor of the rectangular house (Baharell nd; Bernatsik 1935:364; Bernatsik 1939:160; Brandes 1929:289,301,309; C. Miller 1950:192; L. Miller 1941:305).

6. Reasons for the decision to construct the tree-house at Varirata are difficult to ascertain, as there are no extant records. Did the initiative come from Koiari people, other Papuan politicans or bureaucrats in the newly independent government, or from an expatriate victim of the chronology of misrepresentation to which the Lindt photograph gave birth? If the latter, it would be provocative to suggest that these 1970s expatriate sentiments were embedded in the same colonial attitudes of primitiveness and otherness that characterised many authors and publishers at the turn of the century. I would like to thank Bronwyn Douglas for alerting me to this possibility.

'Our ethnological troops in the field': Swedes and museum collecting in Melanesia circa 1900

Hélena Regius

Sweden has in different parts of the world, ethnographical troops in the midst of battle, and in some areas even more troops are being mobilised. Also it is now time that Sweden conduct research in the important and popular study of the history of mankind. So much of the cultural origins are disappearing or being corrupted, and the competition between the civilised nations has increasingly hardened.[1] [*Svenska Dagbladet* 19 June 1913]

In *Svenska Dagbladet*, a contemporary newspaper of 19 June 1913, museum collecting was described in almost warlike terms, with collectors described as troops in the battlefield. According to the article, one of the most important collecting enterprises was to be conducted in the Pacific. Count Birger Mörner had just travelled through Germany to prepare for his trip to the German protectorate of New Guinea. Funding had been provided by the Swedish consul in Rabaul, Rudolph Wahlen, and Mörner had been trained in collecting ethnographic material in German museums.

The task of this paper is to outline how the National Museum of Ethnography in Stockholm acquired most of its collections from Melanesia, especially from the area of former German New Guinea.

In 1992 I was documenting material culture from the Melanesian region in the collection of the National Museum of Ethnography. My task was not only to find the place of origin of the objects, but also to write a small introduction to each collection, including biographical information about each collector. A term for such an exercise in museology is the *biography of things*. I found myself wading into correspondence from the late 19th century, with reports from the field, articles from the major newspapers of the time, and popular travel books. This is how I found the title that in many respects represents that idea surrounding why collecting *ethnographica* was considered essential at the turn of the century.

Today, the press would not bother to keep themselves up to date with new acquisitions in ethnographical museums. So we should ask ourselves what was taking place 100 years ago in the museum world.

The National Museum of Ethnography, Stockholm

Ten per cent of the total collection in Stockholm (around 150 000 objects) comes from the Pacific region. The majority is Melanesian, predominantly from German New Guinea, and was acquired by Sweden between 1880 and 1920.

To understand the context in which the museum acquired most of its Pacific material, it is necessary to go back in the history of the museum. The earliest collections from the area consist of a few New Caledonian and Vanuatu (New Hebrides) clubs dating from Captain Cook's second voyage. These objects were obtained by Anders Sparrman and Daniel Solander,[2] students of Carl von Linné, who travelled with Captain Cook; they became part of the National Academy of Science collections (founded in 1739) and later part of the Natural History Museum (1841).

For many years after Sparrman's and Solander's travels, no major explorations were done by Swedes, and it was not until the *Eugenie* expedition in 1851-53 that any Swedish exploration was carried out in the Pacific. The purpose was to establish trade relations. A few ethnographic objects were brought back, but not for any scientific reason. Most of them were placed in the Natural History Museum and were kept together with other ethnographica in the Department of Vertebrates. Others ended up in private collections. Although not an ethnographic expedition *per se*, the voyage of *Eugenie* stimulated an increasing interest, born out of the study of Swedish cultural history and archaeology, in ethnography.[3]

The development of ethnography in Sweden was the work of Hjalmar Stolpe. He was the catalyst for the changes in attitudes towards the 'other' and for non-European ethnography.

Hjalmar Stolpe was first trained as a zoologist and later as an archaeologist. In 1878, he arranged the first ethnographical exhibition in Stockholm – *Etnografiska utställningen*. Stolpe brought together ethnographica from various private collections, together with pieces at the Natural History Museum. Five years earlier he had established *Antropologiska sällskapet* (the Anthropological Association), together with Gustav Retzius, a natural scientist whose chief interest was physical anthropology. Retzius and Stolpe were influenced by Darwinism and its typological approach to science (Du Rietz 1984:5-20).

Stolpe's exhibition provoked further interest in ethnography. It could be said that the time was right for the Swedish academic world to see the importance of ethnography as a science. The number of artefacts in the museum increased and it was possible to obtain sponsorship for expeditions for scientific purposes. A petition was sent to the Swedish Parliament in 1884 to persuade the government to support ethnography and museum collecting 'for the sake of the study of mankind', especially in the Pacific. It was argued that indigenous cultures in the

Pacific were deteriorating due to influences from the Western world. Collecting had to be done before these cultures disappeared forever (Holmberg 1987:429-30). However, the petition was turned down in parliament. Instead, ethnography was supported by other means through the Academy of Science. This was how the *Vanadis* expedition came about.

Stolpe was the chief ethnographer on the *Vanadis*, which sailed around the world between 1883 and 1885. Apart from Stolpe's archaeological excavations, this was his first encounter with ethnographic field work. Stolpe never conducted field work in a modern sense, but during the journey he felt unhappy about never being able to stay any length of time in one place. He became an avid collector, and his diaries are packed with drawings, field notes and local names for things.

More than 7000 objects from around the world were collected on the *Vanadis* journey [Collection Vanadis 1887.8.1-7565].[4] The *Vanadis* sailed to Hawai'i, where a number of New Guinea objects, including some New Ireland *malagan*, were bought from a dealer. The ship then sailed through Micronesia (Jaluit), where most of the Pacific material (906 objects) was collected or bought from German colonisers. They did not visit Melanesia.

Before the *Vanadis* expedition, Stolpe visited ethnographical museums on the Continent (1880-81). He made friends with ethnographers and natural scientists in Germany (Berlin, Hamburg and Dresden), England, France, the Netherlands and Denmark. In this period, Stolpe published his major ethnographical work, *The Origin of Ornamentation*. On the basis of his study of Pacific objects, he theorised that ornamentation is based on stylised images of animals.

To have a science of ethnography, the museum needed a collection. For this purpose, the museum began exchanging ethnographic objects, and Stolpe used his contacts to push for people to travel and collect worldwide in the name of the museum. For example, he arranged for scientists connected to the Swedish Natural History Museum and the Academy of Science to travel abroad.

Not until the late 19th century was ethnography separated from natural science. In 1900 Stockholm got its own department for ethnography. Before then, most ethnographica lay in storage. Stolpe became the curator of the Ethnographic Department.

Collectors of Melanesian ethnographica

On the basis of the collection at the National Museum of Ethnography, the collectors of Melanesian ethnography operating during the period 1880 to 1920 can be divided into three categories:[5]

- natural scientists, and/or influential academics of aristocratic background;
- administrators in European colonial enterprises in the Pacific;
- Swedish sailors and adventurers in the Pacific.

The kind and the amount of archival material that I have found for the three groups differs considerably. However, Swedish academics and European colonisers had much in common. Their social status was high and they were involved in a sponsoring network, a kind of gift-exchange economy, as we will see later. Particular networks were related to the political situation in Sweden and the country's foreign policy. Ethnographica was collected for scientific but also for business purposes. The ethnographical 'troops' were people from the upper classes and/or scientists. Some were associated with the Natural History Museum or the Academy of Science. In the press, academics who collected were being portrayed as 'crusaders' for the good of Sweden.

Swedish sailors and adventurers, the third category, had travelled to the Pacific for different reasons. These men were of urban working class or agrarian backgrounds, 'restless' young men seeking something more in life than their social status would allow them in Sweden. Sadly we know little about them. Their names rarely figure in any records after they left Sweden.

Many lived a 'nomadic' life by sailing under different flags, working at trade stations all over the Pacific or with less honourable activities such as blackbirding.[6] Occasionally the museum received donations of a few items, often many years later, from relatives in Sweden who had been given them as proof of these men's adventures in the South Seas. Adventures among cannibals and other fantastic tales were popular themes if anything was published (usually exaggerated by sensational journalism).

Letters home often told a different story. Life was difficult, with tropical fevers and other dangers at far-off trade posts. While the colonisers and their aristocratic guests lived safely in the colonial centres, people of lower-class background lived in the 'bush' with local people.

Through trade and other contact with villagers, they obtained ethnographic material and supplied the upper class with collections. They provided the colonisers with the means to elevate their social status.[7]

Let us examine a typical area where some of these Swedes lived and worked. Germany annexed the northeast portion of New Guinea and the Bismarck Archipelago in 1884. The colony was divided into two regions that developed somewhat differently because of different natural constraints.

The successful region consisted of New Britain, with its colonial centre in Herbertshöhe, the Duke of York Group and Witu Islands, New Ireland, New Hanover, St Matthias, the Admiralty Islands, and the Polynesian outliers. The soil was generally better for plantations and the region less affected by malaria. Many sailors came to work in the Bismarck Archipelago and the expatriate community was of mixed nationality.[8]

Kaiser Wilhelms Land (mainland New Guinea), by contrast, was a failure (Firth 1986:21-43). Badly administered from Berlin, the Germans tried to create a perfect colony. It failed because the colonisers did not accept the natural constraints. Many labourers died of disease, as did many expatriates (mainly German) who had come to seek their fortunes in the model colony.

The 'troops' in the name of science

Erik Nyman in Kaiser Wilhelms Land in the era of Die Neu Guinea Companie

In 1897, Erik Nyman, Swedish botanist at the Academy of Science, journeyed to the Pacific to travel and collect for the museum. It was through Stolpe's contacts that Nyman's travels became possible. He first stayed on Java

21.1   Potters in front of a house, Bili-Bili (Bilbil), German New Guinea, 1899. Gift from Frederich Wandres to Eric Nyman. Collection 15:10. (Copyright National Museum of Ethnography, Stockholm.)

at Buitenzorg, a place where many European botanists and other natural scientists stayed. Nyman asked for money to go to New Guinea so he could collect properly. At the time there were many links between the German colony and Java. Plantation managers in Java were taken to Kaiser Wilhelms Land to establish the German model colony.

Through his contacts with Germans in Java, Nyman came to Stephanort on the north-east coast of New Guinea in 1898-99. In his early letters to Stolpe he described the situation in the area. Life was dreadful due to fevers. Despite that, Nyman gave pleasant descriptions of some of the Papuan villages he visited and took photographs that are now in the museum collections (fig. 21.1).

Nyman wrote to Stolpe (11 February 1899):

Men wear big wigs, around their waists a small loincloth and apart from that nothing else. Women wear plaited mantillas of plant fibres around their waists, jewellery of shells around their necks.

He also observed that the village had a '*junggesällehaus*' (a special house for bachelors).

Two months later (8 April 1899), Nyman visited another village near Stephanort and noticed that people there had more elaborate body decorations. Tobacco was given as a gift at first contact with the people. Empty tins and colourful wrappings from various European goods also were things the people treasured. Nyman possibly used these materials in exchange for objects.

'In the inner [part] of the house we discovered some pagan fetishes,' wrote Nyman with excitement, as if he were able to acquire these objects. Whether he collected these carvings is not known.

Collecting in the area around Stephanort and Simbang (Finschhafen area) had already become difficult. Just before Nyman arrived in Simbang in September 1899, Lajos Bíró, a Hungarian zoologist and ethnographer, well-financed by his government, had made large collections and little was left. No doubt this was a way for Nyman to point out that Sweden should provide him with greater funding, otherwise Sweden would lose out in the competition. Bíró was described as using dirty tricks to get the best pieces, 'being ruthless' and an 'egoist' wrote Nyman in very lively terms. Bíró 'had totally extinguished anything worth the name ethnographica'. The war metaphor is very obvious.

Yet Nyman did not lose out in the competition. Today we have about 1000 objects from German New Guinea, many from the same area from which Bíró collected, and objects from Java and China [Nyman 1901.21.1-1284]. Nyman noted from where some of the objects had come, and their local names. Other objects were obtained from labour recruiters who went out to the more remote areas.

Later Nyman travelled by boat through the Bismarck Archipelago. However, he did not visit many areas apart from Herbertshöhe and Matupit and was unable to collect himself. Instead he got a collection obtained from Witu Islands and New Britain by Fredrich Wandres [Wandres 1899.1.1-54], a plantation manager employed by the Neu Guinea Compagnie. Collections made by Wandres are also to be found in Switzerland, and possibly other places. He obviously traded in ethnographica, as many colonists in his position did at the time.

Returning to Europe in 1900, Nyman died of tropical fever in Germany. His collection, along with his photographs, arrived at the museum in due course. In a sense, this collection can be said to mark a new era in the Melanesian collections for the museum in Stockholm, for it involved active collecting in the field.

Birger Mörner, Swedish consul in Sydney: Travels in German New Guinea, 1913-14

Count Birger Mörner was one of those Swedish characters we have come to associate with the Pacific. A talented writer and man of the world who spoke many languages, Mörner was the consul in Sydney for improvement of Swedish-Australian relationships, particularly in the matter of trade.

Already by 1906 Mörner had visited New Zealand and the Solomon Islands. In 1913-14 his major expedition to German New Guinea took place. He stayed in Rabaul, visited New Ireland and the Tabar Islands, the Admiralty Islands, Wuvulu and Aua, and went up the Ramu and Sepik rivers.

Mörner was an accomplished writer. He wrote poetry, fiction and tales based on his life abroad. In his book *Arafs tropiska år* (*Arafs Tropical Years*), based on his travels in German New Guinea,[9] he described his experiences in a style between a travel report and fiction. It was during

this journey that Mörner collected for the museum [Mörner 1915.2.1-1385]. There was much debate as to who would sponsor his travels. Hartman, the director of the Ethnographic Department in Stockholm, had tried to use his position with the Academy of Science to obtain funding but failed. Through Mörner's earlier consular work he had contact with the Swedish consul in Rabaul, Rudolph Wahlen. Wahlen became the sponsor of Mörner's expedition, enabling him to obtain a huge collection from various islands of the Bismarck Archipelago.

Sweden avidly followed Mörner's travels in the articles he wrote for the local press (*Vecko Journalen* and *Svenska Dagbladet*). He described the customs of the New Guinea people and the kinds of objects they used. The public was introduced to all kinds of ethnographic information, along with a rather positive account of Melanesian culture.

For example, Mörner described the art from the Ramu River and rather acidly asked why art historians had not yet dealt with it, since 'even Stone Age people make paintings'. In a village he visited on Christmas Day in 1913, he noticed the following:

> Outside the houses hung something that drew my attention. They were paintings of stylised gods or perhaps just decorative. This was art for art's sake! I managed to buy a half dozen of these original artworks. [*Vecko Journalen* 13 May 1917]

Mörner, as a talented writer, was an artist in his own right, and could see values other than the purely scientific in the objects he collected and the cultures he met. He was influential and thus able to push for his ideas in the museum after he returned to Sweden.

Colonial contacts: The collections of Rudolph Wahlen, Maximiliam Thiel and Robert Pullaine

Before Count Mörner's journey of 1913-14, the museum obtained several interesting Melanesian collections. Rudolph Wahlen, who took over the empire of Queen Emma (Emma Forsayth), was the Swedish consul in Rabaul. In 1908 and 1909, the museum received collections from Wahlen consisting of material from the Bismarck Archipelago [Wahlen 1908.4.1-3 and 1909.4.1-137].

Maximiliam Thiel was a high official for the Hernsheim company in Rabaul, and later the Norwegian consul in New Guinea. He served Germany in the Pacific longer than any other official. Thiel made a huge collection of ethnographica. Parts were sold and sometimes donated to different museums in northern Europe. The museums of Hamburg, Berlin, Dresden and Stuttgart in Germany, and Kristiania (Oslo) in Norway, house his collections. Mörner met Thiel at the Colonial Institute in Hamburg before his travels in New Guinea in 1913. Thiel arranged a collection and donated it to the museum in Stockholm [Thiel 1913.4.1-133]. The 133 pieces were very impressive, and the newspaper *Svenska Dagbladet* (23 June 1913) described at length the objects and their uses. We read about the Sulka dance masks of New Britain:

> Human forms and motifs from the natural world are swirling in a confusing manner ... These incredible masks usually have monstrous helmets and ribbons attached to them, which from a sculptural point of view make up the most interesting part of the art of the Pacific.

In 1913, Dr Robert Pullaine in Adelaide offered the Swedish consul general to Australia 'a magnificent and interesting collection' of Melanesian objects. The collection, according to the newspaper (*Aftonbladet* 18 July 1913), contained many rare objects that soon would be prohibited to export. Pullaine had started to collect in the 1870s, and his collection was now too big to manage.

The museum had no money to buy this collection. After a long debate, Rudolph Wahlen offered to pay for it. In 1914 the collection of more than 4000 objects from all over Melanesia and Australia arrived in Sweden [Pullaine 1916.1.1-4098] and it is today the largest collection of Melanesian objects in the museum. It contains objects from the Papuan coast, the Massim area, the north-east coast of New Guinea, the Bismarck Archipelago and Solomon Islands. Pullaine's collection was catalogued in 1917 but not displayed for many years. Because of the size of the collection, a few hundred pieces have since been exchanged for ethnographic material from other museums.[10]

'Living among the natives'

Carl Pettersson, the 'King' of Tabar

In 1904, Carl Pettersson settled on Tabar Islands, off the north-east coast of New Ireland, as a plantation manager. Six years earlier he had started to work for the Neu Guinea Compagnie as a labour recruiter. Pettersson was born outside Stockholm and had become a sailor at an early age. From 1892 to 1898 no records are to be found about

21.2 Carl Pettersson, his wife Singdo Missis, and six of his children, photographed at his Tabar plantation by Edgar Waite, 12 July 1918. (Acc.1839, AP 3812. Copyright South Australian Museum, Adelaide.)

his travels and how he ended up in the Pacific. His name is not mentioned in the German records.

The information we have from Pettersson is scanty apart from a few letters. Instead we can read about his sensational life in various newspapers in Sweden. He was the 'King of Tabar' and married the daughter of a 'cannibal king' on Tabar (Dahlberg 1954:20-33). Of course, we need to take this information with some reserve. We do not know if Pettersson wanted all this publicity or not. It was the writing of Count Mörner that made Pettersson known in Sweden after Mörner's visit to Tabar in 1913.

What is remarkable about Pettersson was his marriage to a local woman, with whom he had nine children, and that he is said to have spoken the local language. In a photo taken in 1918, Pettersson is seen posing with his wife, Singdo Missis, and six of their children, dressed in Swedish folk costumes (fig. 21.2). It was said in the mythology created about him that he was a 'fair and understanding' manager who respected the local customs and ceremonies.

Pettersson organised collections of several fine *malagan* carvings from the villages around his plantation for the museums in Stockholm and Göteborg [Pettersson 1915.15.1-21]. The most spectacular pieces are the set of ten carvings used in one *malagan* ceremony. The story surrounding the acquisition is that Pettersson and Mörner were out for a walk around the beach near the plantation. Mörner saw the newly erected 'shrine' of palm leaves with the carvings in front of the wall. On the wall hung several pig jawbones. According to Mörner, Pettersson exchanged the 'gods' for a pig, and everything (including the wall) was sent to Sweden (*Vecko Journalen* 13 May 1917).[11]

Carl Wilhelm Öberg: Working for 'Queen' Emma

Another adventurer, and a friend of Pettersson, was Carl Wilhelm Öberg who for longer periods managed a trade station in Nusa, New Ireland. He worked for Emma Forsayth first as a labour recruiter but later as a copra trader, and collected ethnographic material.

Like Pettersson, he became a legend in his home town as the South Sea traveller. When he returned to Sweden in the 1920s as a retired sailor, the manager of the local cultural centre, Bernt Hage, wrote down his stories. Hage's version of the stories became extremely exaggerated and nowhere near Öberg's real experiences. Stories about cannibals, strange rituals among the natives, and so on, dominated. His letters home, however, emphasise more the fevers from which he suffered while in the Pacific.

He met Jack London, and it was said that Öberg inspired London to include him as a character in his novels. This was something Bernt Hage frequently wrote about. An even more amusing aspect of this sensationalism was an article in *Vecko Journalen* in 1930. Öberg collected a very tall *malagan* carving (around 4 metres tall). The carving was referred to as the 'totem pole', similar to those of the north-west coast Indians. To make the carving even more impressive, Öberg was photographed outside his cottage in Sweden together with the *malagan*, but the photo was falsified and an addition to the pole was made. The added part was a real Native American totem pole.

So today, in a village of northern Sweden, we can see Öberg's remarkable collection of carvings, weapons, tools, body decorations, and so on, from New Ireland, New Britain, the Admiralty Islands, Nukumanu/Ontong Java and Micronesia. (For conservation purposes, the National Museum of Ethnography houses part of the collection.)

Öberg left some information on what the objects were, their usage and who made them. For example, the tall *malagan* carving was described as a 'family tree' used at funerals; the Nukumanu looms were operated by men, and so on. Included in Öberg's collection are several postcards, produced in Germany, of Melanesian people in various ethnographic situations. The same images can be found in German ethnographic literature of this period.

Swedish society and 'gift exchange' in the museum world

We must now mention the social, political and economic situation in Sweden in relation to foreign countries to explain the way in which collecting was done.

Sweden in the latter part of the 19th century, and until World War II, was a 'little brother' to Germany. The German tradition prevailed in the language and in scientific literature. Leaving aside the politics, academic life in Sweden was also closely connected to Germany. The second language and the academic language were German, and this may serve as one explanation of why Sweden followed the German tradition of methodical collecting to represent each geographical area worldwide. The German *Kulturkries* theory also won many followers among Swedish ethnographers.

Swedish scientists seem to have had a greater personal network with Germans in this field than with the British and French. So when it came to travelling, the German protectorate seems to have been the choice. Therefore our major Melanesian collections are from the German rather than from the British or French territories.

The Ethnographical Department in Stockholm had the privilege of access to medals. As part of the Natural History Museum and its connection to the Academy of Science, Stockholm awarded these medals to people who helped the museum acquire collections. This was a controversy for many years, because the Göteborg Ethnographical Museum had no access to medals and thus had difficulties getting collections. It is not surprising to find that almost every major Melanesian collection involved a 'gift' given by the museum in return.

Eric Nyman, in his travels in German New Guinea, wrote to Stolpe in April 1899 while in Stephanort that he had met Wandres, who had arranged collections from the Bismarck Archipelago and from Java. Nyman added in his letter: 'Since Wandres has donated these precious collections he deserves a medal'.

Later in the same year (15 September 1899), Nyman wrote to Stolpe about his visits to Thiel's home at Matupi in Rabaul:

I … did not get him to talk about his 'museum' he had arranged in the poolroom in a separate building. But the collection of carvings from New Mecklenburg was absolutely marvellous. These objects would have made your mouth water.

Nyman could not possibly ask Thiel for this collection, so he suggested that Stolpe, in a letter to Thiel, should 'stroke him' and that 'the collection is truly worth a couple of medals (Vasa trissor)'.

As we have seen, fourteen years later, Sweden received parts of Thiel's collection. Whether any medal was offered him is not clear, but by 1913 Thiel was consul for Norway, and he obviously had links with Scandinavia (Sweden and Norway had been united from 1814 to 1905). Whether Thiel's collection that went to Berlin, Hamburg and Kristiania was part of any exchange deal is yet to be discovered. Thiel's poolroom was well known in colonial New Guinea, and several other accounts exist about this remarkable set-up. One can only speculate about how extensive the trade in ethnographic material was during the German colonial period.

Stolpe had many contacts, and one of them was Dr Hans Mayer, businessman and patron of the Ethnographical Museum in Leipzig. A couple of years after Stolpe's death (in 1905), Mayer donated to the museum in Stockholm a large collection [Mayer 1907.44.1-613] from Melanesia (172 objects) and Africa in honour of Stolpe. He wrote explaining the intention of his gift, and at the same time proposed that with this generous gift he deserved a medal from the Swedish Academy for his deeds. In Mayer's 'generous' gift, as it was described in the museum annual, there were several *malagan* carvings, *kulap* chalk figures from New Ireland, and other objects from German New Guinea obtained from J.F.G. Umlauff, a Hamburg firm trading in ethnographic and natural-history specimens.

Hartman, Stolpe's successor, was more successful in getting medals from the Academy of Science. The next obvious case where the donor of a Melanesian collection had intentions other than simple generosity is Rudolph Wahlen. In 1913 the museum experienced problems financing Mörner's ethnographic collecting and the purchase of the Melanesian and Australian collection offered by Dr Robert Pullaine of Adelaide. The consul general of Sweden in Australia, van Goës, appealed in the Swedish newspaper *Aftonbladet* (18 July 1913) for a solution to the problem. The following year Hartman had the solution. Wahlen had offered to buy the Pullaine collection and pay for Mörner's travels in New Guinea. Hartman then offered Wahlen the Linnean gold medal, but Wahlen requested a more prestigious medal, the Nordstjernan. Hartman would not arrange this until the collections arrived in Sweden, when he could satisfy himself that it was large enough.

Another aspect of museum collecting can be seen from the point of view of the curatorship of the Ethnographic Department in Stockholm. Stolpe in his pioneering work was influenced by German and British ethnography and anthropological theory, but in collecting and displaying his methods were strictly German. After his death in 1905, there was no formal leader of the department due to internal conflict, and there was a slight decline in the rate of new acquisitions. In 1909, Hartman became the curator. Hartman was even more pro-German than Stolpe in museum collecting and in academic inclination. He was in a stronger position to get grants for the museum to finance new collecting enterprises. This can be seen by the increase in Melanesian collections.

21.3 The first ethnographic exhibition in Stockholm, 1878-79, curated by Hjalmar Stolpe. Objects from the Gilbert Islands. Collection 4:191. (Copyright National Museum of Ethnography, Stockholm.)

The outbreak of World War I in 1914 made it difficult for the Germans in New Guinea and halted medal-giving in Sweden. Wahlen tried hard to use his background as a Swedish consul and his donations to the museum to get help to establish himself in Sweden, but the country was becoming less Germanic and less interested in backing somebody like Wahlen. The number and size of Pacific collections arriving in Sweden decreased. Material arriving after 1920 tended to come from the British territories. I have found no evidence of medal-giving in relations to these collections.

Exhibition style in Sweden

The first ethnographic exhibition in 1878 was a major breakthrough in the field of museum ethnography. Held at *Arv Furstens palats* (the palace of the hereditary royalty), the exhibition showed objects from different parts of the world. They were placed according to geographical area in different rooms. The exhibiting style was weapons arranged in the shape of a fan, pillars covered with grass skirts and other textiles, and rows of clubs laid out in symmetrical patterns. Stolpe had been inspired by ethnographical museums abroad. It is possible to speculate about other influences.

In Sweden, Arthur Hazelius[12] had begun collecting Scandinavian *ethnographica*, and displayed these in Stockholm at the time. Since the 1850s, many world fairs had been staged in European capitals, and a certain style of exhibiting had become prevalent. A few photographs survive from the ethnographic exhibition of 1878, showing a typological layout of the material (fig. 21.3).

Until 1900, when ethnography obtained status as a separate department, the question of a museum building was raised. In 1904, Stolpe arranged temporary exhibitions at the address Walingatan 1. Displays of non-European ethnographic material had not yet begun to provide context, such as dioramas, although this had already begun in Swedish ethnology with the opening of the Nordic Museum and Skansen, the world's first open air museum. Instead, as in the case of Pacific collections, objects were placed in glass cases labelled Polynesia, Micronesia,

21.4 Display of Pacific culture arranged by Stolpe in 1904 at the Walingatan 1 facilities of the Ethnography Department of the Natural History Museum in Stockholm. Collection 117:2. (Copyright National Museum of Ethnography, Stockholm.)

Melanesia, and so on. In the catalogue of the museum, written by one of Stolpe's students, Erland Nordenskiöld (1907:11), the following was said:

> In certain parts of Melanesia the art of woodcarving stands very high. In Melanesian religion ancestral worship is common and the anthropomorphic ancestor carvings prevail. Dancing masks are used and cannibalism is common.

Most of the Melanesian material was from Erik Nyman's collection dating from 1899. Unfortunately we have no photos from that part of the display. However, the New Zealand displays and those of Tahiti and the Poumotu Islands gives some idea of the style of exhibition (fig. 21.4).

Because of the dreadful conditions in this building, the exhibits were eventually closed. The need for a new museum building was a major issue for many years. The collections were moved a number of times, and it was not until 1978 that a satisfactory museum was built. Between 1909 and 1917 the majority of the Pacific material was taken down due to lack of proper display facilities.

Under the curatorship of Hartman, the museum started to publish a series of books about ethnography and anthropological theory for a wider audience. *Populära Etnologiska Skrifter* (popular ethnological writing) was in part compensation for the now-closed museum to educate the public about the world's cultures. A translation of Alfred Haddon's work on Torres Strait and discussion of such anthropological issues as 'the family' were published by the museum and debated in the Swedish press.

A temporary display was held at the Royal Stable when the Tabar *malagans* from Carl Petterson arrived in October 1914. Mörner had staged this exhibition, and wrote, 'I visit daily and pay my respect to Pettersson's shrine of Tabar gods'. According to the museum annual report, many prominent artists visited the exhibition, and great interest was shown in the artistic merit of the objects on display.

A review in *Aftonbladet* (n.d.) about the opening of the exhibition, noted a somewhat different and less understanding remark: 'If one of the stableboys arouse from the dead, he would immediately die of a heart attack at the sight of the horrible fetishes that would stare at him.' Old-fashioned and prejudiced ideas about Melanesian culture still existed, but the public's view was changing.

Again we have no photos from the Royal Stable display that would give us an idea of how the culture of New Ireland and the rest of Melanesia was presented. But the new exhibitions at the address Walingatan 2 in 1917 might give us a clue. Mörner was behind the new displays, which

21.5 Collections of Melanesia with, to the right, a *malagan* display from Tabar Islands. Objects from the collections of Pettersson, Thiel and Mörner at the Walingatan 2 facilities, 1917. (Photo: Oscar Ellquist. Collection 149:45. Copyright National Museum of Ethnography, Stockholm.)

demonstrated his ideas of what a modern ethnographical museum should look like.

For the first time we see an attempt to contextualise the meaning of ethnographic objects. The *malagan* from Tabar were displayed with a palm-leaf backdrop, and sand was put on the floor around the carvings. Pig jaws from

the local abattoir were attached to the wall in the fashion Mörner had seen in Tabar Islands a few years earlier. The display also showed photographs from Melanesia and a mannequin dressed in a New Guinean outfit (fig. 21.5).

The 1917 display at Walingatan 2 was a major breakthrough for the National Museum of Ethnography. Many

21.6 New Guinea display from Mörner's Sepik and Ramu collections, at the Walingatan 2 facilities, 1917. (Photo: Oscar Ellquist. Collection 149:48. Copyright National Museum of Ethnography, Stockholm.)

new museological ideas became reality. Melanesia and the wider Pacific were given plenty of space because of the many recent collections the museum had obtained from this area (fig. 21.6 shows Mörner's collection).

The new museum space was provided with electric lights. A special music room was set up, and concerts of 'exotic music' from all over the world, including Melanesia, were scheduled. Phonogram records were brought from Germany. Visitors could drink coffee in a fashionable lounge decorated with palm trees and plaster models of stone carvings from the non-Western world, served by girls dressed in Swedish folk costumes.

The most progressive aspect of the new museum, however, was the studio set up for artists who wanted to study the collections. In the original plan the museum wanted two additional studios for students of painting, sculpture and textiles from the nearby Academy of Art and the National College of Art but space did not allow that. In the annual report we read: 'A great number of artists use the studio and several of them express their appreciation for the inspiration they get from studying these objects.'

It was another ten years before the first exhibition of non-Western art as 'art' was set up in Sweden. In January 1927, Liljevalchs Konsthall, a prominent art gallery-museum, housed an exhibition of 'exotic art' with material selected from the National Museum of Ethnography. The exhibition catalogue contained little about the meaning of the objects on display, which were exhibited as 'art for art's sake'. Room 4, displaying Melanesian collections, was labelled 'Woodcarvings: religious and profane', and '8 religious carvings from a ceremonial house of the little island of Tabar north of New Ireland. On each side hangs dancing masks used in the same religious ceremony as the Tabar carvings' (fig. 21.7).

Along with social and ideological changes in Swedish society, the type of objects collected in Melanesia and the Pacific changed during the period from 1880 to the 1920s; the way of displaying these collections also changed. During this time, the museum contributed to an increased understanding of Melanesian cultures by the people of Sweden.

Conclusion: The record, the remainder and contexts of Melanesian cultural heritage

The theme for the fifth Pacific Arts symposium was 'Art and Performance' and perhaps this paper has been peripheral

21.7 'Exotic art and craft' exhibition at Liljevalchs Art Gallery, Stockholm, 1927. (Photo: Karl Wallberg. Collection 159:1. Copyright National Museum of Ethnography, Stockholm.)

to that theme. Delving among archives and among old photographs may add cultural information to specific objects in old collections. However, contextualisation of objects and culture, as we know it today, was rare in the early collection enterprises. Those who benefited from the trade in ethnographic collections rarely met the people who made them. The only information available on 'performance' was from those colonists and visitors who lived with the local people; for example, trade-store managers, missionaries and occasional travellers. This means that museums have to delve very deep indeed to find valuable information that provides the context to their collections.

An important issue that is often raised today is the means by which culturally important or sacred objects were acquired. While examples of cultural theft can be identified, in most cases objects were traded after their role in ritual performance had concluded.

The comparatively high proportion of masks and carvings might suggest that these were sacred objects that after their use had to be disposed of (they were deemed dangerous and powerful). The Tabar *malagans* that Pettersson collected for the museum in Stockholm are one example of carvings that must have fulfilled their use, and the people were happy therefore to part with them. On the other hand, it is difficult to find shell money and other valuable heirlooms in collections from the same period.

The interest in placing ethnographic material in its context developed along with other historical changes in the Western world. The history of museum display shows this development. In Stockholm we saw how Mörner introduced a new concept for exhibiting Tabar Island culture after he had seen the indigenous display. Fourteen years earlier we got a description of how people were dressed on the north-east coast of New Guinea from Nyman in his correspondence with Stolpe. Information of this kind probably had an effect on how these objects were perceived and displayed. Mannequins dressed in traditional costumes were used to give a 'live' image of other cultures.

Turn-of-the-century photographs are another record of the 'performance' aspect of cultural material. Photography played a significant role in providing understanding and context for the objects on display. During this time, ethnographic photographs tended to circulate among museums and appear in displays. Mörner complains in his book that most of his glass plates were destroyed so he had to borrow images from the museum in Hamburg for illustrations. At the same time, he laments that he could not record the beautiful songs and dances he experienced on Wuvulu and Aua islands. Öberg, on the other hand, collected German postcards of New Guinea people, perhaps as a visual reminder of the people among whom he lived.

My outline of the acquisition of Melanesian cultural material by Sweden is not an exercise in apologetic history. Rather, it should be seen as providing otherwise inaccessible information. Colonial history and the collecting of other peoples' cultural material are hardly things of which a museum can be proud. It poses a number of moral issues for museum workers today. In telling the history, such as it is from a Western point of view, there is also the danger of telling anecdotes of the past, of lapsing into hagiography.

However, we cannot ignore the hundreds of thousands of objects taken from the Pacific to Europe, Australia and America around the turn of the century. In the late 20th century, these collections still fill our storage rooms. But what we *can* do is search for additional information that can give us more understanding of these objects from different perspectives.

First, museums housing these objects should make available surveys of their collections and information about them, including translations of archival materials, to the people whose ancestors created them. Archival material can give us additional insights about the meaning of these things and who made them. Second, in combining the past with the present we can present this material to the future in a fairer way. Instead of only providing the context of cultural objects, it is time to *recontextualise* them – to add all the *biographies* to be found in our storerooms.

Postscript

After the presentation of this paper in Adelaide in 1993, I had an opportunity to visit an area from which one of our collections came. In June 1993, I went to Tabar Island, New Ireland Province, where I visited the villages where Carl Pettersson's plantation had been. With photographs of Pettersson and of carvings collected by him on Tabar, I conducted an experiment in ethnohistory. Not only did this elicit information on the objects, but also information on the colonial history of the time.

I was interested in the creation of myths surrounding a man like Pettersson, and to get some idea if these myths had any truth to them. Despite the variety of stories I got, in the Tabar villages[13] and from descendants of Carl Pettersson,[14] certain themes started to emerge, such as how the local people were treated by the colonisers, and the importance that old objects today have to the people and to their sense of identity. Museums should pursue relationships with people living in the areas from which their collections came. They may be surprised at how many new ideas they may obtain which can be used in presenting to their public the people of today and their history, and thus at the same time make a more appropriate use of the old material.

Acknowledgements

I would like to thank the Swedish Institute and the National Museum of Ethnography[15] in Stockholm for making it possible for me to participate in the fifth Pacific Arts symposium in Adelaide. Photographs are by courtesy of the National Museum of Ethnography, Stockholm, and the South Australian Museum, Adelaide.

Notes

1. All translations from Swedish to English are my own.
2. There is great uncertainty regarding the origin of Solander's collection as it probably forms part of the material collected by Joseph Banks. These objects ended up in the private collection of Ahlströmer and were not registered until the mid-19th century.
3. An interest in Scandinavian prehistory sprang from concern over the disappearance of folklore because of industrialisation and urbanisation. It became accepted practice to seek the origin of the past either through present-day 'Stone Age people',

or in agrarian societies elsewhere in the world. However, these ideas were in a very early stage of development and could also be related to the romantic movement earlier in the 19th century.
4. The numbers in brackets hereafter refer to the collection numbers in Stockholm unless otherwise stated. They indicate the year that the collection was registered (1887), the number of the collection for that year (8), and sometimes the total number of objects in that particular collection (1-7565).
5. A fourth category could be added – that of secondary collectors: high-ranking military officers, connoisseurs and art collectors who obtained objects through antique dealers, and so on. These collections mainly consisted of weapons and curiosities. I will not be dealing with this category because it is of little importance and because the material is almost entirely undocumented.
6. Blackbirding was the securing of Pacific Islanders against their will as plantation labourers (see Oliver 1975:125-31).
7. This becomes apparent by studying museum archival material. See also Firth (1986).
8. Many were of Scandinavian origin (Sack and Clark 1979).
9. The word *Arafi* derives from the German word *Graf,* which means count. This was the nickname given to Birger Mörner by the people of Wuvulu Island.
10. Three hundred and fourteen items were exchanged for Central American objects from the San Diego Museum of Man.
11. The South Australian Museum also has several *malagan* carvings from Pettersson, obtained from him by Edgar Waite when the latter was collecting for that museum in 1918.
12. Arthur Hazelius was the founder of the Nordic Museum (*Nordiska Museet*) in Stockholm, and the man behind the world's first outdoor museum, *Skansen*. In the 1870s, Hazelius staged an exhibition of Swedish folklore in temporary localities on Drottninggatan in Stockholm.
13. My gratitude goes to Mangap of Maragon village, whose father worked on Pettersson's boat. Mangap generously provided me with a lot of information about the past. Other people who helped me were Edward Sale and Noah Lurang, with contacts and transport. Minimini at Simberi health station and Jogobert at Tatau provided me with accommodation.
14. I would especially like to thank Mrs Elsa Hörle, daughter of Carl and Sindo Pettersson, for allowing me to videotape an interview with her. My appreciation also goes to Mrs Hörle's

brother, Max Pettersson, in Rabaul, for giving me an insight into the life of people of mixed heritage in colonial New Guinea. I would also like to thank Michael and Michelle Chan in Rabaul, and Mrs Hörle's daughters in Australia, Hildergaard Edwards, Edith Hörle and Margerita Pixner, who generously shared information about the history of their family.

15.   At the National Museum of Ethnography I would especially like to thank Ulla Wagner, Per Kåks and Anne Murray for encouraging me to attend the conference. Iréne Svensson, Dagmar Fröland and Anita Utter helped me with collection and archival material, and Sanna Törneman and Cecilia Johansson with photographic material. Karl Erik Larsson provided me a great deal data on the history of ethnography in Sweden. Barry Craig at the South Australian Museum made many useful comments on the first draft of this text. Finally, my gratitude goes to my husband, Julius Rocca, for proofreading my paper.

22 Art of Astrolabe Bay: History of research, results and future research tasks

Gabor Vargyas

Although Astrolabe Bay (fig. 22.1) is one of the earliest-known territories of Papua New Guinea, we have comparatively little information about the culture and art of this area. German colonisation began there in 1884. Colonial and missionary activities resulted in astonishingly rapid culture change and an almost complete loss of traditional cultural property, especially religious art objects. This change must have taken place during the 1890s.[1]

By the end of the last century, most of the traditional material culture, especially masterpieces of the art of the area, had been collected for European (mostly Hungarian)[2] museums, and the impoverished material culture no longer attracted the attention of collectors. The field-work situation was similar. The first long-term research carried out on the island of New Guinea, that of Mikloucho-Maclay in 1871-72 and 1876-77,[3] remained an admirable personal adventure without lasting effect. Over the next thirty years, a modest body of German colonial literature was produced by missionaries, administrators, explorers, natural scientists and collectors, among them the unsurpassable Hungarian, L. Bíró, and a fellow countryman, S. Fenichel.[4] However, this came to an end as a result of World War I when Germany lost its colonies.

There was even less ethnographic interest after Australia took over German New Guinea. This is best reflected in the anthropological field work undertaken in the region. Ward and Lea (1970) identified only six researchers in the area during a period of 100 years.[5] Most of them date from the 1960s, when – following Lawrence's seminal studies[6] – there was renewed interest. But due to their different focus of interest and to the early culture change mentioned above, however important these modern studies are from a general anthropological point of view, they do not greatly advance our understanding of the art of the area. We have only the scanty and fragmentary German colonial literature that dates back to the end of the last century, and that is far from satisfying according to present-day standards. Thus, to quote Bodrogi (1953:92),

> research into the archaic culture of Astrolabe Bay has thus become more and more a study of a historical character that can be pursued only by collecting random notices from the past and chance descriptions, and by examining material of earlier days preserved in ethnographical museums.

Given that most of the ethnographic material is to be found in the Ethnographic Museum of Budapest, it is but natural that such a task was undertaken by Bodrogi.[7] Therefore the history of research coincides in many ways with his activity.

The idea of Astrolabe Bay as an independent style-province goes back to 1894, when A.C. Haddon, in his classic monograph, erroneously classified the art of the area together with that of Finschhafen but distinct from that of the Huon Gulf. A few years later, Preuss (1897, 1898)

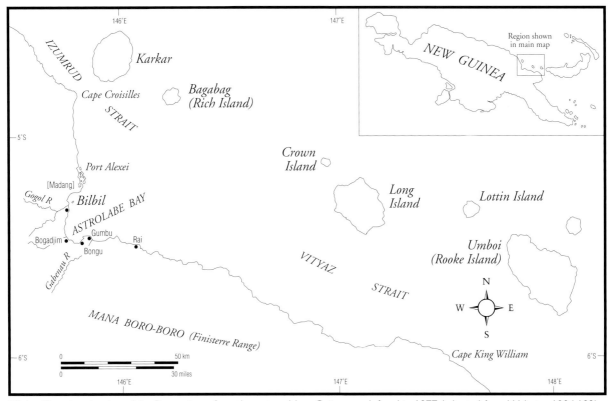

22.1 Map showing Astrolabe Bay region of north-eastern New Guinea, as defined in 1877 (adapted from Webster 1984:192).

divided the territory of German New Guinea into the following provinces:

- Finschhafen, from Parsi Point to Cape Fortification;
- Astrolabe Bay, from Cape Fortification to Cape Croiselles (the island of Rook constituting a transitory area between Finschhafen and Astrolabe Bay, and the islands of Long and Dampier belonging to the latter area);
- the north coast, west to about Berlinhafen (Aitape);
- the German-Dutch border area (Vanimo) west to Taneh Merah;
- the Ramu River region;
- the Sepik River region.

Although Haddon's and Preuss's categories are valid in many respects even today, they were based on relatively little material and contained some errors.

Notwithstanding their results and the identification of the style province of Astrolabe Bay, subsequent researchers forgot about it and neglected this area completely. Thus, it was not even mentioned in Firth's 1936 work, in Linton and Wingert's 1946 pioneer study, or in Kooijman's 1955 summary. The reason for this is probably that German and especially Hungarian museum collections, and the German scientific literature, were at that time not known to the English-speaking world.

Bodrogi, in a seminal study of the initiation rites and ghost cult of Astrolabe Bay (1953), re-established, on a much wider basis, the existence of this style province. Examining the various sources concerning initiation, he summed up in seventeen points the outstanding features of this 'cultic unity'. Some of the most important ones were:

- initiation was the means for indoctrination into the ghost cult (spirit cult or secret society);

22.2 *Ai* masker with spear, Astrolabe Bay; as drawn by Mikloucho-Maclay (1950-54, Vol. 5: plate between pp. 66 and 67).

- circumcision was practised during initiation;
- it was stated that the ghost was an ogre or a monster that bit off the prepuce of the novice at circumcision, swallowed him and, at the end, 'spat him out' when his wounds were healed;
- the return of the novices from seclusion was accompanied by great festivities during which they received gifts; and
- the cult equipment comprised masks, ancestral images, dance swords, and musical instruments such as flutes and bamboo trumpets, bullroarers, ocarinas and rattles.

On the basis of this analysis of the initiation complex and its paraphernalia, Bodrogi concluded that 'Astrolabe Bay is an independent area of decorative style in New Guinea' (1953:140).

This early article contains all we know about the social context and ideological background of the art objects. The fragmentary nature of the data does not allow us to go beyond this. To illustrate this point, I shall quote the only two early descriptions that present the masks and human figures in a functional context. The first is from Mikloucho-Maclay (1950-54 III(1):118):

> In November and December, when Papuans happen to have less work on the plantations, other types of feasts are organized. One of them, where only men are admitted, is called *Ai-mun*; while another, held within the village, and at which women and children are allowed to participate, is known by the name *Sel-mun*. At an *Ai-mun*, specific masquerades take place. Newly painted *aidogans* (very tall wooden figures carved out of one [piece of] timber and having several [human] figures one above the other) that play an outstanding role in the masquerades, are carried to the place of the feast. The *Ai-mun* lasts some days during which men are especially excited. Day and night, without a stop, masquerades, eating, music etc. follow each other. Somewhere it is the *Ai-mun* that plays an outstanding role, somewhere it is the *Sel-mun*. Sometimes the *Ai* wanders from one village to another. On such occasions a sham fight is fought between the invading *Ai* and the men of the *Sel-mun*. I was so much interested in these festivities that once I had almost no sleep during 3 days and 2 nights so that I could witness one of them.

Besides this short description, Maclay provides us with a coloured drawing (fig. 22.2) that, as far as I know, is the only portrayal of a masked dancer from the Astrolabe Bay area.

A somewhat more detailed description is given by Kunze, a German missionary, from Karkar Island (1892:196-207; 1897; 1926:93-9), summed up by Bodrogi twice (1953: 108-9; 1990:12-13). I quote from the last reference:

> Kunze describes an initiation … When he arrived at the festival, the ceremonies had been going on for three or four days … The youths of Kulobob village were lined up in rows. The majority of them had already been initiated and declared mature. The candidates for initiation on that particular occasion were standing with them. A strange figure was walking up and down in front of the line in a stately manner. He had a huge mask on his head, a real wood-carved work of art. Its face was awful, resem-

bling an antediluvian monster rather than a human. A decorated pole some two meters long was attached to the top of the mask. This not only made the mask extremely heavy, but also made it difficult for the wearer to keep his balance … The attire of this figure was rather different from what Papuans usually wear. His body was covered by a shabby European overcoat, on his back hung a *lawalap*, a loincloth made of two colored bandanna handkerchiefs, and in both hands he held boars' tusks. Having, for some time, walked up and down the line of youths with peculiar movements of the head, he presently stopped in front of one of the candidates, glared at him, then hit him on the forehead or on the chest with his fist, and thus declared him 'mature'. During these proceedings, the youths displayed greatest solemnity and attention … Whenever a *Barak* personifier grew tired, he disappeared and another man took his place with the same mask and attire.

From these two descriptions, one can see the limitations of a performance-oriented study of the art of Astrolabe Bay. As for the human figures called *telum* by Maclay (in the Bongu dialect) (fig. 22.3), we do not have even

22.3 *Telum* figure in men's house, Astrolabe Bay, as drawn by Mikloucho-Maclay (1950-54, Vol. 3:101).

that much. Though there exist a few descriptions of them as standing in the men's houses (Bodrogi 1959:44-55), nobody has ever described a ceremony connected with them. Thus the observation of Maclay quoted above ('Newly painted *aidogans* … that play an outstanding role in the masquerades, are carried to the place of the feast') remains the only data hinting at the role and function of these sculptures. No wonder this research orientation could not be pursued any further by Bodrogi.

Some years later, in another pioneer study (1959), Bodrogi set out to describe this style province, based on more than 4000 objects in the Ethnographic Museum of Budapest, and some other smaller German and Russian collections. After treating in detail practically every object type that can be summed up under the heading 'art', he came to the following conclusions:

- As for figurative art, the rendering of the human figure was uniform throughout the whole area and as there was no centre of manufacture for them, 'we are safe to select them as leitmotivs in characterising the artistic style of the province in question. Their geographical distribution gives … the distribution of the style' (p. 96).
- The same holds true for decorative art. Although there are some minor differences in the decorated objects due to different materials and functions, 'their general aspect and decorative motifs betray a close affinity. The most general common feature of the decorative motifs … is their geometrical character: nowhere do we encounter human or animal representations as elements of ornamentation.' (p. 96).
- 'the above arguments and the material presented justify Preuss' early conclusion that the Astrolabe Bay region constitutes a separate style province' (p. 97).
- Although Astrolabe Bay proper extends from Siar Island to Bongu, 'we are not mistaken if we extend this territory to include Karkar Island, the littoral sector between Madang and Cape Croiselles, and, to the east, the Rai Coast as far as the

22.4 (Far left) *Telum*; female figure above male figure. (Ethnographic Museum of Budapest, Reg. No. 11864.)

22.5 (Centre left) *Telum* figure. (Ethnographic Museum of Budapest, Reg. No. 11876.)

22.6 (Left) *Ai* mask. (Ethnographic Museum of Budapest, Reg. No. 8916.)

22.7 (Far left) *Ai* mask. (Ethnographic Museum of Budapest, Reg. No. 8918.)

22.8 (Centre left) *Ai* mask. (Ethnographic Museum of Budapest, Reg. No. 8932.)

22.9 (Left) *Telum*; male figure with counterposed heads on top. (Ethnographic Museum of Budapest, Reg. No. 11861.)

district of Morobe which may be regarded as a link with the province of the Tami style' (p. 97).

With this study, Astrolabe Bay took its place among New Guinean style provinces. From then on, no serious study of the art of New Guinea could omit mentioning it.[8]

The next step was to examine the relationship of art and trade. This was first explored in an article in German on the spear types of the area in which Bodrogi (1975) established that the decorated spears with Janus heads came to Astrolabe Bay by trade from the Gogol hinterland. As an appendix to his article, based on Bíró's notes, Bodrogi provided a list of the trade items of the area.

A systematic analysis of the interconnection of style provinces and trading areas came soon after (Bodrogi 1979). In this highly original paper, Bodrogi examined the geographical distribution of style provinces and trading areas and concluded that, in north-east New Guinea:

there is a clear-cut correlation between the geographical distribution of certain art forms, on the one hand, and

[the] primary mode of intertribal communication (that is, the trade system) on the other. [Bodrogi 1978:271]

Trade and trading relationships, together with the notion of copyright (selling and buying of religious and art objects), and large-scale cult festivals that mobilise the population of broad regions, thus have an integrating effect in artistic production. These conditions favour the diffusion and integration of religious ideas and art forms; that is, the formation of style provinces.

In this article, Bodrogi also elaborated on the notion of style province. His starting point was the difference, within the Astrolabe Bay area, in the style of figurative art on the one hand and of decorative art on the other. The style of each was uniform, but they differed from each other: decorative art was always geometrical. To denote this rather peculiar situation – as against, for example, the unified style, figurative and decorative, of the Huon Gulf area – he coined the term 'art area', a more general term than 'style province'. Astrolabe Bay is thus an 'art area' with two different styles, one figurative and one decorative, while Huon Gulf is an 'art area' with only one style; that is, a 'style province'.

In his later publications, Bodrogi (1981, 1982, 1990) returned to the question of the religious context of the art objects – a problem he first dealt with in 1953. His conclusion, repeated in several ways in several papers, was that this context is different in the case of the masks and of the ancestor figures (*telum*). While masks are connected with initiation and the secret ghost cult (*Asa* or *Ai* cult), *telum* portray culture heroes (mythical figures from the Kilibob-Manub cycle) and various clan ancestors descendant from them. Bodrogi believed that these two traditions were even historically independent of each other, resulting from different waves of migration from somewhere in Indonesia (Bodrogi 1982).

The above interpretation of the *telum* was based on one detail in the rendering of some female figures: a tattoo mark above or around the vulva. This element is a basic motif of the Kilibob-Manub mythical cycle (Schubert 1970; Mennis 1979), according to which one of the antagonistic siblings tattooed his arrow's design onto the vulva

of his brother's wife. This adulterous deed initiated a fight between the two brothers, at the end of which one of them, the one who was light skinned and culturally superior, left the village to found new settlements along the coastline towards the east.[9] In Bodrogi's opinion, this myth reflects historical truth: the eastward migration of an Austronesian-speaking Melanesian population. The *telum*, because of the geometrical, tattoo-like decorations around the vulva of some of the female figures, could be portrayals of these mythical figures.

This ingenious interpretation (put forward as early as 1953) seems to me fairly convincing even if there are some difficulties with it.[10] However, as for the different historical origin of the two 'independent' traditions – that of the masks and that of the *telum* – I have doubts. First, in his posthumously published paper (1990), Bodrogi himself called attention to the description by Mikloucho-Maclay (quoted above) in which Maclay mentions that the newly painted ancestor figures are carried over to the *Ai* places, where they play a role in the *Ai* festivities. This suggests that the two traditions are not at all independent of each other, and that the *telum* play a role during initiation ceremonies.

Moreover, even if we assume their relative independence as traditions, this does not establish different historical origins. Anyway, both traditions are Melanesian in Bodrogi's opinion; he quotes in his 1953 paper indigenous statements according to which the initiation ceremonies were 'given' to the people by Kilibob himself. Thus I do not see any point in maintaining the hypothesis of two waves of immigrants with two separate traditions.

I have looked at the history of 100 years of research and sketched its main results. What else could be done, what directions could be taken in the future? I see two possible approaches. The first is historical-museological. Because the ethnographic material is relatively limited, one should proceed to a systematic inventory and analysis of every available museum piece from the area. This would mean first the publication of Fenichel's collection in the Ethnographic Museum, Budapest, because it is the largest and oldest of its kind. As for Biró's unpublished material, its strengths are in the detailed notes accompanying the objects, and that it illustrates material culture in general, not just the 'art'. Equally urgent is to study in detail the material from the early colonial period in German museums (for example, the Mission-museum in Barmen), as well as the collection of Mikloucho-Maclay in St Petersburg.

In this respect I would like to draw attention to the small number of existing masks and *telum* (for examples, see figs 22.4 to 22.9). Bodrogi (1959) catalogued forty-six *telum* and twenty-six masks (including museum objects, field photographs and drawings). Even if we assume optimistically that future research might double their number, Astrolabe Bay objects may count among the rarest pieces of Papua New Guinea art and of inestimable value. The time has come to make detailed inventories of these works, and to present them in a publication for the scientific world and for the descendants of their makers.

There are other museological approaches. One would be a detailed stylistic analysis, especially of the masks, the formal variations of which seem to show definite clusters. Perhaps it would be possible to trace these variations back to the hands of different carvers, just as Beran has done in the case of a Massim carver, Mutuaga (Beran 1996, and Chapter 18 this volume). Bodrogi's task was more to prove the stylistic unity of the Astrolabe Bay style-province than to deal with minor variations within it.

Another possibility is that some of the pieces, especially the ones made of stone or argil, could have parallels with prehistoric material that may shed new light on them. Nevertheless, however important this research may be, it may not provide much new information on the objects or art. Therefore the other strategy is field work. Notwithstanding early culture change, it seems that thematically directed research could reveal, if not the objects themselves (their making having ceased a century ago), at least their ideological context. My feeling is that the impact of cargo cults and the cultural revival that followed them have been underestimated. My brief visit to Bom (previously Bogadjim) in 1982 (Vargyas 1987) supports this. I arrived there shortly after initiation into the *Asa* cult had finished. In the ten days I spent in the village I was shown the *Asa* house outside the village where initiation took place, the musical instruments connected with the *Asa* cult, and the use of the bullroarers in circumcision and

love magic. I saw some crudely carved figures – the first tentative attempts to reinvent a cultural tradition that had fallen into oblivion. The form and decoration of the *Asa* house, of the musical instruments, and of the bullroarers, and, especially, the importance of the *Asa* cult in social life, was exactly the same as described by Bíró. Moreover, the cult was just as vigorous at Kranket and other places of Astrolabe Bay as at Bom.

Thus it is likely that some of the religious traditions relating to initiation and the ghost cult may still be studied.[11] Long-term field work could turn out to be illuminating and fruitful. The best method would be, however, to combine the two approaches: research on old museum collections and historical documentation on the one hand, and thematically directed long-term field research on the other. In conclusion, I would like to indicate one such possibility: to approach art objects through the study of social structure.

According to Maclay, every *telum* (and, to judge from an indirect hint by him, every mask) has a personal name (Mikloucho-Maclay 1950-54, III(1):102), some of which he recorded. Or, if these sculptures do represent clan ancestors, as they are said to, it should be possible to find out more about them. Being clan founders, their names and the mythical stories connected with them should still be remembered provided there are existing clans connected with them. Thus, a genealogical study in some of the villages in question, together with inquiry into the social structure and related oral history, should allow us to place these pieces in their social context and to give at least a partial answer to the question of their function.

To support my opinion and hint at the feasibility of such a study, I refer to my own field experiences on Tami Islands, Morobe Province (Vargyas 1982). When, in January 1982, I visited Malasiga village,[12] and Wanam and Kalal islands, I showed local people pictures of some of the objects, among them a Janus-faced mask, now in the Ethnographic Museum in Budapest. They were immediately able to identify it and to give its personal name, 'Kumali', though they had never seen it but only heard of it. Then I was shown the cave from where it emerged during ceremonies and was told some of the stories connected with it. This type of Janus-faced mask is not made any more, but its ownership was remembered. Other masks still in use (or, rather, made for sale), too, have personal names and characteristic stylistic features differentiating them from each other. Also, each of them has its own 'stories' and each belongs to different subgroups within the village, called 'family' or 'tribe' (lineage?) in Melanesian Pidgin. Clarifying ownership of the masks in general, I also got a rough outline of the social structure. Thus, formal characteristics of the masks, their personal names, questions of ownership, social structure, mythical stories and oral history go hand in hand; they are different facets of one complex whole. Personal names of sacred art objects may be the first links to the lost social context.

Notes

1.   See Parkinson (1900:18) quoted in Bodrogi (1953:91); and the differences between Fenichel's and Bíró's collections from the same area, only three years apart, as analysed by Bodrogi (1953:91-2).

2.   Hungarian scholars came to German New Guinea as a natural consequence of the general German orientation of the Austro-Hungarian Empire. S. Fenichel spent one-and-a-half years in the area during 1891-93 and died there of blackwater fever. His collection consists of nearly 2500 objects and is unparalleled in many respects. L. Bíró, who spent six years in German New Guinea (1896 to 1901), including nearly two years in the Astrolabe Bay area, followed him. The first part of his collection has been published (Seemayer 1901); the second part awaits publication. The two together would cover nearly 2000 objects (Vargyas 1992).

3.   See Sentinella (1975), Webster (1984).

4.   Bíró's and Fenichel's notes and collections were utilised by Bodrogi in his research (Bodrogi 1953, 1959, 1979).

5.   This includes Karkar Island and the Rai Coast as well: McSwain in 1966-67 and 1968-69 on Karkar Island; Hogg at Amenob in 1968-69; Lawrence among the Garia in 1949-50 and 1953; Miklouho-Maclay in Bongu and the Rai Coast in 1871-72 and 1876-77; McLaren in Bongu and Rereu in 1968-69; and Lawrence among the Ngaing of the Rai Coast in 1953 and 1956. King and Ranck (1982) added two more: McKellin at

Managalasi, Mount Devis, in 1976-77 and Stevenson in Madang in 1965-66 and 1967-68. Even if we count De'Ath in 1977-79 and early 1980s among the Gogol, and the shorter studies of Mennis at the end of the 1970s, we have hardly a dozen researchers interested in this area.

6.   Lawrence 1964, 1984.

7.   From 1948, Tibor Bodrogi was curator of the Pacific collections of the Ethnographic Museum, Budapest; from 1961 to 1968, he was director of that museum.

8.   See Bühler, Barrow and Mountford (1961); Guiart (1963); Schmitz (1969).

9.   Craig (1995:47-8) reports an analogous story among the Sulka of Wide Bay, East New Britain (Eds).

10.   According to the myth, Kilibob ordered all the men in the village to build for him a 'big house', each man to carve a post for it. When, some days later, the posts were ready, he examined their motifs and recognized on one of them the pattern that had been tattooed onto his wife's *mons veneris*. Thereupon he killed the carver and owner of this motif, Manub. On the basis of this detail, Bodrogi assumed that the posts of the mythical house were carved in the form of a human figure. However, this is not certain. It is not clear from the quoted passage whether it was so or not. The tattoo-like pattern could have been carved onto the post as an independent decorative motif, as was the case on Manub's arrow in the myth. Thus a definite link between meeting house and human carving in the myth is missing – even if probable. Other objections can also be made. 'Big house' does not necessarily mean meeting house. Besides, Bodrogi has not quantified his data: we do not know how many of the existing female figures are decorated with 'tattoo marks'. We do not have local data either that would prove that these decorations are really tattoo marks.

11.   This is not to say that the *Asa* cult is necessarily the same as it was a century ago. But one would need field research to decide what remains of it. That elements may have survived should not be excluded; most of the seventeen formal elements mentioned by Bodrogi as characteristic features of the initiation complex may still be found.

12.   Malasiga village is on the mainland, opposite the Tami Islands. This is where today most of the population of these islands live.

PART 4

Pan-Pacific developments

Barry Craig

The two papers in this last section of the book deal with the growth of cultural institutions, and with recent developments in the full range of arts and crafts, covering most of the Pacific region.

Susan Cochrane's paper discusses museums and cultural centres in the Pacific, noting their precursors in traditional cultures. Contemporary museums and cultural centres in the Pacific can be partly differentiated by reference to their activities (museums are more object-oriented, cultural centres more likely to host live performances) and their target audience (cultural centres are keener to attract tourists). Cultural centres may be differentiated according to whether they are national, provincial or local in their scope.

Difficulties facing cultural institutions in the Pacific include insufficient funding to achieve their agreed objectives, lack of appropriately trained staff, and unsuitable buildings. Are these insufficiencies an indication that Pacific governments, and the citizens they represent, see little relevance for museums and cultural centres in their countries? What is the role of these institutions in negotiating the tensions between local desire for cultural integrity and the more abstract imperative for national cultural identity? This last is an issue of great significance for the larger island states such as Papua New Guinea, Solomon Islands, and Vanuatu and has a particular character in the case of New Caledonia and Fiji (and, by extension, though not mentioned by Cochrane, has relevance for Hawai'i, New Zealand and Australia).

Philip Dark's paper concludes the book. It is the third in a series he has given at Pacific Arts symposia dealing with contemporary trends in Pacific arts and crafts. His New York paper is encapsulated in the phrase, 'today's art is tomorrow's heritage'; his Honolulu paper is summed up by the phrase, 'today's heritage, however conceived today, is tomorrow's art'; and the paper for the Adelaide symposium concluded with the phrase, 'These trends will picture tomorrow's history of Pacific art.'

Dark documents 'these trends' in considerable detail under several headings, 'looking at the models on which present productions depend and the extent to which connections with the past result in real or spurious art'. Dark is concerned that the impact of change coming from contemporary Western cultures is not being adequately documented, that there is a tendency for research to be biased in favour of 'traditional' arts. He suspects this bias may be partly the result of the long-held, romanticised view that tribal societies are unchanging, live in harmony with their environment, and are corrupted by Western culture, a view possessed not only by Westerners. And although he does not say so explicitly, there is implicated the snobbishness of the art collector who considers the old 'traditional' carved material of far greater value aesthetically, and therefore monetarily, than anything done in recent times.

It is interesting that Dark identifies among commentators more optimism for the future of 'the performing arts' than for 'the visual arts' of the Pacific. This may be merely an artefact of our ignorance of traditional performing arts, since many more examples of pre-20th century Pacific sculpture, for example, have survived to the present than records of performances from those times, so a more immediate comparison can be made, and a more (unfavourable) qualitative judgement exercised, in the case of changes in the traditions of sculpture than for changes in the traditions of performances.

But this begs the question to which we have been alerted by Schwimmer, as noted in the introduction to this book:

Why do we persist in privileging sculptured objects above other media of artistic expression? And why do we persist in the notion that the various media are somehow distinct modes of expression? As Schwimmer has so convincingly asserted, they are more in the nature of various instruments (for example, painting, ceramics, song, sculpture, dancing, weaving and architecture) in an orchestral whole (the ritual performance), and the art work is the whole performance, not any particular part of it. Are we as researchers bringing too much of our own cultural chauvinism with its value-laden baggage to our research projects, or are we confused about what it is we are researching? Or both?

23

Out of the doldrums: Museums and cultural centres in Pacific Islands countries in the 1990s

Susan Cochrane

Some Pacific Islanders have suggested that museums and cultural centres had precedents in indigenous cultures, although of a different nature to the institutions of today. In 1987 Makiuti Tongia, then director of the Cook Islands Museum in Rarotonga, challenged the notion that museums did not exist in Pacific cultures until they were introduced by Europeans. He pointed out there were Polynesian institutions fulfilling at least some of the roles now undertaken by museums.[1] At the Cultural Heritage in the Pacific Workshop in 1989, Vaine Tutai (1991:201), the assistant director of the Cook Islands Museum, said:

> Going back to pre-contact times, the museum was known as the Are-Vananga, Are-Kariei, Are-Korero and Pia-Atua … Are-Vananga referred to the house of esoteric knowledge, where astronomy was taught and also the history of the people … Are-Kariei was the entertainment house where the art of warfare was also taught … Are-Korero was where history was taught and the Pia-Atua highlighted religion.
>
> The staff who manned these institutions were called Taunga or experts in their own right. They displayed our objects of mana and dressed and fed them on the marae or sacred grounds. The house where these things were kept was tapu just like our storerooms are today. But the open ground of the marae was public and served as a kind of open-air display room.

Other Pacific Islanders have presented concepts of what may constitute a museum different to the ideas prevalent in Western culture. For example, the governor of Easter Island (Rapa Nui), Sergio Rapu Haoa, stated at the Symposium on Pacific Arts (part of the 1992 Festival of Pacific Arts in Rarotonga, Cook Islands), that the entire island of Rapa Nui was an open-air museum. It could be viewed as such not only because it was the site of cultural activities of the ancestors, but also because restoration, conservation, viewing and the other functions of a museum took place out of doors at the *moai* (massive stone figures) sites. Sidney Moko Mead (1984, 1990) and other scholars of Maori traditions (Hanson and Hanson 1990) have stated that the *marae* is the focus of cultural activity for New Zealand Maori. Mead (1990:269) explains that *marae* characteristically belong to a *hapu* that

> is the art-producing and art owning group … identity with this art is strongest, not only with woodcarving, but with traditional dances and music, with cloak-making, basketry and so on … [On the *marae*] tribal art is very close to the individual members of the *hapu* and it forms an essential part of one's sense of being human and cultured.

Although they share with their antecedents a consciousness of the heritage and social value of culture, the types of museums and cultural centres now existing in Pacific countries are very different from the indigenous cultural institutions mentioned above. This paper is concerned with the difficulties encountered by Pacific museums and cultural centres as they continue to develop their role within their local community, and to negotiate their relationships with metropolitan museums, governments, funding agencies and other interested parties. Due to the scope of the subject and the restricted length of the paper, this investigation is selective and comments on particular issues are brief.[2]

There are now three main types of purpose-built institutions for the preservation and celebration of cultural heritage in the South Pacific island nations:

- National museums such as the Fiji Museum and the Papua New Guinea National Museum and Art Gallery. These are funded by national governments, are members of the International Council of Museums (ICOM), and are committed to ICOM objectives. According to one study (TCSP 1990), national museums do not identify foreign visitors as primary targets for their activities.
- National cultural centres such as the Tonga National Centre, Vanuatu Cultural Centre, Sir Geoffrey Henry Cultural Centre of the Cook Islands, and the Jean-Marie Tjibaou Cultural Centre in New Caledonia (fig. 23.1; opened June 1998). These cultural centres are modern developments, generally funded with assistance from developed countries. Tourists, as well as local residents, are target audiences for their activities. Live performances as well as static exhibitions are featured. Cultural centres can also fulfil the function of resource centres with libraries, archives, workshops and educational activities on their premises.
- Provincial cultural centres. Several of Papua New Guinea's nineteen provinces have a cultural centre, a model that is also being followed in the Solomon Islands. Provincial cultural centres are primarily local resource centres. They provide space for artists and craftspeople to work, collect examples of local material and non-material culture, assist by marketing local crafts, and

organise groups from the area to participate in cultural activities.

Nelson Paulius (1991:10-11) identified objectives of museums from the Papua New Guinean perspective, and differentiated them from the roles and objectives of cultural centres:[3]

Museums have five principal roles which include research and documentation, publication, display/exhibition, preservation and conservation, and education.[4]

1. Research and documentation

Research into the traditional arts and crafts. Documentation to be preserved in the museum for safe-keeping from

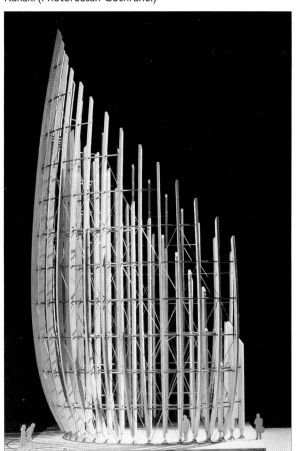

23.1 Model for a component of the Jean-Marie Tjibaou Centre for the Agencie de Développement de la Culture Kanak. (Photo: Susan Cochrane.)

damage for the benefit and enjoyment of current and future generations. Museums will continue to do research and documentation studies for preservation and conservation.

2. Publications

Museum publications be displayed for people to see and read about their cultures. The museum can develop programs on legends and handicrafts for radio to broadcast in the evenings.

3. Display and exhibition

The display or exhibition of art work and artifacts by the museum is an important role. Traditional arts and crafts will be put on display for people to see and appreciate for their real value and significance.

4. Preservation and conservation of cultural property

Museums will preserve and conserve from damage unique arts and crafts.

5. Education

Museums can develop programs and educate our people and foreign tourists about our rich traditional cultural heritage and values.

Principle roles of Cultural Centres

Cultural centres will specialise in housing and preserving special arts and crafts of the local people of each province, district or area. The principal roles of Cultural Centres may include the following:

1. To record, store or preserve local songs, music and legends.
2. To publish and provide publications of local arts and crafts.
3. To develop programs and educate the public about local legends, arts and crafts. Elders can be employed part-time to educate and train children and the public on songs, dances, arts and crafts of the people and the area.

'Cultural centre' is generally the preferred name for the newer institutions. Within their structures, spaces are provided for 'live' performances and workshops.[5] Some national cultural centres (for example, those in Vanuatu and Tonga) also contain the most significant collections of indigenous material culture in the country. The Vanuatu Cultural Centre regards its outreach activities, in particular its oral history recording project using local fieldworkers, to be as important as its museum function.

Commercial cultural centres should not be confused with cultural centres established by national or provincial governments. Hawai'i's Polynesian Cultural Centre is the forerunner of the 'theme park' type of cultural centre built as a tourist attraction, which often reflects foreign visitors' expectations in the types of 'cultural experiences' presented.

At the Cultural Heritage Workshop, hosted by the Papua New Guinea National Museum in 1989, there was considerable debate about rationalising the objectives and roles of museums and cultural centres. The proceedings of the conference noted:

> discussion focussed on the perceived differences between museums and cultural centres … Participants could see no reason why museums could not also function as cultural centres where living aspects of culture are encouraged, and cultural centres might also provide some storage and exhibition facilities in addition to their other functions. [Eoe and Swadling 1991:269]

Difficulties facing museums and cultural centres

There are a number of operational difficulties facing Pacific museums due to budgetary constraints, inadequate staffing, lack of acquisition funds, poor storage facilities, and so on. Sometimes partial solutions have been found to overcome particular problems. But short-term solutions do not resolve many of the fundamental long-term problems facing museums in South Pacific countries.

Museums and cultural centres throughout the South Pacific have relatively small curatorial and other specialist staff, and limited prospects of permanent positions being funded by their respective national governments (Eoe and Swadling 1991; TCSP 1990). The training of museum personnel usually has to be subsidised by aid agencies and assisted by museums overseas. Despite their goodwill in offering training, overseas museums may consider the traditions and values of indigenous people in a different light to that required in the trainee's home country.

Another problem affecting the small number of South Pacific Islanders trained as anthropologists, curators and conservationists is overload. Persons in charge of national cultural institutions are subjected to intense pressures arising out of their positions. Museum directors are sought after to represent their institutions at national and international levels; for example, they are constantly called on to attend conferences and represent their government in cultural matters. Of necessity they are also involved in diplomacy and local politics to acquire and maintain adequate funding levels and project funds for their institutions (Eoe, pers. comm. 1990; Kasarherou, pers. comm. 1995). In many instances it has proved difficult for museum directors to get governments to create new public-service positions to comply with the objectives of the museum.

In most South Pacific nations, there is a lack of appropriately trained personnel to fill museum requirements for research, display and conservation. Volunteer labour does not necessarily provide a solution, as Fergus Clunie, then director of the Fiji Museum, explained of the circumstances there (pers. comm. 1987). Local people could not afford to do unpaid work and, unless expatriate volunteers had special skills and could work unsupervised, the task of supervision further burdened the already overworked staff.

The activities of museums and cultural centres are often limited by insufficient budgets, generally because governments give culture a low priority. Every Pacific Island national museum and cultural centre attending the Cultural Heritage Workshop in 1989 reported crippling financial constraints (see their reports in Eoe and Swadling 1991). Unforseen circumstances (such as the cyclone damage experienced by the Vanuatu Cultural Centre) can bring museum operations to a near halt, sometimes for years, until funds are found for replacement. Museums may also be discouraged from undertaking fundraising activities, or raising revenue by other means (such as by charging entrance fees); for example, the Papua New Guinea National Museum's budget would be reduced by the amount raised, in accordance with government regulations (Eoe, pers. comm. 1993).

It is often difficult for national museums and cultural centres to develop plans for coherent progress. Project funding usually has to come from outside sources. Lawrence Foanaota (1991:110), director of the Solomon Islands National Museum, commented:

> Although the National Museum is a government institution funded through the Ministry of Home Affairs, the annual allocations are not sufficient to cover all the activities and services ... funding for extra projects/programs has come from outside donors such as the British, Australian, New Zealand, USA and Japanese Governments and other agencies like the Gulbenkian Foundation, South Pacific Commission and UNESCO.

Although assistance from aid programs and cultural and philanthropic foundations is welcomed, these sources sometimes have their own priorities to which the museum has to be amenable to get any funds.

A low budget for acquisitions is another difficulty faced by national museums. Fergus Clunie, previously director of the Fiji Museum, commented that museum personnel had to show dedication and initiative to acquire, or obtain repatriation of, important objects that they could not afford to buy on the international tribal-art market. In Clunie's estimation, the Fiji Museum's publication program[6] has been of value in assisting people to recognise and appreciate Fijian artefacts, and has led directly to several donations (pers. comm. 1987).[7]

So far, the most significant repatriation project has been the return of a major portion of the Macgregor Collection to the Papua New Guinea National Museum. Named after the lieutenant governor of British New Guinea who was responsible for its accumulation, the Macgregor Collection was sent to the Queensland Museum for safekeeping, with the intention that it be returned.[8] Papua New Guinea authorities began to investigate the possibility of repatriating the Macgregor Collection from Australia in the early 1970s, and a commitment to return 60 per cent of the collection was negotiated with the Queensland Museum in 1974 and 1975. A new building for the Papua New Guinea National Museum with adequate storage facilities was completed in 1977 and the repatriation program commenced in 1980 (Quinnell 1981; pers. comm. 1990); as at 1996, only one more division of the material remains to be made.

The repatriation of objects dating from early colonial periods fulfils ICOM's ideals and recognises the importance of redressing the imbalance of collections held by metropolitan and post-colonial countries. The objects being repatriated are significant because they represent the cultural heritage of the originating cultures and they reflect the changing relationships between indigenous and non-indigenous cultures. But, whether or not metropolitan museums feel they have a moral obligation to repatriate objects, they are unlikely to do so unless adequate facilities for their storage and preservation exist in the recipient museums.

Separate cultural institutions dedicated to art, like art galleries in Western societies, do not exist in Pacific Islands countries. Some newer Pacific museums and cultural centres, such as the Papua New Guinea National Museum and the Jean-Marie Tjibaou Cultural Centre in New Caledonia, include the function of an art gallery. Most museums and cultural centres, however, are not in a position to acquire, exhibit and otherwise promote the work of contemporary artists.

Eoe (pers. comm. 1989) pointed out that storage and conservation facilities in provincial cultural centres in Papua New Guinea are often inadequate, and in most cases the centres have no funds for acquisitions. When the Papua New Guinea National Museum was built at Waigani between 1975 and 1977, the Australian cultural aid grant included a special acquisition fund for the museum. Some works by contemporary Papua New Guinea artists were collected between 1975 and 1980, but in an unsystematic manner. Barry Craig (Curator of Anthropology, 1980 to 1983) has criticised the then director, Geoffrey Mosuwadoga, for his failure in this regard. Mosuwadoga was an artist who graduated from the Royal Melbourne Institute of Technology and taught for a while at the National Arts School, and, in Craig's view, should have been much more attentive to what his fellow artists were producing (Craig, pers. comm. 1992).

When the new PNG *Museum Act* was passed in 1992, one of the first steps taken by the director of the PNG National Museum, Soroi Eoe, was to reinstate the art-gallery function of the museum. He employed Stalin Jawa as head of the visual-arts section and Martin Morububuna as the first artist-in-residence. A performing-arts program was instituted by the group 'Tambaran Culture', based at the museum.

According to Emmanuel Kasarherou (1995:90), then director-designate of the Jean-Marie Tjibaou Cultural Centre, at the time of the signing of the Matignon Agreements,[9] the Kanak leader Jean-Marie Tjibaou:

> challenged his people to fix their culture firmly in the present and exhorted a place and recognition for Kanaks in the wider society of New Caledonia and beyond. It remains a challenge for Kanak people to affirm and develop their culture, including exploring contemporary forms of artistic expression.

The new cultural centre, which is the largest in the South Pacific, will make a significant contribution to contemporary Melanesian culture. It contains a multimedia facility where the public and researchers have access to an extensive collection of documents, video, audio and other material relating to Kanak and Pacific cultures. The performing-arts complex enables many types of productions to be presented, again accentuating the achievements of Melanesian and other Pacific peoples. The grand pavilion, named *Bwenaado*, is dedicated to Kanak works of art, and that named *Jinu* illustrates the creation myths of the region's indigenous peoples. Behind these, the main exhibition area features the first major public collection of contemporary Pacific art to be established in the Pacific region or elsewhere.

Relevance of museums

What is the relevance of museums and cultural centres for different groups within the communities they serve? How can they assist in the formulation of national cultural identity?

Colonial regimes showed little concern for the likely interests or requirements of indigenous people when they established museums. European interests dominated; for example, the Fiji Museum was established by and for European amateur scholars, and the New Caledonia Museum collected objects of Kanak cultures for overseas exhibitions. Many observers consider that the persistence of European interests over what indigenous people think appropriate for museums is why indigenous attendance at museums was initially poor.

Even after the New Caledonia Museum had been extensively renovated and impressive displays installed featuring aspects of Kanak culture, Kasarhérou (1991:165-6) commented:

> the Museum still attracts few Kanak visitors. The reason is not lack of interest … it indicates that the museum corresponds poorly with the ideas of traditional New Caledonian society … Some of the objects exhibited are very strong and sacred. In traditional society it is a mark of disrespect to show sacred objects to everyone.

The appropriateness of the custodial role of a museum is not being questioned, but rather whether certain objects should be displayed and who has authority to display them.

In Samoa, the idea of a museum setting for displaying Samoan culture seems irrelevant to many Samoans. As Enright (1992:11) points out, institutional support for culture and the arts is not a Samoan concern; 'native Samoans rather naturally resist these well-intentioned attempts to enrol their *fa'asamoa* into … "the administered world", that is, contained within a Western-style built environment and managed by specially trained museum staff'. This may be the case, but Specht (1993:270) comments that UNESCO agreed to assist at least two proposals for setting up a national cultural centre in Western Samoa but neither came about, possibly because of the uncertainty of continuing funding. At the closing ceremony of the 1992 Festival of Pacific Arts in Rarotonga, the leaders of the Western Samoan delegation announced that a cultural centre would be built in Western Samoa in time for the 1996 Festival of Pacific Arts, which it will host. Perhaps a cultural centre was considered a requirement for staging the festival.

When political will drives the building of cultural centres, the interpretation of what is necessary for such a building may differ from what international museological practice may advise. The auditorium of the Sir Geoffrey Henry Cook Islands Cultural Centre can seat 2000, probably an overestimate of audience size when the population of the Rarotonga is only 9000, but perhaps the size reflects the preference for performing arts in Cook Islands culture. The two exhibition halls are generous enough in size, but are not backed up by adequate storage and conservation facilities, and are not airconditioned. This could limit the nature of exhibitions that can be placed there; for example, when metropolitan museums tour exhibitions they require a high standard of climate control and security to be in place in each venue.

In South Pacific museums and cultural centres, cultural objects provide tangible and symbolic evidence of the people who were the original occupants of the land. Where and how such objects are housed can indicate the interests of the regime that is in power for the time being. The context in which objects are presented can promote particular constructs of the indigenous character of the people, or be used to create the impression of a cohesive national identity.

To create an ethos of national identity, political leaders, intellectuals and creative people believe they need to adapt to new ideas while remaining fully conscious of the rich inheritance of their traditional culture. Even where the pre-contact cultural heritage of the people is disparate, as it is in the Melanesian states of Vanuatu, Solomon Islands and Papua New Guinea, that indigenous peoples had established characteristic ways of life long before colonisation can be used as a unifying factor in developing a national cultural identity. Another unifying factor is the experience the indigenous people of a country shared under the period of colonial dominion.

Addressing a tourism convention in Fiji in 1990, the Fijian prime minister, General Sitiveni Rabuka, described Fijian culture in the following terms (TCSP 1990:6):

> Culture is the expression of ethnic identity, the way of life of a community … Culture is the characteristic which

distinctly sets the Fijian people apart from all [others] in the world … Fijian language, Fijian customs and traditions, Fijian values, Fijian religions, Fijian social structure and any other character traits that make a Fijian what he is.

Although 'Fiji' and 'Fijian' are constructs that came into being following Fijian-European contact, it is essential to Rabuka's philosophy to assert Fijian identity and establish a superior position for the indigenous people of the land.

The Fiji Museum has a significant collection of objects that are characteristic of the indigenous peoples. Such objects are identified as 'Fijian' and provide tangible evidence of the material aspects of Fijian cultures over time. The Fiji Museum's collection also encompasses non-material aspects of culture, such as documentation of languages, religions, social structures, and so on. As well as examples of indigenous cultures, the Fiji Museum houses collections, archives and other evidence of post-contact society in Fiji, and of the other ethnic groups – European, Indian, Chinese, and South Pacific Islanders – who have settled there. Collectively, the objects and accumulated knowledge are representative of the country's cultural heritage and ethnic mix.

Although the museum building does not resemble Fijian architecture, and its forms of displaying objects accord with international museum practice rather than Fijian custom, the museum says it can provide a 'Fijian experience'. One example of how this sense of 'Fijian-ness' can be evoked in a museum context is reported (anon. 1991:168):

> Wood carving demonstrations and monthly story telling sessions are two of the most popular activities. Wood carvers produce traditional Fijian artefacts solely by using traditional tools. The monthly story telling sessions are held in the evening. Those present gather around a bowl of ceremonial kava and listen to a gifted orator tell a traditional story. On such occasions the museum is transformed into a Fijian meeting house.

Cultural experiences of Fiji are not only directed at visitors. Fiji is now a multicultural country, and it is considered important to give Fijian citizens of other ethnicities (Indian, Chinese, Rotuman, European) an indigenous Fijian 'cultural experience'. Forty per cent of visitors to the Pacific Harbour Cultural Centre and Marketplace are schoolchildren and members of other local groups, and Manoa Rasigatale, its director, considers the historic re-enactments featured at the centre an important way of informing non-indigenous Fijians about Fijian culture. However, such reconstructions of 'Fijian' culture are limiting unless they reflect the diversity of Fijian cultures of the past and present. But it may suit the present political regime to perpetuate a stereotype of indigenous characteristics 'that make a Fijian what he is'.

Throughout Papua New Guinea, village-based art production sustains the sociocultural needs of the local community. Provincial cultural centres are one avenue through which surplus production can be sold. Some provincial cultural centres, such as those at Wabag and Kainantu, also provide resources, training and marketing for local artists producing traditional or non-traditional objects for outside markets, and encourage traditional and contemporary groups to perform locally and tour. For tourists and other visitors, provincial cultural centres are accessible venues where local cultures are represented and objects may be purchased in a Westernised, familiar type of setting.

In urban centres across the South Pacific, such as Port Moresby, Suva and Auckland, urbanised youths probably have a different perception of the role of museums and cultural centres than do members of their parents' generation. Many Pacific Islanders, such as Samoans and Cook Islanders living in New Zealand, have grown up in cities away from their ancestral homelands. For urban youths, excursions to museums are part of their school education and an important part of the way they learn about their culture. Museums and cultural centres may provide a significant opportunity for the increasing number of urban youths in South Pacific nations to discover the cultural heritage of their forebears. As Kakah Kais (1991:17) notes for Papua New Guinea:

> The trend in the urban areas today is that parents have less and less time to instruct their children properly on cultural values … their children [grow up with] other interests … The introduction of electronic media and advanced

communication systems makes matters even more complicated. We should, therefore, embark on programs of near indoctrination in order to instill into our citizens pride in our cultural heritage and our diverse linguistic groups.

Museums and cultural centres can play an important role in educating local residents and visitors about the country's cultural heritage. The types of visitors a museum or cultural centre attracts, or aims to attract, are related to its perceived mission and the role it plays in society. Visitor studies conducted by the Papua New Guinea National Museum recorded figures of 30 000 to 35 000 local visitors a year between 1985 and 1990, 90 per cent of whom were Papua New Guinea residents, including a high proportion of school groups. A further 5000 tourists from cruise ships or tour groups also visited the museum.

The Pacific tourism authorities generally regard museums as under-utilised assets that should be more attuned to providing cultural experiences for overseas visitors. However, unlike the Cultural Centre and Marketplace of Fiji, most South Pacific museums are not established on an entrepreneurial basis, and feel their primary obligations are towards the people of their country, and to research and scholarship rather than offering cultural experiences for overseas visitors.

In 1990, a review of museums and cultural centres in the Pacific, commissioned by the Tourism Council of the South Pacific (TCSP 1990), examined Pacific museums and cultural centres as existing and potential sites for cultural tourism. The briefing document for the study (TCSP 1990:1) made the following points, among others:

(d) TCSP recognises that museums and cultural centres are first and foremost the natural and proper expressions of the cultural identity of the island populations. National Tourism Organisations (NTOs) wish to increase visitors' sensitivities towards, and appreciation of, their traditional cultural patterns and thus eliminate any adverse socio-cultural effects that tourism may bring about.

(e) NTOs are fully cognisant of the need to take effective measures, on the one hand, to inform tourists about local cultures and, on the other hand, to enhance the overall visitor experience through cultural attractions. In this respect

museums and cultural centres play a vitally important role.

(f) Museums and cultural centres are seen as the main cultural visitor attractions in the region. Sadly, existing centres are generally under utilised … and their contribution to tourism is (thus) diminished.

The TCSP report was compiled by an outside expert, Victor Middleton, who assessed museums and cultural centres for their tourism potential. This contrasts with the focus of the Cultural Heritage Workshop of 1989, where indigenous museum professionals presented papers. The overriding concern of this group was that they often cannot fulfil the basic objectives and obligations of their institutions because of the lack of funding, much less initiate new exhibitions or extensions of their programs (Eoe and Swadling 1991).

Museum professionals, in particular, feel uncomfortable when their institutions come under an umbrella portfolio of 'Culture and Tourism'. As Eoe explained (pers. comm. 1990), the entrepreneurial focus of tourism promoters and bureaucrats is often of limited value to museum operations. They generally want to design and promote spectacular 'cultural experiences', and are not overly concerned with the veracity of the experience. Nor are tourism officials interested in sustained research projects and scholarly pursuits of museums, functions that are a necessary part of the museum's operations but have no public face.

The main problems facing museums and cultural centres in the Pacific are lack of coherent cultural policies and inadequate funding. The recommendations of the Cultural Heritage Workshop (Eoe and Swadling 1991:268-73) called for all governments:

to introduce or revise legislation on cultural matters;
to develop and implement policy statements and guidelines for all areas of cultural activity;
to accept responsibility for adequate funding of the basic functions of their museums and cultural centres;
to permit museums and cultural centres that are able to raise additional funds to use these funds for activities supplementary to their basic functions.

The Cultural Heritage Workshop also assisted the region's museums and cultural centres to identify their problems and clarify their roles.[10] The participants agreed that their institutions could play positive roles in their respective societies:

by acknowledging, and being responsive to, the knowledge of elders;

by developing appropriate displays and custodial arrangements for important objects;

by recognising their responsibilities to youth in an era of rapid socio-cultural change, in particular by organising exhibitions and programs which appeal to, and address, the problems of youth in the country concerned;

by assisting governments to project the nation at home and overseas;

by promoting the achievements of local visual and performing artists in all fields of endeavour.

Further, it was recognised that South Pacific museums and cultural centres could play a more vital role in cultural exchange by providing venues for exhibitions, performances and workshops, especially for artists from within the Pacific region.

Despite their present difficulties, the personnel of the South Pacific region's museums and cultural centres are optimistic. The continuing success of the region's major festival, the Pacific Festival of Arts, is prompting national governments to take cultural events more seriously. One factor is rising popular demand for centralised venues where cultural events can take place. Another significant factor is the growing awareness of cultural politics in the region. Political leaders are realising that they can advantage themselves by emphasising national cultural identity; museums and cultural centres are one way of providing tangible evidence of the government's support for national identity and creative expression.

As far as South Pacific historical collections are concerned, museums and cultural centres are increasingly aware of the sensibilities of people still practising their traditional culture. As in the case of New Caledonia, sensitivity and respect for Kanak culture will replace Francophile preoccupations and interests in the orientation of the Jean-Marie Tjibaou Cultural Centre, and in future displays at the New Caledonia Museum.

Museums and cultural centres now have to be mindful of their social responsibilities to urban youth. As the example of Papua New Guinea shows, where there are high concentrations of urban youth, museums provide one of the few avenues connecting this generation to its cultural background. Cultural institutions in Fiji are already providing different groups with information about Fijian culture, and this role could be expanded.

At the time of making the latest additions to this paper (May 1996), a new dawn seemed to be glimmering for museums and cultural centres in the Pacific. Two cultural centres, the new Vanuatu Cultural Centre and the Cultural Centre in Western Samoa, were to open their doors in 1996 and the Jean-Marie Tjibaou Cultural Centre in New Caledonia was well on its way to completion in May 1997.[11]

For its inaugural exhibition, the Vanuatu Cultural Centre was to welcome back objects collected in the early colonial period of the New Hebrides. This was a joint project of the Vanuatu Cultural Centre, the Museum für Völkerkunde (now the Museum der Kulturen) of Basel, Switzerland, and the Musée des Arts d'Afrique et d'Océanie, of Paris, France. The Cultural Centre of Western Samoa was to be the venue for several important events of the 1996 Pacific Festival of Arts, including the first fully curated contemporary Pacific art exhibition to be held at this renowned festival (Meredith, pers. comm. 1996). The Jean-Marie Tjibaou Cultural Centre was engaged in the second of its preview seasons, featuring visual and performing arts events from many Pacific nations. It fully intends to become a key player in promoting the network of cultural exchange among Pacific nations (Kasarherou, pers. comm. 1996).

In Papua New Guinea, the museum has received a boost of funding and encouragement from the national government. Plans for massive extensions are on the drawing board, including a natural-history park, and separate premises for a museum of modern history and an art gallery. As well, the Papua New Guinea National Museum has been allocated a budget to assist the established provincial cultural centres with project funding, and to provide advice and some seeding funds to provincial governments wishing to establish cultural centres. Simbu Province and New Ireland Province are now taking this initiative (Eoe, pers. comm. 1996). It is to be hoped that this increased recognition of the worth and purpose of Pacific Islands museums is matched by consistent funding.

As museums and cultural centres of the South Pacific region achieve their present objectives, their future will be brighter than their past.

Notes

1.   He also expressed this view at the Pacific Arts Association symposium in Honolulu in 1988, and it has now been taken up by other Cook Islands scholars, most recently in a paper given by Arerangi Tongia, assistant curator, Cook Islands National Museum, at the Fifth Pacific Arts Association symposium, Adelaide 1993. Tongia nominates the pre-contact institutions as Pia-Atua, Are-Korero, Are-Karioi, Are-Pana, Are-Toa and Are-Vananga, and explains their various roles (Tongia 1993:2-3).

2.   Specific problems facing individual museums were reported in contributions to the Cultural Heritage Workshop held in 1989 (Eoe and Swadling 1991); Specht (1993) has examined the lack of appropriate models for Pacific museums more closely, as well as the issues of repatriation and heritage protection.

3.   See Specht (1993:269) on the development of concepts about cultural centres as more appropriate institutions than museums for Pacific countries.

4.   Paulius does not mention collecting, or monitoring national cultural property.

5.   The Papua New Guinea National Museum at Waigani was built with facilities for live performances, but until the new *Museum Act* was passed in 1993 these were rarely used due to lack of funding and insufficient attention paid to the possibilities of such programs. Its art-gallery function also did not operate fully for several years for the same reasons.

6.   As well as the journal *Domodomo*, the Fiji Museum has reprinted early books about Fiji written by missionaries, traders and civil servants. These early histories often have illustrations, as well as text, that can help with the identification of important objects which are in collections outside Fiji.

7.   The most significant of these was the return of a rare figure by the great-granddaughter of an early missionary in Fiji, the Reverend John Hunt. The figure, described as an 'ancestral idol' by Hunt, had been taken by him from a *bure kalou* (gods' house or temple) and kept by the missionary's family until its return was negotiated following the publication of Hunt's journals.

8.   The Queensland Museum held most of the Macgregor Collection, but parts were dispersed to the Australian Museum, the National Museum of Victoria, and the Tasmanian Museum and Art Gallery. Macgregor also sent collections to the university museums in Aberdeen and Cambridge, and to the British Museum in London (Bolton 1980).

9.   The Matignon Agreements between the French Government and the pro-independence and anti-independence movements in New Caledonia (an overseas territory of France) were signed in 1988 following several years of political crisis. The Agencie de Développement de la Culture Kanak was established in 1989, with one of its main aims to initiate a Kanak cultural centre. Following the assassination of Jean-Marie Tjibaou in 1989 it was decided that the new cultural centre would be named after him.

10.   The problems and roles mentioned here are only concerned with cultural heritage, not the environmental or other scientific interests the museums also may have.

11.   The Tjibaou Cultural Centre ultimately opened to the public on 15 June 1998. [Editors]

24 Of old models and new in Pacific art: Real or spurious?

Philip J.C. Dark

The first symposium on the arts of the Pacific took place at McMaster University in Canada in August 1974. The second was at Wellington in 1978, and was the occasion on which the Pacific Arts Association was established. Symposia followed in New York in 1984 and in Honolulu in 1989. This one, in Red Kangaroo Place (Tandanya),[1] was PAA's fifth. At each of the previous symposia I have tried to draw attention to certain major facets of art that are proper to our inquiries into the arts of the Pacific.

At the McMaster Symposium several participants were asked to present general views of the principal features of art in certain areas in a synthesis that would allow of exploration of the lacunae apparent. I was asked to focus on 'The art of the peoples of Western New Britain and their Neighbours' (Dark 1979). The problems I encountered led me to consider what constituted an adequate survey and to propose a methodology for such an inquiry. But the paucity of information for my area – there being no information at all for some cultures in it – led me to the idea of a 'theme as a means of reconstruction'. This is a term used to circumscribe a particular subject – myth, event, custom – and its expression in a set of artistic forms functioning in particular cultural contexts to be found, with variations, in related cultures of an area:

In the different cultures of Western New Britain, the Huon Gulf, and Vitiaz and Dampier Straits, there are a number of cultural features of beliefs, customs and art which are suggestive of parallels and hence of themes common to the area. [Dark 1979:250]

At the Wellington Symposium, I considered what were the factors that made art for the Kilenge. 'What is art and non-art' for them (Dark 1983b:25)? For them 'art is something which is well done', something that is well made. The sense of making, doing something purposefully and well includes the idea of dancing (Dark 1983b:27), of performance. But in all this, what are the ramifications in the doing, in the making, in the creative process? What of creativity?

In New York, I sought to delimit the trends apparent ten or so years ago in the developments of Pacific arts, the changes in creativity, imitation and innovation, and pan-Pacificisation, for today's art is tomorrow's heritage.

At the Honolulu symposium, I was concerned with what changes portended for the future of Pacific arts. In all Pacific countries there appears to be concern for conserving the cultural heritage. In revivals, in re-creations of past arts, when linkages have ceased or are tenuous, style seems to be a major feature of the connections made, but its pertinacity rests with authenticity of imagery and performance: 'today's heritage, however conceived today, is tomorrow's art' (Dark 1993:222).

The nature of art

Over the years, I have tried to draw attention to certain factors at work in all arts, factors that underlie the arts of the Pacific and the nature of the heritage we have received: themes, skill and style, and changes in creativity. An essential factor of themes and style is, of course, form, that which the skill of the craftsman effects. When he or she does this with flair, with imagination, according to the canons of taste of his or her society, we, of the West, and of today, recognise this as art. But it should be remembered that in many Pacific cultures there is not necessarily present a comparable concept, though we seek to approximate it. Among the Kilenge, art is something well made or well done, and the person responsible is recognised by a particular term, *namos*, which we would call artist. In Greek, *arete* is the term for excellence in thought and performance and *ars* in Latin carries a sense of ideas about art as well as the basic concept of practising of skill. In Tongan, *faiva* means skill: 'art was not a category of traditional Tongan culture', Kaeppler (1990:61) reminds us. Teilhet-Fisk (1992b) also noted this and that the skill manifested in a product was not recognised unless the craftswoman was of chiefly rank.[2] Indeed, Kaeppler (1989:213) pointed out that there is no word for art in Polynesian languages, a phenomenon matched in some languages of other regions of the world, such as those of the Inuit, or Eskimo. Further, it should be noted that the forms of art we study today, and view as art, were not so regarded generally at the end of the last century by our forebears, for they were the works of savages or barbarians and were lodged largely in natural-history museums.

There is a danger of misconstruing Kilenge art and the arts of other peoples of Papua New Guinea when one focuses on the thing, for Kilenge appreciation is of the ability to manipulate skill: people admire this, and appreciation has a touch of fear to it, for the sacred and profane are handled by one skilled in their manipulation, whom we call artist, performer, masquerader, dancer (for example, Dark 1974: ills 78-81). Among the Kilenge, the 'maker' is the person who commissioned the piece that the artist made.

It is the creative touch arising from excellence, of doing things to perfection, that stamps the dancer's art (Dark 1974: ills 171, 173), the carver's skill, the execution of craft within the canons of taste of a society. Innovation threatens these, and if the impact is too much, too strong, they will change. In Kilenge in 1966 a traditional singsing was put on at which the youths got drunk on beer and danced to a guitar in the fashion of the bars in the towns. This was met by the traditional chorus of drummers ignoring them: the old and the new continued side by side, at that time.

But what of the creative process in art? What is involved? Knowledge of many things: knowing of the form of the product to be made, of the materials to be used, of the tools, techniques, and so on; knowing the flow of events in execution, the observances necessary for successful completion, such as magic, prayer, use of charms, decoration and secrecy; knowing the canons of taste that permit form, shape, colour and decoration; skill, with the talent, ability and imagination of the artist who brings all these together. The Trobriand Islanders distinguish the artist's insight as consisting of an intellectual creative facility, *kwequvagelu*, and an intellectual ability. The former is inspirational, representing the individual's capability or power to create, or the potential to do so; the latter the ability or talent to execute. It is the intellectual ability of the Trobriand artist that *sopi* (magic) promotes, inspiration deriving from spiritual means (Geoffrey Mosuwadoga, pers. comm. 1978).

Imagination and flair – the natural ability to do something well – when applied with skill, lead to art. In that creative process, being able to envisage formal arrangements and how to execute them is a vital operation, and one in which the maker may have recourse to models of them, images of which are held in the mind or observed in reality. This is not to say that he or she may not envisage new arrangements, make adjustments in the mind's eye, as inspiration takes hold, but art builds on art, and models may assist in or dictate the resulting work; or they may be poorly perceived, get modified and, in execution, be changed or muddled or copied so mechanically that art is seen as a repetition of tastelessness.

Traditional and tourist art

The general scene of Pacific arts presents a considerable variety of activities and trends, the result of rapid changes.

Characterisations of these are differing and can confuse meaning, and many of the images produced are spurious. Nelson Graburn (1983:70-1), in considering what was happening in the Pacific some fifteen years ago, asked for whom are the arts of Oceania created today? 'What formal and symbolic sources are drawn upon?' What contexts are they expressed in? He listed categories accordingly, modifying his previous general classification (Graburn 1976:5-9). He regarded tourism as a ritual, 'the sacred part of modern life in which meaning is to be found' in a life of 'alternating series of work and non-work experiences' (Graburn 1983:76). If tourism is a ritual, then symbolic expressions of it are demanded, hence the production of tourist art, which satisfies the demand. He argues that this process causes revivals of 'traditional arts, symbolic to the modern world of the nostalgic "pre-modern"' (Graburn 1983:77). Today's scene, for Polynesia, Kaeppler (1989: 234-6) sees as consisting of traditional art and evolved forms. Many traditional arts persist though changed; others are reconstructions; others are traditional forms adapted and used to make new ones. Hence there are 'evolved traditional' forms and non-traditional ones, which are 'folk art' and 'airport art' even if traditionally made. She points out that though traditional forms may be reproduced, they are no longer made in the same context (a ritual lodged in supernatural beliefs), but now are factory products made by a native with an imported religion.

I have attempted to put into some sort of order the contemporary scene of Pacific arts (Dark 1990), but recourse to terms like revivals, retentions, innovations, borrowing, transitional and 'the arts of acculturation' (Graburn 1976) are not very satisfactory, for they are open ended. Things are constantly changing in the contemporary scene and in a complex manner, for Pacific Islanders of one country seek out and interact with those of another, making adaptations accordingly, in their search to re-establish their heritage while contending with the tourist culture of America, Europe and Japan, to which they likewise adapt, producing what best suits a cash return. In all this there is also an interchange in the arts among Pacific peoples. Not only subject to the languages and religions of colonisation, they are now, most of them, further exposed to Western stereotypes of people, their behaviour and their material world from the various systems of modern communication that affect their lives daily; and all interact with political and economic changes (Dark 1993). No wonder there is a seeking after the past, an attempt to revive the past, and a belief that the revivals model what once existed. In building artistic bridges between the present and what went before, eclecticism, novelty, new media, new ideas, reinterpretations, all play their part. But what is the nature of that past, of 'newly traditional forms' or of 'new old' ones? (Dark 1993). What is meant by such terms, by 'evolved traditional' and 'non traditional'? What periods or points of time do they embrace? What are the models sought to represent them and how are they used? And are they authentic?

Authenticity

In a recent article by Kasfir (1992:44-5) on African art and authenticity, she makes the point that 'traditional' is equated with 'authentic', which in turn stands for 'good', the negations of these being 'non-traditional' and 'inauthentic', which become synonymous with 'bad'. These distinctions are certainly necessary for the collector and the tourist wanting to know that his memento is authentic, is often reassured in the Pacific by a label that asserts that it is an 'authentic replica'. Kasfir (1992:46) notes that 'authenticity … creates an aura of cultural truth around certain types of African art (mainly pre-colonial and sculptural)', which could also be said of Pacific art. However, as Dutton (1994:6) points out, 'By rendering as somehow inauthentic all later art, it fails to acknowledge the possibility of culture change; this notion of authenticity treats pre-European-contact tribal art as existing in a "timeless past".'

The works of art in the Pacific surviving from pre-European contact times are authentic and traditional, and some may have served as models for others, which were used in similar contexts. Copies are made today of these traditional forms to serve a range of different functions distinguishable as non-traditional (meaning not for traditional ritual uses, not that they don't serve the ritual uses of tourism). The dilemma arises in distinguishing what represents the traditional out of the 'old' if the continuity of the culture has changed so that there are no longer traceable ties. On what can the cultural heritage be modelled?

There are a number of Pacific cultures, such as that of the Maori and many in Papua New Guinea, in which enormous changes have occurred but ties with the past and the continuity of their art forms have not been lost. For these all past art is traditional. But the traditional of the past century for the Maori is different from its forerunner of the 18th century. For traditional dance, the Hawaiian looks to its revival near the close of the last century. Reference to traditional, as a term, needs to carry precision to mark differences. What is produced today can be categorised according to the cultural niche it occupies.

'In the last decade many changes have crept in,' wrote Robert Louis Stevenson (1908) on 14 July 1889, from Butaritari, Kiribati:

> women no longer go unclothed till marriage; the widow no longer sleeps at night and goes abroad by day with the skull of her dead husband; and, firearms being introduced, the spear and the shark-tooth sword are sold for curiosities. Ten years ago all these things and practices were to be seen in use; yet ten years more, and the old society will have entirely vanished. We came in a happy moment to see its institutions still erect and (in Apemama) scarce decayed.

One can thus sometimes mark with precision the points of contact and change in a culture over time, points at which the 'traditional', in part, ceases and is replaced by something else with a new structure, part of which interlocks with tourism. A culture is continuously sorting itself out after each contact, regrouping its values, projecting its heritage, which is always in flux. It is today's ideas about the past that are real and models are made from these to solve current needs of heritage and its expression. This is a repetitive process through time, which one must observe in studying the course of development of art forms and the attitudes to them.

Artists have ideas about forms, patterns, lines, arrangements, movements, spaces, and so on, which guide them in the creative act, and which are learned from the arts repertoire of their culture. Further, the individual learns

to see the results of the creative process as the culture teaches him to. In Tonga, mats 'are beautiful because they are culturally correct' (Teilhet-Fisk 1992a:46). In Tonga, too, Queen Halaevalu Mata'aho made the distinction between handicrafts ('like some of our baskets, beads and carvings, which are mainly utilitarian or decorative but which possess no distinct cultural meaning and play no distinct cultural roles') and cultural property ('traditional goods [that] have distinct cultural significance and play distinct cultural roles' and are not replaceable); the latter is at the heart of the cultural heritage (*Pacific Islands Monthly* 1992).

Performance

The dimensions of performance are extensive. Among the Kilenge of West New Britain, for example, one may consider a variety of activities, such as organisation before and during the event – the people involved, costume, accessories, place, time, duration; gathering together food before for distribution after; and so on. Previous experience provides the organisers and participants with a model to follow, to modify, enlarge or reduce as they will. The performers may be experienced but often require a rehearsal. Some features of a performance may be poorly executed, stumbled over, omitted, because the performers don't know the routine.

In the cycle of dances known as *sia* among the Kilenge, solos and duets were performed as interludes in the choral dancing with drums, though they had been dropped by the mid-1960s (see Dark 1974: ills 169, 171-8 and Dark 1984:21-3). My wife and I did see a remarkable duet of two dancers, representing *saumoy*, a sea-eagle mother teaching her chick to fly, each performer having a palm frond held extended to represent the birds' wings (fig. 24.1). The dance was conducted by a master, a Big Man playing a drum, who directed the steps of the dancers (fig. 24.2). On another occasion, a single dancer imitated a single sea-eagle flying. Both were novel to a number of the villagers. The second performance, however, did not carry the conviction of mime of the first, perhaps because the mimicry lacked observation and, in consequence, authenticity.[3] In times of rapid change, when things tend to be omitted from the artist's repertoire and are no longer performed, an attempt at revival provides invention as a substitute for knowledge; this requires skill for the performance to convince.

The 1960s, when I learned something of Kilenge culture, was a time when certain rituals of the past were still performed, some modified forms were used for entertainment, and some celebrations had ceased altogether under pressure from Christian missionaries. At a singsing given as an entertainment for my wife and me, there were three different performances of traditional celebrative rituals. This led to certain muddles in presentation, in timing and in uncertainty as to what should occur next.[4] The occasion also permitted the miming of a dance of the bush-spirit figure *nausung*, who hadn't been 'summoned' for many years, on a formal occasion of circumcision, from which women and children would have been excluded. The performance by the Big Man and master mentioned above perfectly modelled the rather nervous, hesitant dancing required of the character he was imitating (fig. 24.3).[5] But it occurred as a solo in a round of *sia*, the imitator dressed for the chorus of dancers but distinguished from them by the eye make-up appropriate for the character he was imitating.

Imitative dances are acceptable forms in *sia* performances, but the *nausung* character is normally restricted to his own special ritual. Only a Big Man could take the step of transferring him to a public performance. But the performance was not recognised by most of the audience, only by the older men. Here was change within the culture, old models modified, the transformation of one kind of ceremony into another. It was real in its imitation of the dance, but spurious too – perhaps as a one-off occasion, not to become a part of singsings put on for general entertainment.

A distinction to help clarify the contemporary scene was made recently by Marsha Berman (1990:62) for Papua New Guinea ceremonial occasions. She suggested differentiating such ceremonies into 'rituals' and 'celebrations'. In ritual, variations on a set theme only are possible. Celebrations include all kinds of new events, such as performances for the opening of a new bridge (for example,

24.1 (Top) Duet at Sia: a sea-eagle mother teaching its chick to fly. Waremo, Kilenge, West New Britain. (4.IX.1966: NB23.13.)

24.2 (Above) The duet, as in fig. 24.1, directed by Big Man Tule of Ongaia, West New Britain. (4.IX.1966: NB23.18.)

Holdsworth 1986a:35) or the annual Hagen and Goroka shows. These distinctions allow one to move beyond the restrictions imposed by the notion of 'traditional' and permit all kinds of creativity to be considered.

An example of the commercial use of celebrations in this sense can be found in Rarotonga. The tourist, wishing to learn something of Cook Islands culture, is attracted by advertisements in tourist literature to pay a visit to the Cook Islands Cultural Village, which is situated in Arorangi village on the west side of the island. A visit, which is a

package deal, starts with the visitor being picked up from the hotel. Then:

> A tour of each of the huts in our village includes demonstrations and lessons about our history, Maori medicine, weaving, coconut husking, carving, dancing … and much, much more! Our lunch, served at the end of the tour, has a variety of traditional Cook Islands foods. After lunch, you sit back and relax and enjoy the dance, songs, chants and music of the Cook Islands, as our village artists present an unforgettable show. [*What's On in the Cook Islands* 1990:18]

I visited the Cultural Village with about seventy others. On arrival we were shepherded into a reception room for an introductory talk by a young woman who, with admirable poise, quickly had us in order and treated us like a class of schoolkids. Names? Where from? From the USA, Australia, New Zealand particularly, Canada, Switzerland, Norway and the UK, it turned out. After being told to repeat various Maori phrases, we were given a brief lesson in the geography of the Cook Islands, the fame of Rarotonga for its oranges, of Atiu for vanilla, and of Aitutaki for its mosquitos. There were a few artefacts on the wall, all recent work, as were those we saw on the rest of our visit. Our teacher drew attention to some of these artefacts, notably a club to thrust at the eyes in combat, she said, adding that the notches cut on the side indicated the numbers of victims that had been despatched. Papaya and coconut milk also was served. Then we were treated to various dances by men and women, who included those who had instructed us earlier in the morning. There then followed a short period when members of the audience were persuaded to join the islanders on the dance floor, which was enjoyed by the tourists, no doubt, and treated with friendly playfulness by our hosts. The scene closed with the Cook Islands dancers posing for photographs with and without (fig. 24.4) their visitors.

24.3 (Above left) Tule of Ongaia miming *nausung* at a performance of *sia*. Kilenge, West New Britain. (27.IV.1967: NB160.34.)

24.4 (Left) Cook Islands dancers posing for photographs at end of performance at the Cultural Village, Arorangi Village, Rarotonga. (9.XI.90:9029.5.)

The treatment of visitors by the Cook Islanders at this tourist attraction seemed very professional. The rapport they created was warm and friendly. The Cultural Village is a commercially viable operation and is not sponsored officially, though it was given a small government grant to start it off. The government has built a new museum and cultural centre at Constitutional Park, completed in time for hosting by Rarotonga of the 6th Festival of Pacific Arts (Hall 1992; Moulin 1993). Previously, the National Museum occupied quarters in the Public Library; Makiuti Tongia, director of the National Museum until 1989, provided cultural information for use at the commercial Cultural Village.

Visiting the Cultural Village is highly formalised in terms of time spent on each of the features presented, and the program is no doubt subject to cost accounting, for it has to pay its way, even make a profit. In this it presents a form of 'instant' or 'potted' culture: what is selected for visitors can only run for a certain time so the information imparted is limited. The visitor learns about a particular construct of Cook Islands culture manufactured for tourist consumption. Detailed study of the manner of integration in modern Pacific societies of such constructed forms of entertainment would permit their effects on the development of local art to be traced. Similarly, while there is no doubt that 'Cook Islanders excel at dancing, singing and drumming', which they demonstrate admirably on 'Island Nights' in the various hotel venues on Rarotonga and Aitutaki, performances have to be made to fit locale and a budget. This warrants further inquiry. What are the limits to variations, spontaneity, innovation and further creativity in this facet of the tourist industry?

Connections with the past

Connections with the past differ throughout the Pacific. Those of Hawai'i, for example, have largely been severed by the effects of whalers, missionaries and American colonialism; those of some Papua New Guinea cultures have hardly been interrupted at all; and in other cultures, though considerable changes have occurred, some ties to the past are maintained.

Contact with European cultures has occurred at different times in the past, and with differing results. Though tourism has impacted markedly on all Pacific countries since the 1960s, there have been other major changes stirred by different peoples at different times in the past, indeed from before European contact, and with differing effects. Mention was made above of Robert Louis Stevenson's observation on change and the sale of mementos in Kiribati; this was more than 100 years ago. I read an account in the minutes book of the Athenaeum in Nantucket of a visit made by the Secretary to the Pacific in 1849-50, in which he deplored there being virtually no sign of the 'old' artefacts present in some countries he visited.

Iron tools were introduced into Pacific cultures at very different times with differing effects on their carving arts. For example, along the north-east coast of New Guinea, their introduction in the 19th century was spasmodic; few ships stopped by there until the last twenty years of that century. The Kilenge of West New Britain claimed they received their first iron tool about 1896. The arts in this area changed in consequence but remained 'traditional' from our perspective today.

I will now attempt an overview of the trends of contemporary arts of the Pacific under several headings below. These overlap, in some respects, with ones I have proposed before (Dark 1990) and some I have discussed in different ways more recently (Dark 1993). I will be looking at the question of the models on which present productions depend, and the extent to which connections with the past result in real or spurious art. The topics are: 'The new and the old', 'Old forms as national emblems', 'New syntheses', 'New forms of expression from the old', 'Arts for the visitor and traveller', 'Applied arts', 'Artistic heritages', and 'Muddles or new models?'.

The new and the old

One noticeable phenomenon to be found is the new and the old fitting compatibly side by side (Thompson 1989: 27). The juxtaposition of these two qualities in visual images can be quite startling to the Western observer, providing a sense of incongruity and expressing a local sense of humour (for example, Miller 1983: ill. 110), of protest, of being with the times. Examples can be found in costume, ornament and accessories (Miller 1983: ill. 55), and are manifest in the use of new materials, objects and techniques. Some examples of adaptive costume are: a Dani wearing 'second hand Indonesian army uniform' with two pigs' tusks and a plastic tube through his nose (Thompson 1989:30); a Dani wearing a T-shirt with 'The Space Age is Stone Age' printed on it (Thompson 1989:27); a Kirkenave villager in traditional costume being decorated for a singsing by a woman wearing a Western-style blouse with a *bilum* hanging down her back from her head, and beside her a man, about to take a cigarette from a packet, who is wearing a Goodyear baseball cap and T-shirt with 'Women – A Power to Development' on it (Macintyre 1985:210); an Enga man wearing a letter-printing disc instead of a white shell as a nasal ornament (Miller 1983: ill. 199); a Mount Hagener in 'traditional' costume with an *omak* on his chest and a local government councillor's badge on his headdress (Birnbaum and Strathern 1990: 108). Holdsworth (1986c:55) pictures 'the winner of a highlands beauty contest', in traditional-style costume and decoration, competing 'in a charity fund-raising for the Papua New Guinea Red Cross', an example of the 'old' functioning in a new context.

In adaptations to imposed religious practices, compromises result in juxtapositions or complete subjection to the new practices. For example, in Tonga, paintings in Western-style with Christian themes, and artificial flowers, are placed with graves (Diolé 1976:249);[6] a cross carved at the top of a Vanuatu slit-gong juxtaposes Christian and native symbols (Diolé 1976: 207);[7] young Mekeo girls, in 'traditional' costume, act as altar attendants to Catholic priests at celebrations of mass while the populace dressed in Western style clothing watches (Holdsworth 1986b); in Kiribati, in 1987, I attended a wedding ceremony in the Lutheran church at Bikenibeu, Tarawa, for which the bride, bridesmaids, groom and best man were dressed entirely in a Western style. Artists of considerable skill can execute works satisfactorily in an alien style, as has been done by Kilenge, for example (Dark 1990: figs 18-70).

In practices that have no local precedent, local adaptations would seem to embrace completely the adopted foreign form. For example, the adoption of Western academic dress for graduation at the University of Technology, Lae, Papua New Guinea (Holdsworth 1986a:51, back cover), the only local expression of individuality in the face of conformity being in the choice of tie worn; or the wearing of proper clothing for the game of Rugby football, though tribal dress seems to be essential for those attending the ceremonial line-up before the game starts (Anio 1979).

Examples of the adoption of new materials and their use with ones that have been employed locally in the past are familiar to most, such as the use of beads and plastics for costume ornaments and additions. On Tanna Island, Vanuatu, 'Custom dancers now combine Western and traditional dress, but they still perform their dances and other ceremonies according to instructions handed down through the ages' (*Pacific Islands Monthly* 1991), it is reported. How do they carry out these instructions?

> Most of the Tannese people live a traditional lifestyle and practise the ancient customs of their ancestors, including initiation ceremonies and circumcision rites … Visitors are warmly welcomed to these events – to the extent of participation being encouraged! [*Pacific Islands Monthly* 1991]

The adoption of new materials relates to the use to which they can be put. In the market in Fiji, for example, the now ubiquitous plastic bag is used for smaller products, but for larger ones, such as vegetables and shellfish, the old woven form of basket made so quickly from palm fronds is used. The same solution occurs in Avarua, Rarotonga. The innovator, though, can take the same, 'old' materials and make of them modern forms of hats. Yet, while new materials may be adopted, a change in the old decorative patterns does not necessarily follow; for example, bags women on Manus now make from rice sacks (Sylvia Ohnemus, pers. comm. December 1990).

The change in the modern carver's tool kit, when compared with that of his predecessors, is striking. The adze was the carver's primary tool. Its importance in carving is symbolised rather well by an illustration in the brochure, published by the contingent from New Caledonia to the 6th Festival of Pacific Arts, in Rarotonga, showing an elbow adze with an iron blade in front of a freshly carved light wood piece with, beside it, a similar adze with a stone blade in front of a dark-coloured carving. The title of the brochure is *Who We Are* (Togna 1992). Perhaps, given the drift of the times, it should have been *Who We Were*, for, in a photograph presaging change published by the Papua New Guinea Electricity Commission, the image conveyed is one of the modern carver being a user of a great variety of Western tools, including special carvers' chisels and gauges, among which is one elbow adze with an iron blade.

24.5 Maui Releasing the Sun, by Shige Yamada, Kahalui airport, Maui, Hawai'i. (3.IV.1933:934.0.)

Old forms as national emblems

The prominence of certain forms in cultures can lead to their adoption as national emblems with little alteration to the model from which they are derived. This is the case of the Maori *hei tiki*, which at one time, with very little deviation, was used by Air New Zealand; shaped in plastic, it was given to passengers as a good-luck charm, stamped on an ashtray, fashioned as an aid to dental hygiene in the form of a toothpick, and used as a grip at the top of a stirrer for drinks. A Fijian club form and a stylised Cook Island deity, in plastic, served similar purposes in their respective lands. The shape of the head of a Rarotongan staff god gives its stamp of approval to a plastic bag, just as an image of Tangaroa was used on one face of a Cook Island $1 piece. I have drawn attention to some of these examples before (Dark 1990).

New syntheses

Attention has been drawn by a number of writers to fascinating examples of attempts, with varying degrees of success, by artists and architects to bridge the gap between local or national forms and various Western styles and techniques not in the local repertoire (Dark 1983a, 1990:264-5; Heermann 1979; Simons and Stevenson 1990; Tausie 1980). The new syntheses, as I see them, are works that are essentially eclectic. Some, such as the exciting Papua New Guinea Parliament House (or the Papua New Guinea Banking Corporation building), are remarkably successful despite considerable difficulties in their creation (Rosi 1991).[8] Less successful is the sculpture by Shige Yamada at Kahalui airport, Maui (fig. 24.5), showing Maui releasing the sun:

> The artist researched his work from several sources, including books on traditional Hawaiian sculpture and the work of contemporary Western artists including Lachaise, Moore, and Arp. The figure is definitely not meant to represent traditional Hawaiian sculpture more than to interpret a personal impression of contemporary sculpture. [Enoki 1992:6]

Other recent examples of synthesis are works presented at the 6th Festival of Pacific Arts, such as Tunui Salmon's 2.4-metre-tall female figure, which, Karen Stevenson (1993: 68) recounts, draws on Tahitian mythology and 'modern ideology as well as the strength and importance of women in Polynesian society'. A further example of his was a tuff carving of Ta'ihia, 'a legendary king of Tautira who sailed to Rarotonga' (Moulin 1993:70), a past link between Rarotonga and Tahiti now symbolising a contemporary one. Another was a wooden statue carved by Benjamin Nicholls, *Te Manava Rangatira* (Moulin 1993: fig. 213). Stevenson (1993:68) also refers to the work of the Australian Arone Meek at the festival as drawing for inspiration on Aboriginal mythology and the contemporary world.[9]

The work of several modern Papua New Guinea painters often seems poised between synthetic expressions with forms denoting indigenous ideas juxtaposed with forms from the West – for example, Kauage's *Helicopter* – though many are attempts at new ways of expression as the result of exposure to the Papua New Guinea National Arts School.[10] The tapestries of Alioi Pilioku, the Vanuatuan artist, using a Western medium, seem poised between two worlds, as does the work of some other Vanuatuan artists.[11]

New forms of expression from the old

There are Pacific artists who seem to have perceived the essence of their local styles and moved forward, with great imagination, to new forms of expression that continue their traditions. Their work is original, transcending eclecticism. Examples of modern Papua New Guinea artists are Joseph Nalo, with powerful works such as his *Crucifixion* (Simons and Stevenson 1990:19) and, with similar strength, Taba Silau (Simons and Stevenson 1990:21). Noteworthy, too, is Martin Morububuna who, while retaining his native style, has enlarged it to invent new forms.[12]

Today's Australian Aboriginal artists have been contending with how to express the differences between their past world and that of modern Australia and some seem to have done so successfully by presenting past forms in new media (fig. 24.6), while others have expressed their interaction

24.6 *Bush Tucker and Survival*, depicting lizard, echidna, snake's eggs (representing fertility), spinifex grass and body paint used at ceremonies; acrylic on canvas (76 x 61 cm) by Sammy Petyane, 1991. (937.12.)

with the contemporary scene and their place in it. Transcultural solutions need choices of models, of forms, and of ways of structuring them from both the cultures involved (Poignant 1993).

The Papua New Guinean and Australian artists referred to are 'gallery artists', and there has been increasing general interest in their works for a decade or more, with exhibitions of their art worldwide.[13] These gallery artists have moved successfully into a world of pictorial art dominated by Western views. Yet, in other areas of their arts, craftsmen continue to produce artefacts for ritual purposes as well as for sale to tourists and others; and the performing arts provide a continuing means of expression, whether ceremonial or for entertainment.

The strength of the idiom of Maori art and the continuing understanding of its principles by Maori artists has been such that, while contemporary Maori artists have modified and innovated with old forms intended for new contexts, they have done so successfully, adding to the range of expressions of the style of an object, such as with carvings in bone and whale ivory by Emmitt Aranga (for example, Doig and Davidson 1989: fig. 60) or in greenstone by Hepi Maxwell (Doig and Davidson 1989: fig. 61). Others have ingeniously taken basic forms of the art and produced works that transpose Maori art into a Western context without losing its Maoriness, a successful transcultural solution; for example, a painting by Sandy Adsett (Doig and Davidson 1989: fig. 66). The former two examples, while being made as personal ornaments, can also function as gallery art and have been so exhibited. Sandy Adsett's painting in acrylic on board is meant to be hung.

There are other Pacific artists besides the Maori whose masterly grasp of their native idiom has allowed them to continue its expression with entirely original forms, expanding the indigenous repertoire without transgressing the local style. Some Asmat carvers exemplify this in the face of the strongest of pressures to produce work for dealers and tourists. Schneebaum (1993: fig. 4) reports of a work 'made in the relatively remote village of Damen' in 1991, now in the museum at Agats: 'It is a completely original work, without any relationship to any carving I've seen anywhere in the world.' Similarly, original forms, completely in the bounds of the Asmat idiom yet not for traditional contexts, were being carved twenty or more years ago. The original carvings, depicting ancestors, are amazingly inventive works (for example, Gerbrands 1979: figs 5-28; Hoogerbrugge 1977:131-4; Hoogerbrugge and Kooijman 1976:121-2). Such works are also forms of gallery art.

The problems of developing a new style of expression can be examined in other arts besides painting or carving. Shari Cole (1991), in an account of women's fibre arts of Polynesia, points out that there are a number of factors involved in the development of a new style. There are individual artists' variations in production; what is produced depends on the models that are available, but is also subject to the vagaries of memory and group decisions made under the direction of a *taunga*.

Some artists more than others find themselves with a foot in two worlds, producing works for the tourist trade on the one hand and attempting original creativity on the other. Mike Tavioni, the leading contemporary Cook Islands artist, exploits a variety of media as inspiration comes to him, yet to survive he has to produce works for easy sale. This means printing his designs on T-shirts, carving various sizes of *tiki* figures, and painting small pictures suitable for the tourist trade, which he sells in the Tavioni Arts shop in Cooks Corner, Avarua.

Mike Tavioni does his work in a rambling shed, built around a tree, in front of his home (fig. 24.7). He did not start off as an artist, having trained in New Zealand as a horticulturalist, but too much politicking, he said, drove him to seek a living as an artist. Few people are interested in the arts, he finds, and he is frustrated by having to produce bread-and-butter work and not be able to devote himself full time to the creative work he feels is his natural inspiration. In 1990 he was carving in coral, which is a tricky medium because the coral breaks so easily. He has also carved story boards in a naturalistic style. His most successful work is as an illustrator of local tales and myths (McCarthy 1991).

There are other Cook Islands artists, who set up the Te Pua Neinei Arts and Cultural Society.[14] Of particular interest is the work of Upokoina D. George (Ian George), who established an art department in the national high

24.7 Mike Tavioni's studio, Avarua, Rarotonga. (12.XI.1990: 9033.8.)

school (McCarthy 1990). His drawings and paintings are successful modern presentations of Cook Islands legends and life, as in his painting *The Gods in Conversation* (*Cook Islands Sun* 1992a) and his illustrations for two books of poetry (*Cook Islands Sun* 1992b).[15]

Arts for the visitor and traveller

One effect of tourism is to change the tastes of the culture catering to it. Intrusive and innovative forms alter local ones and change the indigenous style so that they become part of the day-to-day local culture. This is particularly so with material goods such as clothes, designs, and the visual arts and images they project. No longer are the locally produced arts and crafts the sole source of supply of artefacts for the tourists. In the special shops, galleries and emporia given over to tourist arts and crafts will be found the works of many lands. Dealers in the tourist art trade have a wide network of connections to sources of supply in different countries. They have also built up their networks to include the less-accessible destinations that the adventurous tourists seek on expeditions mounted by museums and special exploratory groups. This they have done by making collecting expeditions to some of the remoter parts of some countries, where they act as local stimuli for further production.

The tendency in examining the tourist-art industry is to look at the results, the effects, the changes it has brought about. What is needed are in-depth studies of the production of artefacts, the role of the dealer in distributing them around the Pacific, the economic aspects of production, the effect on the producer and on local production for the community's needs. Most important is the role of the craftsman as an agent of change of local and of public taste. Detailed examination of the performing arts for the tourist should be rewarding, as noted above in the Cook Islands example; the formalisation of some presentations has become very stereotyped and cost-accounted. Under such circumstances, what is the gulf between the host's and visitor's cultures with respect to the images projected of each and the nature of the understanding of each other's cultural values?

The major dilemma for a Pacific country producing crafts for sale and for the community's needs for everyday use is well expressed in the Solomon Islands government catalogue of handcrafts (Austin 1986:3), the preamble to which states:

> The imagination brought to the work is fresh, unaffected by the visual platitudes of the West. The things made are part of everyday life: they are created to be *used*, the notion of selling them being only recent. And they have the dignity of this tradition: even a humble woven basket for rubbish can be beautiful.

Austin continues (1986:5) 'the audience for artifacts is changing from an indigenous to a European or visiting one', with payment made in currency rather than in traditional kind. 'Some changes of artefact have come too'. After discussing the role of the master carvers and the qualities of excellence expected, 'A parallel approach is surfacing, however, encouraged by the less exacting but larger demands of the tourist … there will be a place, and a price, for the humbler artefact' made by the less skilled. 'The dignity of tradition is swept away' (Austin 1986:5) as the 'audience' changes from local to outsider (visitor, traveller, tourist) and artefacts (form and type) change in consequence; furthermore, so does their quality and authenticity, because the 'less skilled' can earn a living at craft production. An increase in tourism leads to increasing blandness of taste and quality.

Tobias Schneebaum (1991:27) drew attention to radical changes occurring among the Asmat of Irian Jaya 'in an effort to bring in a small cash economy'. One trend was reduction in the physical size of carvings, a pan-Pacific phenomenon, to conform to airline transportation restrictions. 'Groups of villages have now banded together to produce new styles, all influenced by the outside world and for the purpose of sales' (Schneebaum 1991:27). The ancestor pole has changed, losing

> its character. It simply became a badly worked carving, with no element of the spirituality that was essential to the older style. As it was it was perfect for rolling in bubble paper or in corrugated cardboard for easy shipping. [Schneebaum 1991:28]

24.8 (Top) Ethnographica in the Asian Connection, Cairns, Queensland. (23.III.1992:9217.12.)

24.9 (Above) Ethnographica in the Asian Connection, Cairns, Queensland. (23.III.1992:9217.3.)

In reference to bowls:

> of course, they fit with perfect ease into a suitcase. Drums have been reduced to 12″ … In spite of these many changes … the carvings that are a part of traditional life remain in traditional forms and are superbly carved. [Schneebaum 1991:28]

Thus it would seem that cultures with powerful art traditions are able to adapt skills to meet the need for cash while continuing the traditional art forms for local use.

A matter of some concern is the recent appearance on the tourist-art market of copies of artefacts characteristic of one country by craftspeople in another. Schneebaum (1993) noted that the work of Asmat carvers was being copied by non-Asmaters for sale in Bali. Rapa Nui artisans living and working in Temuco, Chile, 'the heart of the Mapuche culture' (Ramirez 1992) are producing plates, forks and spoons in the Mapuche style, which, Ramirez noted, they do better than the local craftsmen. Rapa Nui artists living in different towns produce, in addition

> to work in the local style, wooden figures in the Rapa Nui style for local sale. One, who lived in Villarrica, also produced items which mixed the two styles: a classic Mapuche wooden spoon (*huitri*) has handles carved with typical *moai kava-kava* heads. [Ramirez 1992]

The trade in artefacts across the Pacific has reached the stage where the visitor and the local inhabitant are faced with a plethora of styles from many countries shown in a shop as any other goods, massed in an emporium or displayed as gallery art. In Cairns, Queensland, are two principal vendors. One is the Gallery Primitive, 'often likened to a museum', 'Cairns only Primitive Art Specialists'; the 2000 artefacts of the collection displayed in it, mainly from Melanesia, were first obtained in the late 1960s. 'This experience has enabled them to probe deeper into the remote river and swamp systems to collect the unsurpassed quality art that is their trademark' (Australian Tourist Publications 1991). The gallery also displays Aboriginal artefacts. This kind of display, and the objects shown, I have seen elsewhere referred to as 'Fine Primitive Art'.

The other vendor displays his extensive collections in

a vast kind of emporium called the Asian Connection. He makes trips regularly to collect in Papua New Guinea, Irian Jaya, Nias, Bali and South-East Asia, and the material he obtains ranges widely in provenience as well as form: shields, spears, drums (fig. 24.8), bowls, mortuary boards (fig. 24.9), Aboriginal artefacts, betel mortars, masks, baskets, beadwork, ceramics, textiles, T-shirts, sarongs and sandals, and so on.

In Avarua, on Rarotonga, there are two small shops that display only examples of the work of Cook Islanders. One, Tavioni Arts, was mentioned above; the other is the Cook Islands Women's Crafts Centre, which sells mainly local woven items, such as hats, bags and mats.[16] The largest of the shops selling handcrafts is Island Crafts Ltd, which advertises 'For Everything Polynesian'. The shop does include a considerable variety of carvings produced in Rarotonga, particularly figures of Tangaroa in many sizes (fig. 24.10). The smaller figures of Tangaroa are heavily stylised and their proportions severely mechanical: it was impossible to differentiate among twenty figures of the same height. All versions were labelled 'This carving is the Cook Islands god Tangaroa' and:

> Tangaroa was the god of creation, fishing, the sea, carpentry, planting and the weather. He is one of the outstanding in as much that he was present in most islands of the Polynesian Pacific although he varied in different forms.

One version had a penis that could be erected or withdrawn.

Other Cook Island carvings included versions of 'God-staff owned by the Taunga (Witch doctor) of the tribe'; Taringa Nui, the fisherman's god (fig. 24.11); Rongo with his sons; and Pukapukan male and female deities. But the shop contained a good selection of the works of other Pacific cultures. Sepik (fig. 24.11) and other Papua New Guinean carvings, and carvings from the Solomon Islands, are obtained from a dealer in Port Moresby. The carving of storyboards (fig. 24.12) – something Tavioni does – is a new direction for Rarotongan carvers, and mimics Palauan (Belauan) story boards; but they were very fresh and successful executions, all 71 centimetres (28 inches) long.

Island Crafts Ltd is located in a big woodworking shed equipped with lathes, sanders and all the tools necessary

24.10 (Top) Multiple replicas of Tangaroa and other souvenirs in Limmars Island Crafts Ltd, Avarua, Rarotonga. (12.XI.1990:SL9019.12.)

24.11 (Above) Carved replicas of old forms of Cook Islands deities with Sepik carvings in Limmars Island Crafts Ltd, Avarua, Rarotonga (12.XI.1990:9033.4.)

24.12 (Top) Three story boards with various Cook Island replicas in Limmars Island Crafts Ltd, Avarua, Rarotonga. (12.XI.1990:9033.5.)

24.13 (Above) Woman sanding carvings (front) and man working pearl shell in Limmars Island Crafts Ltd, Avarua, Rarotonga. (12.XI.1990:9032.23.)

for mass hand-production of different carvings, and a special room for spray staining. When I visited the factory there were three men and a woman working. I was told that four more were also employed but they were not at work. Of those working, one man and a woman were engaged in making flower arrangements, as it was the Island Flower Week. Two craftsmen were carving wood, the third, wearing a mask, was 'sanding' pearl shell at a lathe, and the woman was sanding carvings (fig. 24.13). Of the two engaged in carving, the younger, Uaongo Williams, was carving letters on a flat board (figs 24.14 and 24.15). He had been working at Limmars Island Crafts for four years. It was a job available when he left school and he applied for it. The elder was Gavin Apatangi, a carver from Mangaia, who was working on several figures of the Rarotongan version of Tangaroa and one Pukapukan one (fig. 24.16), sawing the mango wood with a hacksaw (fig. 24.17), making the same cuts for arms and legs of several figures, one after the other, a process which gives them their grim look of insensibility. Apatangi learned to carve from his father. In a bin, in a corner of the shop, were a number of pieces he had carved some time ago, which served as models. There were representations of Rongo (fig. 24.18) and of male and female Pukapukan deities. The quality of these figures, compared with those he was working on, was very much better. Continual replication according to a formula must be stultifying.

Applied arts

The replication, even though by hand with mechanical means, of many copies of Tangaroa in wood or stamped on a T-shirt, or of the Hawaiian *tiki* version of Kukailimoku reproduced mechanically in many versions, is a form of applied art, it could be argued. Though perhaps not a satisfactory term, there is a whole category of products made for visitors and for local consumption that bear a relationship to the forms and colours of the original models for them, but have been altered in design or colour, shape or size, or space occupied, and are applied to materials quite different to those in which the model was made. Such applied forms of art become part of the generalised

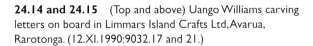

24.14 and 24.15 (Top and above) Uango Williams carving letters on board in Limmars Island Crafts Ltd, Avarua, Rarotonga. (12.XI.1990:9032.17 and 21.)

24.16 (Top right) Gavin Apatangi working on several versions of Tangaroa in Limmars Island Crafts Ltd, Avarua, Rarotonga. (12.XI.1990:9032.11.)

24.17 (Centre right) Two Pukapukan style figures roughed out with hacksaw by Gavin Apatangi in Limmars Island Crafts Ltd, Avarua, Rarotonga. (12.XI.1990:9032.14.)

24.18 (Bottom right) 'Model' of Rongo carved some years before 1990 by Gavin Apatangi in Limmars Island Crafts Ltd Avarua, Rarotonga. (12.XI.1990:9032.30.)

24.19 'Dolphin Dreaming', T-shirt by Churinga Designs, Australia, 1992. (932.5.)

24.20 Six coasters designed by James Galarrwuy Yunupingu, Australia, 1991. (932.4.)

view of a culture's arts, moulding the mental template people have about their art and their folk view of past forms. Though such a view is real, it substitutes the image of the applied form for the one it originated from and misconstrues it. Some applications break all boundaries and become incongruous and manifestations of bad taste. This is one of the areas in which increasing blandness of discrimination and style occurs.

I have referred to the applied arts in the Pacific before (Dark 1990:256-68; 1993). It seems appropriate to draw attention to a few noticeable, and strikingly tasteful, applications of Australian Aboriginal designs on T-shirts, hand prints by Churinga Designs in Australia (fig. 24.19). Each shirt is accompanied by a printed label that states Aboriginal art

> is among the oldest in the world … The styles of Aboriginal art, which developed over thousands of years, appear simple but are in reality a mature, fully-established medium, strengthened by eons of folklore, mythology and custom.

Printing postcards of Aboriginal works in collections, such as the Australian National Gallery does, is a Western trait of gallery art– for example, *Gurramatji* (*Magpie Geese*), 1987, by George Milpurrurru (Australian National Gallery PC No. 00461) – as is the reproduction of Aboriginal paintings on greeting cards, such as the Desert Designs of Jimmy Pike (for example, *Ngampayijarra*), or those printed for the Aboriginal Gallery of Dreamings, Melbourne, such as *Warlu* (*Fire Dreaming*), 1990, by Malcolm Jagamarra, and his *Wana* (*Snake Dreaming*), 1990. The printing of Aboriginal designs on coasters and placemats is another application; for example, six paintings by James Galarrwuy Yunupingu used for a set of coasters (fig. 24.20), and six designs for a set of placemats.

Artistic heritage

I have drawn attention before to the roles of style and authenticity in the recreation of heritage (Dark 1993). Also of concern are the roles for which models can be used. Models capture the past, they carry power and are bound by style, which sets limits on their use in artistic expression, on the one hand, or they may just be copied, on the other. The selection process can be purposeful or spontaneous leading to fads. Lack of perception and/or skill, or an obsessive focus on a fad, lead to a muddled expression.

In Tahiti, there has recently been a revival of tattooing as a way of expressing one's Tahitianness, just as the Samoans have maintained the custom as part of their *fa'a Samoa* (Tsutsumi 1990). 'Apart from its cultural significance, it is intended as a proof of courage' (Aiavao 1990:50). But today electric needles and pain-killers are used. While it may be 'an art that helps survival of an ancient custom' (Aiavao 1990:50), it is subject to change, for Aiavao reports that one design was adopted from a mistake made by the artist.

The revival of tattooing in parts of the Pacific seems to express a concern to seek out the traditional, the custom, the past for display in the present as concrete evidence of the practice as part of the artistic heritage: 'Tattoos a Hawaiian status symbol', the *Maui Beach Press* (1991:A5) assured its readers. As Karen Stevenson has pointed out before, some tattoo artists draw on traditional motifs to create their own designs, and thus they express today's reaction to a traditional art form.

National celebrations stimulate various manifestations of the arts. In Hawai'i, on 11 June the statue of King Kamehameha I is draped profusely with *leis* and decorated with flowers. A parade is mounted, a feature of which is a principal figure and attendant priest, both costumed in feathered cloaks and helmets, with a guard of three warriors with spears in front, and, in the rear, two attendants supporting *kahili*, all riding on a car covered with flowers, greenery and *Cordylines,* and accompanied by gaily dressed riders on horseback. The nature of the costume and the *kahili* rest, in part, on forms surviving from the past, but they are mounted on a means of transport common today. Pride in the heritage is generated, and what might seem a muddle in the models to some is not so to others; what is expressed is a view of the past. The general view that is generated of that past is aided by activities such as the Keiki Tahiti Fete, a Tahitian dance competition for young people, which is in its tenth year. 'The festival is held to stimulate an awareness of Hawaii's Polynesian

affiliations with the peoples of Tahiti' (Ward 1990). But the construction of heritage, with its artistic features, also extends to political contexts where sovereignty, self-determination and the whole nature of 'Hawaiian spirituality' are contended (Keale 1992:22).

Friedman has drawn attention to the total marginalisation of the Hawaiians after the war, under the impact of tourism and the domination in local affairs of the Japanese-Americans. The end of the 1960s saw 'the Hawaiian cultural revival' and led to constructions of the past that are quite different to those generated by Western views of the historical record and process, being 'rooted in a historical distinction between Hawaiian life forms and those that became dominant in the islands' (Friedman 1992:842).

Several national delegations to the 6th Festival of Pacific Arts, in Rarotonga, had information booklets and pamphlets produced. *Who We Are* (Togna 1992) was the title of a New Caledonian glossy sixty-page publication. The Hawai'i Steering Committee's (1992:7) more modest eight-page leaflet on the ten visual artists who were selected to participate in Rarotonga notes:

> [they] were chosen not only for their exceptional knowledge and skill, but for their *aloha* (love) for the Hawaiian culture and way of life … Some of the older practitioners, *kupuna*, were literally 'born into' their work as part of their family's heritage. Those of younger generations have recognised the beauty and importance of their own culture and are committed to learning from the elders, or to conducting research to revive endangered and lost traditions.

The focus here is on the 'Hawaiian life forms' that Friedman distinguished, as noted above. The Sponsorship Proposal (n.d.) of the 6th Festival of Pacific Arts states that the Cook Islanders would 'play their part in defending the cultures of the Pacific'. This sense of threat occurs again in this booklet: 'But as we approach the 21st century the swiftness with which other influences are absorbed threatens the cultural integrity of the Pacific people.'

Futa Helu (1991) has expressed fears that the future of Pacific Islanders will succumb to 'development sponsored by aid donors … precious little of aid is spent on real culture'. He cites the South Pacific Arts Festival as a case in point: 'Exactly how does this festival promote and develop Pacific arts?' All that it does, he argues, is to put money into the hands of the hosts and TV workers, not into the hands of the performers, who only receive

> well rehearsed mouthfulls ... of insecure gratitude! The point is: culture is that which donors must avoid since it takes them into terra incognita, and if they venture there it is only going to gratify their capitalistic aims.

However, the Pacific Arts Council of the South Pacific Commission views the Pacific Arts Festival as a means of conserving the cultural heritage, joining the past and future. Those who put on the festival see it as a means for Pacific Islanders from all three major regions to 'mingle and celebrate their special contributions to the world heritage' (Sponsorship Proposal n.d.). It is the manifestations of their skills and customs in their celebrations that 'make them distinctive and respected in the international community' (Sponsorship Proposal n.d.). It would seem, however, that in practice there are three kinds of manifestations of skills and art that are being contributed by a people to their own heritage: that which is practised at the festival, that which is done at home in the community, and that which receives economic return from visitors and tourists.

The stimulation given to delegations to build canoes to sail to the festival was a means of expressing the sentiments held about past skills in voyaging and navigation, and was a significant contribution to the public image of Pacific Islanders. 'The festival is a great opportunity for us to be able to share and give back to our ancestral families', the Hawaiian navigator, Nainoa Thompson 'enthused' (Festival of Pacific Arts 1992:2).[17]

Muddles or new models?

This grouping includes forms and executions where the 'traditional' model has been wrongly perceived, or misconstrued, or misrepresented. A model is not just an object; it is also a design, something to be imitated, shaped, fashioned. The copier is always concerned that replication of the model is accurate and history is authenticated.

Bishop Museum offers 'The Rare and Genuine in Shop Pacifica' (*Ka 'Elele* 1990:5):

> handsome, hand-crafted replicas of items out of the Polynesian past – work done by contemporary craftsmen willing to share their work with the public ... All of the items are crafted with great attention to detail and historical accuracy.

An advertisement in *Ka Wai Ola O Oha* (September 1990:4) notes that the Royal Feather Company

> is dedicated to the perpetuation of quality Hawaiian featherwork. Materials that are readily available today are used to fashion the beautiful natural and dyed feathers into a *lei hula* for your head, neck or hat.

The advertisement is supported by a drawing of two *kahili* and the phrase *E hana keia la, e pulama ia la aku* (A creation today, a treasure tomorrow). Today's art is tomorrow's heritage.

Diminishing the size of replicas is a common feature of suitcase art, a feature of current production in many Pacific countries; for example, Tino figures, the model for which originates in Nukuoro, are mass carved in Pohnpei. The Cook Islands story boards mentioned above in the Island Crafts shop in Avarua were all 70 centimetres long, thus fitting the larger standard-size suitcase.

In 1967 a master Kilenge artist carved the first *nausung* mask that had been produced for many years (Dark 1974: ills 78–82). At that time there were only two old pre-World War II pieces left in all the Kilenge villages. A man, who was neither carver nor master carver, had a go at carving one, sensing that he might be able to sell it to the resident anthropologists – Adrian Gerbrands, my wife and me. His effort showed that the model he had in mind was erring in form and ill-conceived. The acknowledged carvers were outraged; this was not work 'well done', it was not art. But the occasion of the production of this first 'tourist' piece, together with the master's work, led to other carvers making masks for sale, but carvers who were acknowledged as such. Their results were competent renderings of the Kilenge style of mask (Dark 1974:84, 85). A Kilenge carver shown a postcard of a Tami mask in Field Museum's collections made a fine copy of it, but the press of the Kilenge style led him away from the model into his own idiom (Dark 1974:89-90).

Once a trade can be made for cash, once the demand from 'outside' the local context arises, the traditional model begins to change. Schneebaum (1993:55) writes of the changes in Asmat art:

> the carvings … become more complicated. Handles of drums now have 10 or 11 figures around them over-balancing the visual and physical aspect and making the drum impossible to use. The drum, in fact, is so obscured that it can barely be seen.[18]

The model certainly seems to have been muddled, but then the purpose for which it is intended is now quite different. Under these new conditions, how far does the quality of the style persist?

In the Cook Islands the quality of the representations of Tangaroa appears to be badly eroded. Concern for the quality of carvings, mass-produced in Easter Island for the Polynesian Culture Center in Hawai'i, was expressed by Sergio Rapu. There 'the world's most comprehensive and authentic Rapa Nui exhibit outside Easter Island' was planned for 1992 (*Rapa Nui Journal* 1991). The miniature carvings it was hoped to sell the centre were to number 100 000 *moai*; their quality was to be monitored in Rapa Nui by a local committee, which was to 'provide an authentic seal of approval on all exported items'. Copies of Hawaiian images often have attached labels misrepresenting the qualities claimed for them; for example, 'ALOHA TIKI. Aloha is this tiki's virtue. He'll give you fond memories of Hawaii. ALOHA!' Or on a differently fashioned representation of the same figure: 'LUCKY TIKI. This tiny tiki wishes you an abundance of "POMAIKAI" (po-meye-KAH-i) which means Good Luck and Good Fortune.'

A further potential loss of control of original models lies in the area of conservation of petroglyphs, to which Millerstrom (1992:23-4) has drawn attention – the recarving of rock-art sites in the Marquesas Islands so that tourists can see them better, or outlining them with paint, crayon or chalk as practised in Hawai'i. The embrace of Mammon can lead to the destruction of art, and maybe

all else besides; certainly, in the guise of tourism, he is all-pervading.

When the local demands for an artist's work cease he will seek alternative forms that will bring a return. In the Solomon Islands, carvers produce some objects for the tourist trade for which there are no indigenous models; for example, frogs, herons, seahorses, and eagles with snakes (Austin 1986:26, 27, 30, 33).

Fanciful images of the Pacific and its people persist, and misconceptions are perpetuated. For example, a photograph of a Solomon Islander, tattooed on his forehead, is described as 'Ageless: the face of a Solomons man reveals a life in a country still rich in tradition' (Yates 1992). A postcard showing two hulls joined by a platform with six costumed dancers on it is entitled 'Tahitian Canoe' (Polynesian Cultural Center n.d.). 'Maori dancers demonstrating the art of *poi*-ball twirling' are the subject of an illustration in a booklet on the Polynesian Cultural Center, yet one of the 'Maori' dancers would appear to be illustrated on another page enacting the 'Tahitian legend of Hina and the Eel' (Arioyoshi 1989:5, cf. 40).

A common representation of Hawaiianness is a hula dancer or group of dancers, the costume varying, which can be employed to advertise almost any activity in Hawai'i in the tourist literature; for example, a shopping centre on Kauai, Hawaiian Airlines, or Waimea Falls Park, where 'the spirit of old Hawaii is alive'. A myth of the past and the desire to establish it as part of the cultural heritage may have led to the instalment of the Menehune figure as a tourist attraction at Paradise Cove Luau Park. Menehunes are described as

> small, fun loving yet industrious natives [who] were here long before the Hawaiians arrived … from … the Marquesas Islands. Now four re-creations of these Menehunes joke, play and enjoy the Luau nightly at Paradise Cove Luau Park. Be sure to say 'Hi' to a Menehune and have your picture taken too.

A salacious element is sometimes presented to the tourist, such as a postcard entitled 'Ancient Phallic Rock' and described as 'worshipped as a symbol of generative power by the early Hawaiians … on the island of Molokai'. A girl is posed taking a photograph of it. Postcards are also printed that draw attention to skimpy 'native' dress and to parts of the female anatomy not normally exposed in Hawai'i.

Some misrepresentations can only be categorised as bizarre; for example, an advertisement in *Honolulu* (1992) using an old Bishop Museum photograph of a man holding a surfboard, Diamond Head behind, with the message painted on him: 'The Island Christmas Vest from Canoe Clothing Company, Ala Moana Center'. Or a tourist advertisement urging the reader to 'Wear the True Colours of Hawaii'. Or the concept of Hawai'i can be used to sell pasta by pictures of a parrot, a palm tree, the sun, and the face of a girl with a hibiscus flower behind her ear.

The image of the Pacific as paradise continues (Brown 1982). National Geographic titled a recent book *Blue Horizons: Paradise Isles of the Pacific* (Dunn 1985); Air Niugini's in-flight magazine is entitled *Paradise* (see Dick 1979). The visitor to Hawai'i is told he can go 'Around Paradise in a Day' (Tully 1989). Indeed, there are still some who go to the Pacific 'looking for paradise on earth'. Such a one was the writer and broadcaster John Heminway, but he was told by Bengt Danielson that he was 200 years too late (Grieve 1991); it was a 'lost paradise'. Indeed, this was the title of Ian Cameron's 1987 account of European exploration of the Pacific.

Though it can be claimed that the kinds of representations just given of the Pacific are false, or confusing, they do serve a very practical purpose, and many Pacific Islanders are tolerant of the views projected when they generate needed funds. The mechanism for the promotion of tourism is illustrated by the rear cover of the 'Pacific Arts Festival Programme Issue' of the *Cook Islands Chronicle* (Hall 1992), which shows dancers and drummers costumed for a performance, the sea breaking on the reef behind them, captioned 'Let Images Promote Your Product'. In the 1970s, McGraw Hill used a photograph of a New Guinea Highlander to advertise anthropology films to the educational market in the USA.

Although not common, world tours by Pacific Island dancers and related cultural promotions must lead to stereotyped views of Pacific Islanders; for example, in 1990

there was a European tour by a Papua New Guinea dance troupe (*The Times* 31 May 1990:3) and Hawaiian dancers went to Great Britain (*The Times* 23 July 1990:3); and three Australian Aborigines presented a ritual pole to the Museum für Völkerkunde, Frankfurt, for which 'they were given in return three suitcases' (*The Times* 16 March 1990:10).

The future?

The focus of those interested in researching Pacific arts has tended to be on the arts of the cultures surviving into the near present yet still connected with their past. Are innovations and novelties but frivolities of the moment, or do they get incorporated and last? If so, why? What kind of images are projected by the tourist trade that generate changes in art forms, the attitudes to them, and the values about them? What of the relationship of production to authenticity, to skill, to materials and techniques, and to the models used? What is ephemeral, and what persists and why? What is the effect of economics on production? Does economics determine the benefits of tourism for local peoples? Is it a form of neocolonialism (Crick 1989:319) that people have to bend their ways to decoy and allure the visitor, tempting their tastes with forms that, in consequence, have to be adjusted? How far does tourism really benefit a country and alleviate the inequality between 'tourist-generating and tourist-destination countries'? (Crick 1989: 321).

But perhaps it is an error to think of tourism as a blanket phenomenon affecting Pacific cultures in similar ways, and to think of tourist arts in a similar fashion. For one thing, there are different kinds of tourism functioning in the Pacific and having different effects: these one might distinguish as ecotourism, art tourism and cultural tourism. The West still incongruously exploits the environment of others with its expedition and discovery cruises: 'Polynesia and Peru ... follow "Mutiny and Mystery" ... take the "Passage to Paradise"' (Royal Viking Line); 'The Lure of the South Seas. Follow in the footsteps of Captain James Cook, Robert Falcon Scott and Ferdinand Magellan (But we live to tell the tale)' (Society Expeditions);

and 'An astonishing and colourful voyage to the islands of the South Pacific on the expedition ship *World Discoverer*. 10% of each cruise fare will be donated to the Easter Island Foundation' (Easter Island Foundation). Such visits are encouragement to displays and sales of cash-crop art, and abbreviated performances that give tourists the instant gratification they expect from cultural pursuits.

The changes that beset the Pacific and its peoples have not always been triggered by outsiders from the West. Schmid's botanical ethnography of the Nokopo people (1991:291) exemplifies some of the effects Papua New Guinea peoples have had on their own environment: 'Nokopo people (of Madang and Morobe Provinces) have probably never lived in harmony with nature, as is sometimes claimed for traditional Papua New Guinea cultures or "primitive" non-Western cultures in general.' The Maori had a considerable hand in changing the fauna and flora of New Zealand before the Europeans had a go, and Sinoto's excavations in Oahu in 1976 revealed evidence of the extinction of forty species of birds before the arrival of Europeans: 'These discoveries have not gone down well with native Hawaiians anxious to maintain the myth of the Polynesians as guardians of Paradise' (Mitchell 1990: 194). The Easter Islanders almost eliminated themselves from their volcanic island (Bahn and Flenley 1992).

Paradise is still fragile. At the 22nd South Pacific Forum in Pohnpei, representatives attacked

> driftnetting, French nuclear testing … toxic, hazardous and radioactive waste dumping proposals, U.S. chemical munitions destruction at Johnston Atoll, industrial carbon dioxide emissions which cause global warming and sea-level rise, and environmentally unsound farming, mining and logging practices. [*Washington Pacific Report* 1991]

Under the cloud of apparent gloom cast by the contemporary scene in the Pacific, some Pacific Islanders are seeking their lost heritage as a means of facing the future. Others feel that the effects of changes in their material world are so strong that their arts will no longer persist. In Hawai'i, Rocky Jensen (1990) wrote:

> The art that was Polynesian is very dear to me. The fact that it is quickly mutating into something unrecognizable

is a painful thing to witness, especially when the mutation was never properly understood in the first place.

He decried the lack of art:

> We have virtually nothing to set up to ignite the minds of the young. Nothing established to teach, explain or share in the knowledge of our ancient sculptors … We are a society of knick-knacks.

And from Papua New Guinea John Kolia (1989:69) felt that 'It is hard to see how the destruction of the material past can be prevented in the face of the overwhelming import of foreign artefacts and styles.'

But surely the performing arts, so vital, will prevail and flourish. Yet for those pursuing the study of the visual arts of the Pacific it is important to identify contemporary happenings and trends, to look at past arts where they are continuing, at the attempts of artists and craftsmen to meet economic needs by various sorties into 'applied arts', and at the reactions of those artists trying to find satisfactory means of expressing the contemporary scene of Western culture impacting on their own local one. These trends will picture tomorrow's history of Pacific art.

Notes

1. Called 'Adelaide' by the first white colonists.
2. Teilhet-Fisk (1992:45) quotes Drew Havea, in reference to waist mats: 'I don't look at the *ta'ovala* as an art form. We don't have a word for art. I look at it as to what status or position that particular *ta'ovala* represents … to identify us with a status or social occasion so our society knows what is going on.'
3. See Dark (1974: ill. 176) for a solo dancer imitating *saumoy*, though this was not the occasion referred to in the text, which occurred the year before.
4. This occurred in a version of *agosang*, not performed for a very long time, to the best of my knowledge (see Dark 1974: ills 163-4, 168; 1984:21-3).
5. The dancing of *nausung* on another occasion is illustrated in Dark (1974: ills 74-5). For a complete narration and performance the reader should look at Adrian Gerbrands' excellent 1975 film *Nausung Masks: Performance,* produced and distributed by Stichting Film en Wetenschap, Utrecht.

6. Cf. the work of Tekiraua Urio of Kiribati and his decoration of graves, referred to in Dark (1983a:26; 1990:265).

7. For similar treatment of Christian and Kilenge symbols, see Dark (1990: fig. 18.19).

8. Parliament House is illustrated in Sinclair (1985:126, 149) and the bank building in Simons and Stevenson (1990:36).

9. See also Megaw (1986, 1990); Megaw and Megaw (1993); Ebes and Hollow (1992).

10. See Simons and Stevenson (1990:50ff.) for Kauage's *Helicopter* and other works.

11. See Michoutouchkine (n.d.) for Pilioko, and Douglas (1991) for illustrations of paintings by John Joseph and Juliette Pita.

12. John Kolia (1989:69) rates Joseph Nalo as perhaps the first artist 'who has made an individual breakthrough'. An example of the retention yet remarkable development of a native style is the work of Bill Reid, the distinguished Haida artist (Duffek 1986; Bringhurst and Steltzer 1991).

13. For example, Ebes and Hollow (1992) and 'Australiana' in *Pacific Arts* (1, 2:67-72; 3:29-52) the latter of which includes a number of illustrations.

14. These include Kay George, Claire Higham, Doreen Mellors, Jillian Sobieski, Mike Tavioni, Judith Kunzle, and Ian George.

15. One of these books, *Manakonako: Reflections* by Kauraka Kauraka, was reviewed by Peter Gathercole (1993).

16. A photograph taken by Siers (1977:71) shows the Centre well stocked with locally made crafts and a large carved Tino figure from Nukuoro, Micronesia.

17. See also *Pacific Arts* (5:62).

18. See Muller (1990:135, 139) for two small Asmat shields consistent with Schneebaum's observations.

Contributors

Christopher Anderson is Director of the South Australian Museum in Adelaide. Born in Philadelphia, he has worked as an anthropologist in Australia since 1976. He obtained his PhD in anthropology from the University of Queensland in 1984, based on fieldwork in the tropical north of Australia, studying changes in the political economy of rainforest Aboriginal peoples. Since 1985, Anderson has worked in the deserts of Central Australia on Aboriginal religion and art. An outcome of this was the successful exhibition 'Dreamings', which toured the United States in 1988-89. Anderson's main publications are in the areas of Aboriginal art, Aboriginal history and traditional economy. He is also a specialist in repatriation-related issues, and relations between museums and indigenous peoples. A recent major work is an edited *Oceania* Monograph, *Politics of the Secret* (1995), which examines indigenous Australian secret/sacred objects and their situation in museum and non-museum contexts.

Harry Beran is Senior Lecturer in Philosophy at the University of Wollongong, NSW. After a visit to the Trobriand Islands in 1969, he started collecting and later researching the art of the Massim region of Papua New Guinea. He has made a number of short study visits to the region, and is building a modest resource centre on Massim art. His publications include *Art of the Massim Region of Papua New Guinea* (1980), *Betel-chewing Equipment of East New Guinea* (1988) and *Mutuaga: A Nineteenth-Century New Guinea Master Carver* (1996). He is Foundation President of the Oceanic Art Society, and has curated an exhibition *Oceanic and Indonesian Art: Collectors' Choice* for the society, shown in Sydney July-August 1998; he edited the exhibition catalogue.

Wendi Choulai was born in Wau, Morobe Province, Papua New Guinea, and grew up among her mother's clan in Port Moresby and Central Province. In 1986 she was the first female graduate in Textile Design from the PNG National Arts School, and gained her MA in Textile Design from the Royal Melbourne Institute of Technology in Australia in 1997. She has represented PNG as a textile designer at the Commonwealth Arts Festival in Edinburgh and ESCAP workshop for women in Thailand, exhibited at the Asia Pacific Triennial (Queensland Art Gallery, 1996), and has presented papers to symposia such as the Third Australian Print Symposium (National Gallery of Australia, Canberra, 1997) and the Royal Society of Victoria (Museum of Victoria, 1997). She is interested in showing a meaningful connection between traditional and contemporary design, and demonstrating that contemporary art such as that expressed in her textile design does not have to break with tradition, but can emanate from, and even give added meaning to, ritual.

Susan Cochrane spent eighteen years in Papua New Guinea where her father was a senior government officer in radio broadcasting and her mother was a writer/filmmaker. Cochrane retained her interest in Papua New Guinea and in 1980 decided to study in the area of contemporary indigenous art and cultures, particularly to work with artists of Papua New Guinea and Aboriginal Australia. She gained her MA (Hons) in Art History and her PhD at the University of Wollongong. She is Director of Pacificlink Arts Consultants, and operates as a freelance researcher and curator. She recently completed a consultancy as Head of the Department of Contemporary Kanak and Pacific Art for the Centre Culturel Tjibaou in New Caledonia, where the establishment of a major collection of contemporary Pacific art is a priority. She has published *Contemporary Art in Papua New Guinea* (1997) and is completing the editing of *Aboriginal Art in Australian Museums*. She writes for art journals on contemporary indigenous art, and has curated a number of significant exhibitions of contemporary Pacific and Aboriginal art, including *Luk Luk Gen! Look Again! Contemporary Art from Papua New Guinea* (1990).

Barry Craig obtained his BA (Hons, Anthropology), Dip. Ed. and MA (Hons, Anthropology) at the University of Sydney. His interest in material culture and art of New Guinea was inspired by Bryan Cranstone of the British Museum, and continued with several ethnographic surveys and collecting expeditions in central New Guinea and the upper Sepik in 1964, 1967, 1968, 1969 and 1972-73. His 1969 master's thesis, Houseboards and Warshields of the Mountain-Ok, was published in summary form as *Art and Decoration of Central New Guinea* (1988). Some results from his 1972-3 fieldwork, *Legends of the Amto* and *Legends of the Abau* were published in two issues of *Oral History* (Vol. 8, Nos 4,5) in 1980. In 1980-83 he was Curator of Anthropology at the PNG National Museum, and was appointed Curator of Foreign Ethnology at the South Australian Museum in 1995. In this capacity he is researching and extending the documentation of significant Pacific and African collections, and is planning the refurbishment of the museum's Pacific Gallery. In 1997 he was awarded a PhD in Visual Arts at Flinders University for his thesis

on the collection, documentation and preservation of the material cultural heritage of Papua New Guinea.

Brenda L Croft, of the Kurindji nation, Northern Territory, is an independent curator, artist and writer based in Sydney. Croft was a founding member of Boomalli Aboriginal Artists Co-operative, Sydney, and its General Manager (formerly Co-ordinator) from 1990 to 1996. Croft has a Master of Art Administration from the College of Fine Arts, University of New South Wales. Croft has organised and co-curated exhibitions at regional, national and international levels. Croft's work as an artist encompasses mixed-media installation with a focus on photography, audio, scent, painting and memory. Her work, held in state and federal public collections, has officially represented Australia in 'The Boundary Rider', 9th Biennale of Sydney 1992-93, and the inaugural 'Africus', Johannesburg Biennale, 1995. She has been awarded international residencies including the Australia Council Greene Street Studio, New York, 1996-97; Chicago Artists International Artists Program, 1996; and Banff Center for the Arts, Canada, 1993. Croft's work has been written about in national and international arts magazines, journals and books. As an author, she has written articles and essays for numerous books and national arts publications. Croft has participated as a guest lecturer at national and international tertiary institutions, forums and panels.

Philip J.C. Dark is Emeritus Professor of Anthropology at Southern Illinois University, Carbondale. He holds a diploma from the Slade School of Fine Art, University of London, and an MA and PhD from Yale University. His field research was conducted in West Africa, Irian Jaya, Papua New Guinea, Micronesia, and the central Pacific. Among his publications on Oceanic art are *Kilenge Art and Life: A Look at a New Guinea People* (1974) and contributions to each of the publications (1979, 1983, 1990, 1993) arising from Pacific Arts Symposia, including the editing of, and a paper for, *Development of the Arts in the Pacific* (1984). From 1975 to 1989, Dark has been editor of *Pacific Arts Newsletter*, and of *Pacific Arts* from 1990.

He was awarded the Manu Daula Frigate Bird Award by the Pacific Arts Association in 1984.

Soroi Eoe was born in Horevavo village, eastern Gulf Province, PNG. He received his BA at the University of PNG in 1978, majoring in Anthropology. He immediately commenced employment at the PNG National Museum as Assistant Research Officer, was promoted to Assistant Curator of Anthropology in 1979 and to Curator of Anthropology in 1983. Since 1986 he has been Director of the National Museum. His major fieldwork, during 1978-79, was carried out in the middle and lower Ramu River, Madang Province. During the early 1980s he carried out several field surveys in the Sepik River area, in 1983 he did three months research in Gulf Province, and in 1996 he spent three months in Central Province studying *hiri* trade objects. Eoe has represented PNG at UNESCO General Assemblies, is a member of the National Committee of ICOM, and of the International Advisory Committee for the Jean-Marie Tjibaou Cultural Centre in New Caledonia, and is current President of the PAA.

Roderick Ewins is a practising artist and a sociologist. He is an Honorary Research Associate of the School of Art at the University of Tasmania, from which he retired recently as Associate Professor and Head of Department. In addition to his art practice and exhibition, and research and writing about art and education, for eighteen years he has been conducting research and undertaking regular field work concerning the indigenous art of his home country, Fiji. In addition to short papers, book-review articles, and a video on Fijian ceramics, his most notable publications are the books *Fijian Artefacts* and *Matweaving in Gau, Fiji* (both 1982), and the art-and-prehistory paper 'Proto-Polynesian Art? The Cliff-paintings of Vatulele, Fiji' (*Journal of the Polynesian Society* 1995, 104(1):23-74). Current research concerns the use in Fiji of art and ritual as devices for indigenous identity construction and the mitigation of externally imposed change.

Deane Fergie is Lecturer in Anthropology at the University of Adelaide. Trained at the University of Papua New Guinea, Australian National University and the University of Adelaide (where she was awarded a PhD), she has undertaken ethnographic fieldwork in island and coastal Melanesia (of note here a detailed study of the corpus of public ritual of the Tabar Islands, New Ireland Province, PNG) and Australia (particularly the complex communities of the Marree-Birdsville Track district). The analysis of cultural practices and media by which people 'come to know' forms an enduring thread through Deane Fergie's research and publications. Reflecting this problematic, her publications range from analyses of the cultural significance of manners, to makeup and the cultural construction of gender in contemporary Australia, ritual performance, prophecy, and popular representations. She has also engaged in public debate about national identity and heritage protection in Australia. The paper published in this volume presents ideas that have developed into 'the North Terrace Precinct Research Project' under whose critical gaze the premier institutions of public pedagogy and governmentality in Adelaide have come.

Juno Gemes, born in Budapest, is an artist who combines a background in multimedia and cross-cultural arts with her career as a photographer since 1969. In 1978 she received a grant from the Arts Council of Great Britain to attend the Oxford Photographic Workshop with Aaron Siskind, and in 1979 participated in *Incontri Personali* with Lisette Model at la Fotografia, the International Center for Photography in Venice. She has had seven one-woman exhibitions, including 'Under Another Sky' at the Australian Embassy in Paris, and at the Muscarnok, Budapest. During the 1980s she established the Camera Futura photography studio, was a member of the Australian Journalists Association Freelance Committee, and Arts Editor of Paper Bark Press, Brooklyn, NSW. She has worked extensively with Aboriginal communities, and in 1994 was awarded a fellowship by the Australian Institute of Aboriginal and Torres Strait Islander Studies to document her photographic archive, *In Our Time: Photographs and Texts from the Movement 1969-1995*. Her latest major project was *The Language of Oysters – Poems by Robert Adamson, Photographs by Juno Gemes*, published by Craftsman House, launched at the Sydney Writers Festival in January 1997 and Australia House, London, in June 1997.

Michael Gunn is Associate Curator of Oceanic Art at the Metropolitan Museum of Art, New York, where he has worked since 1994. Previously he was Curator of Oceanic Art and Archaeology at the Northern Territory Museum in Darwin, Australia. He received an MA and PhD from the University of Otago, New Zealand. His field research has focussed primarily on the art traditions of Tabar Islands in New Ireland Province, Papua New Guinea. He has also worked with the Yali of the highlands region of Irian Jaya, on Pulau Atauro in the eastern archipelago region of Indonesia, and in the settlement of Balgo in the Great Sandy Desert of Western Australia. His publications include *Ritual Arts of Oceania: New Ireland* (1997).

Vilsoni Hereniko is Associate Professor of Pacific Studies at the Center for Pacific Islands, University of Hawai'i. Originally from Rotuma, he was educated in Fiji, England and the United States. His latest book, *Woven Gods: Female Clowns and Power in Rotuma*, was published by the University of Hawai'i Press in 1995. His latest play, *Fine Dancing*, was produced on Magic Island Beach, Honolulu, in 1997 by the Network for the Promotion of Asia Pacific Cinema. He is currently working on a screenplay.

Christopher Issac is Principal Research Officer of Cultural Services Development, National Cultural Commission, Papua New Guinea. He worked previously with the Anthropology Department of the PNG National Museum and Art Gallery as a Collection Manager from 1979 until 1990, transferring to the J.K. McCarthy Museum in Goroka, Eastern Highlands, where he worked as a research officer until 1996. In 1989 he did several months work experience in the National Museum of Australia, Canberra, and the South Australian Museum, Adelaide. In 1990 he was sponsored by the Australian government and a UNESCO grant to assist with the documentation of the Melanesian collections of the National Museum of Australia, and gained further experience in the South Australian Museum. His research has focused on the masks of his people, the Sulka

of Wide Bay, East New Britain Province. He has also researched the *iniet* figures of the Gazelle Peninsula, and the material culture of the Herowana, carried out a survey of handcrafts of the New Guinea islands and of culturally significant sites in the Eastern Highlands, and worked with cultural-historical photographs of the Eastern Highlands. Currently he is researching the relationships and economic benefits involved in the buying and selling of betel nut, and assisting with research for a film on the making of clay pots at Yabob, Madang Province.

Bernie Kernot recently retired from Victoria University of Wellington, where he taught anthropology and Maori studies for thirty years, and where he retains an honorary research associateship. After graduating MA from Auckland University in 1963, he spent nearly four years teaching at Ngata Memorial College, Ruatoria, in the heartland of the Ngati Porou people. While there he came under the influence of the great Ngati Porou master-carver Pine Taiapa. His long interest in Maori art dates from this association. He has published widely on Maori politics, art and religion. In 1972 he published the monograph *People of the Four Winds*. With S.M. Mead he edited the papers from the second PAA international symposium under the title *Art and Artists of Oceania* (1983).

Junko Konishi, who teaches ethnomusicology at Osaka College of Music and Kobe Yamate Women's College, received her BA from Osaka College of Music, her MA from Kyoto City University of Arts, and recently her Doctor of Letters from Osaka University. Her dissertation, Voices from the island of Stone Money: An ethnography of music history in Yap (in Japanese with English summary), dealt with dance and music in Yap from 1985 to 1993 and previous written and recorded materials, referring to their cultural and historical context and challenging the authority of the researcher/writer. Her research interests include the popular music that emerged on Yap in the 1930s under Japanese influence, as well as 'traditional' dance, music and soundscape.

Jacquelyn Lewis-Harris was until recently the assistant curator of the arts of Africa, Oceania and the Americas at the St Louis Art Museum, Missouri, and is now Director of the Center of Human Origins and Cultural Diversity at the University of Missouri, St Louis. She received her BFA from St Mary's College, Notre Dame, Indiana, and her MA in anthropology from Washington University, St Louis, where she is presently completing her dissertation research on Papua New Guinean artists in Australia. She spent six years in Papua New Guinea as an art consultant and exhibition developer, working with the National Museum and Art Gallery of Papua New Guinea. Her previous work included two years in Liberia, West Africa, as an art-and-crafts consultant and university lecturer. She has developed exhibits in Papua New Guinea, Canada, and the United States. She has published and lectured widely on several areas of art from the Pacific, Africa and the Americas, with an emphasis on Australia and the Pacific. Her most recent exhibitions include, *Art of the Papuan Gulf, Ceramic Gestures: New Vessels by Magdalene Odundo*, and *Art of the Brazilian Rainforest*.

Noah Lurang is from Tabar Island, New Ireland Province, Papua New Guinea. He received his Teachers Certificate in 1968 and commenced high-school teaching. He studied Public Administration at the University of PNG for a year in 1986, and participated in a Tourism Executive Development Program in 1996. Since the early 1990s he has been employed by the New Ireland Provincial Government, initially as a Youth Coordinator and then as a Culture and Tourism Coordinator. His tasks have included activities aimed at cultural preservation and tourism promotion. Currently he is developing an integrated plan for a Provincial Museum and Cultural Centre for Kavieng, New Ireland.

J.V.S. (Vincent) Megaw is currently Professor of Visual Arts and Archaeology in the School of Humanities of Flinders University in Adelaide. Trained in Prehistoric Archaeology and Fine Art at the University of Edinburgh, in 1961 Vincent Megaw moved to the University of Sydney, where he was successively Lecturer and Senior Lecturer in European Archaeology before being appointed in 1972 Professor and Head of the Department of Archaeology

at the University of Leicester. In 1981 he began teaching at Flinders University where, together with his wife Dr M. Ruth Megaw, he continued to develop an interest in the culture, past and present, of indigenous Australians, which had been engendered during the 1960s. Vincent Megaw has published some 200 books and papers, many in conjunction with his wife, among which are (with Michael Greenhalgh) *Art in Society: Studies in Style, Culture and Aesthetics* (1978) and (with Jane Hardy and M. Ruth Megaw) *The Heritage of Namatjira: The Watercolourists of Central Australia* (1992). In 1992 he was awarded a DLitt by the University of Edinburgh in recognition of his contributions to the study of early Celtic art.

M. Ruth Megaw read history at the University of Glasgow, where she obtained an MA with First Class Honours. Subsequently she joined the United Kingdom Diplomatic Service. Moving to Sydney in 1961 with her husband, Vincent Megaw, she first took a PhD in American-Australian cultural, economic and political relations, after which she taught American History at the universities of NSW and Sydney. Returning to England in 1972, she became Senior Lecturer and Head of American Studies at the Nene College, Northampton. Since settling in Adelaide in 1984, Ruth Megaw has been instrumental in devising the first university courses in Australia to be devoted to indigenous Australian art. She has collaborated with Vincent Megaw in writing on the pre-Roman Celtic art of Europe, and on aspects of contemporary indigenous art.

Regina Meredith (Malala), after receiving her Master of Fine Arts degree from San Diego State University in California in 1988, returned home to American Samoa to teach. She is currently teaching at the American Samoa Community College, and is the Department Chairperson for the Fine Arts Division. Some of her endeavors include being highlighted in *The Samoan Heart*, a twenty-seven-minute video from the Pacific Diaries series by the Pacific Islanders in Communications for the Public Broadcasting System, and illustrator for the *Samoan Word Book* by Aumua Matatusi and Fata Simanu Klutz (Bess Press, Honolulu).

Nancy Pollock teaches Anthropology at Victoria University of Wellington, with special interests in gender issues, development anthropology, and Pacific society and culture. Her research has focused on various aspects of the anthropology of health, beginning with food, diet and nutrition, leading to concerns of food security, alongside conceptualisations of the body from various cultural perspectives. She has published widely in these areas; for example, *These Roots Remain* (1992) as the background to food habits in the Pacific, and *Social Aspects of Obesity*, which she co-edited with Igor de Garine. *The Power of Kava*, a *Canberra Anthropology* special number, was edited by her to bring forward papers on Kava rituals in the central and eastern Pacific. The body in both gendered and cultured perspectives is thus a theme that cuts across much of her research. She has worked in various islands of Micronesia and Polynesia, including Wallis and Futuna, as well as Nauru. Her main field work has been in the Marshall Islands over a twenty-five-year period.

Max Quanchi is Senior Lecturer in the School of Humanities at Queensland University of Technology in Brisbane, Australia. He holds a TTPC, BA (Hons) and MA from Monash University, and a PhD from the University of Queensland. His research on photography is concentrated on illustrated newspapers and magazines, colonial propaganda, the portrayal of pastors in missionary photography, and the wider imaging of 'Papua' in the period up to 1930. He is also writing on the photographer Thomas McMahon's work in the Pacific in the 1920s. He edited *Photography, Imaging and Representation*, a special issue of the journal *Pacific Studies* (1998) and wrote of several articles and textbooks on Pacific and Australian South Sea Islander history. He teaches Pacific history in Brisbane, is joint coordinator of a five-year regional teaching project on Pacific Islands history, is co-editor of the *Newsletter of the Pacific History Association*, and was joint convenor of the 1998 PHA conference in Honiara, Solomon Islands.

Héléna Regius has been studying Melanesian ethnographic collections since 1992 as an affiliated researcher at the National Museum of Ethnography in Stockholm, Sweden. She has a BA in Social Anthropology and Museology, and a BFA in Sculpture, from Stockholm University. She also has a Diploma in Textile Art from the National Arts School in Papua New Guinea, and an MA in the Anthropology of Art from the Sainsbury Research Unit, University of East Anglia. She is presently completing a PhD in Social Anthropology at the University of Cambridge, based on two years of field research on the Willaumez Peninsula of West New Britain, Papua New Guinea. A German research grant enabled her to work at the Museum für Völkerkunde, Berlin, in preparation for this research. Her thesis concerns visual expression of culture in the interface of traditional culture and the Catholic Church.

Dirk Smidt is Curator of the Department of Oceania at the Rijksmuseum voor Volkenkunde in Leiden. He graduated from the University of Leiden, where he studied Anthropology, specialising in the art of New Guinea. From 1970 to 1980 he held several positions at the National Museum and Art Gallery in Port Moresby, Papua New Guinea. He has undertaken field work in various areas of New Guinea, especially among the Kominimung and neighbouring peoples in the Middle Ramu River region, the Abelam (Papua New Guinea), and the Asmat (Irian Jaya). He has published articles in all the symposium volumes of the Pacific Arts Association: 'Establishing Museums in Developing Countries' (1979); 'Kominimung Shields' (1983); 'Kominimung One-legged Figures' (1990), and, with Noel McGuigan, 'An Emic and Etic Role for Abelam Art' (1993). He edited *Asmat Art* (1993), with Pieter ter Keurs, *The Language of Things* (1990), and, with Pieter ter Keurs and Albert Trouwborst, *Pacific Material Culture* (1995). His most recent publications include 'Neue Entwicklungen in der Kunst der Asmat und ihre Darstellung in Museen' (1995) and several contributions in *The Object as Mediator: On the Transcendental Meaning of Art in Traditional Cultures* (1996).

John E. Stanton has extensive experience and involvement in the area of Aboriginal arts, which he has developed primarily since his appointment in 1980 as Curator of the Anthropology Research Museum (renamed Berndt Museum of Anthropology in 1992). His research includes field work among fringe-dwelling Aboriginal groups in south-western New South Wales in 1971, resulting in an MA in Social Anthropology. In 1974 he transferred to Perth to commence a PhD focusing on aspects of social change in a small Aboriginal community on the fringe of the Western Desert. Since his museum appointment, he has collaborated in several publications with R.M. and C.H. Berndt, and mounted five major exhibitions. His research since 1985 in thc Kimberley region of north-west Western Australia and in the south-west of that state has assisted Aboriginal communities to establish local Keeping Places and Cultural Centres. This involved the training of Aboriginal people in curatorial and exhibition techniques, and oral-history recording. Several other projects are being developed in collaboration with members of other Aboriginal communities, urban and remote, as part of the long-term research, teaching and public-relations activities of the Berndt Museum of Anthropology at the University of Western Australia.

Karen Stevensen is Lecturer in Pacific Arts at the University of Canterbury, Christchurch, New Zealand. She received her PhD in Oceanic Art History from the University of California at Los Angeles in 1988. Since then she has been a Rockefeller Fellow at the Center for Pacific Studies at the University of Hawai'i and a Mellon Research Fellow in association with the St Louis Art Museum. Her writings and research have focused on the politicisation and institutionalisation of art and culture, art and identity, Pacific Islanders in film, and the Festival of Pacific Arts. Currently she is working in the area of contemporary art, particularly art production stemming from the urban Pacific phenomenon in New Zealand.

Gabor Vargyas is Senior Research Fellow at the Institute of Ethnology, Hungarian Academy of Sciences, and (part time) Associate Professor of Anthropology at the Department of Ethnology, Janus Pannonius University, Pécs, Hungary. He received his Diploma and PhD at the Loránd Eötvös University, Budapest. From 1979 to 1984 he was Curator for Pacific Collections at the Ethnographic Museum, Budapest. In his unpublished PhD dissertation he dealt with the Massim collections (assembled by, among others, the Hungarian psychoanalytical anthropologist Géza Róheim) of that museum. As a museum anthropologist, Vargyas focused mainly on material culture and art, but also on the colonial history of, and history of ethnographic research in, New Guinea and related areas. In 1981-82, Vargyas made a three-month trip in New Guinea, visiting the places from where the Ethnographic Museum of Budapest's collections originated. His publications include a volume about colonial life in German New Guinea based on the popular writings of Lajos Bíró, a Hungarian naturalist and ethnographer at the turn of the century, and another about the role of the Hungarian geologist H.von Bandat, in the first international petroleum searching expedition in Western New Guinea. A third consists of his 1982 field notes from Astrolabe Bay, Madang Province. Since 1985, he has been conducting intensive field research in the social structure, religion and oral history of a Mon-Khmer speaking 'Montagnard' group, the Bru (Van Kieu), of the Central Vietnamese Highlands.

References

Introduction (Craig)

Bertani, P. 1993. The Message Sticks. '88 and Beyond. *Meanjin.* 52(4):703-4a.

Brook, D. 1977. *The Social Role of Art.* Adelaide: Experimental Art Foundation.

Chance, I., and P. Zepplin. 1993. Cannibal Cultures: The (Un)making of the Modern Museum. *Broadsheet.* 22(2): 12, 13.

Choulai, W. 1996. Art and Ritual: Aina Asi a Mavaru Kavamu. *Artlink.* 16(4):46.

Craig, B. 1993. Letters: Cannibal Critics. *Broadsheet.* 22(4):12

———. 1995. Following the tracks of Edgar Waite in New Guinea for the Pacific Arts Symposium in Adelaide. *Records of the South Australian Museum.* 28(1):33-52.

Dutton, D. 1994. Authenticity in the Art of Traditional Societies. *Pacific Arts.* 9 & 10:1-9.

———. 1995a. Mythologies of Tribal Art. *African Arts* 28(3):33-43, 90-1

———. 1995b. Review of J. Weiner (ed.) 1994. Aesthetics is a Cross-cultural Category. *Pacific Arts.* 11 & 12:139-41.

Fergie, D. 1994. Letters: The cost of curiosity cabinets. *Broadsheet.* 23(1):8.

Forge, A. 1966. Art and Environment in the Sepik. *Proceedings of the Royal Anthropological Institute of Great Britain and Ireland for 1965.* pp. 23-31.

Gemes, Juno. 1993. 'Money is not Time'. *Meanjin.* 52(4): 704a-4b.

Hereniko, V. 1994. Clowning as Political Commentary. Polynesia: Then and Now. *The Contemporary Pacific.* 6(1):1-28.

Levi-Strauss, C. 1950. 'Introduction' in *Sociologie et anthropologie.* Marcel Mauss. Paris: Presses Universitaires de France. pp. ix-lii.

Megaw, R., and V. Megaw. 1993. Pacific Encounters. Visual Arts Exhibitions and the Fifth Pacific Arts Association Symposium. *Artlink* 13(2):74-6.

Schwimmer, E. 1990. 'The anthropology of the ritual arts' in *Art and Identity in Oceania.* Edited by A. Hanson and L. Hanson. Honolulu: University of Hawai'i Press. pp. 5-14.

Stevenson, K. 1996. Polynesian Tattoo: A Shift in Meaning. *Artlink.* 16(4):32-3.

Weiner, J. (ed.). 1994. *Aesthetics Is a Cross-cultural Category.* Manchester: Group for Debates in Anthropological Theory.

Zepplin, P. 1993. Pacific Arts Symposium. *Art and Asia Pacific.* 1(1):15-18.

PART I (Kernot)

Kaeppler, A. 1989. 'Art and Aesthetics' in *Developments in Polynesian Ethnography.* Edited by Alan Howard and Robert Borofsky. Honolulu: University of Hawai'i Press. pp. 211-39.

Chapter I (Konishi)

Anefal, Sebastian L. n.d. Walathol. *Kakrom* (Yap High School eds). pp. 51-66.

Born, L. 1903. Einige Bemerkungen über Musik, Dichtkunst und Tanz der Yapleute. *Zeitschrift für Ethnologie* 35:134-142. Berlin: Verlag von A. Asher and Co. HRAF (Human Relations Area Files, as set forth in 1963 by George Peter Murdock's *Outline of World Cultures*) OR22-17.

Brooks, Jean. 1988. Ours is the dance – a source and demonstration of power on the island of Yap in the Caroline Islands of Micronesia. MA thesis. University of Victoria.

Crowe, Peter. 1990. Dancing backwards? *World of Music.* xxxii(1):84-98.

Feld, Steven. 1987. Dialogic editing: Interpreting how Kaluli read sound and sentiment. *Cultural Anthropology.* 2(2): 190-210.

Furness, William Henry. 1910. *The Island of Stone Money: Uap of the Carolines.* Philadelphia and London: J.B. Lippincott Company. HRAF OR22-10.

Iwata, Junko. 1985. An anthropological study of Yapese music. BA dissertation (in Japanese).

———. 1987. Dance performances in Yap: Their occasions and musical aspects. *Music Research.* 5:95-113. (In Japanese, summary in English.)

Jensen, John Thayer. 1977. *Yapese-English Dictionary.* Honolulu: University Press of Hawai'i.

Kaeppler, Adrienne L. 1971. Aesthetics of Tongan Dance. *Ethnomusicology.* 15(2):175-85.

———. 1992. Epilogue: states of the arts. *Pacific Studies.* 15(4):311-18.

Kennedy, Raymond F. 1980. 'Dance and music in Chamorro' in *The New Grove Dictionary of Music and Musicians.* Edited by Stanley Sadie. Micronesia 4. Mariana Islands (i). London: Macmillan. p. 277.

Kiener, Robert. 1978. Yap between the Lines. *Glimpses of Micronesia and the Western Pacific.* 18(2):31-5.

Konishi, Junko. 1995a. Wavy melodies are new but old: A study of Yapese popular songs from the 1930s-1990s. Paper presented at the 33rd World Conference, International Council for Traditional Music, Canberra, Australia.

———. 1995b. Reconsideration of earlier recordings: A case study of Yapese songs recorded by Muranushi in 1936. Paper presented at the meeting of the Study Group on Music of Oceania, International Council for Traditional Music, Canberra, Australia.

———. In press. 'A common feature in the vocal style of traditional and popular female songs in Yap, Federated States of Micronesia' in *Dynamics of Asian Music-Tradition and its Modification* (tentative title). Asian-Pacific Society for Ethnomusicology.

Labby, D. 1976. *The Demystification of Yap: Dialectics of Culture on a Micronesian Island.* Chicago: Chicago University Press.

Lawson, Mary Elizabeth. 1989. Tradition, change and meaning in Kiribati performance: An ethnography of music and dance in a Micronesian society. PhD thesis, Brown University.

Lingenfelter, S. 1975. *Yap: Political Leadership and Culture Change in an Island Society.* Honolulu: University of Hawai'i Press.

Marshall, Deidre P. 1994. Change and loss in Yapese musical culture: A study of the impact of colonial and Micronesian cultures on the music and musical life of Yap Islands (Micronesia) from 1903 to 1993, with special references to the genres of *tang* and *churu.* MA thesis, Monash University, Melbourne, Australia.

McKnight, Robert Kellog. 1968. Proverbs of Palau. *Journal of American Folklore.* 81(1):1-33.

Montes de Oca, José. 1893. Carolinas Occidentales. *La Isla de Yap sociedad Geigráfica de Madrid.* Boletin 34:251-79. HRAF OR22-15.

Müller, Wilhelm. 1917. *Yap.* Hamburgische Wissenschaftliche Stiftung, Ergebnisse der Expedition 1908-1910, II. Ethnofraphie: B. Mikronesien, Vol. 2, HRAF-Vol. 1. Hamburg: L. Friederichsen & Co. HRAF OR22-6.

Pinsker, Eve C. 1992. Celebrations of government: Dance performance and legitimacy in the Federated States of Micronesia. *Pacific Studies.* 15(4):29-56.

Senfft, Arno. 1903. Ethnographische Beiträge über die Karolineninsel Yap. *Petermanns Mitteilungen.* 49:49-60, 83-7. Gotha, Justus Perthes' Geographischer Anstalt. HRAF OR22-5.

Smith, Barbara B. 1980. 'Yap Islands' in *The New Grove Dictionary of Music and Musicians.* Edited by Stanley Sadie. Vol. 12. London: Macmillan. p. 275.

Strathern, Andrew. 1995. Chant and spell: Sonemic contrasts in a Melpa ritual sequence. *Ethnomusicology.* 39(2):219-27.

Tambiah, Stanley J. 1968. The magical power of words. *Man.* 3(NS):175-203.

Tatar, Elizabeth (ed.). 1985. *Call of the Morning Bird: Chants and songs of Palau, Yap, and Ponape, collected by Iwakichi*

Muranushi, 1936. Honolulu: Anthropology Department, Bernice Pauahi Bishop Museum.

Ushijima, Iwao. 1982. Yap tô no dentôteki shakai kôzô to son'rakukan no kairo; Fanif kan'ku o chûshin ni. (The traditional social structure and communication system between villages in Yap island). *Mikuronesia no bun'kajinruigakuteki kenkyû; nishi karolin no gengo, shakai, sen'shi bunka.* Tokyo: Kokusho Kankô-kai. pp. 39-108. (In Japanese.)

———. 1987. *Yap tô no shakai to koukan* (Society and Change in Yap Island). Tokyo: Kôbundô. (In Japanese.)

Volkens, G. 1901. Über die Karolinen-Insel Yap. *Verhandlungen der Gesellschaft für Erdkunde zu Berlin.* Vol. 28. Berlin: W.H. Kuhl. HRAF OR22-14. pp. 62-76.

Yamaguti (Yamaguchi), Osamu. 1986. Music of Belau (Palau) in the 1860s – An historical observation based on a verbal description by a cultural outsider and non music-specialist. *Shominzoku no oto.* 577-589. (In Japanese, summary in English.)

Chapter 2 (Hereniko)

Andersen, Johannes C. 1969. *Myths and Legends of the Polynesians.* Rutland: Charles E. Tuttle Company.

Angas, F.L.S. 1866. *Polynesia: A Popular Description of the Islands of the Pacific.* London: Society for the Promotion of Christian Knowledge.

Arno, Andrew. 1992. *The World is Talk: Conflict and Communication on a Fijian Island.* Norwoe: Ablex.

Babcock, Barbara. 1978. 'Introduction' in *The Reversible World: Symbolic Inversion in Art and Society.* Edited by Barbara A. Babcock. Ithaca: Cornell University Press.

Bakhtin, Mikhai. 1968. *Rabelais and His World.* Translated by Helene Iswolsky. Cambridge: Harvard University Press.

Britton, Henry. 1884. *Loloma, or Two Years in Cannibal Land: A Story of Old Fiji.* Melbourne.

Caputi, Anthony. 1978. *Buffo: The Genius of Vulgar Comedy.* Detroit: Wayne State University Press.

Clunie, Fergus, and Walesi Ligairi. 1983. Traditional Fijian spirit masks and spirit masquers. *Domodomo: Fiji Museum Quarterly.* 1:46-71.

Dana, Richard Henry. 1959. *Two Years before the Mast.* New York: Bantam Books.

Eagleton, Terry. 1981. *Walter Benjamin: Towards a Revolutionary Criticism.* London: Verso.

Eco, Umberto. 1984. 'The frames of comic freedom' in *Carnival!* Edited by Thomas A. Sebeok. Berlin: Mouton. pp. 1-9.

Ellis, William. 1834 [1829]. *Polynesian Researches, During a Residence of Nearly Six Years in the South Sea Islands.* 2nd ed. London: Fisher, Son and Jackson.

Emerson, Nathaniel. 1965. *Unwritten Literature of Hawai'i.* Vermont: Charles E. Turtle Company.

Forster, R. 1777. *Observations Made During a Voyage Round the World On Physical Geography, Natural History and Ethnic Philosophy.* London: Robinson.

Gifford, Edward Winslow. 1929. *Tongan Society.* Bulletin 61. Honolulu: Bernice P. Bishop Museum. p. 16.

Gluckman, Max. 1965. *Custom and Conflict in Africa.* Oxford: Blackwell.

Hau'ofa, Epeli. 1987a. *Kisses in the Nederends.* Auckland: Longman Paul.

———. 1987b. 'The new South Pacific society: Integration and independence' in *Class and Culture in the South Pacific.* Edited by Antony Hooper et. al. Suva: Centre for Pacific Studies, University of Auckland and Institute of Pacific Studies, University of the South Pacific. pp. 1-11.

———. 1988. Interview With Epeli Hau'ofa. With Subramani. *Landfall.* 43(1):35-51.

Henry, Teuira. 1928. *Ancient Tahiti.* Bulletin 48. Honolulu: Bernice P. Bishop Museum.

Hereniko, Vilsoni. 1977. *Dance as a Reflection of Rotuman Culture.* South Pacific Social Sciences Association and Institute of Pacific Studies.

———. 1990. Polynesian clowns and satirical comedies. PhD thesis. Suva: University of the South Pacific.

———. 1992. 'When she reigns supreme: Clowning and culture in Rotuman weddings' in *Clowning as Critical Practice: Performance Humor in the South Pacific.* Edited by William Mitchell. Pittsburgh: University of Pittsburgh Press. pp. 167-91.

Hereniko, Vilsoni, and Teresia Teaiwa. 1993. *Last Virgin in Paradise.* Suva: South Pacific Creative Arts Society.

Howard, Alan. 1986. Cannibal chiefs and the charter for rebellion in Rotuman myth. *Pacific Studies.* 10:1-27.

———. 1993. Ritual status and power politics in modern Rotuma. Paper presented at ASAO Meeting, Kona, Hawai'i.

Huntsman, Judith, and Antony Hooper. 1975. Male and female in Tokelau culture. *Journal of the Polynesian Society.* 84(4):415-30.

Jersey, M.E. 1893. Three Weeks in Samoa. *19th Century Review.* January.

Kneubuhl, John. 1993. Interview with John Kneubuhl. *Manoa.* 5:1.

Kneubuhl, Victoria. 1987. Traditional performance in Samoan culture: Two forms. *Asian Theatre Journal.* 4:166-76.

Kristeva, J. 1980. *Desire in Language.* Edited by L. S. Roudiez. Translated by T. Gora, A. Jardine and L.S. Roudiez. New York: Columbia University Press.

Lal, Brij. 1992. *Broken Waves: A History of the Fiji Islands in the Twentieth Century.* Pacific Islands Monograph Series, No. 11.

Levy, Robert I. 1971. The community function of Tahitian male transvestism: A hypothesis. *Anthropological Quarterly.* 44(1):12-21.

———. 1973. *Tahitians: Mind and Experience in the Society Islands.* Chicago: University of Chicago Press.

Luomala, Katherine. 1973. Moving and movable images in Easter Island myth. *Journal of the Polynesian Society.* 82:28-46.

———. 1984. *Hula Ki'i: Hawaiian Puppetry.* Honolulu: The Institute of Polynesian Studies.

Mageo, Jeannette Marie. 1992. Male transvestism and cultural change in Samoa. *American Ethnologist.* 19(3):443-59.

Mitchell, William (ed.). 1992. *Clowning as Critical Practice: Performance Humor in the South Pacific.* Pittsburgh: University of Pittsburgh Press.

———. 1992a. 'Introduction' in *Clowning as Critical Practice: Performance Humor in the South Pacific.* Edited by William Mitchell. Pittsburgh: University of Pittsburgh Press. pp. 3-58.

———. 1992b. 'Horrific humor and festal farce: Carnival clowning in Wape society' in *Clowning as Critical Practice: Performance Humor in the South Pacific.* Edited by William Mitchell. Pittsburgh: University of Pittsburgh Press. pp. 145-66.

Nelson, T.G.A. 1990. *Comedy: An Introduction to Comedy in Literature, Drama, and Cinema.* Oxford: Oxford University Press.

Oliver, Douglas. 1974. *Ancient Tahitian Society.* 3 vols. Honolulu: University Press of Hawai'i.

Pritchard, William T. 1866. *Polynesian Reminiscences; or, Life in the South Pacific Islands.* London: Chapman and Hall.

Schweder, Richard. 1991. *Thinking Through Cultures.* Cambridge: Harvard University Press.

Shore, Bradd. 1977. A Samoan theory of action: Social control and social order in a Polynesian paradox. PhD thesis. Chicago: University of Chicago.

———. 1978. Ghosts and government: A structural analysis of alternative institutions for conflict management in Samoa. *Man.* 13:175-99.

———. n.d. The absurd side of power in Samoa. Paper presented in honor of Sir Raymond Firth on the occasion of his 90th birthday, London, December 1991.

Sinavaiana, Caroline. 1992a. Traditional comic theater in Samoa: A holographic view. PhD thesis. Honolulu: University of Hawai'i at Manoa.

———. 1992b. 'Where the spirits laugh last: Comic theater in Samoa' in *Clowning as Critical Practice: Performance Humor in the South Pacific.* Edited by William Mitchell. Pittsburgh: University of Pittsburgh Press.

———. 1992c. Comic theater in Samoa as indigenous media. *Pacific Studies Special Issue: The Arts and Politics.* 15(4):199-210.

Sloan, Donald. 1941. *Polynesian Paradise: An Elaborated Travel Journal Based on Ethnological Facts.* London: Robert Hale.

Stair, John B. 1897. *Old Samoa.* Papakura: R. McMillan.

Stallybrass, Peter, and Allon White. 1986. *The Poetics and Politics of Transgression.* London: Methuen.

Turner, George. 1884. *Samoa: A Hundred Years Ago and Long Before.* London: Macmillan.

Turner, Victor. 1982. *From Ritual to Theatre: The Human Seriousness of Play.* New York: Performing Arts Journal Press.

Webster, Hutton. 1968. *Primitive Secret Societies: A Study in Early Politics and Religion.* 2nd. ed. New York: Octagon Books.

Wendt, Albert. 1973. *Sons for the Return Home.* Auckland: Longman Paul.

———. 1979. *Leaves of the Banyan Tree.* Auckland: Longman Paul.

———. 1993a. An interview with Albert Wendt. *The Contemporary Pacific: A Journal of Island Affairs.* 5(l):112-31.

———. 1993b. An interview with Albert Wendt. *Manoa.* 5(1).

Williams, John. 1984. *The Samoan Journals of John Williams.* Edited by R.M. Moyle. Canberra: Australian National University Press.

Chapter 3 (Stevensen)

Beaglehole, J.C. (ed.). 1962. *The Journal of Captain James Cook, The Voyage of the Endeavour, 1768-1771*. Cambridge: Hakluyt Society.

Carell, Victor. 1992. The purpose, origin and future of Festivals of Pacific Arts. *Pacific Arts*. 5:1-5.

Clifford, James. 1988. *The Predicament of Culture*. Cambridge: Cambridge University Press.

Cook Island News. 1992. 22 October.

Dutton, Denis. 1994. Authenticity in the art of traditional societies. *Pacific Arts*. 9 & 10:1-9.

Epstein, A.L. 1978. *Ethos and Identity: 3 Studies in Ethnicity*. London: Tavistock.

Falassi, Alessandro (ed.). 1987. *Time Out Of Time: Essays on the Festival*. Albuquerque: University of New Mexico Press.

Hammond, Joyce. 1986. *Tifaifai and Quilts of Polynesia*. Honolulu: University of Hawai'i Press.

Handler, Richard, and Joycelyn Linnekin. 1984. Tradition, genuine or spurious. *Journal of American Folklore*. 97:273-90.

Hanson, Allan. 1989. The making of the Maori: Culture, invention and its logic. *American Anthropologist*. 91(4):890-902.

Henry, Teuira. 1928. *Ancient Tahiti*. Bishop Museum Press Bulletin 48. Honolulu: Bishop Museum Press.

Hereniko, Vilsoni. 1980. *Art in the New Pacific*. Suva: Institute of Pacific Studies.

Hobsbawm, Eric, and Terence Ranger (eds.). 1986. *The Invention of Tradition*. Cambridge: Cambridge University Press.

Jolly, Margaret. 1982. 'Birds and banyans of South Pentecost: Kastom in anti-colonial struggle' in *Reinventing Traditional Culture: The Politics of Custom in Island Melanesia*. Edited by Keesing and Tonkinson. *Mankind* Special Issue 13(4): 338-56.

Kaeppler, Adrienne. 1977. 'Polynesian Dance as "Airport Art"' in *Asian and Pacific Dance: Selected Papers from the 1974 CORD-SEM Conference*. Dance Research Annual VIII.

———. 1987. 'Pacific festivals and ethnic identity' in *Time Out Of Time: Essays on the Festival*. Edited by Alessandro Falassi. Albuquerque: University of New Mexico Press. pp. 162-70.

———. 1988. *Com Mek Me Hol Yu Han. Impact of Tourism on Traditional Music*. Jamaica: Jamaica Memory Bank.

Kasfir, Sidney. 1992. African art and authenticity: A text without a shadow. *African Arts*. 25(2):41-53.

Kauraka, Kauraka. 1993. The 6th Festival of Pacific Arts: a personal story. *Pacific Arts*. 8:25-7.

Keesing, Roger. 1989. Creating the past: Custom and identity in the contemporary Pacific. *The Contemporary Pacific*. 1(1-2): 19-42.

Keesing, Roger and Robert Tonkinson (eds). 1982. *Reinventing Traditional Culture: The Politics of Custom in Island Melanesia*. *Mankind* Special Issue 13(4).

Larcom, Joan. 1982. 'The invention of convention' in *Reinventing Traditional Culture: The Politics of Custom in Island Melanesia*. Edited by Keesing and Tonkinson. *Mankind* Special Issue 13(4):330-7.

LeHartel, Manouche. 1989. Artistic Heritage in a Changing Pacific. Paper presented to the Pacific Arts Association 4th International Symposium, Honolulu, 6 to 12 August 1989.

Lewis-Harris, Jackie. 1994. The 6th Pacific Arts Festival. *Pacific Arts*. 9/10:10-20.

Linnekin, Jocelyn. 1983. Defining tradition: Variations on the Hawaiian identity. *American Ethnologist* 10:241-52.

———. 1990. 'The politics of culture in the Pacific' in *Cultural Identity and Ethnicity in the Pacific*. Edited by Jocelyn Linnekin and Lin Poyer. Honolulu: University of Hawai'i Press. pp. 149-73.

Linnekin, Jocelyn, and Lin Poyer (eds). 1990. *Cultural Identity and Ethnicity in the Pacific*. Honolulu: University of Hawai'i Press.

Marion, Virginia. 1988. Kiribati adaptation of dance for the 3rd South Pacific Arts Festival. *Com Mek Me Hol Yu Han*. pp. 139-44.

Myers, Doug. 1989. 5th Festival of Pacific Arts. *Australian Aboriginal Studies*. 1:59-62.

Oliver, Douglas. 1974. *Ancient Tahitian Society*. 3 vols. Honolulu: University of Hawai'i Press.

Rose, Roger. 1971. The material culture of ancient Tahiti. Unpublished thesis. Harvard University.

Simons, Susan Cochrane. 1989. The 5th Festival of Pacific Arts. *Oceania*. 59(4):299-310.

Sissons, Jeffrey. 1995. National movements: Dance and nationhood in the Cook Islands. *Sites*. 30:153-64.

South Pacific Arts Festival. 1972. *Souvenir Booklet*.

Stevensen, Karen. 1987. The fete: Tradition and tourism. Paper given at 12th Annual Pacific Island Studies Conference, Honolulu.

———. 1988. Dispelling the myth: Tahitian adornment and the maintenance of a traditional culture, 1767-1819. Unpublished PhD thesis. University of California at Los Angeles, Department of Art History.

———. 1990. Heiva: Continuity and change of a Tahitian celebration. *Journal of the Contemporary Pacific.* 2(2):255-78.

———. 1992. Politicization of *La Culture Ma'ohi*: The creation of a Tahitian cultural identity. *Pacific Studies.* 15(4):117-36.

———. 1993. The 6th Festival of Pacific Arts. *Pacific Studies.* 6:67-9.

Stillman, Amy. 1988. Images and realities: Visitors' responses to Tahitian music and dance. *Com Mek Me Hol Yu Han.* pp. 145-66.

Takau, Kathy. 1992. *Cook Island News.* 13 October.

Tonkinson, Robert. 1982. 'National identity and the problem of *kastom* in Vanuatu' in *Reinventing Traditional Culture: The Politics of Kastom in Island Melanesia.* Edited by Roger Keesing and Robert Tonkinson. *Mankind* Special Issue 13(4):306-15.

Chapter 4 (Kernot)

Anderson, Benedict. 1983. *Imagined Communities.* London: Verso.

Bassett, Judith. 1987. A thousand miles of loyalty: The Royal Tour of 1901. *NZ Journal of History.* 21(1):125-38.

Benedict, Burton. 1983. 'The anthropology of World's Fairs' in *The Anthropology of World's Fairs: San Francisco's Panama Pacific International Exposition of 1915.* Benedict et al. Berkeley: Lowie Museum of Anthropology & Scholar Press.

———. 1991. International exhibitions and national identity. *Anthropolgy Today.* 7(3):5-9.

Blythe, Martin John. 1994. *Naming the Other: Images of the Maori in New Zealand Film and Television.* Metuchen: Scarecrow Press.

Corbey, Raymond. 1995. 'Ethnographic showcases, 1870-1930' in *The Decolonization of Imagination. Culture Knowledge and Power.* Edited by Jan Nederveen Pieterse and Bhikhu Parekh. London: Zed Books.

Cowan, James. 1910. *Official Record of the New Zealand International Exhibition of Arts and Industries.* Wellington: Government Printer.

Davidson, Janet. In press. Cook Island material culture from the Christchurch exhibition of 1906-1907: Rediscovering a forgotten collection. *Baessler-Archiv.* Vol. 45. Special issue. Edited by Klaus Helfrich and Markus Schindlbeck.

Gorst, Sir John. 1908. *New Zealand Revisited: Recollections of the Days of My Youth.* London: Pitman.

Hector Library, Museum of New Zealand Te Papa Tongarewa. New Zealand International Exhibition 1906-07 File (NZIE 1906-07 File).

Kernot, B. In press. 'Maoriland metaphors and the Model Maori Pa' in *Farewell Colonialism.* Edited by John M. Thomson. Palmerston North: Dunmore.

Orbell, Margaret. In press. 'Maori writing about the exhibition' in *Farewell Colonialism.* Edited by John M. Thomson. Palmerston North: Dunmore.

Neich, Roger. 1977. Historical change in Rotorua Ngati Tarawhai woodcarving art. MA thesis. Victoria University of Wellington.

———. 1983. 'The veil of orthodoxy: Rotorua Ngati Tarawhai woodcarving in a changing context' in *Art and Artists of Oceania.* Edited by S.M. Mead and B. Kernot. Palmerston North: Dunmore.

———. 1991. Jacob William Heberley of Wellington: A Maori carver in a changing world. *Rec. Auckland Inst. Mus.* 28:69-148.

Phillips, J.O.C. 1983. Musings in Maoriland – or was there a *Bulletin* school in New Zealand? *Historical Studies.* 20(81):520-35.

Te Aute College Students' Association Conference Reports. 1897-1910. (TACSA Reports).

Te Pipiwharauroa, No. 95, Pepuere 1906; Nos 104-6, Nowema 1906 to Hanuere 1907. Translated by Margaret Orbell.

Te Puke ki Hikurangi. 1901. Translated by Margaret Orbell. 15 April.

The Weekly Press. Christchurch. 21 March to 31 December 1906, January to May 1907.

Chapter 5 (Meredith)

Allaridge, R.W. 1989. *A Simplified Dictionary of Modern Samoan.* New Zealand: Polynesian Press.

American Samoa Community College Catalogue. 1991. Pago Pago.

Arbeit, Wendy. 1990. *Baskets in Polynesia.* Honolulu: University of Hawai'i Press.

Barrow, T. 1972. *Art and Life in Polynesia*. Vermont: Charles E. Tuttle Company.

Buck, Peter H. (Te Rangi Hiroa). 1930. *Samoan Material Culture*. Bulletin 75. Honolulu: Bernice P. Bishop Museum.

Handy, E.S., Craighill and Willowdean Handy. 1924. *Samoan Housebuilding, Cooking and Tattooing*. Bulletin 15. Honolulu: Bernice P. Bishop Museum.

Hatcher, Evelyn Payne. 1985. *Art As Culture*. Lanham: University Press of America.

Kramer, Augustin. 1985. *Salamasina: Scenes from Ancient Samoan Culture and History*. Pago Pago: Assoc. of Marist Brothers Old Boys.

Leonard, Anne, and John Terrell. 1980. *Patterns of Polynesia*. Washington DC: Field Museum of Natural History.

Marquardt, Carl. 1984. *The Tattooing of Both Sexes in Samoa*. Papakura: R. McMillan.

National Endowment for the Arts. 1988. *Towards Civilization: A Report on Arts Education*. Washington DC: NEA.

Price, Christine. 1979. *Made in the South Pacific*. London: Bodley Head.

Pritchard, Mary J. 1984. *Siapo: Bark Cloth Art of Samoa*. American Samoa: American Samoa Council on Culture, Arts and Humanities.

Stanley, David. 1986. *South Pacific Handbook*. Chico: Moon Publications.

Tausie, Vilsoni. 1980. *Art in the New Pacific*. Suva: Institute of Pacific Studies.

Turner, George. 1884. *Samoa: One Hundred Years Ago and Long Before*. London: McMillan.

Chapter 6 (Pollock)

Baker, P., and T. Baker. 1986. *The Changing Samoans*. London: Oxford University Press.

Banks, Joseph. 1769. *The Journal of Sir Joseph Banks*. Edited by Sir Joseph Hooker. Reprinted 1896. London: Macmillan.

Beaglehole, J.C. (ed.). 1967. *The Voyage of the Resolution and Discovery, 1776-1780,* Parts I and II. Cambridge: Cambridge University Press for Hakluyt Society.

Bray, G. 1990. Obesity: Historical development of scientific and cultural ideas. *International Journal of Obesity.* 14(11):909-26.

de Garine, I., and Nancy J. Pollock (eds). 1995. *Social Aspects of Obesity*. New York: Gordon and Breach.

Delaporte, P., and Mrs Delaporte. 1920. The men and women of Old Nauru. *Mid-Pacific Magazine.* 19:153-6.

Ellis, William. 1829. *Polynesian Researches*. 3 vols. Reprint, 1977. Vermont: Charles E. Tuttle Company.

Fabricius, W. 1992. *Nauru 1888-1900*. Edited and translated by Dymphna Clark and Stewart Firth. Canberra: Division of Asian and Pacific History, RSPS, Australian National University.

Feher, M. (ed.). 1989. *Fragments for a History of the Human Body.* 3 vols. Zone: MIT, Urzone.

Gordon, Tamar. 1993. Body size in Tonga. Paper read at 1993 ASAO meetings.

Hambruch, P. 1914-15. *Nauru*. Band I. Halband I and II. Hamburg: Ergebnisse.

Jackson, Michael. 1989. 'Knowledge of the body' in *Paths toward a Clearing*. Bloomington: Indiana University Press.

Kaeppler, A. 1989. 'Art and Aesthetics' in *Developments in Polynesian Ethnology*. Edited by A. Howard and R. Borofsky. Honolulu: University of Hawai'i Press. pp. 211-40.

Kayser, P.A.L. 1934. Der Pandanus auf Nauru. *Anthropos* 29(5/6):775-791.

Kretzschmar, K.E. 1913. *Nauru 1888-1913*. Private circulation.

Moerenhout, J.A. 1837. *Voyages aux iles du Grand Ocean*. 2 vols. Reprinted 1959. Paris: A. Bertrand.

Oliver, Douglas. 1974. *Tahitian Society*. 3 vols. Honolulu: University of Hawai'i Press.

Orbach, S. 1978. *Fat is a Feminist Issue*. New York: Berkley Books.

Pollock, Nancy J. 1991. 'Nauruans during World War II' in *Remembering the Pacific War*. Edited by G. White. Honolulu: Center for Pacific Island Studies.

————. 1992a. 'Food dependency in the Pacific revisited' in *Development that Works*. Edited by C. Walsh. Palmersto: Massey University.

————. 1992b. *These Roots Remain*. Honolulu: Institute for Pacific Studies and University of Hawai'i Press.

————. 1992c. 'The mining of Nauru and its aftermath' in *Pacific History*. Edited by Don Rubinstein. Mangilao: University of Guam Press.

————. 1993. Fat is good, fat is bad. Paper read at ASAP meeting, Kona, Hawai'i.

————. 1995a. Obesity and the thrifty genotype. In press. *Australasian Journal of Clinical Nutrition*.

———. 1995b. 'Social fattening patterns in the Pacific' in *Social Aspects of Obesity*. Edited by I. de Garine and Nancy J. Pollock. New York: Gordon and Breach.

Rhone, R. Dobson. 1921. Nauru, the richest island in the South Seas. *National Geographic*. XL(6):359-90.

Shilling, Chris. 1993. *The Body and Social Theory*. New York: Sage.

Teilhet-Fisk, J. 1994. Rank, status and symbolism in hairstyles of Fiji, Tonga and Samoa. Paper read at Linking Our Sea of Islands Conference, Auckland.

Stephen, Ernest. 1936. Notes on Nauru. *Oceania*. 7(1):34-63.

Strathern, A., and M. Strathern. 1985. *Self Decoration in Mount Hagen*. London: Blackwell.

Turner, Bryan. 1984. *The Body and Society*. Oxford: Blackwell.

Wedgewood, C. 1936-37. Report on research work in Nauru Island, Central Pacific. *Oceania*. VI(4):359-91 and VII(1):1-33.

Chapter 7 (Megaw and Megaw)

Batty, P. 1993. Who told you we wanted to make our own TV? *Artlink*. 13(1):22-4.

Britton, S., and F. Wright (eds). 1990. Contemporary Australian Aboriginal art. *Artlink*. 10 (1,2). Special double issue.

Giles, K., M.R. Megaw, and J.V.S. Megaw. 1988. *The Cutting Edge: New Art from the Third and Fourth Worlds*. Bedford Park: Flinders University.

Hardy, J., J.V.S. Megaw and M.R. Megaw. 1992. *The Heritage of Namatjira: The Watercolourists of Central Australia*. Port Melbourne: William Heinemann Australia.

Hogan, J. (ed.). 1990. *Balance 1990: Views, Visions, Influences*. Brisbane: Queensland Art Gallery.

Lendon, N. (ed.). 1996. *Groundwork: Aboriginal Artists' Prints from the Canberra School of Art*. Canberra: Canberra School of Art.

Marrie, A. 1980. The informal art of the Pitjantjatjara people of Indulkana, BA thesis, part 1. Bedford Park: Discipline of Visual Arts, Flinders University.

———. 1982. The informal art of the Pitjantjatjara people of Indulkana. BA thesis, part 2. Bedford Park: Discipline of Visual Arts, Flinders University.

Maughan, J. 1986. Indulkana prints. *Imprint*. 21:3-4, 16-7.

Maughan, J., and J.V.S. Megaw. 1986. *The Dreamtime Today: A Survey of Contemporary Aboriginal Arts and Crafts*. Bedford Park: Flinders University.

Maughan, J. and J. Zimmer (eds). 1986. *Dot & Circle: A Retrospective Survey of the Aboriginal Acrylic Paintings of Central Australia*. Melbourne: RMIT Communications Services Unit.

Megaw, J.V.S. 1980. Artists-in-residence: Subjects or objects? Some first reactions to the Aboriginal Artists-in-Residence programme at the Flinders University of South Australia. *Newsletter, Australian Institute of Aboriginal Studies*. NS. 15:50-62.

———. 1984. *Painters of the Western Desert, Contemporary Australian Art Exhibitions*. Adelaide: Adelaide Festival of Arts.

———. 1990. 'Art as identity: Aspects of contemporary Aboriginal art' in *Art and Identity in Oceania*. Edited by L. and A. Hanson, 282-92. Honolulu: University of Hawai'i Press. pp. 282-92.

Megaw, Ruth, and Vincent Megaw. 1997. Ngarrindjeri soldier: Kerry Giles ('Kurwingie') 1959-97. *Artlink*. 17(3):81-2.

Ryan, J. 1989. *Mythscapes: Aboriginal Art of the Desert from the National Gallery of Victoria*. Melbourne: National Gallery of Victoria.

Sutton, P. (ed.). 1988. *Dreamings: The Art of Aboriginal Australia*. New York: George Braziller.

Chapter 9 (Gemes)

Gemes, J. 1982. *We Wait No More*. Hogarth Gallery, Sydney, and Bitumen River Gallery, Canberra.

Harris, R. 1968. *The Desert Chrysalis: A Cloud Passes Over*. Sydney: Angus & Robertson.

Langton, M. 1981. 'The social scientists' great deception' in *Black Alternatives in Australia*. Special issue of *Social Alternatives*. 2(2):25-7.

De Lorenzo, C. 1981. An Interpretation of Some Photographs of Australian Aborigines. Photo discourse. Sydney: Sydney College of the Arts.

Ruby, J. 1991. Eric Michaels: An appreciation. *Visual Anthropology*. 4:328.

Chapter 10 (Fergie)

Anderson, B. 1983. *Imagined Communities: Reflections on the Origin and Spread of Nationalism*. London.

Carter, P. 1987. *The Road to Botany Bay: An Essay in Spatial History.* London: Faber and Faber.

Dicks, S. and J. Lambert (eds). 1992. Adelaide's North Terrace. Explore our cultural mile. An official South Australian Tourist Map, North Terrace Action Group, Adelaide.

Fergie, D. 1991. The state of racism and the racism of the state: Precincts of power and structures of everyday thought in South Australia. Paper presented to the Annual Conference of Museum Anthropologists, Adelaide, 1991.

Chapter 11 (Stanton)

Ames, M.A. 1992. *Cannibal Tours and Glass Boxes: the Anthropology of Museums.* Vancouver: University of British Columbia Press.

Berndt, R.M. 1979. Aboriginal art of Western Australia. *Art and Australia.* 16:372-6.

Boas, F. 1907. Some principles of museum administration. *Science.* n.s. 25(650):921-33.

Burridge, K. 1973. *Encountering Aborigines. A Case Study: Anthropology and the Australian Aboriginal.* New York: Pergamon.

Clifford, J. 1988. *The Predicament of Culture.* New York: Center for African Art.

Edwards, R., and J. Stewart (eds). 1980. *Preserving Indigenous Cultures: A New Role for Museums.* Canberra: Australian Government Publishing Service.

Elkin, A.P., R.M. and C.H. Berndt. 1950. *Art in Arnhem Land.* Melbourne: Cheshire.

Graburn, N.H.H. 1976. *Ethnic and Tourist Arts: Cultural Expressions from the Fourth World.* Berkeley: University of California Press.

Hawke, S., and S. Gallagher. 1989. *Noonkanbah: Whose Land, Whose Law.* Fremantle: Fremantle Arts Centre Press.

Lavine, S.D., and I. Karp. 1991. 'Introduction: Museums and multiculturalism' in *Exhibiting Cultures: The Poetics and Politics of Museum Display.* Edited by S.D. Lavine and I. Karp. Washington: Smithsonian Institution. pp. 1-9.

Miller, M.D., and F. Rutter. 1952. *Child Artists of the Australian Bush.* Sydney: Australasian Publishing Co.

Stannage, T. 1991. Into the Twenty-First Century: Report of the State Task Force for Museums Policy, Western Australia. Unpublished report. Perth: Department for the Arts.

————. 1992. *Into the Twenty-First Century: Report of the State Task Force for Museums Policy, Western Australia.* Perth: Department for the Arts.

Stanton, J.E. 1989. *Painting the Country: Contemporary Aboriginal Art from the Kimberley Region, Western Australia.* Perth: University of Western Australia Press.

————. 1992. *Nyungar Landscapes. Aboriginal Arts of the South-West: The Heritage of Carrolup, Western Australia.* Occasional Paper No. 3. Perth: The University of Western Australia Berndt Museum of Anthropology.

Stocking, G.W. (ed.). 1985. *Objects and Others: Essays on Museums and Material Culture.* Vol. 3. *History of Anthropology.* Madison: University of Wisconsin Press.

Chapter 12 (Anderson)

Anderson, C. 1988. Letter to Christopher Hodges, November 1988. Anthropology Archives, South Australian Museum, Adelaide.

Hodges, C. 1988. Letter to Peter Sutton, November 1988. Anthropology Archives, South Australian Museum, Adelaide.

Kean, J. 1989. Aboriginal artists in New York. *Art and Australia.* 26(4):571-4.

Lauer, P. 1975. *Catalogue Accompanying Mornington Island Exhibition.* Brisbane: University of Queensland Anthropology Museum.

Sutton, P. 1988. Letter to Christopher Hodges, November 1988. Anthropology Archives, South Australian Museum, Adelaide.

Trigger, D. 1975. The politics of Aboriginal material culture: The material domain as resources for 'cultural revitalisation' or political action? Unpublished MS. Brisbane: University of Queensland.

PART 3 (Craig)

Beran, H. 1996. *Mutuaga: A Nineteenth-Century New Guinea Master Carver.* Wollongong: University of Wollongong Press.

Craig, B. 1995. Following the tracks of Edgar Waite in New Guinea for the Pacific Arts symposium in Adelaide. *Records of the South Australian Museum.* 28(1):33-52.

Dutton, D. 1995. Mythologies of Tribal Art. *African Arts.* 28(3):33-43, 90-1.

Gerbrands, A. 1967. *Wow-ipits. Eight Asmat Woodcarvers of New Guinea.* The Hague: Mouton & Co.

Niles, D. 1983. Why are there no garamuts in Papua? *Bikmaus.* IV(3):90-104.

Swadling, P., B. Hauser-Schaublin, P. Gorecki and F. Tiesler. 1988. *The Sepik-Ramu: An Introduction.* Boroko: PNG National Museum

Vargyas, Gabor. 1992. A short history of the Pacific collections of the Ethnographic Museum, Budapest. *Pacific Arts.* 5:24-32.

Chapter 13 (Smidt and Eoe)

Barlow, Kathleen. 1985. The role of women in intertribal trade among the Murik of Papua New Guinea. *Research in Economic Anthropology.* 7:95-122.

———. 1992. '"Dance when I die!": Context and role in the clowning of Murik Women' in *Clowning as Critical Practice: Performance Humor in the South Pacific.* Edited by William E. Mitchell. Pittsburgh: University of Pittsburgh Press. pp. 58-87.

Barlow, K., L. Bolton and D. Lipset. 1986. Trade and society in transition along the Sepik Coast (An interim report on anthropological research in the East Sepik and Sundaun Provinces, P.N.G., July-August 1986). Mimeograph. Sydney: The Australian Museum.

Beier, Ulli and Peter Aris. 1975. Sigia: Artistic Design in Murik Lakes. *Gigibori* 2(2):17-36.

Berman, Marsha. 1988. Papua New Guinea: behoud van traditionele cultuur. *Culturen.* 2(5):12-15.

———. 1990. *Singsing Tumbuan Bosmun.* Video document. 83 min.

———. 1991. *Singsing Tumbuan at Boroi.* Video document, 58 min.

———. 1995a. *Singsing Tumbuan (Mask Dance).* Cultural documentary in three parts. Videofilm, 170 min. Directed by Marsha Berman. Produced by Asples Productions, Boroko.

———. 1995b. *Singsing Tumbuan (Mask Dance).* Cultural documentary. Videofilm, 140 min. Directed by Marsha Berman. Produced by Asples Productions, Boroko.

———. 1995c. *Singsing Tumbuan (Mask Dance).* Television documentary. Videofilm, 50 min. Directed by Marsha Berman. Produced by Asples Productions, Boroko.

———. 1995d. *Singsing Tumbuan (Mask Dance).* Videofilm brochure. Boroko: Asples Productions.

Birket-Smith, Kaj. 1965. Feasts of merit in East Asia and Oceania. *Folk.* 7:23-37.

Blackwood, Beatrice. 1951. 'Some arts and industries of the Bosmun, Ramu River, New Guinea' in *Südseestudien/Études sur l'Océanie/South Seas Studies (Gedenkschrift zur Erinnerung an Felix Speiser).* Edited by Hans-Georg Bandi, Roland Bay and Hans Dietschy. Basel: Museum für Völkerkunde und Schweizerischen Museums für Volkskunde. pp. 266-88.

Böhm, Karl. 1983. The life of some island people of New Guinea: A missionary's observations of the volcanic islands of Manam, Boesa, Biem, and Ubrub. With an introduction by Nancy Lutkehaus. *Collectanea Instituti Anthropos* 29. Berlin: Dietrich Reimer Verlag.

de Grunne, Bernard. 1979. *Art Papou.* Bruxelles: louis musin éditeur.

Falassi, Alessandro. 1987. 'Festival: Definition and Morphology' in *Time out of Time: Essays on the Festival.* Edited by Alessandro Falassi. Albuquerque: University of New Mexico Press. pp. 1-10.

Fukumotu, Shigeki. 1976. *Melanesian Art.* Tokyo: Kyúryúdó.

Gell, Alfred. 1992. 'Inter-tribal commodity barter and reproductive gift-exchange in old Melanesia' in *Barter, Exchange and Value: An Anthropological Approach.* Edited by Caroline Humphrey and Stephen Hugh-Jones. pp. 142-168.

Gourlay, K.A. 1975. Sound-producing Instruments in Traditional Society: A Study of Esoteric Instruments and their Role in Male-Female Relations. *New Guinea Research Bulletin* 60. Port Moresby and Canberra.

Haberland, Eike, and Meinhard Schuster. 1964. *Sepik: Kunst aus Neuguinea.* Frankfurt am Main: Städtisches Museum für Völkerkunde.

Hauser-Schäublin, Brigitta. 1984. Schweinefleisch und Totenseele: Zur Bedeutung des Schweines in der Kultur der Abelam, Papua Neuguinea. *Verhandlungen der Naturforschenden Gesellschaft Basel.* 94:335-65.

Hogbin, Ian. 1970. *The Island of Menstruating Men: Religion in Wogeo, New Guinea.* Scranton: Chandler Publishing Company.

———. 1978. *The Leaders and the Led: Social Control in Wogeo, New Guinea.* Carlton: Melbourne University Press.

Höltker, Georg. 1962. Aus dem Kulturleben der Kire-Puir am

unteren Ramu (Neuguinea). *Jahrbuch des Museums für Völkerkunde zu Leipzig (Berlin)* 19:76-107; Tafeln VI-VIII.

———. 1964. Die Nubia-Awar an der Hansa-Bucht in Nordost-Neuguinea. *Jahrbuch des Museums für Völkerkunde zu Leipzig (Berlin)* 20:33-70, Tafeln IX-XVI.

———. 1966. Das Geisterhaus bei den Bosngun am Unteren Ramu River, Neu Guinea. *Jahrbuch des Museums für Völkerkunde zu Leipzig (Berlin)* 22:17-39, Tafeln I-VIII.

———. 1968. Sakrale Holzplastik der Nor-Papua in Nordost-Neuguinea. *Ethnologica (Köln)* N.F. 4:455-493, Tafeln XXVIII-XXXV.

Huber, Peter B. 1990. 'Masquerade as artifact in Wamu' in *Sepik Heritage: Tradition and Change in Papua New Guinea*. Edited by Nancy Lutkehaus et al. Bathurst: Crawford House Press. pp. 150-9.

Independent, The. 1997. PNG Tumbuan masks festival. 16 May.

Josephides, Sasha. 1990. 'Seventh-Day Adventism and the Boroi image of the past' in *Sepik Heritage: Tradition and Change in Papua New Guinea*. Edited by Nancy Lutkehaus et al. Bathurst: Crawford House Press. pp. 58-66.

Kaufmann, Christian. 1985. 'Postscript: The relationship between Sepik art and ethnology' in *Art of the Sepik River, Papua New Guinea: Authority and Ornament*. Edited by Suzanne Greub. Basel: Tribal Art Centre/Edition Greub. pp. 34-47.

———. 1993. 'Mélanésie (section 'Principaux groupes culturels d'Océanie')' in *L'art océanien*. Edited by Adrienne L. Kaeppler, Christian Kaufmann, and Douglas Newton. Paris: Citadelles & Mazenod. pp. 552-612

Kelm, Heinz. 1968. *Kunst vom Sepik III*. Berlin: Museum für Völkerkunde.

Laufer, B. 1922. 'The Joseph N. Field Hall' in *New Guinea Masks*. Albert B. Lewis. Leaflet 4. Chicago: Field Museum of Natural History.

Lewis, A.B. 1922. *New Guinea Masks*. Leaflet 4. Chicago: Field Museum of Natural History.

Lipset, David. 1985. Seafaring Sepiks: Ecology, warfare, and prestige in Murik trade. *Research in Economic Anthropology*. 7:67-94.

———. 1990. 'Boars' tusks and flying foxes: Symbolism and ritual of office in the Murik Lakes' in *Sepik Heritage: Tradition and Change in Papua New Guinea*. Edited by Nancy Lutkehaus et al. Bathurst: Crawford House Press. pp. 286-97.

Lutkehaus, Nancy. 1985. Pigs, politics, and pleasure: Manam perspectives on trade and regional integration. *Research in Economic Anthropology*. 7:123-41.

———. 1990a. 'The Tambaran of the Tanepoa: Traditional and modern forms of leadership on Manam Island' in *Sepik Heritage: Tradition and Change in Papua New Guinea*. Edited by Nancy Lutkehaus et al. Bathurst: Crawford House Press. pp. 298-308.

———. 1990b. Hierarchy and 'heroic society': Manam variations in Sepik social structure. *Oceania*. 60(3):179-97.

Meiser, Leo. 1955. The 'platform' phenomenon along the northern coast of New Guinea. *Anthropos*. 50:265-72.

Meyer, Heinrich. 1943. Das Parakwesen in Glauben und Kult bei den Eingebornen an der Nordostküste Neuguineas (with an introduction by Georg Höltker). *Annali Lateranensi*. 7:95-181.

Mihalic, F. 1971. *The Jacaranda Dictionary and Grammar of Melanesian Pidgin*. Milton: Jacaranda Press.

Mitchell, William E. 1992. 'Introduction: Mother Folly in the Islands' in *Clowning as Critical Practice: Performance Humor in the South Pacific*. Edited by William E. Mitchell. Pittsburgh: University of Pittsburgh Press. pp. 3-57.

Neuhauss, R. 1911. *Deutsch Neu-Guinea I*. 3 vols. Berlin: Verlag Dietrich Reimer (Ernst Vohsen).

Parker, Susan B. 1978. New Guinea adventure: Sketch of a working anthropologist. *Field Museum of Natural History Bulletin*. 49(5):4-8.

Ruff, Wallace. 1987. *Villages and Sites of Murik Lake, Papua New Guinea, 1981*. Lae: Department of Architecture and Building, Papua New Guinea University of Technology.

Ruff, Wallace M., and Ruth E. Ruff. 1990. 'The Village Studies project for the recording of traditional architecture' in *Sepik Heritage: Tradition and Change in Papua New Guinea*. Edited by Nancy Lutkehaus et al. Bathurst: Crawford House Press. pp. 568-86.

Schmidt, P.J. 1923-24. Die Ethnographie der Nor-Papua (Murik-Kaup-Karau) bei Dallmannhafen, Neu-Guinea. *Anthropos*. 18-19:700-32.

———. 1926. Die Ethnographie der Nor-Papua (Murik-Kaup-Karau) bei Dallmannhafen, Neu-Guinea. *Anthropos*. 21:38-71.

———. 1933a. Neue Beiträge zur Ethnographie der Nor-Papua (Neuguinea). *Anthropos*. 28:321-54.

————. 1933b. Neue Beiträge zur Ethnographie der Nor-Papua (Neuguinea). [Schluss] *Anthropos.* 28:663-82.

Schwartz, T. 1963. Systems of areal integration: Some considerations based on the Admiralty Islands of northern Melanesia. *Anthropological Forum.* 1(1):56-97.

Shurcliff, Sidney Nichols. 1930. *Jungle Islands: The 'Illyria' in the South Seas.* New York: Putnam's Sons.

Simet, Jacob. 1976. From a letter by Jacob Simet. *Gigibori.* 3(1):1-2.

Smidt, Dirk. 1975. *The Seized Collections of the Papua New Guinea Museum.* Port Moresby: Creative Arts Centre.

————. 1990. 'Catalogus Oceanië/Catalogue Oceania' in *Sculptuur uit Afrika en Oceanië/Sculpture from Africa and Oceania.* Edited by Toos van Kooten and Gerard van den Heuvel. Otterlo: Rijksmuseum Kröller-Müller. pp. 218-371.

————. 1996. 'Sepik art: Supernatural support in earthly situations' in *The Object as Mediator: On the Transcendental Meaning of Art in Traditional Cultures.* Edited by Mireille Holsbeke. Antwerp: Etnografisch Museum. pp. 61-7.

Somare, Michael. 1974. Initiation at Murik Lakes. *Gigibori.* 1(1):30-3.

————. 1975a. *Sana: an Autobiography of Michael Somare.* Port Moresby: Niugini Press.

————. 1975b. 'Foreword by the Prime Minister, Mr. Michael Somare' in *Papua New Guinea.* Edited by Chris Ashton. Port Moresby: Office of Information, Papua New Guinea Government.

Stichting Ophraeis. 1996. *Singsing Tumbuan: Maskerdans uit Papoea Nieuw-Guinea.* Een film van Marsha Berman. Amsterdam: Stichting Ophraeis.

Swadling, Pamela, et al. 1988. *The Sepik-Ramu: An Introduction.* Boroko: National Museum.

Terrell, John, and Robert L. Welsch. 1990. Trade networks, areal integration, and diversity along the north coast of New Guinea. *Asian Perspectives.* 29(2):155-65.

Tiesler, Frank. 1969. Die intertribalen Beziehungen an der Nordküste Neuguineas im Gebiet der Kleinen Schouten-Inseln. *Abhandlungen und Berichte des Staatlichen Museums für Völkerkunde Dresden.* 30:1-122.

Tiesler, Frank. 1970. Die intertribalen Beziehungen an der Nordküste Neuguineas im Gebiet der Kleinen Schouten-Inseln. *Abhandlungen und Berichte des Staatlichen Museums für Völkerkunde Dresden.* 31:111-95.

Tranel, Wilhelm. 1952. Völkerkundliche und sprachliche Aufzeichnungen aus dem moándo-Sprachgebiet in Nordost-Neuguinea. *Anthropos.* 47:447-73.

van Bakel, Martin A., Renée R. Hagesteijn and Pieter van de Velde. 1986. *Private Politics: A Multi-Disciplinary Approach to 'Big-Man' Systems.* Studies in Human Society 1. Leiden: E.J. Brill.

van den Berg, Paula. 1990. Singsing tumbuan: Het produktie-proces van een videofilm. *Oceania Newsletter (Nieuwsbrief)* 8. Nijmegen: Centrum voor Studies van Australië en Oceanië, Katholieke Universiteit Nijmegen.

————. 1992. *Singsing Tumbuan (Mask Dance).* Boroko: Asples Productions (in cooperation with the PNG National Museum and Art Gallery).

van Gennep, Arnold. 1909. *The Rites of Passage.* London: Routledge and Kegan Paul.

Vormann, P. Franz. 1911. Tänze und Tanzfestlichkeiten der Monumbo-Papua (Deutsch-Neuguinea). *Anthropos.* 6:411-27.

Wardwell, Allen. 1971. *The Art of the Sepik River.* Chicago: The Art Institute of Chicago.

Webb, Virginia-Lee. 1996. Framing time: Photographs of New Guinea from the Crane Pacific Expedition, 1928-29. PhD thesis. New York: Columbia University.

Wedgwood, C.H. 1934. Report on research in Manam Island, Mandated Territory of New Guinea. *Oceania.* 29:239-56.

Welsch, Robert L., John Terrell and John A. Nadolski. 1992. Language and culture on the north coast of New Guinea. *American Anthropologist.* 94(3):568-600.

Williams, F.E. 1940. *Drama of Orokolo: The Social and Ceremonial Life of the Elema.* Oxford: Oxford University Press.

Wurm, S.A. 1981. 'Madang Province, with Eastern Highlands, Chimbu (Simbu), Western Highlands and Morobe Provinces (Papua New Guinea)' in *Language Atlas of the Pacific Area. Part I New Guinea Area, Oceania, Australia.* Edited by S.A. Wurm and Shirô Hattori. Map 7. Pacific Linguistics C 66. Canberra: The Australian Academy of the Humanities in collaboration with the Japan Academy.

Z'graggen, J.A. 1975. The languages of the Madang District, Papua New Guinea. *Pacific Linguistics* B-41. Canberra: Australian National University (Department of Linguistics, Research School of Pacific Studies).

Chapter 14 (Issac and Craig)

Corbin, George. 1990. 'Salvage art history among the Sulka of Wide Bay, East New Britain, Papua New Guinea' in *Art and Identity in Oceania*. Edited by Alan Hanson and Louise Hanson. Bathurst: Crawford House Press. pp. 67-83.

———. 1996. Continuity and change in the art of the Sulka of Wide Bay, East New Britain, Papua New Guinea. *Pacific Arts*. 13, 14:1-26.

Craig, Barry. 1993. Sulka danced sculpture. *Artlink*. 13(2):46-9.

———. 1995. Following the tracks of Edgar Waite in New Guinea for the Pacific Arts symposium in Adelaide. *Records of the South Australian Museum*. 28(1):33-52.

Hill, Rowena. 1982. *Field Trip to Sulka Area of Wide Bay, East New Britain Province*. Waigani: Conservation Department, PNG National Museum & Art Gallery.

Chapter 15 (Lurang)

Helfrich, K. 1973. *Malanggan. 1. Bildwerke von Neuirland*. Berlin: Museum für Völkerkunde.

Lincoln, Louise (ed.). 1987. *Assemblage of Spirits: Idea and Image in New Ireland*. New York: George Braziller, in association with the Minneapolis Institute of Arts.

Chapter 16 (Gunn)

Albert, Steven. 1986. 'Completely by accident I discovered its meaning': The iconography of New Ireland. *Malagan. Journal of the Polynesian Society*. 95(2):239-52.

Brouwer, Elizabeth C. 1980. A *malagan* to cover the grave – funerary ceremonies in Mandak. PhD thesis. St Lucia: University of Queensland.

Bühler, Alfred. 1933. Die Totenfeste in Nord Neuirland. *Verhandlungen der Schweizerischen Naturforschenden Gesellschaft*. 114: 243-70.

Clay, Brenda J. 1987. 'A line of *Tatanua*' in *Assemblage of Spirits: Idea and Image in New Ireland*. Edited by Louise Lincoln. New York: George Braziller. pp. 63-73.

Corbin, George A. 1979. 'The art of the Baining, New Britain' in *Exploring the Visual Art of Oceania*. Edited by S. M. Mead. Honolulu: University Press of Hawai'i. pp. 159-79.

Derlon, Brigitte. 1991. L'Objet malanggan dans les anciens rites funéraires de Nouvelle Irlande. *Res*. 19/20:178-210.

Eco, Umberto. 1976. *A Theory of Semiotics*. Bloomington: Indiana University Press.

Fergie, Deane. 1985. Being and becoming – ritual and reproduction in an island Melanesian society. PhD thesis. Adelaide: University of Adelaide.

———.1989. Limits of commitment: The resilience of a ritual system in island Melanesia. *Canberra Anthropology*. 12(1,2): 99-119.

Gifford, Philip C. Jr. 1974. Iconology of the Uli figure of central New Ireland. PhD Thesis. New York: Columbia University.

Groves, William. 1932-34. The rough notes and diaries of Tatau fieldwork. MS 6069. Microfilm. Excerpts from field notes: (i) vinevinatak (origin legends of *malagan*); (ii) Death of Limawok, 15 October 1933; (iii) gitekowngi (putting paint on *malagan*, 9 October 1933); (iv) steps in circumcision; (v) circumcision of Songeis and Tulu, October 1933.

———. 1934-35. Tabar today: A study of a Melanesian community in contact with alien non-primitive cultural forces. *Oceania*. 5(2):224-40; 5(3):346-60; 6(2):147-57.

Gunn, Michael J. 1983. *Tabar Malagan 1982 – A Report on Fieldwork May & June 1982*. Darwin: Museums and Art Galleries of the Northern Territory.

———. 1984. 'Tabar *malagan*, an outline of the emic taxonomy' in *Developments in the Arts of the Pacific*. Edited by Philip J.C. Dark. Pacific Arts Association Occasional Papers No. 1. pp. 81-92.

———. 1986. Rock art on Tabar, New Ireland Province, Papua New Guinea. *Anthropos*. 81:455-67.

———. 1987. 'The transfer of *malagan* ownership on Tabar' in *Assemblage of Spirits: Idea and Image in New Ireland*. Edited by Louise Lincoln. New York: George Braziller. pp. 74-83.

———. 1988. Transformers and terrorists – the usage of *malagan* masks on Tabar, New Ireland, Papua New Guinea. *The Beagle – Occasional Papers of the Northern Territory Museum of Arts and Sciences*. 5(1):175-83.

———. 1990. A brief note on the *malagan* Curvunavunga from Tabar, New Ireland Province. *The Beagle – Occasional Papers of the Northern Territory Museum of Arts and Sciences*. 7(2):83-8.

———. 1992. Malagan ritual art on Tabar, New Ireland. PhD thesis. Otago: University of Otago.

Heintze, Dieter. 1969. Ikonographische Studien zur Malanggankunst Neuirlands. Untersuchungen an ausgewählten Vogeldarstellungen. Inaugural dissertation. Tübingen Schwitalla Himmelsthür.

———. 1987. 'On trying to understand some *malagans*' in *Assemblage of Spirits: Idea and Image in New Ireland*. Edited by Louise Lincoln. New York: George Braziller. pp. 42-55.

Helfrich, Klaus. 1973. *Malanggan 1: Bildwerke von Neuirland*. Berlin: Museum für Völkerkunde.

———. 1985. Zeremonialschädel aus Mittel-Neuirland. *Baessler-Archiv*. Neue Folge, Band XXXIII:123-88.

Jessep, Owen D. 1980. Land and spirits in a New Ireland village. *Mankind*. 12(4):300-10.

Krämer, Augustin. 1925. *Die Malanggane von Tombara*. Munich: Georg Muller.

———. 1927. Tombarisisches, Altes und Neues. *Anthropos* 22:803-810.

Krämer-Bannow, Elisabeth. 1916. *Bei kunstsinnigen Kannibalen der Südsee. Wanderungen auf Neu-Mecklenburg 1908-1909*. Berlin: Dietrich Reimer.

Küchler, Susanne. 1985. Malanggan: exchange and regional integration in northern New Ireland. PhD thesis. London: London School of Economics.

———. 1987. Malangan: art and memory in a Melanesian society. *Man*. (NS). 22:238-55.

———. 1988. Malangan: Objects, Sacrifice and the Production of Memory. *American Ethnologist*. 15(4):625-37.

———. 1992. 'Making skins: *Malangan* and the idiom of kinship in northern New Ireland' in *Anthropology, Art, and Aesthetics*. Edited by Jeremy Coote and Anthony Shelton. Oxford: Clarendon Press. pp. 94-112.

Lamers, Father John. 1928-38. Notes and working dictionary of Madara language of Tabar. Manuscript.

Lewis, Phillip H. 1969. The social context of art in northern New Ireland. *Fieldiana Anthropology*. 58.

Lincoln, Louise (ed.). 1987. *Assemblage of Spirits: Idea and Image in New Ireland*. New York: George Braziller.

Neuhaus, Karl. 1962. *Beitrage zur Ethnographie der Pala, Mittel Neu Irland*. Köln: Kölner Universitats Verlag.

Parkinson, Richard H.R. 1907. *Dreissig Jahre in der Südsee*. Stuttgart: Strecker & Schröder.

Peekel, P. Gerhard. 1910. *Religion und Zauberei auf dem Mittleren Neu-Mecklenburg, Bismarck-Archipel, Südsee*. Parts 1,2. Münster: Anthropos-Bibliothek 1,3.

———. 1926. Die Ahnenbilder von Nord-Neu-Mecklenburg. Eine kritische und positive Studie. *Anthropos*. 21:806-24.

———. 1927. Die Ahnenbilder von Nord-Neu-Mecklenburg. Eine kritische und positive Studie. *Anthropos*. 22:16-44.

———. 1928. 'Lang-Manu. Die Schlussfeier eines *Malagan-* (Ahnen-) festes auf Nord-Neu-Mecklenburg' in *Festschrift für P.W.Schmidt*. Edited by W. Koppers. Wien. pp. 542-55.

———. 1929. Das Zweigeschlechterwesen. *Anthropos*. 24:1005-72.

———. 1931. Religiöse Tänze auf Neu-Irland (Neu-Mecklenburg). *Anthropos*. 26:513-32.

———. 1932. Uli und Ulifeier; oder, vom Mondkultus auf Neu Mecklenburg. *Archiv für Anthropologie*. N.F. 23:41-75.

Powdermaker, Hortense. 1931a. Report on field-work in New Ireland. *Oceania*. 1:355-65.

———. 1931b. Mortuary rites in New Ireland. *Oceania*. 2:26-43.

———. 1932. Feast in New Ireland: The social functions of eating. *American Anthropologist*. 43:236-47.

———. 1933 (1979). *Life in Lesu*. London: Williams & Norgate.

Walden, Edgar, and Hans Nevermann. 1940. Totenfeiern und *Malagane* von Nord-Neu-Mecklenburg – nach aufzeichnungen von E. Walden. *Zeitschrift für Ethnologie*. 72:11-38.

Wilkinson, Nick. 1978. 'Carving a social message: The Malanggans of Tabar' in *Art in Society*. Edited by M. Greenhalgh and J.V.S. Megaw. London: Duckworth. pp. 227-41.

Chapter 17 (Ewins)

Deane, Wallace. 1911. The Lali. *Transactions of the Fijian Society*. 11 January 1911.

Ewins, Rod. 1986. Lali: The drums of Fiji. *Domodomo*. 4(4): 142-69.

Wilkes, Captain Charles. 1845. *Narrative of the United States Exploring Expedition during the Years 1838-1842*. Vol. 3. Philadelphia: Lee & Blanchard.

Williams, Thomas. 1982 (1858). *Fiji and the Fijians*. London edition. Suva: Fiji Museum.

Chapter 18 (Beran)

Abel, Russell. 1934. *Charles W. Abel of Kwato*. New York: Fleming.

Baltimore Museum of Art. 1956. *The Alan Wurtzburger Collection of Oceanic Art*. Baltimore.

Beran, Harry. 1988. *Betel-chewing Equipment of East New Guinea.* Aylesbury: Shire Publications.

———. 1996. *Mutuaga: A Nineteenth-Century New Guinea Master Carver.* Wollongong: University of Wollongong Press.

———. 1997. Massim lime spatulas by the Master of the Prominent Eyes. *The World of Tribal Arts.* III:68-76.

Biebuyck, Daniel (ed.). 1973. *Tradition and Creativity in Tribal Art.* Berkeley: University of California Press.

Black, P.G. Diaries. In possession of the Buffalo Museum of Science.

Bounoure, Vincent. 1992. *Vision d'Océanie.* Paris: Musée Dapper.

Bourgoin, Philippe. 1994. Lime spatulas from Massim. *The World of Tribal Arts.* 1:35-46.

Brizzi, B., ed. 1976. *The Pigorini Museum.* Rome: Quasar.

Brown, George. 1908. *George Brown, D.D. Pioneer-Missionary and Explorer: An Autobiography.* London: Hodder & Stoughton.

Catalogue of P.G. Black's Ethnographical Collection, May 1901. Compiled by Chas. Hedley, Sydney. In possession of the Australian Museum, Sydney, and the Buffalo Museum of Science.

Catalogue Ethnographic Collection P.G. Black, 1 January 1914. In possession of the Australian Museum, Sydney, and the Buffalo Museum of Science.

Chauvet, Stephen. 1930. *Les Arts Indigènes en Nouvelle-Guinée.* Paris: Société D'Éditions Géographiques, Maritimes et Coloniales.

Christie's London. 1982. *Primitive Art.* 7 July.

Christie's South Kensington. 1988. *Tribal Art.* 22 November.

Fagg, William. 1963. *Nigerian Images.* London: Lund Humphries.

———. 1965. *Tribes and Forms in African Art.* London: Methuen.

Fischer, Eberhard. 1963. Künstler der Dan. *Baessler-Archiv.* Neue Folge X:161-263.

Force, R.W., and M. Force. 1971. *The Fuller Collection of Pacific Artefacts.* London: Lund Humphries.

Gathercole, P., A.L. Kaeppler and D. Newton. 1979. *The Art of the Pacific Islands.* Washington: National Gallery of Art.

Gerbrands, Adrian. 1967. *Wow-Ipits.* The Hague: Mouton.

Holm, Bill. 1981. 'Will the real Charles Edensaw please stand up? The problem of attribution in northwest coast Indian art' in *The World is as Sharp as a Knife.* Edited by Donald N. Abbott. Victoria: British Columbia Provincial Museum.

———. 1983. *Smoky-Top: The Art and Times of Willie Seaweed.* Seattle: University of Washington Press.

Lawes, W.G. n.d. Photographs of New Guinea, 1874-1890. In possession of Mitchell Library, Sydney.

Neich, Roger. 1991. Jacob William Heberley of Wellington: A Maori carver in a changed world. *Records of the Auckland Institute and Museum.* 28:69-148.

Newton, Douglas. 1975. *Massim.* New York: The Museum of Primitive Art.

Papuan Villager 1,1. 15 February 1929. 'Suau Wood Carving.' Probably by F.E. Williams.

Papuan Villager 3,4. 15 April 1931. Drawing of lime spatula. Probably by F.E. Williams.

Rubin, William (ed.). 1984. *'Primitivism' in 20th Century Art: The Affinity of the Tribal and the Modern.* 2 vols. New York: Museum of Modern Art.

Thompson, Robert. 1973. 'Àbátàn: A master potter of the Ègbádò Yorùbá' in *Tradition and Creativity in Tribal Art.* Edited by D. Biebuyck. Berkeley: University of California Press. pp. 120-82.

Wingert, Paul S. 1953. *Art of the South Pacific Islands.* London: Thames & Hudson.

Chapter 19 (Choulai and Lewis-Harris)

Barker, J., and A.M. Tietjen. 1990. Women's facial tattooing among the Maisin of Oro Province, Papua New Guinea: The changing significance of an ancient custom. *Oceania.* 60:217-34.

Bateson, G. 1958 (1936). *Naven.* Stanford: Stanford University Press.

Beattie, W. 1973. *Iris the Tapa Cloth Maker.* Goroka: Goroka Teachers' College.

Berman, M. 1990. 'Samting Tru, or Samting Nating? What is Contemporary Melanesian Art?' in *Luk Luk Gen! Look Again!* Edited by S. Simons and H. Stevenson. Townsville: Perc Tucker Regional Gallery. pp. 59-63.

Brumbaugh, R. 1990. '"Afek Sang": The old woman's legacy to the Mountain-Ok' in *Children of Afek: Tradition and Change Among the Mountain-Ok of Central New Guinea.* Edited by B. Craig and D. Hyndman. Oceania Monograph 40. Sydney: University of Sydney. pp. 54-87.

Choulai, W. 1993. Women and the Fiber Arts of Papua New Guinea. Paper presented jointly with Jackie Lewis-Harris at the fifth Pacific Arts symposium, Adelaide, April 1993.

Chowning, A. 1987. '"Women are our business": Women, exchange and prestige in Kovein' in *Dealing with Inequality*. Edited by M. Strathern. Cambridge: Cambridge University Press. pp. 130-49.

Christensen, R. 1981. Fiber plants used in Papua New Guinea regions. Field notes.

Dark, P.J.C. 1993. 'The future of Pacific arts: A Matter of Style?' in *Artistic Heritage In a Changing Pacific*. Edited by P.J.C. Dark and R. Rose. Bathurst: Crawford House Press. pp. 206-22.

Forge, A. 1966. Art and environment in the Sepik. *Proceedings of the Royal Anthropological Institute of Great Britain and Ireland for 1965*. London: Royal Anthropological Institute. pp. 23-31.

Gerbrands, A. 1990. 'Made by man' in *The Language of Things*. Edited by P. Ter Keurs and D. Smidt. Leiden: Rijksmuseum voor Volkenkunde. pp. 45-76

Gunn, M. 1993. Taxonomic structure and typology in the *malangan* ritual art tradition of Tabar, New Ireland, Papua New Guinea. Paper presented at the fifth Pacific Arts symposium, Adelaide, April 1993.

Leonard, A., and J. Terrell. 1980. *Patterns of Paradise*. Chicago: Field Museum of Natural History.

Lewis-Harris, J. 1993. The Sixth Pacific Arts Festival. *Pacific Arts* 9, 10:76-85.

———. 1994. Printed, beaten and coiled: Continuing tradition through textiles. *Arts and Asia Pacific*. 2(2):76-83.

MacKenzie, M. 1991. *Androgynous Objects: String Bags and Gender in Central New Guinea*. Chur: Harwood Academic Publishers.

Narokobi, B. 1980. *The Melanesian Way*. Edited by H. Olela. Boroko: Institute of Papua New Guinea Studies.

Pepena, R. 1994. 'Bilum making in the Western Highlands' in *People and Places of Mount Hagen*. Mount Hagen Town Authority.

Post-Courier 1979. Special Edition. *Handcrafts of Papua New Guinea*. 9 September. Port Moresby.

Simons, S. 1990. 'Commercial orientations in Papua New Guinean art' in *Luk Luk Gen! Look Again!* Edited by S. Simons and H. Stevenson. Townsville: Perc Tucker Regional Gallery. pp. 39-45.

———. 1993. 'Strong ai bilong em: A comparison of Papua New Guinean urban artists and Australian Aboriginal urban artists' in *Artistic Heritage in a Changing Pacific*. Edited by P.J.C. Dark and R. Rose. Bathurst: Crawford House Press. pp. 173-84.

Simons, S., and H. Stevenson. 1990. 'Art in public places' in *Luk Luk Gen! Look Again!* Edited by S. Simons and H. Stevenson. Townsville: Perc Tucker Regional Gallery. pp. 33-8.

Stevenson, H. 1990. 'Structuring a new art environment' in *Luk Luk Gen! Look Again!* Edited by S. Simons and H. Stevenson. Townsville: Perc Tucker Regional Gallery. pp. 23-31.

Strathern, M. 1972. *Women in Between: Female Roles In a Male World, Mt. Hagen, New Guinea*. London: Seminar Press.

Teilhet, J. 1983. 'The role of women artists in Polynesia and Melanesia' in *Art and Artists of Oceania*. Edited by S. Mead and B. Kernot. Mill Valley: Ethnographic Arts Publications. pp. 45-56.

Ter Keurs, P. 1990. 'Tami art and the Siassi trade network' in *The Language of Things*. Edited by P. Ter Keurs and D. Smidt. Leiden: Rijksmuseum voor Volkenkunde. pp. 113-30.

Thomas, N. 1995. *Oceanic Art*. London: Thames and Hudson.

Weiner, A. 1988. *The Trobrianders of Papua New Guinea*. New York: Holt, Rinehart & Winston.

———. 1989. 'Why cloth? Wealth, gender and power in Oceania' in *Cloth and Human Experience*. Edited by A. Weiner and J. Schneider. Washington: Smithsonian Institute Press.

Winter, J. n.d. *Traditional Weaving in Papua New Guinea*. Waigani: National Arts School.

Chapter 20 (Quanchi)

ATP/AR. 1909. *Australian Territory of Papua: Annual Report*. Port Moresby: Government Printer.

———. 1912. *Australian Territory of Papua: Annual Report*. Port Moresby: Government Printer.

Baden-Powell, B.F.S. 1892. *In Savage Isles and Settled Lands*. London: Richard Bentley.

Baharell, C. n.d. Photograph collection, UPNG R7-22, ALX 19-2 28.

Baildon, M. 1895. A trip to New Guinea. *Proceedings of the Royal Colonial Institute*. 1895-96:716.

Beaver, W.N. 1920. *Unexplored New Guinea*. London: Seeley, Service & Co.

Bernatsik, H. 1935. A flight into the stone age: Life in unexplored New Guinea. *The Geographic Magazine*. 11(2):53-66.

———. 1939. *Sudsee: Travels in the South Seas*. London: Wein Seidel.

Bevan, T. 1890. *Toil, Travel and Discovery in British New Guinea*. London: Keagan Paul, Trench & Trüber.

BNG/AR. 1887. *British New Guinea: Annual Report*. Brisbane: Government Printer.

———. 1901. *British New Guinea: Annual Report*. Brisbane: Government Printer.

Brandes, E.W. 1929. Into primeval Papua by seaplane. *National Geographic* 56:235-42.

Chalmers, J. 1887. *Pioneering in New Guinea*. London: Religious Tract Society.

———. 1895. *Pioneer Life and Work in New Guinea*. London: Religious Tract Society.

Chalmers, J., and W.W. Gill. 1885/1903. *Work and Adventure in New Guinea, 1877 to 1885*. London: Religious Tract Society.

———. 1885. *Neuguinea Reisen und Missionstatigfeit 1877 zu 1885*. Leipzig: Brodhaus.

Chester, H.M. 1880. 'Extracts from a diary' in *British New Guinea, Annual Report 1897-1898*. Brisbane: Government Printer. pp. 7-8.

Coutts, M.N. 1992. *Looking Back: A Selection of Old Photographs from Papua New Guinea 1880-1960s*. Port Moresby: South Pacific Magazine.

Delbos, G. 1984. *Cent ans chez les Papous*. Paris: Issoudin [Published in English as *The Mustard Seed: From a French Mission to a Papuan Church 1885-1985*. Port Moresby: Institute of Papua New Guinea Studies.]

Doussett, R., and E. Taillemite. 1974. *The Great Book of the Pacific*. London: Beacon.

English, D.E. 1983. W.H. Jackson: Western commercial photographer. *Colorado Heritage*. 1-2:60-88.

Fleming, P.R., and J. Luskey. 1988. *The North American Indian in Early Photographs*. London: Dorset Press.

Fox, F. 1911. *Peeps at Many Lands: Oceania*. London: Charles Black.

Goetzemann, W.H., and W.H. Goetzemann. 1986. *The West of the Imagination*. New York: W.W. Norton.

Hatton-Richards, T.H. 1892-93. British New Guinea. *Proceedings of the Royal Colonial Institute*. XXIV:296.

Huntsman, J. 1992. Matagi Tokelau into print and afterwards. Paper presented at the Ninth Pacific History Association Conference, Christchurch.

Hurley, F. 1924. *Pearls and Savages*. New York: Putnam.

Jammes, A., and R. Sobieszek (eds). 1970. *French Primitive Photography*. New York: Aperture.

Legge, F., and T. Hurley. 1966. *Once More on My Adventure*. Sydney: Ure Smith.

Lennox, C. 1903. *James Chalmers of New Guinea*. London: Melrose.

Lindt, J.W. 1887. *Picturesque New Guinea*. London: Longmans.

Lovett, R. 1902a. *James Chalmers: His Autobiography and Letters*. London: Religious Tract Society.

———. 1902b. *Tamate: The Life and Adventures of a Christian Hero – A Book for Boys*. London: Religious Tract Society.

Lyne, C. 1885. *New Guinea: An Account of the Establishment of the British Protectorate over the Southern Shores of New Guinea*. London: Sampson Low.

Macfarlane, J.S. 1888. *Among the Cannibals of New Guinea: Being the Story of the New Guinea Mission of the LMS*. London: London Missionary Society.

Macgregor, W. 1891. 'Despatch reporting visit of inspection to the Koiari District' in *British New Guinea: Annual Report 1890-1891*. Brisbane, Government Printer. pp. 26-7.

Martin, G.C. 1908. *The New Guinea Mission*. London: London Missionary Society.

Millar, D.P. 1984. *From Snowdrift to Shellfire*. Sydney: David Ell.

Miller, C. 1950. *Cannibal Caravan*. London: Museum Press.

Miller, L. 1941. *Cannibals and Orchids*. New York: Sheridan.

Moore, C.R., J. Griffin and F. Griffin. 1984. *Colonial Intrusion: Papua New Guinea 1884*. Port Moresby: Papua New Guinea Centennial Committee.

Mulvaney, J. 1989. *Encounters in Place*. Brisbane: University of Queensland Press.

Murray, H.P. 1925. *Papua of Today*. London: King.

Nelson, H. 1977. *Black, White and Gold*. Canberra: Australian National University Press

Newton, G. 1979. *Australian Pictorial Photography*. Sydney: Art Gallery of New South Wales.

Office of Tokelau Affairs. 1991. *Matagi Tokelau*. Apia, Western Samoa.

O'Reilly, P. and J. Poirier. 1959. *Nouvelle-Calédonie documents iconographiques anciens*. Paris: Nouvelles ditions Latines.

Robson, W. n.d. *James Chalmers: Missionary and Explorer of Rarotonga and New Guinea*. Kilmarnock: Ritchie.

Romilly, H.H. 1893. *Letters from the Western Pacific and Mashonaland 1878-1891*. London: David Nutt.

Ryan, J. 1969. *The Hot Land: Focus on New Guinea*. South Melbourne: Macmillan.

Saville, W.J. 1928. *Papuan School Reader*. Port Moresby: Government Printer.

Seton, W. n.d. *Chalmers of New Guinea: The Martyr Missionary*. London: Sunday School Union.

Severin, T. 1973. *Vanishing Primitive Man*. London: Thames & Hudson.

Snow, Philip, and Stefanie Waine. 1979. *The People from the Horizon*. Oxford: Phaidon.

Staniforth-Smith, H. (compiler). 1909. *Handbook, Territory of Papua*. Port Moresby: Government Printer.

Thomas, N. 1991. *Entangled Objects*. Cambridge: Harvard University Press.

Thompson, J.P. 1892. *British New Guinea*. London: Philip & Sons.

Time-Life. 1989. *The World We Live In*. Hong Kong: Time-Life.

Chapter 21 (Regius)

Aftonbladet. 1913. Sverge i Australien; En intervju med konsul von Goës. 18 June.

Anon. 1981. Söderhavsfararen Carl Wilhelm Öberg. Stora Skedvi Hembygdsförening. Säters Kommun.

Årsberättelser. 1900-1920. Etnografiska Afdelningen. Stockholm: Naturhistoriska Riksmuseet.

Broberg, Gunnar. n.d. 'Darwinism och utvecklingsläran' in *17 Uppsatser i Svensk idé och lärdomshistoria*. Bokförlaget Carmina.

Dahlberg, Elvira. 1954. Carl Pettersson, Sollentunapojke-Kung av Tabar. *Sollentuna Hembygds Förenings Skrifter*. 5:20-33.

Du Rietz, Rolf. 1984. 'Hjalmar Stolpe och etnografins framväxt i Sverige' in *Resa med Vanadis: Hundraårsminnet av en världsomsegling*. Stockholm: Etnografiska Museet. pp. 5-20.

Firth, Stewart. 1986. *New Guinea under the Germans*. Port Moresby: Web Books.

Holmberg, Åke. 1987. *Världen bortom västerlandet: Svensk syn på fjärran länder och folk från 1700-talet till första världskriget*. Humaniora 28, Kungl. Göteborg: Vetenskap-och Vitterhets-Samhället.

Larsson, Karl Erik. 1967a. *Malanganer*. Örebro Läns Museum.

———. 1967b. 'Birger Mörner-Konsul, Resenär och Samlare' in *Samfundet Örebro Stads- och länsbiblioteks vänners meddelande XXXIV*.

———. 1975. 'Birger Mörner- och den infödda befolkningen i Söderhavet' in *Mot Fjärran land: Berömda svenska upptäckare*. Läckö Slott.

Liljevalchs Konsthall. 1927. Kortfattad vägledning över utställningen Exotisk konst och konsthantverk. January: 8-30.

Mörner, Birger. 1914. *Arafis tropiska år*.

Nordenskiöld, Erland. 1907. *Kortfattad handledning för besökande af Riksmuseets Etnografiska Afdelning 1*. Uppsala: Samlingarna Wallingatan 1.

Oliver, Douglas L. 1975. *The Pacific Islands*. Revised ed. Honolulu: University of Hawai'i Press.

Sack, Peter, and Dymphna Clark (eds). 1979. *German New Guinea: The Annual Reports*. Trans. by Peter Sacks and Dymphna Clark. Canberra: ANU Press.

Stolpe, Hjalmar. 1890. 'Utvecklingsföreteelser i naturfolkens ornamentik' in *YMER*.

Svenska Dagbladet. 1913a. Grefve Birger Mörner redan i samlartagen: En etnografisk samling från Söderhavsöarna i dagarna anländ till Stockholm. 3 June.

———. 1913b. Yorrick: Våra etnografiska trupper uti i fält. 19 June.

Vecko Journalen. 1917. Birger Mörner: När Birger Mörner fick ett tempel för en gris. 3 May.

———. 1930. Bernt Hage: Dalmasen som blev Kannibalhövding. 6 October.

Chapter 22 (Vargyas)

Beran, H. 1993. The Woodcarvings of Mutuaga, a Nineteenth-Century Artist of the Massim Region of New Guinea. Paper presented at the 5th International Symposium of the Pacific Arts Association, Adelaide, 12-17 April.

———. 1996. *Mutuaga: A Nineteenth-Century New Guinea Master Carver*. Wollongong, NSW: University of Wollongong Press.

Bodrogi, T. 1953. Some notes on the ethnography of New Guinea. I. Initiation rites and ghost-cult in the Astrolabe Bay region. *Acta Ethnographica*. III:91-144.

———. 1959. 'New Guinean Style Provinces. The Style Province "Astrolabe Bay"' in *Opuscula Ethnologica Memoriae Ludovici Bíró Sacra*. Edited by T. Bodrogi and L. Boglár. Budapest: Akadémiai K. pp. 39-99.

———. 1975. Speere aus der Astrolabe-Bai (Nordost-Neuguinea). *Abhandlungen und Berichte des Staatlichen Museums für Völkerkunde, Dresden* 34:507-23.

———. 1979. 'Style provinces and trading areas in north and northeast New Guinea' in *Exploring the Visual Art of Oceania*. Edited by S. Mead. Honolulu: University Press of Hawai'i. pp. 265-77.

———. 1981. *Törzsi mûvészet* [*Tribal Art*]. I-II. Budapest: Corvina. [German edition, 1982, *Stammeskunst* I-II. Budapest.]

———. 1982. Mûvészet Észak-Uj-Guineában, az Astrolabe-öböl térségében [Art in northeast New Guinea, in the Astrolabe Bay area]. *Mûvészet* XXIII(10):39-43.

———. 1990. 'Between the invisible and the tangible: The role of art in communication between the two realms. An example from Papua New Guinea' in *Art as a Means of Communication in Pre-Literate Societies*. Edited by D. Eban. Jerusalem: The Israel Museum. pp. 7-26.

Bühler, A., T. Barrow and C.P. Mountford. 1961. *Ozeanien und Australien. Die Kunst der Südsee*. Baden-Baden: Holle & Co.

Craig, B. 1995. Following the tracks of Edgar Waite in New Guinea for the Pacific Arts symposium in Adelaide. *Records of the South Australian Museum*. 28(1):33-52.

Firth, R. 1936. *Art and Life in New Guinea*. London: The Studio Ltd.

Guiart, J. 1963. *The Arts of the South Pacific*. New York: Golden Press.

Haddon, A.C. 1894. *The Decorative Art of British New Guinea: A Study in Papuan Ethnography*. Cunningham Memoirs No. 10. Dublin: Royal Irish Academy.

King, D., and S. Ranck (eds). n.d. *Papua New Guinea Atlas: A Nation in Transition*. Waigani: Department of Geography, University of Papua New Guinea and Robert Brown & Associates.

Kooijman, S. 1955. *De Kunst van Nieuw-Guinea*. The Hague: Servire.

Kunze, G. 1892. A letter from the Island Karkar. *Rheinische Missionsberichte*. XLIX(6):196-207.

———. 1897. Allerlei Bilder aus dem Leben der Papua. *Rheinische Missionsschriften*. Heft 3.

———. 1926. *Bilder aus dem Leben der Papua*. 3. Auflage Barmen.

Lawrence, P. 1964. *Road Belong Cargo*. Melbourne: Melbourne University Press.

———. 1984. *The Garia*. Melbourne: Melbourne University Press.

Linton, R., and P.S. Wingert. 1946. *Arts of the South Seas*. New York: Museum of Modern Art.

Mennis, M. 1979. The Kilibob and Manup myth found on the north coast of PNG. *Oral History*. VII(4): 88-101.

Mikloucho-Maclay, N.N. 1950-54. *Sobranie Sochinenii* [*Collected Works*]. 5 vols. Moscow-Leningrad: Academy of Sciences.

Parkinson, R. 1900. Die Berlinhafen-Section. Ein Beitrag zur Ethnographie der Neu-Guinea-Küste. *Internationales Archiv für Ethographie*. XXXVIII:93-9.

Preuss, K.Th. 1897. Künstlerische Darstellungen aus Kaiser-Wilhelms-Land in ihrer Bedeutung für die Ethnographie. *Zeitschrift für Ethnologie* XXIX:77-141; XXX:74-125.

———. 1898. Künstlerische Darstellungen aus Kaiser-Wilhelms-Land in ihrer Bedeutung für die Ethnographie. *Zeitschrift für Ethnologie* XXIX:77-141; XXX:74-125.

Schmitz, C.A. 1969. *Oceanic Art: Myth, Man and Image in the South Seas*. New York: Abrams.

Schubert, R. 1970. *Methodologische Untersuchungen an ozeanischen Mythen-material*. Wiesbaden: Studien zur Kulturkunde 14.

Seemayer, V. 1901. *Beschreibender Catalog der ethnographischen Sammlung Ludwig Biró-s aus Deutsch-Neu-Guinea (Astrolabe-Bai)*. Budapest.

Sentinella, C.L. 1975. *Mikloucho-Maclay: New Guinea Diaries 1871-1883*. Madang: Kristen Press.

Vargyas, G. 1982. Unpublished field notes from Malasiga village and the Tami Islands, Morobe Province, PNG.

———. 1987. Field notes from the Astrolabe Bay. *Occasional Papers in Anthropology No. 2*. Budapest: Ethnographical Institute of the Hungarian Academy of Sciences.

———. 1992. A short history of the Pacific collections of the Ethnographic Museum, Budapest. *Pacific Arts*. 5:24-32.

Ward, R.G., and D.A.M. Lea (eds). 1970. *An Atlas of Papua and New Guinea*. Waigani: Department of Geography, University of Papua and New Guinea and Collins, Longman.

Webster, E.M. 1984. *The Moon Man*. Carlton: Melbourne University Press.

Chapter 23 (Cochrane)

Anon. 'The Fiji National Museum' in *Museums and Cultural Centres in the Pacific*. Edited by S. Eoe and P. Swadling. Port Moresby: PNG National Museum and Art Gallery. pp. 168-9.

Bolton, L.M. 1980. *Oceanic Cultural Property in Australia*. Canberra: Australian National Commission for UNESCO.

Enright, John. 1993. The field as home: An American folklorist in American Samoa. *Pacific Arts*. 8:29-30.

Eoe, Soroi. 1991. 'The role of museums in the Pacific: change or die' in *Museums and Cultural Centres in the Pacific*. Edited by S. Eoe and P. Swadling. Port Moresby: PNG National Museum and Art Gallery. pp. 1-4.

Eoe, S., and P. Swadling (eds). 1991. *Museums and Cultural Centres in the Pacific*. Port Moresby: PNG National Museum and Art Gallery.

Eritaia, B. 1988. A report on the cultural heritage of Kiribati: Present activities in the cultural division. *Pacific Arts Newsletter*. 27:27.

Foanaota, Lawrence. 1991. 'The Solomon Islands National Museum' in *Museums and Cultural Centres in the Pacific*. Edited by S. Eoe and P. Swadling. Port Moresby: PNG National Museum and Art Gallery. pp. 107-12.

Hanson, A., and L. Hanson (eds). 1990. *Art and Identity in Oceania*. Bathurst: Crawford House Press.

Kais, Kakah. 1991. 'How museums will be funded and established in PNG' in *Museums and Cultural Centres in the Pacific*. Edited by S. Eoe and P. Swadling. Port Moresby: PNG National Museum and Art Gallery. pp. 15-18.

Kasarherou, Emmanuel. 1991. 'The New Caledonian Museum' in *Museums and Cultural Centres in the Pacific*. Edited by S. Eoe and P. Swadling. Port Moresby: PNG National Museum and Art Gallery. pp. 161-7.

———. 1995. Men of flesh and blood. *Art and Asia Pacific*. 2(4):90-5.

Mead, S.M. (ed.). 1984. *Te Maori: Maori Art from New Zealand Collections*. New York: Harry Abrams and American Federation of Arts.

———. 1990. 'Tribal art as symbols of identity' in *Art and Identity in Oceania*. Edited by A. Hanson and L. Hanson. Bathurst: Crawford House Press. pp. 269-81.

Paulius, Nelson. 1991. 'The cultural heritage of the Pacific: Preservation, development and promotion' in *Museums and Cultural Centres in the Pacific*. Edited by S. Eoe and P. Swadling. Port Moresby: PNG National Museum and Art Gallery. pp. 5-14.

Quinnell, M. 1981. The return of ethnographic material to Papua New Guinea. *Pacific Arts Newsletter*. 12:6.

Specht, Jim. 1993. 'Museums and cultural heritage of the Pacific Islands' in *A Community of Culture: The People and Prehistory of the Pacific*. Edited by M. Spriggs et al. Canberra: Department of Prehistory, ANU. pp. 266-80.

Tongia, Arerangi. 1993. Cook Islands National Museum. Paper presented at 5th International Symposium of the Pacific Arts Association, Adelaide, South Australian Museum.

TCSP (Tourism Council of the South Pacific). 1990. *Review of Museums and Cultural Centres in the Pacific*. Suva: Tourism Council of the South Pacific.

Tutai, Viane. 1991. 'The Cook Islands Museum' in *Museums and Cultural Centres in the Pacific*. Edited by S. Eoe and P. Swadling. Port Moresby: PNG National Museum and Art Gallery. pp. 201-4.

Chapter 24 (Dark)

Aiavao, Ulafala. 1990. Needles of Courage. *Pacific Islands Monthly*. 12:49-50.

Anio, Prama. 1979. 'The 'Greatest Game of All'' in *Paradise Plus*. Edited by Gerry Dick. Sydney: Pacific Publications. Pp. 109-12.

Arioyoshi, Rita. 1989. *Polynesian Cultural Center*. Laie: Polynesian Cultural Center.

Austin, Robert. 1986. *Handcrafts of the Solomon Islands*. Honiara: Ministry of Trade, Government of the Solomon Islands.

Australian Tourist Publications. 1991 *Magazine* (Cairns). October 1991-April 1992.

Bahn, Paul, and John Flenley. 1992. *Easter Island Earth Island*. London: Thames & Hudson.

Berman, Marsha. 1990. 'SAMTING TRU, OR SAMTING NATING? What is contemporary Melanesian Art?' in *Lukluk Gen! Look Again, Contemporary Art from Papua New Guinea*. Edited by Susan Cochrane Simons and Hugh Stevenson. Townsville: Perc Tucker Regional Gallery. pp. 58-63.

Birnbaum, Phil, and Andrew J. Strathern. 1990. *Faces of Papua New Guinea*. Darlinghurst: Emperor Publishing.

Bringhurst, Robert, and Ulli Steltzer. 1991. *The Black Canoe, Bill Reid and the Spirit of Haida Gwaii.* Seattle: University of Washington Press.

Brown, Desoto. 1982. *Hawaii Recalls, Selling Romance to America, Nostalgic Images of the Hawaiian Islands 1910-1950.* Honolulu: Editions Ltd.

Cameron, Ian. 1987. *Lost Paradise, The Exploration of the Pacific.* London: Century.

Cole, Shari. 1991. Women's Fiber Arts Extend the Polynesian Social Fabric. *Pacific Arts.* 4:14-16.

Cook Islands Sun. 1992a. Pacific Arts Extravaganza. *Cook Islands Sun, Souvenir Guide.* 5(1):1.

———. 1992b. Ian George – painter and bonecarver, contemporary Cook Islands artist. 5(1):5.

Crick, Malcolm. 1989. Representations of international tourism in the social sciences: Sun, sex, sights, savings, and servility. *Annual Review of Anthropology.* 18:307-44.

Dark, Philip J.C. 1974. *Kilenge Life and Art: A Look at a New Guinea People.* London: Academy Editions.

———. 1979. 'The art of the peoples of Western New Britain and their neighbours' in *Exploring the Visual Art of Oceania.* Edited by Sidney M. Mead. Honolulu: University Press of Hawai'i. pp. 130-58.

———. 1983a. Shop signs in Kiribati: Today's folk art. *Pacific Arts Newsletter.* 17:25-6.

———. 1983b. 'Among the Kilenge "Art is something which is well done"' in *Art and Artists of Oceania.* Edited by Sidney M. Mead and Bernie Kernot. Palmerston North: Dunmore Press. pp. 25-44.

———. 1984. *The Kilenge of Papua New Guinea.* London: Royal Anthropological Institute.

———. 1990. 'Tomorrow's heritage is today's art and yesteryear's identity' in *Art and Identity in Oceania.* Edited by Allan Hanson and Louise Hanson. Bathurst: Crawford House Press. pp. 244-68.

———. 1993. 'The future of Pacific arts: A matter of style' in *Artistic Heritage in a Changing Pacific.* Edited by Philip J.C. Dark and Roger G. Rose. Bathurst: Crawford House Press. pp. 206-22.

Dick, Gerry. 1979. *Paradise Plus: A Selection of Stories from Air Niugini's In-flight Magazine.* Sydney: Pacific Publications.

Diolé, Philippe. 1976. *The Forgotten People of the Pacific.* London: Cassell.

Doig, Fiona, and Janet Davidson. 1989. *Taonga Maori, Treasures of the New Zealand Maori People.* Sydney: The Australian Museum.

Douglas, Ngaire. 1991. Vanuatu: state of the arts. *Pacific Islands Monthly.* 61(1):43-4.

Duffek, Karen. 1986. *Bill Reid, Beyond the Essential Form.* Museum Note No. 19. Vancouver: University of British Columbia Press/University of British Columbia Museum of Anthropology.

Dunn, Margery G. (ed.). 1985. *Blue Horizons: Paradise Isles of the Pacific.* Washington, DC: National Geographic Society.

Dutton, Denis. 1994. Authenticity in the Art of Traditional Societies. *Pacific Arts.* 9,10:1-9.

Ebes, Hank, and Michael Hollow. 1992. *Modern Art – Ancient Icon: A Gallery of Dreamings from Aboriginal Australia.* Melbourne: The Aboriginal Gallery of Dreamings.

Enoki, Estelle (ed.). 1992. Maui Commissions celebrate the Spirit of Art and Man. *Hawai'i Artreach.* 8(6):1,6-7.

Festival of Pacific Arts. 1992. *Festival No. 2.* Rarotonga: Festival of Pacific Arts.

Friedman, Jonathon. 1992. The past in the future: History and the politics of identity. *American Anthropologist.* 94(4):837-59.

Gathercole, Peter. 1993. Review of 'Manakonako: Reflections' by Kauraka Kauraka., n.d. [1991]. *Pacific Arts.* 7:84-5.

Gerbrands, Adrian A. 1979. 'The art of Irian Jaya: A survey' in *Exploring the Visual Art of Oceania.* Edited by Sidney M. Mead. Honolulu: University Press of Hawai'i. pp. 111-29.

Graburn, N.H.H. (ed.). 1976. *Ethnic and Tourist Arts: Cultural Expressions from the Fourth World.* Berkeley: University of California Press.

———. 1983. 'Art, ethno-aesthetics and the contemporary scene' in *Art and Artists of Oceania.* Edited by Sidney M. Mead and Bernice Kernot. Palmerston North: Dunmore Press. pp. 70-9.

Grieve, Ken. 1991. *The Land of Man.* Film Broadcast on Independent Television (Channel III), in UK, 20 March.

Hall, Corlin (ed.). 1992. *Cook Islands Chronicle No. 002, October.* Rarotonga: Chronicle Publishing, Cook Islands Chronicle.

Hawai'i Steering Committee. 1992. *6th Festival of Pacific Arts, Visual Arts of Hawaii.* The Hawai'i Steering Committee for the 6th Festival of Pacific Arts.

Heermann, Ingrid (ed.). 1979. *Tingting bilong mi, Zeitgenössische Kunst aus Papua Neuguinea.* Stuttgart: Institut für Auslandsbeziehungen.

Helu, Futa. 1991. Aid aiding corruption. *Pacific Islands Monthly.* 61(10):39.

Holdsworth, David. 1986a. *Lae and Morobe Province.* Papua New Guinea Series. Bathurst: Robert Brown & Associates.

———. 1986b. *The Central Province.* Papua New Guinea Series. Bathurst: Robert Brown & Associates.

———. 1986c. *The Highlands.* Papua New Guinea Series. Bathurst: Robert Brown & Associates.

Honolulu. 1992. 'Dress like you live here.' Advertisement. XXVII(6):5.

Hoogerbrugge, Jac (ed.). 1977. *The Art of Woodcarving in Irian Jaya.* Jayapura: Regional Government of Irian Jaya/United Nations Development Program.

Hoogerbrugge, Jac, and Simon Kooijman. 1976. *70 Years of Asmat Woodcarving.* Breda: Rijksmuseum voor Volkenkunde.

Jensen, Rocky Ka'iouliokahihikolo 'Ehu. 1990. Makaku. *Ka Wai Ola O Oha.* 7(9):19.

Ka'elele. 1990. *Ka'Elele.* September-October. Honolulu: Bishop Museum.

Kaeppler, Adrienne L. 1989. 'Art and Aesthetics' in *Developments in Polynesian Ethnography.* Edited by Alan Howard and Robert Borofsky. Honolulu: University of Hawai'i Press. pp. 211-39.

———. 1990. 'Art, aesthetics, and social structure' in *Tongan Culture and History.* Edited by Phyllis Herda, Jennifer Terrell and Niel Gunson. Canberra: Australian National University Press. pp. 59-71.

Kasfir, Sidney Littlefield. 1992. African art and authenticity, a text with a shadow. *African Arts.* XXV(2):41-53, 96.

Keale Sr, Moses. 1992. Trustees' views. *Ka Wai Ola O Oha.* 9(8):22.

Kolia, John. 1989. Aspects of cultural life in New Guinea. *Ethnies.* 8,9,10:68-73.

Macintyre, Michael. 1985. *The New Pacific.* London: Collins.

McCarthy, Angela. 1990. Adding colour to life in Rarotonga. *Pacific Islands Monthly.* 60(5):21-2.

———. 1991. Carving a path for Art. *Pacific Islands Monthly.* 61(1):49-50.

Maui Beach Press. 1991. Tattoos a Hawaiian status symbol. 9-15 December:A5.

Megaw, J. V. S. 1986. Contemporary Aboriginal art, Dreamtime discipline or alien adulteration. *Bulletin of the Conference of Museum Anthropologists.* 18:31-49.

———. 1990. 'Art and identity: Aspects of contemporary Aboriginal art' in *Art an Identity in Oceania.* Edited by Allan Hanson and Louise Hanson. Bathurst: Crawford House Press. pp. 282-92.

Megaw, Ruth, and J. V. S. Megaw. 1993. 'Black art and white society, some observations on contemporary Australian Aboriginal Art' in *Artistic Heritage in a Changing Pacific* Edited by Philip J.C. Dark and Roger G. Rose. Bathurst: Crawford House Press. pp. 162-172.

Michoutouchkine, Nicolai. n.d. *Aloi Pilioko, Artist of the Pacific.* Suva: South Pacific Social Science Association/Institute of Pacific Studies.

Miller, Brian. 1983. *The Highlands of Papua New Guinea.* Bathurst: Robert Brown & Associates.

Millerstrom, Sidsel. 1992. Report on the Marquesas Islands Rock Art Project. *Pacific Arts.* 6:19-25.

Mitchell, Andrew. 1990. *A Fragile Paradise. Nature and Man in the Pacific.* London: Collins.

Moulin, Jane. 1993. The VIth Festival of Pacific Arts, Rarotonga, Cook Islands, October 17-27th, 1992. *Pacific Arts.* 7:69-71.

Muller, Kal. 1990. *Indonesian New Guinea, Irian Jaya.* Berkeley: Periplus Editions.

Pacific Islands Monthly. 1991. Minefield of adventure found in Vanuatu. 61(2):40.

———. 1992. Natural, national treasure. 62(3):28-9.

Poignant, Roslyn. 1993. Review of 'The Heritage of Namatjira: The Watercolourists of Central Australia' edited by Jane Hardy, J. V. S. Megaw and M. Ruth Megaw, Australia: William Heinemann, 1992. *Pacific Arts.* 7:86-90.

Polynesian Cultural Center. n.d. 'Tahitian Canoe.' *14 Picture Souvenir Album.* Laie: Polynesian Cultural Center.

Ramirez, José Miguel. 1992. Some notes about recent Rapanui-Mapuche connections. *Rapa Nui Journal.* 6(4):73-4.

Rapa Nui Journal. 1991. Rapa Nui and the Polynesian Cultural Centre. 5(1):16.

Rosi, Pamela C. 1991. Papua New Guinea's new Parliament House: A contested national symbol. *The Contemporary Pacific.* 3(2):289-324.

Schmid, Christin Kocher. 1991. *Of People and Plants: A Botanical Ethnography of Nokopo Village, Madang and Morobe Provinces, Papua New Guinea.* Basler Beiträge zur Ethnologie Band 33. Basel: Ethnologisches Seminar der Universität und Museum für Völkerkunde. In Kommission bei Wepf and Co. AG Verlag.

Schneebaum, Tobias. 1991. Tourism and art. *Pacific Arts*. 3:27-28.

———. 1993. Touring Asmat. *Pacific Arts*. 7:52-6.

Siers, James. 1977. *Rarotonga*. Wellington: Millwood Press.

Simons, Susan Cochrane, and Hugh Stevenson. 1990. *Lukluk Gen! Look Again, Contemporary Art from Papua New Guinea*. Townsville: Perc Tucker Regional Gallery.

Sinclair, James. 1985. *Papua New Guinea: The First Hundred Years*. Bathurst: Robert Brown & Associates.

Sponsorship Proposal. n.d. *Sixth Festival of Pacific Arts, Rarotonga, Cook Islands, October 16-27, 1992*. Lindsay Missen Design and Production.

Stevenson, Karen. 1993. The VIth Festival of Pacific Arts, Rarotonga, Cook Islands, October 17-27th, 1992. *Pacific Arts*. 7:67-9.

Stevenson, Robert Louis. 1908. *In the South Seas*. London: Chatto & Windus.

Tausie, Vilsoni. 1980. *Art in the New Pacific*. Suva: Institute of Pacific Studies/South Pacific Commission.

Teilhet-Fisk, Jehanne. 1992a. Clothes in tradition: The *Ta'ovala* and *kiekie* as social text and aesthetics markers of custom and identity in contemporary Tongan society, Part I. *Pacific Arts*. 5:44-52.

———. 1992b. Clothes in tradition: The *Ta'ovala* and *kiekie* as social text and aesthetics markers of custom and identity in contemporary Tongan society, Part II. *Pacific Arts*. 6:40-65.

Thompson, Liz. 1989. Land of the Dani. *Pacific Islands Monthly*. 59(18):27-30.

Togna, Octave. 1992. *Who We Are*. Delegation of New Caledonia, VIth Festival of Pacific Arts, Rarotonga, Cook Islands. Nouméa: Comité du Festival/ADCK.

Tsutsumi, Cheryl Chee. 1990. Fa'a Samoa. *Hawaiian Airlines Magazine*. 1(3):18-22.

Tully, Janine. 1989. Around Paradise in a day. *Outrigger Hotels Hawaii*. 7(2):70-1.

Ward, Deborah Lee. 1990. Iaorana! Island *keiki* dance to the drums of Tahiti! *Ka Wai Ola O Oha*. 7(5):12-13.

Washington Pacific Report. 1991. 22nd South Pacific Forum in Pohnpei. 9(21):1.

What's on in the Cook Islands 1990, Free Visitors' Guide. 1990. Auckland: The Publishing Group/Cook Islands Tourist Authority.

Yates, John. 1992. Photograph, 'Ageless.' *Pacific Islands Monthly*. 62(4):62.